MULRONEY

THE POLITICS OF AMBITION

BY JOHN SAWATSKY

Men in the Shadows (1980)

For Services Rendered (1982)

Gouzenko (1984)

The Insiders (1987)

MULRONEY

THE POLITICS OF AMBITION

John Sawatsky

RESEARCH ASSOCIATE

HARVEY CASHORE

Macfarlane Walter & Ross

Toronto

MACFARLANE WALTER & ROSS
37A Hazelton Avenue
Toronto, Canada M5R 2E3

Canadian Cataloguing in Publication Data
Sawatsky, John, 1948-
Mulroney: the politics of ambition

Includes index.
ISBN 0-921912-06-4

1. Mulroney, Brian, 1939- . 2. Canada - Politics and
government - 1963-1984.* 3. Prime ministers - Canada -
Biography. I. Title.

FC631.M84S3 1991   971.064'7'092   C91-094616-7
F1034.3.M84S3 1991

Printed and bound in the United States of America

FOR MY DAUGHTER

LARISSA

WITH THANKS TO THE CARLETON UNIVERSITY SCHOOL
OF JOURNALISM FOR ALLOWING THIS PROJECT
INTO ITS CLASSROOMS

AND SPECIAL THANKS TO MY STUDENTS FOR HELPING
WITH THE EARLY RESEARCH

Stephanie Barrett Louisa Battistelli Kanina Bhatnagar
David Blais Jill Marie Burke Sandra Burkholder Anita Chan
Yves Cossette Hélène Côté Sara Darling Marlene Davis
Christine Endicott Jos Erzetic Marcea Fairbairn
Beth Gallagher Jim Gibbs Margaret Gural Jackie Holden
Doug Le Faive Fiona Miller David Noble Tanya Offereins
Diane Paquette Rita Parikh Anne Patry Kathy Pendergast
David Scanlan Keith Schaefer Sarah Sloan Sharon Stanford
Angela Stelmakowich Louise Yako Lydia Zajc

CONTENTS

AUTHOR'S NOTE   xi

PART ONE: THE SEEDS OF AMBITION   1

1 The Company Town   3

2 An Introduction to Politics   19

3 The Chief   32

4 The Prime-Ministerial Itch   56

5 The Missing Year   74

6 Comeback   108

7 A Quebec Base   129

PART TWO: AMBITION DENIED   157

8 Legal Hurdles   159

9 The Civil War   176

10 Dealmaker   195

11 The Wagner Recruitment 217

12 The Perfect Wife 233

13 Crimebuster 248

14 The Cadillac Candidate 262

15 Opportunity Lost 289

PART THREE: ASCENT TO POWER 315

16 Aftermath 317

17 The New Man 342

18 The Guerrilla War 375

19 The Battle of Winnipeg 432

20 Leadership Gained 458

21 Inside the Tent 491

22 The Fruits of Ambition 523

INDEX 559

AUTHOR'S NOTE

THIS BOOK BEGAN life in the fall of 1987 as a project for the investigative journalism course I teach at Carleton University. During the subsequent journey of more than three years I have travelled farther and discovered more intriguing material than I would ever have imagined possible.

In all, my students and I conducted more than six hundred in-depth interviews and conversations. It has long been my policy not to reveal who was interviewed and who was not. This anonymity both protects the interviewee and encourages frankness. The only exception I will make here is to say that Brian Mulroney himself was not one of our interviewees. We made requests for an interview both orally and in writing but the prime minister never responded. Fortunately few others turned us down.

For the interview process, Mr. Mulroney's life was broken down into distinct chronological periods, starting with his childhood in Baie Comeau and finishing with his second term as prime minister. We then devised an exhaustive list of neutral, open-ended questions for each of these periods, which became the basis for all the interviews we did. The majority of interviews were taped, then indexed on computer and cross-referenced by subject and time period. Concurrently we entered the names of the people in Brian Mulroney's life into a separate data base for the purpose of disentangling his various networks and to help us define our interviewing priorities. Given the extraordinary number of his friends, this task in itself proved quite an undertaking. (Of the three biographical works on Mr. Mulroney published previously, by far the most helpful was L. Ian MacDonald's *Mulroney: The Making of the Prime Minister*. It provided, in the words of journalist Stevie Cameron, a "road map" to his friends and networks.) Eventually it became clear that the last five time periods — dealing with how he handled power as opposed to how he acquired it — belonged to a different story, one that is still unfolding. Mr. Mulroney's election as prime minister in 1984 formed the natural conclusion to this work.

This book has proved to me what a wonderful journalistic tool the computer has become. Without a data base, I would have drowned in the morass of names of Brian Mulroney's legion of friends and never known where to start and finish the interviews. Without an electronic indexing program, many important developments in the story would have been lost in the thousands of transcript pages. However, human help was still the most important component of my research. Never before have I written a book to which so many people have contributed.

For allowing me to involve my students in this research as part of their course work, I would like to thank Stuart Adam, Peter Johansen, and particularly Anthony Westell of the Carleton University School of Journalism. All of them at one time or another sat in the director's chair, and all consistently supported me. Once again Professor Joe Scanlon deserves to be singled out for special thanks.

One of the joys of a project like this is the opportunity of encountering people like Lydia Zajc, a student volunteer who not only did some exceptional research but brought an infectious enthusiasm to the work. Ralph Curtis programmed my computers to do exactly what they were supposed to do, and always saved the day when things went awry. Peter Jermyn of CTV was very cooperative in helping me search for film footage, and his employer was most accommodating. At the CBC, Jean Ménard of *The Journal* deserves particular recognition. Other individuals to whom I am indebted are

Michel Cormier, Jean Bourguignon, Amanda Pelham, Harold Shea, Norma Reveler, Anne McKague, Louise Crandall, Larry McDorman of the *Fredericton Daily Gleaner*, Michael Stewart of Public Archives Canada, and Dave Bullock of the City of Ottawa Archives.

The staff of the Library of Parliament, one of Ottawa's most cherished institutions, went out of their way to be helpful, as they have been during my sixteen years as a reporter on Parliament Hill. In particular, I wish to thank Carole Lefebvre and Louise Latour.

Macfarlane Walter & Ross has been a wonderful and most supportive publisher. When I fell behind schedule, Jan Walter remained patient and understanding. Rick Archbold, a demanding but superb editor, advanced the manuscript immeasurably. Barbara Czarnecki saved us from countless errors, large and small.

The last word I am reserving for the person who made by far the greatest contribution of all, Harvey Cashore. The most rewarding decision I made during the entire project was to bring Harvey into it. He started with me in the fall of 1987 as a researcher and finished as my associate, all the time working cheerfully, persistently, and brilliantly. This is a far better book for his efforts.

John Sawatsky
Parliamentary Press Gallery, Ottawa
July 1991

PART ONE

THE SEEDS
OF AMBITION

CHAPTER ONE

THE COMPANY TOWN

THE MOVE TO THE duplex at 99 Champlain Street in Baie Comeau had definitely boosted Benedict Martin Mulroney a step up in the world. With World War II reaching an end, Ben had recently become chief electrician at the local paper mill and could afford to move his young family from a smaller house at 132 Champlain. By the standards of the place, the Mulroneys were middle-class, but this was as high on the social and economic ladder as they would ever climb. Ben still got paid by the hour and would remain an hourly electrician for as long as he worked for the Quebec North Shore Paper Company.

Still, he couldn't complain. The mill paid top dollar. When the rest of the world was earning $75 a week, the basic wage in Baie Comeau was $100. And by the time the world had caught up, the mill had jumped ahead to $125. As chief electrician, Ben Mulroney did better than most of the workers, but his paycheque barely covered the family's expenses. Nonetheless, his modest table never lacked food and the house's simple furnishings included an old Willis piano. (Ben even managed to provide piano lessons for several of the children.)

Punctually at 3:00 P.M. each Thursday, the mill issued weekly pay envelopes filled with cash. Often, Ben did not bring home his wages himself. This honour belonged to his eldest son, Martin Brian. As soon as school was out, Brian would meet his father at the mill and then carry the envelope straight to his mother, Irene. He didn't have far to go: from the mill to the Mulroney house was a little over half a mile along Champlain Street, the town's main thoroughfare.

Brian had always assumed special duties and responsibilities in the household. As the first surviving son after two daughters, he received special treatment. His birth on March 20, 1939, the family's first in Baie Comeau, had brought great joy. (The Mulroneys' first child had been a boy, but he had died at birth in 1935.) Ben Mulroney revered his son; in return, Brian worshipped his father's very shadow.

Otherwise they seemed to have little in common. A neighbour from these days recalls wondering how Ben Mulroney had produced a son so unlike him. The elder Mulroney was modest and unassuming; the son was outspoken, self-assured, even cocky. The father viewed the majority French population of Baie Comeau with caution; the son saw them as potential friends. And while Ben Mulroney quietly accepted his second-class station in Baie Comeau society, Brian did not.

Neither did he inherit his outgoing personality from his mother, who was quiet and painfully shy. Irene Mulroney was ten years younger than her husband. Her ancestors, tenant farmers in Ireland, had come to Canada in the 1820s, and she grew up in the Irish community of Shannon, about twenty miles north of Quebec City. Ben and Irene had met in his home town of Sainte-Catherine-de-Portneuf, another Irish community just a few miles to the west. Ben spotted Mary Irene O'Shea one day at Mass and courted her, and in 1934 they were married. He was thirty-one and his bride just past twenty. She was lovely to look at, smiled easily, but was delicate and demure, rarely raising her voice and never knowingly offending anyone. When there was work to be done, she always lent a willing hand. She was also strongly religious, uttering a quiet prayer whenever

4

something went wrong. In many ways a typical woman of her era, perhaps; but, like her husband, she was ambitious for her children, determined that they would rise higher in the world than she had.

Ben also came from thoroughly Irish stock. His ancestors had emigrated from Ireland during the nineteenth-century potato famine and had worked hard to prosper in their adopted land. As a young man Ben took a correspondence course in electricity and became an electrician who hired on at construction projects throughout Quebec, moving from site to site. In 1936 he had left his pregnant wife and infant child in Sainte-Catherine-de-Portneuf and travelled east along the St. Lawrence in search of work. He found it on the site that would become Baie Comeau the following year. For months he lived in a tent, labouring through the fall and the bitter winter, away from his family. When the ice thawed the following spring, Ben Mulroney's young family sailed into Baie Comeau and settled into their first house at 132 Champlain Street. Ben took a permanent job with the mill and put down roots in the newly incorporated town.

Brian Mulroney grew up in a home where hard work was the norm. His mother seldom rested, what with six children to look after. Ben was known as a tireless worker; he sometimes worked an extra shift, an extra day a week, in the mill, or took other jobs at night, installing electricity in new homes or replacing coal furnaces with oil burners. He ran an electrical fix-it shop out of his basement, where he could frequently be found well past midnight.

Ben Mulroney may have been an hourly worker, but one thing he did not do was carry a lunch pail. Every day at noon he drove home for lunch. The bosses went home too, and when they did Ben Mulroney walked out the front door with them, his coveralls left behind and his greying hair immaculately groomed.

Neighbours regarded Ben Mulroney as an ideal citizen who, whatever his aspirations, had a sense of his own modest place in the company town. Never pushy and always approachable, he did not hesitate to chat with fellow employees and would talk comfortably about sports or fishing or municipal politics. But he remained a very private man who kept his problems to himself. And he could be stubborn. He demanded much of himself but also expected much of others. Apprentices called him "Mr. Mulroney"; he insisted on it. He believed they had to learn their craft from the bottom up, beginning with mopping the floor. Fellow workers might complain of his cantankerous nature, but inwardly they thought of him as solid and decent.

Above all else, Ben Mulroney was a dedicated family man who doted on his children. In addition to Brian there were four girls and one boy: Olive (born in 1936), Peggy (born 1937), Doreen (born 1942), Gary (born 1943), and Barbara (born 1948). During Ben's precious non-working hours, he was seldom seen in public, and he rarely stopped at the tavern for a beer after work. His social life was his home life. The family went to church together and on occasion would pile into the car and go for a Sunday-afternoon drive. Ben Mulroney took the role of family patriarch. He would say a prayer before meals, and no one dared start eating before he did. After dinner he might sit and rest in the La-Z-Boy chair in the living room. The Mulroneys were a warm, close-knit family, but that did not stop Brian from fighting with his sisters and particularly with his younger brother, Gary.

When Brian was growing up, Baie Comeau presented a very particular view of the world. The town began and ended at the mill, operated by the Quebec North Shore Paper Company, a subsidiary of the Tribune Company, which owned the *Chicago Tribune* and its sister publication, the *New York Daily News*. The *News*, which boasted the biggest circulation in the United States, consumed newsprint as fast as the mill — which housed the fastest newsprint machines in the world — could roll it out.

The most striking feature of the mill building was the name painted in huge block letters across the wall facing the water: Colonel Robert R. McCormick. Colonel McCormick was the American owner of the Tribune Company and therefore of the mill. Building a paper mill and founding a town in this desolate spot had been his vision, and he was Baie Comeau's absentee feudal lord, the most powerful man in Brian's universe. Two columns of lesser names appeared under McCormick's, but with the exception of Tibasse, a native guide who led the colonel on hunting and exploration expeditions in the surrounding bush, the names were all business associates of the colonel, most of whom had no relationship with the people of Baie Comeau.

Champlain Street made a loop in front of Colonel McCormick's mill, then meandered for a little more than a mile along the north shore of the St. Lawrence River. The town proper began five hundred feet from the mill. The community centre was right next to the No. 4 paper shed and close to the Deninger Hotel, just beyond the mill grounds. Sainte-Amélie Church, where the Mulroneys attended Mass each Sunday, was just inland and uphill. Next came the company-owned Boisvert Memorial Hospital, with fifty beds and a nursery, the same hospital where Brian had been delivered by Dr. Thurber.

About fifteen hundred feet from the mill Champlain Street began to climb a hill, which, although not much more than a hundred feet high, loomed large in the local consciousness. Its height was sociological rather than topographical: it was Baie Comeau's yardstick for measuring the status of its citizens. In general, the higher up the hill, the larger the homes and the more lofty the station of their residents. First came a few four-plex and duplex houses and a few single homes, occupied by lower management. It was one of these dwellings that Brian's father aspired one day to possess. Near the top lived the company doctor, the woodland manager (who supervised inland operations), and the mill's production manager. These residences afforded a fine view of the mill and the bay.

At the summit, where the land flattened into a small plateau, Champlain Street divided in two. The right fork continued straight on and was lined with more houses. The fork that looped to the left followed the bluff overlooking the St. Lawrence and led to two impressive buildings. The more magnificent was the posh company-owned hotel. The Manoir, replete with six-foot-high turret windows, wood-panelled lounge, and sumptuous dining room, was surrounded by trees and encircled by a fence.

The other significant building on the summit was the residence of the mill manager, the chief administrator of the company's operations in the area and the most important man in the town of two thousand people. The manager's house had six bedrooms, a spacious dining room, and a party room that could easily accommodate a hundred people. The well-kept grounds were tended by his personal gardener. The mill manager saw himself very much as an aristocrat and the workers as vassals. He seldom fraternized with them; in fact he spoke not a word of French, the language of 80 per cent of his employees. (He took translators with him to company events.)

Looking from the steps of the Manoir, one's view was dominated by the mill, its three 160-foot-high chimneys spewing the exhaust from the burning coal. Visible beyond it was a sheltered cove called English Bay, which was often choked with four-foot logs that had been boomed on the Manicouagan River nine miles away and floated down in a flume. Just in from the grey, rocky shoreline one could see the mill yard crowded with stacks of these logs waiting to be stripped and fed into the pulping machines.

The Manoir also afforded a breathtaking view of the St. Lawrence River where it broadens into the Gulf of St. Lawrence. Here the widening expanse of water is really a sea, more salt than fresh, with tides that rise and retreat. During the summer small beluga whales swam by in search of food, and fishing boats dotted the horizon. To the south and east the mountains of the south shore were visible on a clear day. To the north lay an endless wilderness of forests, lakes, and granite mountains. The nearest city of any size was Quebec, 260 miles to the southwest. For Brian, as a native of Baie Comeau, its horizons were the horizons of his world.

These horizons shrank in winter into a numbing isolation. There was no railroad and only one seldom-travelled road out of the town. Normally the trip to Quebec City started with a four-and-a-half-hour boat ride to Rimouski and ended with a six-hour drive by car. In winter the ice closed down this lifeline; when the last boat left in late autumn it did not return before spring.

Despite the smallness of Baie Comeau, it contained much for a boy to explore. Its heart lay down the "back slope" of the hill, away from these broad vistas, where Champlain descended away from the mill. Here status declined more quickly than altitude. Single-family houses became smaller and boxier, then gave way to semi-detached duplexes. The inhabitants of these houses were still mostly English, with names like Smith, Goodfellow, Neil, Malloy, Dawson, Scott, and Hall — and Mulroney.

On the back slope inland from Champlain lay Laval Street, the residents of which seldom mixed with the people who lived on Champlain. Laval was French, and the anglophones on the back slope of Champlain Street spoke little or no French, but in Baie Comeau that was acceptable. The mill management stood behind them, keeping the English language secure and supreme, and for good reason. Without this anglophone buffer on the back end of Champlain Street, the English-speaking bosses on the top of the hill were hopelessly outnumbered.

Like most anglophones in Baie Comeau, Ben and Irene Mulroney spoke little French and lived in an English-language cocoon. Even so, they could not escape the sociological realities of the place. The local pecking order affected them deeply and held them back in ways that did not confine most of the English-speakers around them. The Mulroneys were anglophones, but a different breed of anglophones, one suffering its particular form of cultural apartheid. They were Anglo-Catholics.

French and English were Baie Comeau's spoken languages, but the cultural make-up of the town was more complex. French Catholics accounted for four-fifths of the population; English Protestants made up most of the rest. The small cluster of Anglo-Catholics were poised between these two. In effect they were English by language and French by religion. In theory the combination should have opened the doors to each world, but more often it cut them off from both. They went to the French Catholic church but could not communicate with their fellow parishioners. Neither the English Protestants nor the French Catholics entirely welcomed them. They lacked status, a sense of belonging, and, most of all, true acceptance. They were a minority within a minority. In a town with two solitudes, they occupied the lonely centre.

The English Catholics played a middleman role in the town, seeking to become the indispensable bridge between the two predominant groups. In part they succeeded. The citizens of Baie Comeau accepted their presence, and the mill gave them jobs and permitted them housing on Champlain Street. They settled into the community, but they harboured no illusions about their true status. They were Catholics and for that they paid a price: Catholics seldom advanced at the mill.

The uneasy position of the English Catholics was nowhere more evident than in the school system. Protestant children attended Baie Comeau High School, a beautiful old building on the hill. French children took their schooling at nearby Sainte-Amélie, a Catholic school. There was no school for the children of the English-speaking Catholics. Their parents could send them either to Baie Comeau High for schooling in the wrong denomination or to Sainte-Amélie for schooling in the wrong language. Knowing that other families faced no such dilemma, English Catholics swallowed hard and sent their kids to Sainte-Amélie, where occasionally some courses in English were offered. Brian also took math and history at the Protestant school, but when religion and language collided, religion won.

Although French and English seldom mixed socially, they lived together quite peacefully. After all, the two groups had both arrived during the Depression, when the town consisted of nothing more than a gravel road and a few tents pitched in the wilderness. They had built Baie Comeau side by side, and most of these pioneer founders were still living, and equally proud of their creation. They worked at the same mill, frequented the same tavern, suffered the same black flies each spring and endured the same long, cruel winters. As a result, although there was the occasional skirmish, there was no real feuding and surprisingly little animosity. The harmony contrasted with the uneasy coexistence of French and English in the older towns of Quebec, where the economies were still dominated by a handful of old Anglo-Saxon families. In the town of New Carlisle, 125 miles away on the Gaspé Peninsula, where René Lévesque had grown up in the thirties, English and French kids regularly skirmished in the streets. That sort of thing did not happen in Baie Comeau.

Although an invisible barrier seemed to separate Champlain Street from Laval Street, by the time Brian was six or seven he was not afraid to cross it. Even before he started attending Sainte-Amélie, where classes were in French, he began to learn the language from his playmate Gilles Lachance, one of the few francophones who lived on Champlain. Lachance would speak in French and Brian would reply in English, giving each a working knowledge of the other's mother tongue. Most anglophone children learned some French in the streets, but few as quickly as Brian — although it was obvious from his accent that his French was not native.

Even though Brian became a member of the English-speaking gang known as "la gang de la rue Champlain," he continued to mix with the Laval Street crowd and moved effortlessly back and forth from neighbourhood to neighbourhood and from culture to culture. He was extraordinarily personable and outgoing at a very young age, with an amazing talent for friendship.

He was an attractive boy with a broad face and a square jaw. Although he was short for his age, that deficiency was almost forgotten because of his remarkable self-possession. Head held high, he did not walk so much as strut. He loved to tell jokes; he knew all the Irish songs along with many others, and was always ready to jump up and belt out a tune. But he also had an Irish temper and was sometimes sensitive and touchy. In particular he took Irish jokes badly; his friends all knew this weak point and sometimes used it to goad him.

Above all, he was loyal to his friends and expected loyalty in return.

But he also liked to win, and sometimes his desire to win collided with his code of loyalty. When an injured goaltender on his hockey team needed replacing, Brian took charge and asked a buddy, Butch Lavoie, to take over in net. Lavoie protested, claiming he could not play goal, but Mulroney convinced him he was a fine goalie and persuaded him to put on the pads. The team lost, 24 to 6, with Lavoie in the net, and Brian never asked Lavoie to play goal again.

As a youngster he was uncommonly skilled at manipulating people through flattery, and had a sure instinct for whom to flatter. He possessed an uncanny knack for being with the right people at the right moment, and he appeared on the scene whenever something important was brewing in town. He simply made it his business to be there. Among his childhood friends were the Ferguson twins, Ann and Barbara, whose father, Ernest Ferguson, was the woodland manager at the mill, only one rung below the mill manager himself. Ernest Ferguson was a gregarious character, and his position required him to entertain a great deal. And, it seemed, whenever a visiting VIP was being fêted at the Ferguson home, Brian appeared. He was always welcome and invariably he put on a show that endeared him to the adults present. He met industrial barons and VIPs who came through town, among them John Fisher, the CBC broadcaster whose thrice-weekly show, *John Fisher Reports*, had made him a famous figure and who later became known as "Mr. Canada." When John Fisher was in Baie Comeau to speak at the Manoir, Mulroney leapt up on stage with Fisher and sang "When Irish Eyes Are Smiling" and "Danny Boy."

Of all the visiting notables, the one with whom Brian scored his greatest success was none other than Colonel McCormick himself. Nothing caused more commotion in the town of Baie Comeau than a visit from the colonel, an event that happened at least once every year, usually in July, for his birthday. One time the colonel brought with him an entertainment troupe of 150 performers. Whatever the manner of his arrival, the entire town was polished up for the occasion.

The colonel genuinely liked Baie Comeau and, in the best American tradition of paternalistic capitalism, regarded its residents as children of the Tribune family. The mill made money — tons of it — never went on strike, and contributed significantly to the colonel's empire. In return he treated the workers well, paid them premium wages, and showered Baie Comeau with gifts that few towns enjoyed. The colonel supplied the townsfolk with inexpensive power from the company's hydro dam on the Manicouagan. He built a community centre that was probably the best in the province, providing facilities for bowling, skating, curling, squash, indoor tennis, hockey, and badminton. He built and stocked a community library. When the citizens pressed for a ski hill, he sent in a crew and created one. Colonel McCormick looked after everything and served it on a platter.

When Colonel McCormick flew in from Chicago, the town, prodded by the colonel's underlings, opened its arms.

Young Brian donned a white shirt and black tie and was on hand at the Manoir when Colonel McCormick arrived. Using his charm, Brian endeared himself with the colonel just as he had with the kids on Laval Street and the VIPs at the Ferguson house. The Catholic bishop never failed to stage a special program for the colonel. And when Sainte-Amélie assembled a choir to perform for him, Brian was in the middle of it, singing his heart out. Sometimes the organizers literally had to yank him off the stage.

Years later, Mulroney described to his friend L. Ian MacDonald how the colonel asked for him personally when he visited Baie Comeau. "Any time he came to Baie Comeau," MacDonald quotes Mulroney in his biography, *Mulroney: The Making of the Prime Minister*, "he asked for me, and I'd go sing. I'd perform any song that he'd want. He'd just name them and I knew them." Other residents say that Colonel McCormick's requests for Mulroney came only after the young man had first sought the colonel's attention.

After Brian completed elementary school, his parents moved him out of Sainte-Amélie and into a newly created English-Catholic institution that offered Grade 9 and 10 classes. It was a school of sorts, founded as a result of an alliance between francophone parents who wanted their children to learn English and English Catholics who could accept the local education set-up no longer. Ben Mulroney himself sat on the new school's board. It was a makeshift establishment at best; it had few students, no building — classes were held in a church basement or in the community centre or wherever space could be found — and its curriculum was full of holes. It relied on the goodwill of Sainte-Amélie to fill the gaps.

In June 1953, Brian finished Grade 10, and once again his parents faced the familiar dilemma. English Catholics who wanted to take Grades 11 and 12 were forced to choose between French-Catholic Sainte-Amélie and English-Protestant Baie Comeau High. Ben and Irene liked neither option yet insisted that Brian finish school.

Had Brian left school altogether, he would have faced a lifetime job at the mill. He once spoke of joining the mill's apprenticeship program for workers' sons and becoming an electrician like his dad, but Ben Mulroney would hear none of it. His son was not going to get stuck in the same rut as he, labouring at two or three jobs, his path to promotion blocked by religious prejudice. "Listen, Brian," Mulroney would remember his father saying, "the only way out of a mill town is through a university door."

Since Protestant schooling was unthinkable, Sainte-Amélie appeared to be the only choice. But Sainte-Amélie had lower standards than Baie Comeau High. Worse, it might lock his son into a francophone ghetto and ruin his chances of success. Brian already spoke too much French as far as Ben was concerned. The clincher came one day when Brian could not recall the English word for butter. The Mulroneys decided then and there that their son would complete high school in an English-Catholic boarding school, no matter the cost or how much moonlighting Ben Mulroney would have to do to finance it.

Finding an English-Catholic school that fit the family pocketbook was not easy. Good schools existed, but in virtually every case the price of admission was beyond the Mulroneys' reach. Budget boarding schools for hard-pressed English Catholics were scarce. In fact the Mulroneys knew of none until they learned from other parents of an all-boys school in Chatham, New Brunswick, that was run by priests.

St. Thomas High School offered a satisfactory program and had the added advantage of being relatively close to Baie Comeau and located in a town not much larger. But its main attraction was its incredibly low cost: tuition was $25 a semester. Other fees included $10 for laundry, a $5 athletic fee, $5 "caution money" (a deposit on textbooks), and $4.25 for medical and surgical services. Room and board was $160. The school year comprised two semesters, bringing the cost of housing, feeding, and educating Brian for ten months to a grand total of $418.50.

It was a lot of money, but the Mulroneys could just manage it. Brian's two older sisters, Olive and Peggy, were already attending the Iona Academy in eastern Ontario, and the expense of his education tightened the family belt another notch. But his parents accepted the sacrifice without complaint. The hardest part was living without their fourteen-year-old son for ten months. During that span he would return only for a couple of weeks at Christmas. Brian was still a boy, but if he fulfilled the ambitions they had for him, he would never again spend a winter in Baie Comeau.

Brian Mulroney arrived at St. Thomas in September 1953 and soon understood how the school could afford to take students for so little. The main school building, architecturally beautiful but in need of repair, sat behind an unpaved schoolyard. Behind it sat an old military building that had been donated to the school and converted into classrooms. There was also a wooden gymnasium and a spartan dormitory filled with bunk-beds, barracks style. The entire campus of tiny St. Thomas College, a post-secondary institution with eighty students, was right next door. It awarded fourteen bachelor of arts degrees the year Mulroney arrived. Also next door was the school farm, which produced potatoes, vegetables, and pork for the in-mates — a school priest was frequently seen on a tractor ploughing the fields. Most of the teachers were priests paid a subsistence salary. The combination of frugal facilities, home-grown food, and under-paid faculty allowed St. Thomas to operate on a shoestring.

This unimpressive institution followed the basic New Brunswick

Department of Education high school curriculum: English, French, history, physics, chemistry, and mathematics, adding a course on religion and offering Latin as the single option. The school lived by the motto "Teach me goodness, discipline, and health," with the accent squarely on discipline. "The object of discipline," the school calendar warned, "is to aid the student to acquire habits of regularity, promptness and intelligent obedience, as well as to develop a high moral sense and a taste for propriety." Despite its religious trappings, St. Thomas leaned towards the military style.

Each morning at precisely 6:30 a school bell rousted Brian out of bed and gave him exactly half an hour to dress, use the washroom, make his bed, and get to chapel for morning prayers. At 7:40 he lined up for breakfast. Talking was forbidden until grace was said, and then students could talk only until 8:00, when the bell silenced them again. Then they filed quietly outside for recreation, where conversation resumed. At 8:15 Brian had to button his lip once more for a compulsory study session, the first of several in the day. For forty-five minutes he and his classmates sat at long rows of desks in a large study hall, staring at their textbooks and silently working on assignments. Classes followed from 9:00 to noon. Then came lunch and a brief half-hour of free time, followed by more classes from 1:30 to 3:30. Sports followed. Then another study session started at 5:00, and supper was served at 6:00. He had more supervised study from 8:30 to 9:00 and then went promptly and quietly to bed.

Weekends were mostly free, but there wasn't much to do in Chatham. Like Baie Comeau it was a one-industry town; in this case the industry was the air force base nearby. On Saturday the college football or hockey team might be playing. In winter there was ice skating. Otherwise Mulroney and his friends often went downtown and hung around the MicMac Restaurant, where they ordered Coke and talked for hours. It was about the only place to meet girls from the girls' school down the hill.

Brian never complained about life at St. Thomas; in fact, he adapted well to the school. The priests demanded discipline, but the regimen was not unusual in the 1950s. The place was strict but also fair, and on occasion even compassionate. It routinely waived fees for students who could not pay, a practice that later almost caused it to fold. Rescue came from the provincial government, which incorporated the college section into the University of New Brunswick.

At fourteen, Brian was under-age for Grade 11, where the norm was fifteen or sixteen, and he was still short for his age. And for the first time in his life he was away from home and living among strangers. But if he could make friends with the gang on Laval Street and thrive as a member of a minority in Baie Comeau, he could survive at St. Thomas. It also helped that he arrived along with a couple of friends from home — Andy Morrow, David Goodine, and Frank Buggie. Tom Buggie came the following year.

As a new boy Mulroney never hung his head or looked the other way when fellow students passed by in the hall. He was quick to say hello, just as he had done back in Baie Comeau. In a group, he had a knack for projecting his presence that overcame his shortness and youth. He talked constantly and confidently; students could not help but notice his smoothness. He could sweet-talk almost anyone, including teachers. Whenever things got a little dicey or the prospect of conflict loomed, Brian was the one to defuse the crisis with comforting assurances. He was a natural conciliator. His classmates soon realized that they were watching a charmer.

In class Brian got good marks, and he worked at least as hard as the other students. When he entered Grade 11 he had to choose between math and Latin. He chose the latter, although unlike the rest of his class he had taken no Latin before. Catching up turned out to be tougher than he thought, but not insurmountable. Nothing was insurmountable. Brian turned to one of his fellow students — Michael Nowlan, one of the top Latin students — and asked for help with his verb tenses. With Nowlan's tutoring, Mulroney recovered lost ground and went on from there, eventually to the head of his class. When he graduated from St. Thomas in 1955 he was awarded the Reverend B.F. McMahon Prize as top student in Latin.

With high school over, Brian had to decide what to do next, but he now knew that Baie Comeau would not figure in his future. He was not going back to work in the mill, and Baie Comeau offered not much else. The next step was university, that much was decided, but the question again was where to go and how to pay for it. Student loans had not yet been invented in Canada, and the Mulroney household budget was tight. Not all of the Mulroney children could be sent to university. Olive, the oldest, was bright, and Peggy, the next-oldest, needed university to become a teacher. Doreen, three years younger than Brian, was gifted, even brilliant. But Brian was the chosen one. He would go to university and Doreen, when the time came, would settle for nursing school.

As with high school, the Mulroneys had few options in selecting a university. Brian could stay at St. Thomas and join about twenty other freshmen in the first-year post-secondary program, but the college offered a painfully limited curriculum. Ben Mulroney wanted a first-class education for his son. An obvious choice lay in Montreal at Loyola College, an English-Catholic university with Jesuit roots, or maybe the prestigious but non-religious McGill University. Both these alternatives were beyond their means.

The Mulroneys finally settled on St. Francis Xavier University in Antigonish, Nova Scotia. It was a working-class Catholic university, yet it enjoyed a prominent name and a good reputation. A full year of St. FX, as it was popularly known, would cost $680, including room, board, tuition, and medical and student union fees. Textbooks, at $3.95 each, would bring the sum to about $700. It would not be easy, but Ben Mulroney would manage somehow.

CHAPTER TWO

AN INTRODUCTION TO POLITICS

Brian Mulroney arrived on the St. Francis Xavier campus in September 1955, proudly wearing his green, gold-crested St. Thomas jacket and brimming over with excitement. He looked completely out of place. He was only sixteen, and his fresh, boyish face and tightly cropped brushcut made him seem even younger. Brushcuts were popular with many boys in 1955 but his stood out. Instead of going flat like a normal brushcut, it followed every contour on the top of his head. He had hardly grown since St. Thomas and was still short for his age, which only underscored his youthfulness. His clothes looked as if they came from the boys' department.

Arriving at St. Thomas two years earlier with several buddies from Baie Comeau had been different. Including part-timers and women from nearby Mount St. Bernard, the affiliated women's college, St. FX had a thousand students, small by most university standards but huge compared with boarding school. Mulroney knew not a soul.

St. FX had opened as a seminary in 1853 and gained full university status in 1866. It had achieved its renown in the 1920s and 1930s when the Extension Department, under the direction of Father Moses Coady, brought the gospel of self-help to the depressed Maritimes and thereby founded the Antigonish Movement, which encouraged local groups to seek social and economic self-improvement. Organizers visited communities, held public meetings, created study clubs, and taught local citizens how to organize and run their own cooperatives and credit unions. The Antigonish Movement spread across the Maritimes and later into the Third World. By the time Mulroney arrived on the scene, the university was teaching courses on the Antigonish method to educators from around the world. Father Coady, now retired and in his mid-seventies, and much decorated with awards and honorary degrees, appeared occasionally on campus, strolling the square with a cane. Like Father Coady, Antigonishism had grown old and had lost its activist thrust.

But there was much St. FX had not lost, especially its religious diligence. The place was only slightly more tolerant and progressive than St. Thomas. It was still run by priests, as it had been since its founding, and students were expected to appear at Mass at 7:00 every morning and again at chapel for fifteen minutes of prayer before dinner. Once a year the entire student body attended a three-day religious retreat during which they could not speak and spent hours listening to a fire-breathing preacher who tried to scare them witless. Students who arrived in the fall with a car were required to turn in their keys for the term. Liquor was forbidden on or off campus. St. FX got some cosmopolitan flavouring from the two dozen or so students who had come from around the globe to study the co-op movement, plus a handful of Americans, mostly from Maine and Massachusetts, who arrived in their khaki outfits for a cheap education. But most of the students came from Canadian working-class backgrounds and, like Mulroney, lived in dormitories on campus.

As a freshman, Mulroney was assigned to MacPherson House. That first day when he located his room and opened the door he discovered a compact rectangular space with two army-type metal cots, a double desk with a partition down the centre, and a tiny closet. Still, compared with the bunk-bed barracks at St. Thomas, it was a veritable suite.

The main student residence was a monolithic block divided into four areas called houses, each containing twenty-five double rooms. Each house was identical, with identical floor plans and identical furnishings. Women were forbidden from setting foot inside. Each house had a live-in priest and several student prefects. Lights went out at 11:00 sharp; only the washrooms remained lit. When final exams came around each year, the bathrooms became almost impassable as students, textbooks in hand, occupied every square inch, blocking the paths of those in urgent need.

After dumping his luggage at his room Mulroney wandered off in the direction of Morrison Hall, the main dining room and one of the chief gathering points on campus. He paid no more attention to the social traditions of St. FX than he had to the cultural boundaries of Baie Comeau. He was excited and impatient, itching to make friends, and protocol would not get in his way. He reached the footpath in front of MacPherson House and flagged down the first passing student.

"Hi," he beamed, "I'm Brian Mulroney."

The ambush caught the unsuspecting student off guard. Mulroney's action had breached custom — here was a mere freshman, a kid at that, acting chummy with a senior student.

The previous year St. FX had banned the annual ritual of hazing, the initiation rite that compelled freshmen to wear funny clothing, act as servants for upper classmen, and endure a hundred silly pranks during the first week of classes. Hazing had gotten out of hand, but the university could not prevent the returning students from ignoring or even ostracizing new arrivals. A gulf still separated upper classmen from the scruff, as freshmen were called.

Mulroney's target was no ordinary senior. He turned out to be Pat MacAdam, the editor-in-chief of the *Xaverian Weekly*, the campus newspaper. MacAdam was momentarily taken aback, but he did not take offence at Mulroney's audacity. The son of a Glace Bay coal miner, MacAdam had worked for a year to scrape together the money to get to college, and he was not the kind to stand on ceremony. Amused, he stopped and talked. What surprised MacAdam was not Mulroney's boldness, but his voice. It was very deep and it positively resonated. MacAdam could not believe that someone so small could produce such a sound. Nor could he believe someone so young could be so poised and confident. He soon came to like this cocky little guy.

MacAdam had been heading to Morrison Hall for lunch, and Mulroney accompanied him. When they arrived MacAdam made his way to the second floor at the front, where he took his position at the head table alongside the student union president and other campus big shots. As a freshman Mulroney was consigned to one of the first-floor tables in the corner by the doorway. Morrison Hall was no modern cafeteria, but a huge, old-fashioned two-storey dining room crammed with heavy Formica tables on metal pedestals. The place fed just about everybody on campus in one sitting, three times a day. While people took their places, student waiters carried tin trays from the kitchen and plunked down bowls and dishes. Then Bobby Higgins, the student union president, signed on to the PA system and delivered the benediction: "Blessed O Lord, for these thy gifts, which from thy bounty we are about to receive, through Christ Our Lord. Amen. Let's eat."

Each table seated eight students who divided the food among themselves. Mulroney, like other freshmen, had picked his table more or less randomly, but it automatically became his spot for the rest of the year. It turned out that half his tablemates came from New Brunswick and he lost no time touting his own New Brunswick connection through St. Thomas. There was Gordie Weeks, "the Duke," from Moncton, Sam Wakim, Mike Jennings, and Brian McGoughty. The others at the table were Red MacGillivray and Cliff Marchand, both from Nova Scotia, and Gene Neury from the Caribbean. Mulroney befriended them all but hit it off best with

Wakim from Saint John, a swarthy, bushy-browed young man of Lebanese ancestry.

Mulroney and Wakim were unlikely companions; on the surface they had little in common. Mulroney was smooth, self-assured, and articulate. Wakim was physically awkward and prone to malapropisms, the target of much ribbing. He couldn't catch a football and once referred to squid tentacles as "testicles." Mulroney was a commerce student, enrolled in general arts, while Wakim was taking science, because his mother wanted him to be a doctor. But there were deeper similarities. Wakim always wore a smile, loved to laugh, and loved repartee, as did Mulroney. Like Mulroney, Wakim had grown up in a big working-class family and had chosen St. FX because it was Catholic and affordable. They became best friends.

The Mulroney-Wakim table got along famously from that very first day, and in the weeks that followed they debated everything under the sun. No topic sparked more discussion and argument than politics. Each September the campus political clubs launched drives to recruit new members. The big three parties — the Liberals, Conservatives, and CCF (the forerunner of the NDP) — plus a fourth, the anti-monarchist National Republic Party, plastered the campus with posters and filled the Morrison Hall PA system with announcements. One of the parties would form a government in the St. FX Model Parliament to be elected in November. The student parliament sat only one day a year, not until well after Christmas, but the election that fall was the rage on campus. Mid-fifties college life went wild during the campaign. It had nothing to do with the student council, the only real student power on campus. Model Parliament imitated every detail of the federal parliament in Ottawa, right down to the carrying of the ceremonial mace.

Mulroney was determined to make his mark on campus in some fashion and concluded that the route for him was not through sports. He played hockey well enough to excel in intramural games, but he never even tried to make the varsity team. However, at St. FX politics rated almost as highly as athletics and was just as competitive. Mulroney set his sights on one of the thirty-three seats in Model Parliament. Given the number of candidates, it would take extraordinary effort to land one, but Mulroney believed he could do anything he set his mind to.

The first step was to join one of the political parties, but the choice was not obvious. Prior to St. FX, Mulroney had given politics no more thought than the average teenager. Elections had always placed the good citizens of Baie Comeau in an awkward position. They were caught between two feuding and unforgiving political machines, the Union Nationale and the Liberal Party. The mill in Baie Comeau had a cosy alliance with the Union Nationale, which did not hesitate to punish areas that voted Liberal, and made it clear its employees were expected to vote accordingly in provincial contests. But the Union Nationale was not on the federal ballot. When a federal election rolled around, the townspeople quietly switched to the Liberals. This juggling of loyalties meant that the people of Baie Comeau did not discuss politics much on the streets or in the coffee shops.

Given the discrimination that had held back his father, Mulroney should have been drawn to the CCF, but in fact he never gave it a moment's thought. The CCF may have spoken to his labour roots, but it did not represent his aspirations; he did not plan on remaining in the working class very long. Besides, the CCF regularly slammed big corporations and showed tinges of anti-Americanism; Mulroney, coming from the paternalistic world of Colonel McCormick, thought big corporations were just fine and regarded the United States as the ideal neighbour. Moreover, the CCF was stodgy and ideological. Mulroney wanted excitement rather than political doctrine.

Equally unappealing was the anti-monarchist National Republic Party, which operated on the political fringe and showed more interest in spoofing the system than winning elections. The unconventional NRP was not the place for someone who wanted to join the establishment. Besides, the party could be counted on to win only a few seats, and the purpose of the exercise was to get into Parliament, not to make a point.

That left the Liberals and the Progressive Conservatives. Intuitively Mulroney leaned to the Liberals; they seemed the natural choice for a Catholic from Baie Comeau. The Tories had been virtually extinct in Quebec since being merged with the Union Nationale by Maurice Duplessis in 1935. Mulroney knew little about the Tories, and what he knew he did not like. In his mind Conservatives were Protestants; Mulroney, a staunch Catholic, believed that Protestants had historically oppressed the Catholics. Tories were just fat-cat WASPs from Toronto.

In addition Mulroney tilted towards the Liberals because of family tradition. His father had voted Liberal in every federal election he could remember. Mulroney was superficially familiar with the Liberal Party, felt comfortable with it, and seemed temperamentally suited to it. The St. FX Liberal Party had no overt ideology; neither did he. He came from a lower-middle-class background and associated Liberals with ordinary people.

Mulroney was not the only freshman who gravitated towards the Liberals. Career-minded students knew that joining the Liberal Party meant joining the mainstream and, ultimately, the government pipeline. The Liberal Party dominated the campus and was entrenched across the province of Nova Scotia. Sections of the Maritimes resembled the old American South: people belonged to a party because their parents had, and ridings almost always voted the same way, so winning the right nomination meant winning the election. In 1955, everywhere he looked, Mulroney saw nothing but Liberals. Ottawa had been Liberal for the last twenty-one years, Nova Scotia for the past twenty-two years, and St. FX for as long as it had played at party politics.

St. FX had held its first Model Parliament election in 1948. The Liberal Party had won it handily, and had won every election since. The seats were allocated by a proportional system. If a party won one-third of the vote, it took one-third of the seats. The party leaders arbitrarily chose the lucky club members to fill their party's allotment of seats. Since the Liberals always won the biggest share of the vote and formed the government, they always had the largest number of seats to distribute among their members. Overall, Mulroney's best shot lay with the Liberals, and joining the Liberal Party would be a mere formality. In nine years out of ten he would have done exactly that. But 1955 was different. Two factors that fall prevented Mulroney's rendezvous with the Liberals.

To the astonishment of everyone on campus, the wheels had suddenly come off the magnificent Liberal machine. That year the party elected as its leader Danny MacLennan, a small, abrasive Cape Bretoner, the proverbial outsider. The election of MacLennan riled the party's old guard, who quickly ousted him on the pretext that he was running the party like a private clique. MacLennan, no quitter, mounted a counter-coup and a week later regained power at a stormy meeting, polarizing the party between Cape Bretoners and mainland Nova Scotians. The Liberals' civil war became the talk of the campus, and the other political parties could not suppress their glee over this public disembowelment, nor did they hesitate to exploit it for partisan gain. In a matter of weeks the Liberal Party was reduced to a shell. It was no time to join the Grits.

There was also the Wakim factor. Mulroney's tablemate and new friend Sam Wakim shared more with him than a gift for repartee. Both were fascinated by politics, Wakim even more so than Mulroney. Wakim was already a certifiable political junkie who had first worked as a volunteer in the 1953 federal election, before he was old enough to hold a driver's licence. As a working-class Catholic from New Brunswick, Wakim should have been a Liberal; instead, he was a thoroughly committed Tory. In fact Wakim's whole family was Tory, which defied Mulroney's stereotyped image of the Conservatives as rich Protestants from Ontario.

Early that fall Wakim invited Mulroney to a meeting of the campus PC club and got him thinking about joining the Tories. Some of the eggheads on campus formed political affiliations on the basis of issues. Mulroney, only sixteen and impressionable, saw the world in terms of friendships and personalities rather than philosophies and ideas. So if he chose the campus Tories he would really be opting for his friendship with Sam Wakim and for a small club that readily accepted him. Moreover it looked like they had a real shot at winning more seats than ever before.

Before the Liberal infighting, the Tories had been perennial also-rans in campus elections. Two years earlier they had even fallen into third spot behind the NRP. At that point, Lowell Murray, an arts student from Cape Breton, took over, only to see the party tumble further in the 1954 election into fourth and last place, with only three seats, behind both the NRP and the CCF. However, Murray had stayed on for another year, and by the time Mulroney arrived on campus he had emerged as an exceptional leader. Murray possessed an authority beyond his years, and he seemed able to rise above the fray. On campus he was widely respected and admired even by his opponents. Now, while the Liberals were tearing themselves apart, the Tories, led by Murray, were finally marching forward.

A few weeks before the Model Parliament elections, Mulroney spotted Murray crossing the campus square and raced over to stop him. The eager freshman announced that he wanted to join the Tory club and would help out any way he could. As leader of a political underdog, Murray did not question offers of support, especially those proffered with such enthusiasm. He welcomed Mulroney to the party and gave him his first assignment on the spot: to canvass first-year students for the upcoming election. Mulroney started that afternoon.

Mulroney took his political duties seriously and discovered right away that he loved campaigning. It made him feel important and gave him a kick. Mulroney had always gone out of his way to meet people and win friendships, and canvassing was merely an extension of something he had been doing all his life. He proved to be exceptionally good at it.

Soon he knew every freshman on campus and was better known

himself than most seniors. Whenever he ran into someone he knew, he turned his full charm onto him. He started with an irresistible "Hi, how are you?" and followed it with chatty conversation, making his new friend feel like the only person in the world who mattered. Mulroney threw himself into every passing relationship. Occasionally he overreached and ruffled a few feathers — he could come across as a squirt with a motor mouth — but that did not happen often. He was too good. Politics was people, and campaigning was making friends along the way.

The federal parties in Ottawa wanted to win the Model Parliament elections almost as badly as the students. The elections revealed political trends on Canadian campuses and were the public opinion polls of their day. All parties kept score and touted their victories. Since electoral prospects for the St. FX Tories were better than ever, Murray pulled out all the stops with a razzle-dazzle campaign that featured posters, a rally, a one-float parade, and a two-man band. In the days leading up to the election a loud-hailer mounted in a residence window constantly proclaimed the virtues of voting Conservative. But despite these efforts and Mulroney's tireless canvassing, most people assumed the Liberals would hang on to win.

The polls opened at 9:00 A.M. on November 28 and closed at 4:30. Over dinner in Morrison Hall that evening the student body listened to the stunning results: Tories 13 seats, Liberals 11, NRP 5, and CCF 4. In one year the Conservatives had gone from last place to first and for the first time had beaten the Liberals. Murray, the newly designated prime minister, declared the victory the greatest day in the history of St. FX student politics and immediately announced the appointment of four ambassadors. In fact, the Tories had squeaked in with a minority victory, one so thin that a switch of fewer than two dozen votes would have locked the Liberals and Conservatives in a tie. Voter turnout had dropped to 76.6 per cent, the lowest in campus history, a development the *Xaverian Weekly* attributed to abstentions from disgruntled Liberals. Most students felt that the results would have been different had popular Bobby Higgins been

Liberal leader. But whatever the reason, it was a great day for the Conservatives.

With the election over, Murray had to pick the twelve Tories to join him as members of Parliament. Selecting a caucus was any leader's toughest task, and Murray found it no different. After faithfully sticking with the party through the lean years, senior club members expected to be rewarded. Six or seven dozen party stalwarts wanted a seat, including a number of other upper classmen. Freshmen would have to wait their turn in future years. However, Mulroney had campaigned like nobody else. He could take credit for having moved votes. In addition, he had tagged along with Murray during the campaign, proving extremely capable and becoming a de facto executive assistant. To the surprise of many, when Murray presented his caucus list, Mulroney's name was on it. Mulroney was elated.

Things remained quiet on the political front until after the Christmas break, when the Students' Political Association, the organization that ran Model Parliament, met to iron out some administrative details before the upcoming session. Everybody expected the February 1 meeting to be short and uneventful. Murray had business off campus and did not attend, sending party whip Paul Creaghan in his place. The event started quietly and seemed to be unfolding as expected, until Gerry Campbell of the CCF announced that the coming session needed some fireworks to give it flavour. He was followed by Steve Berry of the Liberals, who inquired about the "pyrotechnic" quality of Creaghan — in other words, how vulnerable he was to a coup d'état.

With mounting consternation Creaghan realized that the Liberals, the CCF, and the NRP planned to overthrow the Tory government on the spot, a month before Parliament was due to convene. Spokesmen from all three parties in the anti-Tory coalition claimed they should not have to wait for Parliament on March 3 to be recognized as a government, since their alliance already outnumbered the Tories twenty to thirteen. The coalition put forward Dan MacLennan, the controversial Liberal leader, as prime minister. At this, Creaghan jumped to his feet hollering "Unconstitutional" and "Out of order," but he was shouted down.

In the end the SPA sided with the Tories, but the opposition coalition refused to accept the verdict. For the next week the political crisis played itself out as Murray and MacLennan wrestled for the right to be called prime minister. The dispute came to a head when MacLennan and his coalition partners appealed to the SPA's executive council. With a crowd of spectators packing the room, the coalition contended the Tories should not be recognized as the government because they could not possibly conduct a Parliament with a minority of seats. Murray countered that the people had spoken and had chosen a government. He argued that the Tories could be unseated only by a vote of non-confidence on the floor of the House of Commons. After wringing its hands the SPA supported Murray, but the coalition remained rebellious, threatening to impeach the SPA president and even walk out of Parliament. Ultimately the Governor General — Bobby Higgins, the popular Liberal — ruled in Murray's favour. After much cajoling, the opposition sullenly accepted the decision while vowing to overthrow the Murray government the moment Parliament met.

Once confirmed as prime minister, Murray named his cabinet ministers. He did so with diplomacy, taking care not to bruise egos. Although everybody in the caucus made the cabinet, the plum posts such as External Affairs and Finance went to respected elders. Mulroney, as the lone freshman, became minister of fisheries. "If the sawdust triplets wish to conduct an orthodox Parliament," Murray announced as he unveiled his cabinet, "we have appointed cabinet members of sufficiently high ability to make the opposition look like a gang of sixth-rate nincompoops. If, on the other hand, the 'majority' coalition attempts to hold a Parliament more in accordance with their own propensities, we have a sufficient number of cutthroats to slay them on the spot."

The opening of Model Parliament in Immaculata Hall, the women's residence at nearby Mount St. Bernard College, was always a major campus event. Students donned their best jackets and ties and many of the faculty came to watch. The make-believe MPs sat opposite one another behind long tables, and spectators watched from a bleacher above while Governor General Higgins, in red tunic and busby, ceremonially arrived to read the throne speech.

Lowell Murray prepared a throne speech that he had boasted in advance was wholly original, not lifted out of Hansard as his Liberal predecessors had done in years past, but the packed galleries paid scant attention to its content. Everybody was waiting for the fireworks after the speech. The only issue on Parliament's mind was how long Murray's government would survive.

Opposition leader MacLennan led off the debate on the throne speech by moving a motion of non-confidence. His motion was supported by several speeches from the opposition benches, then the House divided for a formal vote. To no one's surprise, the Murray government went down to defeat. As a junior minister, Mulroney could only sit in the background and watch as his brief parliamentary tenure as a cabinet minister came to an abrupt end, without even the opportunity to speak. With the defeat of the government, Parliament adjourned briefly. When it reconvened the Tories were back on the opposition side. Mulroney had received his baptism in hardball politics.

CHAPTER THREE

THE CHIEF

O N APRIL 26, 1956, the St. FX Conservative Party gathered for the last time during Brian Mulroney's first year at university. The party had one piece of business on its agenda: Lowell Murray was graduating, and that meant the party had to elect a new leader. The Tories met in the Old Assembly Hall, where all the clubs conducted their business. The hall had acquired a nickname — "the Railroad Station" — because everything that happened inside its walls seemed the result of a brokered deal. No matter the club or the issue, the winning candidates always seemed to be railroaded through. True to tradition, the Tories selected Paul Creaghan as their new leader.

Creaghan was a commerce student from Moncton, and a Tory stalwart in the last two Model Parliaments. A straight-A student, he easily surpassed student politicians from all parties in raw intellect and was among the two or three top academic achievers in the entire student body. He also participated in virtually every extracurricular activity on campus. On paper Creaghan was the perfect leader; in reality, he was a disappointment after Murray, and a potential disaster for the Tories.

In the parlance of the day, Creaghan was an egghead. He telegraphed an earnest intellectualism that was altogether wrong for the Conservative Party on campus, an image that jeopardized the hard-won gains the party had made in broadening its base under Murray. Creaghan was barely nineteen but already wore the mien of an old-line Tory: stodgy, wooden, and instinctively cautious. His persona hurt him on the stump, but his problems went deeper than that. He came from a well-to-do merchant family in Moncton, and students, fairly or not, dismissed him as a rich boy. He was tagged with the fat-cat label, and his personality simply confirmed the prejudice. The Conservative Party did not need such a leader when it had hopes of outpolling the Liberals again.

Later the Liberal Party chose Russ Pellerin as its leader. Under his direction the club's rival factions settled their differences and the Liberals soon recovered their smug confidence. The CCF was on the march as well. It was about to correct its lacklustre style with an energetic new leader, Leo Nimsick, the son of a British Columbia MLA. The two other main parties were moving forward while the Tories seemed to be stalled.

Mulroney returned to campus in the fall of 1956, now a sophomore with a measure of seniority. At the first Conservative club meeting of the year he was elected party whip, a fitting promotion for a rising star, and one that augured well for his political future. Being party whip placed him in the thick of operations (not that he had ever languished on the periphery), secure in his position by virtue of his post. He no longer owed his status to an ability to hang onto the leader's coat-tails. Furthermore, party whips made strong leadership contenders, as Paul Creaghan well knew, since Creaghan had served as whip the previous year.

Classes were nicely under way when Henry Hicks, the Liberal premier of Nova Scotia, dissolved the provincial legislature and called an election for October 30, creating headaches for all the political clubs. The province-wide campaign would overlap with St. FX's preparations for Model Parliament, drawing the leading activists off campus just as the student campaign was getting started. The Students' Political Association decided to shorten the time usually allowed for the Model Parliament campaign. It was good news for Mulroney. He had accompanied Lowell Murray to the local PC constituency meeting the previous March and had watched Bill

MacKinnon win the nomination as PC candidate for Antigonish. Ever since, he had been eager for the Nova Scotia campaign to begin.

No sooner had Premier Hicks called the election than Mulroney headed over to the Tory campaign headquarters on Main Street to volunteer his help. Gillis Brown, the campaign manager, was delighted to accept it. The Conservative Party in Antigonish had never before received any support from St. FX; local Tories knew the campus was a Liberal stronghold and had traditionally written it off as a lost cause. Mulroney confidently told Brown that Tory votes were to be had at St. FX, and he offered to organize the effort. Brown was pleased that something might be done, but he did not hold out much hope, nor did he expect much of a campaign from Mulroney. He soon learned otherwise. Mulroney rounded up a handful of student volunteers to work for Bill MacKinnon. He checked into the Main Street headquarters every day, after class or in the evening, and tackled every assignment cheerfully and tirelessly. He took the initiative and hardly had to be told what to do. Tory headquarters was kept busy keeping Mulroney busy.

Mulroney's deep voice and mellifluous delivery won him the role of narrator for MacKinnon's radio commercials. Ironically, the candidate he was touting was himself a radio announcer at CJFX and a popular celebrity. That fact should have made him a contender, but MacKinnon was challenging the Liberals in one of the safest Liberal seats in all Nova Scotia. Antigonish had voted Liberal for forty years; it was represented in the legislature by a cabinet minister. MacKinnon's chances were slim, but the odds did not daunt Mulroney. Election campaigns were driven by partisanship, zeal, and hard work, and Mulroney displayed plenty of all three. He predicted that on October 30 Bill MacKinnon would teach everyone a lesson about politics.

As it happened, the Conservative Party itself scored an historic upset. Tory leader Robert Stanfield won a majority of seats across the province and put an end to twenty-three years of Liberal rule. The campus vote at St. FX remained loyal to the Liberal Party, but as

Mulroney had predicted, MacKinnon captured Antigonish. Jubilant supporters marched through the streets of the riding in triumphant procession while cars and trucks blared their horns to mark the new era. Mulroney celebrated the biggest victory of his young political life.

Even before the polls closed, he had left a note at headquarters advising officials that his St. FX volunteers would be dropping in that night to watch the vote returns, and asking that they be given "anything they want." In other words, supply them with booze. Mulroney was playing the role of party boss, generously rewarding his followers, and liquor was real booty. Not only was drinking strictly forbidden at St. FX, on or off campus, but offenders were punished harshly. The penalty for a first offence was an official letter to the culprit's parents. A second violation meant expulsion for the rest of the semester. Students who bought a quart at the local liquor store risked an encounter with Father O'Keefe, who was known to patrol the area in his Oldsmobile, hunting violators. Mulroney had suffered the disgrace of a letter to his parents but was never caught a second time. However, Tory headquarters was safe ground. On election night the booze was plentiful and Mulroney's troops joined whole-heartedly in the victory celebration.

After the exhilaration of the provincial election, the St. FX campaign for Model Parliament was anti-climactic. Mulroney might have been forgiven for letting up, but an election was an election. He believed the Tory party could repeat on campus what it had accomplished across the province, and he was no less aggressive in his efforts. Unfortunately, the rejuvenated Liberals returned to form, and Creaghan, so able in other ways, lacked Lowell Murray's standing as a leader. The Liberals scored their biggest victory in the history of St. FX Model Parliaments and for the first time captured an absolute majority of seats, an unheard-of achievement under the proportional electoral system of a Model Parliament. In a single year, the St. FX Tories had been both triumphant victors and shell-shocked losers.

Pretend politics did not provide the only outlet for Mulroney's developing oratorical skills. Every Sunday St. FX held a public speaking contest.

Sundays were slow on campus. The morning began with a compulsory late Mass followed by a brunch of French toast and bacon at Morrison Hall. Afterwards there was time to relax. Some students lingered in the dining hall over casual conversation, others wandered off in different directions, and others still headed to the Old Assembly Hall.

The speaking contest held there was the Sunday-morning equivalent of amateur talent night. Participants enjoyed the opportunity to strut their oratorical stuff. Each contestant spoke for two or three minutes on a subject of his choice, and a panel of judges picked a winner. Once a year the debating society held a major oratorical competition. Anyone could enter the Oratorical Contest merely by showing up with a ten-minute speech on any topic. The winner walked away with $10, and second- and third-place finishers picked up $5 and $2.50 respectively, significant pocket money in 1956. But the real first prize was almost certain membership in the intercollegiate debating team: the top six debaters on campus won the honour of representing St. FX against other universities across the Maritimes. Mulroney had been debating at the inter-class level all through his freshman year, and loved it. The previous spring, in April 1956, he had been elected secretary-treasurer of the debating society. Save politics, no other extracurricular activity meant as much to him, and he dearly wanted to make the debating team.

After brunch on the morning of October 21, Mulroney presented himself at the Old Assembly Hall as a contestant in the Oratorical Contest. When his turn came, he strode purposefully to the small lectern and launched a thundering attack against the corrupt political machine in Quebec. For ten minutes he blasted the government of Premier Maurice Duplessis and the Union Nationale party, declaring that Quebec politics needed a thorough house-cleaning. The message was flawlessly delivered, without hesitation or slips. The audience was transfixed by the confidence, poise, and conviction of the seventeen-year-old sophomore. Other contestants followed

Mulroney, including Gerry Doucet, the previous year's winner in a field of twenty candidates, but the outcome was known long before the judges formally crowned Mulroney the winner.

Only one question was left unanswered about Mulroney's dazzling performance: What would Brother Bert think? Bert Lavoie was one of his political confidants, a co-worker on Bill MacKinnon's campaign, and a close friend. Together they had smuggled booze onto the campus more than once. Mulroney called him "Brother Bert," and it was Lavoie who first tagged the skinny Mulroney with the nickname "Brother Bones," or just plain "Bones," a moniker that would stick for life. Brother Bert was a portly Quebecker and a classic pork-barreller who carried a paid-up membership card in the Union Nationale. He devoted his summers to the party, working as an organizer, and he personally admired Maurice Duplessis, so much that he would later miss school for his funeral. Lavoie was bound to find out about Mulroney's ringing denunciation of the Union Nationale; it was reported in the *Xaverian Weekly* and widely discussed. No one could explain how Mulroney stickhandled his way around this complication, but somehow he did; his friendship with Lavoie did not skip a beat.

As expected, Mulroney made the intercollegiate team. But oratorical contests were one thing and debates another, as Mulroney knew from his experience in inter-class contests. Debating required him to think on his feet and rise to rebuttal in hopes of undermining the opponent; he had already proven himself capable at both.

The debate format was made to order for Mulroney, a naturally polished speaker who used the English language well and was never at a loss for words. He could sense opportunities and pounce with lightning speed, all the while appearing relaxed and at ease, an advantage in rebuttal. He possessed a quick wit and knew how to perform on stage, which helped him through weak moments. Perhaps his greatest gift was his voice. That deep timbre coated his words like rich cream and was unforgettable to those who heard it.

Above all he showed extraordinary self-confidence. Most teenagers dread the prospect of public speaking, of being scrutinized by every eye in the room. Mulroney welcomed it. He seemed to crave recognition and to know instinctively how to attract it. He stood on stage assured and unruffled, his composure hinting at arrogance, never doubting that he had the right stuff.

By virtue of making the intercollegiate debating team, Mulroney was now one of the top six debaters on campus, but no one, not even Mulroney himself, placed him at the very top. That position undeniably belonged to Rick Cashin, an arts student from Newfoundland and a true crowd-pleaser in the mould of the stereotypical Irish orator. The histrionics of a Cashin oration were something to behold. His stemwinders, filled with fire and poetic turns of phrase, made him perhaps the best orator St. FX had ever seen. Cashin and Mulroney were on good speaking terms and were friends of sorts, but they were also rivals, whether they were competing in Model Parliament or auditioning for roles in theatrical productions. That rivalry dominated their relationship.

The two could hardly have been more different on stage. Mulroney was logical, self-possessed, pragmatic, and dispassionate. He liked to work out sensible arguments in advance and deploy them deftly, always looking to score debating points. Despite his skills as an extemporaneous speaker, Mulroney came well prepared; often he would appear to be winging it when in fact he had carefully planned his remarks in advance.

Cashin, on the other hand, was a romantic who advocated causes at full throttle, arms flailing and voice swelling. Mulroney could spit fire too, but the conviction often seemed contrived rather than heartfelt. Cashin spoke for the little guy and the downtrodden; nobody could pin much of a philosophy onto Mulroney. Cashin had cast his fortunes with the hapless National Republic Party, a rump group that held ideals but little political strength and had no chance of winning. After it failed, he flirted with other fringe parties before reluctantly joining the Liberals. Fate had dropped Cashin into the wrong era: he should have been a student in the protesting sixties; instead, he was stuck in the staid and conformist fifties.

Whether by chance or evasion, Mulroney and Cashin never faced each other as contestants in a debating match. Mulroney took on all comers, yet somehow never went head to head with Cashin. Occasionally they joined the same small group up in the dormitory at night and talked politics, and sometimes their exchanges quickened into impromptu sparring. Mulroney, as good as he was, could not keep up with the passionate Newfoundlander.

St. FX hosted three intercollegiate debates a year. The six members of the debating squad were divided into three two-man teams, each team appearing in one debate in that school year. Mulroney's turn came up in the second debate of the season, a home encounter on December 2 when he and partner Charles Keating, a second-year engineering student from Dartmouth, argued the negative side of the resolution "That compulsory military training should be inaugurated in Canada." The debate held sentimental value for Mulroney: he was squaring off against a team from the college wing of his old high school, St. Thomas. It was an occasion that put him face to face with his past. Mulroney possessed an acute sense of his roots and an abiding awareness of his accomplishments; this was a perfect occasion to review where he had been and measure how far he had come. The exercise was reassuring.

Mulroney performed impressively against his old school, as did his partner Keating; together they scored a unanimous victory for St. FX. But Keating had outshone his teammate and outscored him with the judges. Consequently it was Keating who was picked for the select team that would participate in the upcoming McGill Winter Carnival Debating Conference in Montreal. However, another trip was in the offing, one that Mulroney coveted even more.

George Drew, the national leader of the Conservative Party and loser of the last two federal elections, had announced that he was stepping down for health reasons. The party would pick his successor in mid-December when more than thirteen hundred Tories would converge in Ottawa for the largest Tory convention in history. St. FX, like other campus clubs across Canada, could send two voting delegates at party expense.

Few of the Tory club members had been to Ottawa before; most had never travelled west of the Maritimes. A trip to Ottawa would be the highlight of their university careers. Creaghan, as club president, would go, of course, but who would accompany him? There were many deserving candidates. Pat MacAdam, who had graduated but returned for another year, was the senior Tory on campus, having loyally soldiered through the bad years. Gerry Doucet and Dave McKee also warranted recognition for their hard and faithful work, as did several others. Mulroney was in the running, but he was only a sophomore and a prize of this calibre had "upper classman" written all over it. Nonetheless, when the club meeting was called and the selection made, the triumphant winner was Mulroney.

For a seventeen-year-old comer with one foot planted firmly on the bottom rung of the party ladder, nothing could match a trip to the country's political Mecca for a national leadership convention. The youth delegates alone would number in the hundreds. Mulroney could hardly contain his excitement.

The leadership convention excited all Tories. It offered the hope of a fresh beginning for the snake-bitten party and an end to the straitjacket of permanent opposition. A new leader could arouse the nation and break the Liberals' indomitable grip on the country. Three Tory MPs offered themselves as saviours: John Diefenbaker, the sixty-one-year-old criminal lawyer from Prince Albert, who was already a national figure; Donald Fleming, the successful Toronto corporate lawyer who carried the blessing of the business world; and E. Davie Fulton, also a lawyer, a young former serviceman and Rhodes Scholar with the image of Mr. Clean. Mulroney perused the alternatives with Lowell Murray and gravitated naturally towards Fulton. The Kamloops MP was already one of his political heroes; he admired Fulton above any other politician, with the exception of

Robert Stanfield. The difference in philosophy between Fulton and his two rivals was a matter of shading, but Mulroney too wanted to be a lawyer, and he saw Fulton as the quintessential advocate, master of the logical argument. With Murray's encouragement, Mulroney went to Ottawa a Fulton supporter. (Murray had to pass up the trip. He was still convalescing from a broken pelvis suffered in a recent car accident. The driver, Pat MacAdam, had escaped with only a few bruises.)

A university that blacked out the campus each night at 11:00 did not allow students to be absent without permission, and Creaghan and Mulroney required a series of official approvals before they could board the train for Ottawa. But these were duly given, even though the trip meant missing classes. With transfers the journey lasted the best part of two days: Antigonish to Truro, Truro to Moncton, Moncton to Montreal, Montreal to Ottawa. Virtually all delegates arrived by train, and when the St. FX delegates stepped onto the platform in Ottawa they were greeted by arctic temperatures and mounds of snow.

Sniffing the political winds in the sub-zero capital, Mulroney quickly realized where the convention was heading: Diefenbaker had emerged as the most exciting figure in the contest and showed every sign of being unstoppable. Not only could Diefenbaker win, but he could do it on the first ballot, despite the fact that he was distrusted by the Toronto establishment that ruled the party and had been rejected twice previously, first in 1942 and again in 1948. The old guard had tried to block his third attempt, but the momentum had shifted Diefenbaker's way and now delegates were lining up behind him. The party was tired of losing and many believed that Diefenbaker could dislodge the Liberals. Even the reluctant old guard was beginning to accept political reality.

Diefenbaker's aura had enraptured the youth delegates in particular. The splashy show of student strength was orchestrated by the Youth for Diefenbaker organization, also known as Rogers' Raiders because of its chairman, Ted Rogers. Mulroney sought him out.

Rogers had never heard of Mulroney before, but he needed a volunteer to look after the Maritimes, and a quick appraisal told him Mulroney was his man. Rogers introduced Mulroney to David Walker, a senior strategist in the Diefenbaker hierarchy, who immediately proclaimed Mulroney vice-chairman of Youth for Diefenbaker. Within hours of arriving in Ottawa, he was sporting a Diefenbaker button and had forgotten Davie Fulton.

Everyone in the Youth for Diefenbaker organization outranked him in age and experience. Ted Rogers, the well-to-do son of Toronto broadcasting pioneer Edward Samuel Rogers, was seven years older and had been seasoned so long that people called him a veteran youth leader. His sidekick, Hal Jackman, was also seven years older, and already a law school graduate. Jackman was the son of a Toronto investment dealer who had made his fortune during the Depression. Mulroney was vice-chairman in title, but served more as a gofer. When something had to be done, Mulroney got up and did it, and usually he did more than was asked. Rogers had assigned him to organize the Maritime youth, and with his characteristic gusto, he tracked down every Maritime youth delegate on his list. He returned to Youth for Diefenbaker headquarters in the Château Laurier to volunteer for more duty. "What do I do next?" he asked. "Brian," Jackman quipped, "if you're really keen, why don't you go out and hang up more signs out in the Cow Palace." Jackman had not really meant it: the hour was late and the weather bone-chilling, but no matter. Mulroney dashed outside, boarded a bus down to the convention hall, and posted more signs. When he returned later to ask what else there was to do, Jackman could not believe it.

Mulroney had heard much about Diefenbaker, especially about his oratory, but he had never seen him on the stump and only now got a chance to watch him perform. What he saw stirred him up. Diefenbaker came on like an avenging angel, burning with more dynamism and inspiration than Mulroney had ever seen before. He worked an audience better than any English-speaking politician in Canada, except maybe Tommy Douglas, raising passions and winning followers wherever he spoke. Mulroney had never seen anybody eat Grits alive the way he did. Seeing Diefenbaker in action, piled on top of the general stimulation of the convention, swept Mulroney away. Although he joined the bandwagon late, he became a complete convert, a true believer. He had faith that Diefenbaker would smash the Liberals.

Diefenbaker's supporters worked the convention as if marching to the Hallelujah Chorus. Diefenbaker stood squarely for un-hyphenated Canadianism, a bill of rights, and unfettered patriotism. "I have but one love — Canada. I have but one purpose — its greatness. I have but one aim — unity from the Atlantic to the Pacific," he thundered. No other politician wore his heart on his sleeve like Diefenbaker, and no other politician could arouse an audience's fervour the way he could. Diefenbaker had lived the life of a political underdog, first as a defence lawyer who embraced formidable cases, then as a lonesome Tory in Liberal Saskatchewan, and finally as a leadership outsider who overcame the party élite. He represented the farmer, the fisherman, the veteran, the little guy. More pointedly, Diefenbaker did not represent Bay Street; in fact, he distrusted Bay Street and the whole Toronto crowd. Diefenbaker had small-town roots, just like Mulroney, but there was one funda-mental difference: Diefenbaker expected to challenge the establish-ment while his young devotee hoped to join it. And at that moment, Diefenbaker appeared to offer his best opportunity. The tantalizing prospect of Tories in power swept Mulroney off his feet.

Wherever Diefenbaker put in an appearance, on the convention floor or at the Château Laurier, Mulroney showed up to cheer him on. A photograph of Mulroney standing behind Diefenbaker in a throng of admirers was published in the *Ottawa Journal* that week. He had joined the entourage. And as he had done with Colonel McCormick back in Baie Comeau, Mulroney managed to attract the personal attention of Diefenbaker. Diefenbaker warmed to Mulroney and gave him his paternal blessing, as he did for many other young Tories, and posed beside him for a special photo. Dief liked young people and sought to identify with them, and nobody from the Youth for Diefenbaker organization showed as much enthusiasm and *esprit de corps* as Mulroney.

The convention had formally opened on Wednesday afternoon, and it was not long before word of Mulroney's support of Diefenbaker reached the ears of George Nowlan, the senior MP from Nova Scotia. On Thursday morning, the day before the vote, Nowlan summoned the Nova Scotia delegates to a closed-door session in the Château Laurier. Nowlan had been publicly toying with the idea of running for leader himself, but he was merely posturing for strategic purposes. Members of the Nova Scotia delegation were about 80 per cent in favour of Diefenbaker, but Nowlan disliked the prairie firebrand and wanted to slow his bandwagon. Nowlan and his close associates had arrived at the convention wearing huge buttons with the words "Nova Scotia," followed by a question mark, a not-so-subtle show of resistance to the tide. On Thursday morning in the Château Laurier, Nowlan counselled the Nova Scotia delegates to remain neutral in the hours leading up to the vote, and not to work for any particular candidate. The clear message was: Don't work for Diefenbaker.

Virtually every delegate from Nova Scotia heard the message. Mulroney and Creaghan were at the meeting, as were two delegates each from Acadia University, Dalhousie, King's College, St. Mary's, and Mount St. Vincent. Premier Robert Stanfield and almost the entire provincial caucus were there, along with the PC women's organization, a group of delegates at large, and the riding delegates themselves, in all between eighty and ninety individuals. Mulroney had arrived sporting a "Nova Scotia for Diefenbaker" button and was the obvious target of Nowlan's remarks. Mulroney could have removed the button, but Diefenbaker had become his hero, and Nowlan was behaving in an unfriendly manner. With no apparent hesitation, Mulroney rose in rebuttal. Mulroney noted that many Nova Scotians were working for specific candidates and, referring indirectly to Nowlan himself, alleged that some who were supposedly neutral were in fact working against Diefenbaker. He added that he was supporting Diefenbaker and would continue to do so publicly. Diefenbaker, he declared, would be the next prime minister of Canada. Then he sat down. Nowlan, one of the finest parliamentary debaters of his generation, simply let the matter drop. When the session broke up it was understood that delegates were free to go any way they wished, and most went straight to the Diefenbaker camp.

There was only one weak spot in the Diefenbaker campaign, and that was Quebec. Like those of other provinces, Quebec's delegates were ready to fall into line behind Diefenbaker, but they had to be courted. In formulating his convention strategy Diefenbaker had departed from the tradition of having a French-Canadian mover or seconder to his nomination: he picked New Brunswick premier Hugh John Flemming to nominate him and British Columbia MP George Pearkes to second the nomination.

Léon Balcer, the party president and one of only four Tory MPs from Quebec, accused Diefenbaker of sending the wrong message. An unsympathetic and stubborn Diefenbaker explained that he had chosen the two anglophones to symbolize support from the Atlantic to the Pacific. Several leading anglophone Tories, including Manitoba leader Duff Roblin and convention chairman Dick Bell, urged Diefenbaker to change his mind, but Diefenbaker refused to budge. Faced with this snub, Balcer and other Quebeckers moved to Donald Fleming.

The defection of Quebec gave Fleming an eleventh-hour boost but could not alter the outcome. On Friday afternoon, victory came on the first ballot: Diefenbaker, 774; Fleming, 393; Fulton, 117. While Fleming and Fulton were jointly raising arms with Diefenbaker on stage, the Quebec delegation, led by Balcer, quietly walked out. Their protest went largely unnoticed by the crowd cheering Diefenbaker's victory speech. "We have an appointment with destiny," he told them.

The walk-out attracted so little attention, and lasted so briefly, that it seemed insignificant at the time. Relations were soon mended, and

Balcer returned to the fold. Mulroney dismissed the spat as a misunderstanding and refused to allow it to dampen his delight with the outcome. He boarded the train back to Antigonish confident in the belief that the Liberal government was on its way out. Many others shared his belief.

Mulroney left Ottawa knowing more Tories than did many old-time party stalwarts. He networked non-stop from the moment he arrived, charming people everywhere he went. Rogers' Raiders had opened the Diefenbaker organization to him and introduced him to contacts from the West, the core of Diefenbaker's strength. At the same time he had consolidated his base in Nova Scotia, enlarged his circle of acquaintances across the Maritimes, strengthened his ties with Tories in Quebec, his home province, and made new friends in Ontario. In under four days he had met and exchanged pleasantries with perhaps five hundred individuals. Operating on only a few hours of sleep a night, he was exhausted by the hectic pace of the convention, but before leaving Ottawa he found the energy to make one last connection. Gary Quinn, a younger kid from Baie Comeau, was attending Ashbury College in Ottawa. Mulroney phoned Quinn at school, invited him over to the Château Laurier, and gave the fourteen-year-old a feel for the political big time. He had nothing to gain from this, at least in the immediate future. He was simply doing a favour for a friend of the family. Such acts seem to have always given him genuine pleasure.

Those who had met the junior delegate from St. FX invariably liked his chutzpah. Still, one person remained singularly uncharmed. Mulroney's raw ambition and unabashed aggressiveness left Paul Creaghan fuming. The circumspect Creaghan believed in proper behaviour and thought Mulroney had crassly overreached. Two years older, a year ahead in university, and a lot smarter, Creaghan seethed at the spectacle of Mulroney ingratiating himself with the party bosses, and he never forgave him.

There was no demand for a formal report back at St. FX, and there was no need. Mulroney had returned to declare that Diefenbaker

46

would sweep the next election. The convention and the new leader dominated his conversations; indeed, he was still nattering on about both when he returned to Baie Comeau for Christmas the following week. Thanks to his proselytizing, Diefenbaker won another convert in short order. Ben Mulroney had voted Liberal all his life, but he had become intrigued by this reputed Messiah from Saskatchewan after listening to his son. He spotted Diefenbaker on television during the holiday break, watched him closely, and liked what he saw. Diefenbaker's quasi-populism appealed to him. "I can vote for that guy," the elder Mulroney said, "because he knows exactly the way I feel. He knows how tough it is." Ben Mulroney would later become committed for life when Diefenbaker sent him a letter extolling the talents of his son. Ben voted Conservative ever after.

At the end of 1956 Mulroney could not have imagined that recent events in far-off Europe would soon touch him personally. Soviet tanks had rolled into Hungary and quelled a popular insurrection, prompting a mass exodus of citizens. Almost a third of the 37,500 refugees landing in Canada were students who had abandoned their classes to take flight. In a display of humanitarianism, universities across the country raised money to help at least some of these displaced students finish their education. But St. FX, home of the Antigonish Movement, the helping hand that had served so generously over the years, lagged behind other institutions and offered only a pittance in comparison — two scholarships of free tuition. The recipients would be left to their own devices for room and board and other expenses.

Most of the students at St. FX soon forgot about the plight of the Hungarian refugees, but not Mulroney's friend Sam Wakim. In early March he passed the hat at a student council meeting. Every council member contributed and when the hat came full circle a total of $29 had been raised. Moved by the spirit of its own generosity, student council decided to pass the hat, literally, around the entire campus. A committee was struck to mount a fundraising campaign: the goal was $1,100, an ambitious target in 1957. Mulroney was one of the members of the fundraising committee; in short order, he emerged as chairman, running the show. He notified the *Xaverian Weekly* that the drive would start the following week, and would feature a door-to-door canvass. That much he knew; the rest had to be worked out. Mulroney intended to raise $1,100 from a working-class student body, and he needed a strategy.

The next edition of the *Xaverian Weekly* featured a photograph of Mulroney clutching a handful of dollar bills beside a United Way-type thermometer. The Freedom Fund — a name designed to capitalize on the Cold War mood of the fifties — was launched with a canvassing blitz. The whole scheme was conceived and directed by him from start to finish.

The campaign peaked on "Hungary Day" with a giant rally in the university auditorium featuring a gala of imported stars: the reigning Miss Purdy Cup, Carrie Ann Matheson of Dalhousie University, a Hungarian refugee student from Dalhousie performing a classical and popular piano recital, and a student from Acadia University who parodied piano comedian Victor Borge. They were joined by a cast of local campus entertainers. A celebrity auction offered an array of prized items, including a basketball autographed by the St. FX varsity team, the Maritime champions; an autographed stick from the hockey team; a hat belonging to Dr. H.J. Somers, the university president; a half-dozen fine cigars from C.R. Chadwick, the university accountant; and the hottest item of all, a chance to throw a lemon pie into the face of student union president Peter Lesaux.

In the twenty-four hours prior to this extravaganza, Freedom Fund canvassers blitzed the campus for a second time. A minimum 25-cent contribution earned donors a numbered ticket for the grand draw at the rally. The lucky winner enjoyed a formal dinner at the Royal George Hotel with Miss Purdy Cup as his date, limousine service afterwards to Memorial Rink, and box seats for the hockey final between St. FX and the University of New Brunswick.

Hungary Day was a hit. It raised $310 in cash and $250 in pledges, and boosted the thermometer to $750. A skating party and jazz concert featuring the A-men of Note was expected to push the fund over the top. Mulroney had created the Freedom Fund, promoted it with pizzazz, and made it pay off.

The episode revealed a great deal about Mulroney, not least of which was that he had a heart, and that it was large and generous. There is no doubt that he possessed a social conscience and a sensitivity to the less fortunate. The refugees needed help, and he had jumped to their aid with compassion and gusto. The following year, the arrival of two Hungarian students gave him real satisfaction.

His handling of the Freedom Fund campaign also displayed a genuine capacity for leadership and an innate ability to inspire others. His extravaganza relied on volunteers; he had assembled a small army of them and had kept them motivated and working. It showed too a hankering for the big event. Mulroney thought in grandiose terms and loved the grand gesture.

He possessed a flair for promotion that can only be described as a natural gift: the catchy name "Freedom Fund," the thermometer, the rally, the celebrity auction, the raffle, and the campus blitz sounded more like the creations of Madison Avenue than the schemes of a second-year student at a small Catholic university in the Maritimes. Where the glitz originated is not clear; he had not learned it in Baie Comeau.

Furthermore, he loved attention; indeed he seemed to crave it. A brassy campaign such as the Freedom Fund trained the spotlight directly on him and allowed him to play the role of star. There was, however, the danger that he could not separate himself from the cause he was promoting, that his grand personal ambitions would simply take over. In later life this tendency would sometimes manifest itself in peculiar swings between selfishness and altruistic acts of charity.

Above all, the Freedom Fund experience met a deeply felt need for action and adulation: its success rewarded him with applause for his efforts on behalf of a humane cause. The most important thing in the world to Mulroney was that he be liked — by everyone — and his quest for public affirmation and even adoration bordered on obsession. Seeing one person outside the fold bothered him. It explained the continual rush to make friends, and the non-stop networking. It explained in part why he needed so many friends in the first place: friends gave him much more than companionship; they provided a steady and reliable reservoir of recognition for these accomplishments. It explained the delight he derived in helping others with unsolicited good deeds and favours. It explained his eagerness to stand up before an audience, and why he played for applause. Beneath everything, it explained his irresistible attraction to politics.

This need for admiration was both a strength and a weakness, with consequences good and bad. It made him a chronic do-gooder. When something went wrong in someone's life, he dropped by with a word of understanding and encouragement, a hand on the shoulder. His concern was authentic. But he also seemed on the lookout for opportunities to offer comfort, even to those who were not especially close friends. Helping others always gave him a vicarious thrill; on one occasion he took a nervous Terry McCann into an empty auditorium and coached him for an intercollegiate debate, demonstrating how to use emphasis and gestures effectively, when to pause for dramatic effect, and even when to take a drink of water. McCann, who would go on to become mayor of Pembroke, Ontario, became a friend and political supporter for life. When Mulroney ran for leader of the Conservative Party almost two decades later the first contribution to his campaign was a $500 cheque from McCann.

It followed that if he loved being adored, he hated being criticized. The armour protecting his ego was tissue-thin, and brittle. It shattered easily. The slightest personal rebuke cracked his customary composure and triggered the urge to retaliate. He could coolly withstand a stinging condemnation on practically any political issue and intellectual criticism hardly fazed him, but an attack on his own character or motives set off a display of fireworks. He clenched visibly, tightening up at the first sign of a put-down, and swallowed the bait. People like Rick Cashin could become charged with emotion without becoming vindictive. Mulroney became overheated and launched a search-and-destroy mission. Criticism or ridicule hurt him like nothing else. He could not stand being the butt of jokes, even harmless ones.

Repressed insecurities defined his character more than the familiar outward confidence would ever allow him to admit. He was overly conscious of his image and understood that he would be judged on appearances. Despite his working-class background and his frugal living allowance, he always dressed impeccably. Most St. FX students knocked about campus in windbreakers and open-necked shirts; Mulroney always wore a sports jacket and tie. Paul Creaghan, befitting his image as a rich kid, wore an expensive Harris tweed jacket; Mulroney rearranged his finances until he had one too. Other students drank Black Diamond rum — facetiously called Black Death rum — bottled by the government of Nova Scotia at $3 a bottle; Mulroney and friends Brother Bert Lavoie, Max MacEwen, and Myles Mills flashed a bottle of Bacardi. Mulroney was as poor as the rest, but he always went first class, or so it seemed.

His desire to impress people affected even his speaking style: he shamelessly inflated his rhetoric and often took flight into hyperbole. He exaggerated automatically and constantly. His friends dismissed it as Irish blarney, but there was more to it than that. It was not only how he spoke but what he said. His appetite for approval led him to say the things that people wanted to hear. He rarely took a political stand without first testing the waters, reading the signs. His positions on issues usually depended on where he found the most support. He never lacked opinions and never hesitated to express them, but how deeply he held them and at what cost he would defend them was another matter.

The Freedom Fund was not the only preoccupation for Mulroney in March of 1957. In the middle of fundraising, he auditioned for the St. FX dramatic society production of *Everyman* and won the role of Fellowship, one of the personified attributes who help transform the life of the main character, Everyman, from vice to virtue. And just as the Freedom Fund was shifting into high gear, St. FX kicked off its annual exercise in mock government, Model Parliament.

The Conservatives were back in opposition following the majority victory scored by the campus Liberals in the fall election, and Mulroney, listing himself as the MP for Quebec West, performed his role as party whip. The National Republic Party had folded soon after Rick Cashin became its leader, and now Cashin sat across the aisle as a member of the Liberal cabinet. The Conservatives performed weakly under Creaghan, although the session hit a high moment when Tory MP Sam Wakim introduced a conscience vote abolishing capital punishment. The bill did not threaten the government and squeaked through by two votes. Mulroney had supported Wakim's bill and stood squarely behind him; in fact, the bill was more Mulroney's than Wakim's.

Opposition to capital punishment was one of the very few items in Mulroney's slender catalogue of political absolutes. For him politics remained a question of building bridges, forging alliances, and winning elections. Mulroney was the quintessential pragmatist who took moderate positions in search of a compromise, avoiding the hard and fast wherever he could. But he opposed the death penalty straight out and never looked for middle ground. To him the death penalty was a moral issue, outside the barter of everyday politics, and his convictions against it came from the heart.

The session had scarcely finished when Paul Creaghan announced he was stepping down as party leader. There was little mystery surrounding the identity of his successor. Mulroney had been front and centre with the Freedom Fund, and only days after the staging of the giant rally with its gala concert, celebrity auction, and raffle, the PC club was to pick its new leader. The timing could not have been better. Mulroney easily commanded the highest profile of any Tory on campus, and as the end of his sophomore year approached, he even looked like a leader. An amazing spurt in growth had added six inches to his height. Seemingly overnight, he was tall; at six feet and still skinny, his new lanky look more than ever justified the nickname Bones.

The campus Conservatives met on March 21 in the Old Assembly

Hall to choose their new president. Pat MacAdam, former editor-in-chief of the *Xaverian Weekly* and elder statesman of the club, formally nominated Mulroney and for five minutes enthusiastically outlined his record of achievement. The young man from Baie Comeau was a multifaceted individual, he said, who had been active in extracurricular activities and had done a lot for the party in the two years just past. He would do a lot more in the two years to come; Mulroney possessed the energy, the know-how, and the sparkle to propel the Tories on to victory.

Only one other candidate stood in Mulroney's way, and that, oddly enough, was his friend and soon-to-be roommate, Sam Wakim. Wakim's candidacy defied explanation. No one saw the easygoing Wakim as a serious contender: he lacked the drive for political leadership and moreover was widely regarded as Mulroney's toady. He brought verve and enthusiasm to the party, but not much substance. Wakim's idea of a political challenge was to sneak a case of beer into the club's bash on Saturday night without getting caught.

Wakim had jumped into the race at the last minute, and in later years would actually forget that he had run at all. It all sounded too improbable, and maybe it was. Mulroney was not beyond juicing up a humdrum acclamation by injecting a little drama into the proceedings. With the academic year almost over, essays piling up, and exams lurking around the corner, some observers later speculated that the contest was designed to lure club members to an otherwise routine meeting so that a larger audience would witness Mulroney's moment of triumph.

Whatever the truth, when the votes were cast, Mulroney rolled over Wakim and was duly declared party leader. He showed only momentary jubilation and accepted his victory with quiet humility. When he took the stage as the party boss, he soberly thanked club members for their support and stressed the need to elect a strong club executive in the fall. He said he looked forward to battling the Grits next year and would work to bring the party into fighting shape. "The Achilles' heel of the Progressive Conservative Party this year has been

Mount St. Bernard, where we didn't draw too well," he said, referring to the nearby women's college. "Next year we will try to do better there." Mulroney had become leader of the St. FX Progressive Conservative Party the day after his eighteenth birthday.

However, he didn't have much time to savour his victory. Prime Minister Louis St. Laurent was entering the fourth year of his mandate and was expected to call an election at any time. The Conservatives in the local riding of Antigonish-Guysborough had jumped the gun and nominated their candidate, Angus R. MacDonald, a town merchant, back in February. Given the history of the riding, the Tories needed a head start: the last Tory to win had eked out a 143-vote victory in 1926, but had died before taking office. The Liberals won the by-election that followed. The last Tory to sit in the Commons on behalf of the constituency was elected in 1891. In 1957 the Liberal incumbent was J. Ralph Kirk, a well-known Antigonish businessman who had held the seat for twenty years and was planning to run again. The prospects looked bleak, but that had not prevented Mulroney from turning out for the nomination and predicting a PC victory in Antigonish-Guysborough.

On April 11 St. Laurent announced the election for June 10. Diefenbaker had been criss-crossing the country, campaigning unofficially, ever since his election as party leader the previous December. Three weeks after the start of the formal campaign, Diefenbaker was in Antigonish for an evening rally at the Capitol Theatre, but first he dropped by St. FX for a private visit with President H.J. Somers. Diefenbaker, his wife, Olive, and his aide Derek Bedson arrived on campus that afternoon and stopped student Jim Conrad to ask directions to the president's office. Conrad was not sure. "It's over there some place," he said, pointing in the general direction. At that moment Mulroney appeared out of nowhere and successfully escorted the Diefenbaker entourage to Dr. Somers's office. (Unlike Conrad, Mulroney knew exactly where to find the president's office. Once a month or so, on a Friday afternoon, President Somers invited a select handful of students into his office for informal chats, and

Mulroney was a charter member of this élite group.) The leader was by this time quite familiar with his new acolyte. The two had met just five weeks earlier at a luncheon reception at Angus MacDonald's home. Mulroney took every opportunity to see Diefenbaker and foster the relationship.

Six weeks later, while Mulroney was home for the summer in Baie Comeau, Diefenbaker won the election and was sworn in as Canada's thirteenth prime minister. Even Antigonish-Guysborough, that Liberal bastion, joined the Diefenbaker swing and elected a Tory by 197 votes. Mulroney was ecstatic. Twenty-two years of Liberal arrogance had been ended, and his idol was running the country. His other hero, Davie Fulton, was sworn in as minister of justice. The school year had opened with Stanfield's surprise victory in Nova Scotia; it ended with Diefenbaker's triumph in Ottawa, not to mention Mulroney's election as campus PC leader. These were heady times for the Progressive Conservative Party of Canada, and for Brian Mulroney.

CHAPTER FOUR

THE
PRIME-MINISTERIAL
ITCH

IN SEPTEMBER 1957, Mulroney returned to St. FX for his third year, exuding his characteristic snap and hustle. Now leader of the campus PC Party, he directed his energies into making the Tories the government party in Model Parliament. His dream was to repeat the Diefenbaker miracle: uproot the tired and arrogant Liberals at St. FX just as Diefenbaker had done in Ottawa. If the campus Liberals harboured any worries about their new opponent, they hid it well. By early October they had not yet picked a leader for the year, a manoeuvre that infuriated Mulroney. Hunting Grits was hard without a target to shoot at: "Having proven themselves apathetic and lethargic, their interest in the students is aroused only at election time," Mulroney charged. "With the elections only five weeks away, they have yet to elect a leader — or show the least sign of life." Other than that there was little he could do.

The Liberals wanted Rick Cashin as their leader, but Cashin was not a party man at heart; his interest went no further than participation in

Model Parliament. The party finally chose its standard-bearer at the end of October, and did so by acclamation. Don Keenan was a third-year engineering student, a member of the prestigious Exekoi Society of élite academic achievers, and a respected campus personality. Yet his election as party leader was a singularly opportunistic and cynical act on the part of the Liberals. In conventional political terms Keenan did not belong in the same league with Mulroney or Cashin, or even Creaghan. He was an acceptable public speaker who delivered his lines adequately, but he had never participated in an oratorical contest or belonged to one of the debating teams. His assets were of a different sort. Keenan was a hockey star, the stand-out goalie for the St. FX X-Men, and the best collegiate net-minder in all Nova Scotia. He also happened to be a heartthrob. The Liberals had picked a handsome, clean-cut, agreeable jock for the express purpose of winning the election.

The Liberals could not have selected a leader more unlike Mulroney. Keenan came from an upper-class Toronto family with longstanding ties to the Liberal Party. His father was a vice-president at General Electric. Mulroney had plotted his way to the top of his party; Keenan was offered the position on a platter, took a week to think about it, and even then accepted only on condition that someone else do all the work. Cashin promised to carry the load in Parliament.

Keenan's campaign strategy was simple, even contemptuous: he said and did next to nothing. The Liberals had deployed the same kind of non-campaign against Creaghan the year before and had walked away with their biggest win ever; Keenan was sticking with a proven formula. He offered no platform to speak of, and did little more than put up posters and distribute the pamphlets provided by the Liberal Party in Ottawa, hoping to ride to victory on the coat-tails of his personal popularity and the innate strength of the St. FX Liberal Party.

Mulroney, by comparison, started campaigning early and aggressively. His high profile was given another boost when he won the Oratorical Contest for a second year with a five-minute speech about, as he put it, the "dictatorial dealings of Premier Duplessis with regard to the Murdochville and Arvida strikes" in which he alleged that "the Quebec workers were under the domination of the Union Nationale party." His name and face were everywhere, but the campaign was not working. He attempted to provoke Keenan, engage him in debate, and thereby expose his weaknesses. But Keenan was cagier than expected and refused to rise to the bait. Mulroney had no trouble locking horns with CCF leader Leo Nimsick, who was running a feisty and substantive campaign, but Nimsick was not the candidate to beat. Try as he might, Mulroney could not draw blood from the bloodless Liberals.

With two weeks to go, he gathered his party executive for a policy meeting. Somehow the PCs had to land a knockout punch. Mulroney had a plan, and he emerged from the executive meeting with a comprehensive platform that he boasted was wholly original. Original it was. Mulroney unveiled five key planks: (1) the appointment of an ambassador to the Vatican; (2) the creation of a Ministry of Engineering to be manned by St. FX engineers; (3) raising student income tax exemptions to $2,000 per year; (4) official government recognition of the National Federation of Canadian University Students as the voice of Canadian students; and (5) the introduction of a "sparkling new scholarship plan." The consensus was that the platform went beyond original all the way to blatant and crass.

Mulroney's ploy finally smoked out Don Keenan, who surfaced just long enough to attack it, briefly igniting the campaign. Keenan accused Mulroney of desperation tactics and of making "rash and cheap promises" in an attempt to buy votes. Mulroney had achieved his short-term aim, but in the long run his controversial platform back-fired. Charges of opportunism and doubts about the PCs' fundamental convictions pricked the Tories and robbed them of some of their credibility. The controversy allowed the Liberals to take the high road and pretend to principles and virtues that they did not possess.

Nevertheless, Mulroney had made an impact, and as voting day approached, optimism ran high in the Tory camp. The leader sounded confident and credible in claiming that first-year students were shifting to the Conservatives. "We feel that our support has never been as well rounded as it is this year," Mulroney crowed. "Students from all parts of many different countries are really coming out in force behind the party. Things look fine." Except for Mulroney's contentious platform, the campaign had been listless, thanks to the Liberal strategy. The voters were listless too, and were not communicating their mood. Mulroney believed he was going to win, as he always did, while the heretofore confident Liberals were privately hedging their forecasts. Possibly they had stretched their peekaboo strategy too far.

Both the Liberals and Tories expected a close vote and both were surprised by the results. The students showed up in force — better than 80 per cent turned out — and voted strongly for Keenan, giving the Liberals their second consecutive majority. The Liberals picked up seventeen of the thirty-three seats; Mulroney limped in with thirteen. Despite his energetic leadership and the momentum of Diefenbaker's conquest in June, Mulroney had bettered Creaghan by only two seats, stealing one each from the Liberals and the CCF. Mulroney lost all three polling stations, including Mount St. Bernard, the Achilles' heel he had worked to turn around. The Tories were surging on campuses across the country, but not at St. FX.

The results forced Mulroney to accept the unpleasant reality that he would not be the prime minister in Model Parliament. The Liberal victory meant more than the simple triumph of one leader over another, or the success of one platform over another. No matter what Mulroney might have done, the win was not there to be had. He might run again next year, but the latest results strongly suggested that Lowell Murray's victory two years earlier had been just an aberration, a freak accident while the Liberals were momentarily vulnerable. As long as Maritime Catholics voted Liberal, the PC club simply lacked the base to win an election at a Catholic university like St. FX. Mulroney faced the prospect of forever staring across at the smug Liberals from the opposition side of the aisle.

Unknown to him, deliverance was at hand. At the very moment that his prime-ministerial hopes looked the most bleak, his friend Gerry Doucet was promoting an ambitious project that, although not designed to make an end run around the St. FX Liberals, could do precisely that. Doucet, the son of a poor Acadian fisherman, graduated from a second-rate school system in Cape Breton and landed at St. FX in 1954. His written English was passable, but his English vocabulary was limited; he chose St. FX and majored in English in order to learn the language. His first science exam netted him a mark of 10 per cent, but dedicated study and an extraordinary determination to overcome humble roots drove him on. With his thick accent, he had little hope of winning the Oratorical Contest, but he entered anyway, preparing diligently. He pulled off a surprise victory the year before Mulroney won it, and went on to be elected secretary of student council while his marks rose to the top level.

Doucet set his sights high and always succeeded, until he reached for the highest office, student council president. He finished in third place. He then ran for the next most prestigious post, senior class president, and lost again. Devastated by two consecutive losses, he settled for the far less glamorous post of debating society president, a much less significant office that was his for the taking. Determined to prove himself to the student body that had twice rejected him, Doucet set out to make the most of the debating society position. His ambition to make his mark would offer Mulroney his biggest break as a student politician.

Doucet settled on an intercollegiate Model Parliament, hosted by St. FX and drawing students from across the Maritimes, as his pet project. Dalhousie University had staged a Maritimes-wide Model Parliament several years earlier, but Doucet intended to mount an event that would be second to none. He called meetings and prepared lists, and ultimately recruited more than 150 students to serve on committees under his direction.

Doucet invited real-life political heavyweights to sit in the chamber with the students to advise on strategy and help with the debate:

W.S.K. Jones, the venerable Speaker of the Nova Scotia legislature, agreed to preside as Speaker, and Richard Donahoe, the attorney general, and several other Nova Scotia MLAs accepted invitations to participate. From Ottawa he bagged Allan MacEachen, the young Liberal MP who sat for nearby Inverness, and CCF MP Doug Fisher, the giant-killer who had knocked off the legendary C.D. Howe in the recent Diefenbaker win. He almost collared Lester Pearson, the fresh new leader of the Liberal Party, but settled for his runner-up, Paul Martin, the former minister of health. And there was some early hope of landing the Chief himself. When that prospect fell through, Doucet set his sights on Davie Fulton, Diefenbaker's minister of justice, but that too fizzled, and after a while he had exhausted his short list. The federal Conservative Party was not coming through with anyone; with less than two weeks to go, he had not a single big-name Tory from Ottawa.

Meanwhile, Mulroney was preparing for a trip to the capital. That winter more than five hundred young Conservatives from across Canada were gathering for the annual meetings of the two national Tory youth groups, the Progressive Conservative Student Federation and the Young Progressive Conservatives. Mulroney was attending as the representative from St. FX. Before he left, he volunteered to lobby Ottawa on Doucet's behalf.

The meeting of Conservative youth was the first large party gathering since the leadership convention. Mulroney travelled to Ottawa for the second time in fourteen months, anticipating the pleasure of watching Diefenbaker perform on three occasions in one weekend. The first opportunity would come on Friday evening when the young Tories were to present the prime minister with a wagon-sleigh that had been built sixty years earlier in his grandfather's wagon shop. Then on Saturday morning Diefenbaker was back again for a short talk. But the main event was the banquet in the ballroom of the Château Laurier on Saturday night, with Diefenbaker as the featured speaker. Three appearances by Diefenbaker meant three chances to meet the prime minister.

There was nothing elaborate about Mulroney's technique: the first chance he got he simply followed Diefenbaker into an elevator and stood between him and the door. Diefenbaker recognized Mulroney instantly and invited him to his office. It seemed odd that the prime minister would take time to talk to an eighteen-year-old university student from Antigonish, but Diefenbaker did that sort of thing. He was surprisingly easy to reach given the office he held, the most accessible prime minister of his or any subsequent generation. Diefenbaker prided himself on knowing ordinary Canadians, lots of them, and made a point of regularly touching base with common folk across the country. It was his way of keeping track, his personal form of polling before polling took over politics. And at sixty-two, he loved having young people in his orbit. While Diefenbaker regaled visiting young people with stories inside his office, his staff might be wrestling with a crisis on the other side of the door. Diefenbaker was known to invite young Tories into his office for a private talk, and that weekend he gave Mulroney a half-hour personal conference.

Together in the East Block office, Diefenbaker, the prime minister, and Mulroney, the third-year arts student, established an immediate rapport. Diefenbaker wanted constant stroking, and Mulroney knew how to turn on the praise. Diefenbaker always required an audience — he refused to use a Dictaphone because he needed someone in the room to respond to his lines — and Mulroney proved the consummate cheerleader. Diefenbaker was a populist who avoided the tangled and complex, who liked his truths to be simple; Mulroney was a true believer who hung on every word. Their relationship had chemistry; they related well to each other — or, to be precise, Mulroney related well to Diefenbaker. The prime minister soon came to take a personal interest in Mulroney's future.

The interview that weekend gave Mulroney an opportunity to solicit Diefenbaker for the St. FX Model Parliament. It was one of the first items he raised and it proved a taller order than he had originally expected. Unknown to Mulroney, or anyone else in Nova Scotia, Diefenbaker was on the verge of calling a snap election; the

Tories were about to go into battle and were reluctant to tie up their troops. Nor did they want to get caught playing a "let's-pretend" parliament when at any moment they might be engaged in a real political fight. But Mulroney was a salesman and knew how to play to Diefenbaker's vanities; he presented the St. FX case and sold it well. Diefenbaker agreed to send Gordon Churchill, the minister of trade and commerce.

It was only after Mulroney arrived in Ottawa that he heard the rumours of a sudden vote. Diefenbaker was riding high in public esteem and was known to be looking for an opportunity to dissolve Parliament and call an election in search of a majority. Lester Pearson had been named Liberal leader only three weeks earlier and an election was the last thing the Grits wanted, particularly since they were likely to succumb to a Tory landslide. Diefenbaker himself fanned the flames on Saturday morning by apologizing for not spending more time with the Young PCs. "Unfortunately some things have to be done today," he hinted broadly. "There are questions that have to be answered. For some reason or other, there are so many who want an answer to a particular question. We don't think the answer is far removed."

Diefenbaker satisfied their curiosity soon enough. After leaving the session, he boarded a government Viscount for a quick trip to Quebec City where the Governor General happened to be visiting. When he returned to the Château Laurier for the banquet that evening, the deed had been done. The boisterous young audience greeted his arrival with shouts, whistles, and the banging of silver serving trays, grabbed out of the hands of surprised waiters and used as cymbals. Less than two hours earlier, Diefenbaker had dissolved Parliament and called an election for March 31. He launched his re-election campaign with his dinner speech that night. He could hardly finish two sentences without being interrupted by cheers and applause; he fired up the delegates as only he could do, and appealed to them to return to their ridings and work for a victory. "The campaign begins tonight," he thundered.

It was an electric moment for all who witnessed it. Sitting on the ballroom podium, off to the side but very much on stage, was Mulroney. Just prior to Diefenbaker's address, the PCSF had held its annual elections; Mulroney was elected to the executive as Maritimes vice-president, and now had a spot on stage with the leader. The post represented another breakthrough for the rising young party stalwart; it gave him an entrée to the national Tory scene. Hereafter he would attend executive meetings and enjoy a regular ticket out of Antigonish. He would visit Ottawa frequently and have formal access to Diefenbaker.

Back at St. FX, Doucet's project had escalated into the event of the school year. Gordon Churchill was no celebrity like Davie Fulton, and had never graced Doucet's wish list, but he added weight to an already weighty list. As a senior cabinet minister, Churchill had the ear of Diefenbaker and that gave him a lot of backroom clout. Churchill was the author of Diefenbaker's "We can win without Quebec" strategy, and he had been the one to carry the message that Diefenbaker would not accommodate Léon Balcer's wish for a Quebec seconder at the 1956 leadership convention. He was a mover and shaker in the corridors of power and represented quite a catch.

The sheer size of the gathering had pushed the venue off campus and into the Antigonish Recreation Centre. St. FX's regular Model Parliament had been dramatically overshadowed and finally scrapped for the year; now Mulroney had a second chance to become prime minister and this time the odds were in his favour. Whether the government would be Conservative or Liberal depended on the formal posting of delegates from the various campuses. Delegates would attend from eleven colleges across the Maritimes, most of which had voted Tory.

The partisan alignment unfolded slowly as the names of delegates and their party affiliations trickled in by mail. Everybody on campus awaited the result, and few paid closer attention than Mulroney, who stopped by every day to check the emerging count. As it turned out, the vote was true to the mood of the country. The final tally was 25

Tories, 18 Liberals, 5 CCF, and 3 others. The Tories had more than enough to form a government and came within one seat of an outright majority.

With all fifty-one delegates picked and posted and on their way, only one important preliminary remained unresolved, and that was the selection of party leaders by their caucuses, with the Conservative winner becoming prime minister. Here Mulroney had the advantage. As a member of the host organizing committee, he knew who the Conservatives were, and when and where they were arriving. He started his campaign for party leader with the arrival of the first Tory delegate.

Whether delivered by train, bus, or car, the PC delegates were greeted on arrival by Brian Mulroney. He welcomed them to the university, gave briefings, showed them their lodgings, and made sure they were comfortable. After all delegates had registered and picked up their credentials, he showed the Tories to the first caucus meeting and introduced them to their party colleagues. Liberal delegates chose Dan Hurley of the University of New Brunswick law school as their leader, and CCF members selected Leo Nimsick from St. FX. The Tory vote was a foregone decision. Thanks to his networking blitz, Mulroney was the only Tory every caucus member knew, and the only logical leader. There were no other contenders. Hard work, alert performance, and above all great good luck made Mulroney prime minister at last.

Mulroney appointed a nineteen-member cabinet and lifted his throne speech almost word for word from Diefenbaker's throne speech of four months earlier. In fact, he shaped his entire government in the Diefenbaker mould. But would Mulroney's minority survive the weekend? The opposition parties could topple the Tories on the floor of Parliament if they were so inclined, and the Liberal Party, looking to boost its sagging fortunes across the country, longed to start the national campaign with a victory of some sort. The parties were still caucusing when Paul Martin took aside CCF leader Leo Nimsick to propose an alliance. Inside the CCF caucus, Martin's overture received a frosty reception, mostly from Doug Fisher. "No way," counselled Fisher, mindful of the national election campaign. "That will just play right into the Liberals' hands." The CCF caucus did not bother with a vote, and later went a step further, abstaining on some votes to save Mulroney's government from defeat. With opposition collusion unlikely, Mulroney was safe.

At 8:00 on the evening of February 7, 1958, all members of Parliament, both student and genuine, marched into the chamber behind the Sergeant-at-Arms, who carried in the mace. The student Governor General arrived in full regalia and, after a salute from a navy guard, commenced reading the throne speech. Youthful pages in white shirts, black bow ties, and black trousers hovered everywhere on the chamber floor. The national press showed up in force, and so did the citizens of Antigonish. A standing-room-only crowd of nearly nine hundred jammed the bleachers up above, and only fire regulations kept out others. More than two thousand people squeezed their way in before the two-day event ended. The town of Antigonish, population 4,500, had never seen anything like it.

Mulroney, wearing a double-breasted gabardine suit that hung a bit heavily on his thin frame, sat erect in the prime minister's chair. Beside him were Gordon Churchill and Churchill's parliamentary secretary, Tom Bell, the MP from Saint John, New Brunswick. Directly across the aisle was opposition leader Dan Hurley, flanked on either side by Liberals Paul Martin and Allan MacEachen, and by Don Keenan and Rick Cashin. Down the aisle, CCF leader Leo Nimsick sat next to Doug Fisher, who towered over everyone like a friendly bear. A few representatives of the Canada First Party at Dalhousie were stuck at the very end.

Following the reading of the throne speech, Mulroney rose to speak. He always made an impression when he got to his feet, and this time was no different. Despite the stiff formality of the occasion, he seemed at home, as if he had been schooled in Parliament, though his parliamentary experience was no greater than that of most of the others. The baritone voice served him especially well on this stately occasion.

Conscious of his role as prime minister, he spoke soberly and earnestly, and for the most part delivered his message well, embellished as it was with frequent references to Diefenbaker and Sir John A. Macdonald. Then Mulroney caught Parliament by surprise and did something neither of those gentlemen could do: he repeated part of his speech in French, an unprecedented act in the pre-bilingual fifties. That inspired gesture won admiration in every quarter.

Hurley, the Liberal leader, launched a conventional opposition attack and wasted little time trying to bring down the government with an amendment to the throne speech. Paul Martin, his seconder, attacked the government too, but instead of firing at the Mulroney government in Antigonish he trained his sights on the Diefenbaker administration in Ottawa, singling out in particular Churchill's trade policy. He accused Churchill of causing much of Canada's high unemployment. "The government is not facing up to the problem," Martin charged. "This is the first and foremost issue, and the government must not be allowed to escape from it."

The audience relished the attack, but Martin had committed a serious breach of etiquette. The real MPs were meant to advise and assist, and even participate, but they were not to perform, much less stop the show the way Martin had done. Furthermore, guests were not supposed to be partisan, and he had been blatantly partisan, using Model Parliament as a launching pad for the election campaign.

Across the aisle, Churchill, a gentle, unassuming man who was slow on his feet and lacking any oratorical fire, was caught completely off guard and mustered only a feeble reply. He mumbled something about believing that he thought the "function at this event would be different" and that he never dreamed of being drawn into a campaign debate. He lamely tried to "correct" some of Martin's "inaccuracies" but mouthed his words so softly that they died before reaching the ears of the audience.

The Tory students sitting around Churchill rose to his defence, particularly Mulroney, who quickly forgot prime-ministerial decorum and got in some old-fashioned heckling. He was coming to the aid not only of Churchill, but of Diefenbaker and the Conservative Party, and he carried on sniping at Martin well into the next day. With the cockiness of a teenager Mulroney taunted Martin and boasted that the Liberals would be finished after March 31. Was there, he asked impertinently, any unemployment insurance for former cabinet ministers? "My dear young man," Martin scoffed patronizingly, "if you were a real prime minister you would shortly find out for yourself." The audience laughed. Mulroney had been outquipped, but he remained unchastened and kept badgering Martin until he finally scored a hit that momentarily stopped him. "If you were on television," Martin declared, "I would turn you off." The audience laughed again, but this time Mulroney was ready. "We're going to turn you off," Mulroney shot back, referring again to the election campaign. "We're going to shut you fellows down for good." This time the audience cheered for Mulroney. He had not been especially witty, but had showed some spunk. He had traded punches with a wily political veteran and survived.

In fact Mulroney had more to fear from Cashin than from Martin. Cashin, speaking behind both Hurley and Martin, cut the widest swath of all and soon took over the show. His ringing delivery and grandiloquent phrasing made him the most colourful speaker by far and a joy to hear. Mulroney could return the artillery as fast as it came in, but a one-on-one shooting war with Cashin usually left Mulroney one gear behind. Although Cashin was generally agreed to have won the opening debate, many felt that Mulroney proved himself the better parliamentary strategist.

Mulroney successfully won approval for his main piece of legislation, a $5-million fund for university scholarships and bursaries. The CCF tried to boost the figure to $100 million, but the amendment died when the Speaker ruled it out of order. The students also passed a bill of rights "to guarantee freedom of speech and worship, right of lawful assembly, association and organization, equal treatment before the law and enjoyment of all rights without distinction of sex, race, religion or language." But not with Mulroney's approval. The bill was moved by the CCF and supported by the Liberals, while the Tories abstained. It would be another two years before Diefenbaker brought in his own bill of rights.

Oddly enough, Mulroney's biggest headache came not from the Liberals or the CCF, but from the pesky Canada First Party at the far end of the chamber. Its leader, Bobby Carleton, introduced an omnibus bill proposing a distinctive national flag, the adoption of "O Canada" as the national anthem, a more bilingual Canada, a national pension plan, and universal medicare — all measures that Ottawa would implement in the coming decade. Model Parliament treated the bill as a joke and shelved it, but the press paid attention and crowded around the two Canada First delegates while Mulroney glared on. The Canada First Party members had temporarily stolen his limelight, and for the rest of the session Mulroney gave them the cold shoulder.

Cashin and the upstart Canada First Party aside, Mulroney had sparkled in the intercollegiate Model Parliament and seemed completely at home in his role as prime minister. Moreover, he loved it. Leading his pretend government gave him the same feeling of adoration that his triumph with the Freedom Fund had given him a year earlier, only more so.

As soon as the intercollegiate parliament was dissolved Mulroney plunged himself into the federal election campaign already under way.

The calling of a snap election had caught not only the Liberals off guard, but also the Tories in Antigonish-Guysborough. Angus R. MacDonald, the local Tory who had upset the Liberals the previous year, had collapsed in Ottawa a few weeks before the writ was issued, and now, with the campaign starting, lay partially paralyzed in hospital with a stroke. The Tories needed a new candidate in a hurry and quickly nominated MacDonald's campaign manager, Clem O'Leary, a local insurance broker. Half a dozen speakers took the stage at the nominating meeting, including Minister of Revenue George Nowlan and other political VIPs, but the speaker who packed the most pep and enthusiasm was Brian Mulroney.

Early in the campaign Mulroney brought O'Leary onto the

campus and took him from room to room, but even in 1958, when Diefenbaker was expected to sweep to victory, St. FX remained cold and miserly to the Tories. Mulroney was handicapped by his candidate, an unknown backroom boy, while the Liberal Party was running Al Graham, the popular sports director of local radio station CJFX. And the Liberals had a highly capable campus campaign manager in the person of Rick Cashin, who was not going to let Mulroney outdo him. Mulroney managed to bring Davie Fulton into the St. FX auditorium, but Cashin went one better and produced Lester Pearson, the Liberal leader.

This time around, the St. FX campus was not big enough for Mulroney and could not satisfy his appetite for campaigning. Before long he was working across the entire constituency. The riding had several French communities, and Mulroney and Bert Lavoie visited them all, accompanying the English-speaking O'Leary and introducing him in French.

Not even Antigonish-Guysborough could contain Mulroney's zest for campaigning as he routinely ventured into neighbouring constituencies, always offering to lend a helping hand. He hitched rides with senior Tories to countless campaign rallies. He could not be held back or even slowed down. "I can help," he claimed eagerly. "Let me help." Soon Mulroney was popping up all over eastern Nova Scotia, endearing himself to local organizations at every stop. They needed a youth spokesman, and Mulroney quickly demonstrated what a dynamite warm-up act he could be. He knew how to play the endearing role of the youngster representing the future of the country. A few minutes of his exuberance softened the crowd and paved the way for the heavy hitters behind him. And his facility with French made him invaluable to an English-speaking party that had been historically shut out of Catholic and French communities. Whether French or English, audiences witnessed an eighteen-year-old, about to turn nineteen, confidently belting out a partisan message with the unbridled enthusiasm of youth.

Diefenbaker bestrode the country like a giant during the 1958 campaign, and on election night swept to victory. The only surprise was the magnitude of the win: 208 seats out of 265, the greatest landslide in Canadian history. Antigonish-Guysborough went Tory by an astounding 931 votes, although the campus vote had stubbornly clung to the Liberals. Across the country Liberal and CCF candidates melted away like the spring snow. That night Mulroney phoned Diefenbaker to offer congratulations. And at local celebrations later that evening he boasted that some day he too would be prime minister.

Mulroney's proudest possession in all the world was his eight-by-ten glossy of Diefenbaker standing radiantly beside him at the 1956 leadership convention in Ottawa. The picture hung in his room for all to see. Just him and Dief, and Dief's personal autograph. "See that picture?" Frank Buggie told his friends. "The roles are going to be reversed sometime."

High political office had not been a serious prospect for Mulroney before St. FX, or before Diefenbaker. He had wanted to go as far as he could, without knowing precisely how and where. St. FX had introduced him to politics, and as much as he always aimed for the top, becoming a Conservative prime minister seemed too far-fetched. Running at St. FX had been tough enough; his home province of Quebec was even more solidly Liberal. Nonetheless, the Maritime Model Parliament had given him the prime-ministerial itch, and the Diefenbaker landslide of 1958 convinced him that he could do it. Diefenbaker always joked that when he started his political career in Saskatchewan the Conservatives were so unpopular across the Prairies, the only thing protecting him was the game laws. Diefenbaker had first run for Parliament in 1925, and lost. He ran four more times for political office before finally squeaking into the Commons in 1940 by 280 votes. Now, sixteen years later, after three runs at the party leadership, Diefenbaker had proved a Tory could become prime minister in a Liberal country. He had raised the Conservative Party above its Ontario WASP base and had made it a national force — politically and geographically. Diefenbaker had even swept Quebec.

71

St. FX had opened the door to politics for Mulroney, and Diefenbaker showed him how far he really could go. Diefenbaker had an absolute belief in his personal destiny. He was going to give his life to his country and was sustained by an unshakeable faith that the greatness of Canada rested on his shoulders, that he would prevail despite all the setbacks. Mulroney now admired Diefenbaker more than ever. He admired his perseverance. He admired the historic breakthrough in Quebec and the West. Diefenbaker inspired Mulroney to believe he could achieve anything he wanted, if only he wanted it badly enough.

Sam Wakim, Mulroney's roommate, friend, and follower, never doubted that Mulroney would one day lead the Conservative Party. He had watched Mulroney in their tiny room in MacPherson House read the *Fathers of Canada* book series, and Wakim figured the fire burned within him. Yet Mulroney said little about his political ambitions; he was too astute about his image and too much in need of approval to risk derision. But once in a while, in moments of excitement, he could not contain himself and boasted that one day he would be prime minister of Canada. The jubilant night of March 31, 1958, was such a moment.

However circumspect he might be about his personal aspirations, he did not hesitate to let the world know about his close relationship with Diefenbaker. He frequently mentioned that he was on speaking terms with the Chief and that he could dial the prime minister whenever he wanted. That claim was too much to swallow for some of the sceptics at MacPherson House. On one occasion, they called his bluff. "Look, Mulroney," somebody said, pointing to a telephone next to the stairway, "there's a phone. Call him."

Oozing confidence, Mulroney walked over to the phone and lifted the receiver. A small crowd gathered around. He knew the number to dial and got through quickly to the prime minister's office, but then he hit a snag. The crowd watched as he got tied up by various secretaries, or maybe it was the same secretary, nobody knew for sure. Whatever was happening, Mulroney was in trouble. The taunts and snickers started. Mulroney tightened a little but remained unflushed. "Look it," Mulroney finally blurted out, "do you know who this is? This is Brian Mulroney calling." There was a pause, and a minute later Mulroney said, "Hello, Chief." A gasp came from his audience. Mulroney, on top of the world, was talking to Diefenbaker in front of his dumbfounded friends. Amazed and chastened, they shrank away. No one challenged him about Diefenbaker again.

CHAPTER FIVE

THE MISSING YEAR

IN THE FALL OF 1958 Mulroney returned to St. FX for his fourth and final year with an impressive list of credentials. He had become a student leader, a first-rate debater, a Tory apparatchik in youth circles, and a businessman of sorts. As the newly elected president of the Student Co-op, he was in charge of the biggest business on campus next to the university itself, the student-owned enterprise that managed the canteen and bookstore, which sold not only books and course texts but also jackets, T-shirts, and university souvenirs, and had annual gross revenues of nearly $100,000. Presiding over the operations was an administrative job that required organization and an understanding of financial statements. He also captured the Oratorical Contest for an unprecedented third consecutive year and won another intercollegiate debating victory, this time against the University of New Brunswick; he would graduate undefeated in inter-varsity competition.

Flushed with the success of the Maritime Model Parliament, Mulroney had already stepped down as Tory leader at St. FX. He campaigned for his successor, Ray Guerrette, but his political interest had moved beyond boyish games. Not long before graduating, Mulroney chaired a PC Student Federation meeting at the Lord Nelson Hotel in Halifax featuring both Robert Stanfield and Alvin Hamilton, the federal minister of northern affairs.

St. FX had done much for him since his arrival four years earlier as a wide-eyed sixteen-year-old. It had introduced him to politics, given him a goal, and provided him with a circle of friends to help him reach that goal. But St. FX had not noticeably shaped his political thinking — despite its largely working-class student body and the remnants of the Antigonish Movement. Mulroney paid lip service to the movement's underlying doctrine, but he was not moulded by it.

Long before graduation he was thinking about his next move. Late in the fall term, just before the Christmas break, he appeared unannounced in Halifax and telephoned Pat MacAdam. Each had come a considerable distance since a brash freshman named Brian Mulroney had buttonholed the editor of the *Xaverian Weekly*. MacAdam was now a civil servant in Nova Scotia's Department of Education. Mulroney was Maritime vice-president of the student federation, visiting Halifax often for regional meetings. But this trip had nothing to do with party politics.

"Can I come up this evening," Mulroney asked, "and come to dinner?"

"You certainly can."

"Are you sure?"

"I'm positive."

A free meal was nice, but Mulroney had not invited himself to dinner for the food. He was there for some coaching in formal dining etiquette, the kind not normally available to kids growing up at the back end of Champlain Street. That evening MacAdam, who had learned the rules during two summers in army officer training, showed Mulroney which fork to use and when. The next day Mulroney put his new-found skills to work at a stuffy lunch in an old club on Barrington Street in downtown Halifax, hosted by the Rhodes Scholarship selection committee. Mulroney was one of half a dozen or so candidates in Nova Scotia applying for a three-year all-expenses-paid pass to Oxford University.

Applying for a Rhodes Scholarship with his record was an act of cheeky bravado. The award demanded excellence in academics and athletic accomplishment, and Mulroney did not qualify on either count. The selection committee did not insist that the winner sit at the very top of the class, but it made sure that the successful candidate came — as one of the judges put it — "pretty damn close." Mulroney would graduate at the *cum laude* level, 75 to 80 per cent, which was above average but not outstanding, and a long way from the top of his class. Given all his extracurricular activity, Mulroney had compiled a most respectable academic record, but Rhodes Scholarship calibre it was not. As for sports, he was a good hockey player and a fierce competitor, but had never tried out for the varsity team. His father had told him there was no money in sports, and Mulroney had taken that bit of advice to heart. Brian Mulroney was no more a Rhodes Scholar than Robert Stanfield was a fire-breathing populist, but in 1959 anybody who applied for a Rhodes Scholarship received the courtesy of an interview, and Mulroney never lacked for chutzpah. He unleashed his charm and enthusiasm on the selection panel but could not overcome his lack of qualifications.

His chance of Oxford dead, Mulroney looked elsewhere. He had started at St. FX as a commerce student, intending to go into business. A degree in commerce was to be his ticket out of the working class and up the corporate ladder, but after two years he changed his major to political science. He had not ruled out business, but he had set his sights on a law degree. He had demonstrated a natural talent for debate, and law provided a forum to showcase that talent. Law paid well, and more politicians were lawyers than anything else. Besides, as he once told his friends, the most successful businessmen in Canada had law degrees. In short, the study of law did not interest him as much as the opportunities the law afforded.

It remained only to choose an appropriate law school. He could go to Dalhousie University down the road in Halifax, or move over to McGill University in Montreal, or even accompany his buddy Sam Wakim to the tiny law school at the University of New Brunswick. Instead he chose to enrol at historic Laval University in Quebec City, and for valid reasons. Laval would put him back in Quebec, his native province, and bring him closer to Baie Comeau, where he planned to establish his law practice and a political presence before running for office. Laval would give him the French-Canadian connection, and perhaps help him do for the Conservative Party in Quebec what John Diefenbaker had done in the Prairies. He had spent the past six years — nearly one-third of his life — in the Maritimes, and each year made him more a Maritimer and less a Quebecker. He felt it was time to return home. "Future plans point to Laval University and a career in Law," read the caption under Mulroney's picture in his graduating yearbook.

Underlying his sentimentality about his Quebec roots was hard political reality. Six years of life in English Canada had dulled his French; the creeping loss of fluency had been noticed a little more each summer by the folks back home in Baie Comeau. He needed to spruce up his second language if he wanted to represent that part of Quebec, and Laval, a French-speaking university at which all courses were taught in French, would do precisely that.

His career planning showed remarkable foresight and maturity for someone who had not quite turned twenty. He had delineated his targets and plotted his route carefully. But he was still a kid, and had not shaken off the whims and whimsy of youth. Second thoughts overcame him even before he left St. FX. At the last minute, in the spring of 1959, a new factor entered his life, one that he had not anticipated.

With graduation around the corner, Mulroney looked for a date to the graduation dance. On a campus where men outnumbered women five to one, social life was constricted and the school's Victorian rules did nothing to help. Women had to be in their dorms by 10:00 — 7:30 for first-year women — and by 10:30 on weekends. For the undergraduate Mulroney, there had been an additional handicap. At a dance he attended as a freshman he spotted the most striking girl in the crowd sitting alone in the bleachers. He boldly marched up to ask for a dance. Everything was fine until she stood up. The young woman was Helen Lane, a senior, four years older and, at five-foot-ten, almost six feet in heels. Mulroney, then the proverbial pint-sized shrimp, looked up at her. "Well," he said, without missing a beat, "I think I'd better grow up a little and come back." He walked away unruffled.

His pee-wee days were long behind him now. He had grown tall and handsome and could attract girls if he wanted to, but women were not a priority, and never had been. Since leaving Baie Comeau at fourteen, he had spent two years at an all-boys school and four years at a predominantly male university. He'd had less exposure to the opposite sex than a typical nineteen-year-old, dating sporadically and avoiding entanglements.

However, the woman he most admired was beyond reach because she was dating the college quarterback. This was Rosann Earl, a bright-eyed student from Newfoundland who had first caught his eye when they were both freshmen. Mulroney demanded chiefly one thing of women, and that was physical beauty. On that score, Rosann met and exceeded the most exacting standards. A beauty queen, she would later be described as a cross between Jacqueline Onassis and Margaret Trudeau.

But late in the year, just as Mulroney was casting about for a graduation date, news reached him that Rosann had broken up with the quarterback and was free for the big dance. Mulroney could charm birds out of trees and had no difficulty speaking to the president of the university or the prime minister of the country. But asking Rosann for a date was different. In first year he and Rosann had both taken English II — advanced English for students who scored well on their placement tests in literature. Then Rosann had dismissed him as a smart aleck trying to look big, and they had had little contact since. Mulroney was afraid that Rosann did not like him, and nothing undermined his self-assurance faster than the possibility of being disliked. Now, as he thought about approaching her, he was nervous at the prospect of rejection and could not bring himself to ask her out.

So he turned for help to the always obliging Sam Wakim, who

would do almost anything he asked, even play the role of Cupid. Wakim agreed to pop the question: Would she go to the dance with Brian if Brian asked?

"Why doesn't he ask me?" she replied, when Wakim delivered the message. "Tell him to ask me." Clearly Rosann had noticed the transformation of the brash freshman into a big man on campus. Her response was as good as a yes. Wakim relayed the message to Mulroney, who screwed up his courage to make his bid. But still he could not ask her face to face, and resorted to the telephone. She accepted.

Graduation was a triumph. Mulroney was resplendent in his tuxedo; Rosann's presence by his side made him the envy of his classmates. He introduced her to his parents, who had come from Baie Comeau for the occasion. Ben and Irene never were prouder, nor felt more rewarded for their sacrifices.

As for Mulroney, he was more than proud; he was seriously in love as never before. Rosann had captivated him; happily, she too was enamoured, and their relationship quickly blossomed into a full-scale romance even though the academic year had ended and they were both graduating. She was returning to Newfoundland and he to Baie Comeau. They would be apart not only for the summer but for a long time after that, it seemed. Rosann was off to the University of Toronto in the fall while Mulroney was heading to Quebec City.

That summer of 1959, more than a thousand miles separated Mulroney in Baie Comeau from Rosann in St. John's. As the weeks dragged by Mulroney wrote letter after letter, telling Rosann about life in Baie Comeau, his summer job, the misery of having his tonsils out, and above all how much he missed her. Her replies only made him more lovesick.

In midsummer, just as Mulroney was beginning to wonder whether he would ever see his beloved again, his luck changed. Rosann wrote to say she would not go to Toronto after all. She had run into a funding problem, had been forced to postpone her plans for a master's degree, and would settle for a teaching diploma. Instead of Toronto, she would attend Mount St. Vincent University in Halifax.

The change caused Mulroney to reconsider his own plans. Dalhousie was in Halifax too, and had been one of the finalists on his short list of law schools. In fact the path from St. FX to Dalhousie Law had recently been taken by grads like Gerry Doucet, Paul Creaghan, and Rick Cashin; he knew he would feel at home there. And Dalhousie was perhaps the top law school in Canada, having produced more than its share of judges and premiers, even a prime minister (R.B. Bennett). But switching to Dalhousie made no strategic sense for a Quebecker bent on a political career. Nonetheless when Rosann altered her course for Halifax, Mulroney did the same. "Nay, I'll not be going to Laval in September," he wrote in a private letter that August. "Following Kent's wedding in Antigonish on the 29th, I'll be off to Halifax and — no, not Holy Heart [a seminary] — Dal Law School. I guess that I'm a real Maritimer at heart and with Rosann going to Mt. St. Vincent this year, we Maritimers will have to stick together!"

Law school represented a considerable step up in stature for Mulroney, but so did the cost: most Dal students budgeted their total costs at $1,200 a year, which put a strain on the Mulroney family budget despite his savings from a well-paying summer job. However, that year Dalhousie introduced a generous new scholarship program, the Sir James Dunn Scholarships, which offered five first-year students $1,500 a year for all three years of law school. Mulroney applied, as did many others, but once again fell short. He ultimately accepted help from the University Aid Fund, which paid tuition fees for "meritorious students who are unable to attend the university without assistance."

In early September 1959, Mulroney arrived in Halifax in time to meet Rosann at the airport in Rick Cashin's car. The reunion was joyous, but the joy was short-lived. Rosann settled into a place six miles out of town, which meant visits were difficult. Moreover, now that they were back together and had time to know each other better, it became apparent that the chemistry was wrong — at least she thought so — and after a couple of months Rosann ended the affair. Mulroney tried to talk her out of it, but she believed the match was not working, and nothing he said convinced her otherwise.

The break-up devastated Mulroney and left him heartbroken; the hurt lingered for months. Mulroney rarely showed weakness, and almost never admitted to a setback, but the loss of Rosann was painful and traumatic. He could not keep it inside, and told Cashin about his hurt.

"For Christ's sake," Cashin would counsel him, "forget her. She's a dizzy dame. . . ."

But Mulroney kept pining. His first big romance had brought him his first big break-up. Nothing like this had ever hit him before, and he continued moaning until Cashin could take it no more.

"Well, Brian," he finally said, "you've got to get on with the rest of your life and your career and everything else."

Cashin's attitude would soon change. He and Rosann came to know each other well the following year, fell in love, and were married after a whirlwind romance. At St. FX Cashin had won the debates; at Dalhousie he would win the girl as well.

In the end, the salve to Mulroney's wounds was found not in Cashin's counsel, but within the walls of his own boarding-house, in the form of the landlady's daughter. Like other Dal students from out of town, Mulroney had looked for rented rooms for $6 to $10 a week in the basements or attics of the old homes surrounding campus. Mulroney teamed up with Joe Khattar, another St. FX grad enrolled in Dal Law, and found attic quarters with the Leach family in an older two-storey house at 325 South Street, a few doors from the university hockey rink, literally on the edge of campus. Space was a bit tight between the slanting walls, but they had enough room for two beds, a little desk, and Mulroney's prized picture of Diefenbaker. And the location was ideal: virtually across the football field from the law building.

By cutting across the football field, Mulroney usually shaved a few seconds off his already-short walk to class. One day the football team was out practising when the ball squirted loose. Mulroney picked up the ball and heaved it back, launching a perfect spiral that soared forever. It was a once-in-a-lifetime feat, a spectacular throw for a skinny law student. The coach later came over and invited him to try out for the team, but Mulroney declined.

The Leach family had two finished rooms in their third-floor attic. One belonged to Mulroney and Khattar, while the one across the hall belonged to Bill Murphy, another law student, and David Ronan, an engineering student at the Nova Scotia Technical College. Mrs. Leach fed them all breakfast each morning but they were on their own for lunch and dinner. Most student boarders ate at a fraternity house for 65 cents a meal or in the university cafeterias, but Mulroney wanted something better that was still economical. He had heard about Mrs. Boutilier, a sweet, elderly widow who lived in the neighbourhood and was reputed to be a great cook, but she refused to take boarders, much less cook for them. Although advised to forget about her, Mulroney phoned her anyway and was politely refused. So he stopped by her house and worked his trademark charm. Captivated by this ever-smiling young law student who looked in need of a good meal, Mrs. Boutilier agreed to serve Khattar and Mulroney lunch and dinner. For $12 a week the boys ate like kings twice a day. Mrs. Boutilier's meals became legendary and other students tried to join the table, but she refused all comers and would cook for no one else.

Meanwhile, Mulroney was taking a different kind of nourishment from his acquaintance with the Leaches' eighteen-year-old daughter, a first-year arts student at Mount St. Vincent. Anne Leach had a sweet demeanour, a magnificent complexion, a great figure, and a mind to match. Moreover she was outgoing and friendly and belonged to the youth wing of the Conservative Party, so they sometimes attended political events together. She liked to date, judging her suitors above everything else on their ability to keep her from being bored. Mulroney happily obliged and she was exactly what Mulroney needed in the wake of Rosann.

First-year law students were freshmen all over again. They met in the same classroom in Dalhousie's old law building — a small, dark, and old-fashioned stone edifice that housed the entire law school, including the law library on the top floor. Mulroney, still with his flattened brushcut, arrived for class in his regular garb, a neatly pressed shirt, sports jacket, and tie. All law students were similarly attired. Horace Read, the dean, tolerated no deviation, or almost none. For some reason, Rick Cashin, then in second year, often showed up for class in a sweater and for some reason seemed to get away with it. Mulroney sometimes departed from the norm too, but always in the other direction, with a dark suit. Their formal attire distinguished the law students on campus — the *Dalhousie Gazette* that year derisively called them the "Blue Suited Boobs" — which suited the law school just fine.

On the opening day of classes nearly fifty students crowded into the first-year lecture room, the largest first-year law class in Dalhousie history. The school's scholarship program attracted academic achievers from across Canada, as did its reputation as the Harvard of Canadian law schools. "Look to the left of you and look to the right of you," warned one professor that first day. "One of you won't be here at the end of the year." The professor had exaggerated the drop-out rate, but not by much. Dal Law had no entrance tests, but after lowering the drawbridge to let in the hordes, the school started culling them out with high demands and a killing workload. About one-fifth of any given class would almost certainly drop out or fail before the next year, unmourned by the faculty.

The university dated back to 1818, the law school to 1883, when it became the first in the British Empire to teach common law. It was an élite institution, and the faculty cultivated the mystique of élitism among the students, wanting them to feel privileged and at the same time not a little scared.

Classes began with the circulation of an attendance sheet; as the mimeographed form moved down the rows, every student signed the blank beside his or her name. This ritual would be repeated every day in every class for the rest of the school year; Dal kept track of who showed up and who did not. The message was that the students would have to work their butts off.

Dal profs did not lecture. They held tutorials and followed the Socratic method of discussion and argument. Law was taught by the case method as developed at Harvard law school: a curriculum of hundreds, even thousands, of legal cases was presented at the beginning of the year, and specific readings assigned each week. The professor introduced the cases in class and called on individual students to outline the facts and analyze the legal principles. The professor would then lead a discussion of the implications of their answers. A case might start off black and white and gradually turn grey all over.

Some students liked to sit back and watch the dialogue unfold, while others jumped into the action. Mulroney needed no prodding and fired off his analysis with speed and assurance, his voice booming with confidence from the back of the room. Insofar as the practice of law was a matter of performance, of rising to one's feet and performing on demand, Mulroney possessed the tools to be an outstanding lawyer, something he showed early in the year.

Socratic dialogue suited him well, but other aspects of Dalhousie's educational approach did not. Mulroney in no way fitted the mould of the classic legal scholar. Law was detailed, pedantic, and ultimately tedious — even a grind — and he lacked patience for chasing down every petty nuance, every fine detail. He was not a detail man and never pretended to be; nor had he much interest in the intellectual side of law. Legal issues bored him, and digging into the minutiae of legal theory bored him silly.

One other feature of the case method also gave him headaches — he could not look up the solution in a textbook. He had to chase down syllabuses, check the statute books, and research the cases themselves. There were no short cuts and no easy answers. Mulroney found the workload shocking — as did all law students, even the devoted ones — and preferred to avoid the library. But that could not be done. Law school was worse than boring, it was gruelling.

Yet not everything about Dalhousie repelled him, certainly not the after-hours life, free from the rigidity of St. FX. At Dal he could roam as far as he wanted and do anything he pleased. He discovered not long into the term that law school could mean either working very hard or hardly at all. He could skip his readings, even cut classes altogether, although a poor attendance record would be duly noted. His fate hung not on how he did in class, but on how he performed in the final exam. The faculty emphasized the classroom tutorials, but graded students on the big test in April. Mulroney figured he would pour it on in the final weeks and pull it all together. Before long he started skipping classes, first a few and then more; eventually his space on the attendance sheet remained blank more often than not.

Classmates wondered what had happened to Mulroney. He never seemed to be around, and when he did appear, he gave the impression of having been very busy, preoccupied by events the details of which no one seemed to know. Some ribbed him about staying home with Anne. Mulroney said nothing and merely grinned the grin of the cat who'd swallowed the canary. Classmates had the impression that he lacked time for class and was not much interested anyway. He seemed unconcerned about Contracts, Procedure, and Torts, courses that were making life miserable for his classmates.

Part, but not all, of the explanation was politics. Mulroney was every bit the political animal he had been at St. FX, only now he operated in the provincial capital, seat of Stanfield's government, and home of the PC Party's provincial headquarters. He participated in both provincial and federal parties as Maritime vice-president of the PC Student Federation and as a member of the Nova Scotia Young Progressive Conservatives, the off-campus Tory youth group for party members not over thirty-five. In no time he became fourth vice-president of the latter, which put him on the executive of both the student federation and the YPCs.

The dual posts gave him two regular tickets to Ottawa, the first of which he used in early December as a delegate to the YPC national convention. The senior party itself happened to be gathering in Ottawa on the same weekend. Mulroney stopped by and, after some lobbying, managed to get himself elected to its constitution committee along with some notable political heavyweights. He had seen Diefenbaker at the Nova Scotia YPC convention in Halifax in November, and now saw him again, the second time in three weeks. Virtually every time he flew to Ottawa he met with the prime minister. He still championed the Chief as much as ever, even though a couple of years of power had dimmed Dief's star in student circles. Diefenbaker and Mulroney remained close, and when the youth groups came to Ottawa, Dief made a point of looking out for him.

Mulroney's profile in the Conservative Party seemed high every-where except, strangely, at Dalhousie. He had joined the law school's PC club in September, but he attended meetings only occasionally. His interest in campus politics jumped, however, when political dignitaries visited the school. That fall Minister of Justice Davie Fulton came to promote the Bill of Rights and it was obvious that Mulroney already knew him. His fellow students had known — or would soon find out — that Mulroney also had connections with other political stars: Alvin Hamilton, Diefenbaker's minister of nor-thern affairs, flew into Halifax to see Stanfield and while there took Mulroney to dinner.

Although politics was a major diversion, his absence from class more often meant he was socializing, or recovering from having socialized the night before. Mulroney settled into Halifax quickly, perhaps too quickly, and soon came to know his way around town. His companion on many a visit to the local taverns was his roommate, Joe Khattar; neither exercised any restraint on the other.

The social life at Dalhousie was lively as well, if a bit clubby, and getting inside — so Mulroney thought — meant joining a fraternity, the only places students could find a drink on campus. Although not accepted as a member at Phi Delta, he still managed to get himself invited to many frat parties, especially the ones at Zeta Xi in an old clapboard house two blocks from where Mulroney lived. Most of the fraternity houses were sparsely furnished and shabby, but Zete, as it was called, was one of the shabbiest and the raunchiest: it was the fraternity most notorious for drinking. Zete had a six-foot beer bottle in the basement as a symbol of its true interest; patrons, so the joke went, had to wear hard hats for protection from falling beer bottles. All kinds of things happened at Zete, but never had anyone called the prime minister of Canada from inside its seedy premises. Mulroney proudly astonished a small audience by doing exactly that.

Mulroney had been anything but a womanizer at St. FX, but Dalhousie was different. Halifax had many more good-looking women than Antigonish and in the aftermath of Rosann, Mulroney soon came to know his share of them. He never boasted about his exploits but had a way of dropping hints. Stories circulated about how he and Anne would take showers together when Mrs. Leach was out of the house. The gossip usually centred on Anne, but she was only one woman in his life. Anne was more playmate than girlfriend, which suited him fine, and her too, it seemed. After all, they passed each other in the hall on their way to brush their teeth in the morning. Anne did not like playing second fiddle to his ambition and detected that he was more interested in his future than in her. As for Mulroney, the scars from Rosann had not yet healed, and he wanted to play the field.

Meanwhile Mulroney's college attendance had deteriorated even further. It was clear that he did not give a damn about class; no one ever saw him upstairs in the library either. The attendance sheet still circulated around the classroom at the start of every lecture, and students still signed it, but the passing months had inspired creativity in the entries. Some jokesters could not resist the temptation to scribble graffiti beside Mulroney's name, or register digs that were sometimes funny, rude, or simply spiteful. Vince O'Donovan, a classmate with a ready laugh and a yen for fun, and Joe Khattar skipped as many classes as Mulroney, attracting their share of wise-cracks on the sheet. O'Donovan once received a standing ovation just for showing up in class, and acknowledged the applause by standing up at his desk, his arms raised like a victorious boxer.

Once, after Mulroney failed to show up for a group project on torts, fellow student Joe Martin asked where he had been. Having lunch with Bob, replied Mulroney. "No, you weren't," Martin shot back, "because Bob was here." Mulroney looked at him smugly: "I'm talking about Bob Stanfield." Word circulated that Mulroney was spending time in Province House, Nova Scotia's legislative complex in downtown Halifax. Whenever faculty members inquired as to his whereabouts they were inevitably told he was tied up on political business. Mulroney had not endeared himself to his law schoolmates the way he had done at St. FX. Many saw him as a young man on the make, too busy hobnobbing with VIPs. He never talked about his ambition, but they could smell it.

While Mulroney ducked out of school, flaunting his indifference, the professors kept piling on the assignments and seemed to delight as students struggled to keep pace. Only those with self-discipline and exceptional talent could juggle serious extracurricular activities without paying the price. Some wondered how Mulroney could be politicking and socializing while they worked past midnight trying to keep their marks up. Mulroney gave the impression that he was above it all, that law studies were a secondary matter.

He bypassed Dalhousie's formal extracurricular activities with the exception of the debating club. He loved debate too much to stay away, and in early November he tried out for Dal's inter-varsity debating team, bringing with him the weapons that had served him so well at St. FX: the stage presence, the facility with language, the self-assurance, the sense of political theatre, the quick rebuttal, and the ability to score in battle. He made the inter-varsity team with ease.

His old nemesis, Rick Cashin, was president of the debating club and had gone from being St. FX's best debater to being Dal's top gun.

Mulroney was paired with fellow first-year law student Brian Flemming; later in November they took on the University of King's College to uphold the resolution "That Canada follow a policy of neutrality in foreign affairs." Mulroney led off the debate by suggesting that Canada should abolish its armed forces, thereby eliminating a "wasteful expenditure," and turn itself into an international mediator between east and west. Dalhousie won the debate and no one laid a glove on the Mulroney-Flemming duo for the rest of the year. They made a superb team: Mulroney performed better on stage, but Flemming prepared the research that helped make him look good. In debating, as elsewhere, Mulroney usually found others to do the digging for him.

That year Mulroney won the Angus L. Macdonald Medal, taking first place in Dalhousie's Oratorical Contest, which when added to his St. FX victories made him the top public speaker at his school for four consecutive years. He also won cash awards for several other public speaking contests around Halifax. Before each performance, the residents of the Leach household would hear him practise his standard speech on the theme of economics, rehearsing the delivery of his favourite lines.

Mulroney returned from Christmas holidays early in 1960 to an icy greeting from the registrar's office. He had done terribly on his Christmas exams. The results shocked everyone. In some ways Mulroney was the least surprised; he could hardly have anticipated much less than a complete débâcle. But it did not matter: his scores did not count. Christmas exams were nothing more than a trial run for the finals at the end of the year. They were intended to give students an idea of where they stood, and what to expect in April, but contributed nothing to their final mark. Nevertheless he realized that the party had to end at some point, and that surviving first year would be tougher than he had thought. He would get to work, but first things first: another Maritimes-wide Model Parliament was in the offing.

This was the first regional gathering since the St. FX extravaganza of two years before — this time hosted by St. Mary's University in Halifax. Unlike the slapdash Dal Law parliament, which nobody took seriously, it promised to be a grand affair, and when it convened on January 30, Mulroney was again Tory leader. But the show that St. Mary's put on fell far short of the St. FX spectacle and, more importantly, Mulroney's Tory caucus came up short in the seat count. This time the Liberals (27 seats) formed the government while the Progressive Conservatives (22 seats) shared the opposition benches with the CCF (5 seats) and Christian Atheists — "Christians broadminded enough to admit atheists" — 2 seats. Mulroney took his seat in the chair of the leader of the opposition and sat directly across the aisle from the Liberal prime minister, Rick Cashin.

During the opening debate Mulroney tried to topple Cashin's minority government. He had lined up the CCF and the Christian Atheists behind him, and the Liberals seemed doomed. The impending calamity, as well as last-minute troubles within Cashin's own ranks, distracted him and he failed to rise to his usual oratorical heights. For the first time in his life, Cashin was trounced in parliamentary debate by Mulroney; he escaped defeat only by adjourning the session to the next day.

Much changed overnight. When Parliament reconvened the next morning Cashin was again firing on all cylinders and the CCF was strangely absent. The Liberals had worked out a deal with the socialists to prop up Cashin the whole weekend, and the CCF was now lying low so it did not have to vote against its own sub-amendment to the Conservative non-confidence motion. The move caught Mulroney by surprise, but he quickly regained his composure and went on the offensive, skilfully using the rules to embarrass the CCF when it finally appeared. But he could not lay a finger on Cashin, who easily survived the rest of the session.

Later that day a Tory backbencher introduced a farcical resolution to cede Sable Island to the United Nations as a supervised international retreat, a "poor man's Pugwash." This drew laughs from both

sides of the chamber, until Mulroney stood up to speak. "In our
levity," he intoned, "we are forgetting the serious principles embodied
in this bill. We should disregard for the moment our political
concerns and realize our human obligation. The world is on the brink
of disaster. We as students should feel responsible for the failure of
the world. To get to the core of the matter, we must show the world
that Maritime university students are willing to struggle for the
welfare of mankind." As Mulroney droned on, the whole chamber
started to react around him. Nobody knew whether Mulroney had
intended to be so pious or had merely been hijacked by his own
rhetoric. The Liberals heckled, and even his own caucus squirmed
uncomfortably, but Mulroney continued. The Speaker, of all people, feigned a series of convulsive contortions and Cashin's barbs
grew more pointed. Finally Mulroney grew stiff and flushed, then
exploded into a tantrum, calling Cashin a "red-haired idiot." What
started as a harmless gag had disintegrated into a partisan slanging
match that cast a pall over the final hours of the session.

Almost as soon as Model Parliament ended, Mulroney rushed off
to Ottawa again, this time for the PC Student Federation annual
meeting. Ted Rogers, leader of Youth for Diefenbaker at the 1956
convention, was stepping down as president and Mulroney was
regarded as his heir apparent. Fellow delegates urged him to run, and
Bob Amaron, the Quebec vice-president, promised to support him;
but Mulroney unexpectedly demurred, even though he could expect
to win in a landslide, and backed Amaron instead. Amaron won
handily while Mulroney became national vice-president by acclamation. People asked why he had backed down, but Mulroney was
evasive. Most assumed the president's workload with its administration and constant travel had scared him off.

Meanwhile Premier Stanfield had entered the fourth year of his
term and political observers were waiting for the election call. All the
conjecture kept Mulroney alert, active, and out of school even more.
Dalton Camp, Stanfield's campaign guru, had already ensconced
himself in a suite in the Lord Nelson Hotel in preparation for the

coming battle. The Lord Nelson was within walking distance of the campus and was one of Mulroney's favourite watering holes. One day he simply showed up at Camp's suite unannounced and introduced himself. Camp had heard about the young man's successes at St. FX but was nonetheless surprised by his political maturity. Camp had never met a student who truly understood how the political process affected society's various vested interests, but clearly Mulroney did. He was also bilingual, which carried little weight in Nova Scotia in 1960 but set him apart nonetheless. Camp sized him up as a comer, and before long invited him to join the election strategy group, which already included Finlay MacDonald and Norman Atkins, both rising backroom Tories.

Soon winter was half gone, and the time was approaching when even the slackest of students rolled up their sleeves for some serious study. Joe Khattar had already come to terms with the inevitable and packed his bags and gone to the United States, leaving Mulroney alone to his room. (Bill Murphy across the hall took Khattar's place at Mrs. Boutilier's dinner table.) Mulroney considered quitting too, but decided to stick it out. However, even an optimist like himself realized the hour was late and that his cramming had better start soon.

Then in late February he fell sick and became too ill to study, despite his good intentions. Earlier in the year he had suffered acute headaches, prompting Mrs. Leach to urge him to have his eyes tested. But this was different; it had nothing to do with headaches or eye strain. He quietly checked into the Victoria General Hospital. Whatever was wrong with him, he told no one.

Illness was the last thing he needed. His schedule for catching up could not accommodate down time, and being sick played havoc with his political activities. First he missed Dal Law's annual PC club elections for next year's slate of executives, and the club went ahead and filled its executive board without him, although he had not been very active and was no longer sure he would return to Dal the following year anyway. More importantly, he missed a trip to Montreal for a critical PC Student Federation executive meeting on March

5, probably the most important gathering of the year since the executive would be allocating its annual budget.

The ailment dragged Mulroney down for weeks and continued to bedevil him after his release from hospital. He was up and about, but his usual pep and vigour were missing. He looked pale, run down, and positively gaunt. The nature of his ailment was known only to him and his doctor. Even the fact that he had spent time at the Victoria General was a carefully guarded piece of news. A few trusted friends had visited him at bedside, but Mulroney managed to keep the word out of general circulation. (In later years many of his classmates, perhaps as many as half, were under the impression he had dropped out after Christmas.) General ignorance allowed Mulroney to suppress his secret — for a while at least — but word of his illness eventually leaked out, and when it did the rumours started spreading.

When people asked, Mulroney passed off his troubles as a virus and let it go at that. No detail was offered, but he incriminated himself by giving different explanations in different circles. One story had him down with mononucleosis, a credible explanation since the affliction was going around campus and would explain his anemic appearance. Another story put him in hospital for a minor surgical procedure, and that seemed true as far as it went, because while there he was circumcised. In fact the bandages had been applied so amply that people would notice the extra bulge in his pants. But Mulroney was not fessing up even to circumcision. Yet another story laid him low with an infection in his urinary tract, which also made sense and could explain the circumcision. Earlier in the year he had talked about the need to see a urologist about a problem with his waterworks.

But another story also made the rounds and if true explained his passion for secrecy. This story had Mulroney attending a fraternity party one night, drinking too much, and being taken to Africville by his companions. Africville was a little shanty town that sat at the tip of the Halifax Peninsula, inhabited mainly by blacks. After 11 P.M., when prudent Halifax closed its taverns and rolled up its sidewalks, anyone wanting a drink headed for Africville, where bootleggers abounded. Prostitutes could be found there as well, and what started out as a student drinking spree turned into a minor sexual escapade, or so the story went. Word had it that Mulroney's alleged sortie in Africville had landed him in hospital with a virulent form of venereal disease. The Africville story was discussed, and people were unsure what to make of it. It made sense given his happy-go-lucky social life but was so scandalous nobody confronted him with it.

When Mulroney returned to campus that spring he looked like anything but the cheery, congenial student of the previous September. He had vainly tried to keep on top of the course work from his hospital bed but found it impossible. The mystery illness and its lingering aftermath had set him still further behind, and now he was worried. He no longer laughed easily and had become uncharacteristically withdrawn. He seemed contemplative and preoccupied, as if grappling with serious decisions. His voice also betrayed his inner turmoil. It had dropped lower, a sure sign of personal distress. Through it all he carried a decidedly hangdog look.

As the weeks passed, he found himself so out of touch with his course material that half the time he had not the foggiest idea what other students were talking about. Reclaiming a squandered year in the final weeks would take a miracle. His confidence and internal resolve had taken a beating, but he did not want others to know he was hurting. It was important to put on his best face.

Mulroney decided he could still salvage the year by going flat out in a concentrated blitz. It would be tough and would require some serious work, but he could still pull it off. He had come from behind in Latin at St. Thomas and ultimately emerged at the top of the class. He had done it brilliantly at St. FX, especially in Sister Veronica's Canadian history course, where he skipped classes half the year and then wrote the finals with the help of Jim Conrad's notes and scored almost as well as Conrad himself. But that was nothing compared with what confronted him now. He would need a strategy, help from other students, and a bloody good set of borrowed notes.

His search for notes took him to Lawrence Hayes, a gold medal student who always hovered at or near the top of the class. He also paid a visit to Vince O'Donovan, who had missed as many classes as he had. O'Donovan happened to have in his possession the notes of Paul Creaghan, the star student who had preceded Mulroney as Tory leader at St. FX, now in his second year at Dal Law. Notes by Creaghan, a Dunn Scholar and a gold medallist, were worth chasing down, and Mulroney lost no time convincing O'Donovan to share his wealth.

But easily the best set of notes in the school belonged to his friend and debating partner Brian Flemming. Flemming had the unusual, almost bizarre habit of typing his notes. At home each evening he arranged the day's lecture topic into a structured outline, pounded the results into a typewriter, and then colour-coded the works. The result was an academic treasure trove, and Mulroney made sure he got his hands on the complete set.

Now that he had notes — lots of them — Mulroney looked for other kinds of help, picking the brains of classmates and getting what he needed through casual conversation. He did it deftly, cannily, even brilliantly, extracting the essentials, filling holes, and scooping up hot tips. For someone so young and mouthy, he listened astutely and knew when to shut up and absorb.

Above all, Mulroney relied on Flemming. Flemming realized that Mulroney did not know the course material, that he lacked even an elementary grasp of the work, but he did not despair. He had watched Mulroney prepare for debates and recognized his intuitive intelligence, his knack for the instant assimilation of facts, and his ability to survive in the crunch. Flemming took it as a challenge to prop him up for the oncoming finals and see what would happen.

He tutored Mulroney, starting with a practical strategy that gave him a fighting chance. It was too late to learn the course; instead, they would examine the examiner and look for clues as to what the final might hold. They treated the exam as a political challenge that required Mulroney to understand the likes and prejudices of the professor and to cling to any advantage to get him through. It represented his only hope at this late stage.

They assembled as many old exams as they could find, searching for recurring themes. After picking out the common threads, Flemming introduced him to the legal principles behind them, laying out the main issues and the kinds of questions that would have to be answered. Meanwhile Mulroney familiarized himself with twenty to thirty key cases so that he could drop some names, hoping to give the appearance of depth. The goal was not to learn law but to pass the exam.

Flemming's coaching brought Mulroney a long way, especially on Criminal Law and Contracts, and helped him make progress on Torts. But Property I and Procedure I were another matter. Mulroney was in no shape to write either exam, especially the nitpicking Procedure I. It was a simple course full of petty — even silly — detail. There were no short cuts, and he hardly had the time to read the material, let alone absorb it. If any course would punish him for past sins, this was the one. His only hope lay in buying extra time and an opportunity to prepare, and that meant postponing the exam, no mean feat since he would need special dispensation from the dean.

It was a feat all right, but not as impossible as it seemed. Mulroney had ingratiated himself with the ruling powers at Dalhousie just as he had done at St. FX and in Baie Comeau before that. He had made himself known to the university hierarchy and specifically to Dr. Alexander Kerr, the president, who thought highly of him. Somehow he had built up goodwill with the faculty, despite his poor attendance records. When he did come to class he often stayed after the lecture and talked with the professor, provoking some classmates to sneer that he was sucking up. Only one other classmate did it as blatantly as he did, and that was Clyde Wells, a first-year student from Newfoundland, but he lacked Mulroney's finesse. "Brian was more sophisticated than just going up and kissing ass," says one classmate. "Brian knew how to kiss ass in an artistic way. Clyde was simple and direct, just like he is today."

Mulroney had been genuinely sick, and that allowed him to build a case for special consideration. The administration recognized that he had fallen down as a student but concluded that extenuating circumstances had robbed him of a fair chance, so the university granted him permission to postpone the writing of Property I and Procedure I, and the course work for Research and Writing.

When Mulroney walked out of the examination room in late April, he felt reasonably confident about Criminal Law and Contracts. Thanks to Flemming's coaching, he had been ready for most of the questions and believed he had answered them satisfactorily. The Torts exam was another matter. Torts dealt with negligence issues and personal injuries such as automobile accidents and libel and slander, and was taught by a young whiz fresh out of Harvard, Professor Ed Harris, nicknamed "Fast Eddie" for his speed at putting students through their paces. Harris demanded precision and thoroughness, and his material did not lend itself especially well to last-minute cramming. The final simply demanded more than he knew, and Mulroney had missed enough to realize that he had blown it. The botched Torts exam had sealed his fate, and nothing depressed him more than knowing he had flunked. The hardest part would be explaining it to his parents.

As Mulroney dragged himself through the last week of exams, Premier Stanfield surprised almost no one by dissolving the Nova Scotia legislature and calling a general election for June 7. With the exams over, Mulroney needed to get away from campus, and the election was his deliverance. Leaving his academic future hanging, he plunged into the campaign. He did not allow study time for his postponed exams, but he no longer cared.

Elections always perked up his spirits, and now that the race was under way his enthusiasm returned. The Lord Nelson crowd knew nothing of the personal travail he had left behind on campus. Mulroney put aside his problems whenever he stepped into the political arena, relieved to have the distraction of more pleasant tasks. When CBC announcer Max Ferguson declined the Tories' invitation to narrate their radio commercials, Mulroney stepped in to record a series of thirty-second scripted spots proclaiming Nova Scotia's need for Stanfield. He delivered his lines well, but the radio ads were just the beginning. A special assignment awaited him up in Dalton Camp's suite.

Camp directed his young aide to travel across the province and drop into small communities to spread the gospel of Robert Stanfield. Mulroney hit the road, opening doors wherever he went. Parish priests, teachers, and local Tory officials were won over by this personable law student and welcomed him into their midst. Camp could not have chosen a better ambassador. But promoting the virtues of the premier was not Mulroney's true mission, which was to gather intelligence. He needed only an hour or two at each stop to pick up the locals' thinking and learn virtually everything that was going on in the community.

He returned regularly to the Lord Nelson Hotel to brief Camp on the details. The entertainment value of his reports alone made them worth listening to, but above all, they provided invaluable information that allowed Stanfield to whistle through those same towns later, aware of the local sensitivities, knowing precisely where to inflame feelings and where to soft-pedal. Mulroney's legwork had introduced modern campaigning to Nova Scotia. He was doing "issue advance work." It was not called that back then, but it would soon grow into a standard campaign practice and a science of its own. In 1960 no provincial campaign had ever used it before.

There was more to Mulroney's countryside ramblings than spreading the gospel and doing advance work — much more. Back in his hotel suite, Camp had tagged him for a clandestine mission that was underhanded or even worse, although quite in keeping with the traditional spirit of Nova Scotia elections.

Stanfield had ousted Henry Hicks as premier four years earlier and now faced him again, and that worried some Tories because Stanfield's 1956 victory over Hicks had been a fluke. The Tories owed their triumph not to the strength of the Conservative campaign, but to the Liberals' disarray after choosing Hicks as their leader. Hicks, a Protestant, had come from behind to whip Harold Connolly, a Catholic, on the fifth ballot. The manner in which it happened had set Catholic against Protestant in a religious gang-up. Catholics had always voted Liberal and had regarded the party as their political turf, but many of them voted Tory or stayed home in 1956, opening the door to Stanfield. In 1960, these Catholics once again held the key to Tory success. Keeping them out of the Liberal fold became part of the Conservative Party's strategy, and the person picked to spread the enmity in this unholy cause was Mulroney.

The Conservatives learned that a prominent Montreal journalist and author named Leslie Roberts had been hired to help Hicks on the campaign, and that gave them some convenient ammunition. Roberts, along with well-known figures like Eleanor Roosevelt, had once sat on the editorial board of a U.S. magazine called *The Protestant.* At the end of the war the magazine had suddenly turned anti-Catholic, and Eleanor Roosevelt and others promptly quit. As far as anyone knew, Roberts had stayed on, and that made Hicks vulnerable to a whisper campaign. Mulroney, one of the few Catholics on the Stanfield team, was given the task of planting suspicions about Roberts and his past associations. While Mulroney was on the road in quest of intelligence, he was also quietly spreading the word among the Catholic faithful as to who Henry Hicks had working for him. It was a classic undercover smear campaign, and Mulroney was the perfect agent to carry it off.

The war was fought above ground too, and sometimes bitterly. In the end Stanfield scored a greater victory than in 1956 and broke the Liberal grip on the province, changing forever the landscape of Nova Scotia politics. The campaign had been exhilarating for Mulroney, but there was no escaping the academic reckoning awaiting him back on campus.

The results of the exams, which had come out during the campaign, confirmed his bleak expectations:

Criminal Law, 65

Contracts, 60
Torts, 42
Property I — incomplete
Procedure I — incomplete
Research and Writing — incomplete

The transcript reduced the academic year to cold reality: two passes; one all-out failure; and three incompletes, which would become failures by the end of summer if he did not do something about them. He had yet to write Procedure I and Property I. Research and Writing had no final exam, but Mulroney had not done his assignments, so it too needed work. He had failed Torts outright, and that was a problem.

Dal Law operated on the all-or-nothing principle, which required students to pass all six courses before moving on to second year. Partial years counted for nothing. Failing one course meant failing the whole year. However, the school, tough as it was, allowed students to write supplemental exams in the summer and reinstate themselves into the program, provided they had not failed more than two subjects and maintained a 55 average. Mulroney had already received dispensation for half his courses and still flunked. A second request for special consideration stretched the spirit of the rule and the generosity of the school, but once again the university took pity on him and gave him the opportunity to rewrite the Torts exam.

Given yet another chance, he had to decide whether he wanted to go through with it after all. Writing the supplementals made no sense if he was quitting, which is what his instincts told him to do. Since breaking up with Rosann, he had wondered what he was doing at Dal anyway; now he was suffering the consequences of an impulsive decision. He wanted out, but it meant walking away from a whole year and starting over again somewhere else. He was no longer sure he wanted to be a lawyer at all. The debate raged within him but rarely surfaced. He was too proud to pour out his inner turmoil.

However, he needed counsel, so he called on Professor Andy McKay. The good-natured McKay was the most approachable professor on the faculty, an easy man to talk to, and anything but a taskmaster. Mulroney had sought him out before and had found him wise and sympathetic. They talked for nearly half an hour, and while leaving much unsaid, Mulroney came as close to unburdening himself as his dignity allowed. He did not hide the simple truth that he was struggling with a difficult decision and was unsure of what to do.

Mulroney said he was considering switching over to the law school at Laval. McKay cautioned him to think carefully about changing law schools, and about dropping common law in favour of civil law. A common law school like Dalhousie offered access to more parts of the country than a civil law school. With a Dalhousie degree, McKay said, he could practise in Nova Scotia or in Ontario or anywhere in the West, for that matter. A civil law school like Laval would tie him to Quebec. Mulroney replied that his roots were in Quebec; he wanted to settle and establish himself there, and he believed that was where his political future lay. Mulroney impressed McKay with the fervour of his commitment to his home province.

Mulroney also revealed that he had half a mind to skip law school entirely and jump straight into politics, that politics really interested him more than law anyway. McKay, in his adviser's role, applauded his commitment to public service but cautioned him about being too hasty, and advised him to establish a professional base before embracing a political career. Mulroney could not dispute McKay's advice. It made sense that he would enjoy a softer landing in politics by securing his law degree first. Mulroney struck McKay as an earnest young man who had gotten into some difficulty and was now trying to sort out his future. The gravity of his circumstances had not erased the old Mulroney charm. When the interview was over McKay was unsure just what his troubled first-year student would ultimately decide.

Mulroney's decision to stay in the Maritimes for the election had stretched his finances to the limit, and he needed to start earning some money for September, whatever it might bring. He could have found summer work in Halifax, but Baie Comeau offered the best-paying jobs, and living at home allowed him to put more into the bank. Baie Comeau also offered a sanctuary where he could lick his wounds in peace. In early June he returned home, as he had done every summer since he first went to boarding school.

Over the previous five summers Mulroney had watched his home grow from a sleepy company town to a thriving centre of enterprise. Colonel McCormick was dead and so was the old Baie Comeau. The mill was disposing of its stock of houses, and in the summer of 1960 one of the buyers who took advantage of the sell-off was Ben Mulroney, who snapped up a house at 79 Champlain Street and moved a little further up the hill, a home-owner at last.

The town had not just grown, it had boomed with the construction of another power dam on the Manicouagan River, an aluminum plant, and new elevators built by Cargill Grain. Each development brought a fresh wave of construction workers from outside, and university students flocked in every summer, landing jobs as soon as they got off the boat. As a local boy, Mulroney had his pick of summer positions, and each summer brought a different job. One year he lived alone in a cabin in the bush five miles out of town, guarding access to a gate for fire protection. The job required his presence twenty-four hours a day. Friends would come up for visits, but it was awfully lonely. Another summer he drove a station wagon and shuttled employees from town to the new aluminum plant job site. The job was classified as that of truckdriver and that allowed him, in later political life, to claim he had been a truckdriver. Another year he worked in the paper mill. Industrial jobs like these paid handsomely.

Despite his long periods away at school Mulroney had not lost his knack for touching base around town. Like the other workers, Mulroney stopped off at the Taverne Aux Amies after work. But unlike the others, he made a detour first. While most headed straight to the tavern, Mulroney sneaked home and washed up and traded his working garb for a fashionable T-shirt and some khaki slacks. It was a touch of American dress that he had picked up from the New England crowd at St. FX. Only after he had spiffed himself up did he head for the tavern.

When Mulroney entered the tavern he wended his way over towards a table of mill old-timers on their second or third round. "Brian, ça va bien?" He knew each one by name and slapped them on the back. They begged him to stay and sit down awhile and tell them how Ben's son was doing at university, and bought him a quart of beer. Mulroney nursed his quart bottle and turned on the charm and got them going. He had not finished half his quart before he was gone and sitting with his collegian friends at another table, taking with him his bottle of beer. If the old-timers caught on to this routine, it doesn't seem to have bothered them.

Mulroney usually strutted around Baie Comeau as if he owned it, dropping in at the Taverne Aux Amies after work, socializing with the regulars at the tennis club. But not in the summer of 1960. After arriving late in the season because of the Nova Scotia election, he seemed unusually quiet and was strangely scarce, and the residents of Baie Comeau could not help but notice. He went back to being a gatekeeper-cum-firewatcher, this time at the newly opened Cargill Grain elevator, and passed his time guarding access to a private road and fighting the occasional brush fire. The job would normally have bored him to death, but it was exactly what he needed; he had all the free time in the world to study for his exams. Sheer boredom would force him to do it, or so he hoped.

He found studying just as tough in summer as in winter, indeed tougher. The study of law interested him no more now than before, and he concluded that the sacrifice of his summer guaranteed him nothing. If he returned to Dal and failed again he would be bounced straight back to first year, and at that late stage have no time to move to another school. "I am again in a quandary as to what university to attend in the fall," he wrote to a friend on August 2. "I have written to quite a few places, making all kinds of inquiries, but have yet to make the decision. It will probably be Laval — or Dal — or Montreal, etc. (See the spot I'm in!)"

Either Mulroney believed he could do anything in the world or he could not be bothered, and at this low point he could not motivate himself to make the effort. He saw no point in writing the exams, and in the summer heat of Baie Comeau, he talked himself out of trying. He also ruled out repeating first year at Dalhousie. Starting over at Dal meant conspicuous failure, sticking out like the dumb kids who repeated their years in grade school. If he had to start over he might as well do it somewhere else, where nobody knew, where he could begin afresh, not only in the minds of his classmates but in his own mind too.

Most students learned about Mulroney's departure the following September when they arrived for the new school year and looked around the class. He was one of eleven first-year students who failed to show up for second year. As the weeks passed, his name surfaced occasionally. One rumour had him taking an important job in Ottawa in the office of Minister of Justice Davie Fulton, but others figured he had just flunked out. Now and then law students in the Lord Nelson tavern lifted a schooner to his memory, and when classmate Bob Scammell graduated in 1962 the caption for his yearbook picture included the puzzling words: "V.-Pres. B. Mulrooney [sic] Memorial and T.G.I.T." Years later students would wonder what T.G.I.T. stood for. Nobody would admit to knowing.

The president of the university took Mulroney's departure more seriously than did his classmates. President Alexander Kerr treated the news with genuine sorrow. Each fall he welcomed the new crop of incoming students in his convocation speech, and his October 1960 address seemed to be written with Mulroney in mind, although he gave no names and mentioned no specifics. The president urged new students — "the children of Dalhousie" — not to go overboard now that they were free from the restraints of home, and to devote themselves to study. He counselled his audience to remember why they had come to university, to subordinate extracurricular interests to the purpose of study, and to consult their teachers if they got into difficulty. "I shall always be glad to see you if you think there is ever anything that I can do to help you."

The president's words were apt. Mulroney had indeed gone overboard. His unhappy career at Dal demonstrated that he could not handle freedom without rules; he needed limits. Although at St. FX he had spent half his time trying to outwit the rules, and had often succeeded, he always knew they were there. Artificial as they were, he needed those imposed restraints, for he had few natural boundaries of his own. His inclination always was to get going, and surge ahead, and strive for more. There was little in his make-up that cautioned him to slow down or hold back. He did not know how to stop, or when. Nature had blessed him with many natural gifts but had forgotten to give him a set of brakes, or the instinct to use them. Mulroney had experienced a painful lesson, namely that his unchecked impulses could drive him down as well as up.

Lack of boundaries helped explain his skill at selling himself up and down the social ladder. It explained his natural facility for relating to everyone from the francophone kids on Laval Street to John Diefenbaker in Ottawa. The huge invisible boundaries that stopped others never stood in his way because he never saw them.

Moral boundaries sometimes escaped his radar system as well. At times he could not separate right from wrong, good from bad. It seemed he lacked a moral rudder. Not that he was immoral. When faced with the need for a Hungarian relief fund, or when in the company of the upright Robert Stanfield, he became virtuous, principled, and outright Christian, and meant it sincerely. He wore the cloak of virtue often and it fit well. However, other clothes hung in his closet and he put them on in the company of drinking companions and fraternity pals and looked equally comfortable. When it came to choosing his friends he could not distinguish between the scrupulous and the sleazy. All looked the same to him, and all influenced him equally. For just as he had a gift for influencing people, he in turn was easily influenced. With no personal code to guide him, he adopted the morality of those around him.

His failure at Dalhousie devastated him, pierced his shield of confidence, and caused him — momentarily — to doubt his own abilities. He had always flown high, defying gravity; never had he crashed like this before, nor been so humbled. Now he had learned that he could fall flat on his face like anybody else, a most unpleasant lesson. In fact, it was a lesson he could not accept; to do so would threaten the foundation of his innermost persona, which was the belief that he could do anything, that nothing could stop him, and that no boundaries could confine his ambition. Dalhousie had proven him wrong. He could not acknowledge his shortcomings and still remain invincible, and largely for that reason Dalhousie confronted him with the biggest crisis of his life to date.

Mulroney allowed old Dal acquaintances to believe that his switch to Laval had everything to do with returning to his Quebec roots and nothing to do with marks. There was no mention of failure, no reference to his real reason for choosing Halifax — Rosann Earl. In later years Mulroney frequently regaled his friends with amusing stories about his college days, but never once mentioned Dalhousie. Dal did not exist in his anthology of anecdotes. It was a missing year, a mysterious gap in his biography. Acquaintances who did not know better assumed he had moved straight from St. FX to Laval, and those who did know better knew better than to ask. Except for his Dalhousie debating partner, Brian Flemming, with whom he would collaborate as a lawyer in the 1970s, no lifelong friendships were born at Dalhousie. He spoke of Cashin, Creaghan, and Gerry Doucet, but only in their St. FX days.

Occasionally circumstances left him no choice but to acknowledge his time at Dalhousie, such as when he was interviewed by the authors of his first two biographies. "I had been in the Maritimes six or seven years," he was quoted as saying in *Brian Mulroney: The Boy from Baie-Comeau* (by Rae Murphy, Robert Chodos, and Nick Auf der Maur), which dismissed Dalhousie in half a paragraph, "and was sort of thinking: 'This is a great place; I might settle down here.' Then I suddenly thought: 'Hell, all my roots are in Quebec. I'd better hightail it back home.'" He flatly told biographer L. Ian MacDonald that he had not failed. "I found out you could transfer, and then I was ill for part of the year," he told MacDonald in *Mulroney: The Making of the Prime Minister.* "By Christmas, I was pretty clear I wanted to transfer. I enjoyed it, but I wanted to get back to Quebec. So at Christmas I went home and decided to transfer to Laval, with a series of accepted credits."

In fact he did not transfer. He enrolled fresh at Laval and started first-year law over again, without any credits from Dalhousie. Transferring credits between the two systems was not possible in 1960, but saying he had transferred allowed him to maintain the façade of unbroken triumph. His statement was nominally directed at L. Ian MacDonald but was really meant for himself, because he needed to convince himself more than anybody else that he had not failed. He resolved his Dalhousie crisis by wiping it from his memory and pretending it never happened.

CHAPTER SIX

COMEBACK

WHEN MULRONEY ARRIVED at Laval University in September 1960, he had traded much more than one provincial capital for another. Pleasant as Halifax was, it could not compare to Quebec City. Quebec simply offered too much charm, too much vitality, and too much history. Its chief enchantment was the beautifully preserved Quartier Latin inside the stone walls of the Old City, which had not changed much from the colonial capital that had fallen to the British two hundred years earlier. The grey stone buildings hugged the streets and left just enough room for two cars to pass. The streets twisted and veered in every direction, and the quarter teemed with restaurants, pubs, cafés — and life. It ranked among the most delightful cities in the world.

Laval University had spent a century in the Quartier Latin but, with the exception of the law school, had recently fled to shiny new quarters in the suburbs. The law school remained in the heart of the Old City in its nineteenth-century premises, waiting until the new campus could digest it. Law students counted themselves lucky to have the run of the quarter and to partake of its exuberant spirit. In coming to Laval University when he did, Mulroney joined the last generation of students to graduate out of the Quartier Latin.

The old campus had no residences. Out-of-town students usually made their living quarters in rooming-houses, which is what Mulroney did. He settled into Au Vieux Foyer at 71 Saint-Louis Street in the heart of the Old City, only seven or eight minutes' walk to class. Au Vieux Foyer was a century-old grey stone building with an elegant staircase, hardwood floors, large mirrors, beautiful chandeliers, and, true to its name, fireplaces in almost every room. For $10 a week Mulroney shared room No. 5, a huge fifteen-by-twenty-foot space on the second floor with a private bath and fireplace. Never before had he lived anywhere so splendid.

One of the delights of 71 Saint-Louis, and one of the reasons why it always had a waiting list, was the landlady, Mademoiselle Fortin, a thin, tallish, and amiable spinster who lived in the basement and came upstairs to banter good-naturedly with her tenants. Students regularly dropped down to her basement flat for a game of cards. She also happened to be a strong Liberal and was not shy about expressing her partisan views.

For an extra fee Mademoiselle Fortin provided dinner in her kitchen, but Mulroney usually caught his meals at little cafés in the neighbourhood. The Quartier Latin was good for that. Tiny eating spots were tucked away in all sorts of nooks and crannies, and three or four of them were cheaper than the rest. A couple of them even sold meal cards for students. At the Café de la Paix Mulroney could get soup, a hamburger steak, and mashed potatoes for 99 cents. A pricey meal would set him back $1.25. He also ate occasionally at the Buade, but favoured a restaurant a couple of hundred yards from the law school that everybody called "the Sweden" because of the brand name emblazoned on its soft-ice-cream machine. Mulroney's cousin, Elmar Kane, was part-owner of this dairy bar and eatery and gave him discounts on meals. His Aunt Jenny worked upstairs in the office of Elmar's restaurant-equipment businesses. Jenny Keenan, his father's sister and now a childless widow, adored her nephew, and Mulroney popped up to see her almost every day. They often dined downstairs together and Aunt Jenny always picked up the bill.

Around 7:50 each weekday morning Mulroney rushed out of 71 Saint-Louis and headed for school, stopping along the way at a smoke shop for coffee and a pack of cigarettes, his only breakfast. Usually he landed at his seat with only a minute to spare before the 8:00 start of classes. But arriving late was no big sin; the professors themselves often came late and the mood was casual. Many showed up carrying coffee, a newspaper, and sometimes a sandwich or doughnut. They could afford to sit back and relax in class since Laval did not teach law by the case method as did Dalhousie. Professors here gave traditional lectures, and as they talked the students munched their breakfast and passed around cigarettes. Everybody was supposed to wear a shirt and tie, but not everybody did, and nobody seemed to mind. Laval could hardly have been more different from Dalhousie.

Another contrast to Halifax for Mulroney was that he knew absolutely no one when he arrived, but that changed soon enough.

"Do you speak English too?" Mulroney asked one classmate on his first day.

"Yes, I do," replied Michael Meighen, who had graduated from McGill.

Mulroney was surprised. He had expected to be the lone English-speaker at Laval. In its 106 years the law school had hardly ever seen an anglophone. He grew more surprised still when he discovered that of seventy-odd law students entering Laval in the fall of 1960, eight came from English-speaking backgrounds. Laval had never seen anything like it. In an age when few English-speaking Canadians bothered to acquaint themselves with Quebec, anglophones who accepted education in French were avant-garde.

Initially the anglophones awkwardly flocked together but Mulroney didn't let this last long. With the Dalhousie experience now behind him, he had reverted to his customary confidence and conviviality. Now, on the first day of classes, he quickly met all the Anglos and introduced himself to the francophones. Soon he was shuttling back and forth between the two groups, just as he had shuttled between Champlain Street and Laval Street in Baie Comeau. The Anglos thought he had a special tie to the francophones, and the francophones thought he was "one of those guys" but liked him. In no time the cultural boundary had melted and everyone in the class got along famously — as it probably would have anyway, only Mulroney speeded the process along.

Several of the sons of the Quebec élite sat in his classroom. Michael Meighen's grandfather was Arthur Meighen, the ninth prime minister of Canada. Jean Comtois's father, Paul, was the minister of mines in Diefenbaker's cabinet, and Jean Bazin's uncle, Marc Drouin, was the Speaker of the Senate. Only one year ahead was Jules Lesage, son of the new premier of Quebec.

But the real story was not so much where the freshman class of 1960 had come from, but where it would go. He found himself among a remarkable group of intelligent and motivated students whose meteoric climb would outstrip all classes before. When Mulroney became prime minister he would pick from that class a cabinet minister, two senators, a chief of staff, and a principal secretary. But the class would still do extraordinarily well without his help, producing several judges, cabinet ministers both in Ottawa and in Quebec, and a string of high-profile lawyers and successful business executives. Almost everyone was destined for success.

Laval law students always stood up when they asked a question in class. "Excuse-moi, monsieur, veux-tu dire . . . ?" Mulroney would begin. He was on his feet a lot and at first always addressed his professors with the casual "tu" instead of the formal "vous." The class smirked a little, and silently cheered him on. No francophone could pull it off, or would even try, but the professors passed it off with a smile. Hardly anyone used "vous" in a mill town like Baie Comeau.

Never before had Mulroney lived in an exclusively French-speaking environment, and it showed. His French had impressed Antigonish and Halifax, but it did not impress Quebec City. Although his accent was good, his usage was unpolished, as would be expected from an anglophone who had picked it up in the streets. By Laval standards he spoke slowly. Often he had to grope for the right word. Sometimes he stopped in mid-flight to ask about nuances and precise meanings, and he frequently made grammatical mistakes. His French improved enormously at Laval, but it was never good enough for the debating team. The closest he came was coaching housemate André Tremblay on technique for the big Villeneuve inter-varsity debating tournament, which Tremblay went on to win.

Apart from the challenge of taking classes entirely in French, Laval law school proved amazingly easy. Morning lectures ended by 10:00 and the next lecture did not begin until 4:00 P.M. Classes finished for the day at 6:00 P.M. The strange hours were designed to accommodate the schedules of the professors, most of whom were practising lawyers. Sometimes a professor interrupted himself in mid-lecture to dash off for an urgent appointment. The faculty did little academic research, published few learned articles, and cancelled a lot of classes. They also gave few work assignments, which spared them the drudgery of marking. As at Dalhousie, everything hinged on the final exam but nobody fretted about exams here. Students could cram in the final weeks and still do well. Compared with McGill, the University of Montreal, or just about any other law school in the country, Laval was a picnic.

With no difficult assignments to carry out, and a six-hour gap to fill, Mulroney could spend the best part of his day any way he pleased. When classes broke at 10:00, students scattered in all directions. A few keeners headed over to the law library, but they were exceptions. Some had part-time jobs; others concentrated on sports and other traditional extracurricular activities. If a good case was coming up, some students wandered off to the courthouse and watched top lawyers perform. But most, especially those in first year, whiled away their mornings doing nothing in particular — and often their afternoons too — seemingly without a care in the world.

Of the idle majority, some wandered over to Couillard Street and parked themselves in Le Cercle des Étudiants, the little student lounge, and ordered toast and played billiards. Others coalesced into small groups and invaded the little neighbourhood cafés where they read newspapers, played cards, and talked about current events.

Mulroney usually tagged along with the café crowd and as often as not steered the gang over to cousin Elmar's restaurant for lunch.

However, when the Quebec legislature was sitting, Mulroney often skipped the café camaraderie and strolled over for question period, often accompanied by friends such as Meighen and Michel Cogger. Cogger was the French-Canadian version of the Pillsbury Dough Boy, short and good-natured. People wanted to poke him in the stomach and watch him giggle. A highly likeable person who wore his heart on his sleeve, he could give off a shrug as expressive as René Lévesque's. When they first met, Cogger acted as Mulroney's tour guide, pointing out the good taverns and restaurants. Although Cogger was a Liberal, and so had some entrée to the governing party, Mulroney did not need much help in finding the corridors of power. In no time he knew the entire press corps, and most of the politicians too.

In the Quartier Latin nothing was easier than meeting a politician. The legislature sat just outside the walls of the Old City, and politicians, journalists, and students all walked the same narrow streets and soon got to know one another. Mulroney made it his business to cross paths with them all. He knew their favourite hang-outs and when to be where. Whenever something important was happening, he appeared on the scene.

On most evenings around 10:00 Mulroney stopped by the Aquarium restaurant on Sainte-Anne Street, where politicians, journalists, and artists ritually gathered for a late-evening snack and a few beers. René Lévesque, Quebec's young minister of hydraulic resources and public works, dropped in regularly. In those days politicians and journalists drank together and shared secrets in complete trust. Mulroney relished the gossip and the backroom revelations and blended in perfectly among the older men, who accepted him as one of them.

Sometimes leaving the Aquarium after midnight, Mulroney might head up the street and around the corner to the Château Frontenac, where he would slip into the bar and manoeuvre himself over to Daniel Johnson, a prominent member of the Union Nationale.

Johnson was a night-hawk who lived in the Château Frontenac and often stopped in for a drink. He loved talking into the night and holding court. At that point Johnson was apparently a has-been, an old-line member of a discredited party, but Mulroney spent many hours with him nonetheless.

In earlier days Mulroney had carved out a minor specialty of winning oratorical contests in which he denounced the Union Nationale under Duplessis, but that did not stop him from drinking with the man who had been Duplessis's parliamentary assistant and one of his cabinet ministers. Making connections won out over differences of party or philosophy any day, although there were times when even Mulroney had limits. "Jesus Christ," he once exploded after listening to Johnson preach about the need for morality in politics, "the Union Nationale party is probably the most corrupt political machine in Christendom. How can you sit there and talk about morality?" Johnson did not blink. "So what, Brian," he said. "Lloyd George was a son of a bitch too." Johnson and Mulroney each had a roguish charm that appealed to the other. When Johnson looked at Mulroney he saw an image of himself as a younger man, someone who had risen from a humble background by massaging egos, building networks, remembering names, and keeping track of where all the dead bodies lay.

Not long after arriving at Laval, Mulroney joined the Union Nationale despite having once vilified it. The Union Nationale was philosophically close to the Tory party, but Mulroney had denounced it too hard and too long for him to blithely embrace it now. He believed everything about the Duplessis era was crooked, and even though Duplessis was dead and his party was out of office, it was being run by an ageing band of his cronies. Still, if Mulroney wanted to muck about in Quebec provincial politics, he had to pick between the Liberals and the Union Nationale. The Liberals disgusted him even more. Although the Quebec Liberal Party was the overwhelming preference of Laval students, it was in bed with the federal Liberals. Mulroney could never cosy up to them. Ever since St. FX, he had hated the party. "Les maudits Libéraux" (Damn Liberals) was one of his favourite expressions. So, unpalatable as he found it, Mulroney joined the Union Nationale and thereby endorsed the party he had repeatedly condemned over the last five years.

Mulroney could not have picked a more electrifying time to show up in Quebec's capital. He had surfaced in Quebec City just ten weeks after Jean Lesage's historic victory over the Union Nationale in June 1960, arriving just in time to see Quebec awaken from a long slumber as the new Liberal government swept away sixteen years of Union Nationale cobwebs. Lesage and his Liberals were turning Quebec upside down with reform. The Catholic clergy was being stripped of its political power, and social reform was in the air. Quebec City was boiling with ideas. Mulroney could watch the politicians walk down to the legislative assembly, then he could pick up a newspaper and read what they had done, then stop by the Aquarium and the Château Frontenac for the inside scuttlebutt. Mulroney had a ringside seat to the Quiet Revolution and could feel events moving around him. It was a fascinating time to be in Quebec City.

The ferment of reform influenced students more than anybody else. They spent hours debating the future of Quebec and trading polemics in the classroom, in the pub, and in the student newspaper. Some of the key issues being bandied back and forth were abolition of the monarchy, patriation of the Constitution, and Canadian bilingualism. Quebec nationalism was growing quickly but few people in the law school advocated separatism. Everybody agreed, however, that Quebec was moving fast and Canada had to give it more room. Mulroney believed that Quebec had a legitimate point of view that needed to be expressed, but he also believed in the federal system, a strong central government, and Diefenbaker's vision of One Canada, which could not countenance the idea of Quebec as an autonomous society, a separate "nation" within the Canadian whole. He did not follow the fine points of the debate, but felt everything could be settled through better communication between French and English. If both sides got together and started talking, it could all be worked out. Most of his colleagues shared this view. Optimism ran high and students then believed anything was possible.

Despite the intellectual hothouse that was Quebec City in 1960, party politics, not political ideas, remained Mulroney's primary passion. And being a Tory at Laval took some conviction, even a little courage. The Liberals could call a party meeting and fill a room without trying, whereas the Tories always had to search for bodies. The Tory club at Laval was nothing to brag about, although Mulroney boosted it any way he could. He sometimes brought Laval friends to Tory meetings in Ottawa. When a cabinet minister travelled to Quebec City, Mulroney would invariably meet him, sometimes even be waiting at the hotel room to welcome him. He kept in touch with the Quebec MPs, particularly Minister of Transport Léon Balcer, whom he accompanied to Baie Comeau later that fall, Noel Dorion, the secretary of state, and Jacques Flynn, the local MP who would later be appointed minister of mines.

Virtually nobody important slipped through Mulroney's net, but his ultimate contact remained John Diefenbaker. The downfall of the Union Nationale government had drawn him even closer to the prime minister. Diefenbaker had swept Quebec in the 1958 election with the help of the still-potent Duplessis machine, but now that Duplessis was dead and the Union Nationale in opposition, Diefenbaker needed other eyes and ears in Quebec. He wanted not only the news but the gossip, the juicier the better, and Mulroney knew how to serve it up. He kept on top of things, seemed to know everything that was going on in Quebec City, and eagerly passed it along. Diefenbaker and Lesage were hardly speaking to each other; Mulroney told Diefenbaker what Lesage was up to, and what was still to come.

The medium that tied Mulroney and Diefenbaker together was the telephone. Diefenbaker had spent years building up his web of contacts and, stretching across the country, it was some network. Before Diefenbaker, Canada's prime ministers had kept in touch with their followers by letter. Diefenbaker was one of the first Canadian politicians to deploy the telephone as a tactical tool. It was also a toy.

He loved making calls and receiving them. He constantly wanted feedback and could never get enough. Diefenbaker was the only prime minister in Canadian history an average citizen could call up with a reasonable chance of getting through. Almost anybody could get him on the line if only he or she was brash enough.

Diefenbaker called up some members of his network more than others. Mulroney happened to be one of his favourites. By the time he reached Laval, Mulroney had almost unlimited access to the prime minister. He could pick up the phone and get him almost anytime. "You know," Diefenbaker mused to his office staff, "that boy is going far. He's so keen." Diefenbaker aides could see that Mulroney and the Chief hit it off. Indeed they were a natural match. Diefenbaker had an insatiable need for praise; Mulroney was the consummate cheerleader. Anybody could cheer with enthusiasm, but Mulroney did it with flourish and conviction. He also knew Dief's love of gossip and could always deliver the latest juicy morsel guaranteed to make him chuckle.

As at St. FX, Mulroney couldn't help bragging about his friendship with the prime minister of Canada. Like his classmates in Antigonish, his Laval colleagues were sceptical. Who could blame them since now Mulroney claimed he actually wielded influence with the prime minister. His friends did not doubt that he had met Diefenbaker, and a few even believed the prime minister recognized him, but nobody swallowed this incredible claim. When Mulroney refused to back down, they challenged him to bring Diefenbaker into class. Diefenbaker was coming to Quebec City in a few weeks, and either Mulroney could produce him or could not. Mulroney self-confidently boasted that it would be no sweat.

The news soon spread across the campus that the prime minister would be dropping by the law school on December 9, 1960, and would be fêted at a formal reception. The Law Students' Association was officially hosting him but everyone knew what had happened; Mulroney had managed to bring Diefenbaker to Laval. And immediately before the wine-and-cheese ceremony, Diefenbaker would drop into the first-year law class just as Mulroney had promised.

When the day finally arrived, Mulroney was ready to make the most of it: from the moment Diefenbaker got off the plane until he left, Mulroney was constantly at his side. Breakfast was at the Château Frontenac. There he and PC Student Federation president Bob Amaron wrapped up final approval for changes allowing students to deduct tuition fees from income tax. The PCSF had been lobbying for the exemption for years but Diefenbaker had dithered. Education was a provincial jurisdiction and he feared stepping on Quebec's toes. But Mulroney had managed to get assurances from the Lesage government to support the exemption. Now, eleven days before a federal budget, he delivered the news to Diefenbaker that the provincial Liberals were onside. It was remarkable evidence of how quickly he had penetrated Quebec politics.

At the reception that afternoon the rector, the vice-rector, the dean, and all the law professors were in attendance as were all the students, even the diehard Liberals. In the centre of things, Mulroney, immaculately dressed as always, beamed with pride as Diefenbaker, in high spirits, treated him like an old friend; he put his hand on his shoulder and called him "Brian." Mulroney on one occasion stunned those around him by calling him "John." "Jesus," whistled one student, "he's close to him." But Diefenbaker had not finished plugging Mulroney yet. "This young fellow," he predicted to Firmin Bernatchez, the leader of the campus Tory club, "is the future prime minister of Canada." The foremost politician in Canada had paid him the ultimate compliment. Mulroney had answered the sceptics and then some. Being seen to have connections was almost as good as having them, and his greatest connection had just been seen and admired by everyone. That afternoon Mulroney grew a full foot in the eyes of his classmates.

"Well, another hectic weekend over!" Mulroney wrote triumphantly to party headquarters a few days later. "As you know, the PM was in town on Friday and arrangements were made for him to pay a visit to Laval; and what a visit! I really believe that he charmed ninety percent of the boys out of their socks, he was that effective. I can't recall having seen him in such good cheer in many, many moons. He really perked things up around here which, in effect, was just what the doctor ordered. If it were possible for him to make occasional sorties onto various campuses in advance of campus elections — the crucial ones — I daresay that our record would improve markedly. I will be sending you some pictures of his visit to the University in the hope that they will be useful for propaganda purposes."

Diefenbaker was not alone in pegging Mulroney as a future prime minister. The Laval law student had also impressed the Quebec editor of *Maclean's* magazine, a young writer with keen journalistic instincts by the name of Peter Gzowski. Gzowski spotted Mulroney as a comer and dispatched a memo to Toronto suggesting an article on future prime ministers, submitting Mulroney's name as his candidate. Blair Fraser, the magazine's editor, sent back a memo to the effect that he had lost count of all the pompous young future prime ministers around. But out of that exchange came the idea for a feature article on young political leaders and what they were thinking. Not long afterwards Peter C. Newman, Ottawa editor for *Maclean's*, and Gzowski sat down at a boardroom table to talk politics with six young men from the three main political parties. An edited transcript of their conversation was published in the March 25, 1961, edition.

Mulroney and Ted Rogers represented the Tories, David Greenspan and Jean David the Liberals, and John Brewin and Jean-Pierre Fournier the CCF. The roundtable interview started with Newman asking each of them how he became interested in politics, and before long Gzowski was chiding them over their lack of ideals and ideas.

Gzowski: Why don't you talk about wanting to do something? I always thought the idea of going into politics was to right a wrong, or to carry a banner, or at least to accomplish something.

Mulroney: When I first got interested in politics, I didn't want to go off on some holy crusade. This was just to get my feet wet, and find out what politics entailed.

Jean David: Personally, when I said that politics is at the root of everything I should have said as well that I have certain ideas I want to sell. I'm a Liberal with a small "l."

Mulroney: The main attraction for me was the fact that we felt we had something to do, and that it could best be done through the Conservative party.

Gzowski: What was the "something"?

Mulroney: Well, to make our own ideas heard.

Gzowski: What ideas?

Mulroney: You will notice that in Mr. Fleming's baby budget there was a reference to the students for the first time in history. We are now permitted to deduct our tuition fees. This is one little idea that has been pushed through the federation, and Ted Rogers came to Ottawa and presented it to the cabinet committee.

Newman: Let's talk about ideas that are bigger than that.

Later Newman asked the group what the politician of the future would think about patronage, and Mulroney jumped in first. "I think," he said, "his attitude is going to be drastically changed from the attitude of those who are in government today. The young people of today are going to strengthen the nation at the cost of partisan politics, and they are going to take a much more idealistic view of things twenty years from now than we do today."

Aside from that answer, which would echo a quarter of a century later, Mulroney and his peers — even the CCFers — showed little vision and less idealism. What would be their "first major crusade" if they became prime minister in the next decade or two, Newman asked. "I would legislate to change the tax structure of Canada," Mulroney replied, "to permit the Atlantic provinces to share equally in the prosperity of the country — and, I should say, the other have-not provinces — something similar to Operation Bootstrap in Puerto Rico." The others weren't much more inspiring.

"Their ideas and ambitions are tested, respectable," *Maclean's* concluded. "They seem to be the most hidebound of the middle-aged young." And Mulroney came across as the most hidebound of the bunch.

Indeed Mulroney was anything but a rebel. He revelled in his role as Diefenbaker's main man in Quebec City. By the spring of 1961 his reach stretched beyond the circle of politics into the legal establishment. He had gotten to know many of the leading lawyers in town and along the way had become friendly with Gérard Corriveau, a local prosecutor. Corriveau had set his sights on becoming a judge, and wanted a judgeship so badly that he was not averse to a little lobbying. After Diefenbaker's visit to the law school, the word about Mulroney's big connection had spread across campus and beyond, and had reached Corriveau's ears. It had also gotten around that Mulroney was on friendly terms with the minister of justice, Davie Fulton. Corriveau concluded that Mulroney was his ticket to the bench.

Improbable as it sounded, Mulroney actually had some pull in such matters. He and Diefenbaker talked about many things, including who in the Quebec City area would make a good judge. Mulroney could brief him on the political allegiance of all the good lawyers in town. In fact Diefenbaker often checked with Mulroney before awarding government legal business to local firms.

Corriveau's lobbying soon paid off. On March 30, 1961, he was appointed a judge on the Quebec Superior Court. When the announcement was made he dropped by the law school and jubilantly took Mulroney and his buddies out for a celebratory drink.

The Corriveau appointment revealed several things. It demonstrated — once again — the depth of Mulroney's relationship with Diefenbaker, and how far he had taken it from their first meeting in December 1956. With his remarkable facility for winning the confidence of older people, Mulroney had gotten about as close to Diefenbaker as Diefenbaker allowed anyone to come. The appointment said almost as much about the way Mulroney operated as it did about Diefenbaker. Moreover, the fact that the prime minister of Canada consulted a twenty-two-year-old anglophone law student about judicial appointments in French Canada demonstrates just how weak the Conservative Party was in Quebec and helps explain its subsequent decline. It also shows how isolated the prime minister was from French Canada, not to mention how little faith he placed in his Quebec ministers. Diefenbaker had built his career by assembling a vast political network of contacts across the country, yet he relied on a law student as one of his most trusted assets in Canada's second most populous province.

Mulroney's status on campus was more than political. He also enjoyed enough success with women to make him the envy of most of his friends. He was far from the handsomest law student at Laval, but few could match his extraordinary record of conquest. One friend, perplexed by his success, asked one of his admirers if she found him physically attractive. No, she answered, but Mulroney was irresistible nonetheless. It was his personality: he always seemed completely at ease and was full of jokes and stories. He made women laugh and usually won them over.

The lax academic schedule left lots of time for a social life, and Mulroney had many casual liaisons during his first year. But there was one liaison that soon became serious. It began one day when Mulroney and Michael Meighen were walking in the Old City. Suddenly Mulroney stopped in his tracks and pointed at a young woman waiting at a bus stop. "Do you know who she is?" he asked his friend. Meighen had no idea, so Mulroney promptly went up and introduced himself.

Her name was JoAnn Ross. She was a student nurse at the nearby Hôtel-Dieu hospital and lived with two aunts on Saint-Cyril Boulevard outside the walls of the Old City. Despite the English-sounding name, she was thoroughly French and spoke little English. She turned out to be vivacious, outgoing, and intelligent, but above everything else, she was tall, blonde, and simply gorgeous — and good looks had always ranked at the top of Mulroney's checklist.

JoAnn seemed taken with Mulroney, too, but there was a catch. She was already dating another law student, René Dussault. Soon after this first meeting, Mulroney saw René and JoAnn dancing together and vowed to win her. For the rest of the year he campaigned relentlessly, and slowly but surely won her over. (By the time Dussault left Laval the following year to study in England, Mulroney had already triumphed.) Not that their relationship was all smooth sailing. It was off one week, on the next, but their mutual attraction was strong and over time grew deeper.

Dalhousie law school's anemic Model Parliament had disappointed Mulroney, but he had yet to taste the one at Laval. In fact Laval had no Model Parliament at all until the year Mulroney arrived, and it was easy to tell. Although the university convened a Model Parliament that year, it skipped the elections and apportioned the seats according to the standings in Ottawa, which was good for Mulroney since the Conservative Party held power. So while campuses across the country were swinging back to the Liberals, Laval, a highly Liberal campus, was saddled with a Tory government that included, not surprisingly, one Brian Mulroney. Later the student newspaper blasted parliamentarians for the quality of debate but singled out Mulroney as one of the exceptions.

Another parliamentarian singled out for exemplary performance was Peter White, the minister of labour. White, one of the eight Anglos in the freshman class, lived at a motel at 51 ½ Saint-Louis, not a hundred yards away from Mulroney's rooming-house. Although White was something of an egghead whose ever-present glasses gave him a bit of a bookish look, he and Mulroney quickly became friends and had dinner together most evenings. White was also a Tory activist. He enjoyed deep intellectual debate as well as grassroots political action, and unlike many fledgling politicos pursued both with equal fervour. Like Mulroney, White thought big and operated on a grand scale. For a summer job in the Eastern Townships, he had bought for one dollar a struggling weekly newspaper called the *Knowlton Advertiser* and now kept it going year-round. Each weekend he drove to Knowlton and helped put his paper to bed, making him the only law student in Canada who also was a bona fide publisher. In keeping with his status as a successful capitalist, he normally dressed as if he were on his way to the stock exchange to trade some shares.

As an undergraduate at McGill, White had been impressed by the university's annual Conference on World Affairs. At Laval he decided there should be something similar on Canadian affairs. In the spring of 1961, he had laid the groundwork and settled on the theme "The Canadian Experiment: Success or Failure." He soon enlisted the help of Michel Cogger and Michael Meighen, and lined up the support of student council. By the fall White's volunteer organization had ballooned into a mini-bureaucracy.

Not interested in organizing an intellectual conference, Mulroney sat on the sidelines through all the early planning. Only in the final month, after the event had mushroomed into a major spectacle, did he jump on the bandwagon. However, once aboard, he quickly emerged as one of the vice-presidents on the organizing committee and helped make an already big event even bigger. The Congress on Canadian Affairs needed more star speakers, so Mulroney started to recruit. It soon became apparent that he loved picking up the phone and calling political contacts every bit as much as Diefenbaker did. He began phoning up people in his network for help and information, the first flowering of a practice that would become his main modus operandi for the rest of his life. First he recruited René Lévesque, the dynamic Quebec minister he had cultivated at the Aquarium. He also pulled in Premier Jean Lesage and the mayor of Quebec City. But the congress needed a national star to kick off the conference as keynote speaker, somebody who could get newspaper headlines, and for that Mulroney tapped Canada's minister of justice, Davie Fulton.

Only one person in Quebec City could have picked up the phone and booked Fulton on the spot, and that was Mulroney. By now he knew Fulton well and had already brought him into the law school for a *vin d'honneur*, as he had with Diefenbaker. Whenever Mulroney visited Ottawa he stopped by Fulton's office, and Fulton always found room in his schedule to see him. Although Fulton had lost to Diefenbaker in 1956, he was still young and ambitious and was making it his business to meet Tories across the country. He particularly wanted to bolster his strength in Quebec, especially in the Quebec City region, so he cultivated Mulroney almost as much as Mulroney cultivated him. They happened to be a good match. Both advocated bilingualism and sympathized with Quebec's concerns, talking for hours about how the Conservative Party could sink roots in the province. Before making important decisions about Quebec, Fulton often touched base with Mulroney. In fact Fulton's entire office treated Mulroney as its man in Quebec City. So when Mulroney called, Fulton readily accepted his invitation.

Now that the big names were all lined up, the congress needed an audience to fill the seats, and here Mulroney helped too. Too many universities had decided not to send delegates. The organizers sent out telegrams to each college, warning that it alone would be missing. The ruse embarrassed most into changing their minds. As an added incentive Mulroney had assembled an exposition of Canadian books that he touted with characteristic exaggeration as the biggest-ever display of books on Canada.

But nowhere did Mulroney help more than in raising money, the need for which had grown steadily as the plans grew ever more grandiose. Formal banquets would both open and close the conference, and all the speakers were being lodged in style at the Château Frontenac. Student council had allocated $10,000 and Quebec's Ministry of Cultural Affairs had kicked in another $1,000, but that seed money was long gone. As the date approached, Mulroney emerged as by far the most successful student bagman, tapping the business community for donations. One of the largest came from the Quebec North Shore Paper Company in Baie Comeau, where his father still worked.

During the final stages of preparation for the congress the Union Nationale held a leadership convention to replace outgoing leader Antonio Barrette. Mulroney missed none of the action, getting himself accredited as a voting delegate from one of the Union Nationale's rotten boroughs. It was difficult for him to decide who to support — Daniel Johnson, his late-night drinking companion, or Jean-Jacques Bertrand, the party's reformer. He personally liked Johnson far more than Bertrand, but Johnson represented the ward-heeling Duplessis tradition while the progressive Bertrand promised to clean up the party and banish its sordid past. Most students supported Bertrand, and ultimately Mulroney did too.

However, that weekend Mulroney learned another lesson in the raw realities of politics. Bertrand, the candidate of the future, offered a better platform, delivered a superior speech, and looked more worthy, but Johnson commanded a more potent political machine. Johnson out-organized his opponent and won the ballot. Progressive ideas were all very well and good, but the superior political mechanic usually won the day.

Certainly it was superior organization that ensured that the Congress on Canadian Affairs would be a success. What happened exceeded even White's and Mulroney's elevated expectations. At the opening banquet the evening of November 15, 1961, in the ballroom of the Château Frontenac, Davie Fulton came through with a block-buster speech announcing that Ottawa had drafted legislation to patriate the Constitution. With reporters scribbling and cameras flashing, Fulton disclosed that he would soon circulate draft amendments to the British North America Act to give Canada control over its constitution and Quebec a charter of French-Canadian rights. In one stroke the congress had grabbed the headlines of every newspaper in the country, and it was guaranteed national press coverage for the remainder of its four days.

And there was a great deal for the reporters to listen to. Historian Murray Ballantyne talked about "What French Canadians have against us," followed by *La Presse* editor Gérard Pelletier on "What English Canadians have against us." André Laurendeau, the editor-in-chief of *Le Devoir*, debated Eugene Forsey, the director of research for the Canadian Labour Congress, under the title "Canada: One nation or two?" René Lévesque incited an outraged response from MP Doug Fisher when he told English Canada that "you need us more than we need you." Fisher lashed back: "I'd be tempted to say that goes double," and then wondered aloud what English Canadians west of Sudbury could admire about Quebec. "Is it your marvellous police tradition we should admire or the tradition of your telegraphers, or your censorship of the goings-on at Jacques-Cartier Bridge? . . . For us the greatest impact of French-Canadian culture has been made by Maurice Richard and Lili St. Cyr." Maurice Richard was a hockey star and Lili St. Cyr a stripper. The Quebec press was livid at these insults. "What Culture? — Fisher" the headline in *La Presse* proclaimed the following day.

Only one thing stirred up more press coverage than Fisher's remarks, and that was the dramatic arrival of Dr. Marcel Chaput, leader of the Rassemblement pour l'Indépendance Nationale, Quebec's fledgling separatist party. What Chaput said did not matter nearly as much as the fact that he had showed up to say it. Chaput was a federal civil servant in Ottawa, and his employer, the Defence Research Board, had ordered him to stay at his desk. When Chaput appeared at the conference anyway, everybody awaited Ottawa's reaction, which came swiftly. Chaput had not finished his speech when the newswire flashed word that he had been suspended from his job. "Separatism so far has been a matter of doctrine," Chaput announced to the encircling press minutes later, "a thing discussed by intellectuals. Now, I think they have personalized it. They have brought it into the realm of fact." The Chaput suspension produced another big headline for the congress.

The final day ended with a speech from Premier Jean Lesage, yet another high point, again not so much for what he said as for the fact that he spoke. The conference's enormous success defied the rule that an intellectual gathering could not attract wide popular interest. In part it was a matter of lucky timing. Quebeckers were beginning to ask profound questions about their place in Canada and the congress had captured their emerging doubts. Never before had Quebec's problematic role in Canada been aired so publicly and so starkly. Many of the novel ideas expressed at the congress would become common currency in the years to come. If there was any criticism to be made, it was that more often than not the speakers stole the show, leaving little time for the small discussion groups where delegates were supposed to thrash out the issues in more detail.

The congress was about ideas — the nature of separatism, the role of the federal and provincial state — but Mulroney left the intellectual debate to others. Instead he took on the role of the ubiquitous organizer, the fixer, the one who greased the squeaky wheels and handled the media big shots. When René Lévesque tried to cancel just before his scheduled appearance, Mulroney made an emergency phone call to Premier Lesage. "Hey, your minister won't come," he complained. "He's too busy up north." Lesage promptly promised to send a government plane, which got Lévesque back in time. When Doug Fisher's rude response to Lévesque sparked an uproar in the Quebec press, it was Mulroney who assured francophone reporters that the CCF MP had been misinterpreted. As a result of the skill with which Mulroney had played this backroom role, his press contacts now included some of the biggest names in Canadian journalism, a network he would carefully nurture in the years to come.

CHAPTER SEVEN

A QUEBEC BASE

IN THE EARLY SPRING of 1962, as Mulroney neared the end of his second year at Laval, Diefenbaker was reaching the end of his mandate. He had said new things in 1958 and had captured the public's imagination with his messianic appeal. But once in office he had failed to carry through, had aged rapidly, showed himself to be weak and indecisive, and no longer spoke with a fresh voice. In short, the Diefenbaker dream had worn thin, particularly in student circles. Now, as Canadians awaited the next election, the Tories were losing Model Parliaments across the country, which usually signalled the coming of electoral trouble.

As the election call drew closer, Diefenbaker phoned Roy Faibish, who was executive assistant to Minister of Agriculture Alvin Hamilton and one of the most capable political operatives on Parliament Hill. "I think I will need you," he announced cryptically. It was Diefenbaker's way of saying that he wanted Faibish working for him on the campaign. Faibish's secondment would deprive Hamilton of his right hand, but a prime minister is the boss and gets whatever he wants. Scrambling to find a temporary replacement to fill in for him, Faibish quickly thought about Mulroney, whom he had first met at the 1956 Conservative convention and by whom he had been instantly impressed. Since then he had watched the young man rise in the party and seen his initial judgement confirmed. So Faibish asked Mulroney if he was interested.

Indeed he was. Mulroney could hardly dream up a better summer job. Posts like this did not usually open for such a short term. And aside from Davie Fulton, Mulroney could not hope to work for a better minister. Hamilton possessed the most fertile mind in the Diefenbaker cabinet and swung as much influence as any of his ministers. He also came from Saskatchewan, and Mulroney had never travelled west of Ontario. The West was just a big wilderness to him, a huge chink in his already impressive political network. Working for a Western cabinet minister would help him plug that gap. Most important of all, working for Hamilton would land him on Parliament Hill, where he could further cultivate his relationships with the country's elected decision-makers while learning a little about the machinery of government and making connections in the civil service bureaucracy. As a bonus, the job would provide a short course in Canadian agriculture, a subject that did not come naturally to an electrician's son from an isolated mill town. An opportunity like this was almost too good to be true.

There was one potential snag, however. Another highly qualified candidate was actively lobbying for the job of Hamilton's temporary assistant, a recent graduate of the University of Alberta named Joe Clark. Clark, who was then working at Tory headquarters producing propaganda for the coming election, held excellent qualifications and had put in an application with Faibish. He had already talked to Hamilton personally about coming onto staff.

In many ways, Mulroney and Clark offered Faibish little to choose between. They were virtually the same age, having been born only seventy-seven days apart, and shared many similar political skills. Both were fast on their feet. Both showed maturity beyond their years. Both had deep orators' voices that they used with tactical efficiency in front of an audience. Clark spoke every bit as impressively and compellingly as Mulroney. He too had won his share of public speaking contests.

Like Mulroney, Clark also became Conservative leader in his undergraduate days, and had distinguished himself in the mock wars of Model Parliament. Both Mulroney and Clark were Red Tories, Catholic, pro-Quebec, and fans of Davie Fulton. Both grew up being called by their middle names; Mulroney's unused first name was Martin, Clark's was Charles. Both saw university as a political door-opener. Both were tremendous tacticians and had a gift for causing events to happen the way they wanted. Both were actively building networks and never forgot a thing. Both had achieved a lot in politics while still in university. People around both of them never doubted that they would sooner or later end up in the House of Commons.

Clark grew up in High River, Alberta, a small town thirty-five miles south of Calgary, then similar in size to Baie Comeau. According to David Humphreys, Clark's friend and biographer, in his book *Joe Clark: A Portrait*, Clark visited Ottawa in 1956 after winning a public speaking award and passed up visits to the art gallery and museum in order to hang around Parliament Hill. He met Diefenbaker (a few months before Mulroney did), was captivated by him, and from then on never missed a chance to meet him, though he did not meet him as often or know him as well as Mulroney.

Clark was even more politically driven than Mulroney. He not only practised politics but studied it. A voracious reader, he was a student of politics in the best sense. He had set his sights on becoming a professional politician and pursued that goal with single-minded devotion.

At the time they both applied for the job as Alvin Hamilton's assistant, Clark and Mulroney had known each other for four years. They first met in 1958 at the Tory youth gathering in Ottawa where Mulroney got Diefenbaker to send Gordon Churchill to the Maritime Model Parliament, and from then on had regularly bumped into each other at party conventions. They also shared a lot of common friends, like Jean Bazin, Lowell Murray, and Pat MacAdam — but here their similarities abruptly ended. Mulroney was best buddies with just about everybody, but not with Clark. They were sort of friends, but no more. Nobody had ever seen Mulroney and Clark put their feet up and talk — and nobody expected to see it. Clark and Mulroney had nothing to say to each other. For despite their similarities, they were as different as their home provinces, Quebec and Alberta.

Their differences started with physical appearance — despite the fact both were tall and thin. People could not help but notice their respective chins, and how unusual and different they both were. Clark's zigged where Mulroney's zagged. Clark had no chin, absolutely none. His face simply disappeared below the mouth, whereas Mulroney's big chin stuck out so far that the middle of his face looked pushed in. With his big forehead and protruding chin, a profile of Mulroney's sunken face resembled a silhouette of a quarter-moon. Clark's pompadour haircut made his hair look long by 1962 standards, whereas Mulroney had only recently let his hair grow barely long enough to lie flat. Clark dressed like a small-town kid from Alberta, whereas Mulroney, always dapper in a blue suit or sharp blazer, looked like an American whiz kid from Boston. People could tell them apart merely by their physical movements. Mulroney moved gracefully and evenly, whereas every movement Clark made was stilted, particularly the way he walked — a jerky motion that looked awkward and lent itself to caricature. People could pick Clark out of a crowd at a distance simply by his gait. Their speaking styles set them apart too. On the stump Mulroney's words oozed like honey, rich and smooth, with never a seam. Clark's words came bursting out like the rat-tat-tat of a machine gun, each word a separate bullet.

In many ways Clark's early success was more remarkable than Mulroney's, for he achieved it without his rival's numerous natural gifts. Clark was totally lacking in social ease. He was shy, earnest, no good with women, and devoid of small talk. At the youth conventions where they met so often over the years, Clark devoted all his energy to debating issues at policy plenums while Mulroney concentrated on being the life of the party. Clark was high-strung, drank Coke by the case, and read widely. With his funny-looking haircut and ill-fitting clothes he was like a Tory boy scout with no room in his life for anything but politics. He was honest to the point of naïveté, having none of Mulroney's street smarts or his gut instinct for survival — a difference that would prove crucial in the years to come.

Clark's rise was due in part to his lack of complexity. Although people thought he was a bit of a square, they respected him, even admired him, and voted for him on the convention floor. And he had one great advantage over Mulroney: he could laugh at himself. Thanks to Clark's wonderfully wry self-deprecating sense of humour, nobody ever accused him of being arrogant. He was something of a misfit, but popular in his own way.

In the spring of 1962, when the job in Hamilton's office opened up, Clark had been working at party headquarters for about six months. He had applied for the job from Europe where he had run out of money in the midst of a self-financed grand tour following his graduation from the University of Alberta. At headquarters on Laurier Street he shared an office with Marjorie LeBreton and Pat MacAdam, who had left the Nova Scotia civil service and landed his job in Ottawa largely on the strength of Mulroney's influence. In those days the political parties fought their campaigns not on television but through pamphlets, and Clark's chief task was to churn these out. He tackled his job with gusto, as he did everything, but working for Hamilton sounded far more appealing.

Although Clark had a head start, he didn't really stand a chance once Mulroney expressed an interest. Faibish had approached Mulroney in the first place because he was ideal for the job. Not only would his easygoing personality mesh well with the energetic Hamilton, he spoke French fluently (Clark had flunked first-year French in university and then dropped the subject). Hamilton was one of the few Diefenbaker ministers who had tried to lure francophones into his department. He had gotten absolutely nowhere, so he commissioned an informal study into the department's working language policy. And this was the job Mulroney and Clark were technically competing for. Nor did it hurt that Hamilton had previously met Mulroney and been impressed, as almost everybody was.

When Faibish formally offered him the job at a salary of $541 a month, Mulroney promised to be there the day after his last exam in April. When he reported to work at Hamilton's office on the fourth floor of Parliament Hill's Centre Block, Diefenbaker had already dissolved Parliament and called a general election. Mulroney arrived to find the whole government operating on a campaign footing.

Before departing for the hustings, Diefenbaker had named Hamilton the acting prime minister for the rest of the campaign, which in effect made Mulroney the chief aide to the head of the government. But Hamilton was too much a political warhorse to stay put during an election campaign. After a few days he hit the road himself, taking his twenty-three-year-old executive assistant with him.

An election campaign put Mulroney into his natural element, and this one proved no exception. He had to be a logistical gymnast to keep his man more or less on schedule, because Hamilton had the incurable habit of talking non-stop to anybody within range of his voice. Each morning Mulroney dashed into Hamilton's hotel room bright and early with a list of urgent decisions from the Department of Agriculture. Once these were dealt with, the rest of the day was non-stop stumping. Wherever Hamilton went, Mulroney remained at his side, or a few steps behind. At the end of each long day, usually hundreds of miles and many towns and speeches later, Mulroney would ask, "Are you finished with me tonight?" Hamilton, exhausted, would wave him off and Mulroney would disappear into the local night-life. Hamilton could usually tell the next morning that he had been up into the wee hours. "My God," the older man would remark, "you didn't get much sleep last night." He hadn't, but that never seemed to slow him down.

In the final weeks of the campaign Hamilton spent all his time covering his own sprawling Saskatchewan constituency, Qu'Appelle. Since the riding could be covered only by car, Mulroney added chauffeur to his list of duties. When Hamilton delivered a speech, Mulroney would sit back and take notes, then disappear. He had gone off to the nearest telephone to call a local radio station. Then, using his best radio voice, he delivered a news report just as if he was a reporter. En route to their next stop, Hamilton and Mulroney would turn on the car radio and listen to Mulroney's glowing account. "This is Brian Mulroney reporting on the meeting of the Honourable Alvin Hamilton, Minister of Agriculture," he would sign off. During this final stage of the campaign more people heard Mulroney's voice than Hamilton's.

While Mulroney was enjoying himself on the hustings, Joe Clark was stuck in Ottawa slogging away at party headquarters. Diefenbaker had lost his magic, and headquarters was having a hard time trying to sell him this time around. But the frustration of it all merely caused Clark to work harder. During the campaign he ran a speakers' bureau for local candidates, dug up research, wrote speeches, produced pamphlets, and did the countless tasks that needed doing in an election. He amazed everybody with his boundless energy and extraordinary stamina.

The campaign went well in Saskatchewan and on election day, June 18, 1962, Hamilton won handily, padding his already fat 1958 margin by another couple of hundred votes. Saskatchewan elected sixteen out of seventeen Tories, just as it had four years earlier. But elsewhere Diefenbaker was in full retreat, ultimately dropping more than 90 seats and falling from the biggest majority in Canadian history to a humble minority with only 116 seats. In the coming session he would need the support of the suddenly emerging federal Social Credit Party to avoid parliamentary defeat.

Unfortunately, Clark's ordeal did not end on election night. The voters of Stormont, in eastern Ontario, had yet to cast their ballots. In that riding the election had been suspended for a month when the Liberal candidate suddenly died of a heart attack twelve days before voting day. When activity resumed, Allister Grosart, the national director of the Conservative Party, dispatched Pat MacAdam and

Clark from headquarters to run the campaign. Headquarters also sent down a wave of politicians to help stump; one of them was Harry Willis, a party veteran who had been appointed to the Senate a week or two before.

"Congratulations, Senator," Clark beamed cheerily when Willis arrived.

Willis, with prominent jowls, seersucker suit, and panama hat, looked like a senator from the old American South, and behaved gruffly. He was more than gruff. He was plain rude.

"Who are you?" Willis barked upon seeing the gangly twenty-three-year-old.

"My name is Joe Clark, sir, Senator."

"What are you doing here?"

"Well, uh, sir, Allister Grosart sent me down here to help on the election."

"Jesus Christ," Willis growled. "Allister Grosart must be out of his mind."

Thereupon Willis turned on his heel and stomped off, leaving Clark devastated.

With the election over, Roy Faibish returned to his old post as Hamilton's executive assistant. Mulroney now became a sort of political handyman. He worked a little on the bilingualism study that he had been formally hired for, and also handled Faibish's overload; he helped Hamilton anticipate questions in Parliament by research-ing the answers in advance. Whatever it was, Mulroney seldom had to wait for instructions. He always seemed to know what to do.

Of his many tasks, the most unusual was as a courier for contra-band bull semen. As minister of agriculture, Hamilton had been trying to import Charolais cattle from France to raise the quality of Canada's breeding stock but had been foiled by the French govern-ment, which refused to share its prized cattle with Canada. However, an American had somehow acquired four of the large white Charolais bulls, which were waiting for clearance on the French island of Saint-Pierre prior to landing in the United States. The Health and

Animals Branch on Saint-Pierre was run by Canada, and that gave Hamilton an opening. He instructed his health officials to administer every possible test before clearing the bulls and to take their time at it. This provided ample opportunity to milk the bulls for as much semen as was needed. Although no law expressly forbade this practice, the civil servants in the Department of Agriculture wanted nothing to do with what was in effect stolen property. So it was Mulroney who delivered the little vials of prized semen to farmers and institutions all over the prairies.

Whatever Mulroney was asked to do, he tackled it with gusto. What a difference a couple of summers had made. Two years earlier he was drowning in depression; now he laughed, sang, and cracked jokes wherever he went. The happy and charming Irish side of his personality was in full bloom. He was dating several women in Ottawa and spending many a weekend in a rented cottage in the Gatineau Hills of Quebec with buddies such as Sam Wakim and Lowell Murray, who also were working as aides on Parliament Hill.

One of the best things about the Hamilton job was the opportunity to expand his network. As he moved through the hallways of Parliament Hill he met countless politicians, political aides, and reporters. He was a regular at the long table in the middle of the fifth-floor cafeteria where MPs and reporters traded gossip and jokes. He made many friends.

One of these was a nervous young Nova Scotia MP named Robert Coates, who would later become president of the party. But the one with whom he clicked best was Arthur Maloney, the famous trial lawyer who represented the Toronto riding of Parkdale. Like Mulroney Maloney was a small-town Irish Catholic in a thoroughly WASP party, and they hit it off immediately. Although Maloney had lost his seat in the 1962 election, Mulroney kept in touch and adopted Maloney as another of his spiritual fathers.

Because the 1962 election had shifted political fortunes, there were many rookie MPs in Ottawa that summer. One of these was a young Liberal lawyer named John Turner. One day when Peter White, his

Laval classmate, happened to be visiting, Mulroney spotted Turner heading his way outside the Centre Block.

"Let's go and say hello," Mulroney said to White.

"What do you want to say hello to him for?" his friend snorted. "He's a Grit from Montreal and no friend of ours."

"He's going to be prime minister one day," Mulroney responded as he went over and introduced himself. As always, he never let political labels get in the way of adding to his list of contacts.

Mulroney also regularly bumped into Joe Clark, who was still working at party headquarters. Their relations remained amiable, but distant. Each saw the other as a rival, a future opponent, and while they continued to collect people for their respective networks, neither tried recruiting the other.

By the end of the summer Faibish had concluded that hiring Mulroney had been an inspired move. The young Quebecker had done everything expected of him and more. Faibish, who had a knack for sniffing out comers, had him pegged as the future Quebec leader of the Conservative Party in the tradition of George-Étienne Cartier and Ernest Lapointe. Of course he had to get through law school first. "If I can be of any help," Faibish told him before he returned to Laval, "let me know."

When Mulroney bundled up his belongings for the trip back to Quebec City, he took care to pack his giant three-month desk calendar. It chronicled the day-to-day events of his time in Ottawa. He was keeping it as a memento of a wonderful summer, and to show his friends in third-year law. Meanwhile Clark was packing too. He was off to Halifax to enrol in Dalhousie law school just as Mulroney had done three years earlier.

By the time Mulroney left Ottawa it was clear that the Diefenbaker government's days were numbered. Although still prime minister, the Chief had already lost his grip on the country and was quickly losing it in Parliament too. He was even beginning to lose his grip on his own party. Rebel camps were forming and knives were being sharpened.

Nowhere had the Tories slid further than in Quebec, and nowhere was the internal bickering so serious and so deeply entrenched. The province had started souring already in 1958 when Diefenbaker brought some of the Quebec caucus's real lightweights into his cabinet. But it was the coming of the Quiet Revolution that really alienated Diefenbaker from Quebec. "Maîtres chez nous" (Masters in our own house) became the rallying cry of the new Quebec under Premier Jean Lesage. The Liberal government wanted to change the Ottawa-Quebec relationship, and Diefenbaker did not. Diefenbaker offered mere gestures — bilingual government cheques, simultaneous translation in the House of Commons, and the appointment of a francophone governor general. He could not grasp the forces that had been unleashed in Quebec, and the province had written him off long before the 1962 election.

Back at Laval, Mulroney soon discovered that even the members of the tiny PC club were openly grumbling about Diefenbaker's leadership, including Anglos like Peter White and Michael Meighen. They cited Diefenbaker's track record in Quebec: nine seats in 1957, fifty in 1958, and now fourteen. "Look," White argued, "he's blown it. He's finished. It's only a matter of time." Most of the Laval Tories agreed, but not Mulroney. He continued to defend his leader and tried convincing others that the Conservative Party had a future, not only in Canada but in Quebec.

Every morning Mulroney and his circle of friends perused *Le Devoir*, the small but influential French-language daily newspaper published in Montreal. As Diefenbaker started to slide, editor-in-chief André Laurendeau stepped up his editorial campaign for a royal commission on biculturalism, the idea that French and English could be represented and could participate in common institutions without sacrificing their own cultures. Mulroney thought Laurendeau's idea made marvellous sense and endorsed it wholeheartedly. He believed it would wake up English Canada to the new Quebec reality. But Diefenbaker rejected the proposal out of hand. Undaunted, *Le Devoir* kept campaigning and whipped up enough momentum to make the prime minister waver. Ultimately, however, Diefenbaker could not accept a commission that challenged his vision of One Canada. After weeks of stalling, on January 18, 1963, he irrevocably announced that the idea had "no place in my thinking."

The next morning a saddened Mulroney read about it in *Le Devoir*. He especially noticed the editorial that said the Conservative Party was falling victim to the tradition of its past, and to the personality of Diefenbaker, and faced oblivion in Quebec. "French Canada is waking up," the editorial said. Everybody in the Laval PC club agreed with Laurendeau's assessment and felt that, if anything, he had been too kind.

Diefenbaker's dismissal of a separate Quebec identity forced Mulroney to face up to the reality that his hero had a blind spot on Quebec, one he could not blithely explain away. Mulroney had to confront the fact that Diefenbaker did not understand his home province, and did not want to. He still clung to Gordon Churchill's theory that the party could win national elections without winning Quebec. Mulroney had recently been converted to exactly the opposite view. He believed the party needed to build up its base in Quebec to assure electoral success — as the Liberal Party had already done.

But despite Diefenbaker's failure of vision, Mulroney continued to admire him, especially for persevering through the lean years in Saskatchewan, for achieving the biggest victory in history, and for his principled stand against capital punishment. Although increasingly in the minority, he still thought of the Chief as a great political leader. Other students sometimes ribbed him about Diefenbaker, but Mulroney was not ready to forsake his idol yet.

In fact, he believed he could still win Diefenbaker over, if not on biculturalism then on Quebec's place in Canada. So he rounded up Peter White and Michael Meighen and together they travelled to Ottawa to lobby on behalf of Quebec. They decided particularly to push for more francophones on royal commissions. Since coming to office, Diefenbaker had named seventeen royal commissions and had put a French Canadian in charge of exactly one. The three students naïvely believed they had a good chance of persuading him to appoint more.

However, the door to Diefenbaker's office no longer swung wide open for Mulroney. Since his near defeat, the prime minister had begun withdrawing into himself and showing signs of paranoia. With his government teetering, he became suspicious of anybody who was not a sycophant, including members of his own caucus and party hierarchy. Mulroney could no longer breeze into his office for a casual visit, and on this particular trip he could not swing a meeting at all.

After this rebuff, Mulroney and his friends redirected their lobbying to the powers behind Diefenbaker, particularly Gordon Churchill, now minister of veterans' affairs. In some ways Churchill was the biggest stumbling block of all, even more than Diefenbaker himself, since he had been the author of the "We can win without Quebec" strategy and continued to push it. Churchill gave the Mulroney delegation some of his time but refused to budge an inch. The Mulroney group also met with Alvin Hamilton and made some progress, but at the end of the day they were forced to conclude that the Diefenbaker government really was intractable and not interested. They returned home more disillusioned than before.

That spring the Tory vote in the Laval Model Parliament fell to an abysmal 9 per cent, one more sign of the party's fading fortunes in Quebec. Raynold Langlois, the Liberal prime minister with 49 per cent of the vote, teased the Tories in Parliament over why they did not establish an inquiry into the causes of their electoral disaster. But nobody at Laval needed an inquiry to learn what was bedevilling the Conservative Party. Whenever campus Tories got together, sooner or later their conversation always drifted back to the same thing — Diefenbaker. Secretly they hoped Diefenbaker would resign before he destroyed the party. They all believed that with a new leader they could still stage a comeback.

Mulroney still defended Diefenbaker, but he no longer boasted about the Chief's greatness. Now when he spoke up at all it was by way of explanation, quietly and almost defensively, as if asking for patience and understanding. Gone completely was the ring of authority, and the conviction of certainty. He was looking elsewhere for role models.

Ironically, in the last year or two Mulroney had begun patterning himself on U.S. president John F. Kennedy, whom Diefenbaker hated with a passion. He admired Kennedy's style and grace and his ability to inspire his citizenry after taking office, something Diefenbaker had failed to do. Mulroney idolized Kennedy. He carried with him the Camelot factor and the admiration of a country, and this clearly fascinated him. When Theodore White's landmark book *The Making of the President — 1960* was published, Mulroney devoured every word, then read it a second time. He saw Kennedy as the ultimate politician and wanted to be just like him.

It had been longer than anybody realized since Mulroney had last contested an election. He had never run for anything at Laval, which explained why he had never become Tory leader even though he was the most high-profile Tory on campus. During his year at Dalhousie he had bypassed the national presidency of the PC Student Federation, opting for the lesser slot as executive vice-president, which was his by acclamation. In fact since leaving St. FX in 1959 he had stopped running, period, and would never again compete in a party election until he ran for national leader in 1976. Mulroney had a normally unspoken policy — he actually revealed it once or twice — of not allowing his name to stand for any office that he could not win by acclamation. When his term as executive vice-president of the PCSF expired in 1961, he stayed exclusively in the backrooms. He now spent most of his time with the YPCs, the older Tory youth group made up mostly of people who had already graduated.

Avoiding office allowed him to sidestep the increasingly pesky Diefenbaker issue, but his distaste for elections went deeper than that: he hated losing. As a student federation veteran, he had once almost fallen victim to an anti-establishment purge attempt from some dissident Young Turks. Political office rarely came easily and was often easily lost in the Tory youth. And Mulroney did not want a defeat on his record. Moreover, he figured he did not need to run for office in order to be a player. In fact in many ways he wielded more influence as an unelected backroom operator.

Joe Clark had chosen the opposite approach: he contested every youth election and inexorably worked his way up through the ranks, building his network along the way. While Mulroney was visiting a cabinet minister upstairs in his hotel suite, Clark would be bulldozing his way through the resolutions on the convention floor down below. He believed that discussion and debate were the ways to develop policies that were inherently right for the country. His perseverance paid off at the PC Student Federation convention in January 1963, which Mulroney attended as a delegate. For at that convention the student federation, after harassing Diefenbaker for his dithering over the question of nuclear warheads for Canada, elected Clark as its national president.

One did not get to be student president without knowing what young Tories were thinking about Diefenbaker. Clark was well aware of the widespread estrangement and fundamentally agreed with it. "We appear to have alienated the suburban 'sophisticated' voter and the young voter," Clark wrote in a memo to party headquarters not long after becoming president. "In some quarters, we are branded an anti-intellectual 'Peasants' Party.' Without sacrificing the support we now have, we could build strength in the suburbs and among the young by showing a new interest in the ideas of these groups." Clark knew that Diefenbaker was the wrong leader for the 1960s and supported the concept of periodic leadership review, but he never sniped at the prime minister. He came from Alberta and prairie Tories did not turn their backs on Diefenbaker quickly, so he remained loyal and stayed as far away as he could from the anti-Diefenbaker plotting. Straight, honest, and always a team player, Clark set aside his doubts about the leader in order to promote harmony within his organization. He was the upholder of the established order whose duty it was to smooth over dissent.

As student president, Clark automatically sat on the national executive of the senior party, which put him in direct touch with the real political heavyweights. The senior party also invited him to speak to its big convention. In his clipped way, Clark could unleash a real stemwinder, and on this particular occasion he delivered an awesome speech that had the older Tories nodding in amazement.

By this time it was obvious to everyone that both Clark and Mulroney had set their sights on a career in the House of Commons. But Clark stood out as the more ambitious. He pursued politics single-mindedly and was too obvious in his efforts at knitting together a network that covered every region.

At this stage Mulroney struck outsiders as being more interested in a good time than in scaling the political heights. After leaving St. FX, he rarely talked about his prime-ministerial ambitions. Only the people close to him knew that the flame first ignited in the 1958 Maritime Model Parliament still burned within him. They knew that his desire to lead, his fascination with power and its trappings, his need for the limelight were all evidence of an unquenchable ambition. They knew Mulroney could never be satisfied sitting in the House of Commons as a backbencher. "As you look around the country," Peter White once asked him, "do you see anybody who would be a serious rival to you as leader of the party, and as prime minister?" The question stopped Mulroney for a moment. After pausing, he simply said no and let the matter drop. He knew exactly what Clark was doing but did not consider him a competitor.

At Dalhousie, Clark skipped classes to pursue politics, much as Mulroney had done three years earlier. But unlike Mulroney he became Dalhousie Law's Conservative leader — a rare achievement for a first-year student. However, he devoted most of his time to the national student federation. Clark treated the presidency of the federation as a full-time job, touring campuses, organizing new clubs, and doing whatever he could to build the organization. This strengthened his network to the point where it rivalled even Mulroney's. In later life Clark's and Mulroney's respective supporters would debate which one knew more young Tories in their student days.

Having neglected his studies for most of the year, Clark would learn the same hard lesson Mulroney had. He crammed furiously for the final exams, wrote them all, and finished near the bottom of the class. However, he managed to pass all but one course: Procedure I, which dealt with elementary legal mechanics and happened to be the easiest course on the first-year curriculum. It also happened to be the most boring. The professor tolerated some absenteeism but dealt harshly with hard-core no-shows such as Clark, giving them an automatic grade of 40 no matter how well they scored on the final exams. But although Clark had failed his year, it was a technical failure — a warning from the professor to get serious. He could move on to second year by writing a supplemental exam.

Both Mulroney and Clark spent much of the fall of 1962 monitoring the shaky pulse of the Diefenbaker government. The pulse grew less steady month by month, and as cabinet ministers began quitting one after another, the only question left unanswered became what would topple Diefenbaker first — a gang-up of opposition parties in Parliament or a gang-up of anti-Diefenbaker ministers in cabinet. The answer arrived in February 1963 when the Liberals, the NDP, and Social Credit got together on the floor of the House of Commons to bring down the government. Diefenbaker called an election for April 8, 1963, and set out across the country by train, claiming at one stop after another that he had been betrayed and thwarted at every turn.

As Diefenbaker's campaign train rolled into Quebec and along the St. Lawrence, Mulroney, Meighen, and other young Tories — although still in school — hopped aboard. When very few people awaited the prime minister at a small whistle stop, they and others on the train formed an instant crowd that cheered wildly. But their efforts were in vain. What started as a campaign tour turned into a wake before the death certificate was signed. On election day Diefenbaker dropped another twenty-one seats, narrowly denying Lester Pearson and the Liberal Party a majority. In April 1963 he duly relinquished power but refused to vacate the office on the fourth floor of Centre Block that traditionally belonged to the prime minister; the gentlemanly Pearson never kicked him out.

The demise of the Diefenbaker government killed Mulroney's

chance for another summer job in Ottawa. In opposition the Conservative Party had few to give out. He applied as an announcer at CBC Radio and received a studio test, but wasn't hired. He ended up working as a legal assistant in the Montreal head office of the Quebec North Shore Paper Company, which owned the paper mill in Baie Comeau where his father still worked as chief electrician. Mulroney got the job through an old connection; he had kept up his home-town network and now it paid off.

In the third year at Laval, Mulroney shifted some of his political attention from the crumbling Conservative Party to student council politics. He was appointed to the five-member campus executive council. Sitting on student council was a first for him, and he delved into his duties so deeply that Yves Pratte, the new dean of law, called over Claude Frenette, the student president, and asked him to put on the brakes. Pratte was worried that Mulroney was missing too much class.

Committed as he was, Mulroney still missed more than his share of student council meetings. He had unlimited energy for pursuing plans and making deals all week long, yet could hardly bring himself to attend the formal sessions. The endless debate as students split hairs over petty detail bored him silly. Often he left early or arrived late or simply failed to show up at all. This spotty attendance record became well enough known that Mulroney's apparent absence from the annual student parade was noted in *Le Carabin*, the student newspaper, with the sarcastic suggestion that he must have mistaken it for a student council meeting. Mulroney shot back a letter the next week:

Excuse me, I was in the calèche . . .

Dear Mr. Editor,
In your last issue you spoke of my "absence" from the Executive calèche [carriage] during the students' parade.
 Not guilty, sir: I was there! Me and Nicole and Claude and

Henri and the other Claude, and Miss Rouge-et-Or, we were all there — with a driver, a horse and forty ounces of scotch!

I bitterly regret that you didn't see me, sir. Nevertheless I even waved at you (corner of de Salaberry and St. Jean) and I yelled "Hello, Mr. Editor!" Unless you took me for the horse.... (Ah, cursed drink!)

Regarding my "absences" (again!) from Executive Committee meetings: in fact my attendance at meetings isn't perfect. Of a total of more than fifty meetings of the Executive since we took office, I have been absent about six times. *Peccavi!*

I even missed a meeting of the Grand Council. *Mea culpa!*

And, do you know, sir, that things are getting a bit worse all around the university. For example, *Le Carabin*, which formerly was faithful to a Thursday-morning publication, now appears on Friday . . . and sometimes Saturday . . . and alas, even once on Monday! Ah, human weaknesses! *Ora pro nobis.*

My best wishes, sir. Till the next parade!

BRIAN MULRONEY

Campus politics did not keep Mulroney from the major Tory political event of the year. In early February 1964 the national party, the student federation, and the YPCs all held conventions in Ottawa. The nation's capital was awash with Tory conventions, and everybody — supporters and opponents alike — was talking about the same thing, namely Diefenbaker's leadership. Everybody, that is, except Mulroney, who had grown discreet on the subject. He showed up in Ottawa as a YPC delegate as usual but this time kept mostly out of sight.

Mulroney's Quebec friends were a different story, particularly Peter White and Michael Meighen. White had assembled an anti-Diefenbaker coalition and arrived in Ottawa actively campaigning for a formal leadership review. They were far from alone. The Tory students were hatching all kinds of schemes in the Château Laurier that weekend, and nobody could predict what damaging resolutions their convention might adopt.

The fact that all three conventions were voting on Diefenbaker's leadership made the pro-Diefenbaker forces decidedly nervous, but they had a trick or two up their sleeves. The Diefenbaker faction's strategy was to undermine the whole review process by scuttling plans for a secret ballot, thus forcing delegates to stand up and declare themselves publicly. They were betting that many anti-Diefenbaker delegates lacked the courage to oppose him in a fishbowl. At both the national party and the YPCs the ploy worked, allowing Diefenbaker to escape repudiation.

However, across town at the Bruce MacDonald Motor Hotel, where the student federation was holding its convention, events unfolded differently. The students, the first group to fall away from Diefenbaker, stubbornly refused to go along with an open vote. After the secret ballot, delegates knew something had gone awry when the student brass declined to announce the outcome, refusing to budge even after a floor fight. However, the delegates managed to wring out one concession: if they were not to be informed of the result, then at least Diefenbaker should be. The convention executive agreed to communicate the result directly to Diefenbaker on a confidential basis. Joe Clark, who had just been acclaimed for a second term as the federation's president, was trying to put the best front on a bad situation and save Diefenbaker some face. He knew the vote was thirty-one to thirty in favour of Diefenbaker with an embarrassingly high number of abstentions.

Since no one was volunteering to deliver Diefenbaker the grim news, the task fell to Clark, who grumbled a bit but dutifully trudged out to Stornoway. Mulroney could have sugar-coated the news but Clark, stiff and awkward at the best of times, lacked this knack. The Tory leader wanted to hear only good news, and he took the results badly, confusing the message with the messenger. Forgotten was the fact that Clark had loyally supported him and managed to bottle up the dissent within the student federation since the 1963 election. To his grave, the Conservative leader classified Clark as a traitor and never forgave him. In later years, when Diefenbaker ranted against Clark, what he would remember was the young man's deportment that day at Stornoway. He had arrived on a Sunday afternoon — Diefenbaker's day off — and then compounded the error by asking for tea when his wife, Olive, had already made coffee, thus forcing her to make both.

Mulroney's fourth and final year at Laval offered him almost certain victory as student law school president. The only obstacle holding him back was his own reluctance to fight an election. For the first time in their history Laval students were electing their student council. Faced with the possibility of losing he quickly backed off and urged Paul Fortin — a Liberal — to run instead. "I'll organize for you," Mulroney promised. However, Fortin was transferring to the University of Montreal and urged Mulroney himself to run. But to no avail. Sticking to his policy of not contesting elections, Mulroney refused to let his name stand.

The youth revolution arrived on campus that fall of 1964, and Laval's first-ever student council election became polarized between warring factions of left and right. The two sides battled it out across campus, except in the law school, which still had no candidate for president. At the final moment, with victory assured, Mulroney declared his candidacy and won by acclamation.

During the campaign Mulroney had officially aligned himself with the right-wing slate (led by friend and fellow Tory Jean Bazin), but after the election he adopted the role of the *éminence grise* who floated above the partisan fight. The student politicians at Laval took strong positions on almost everything and continually tried to thwart their opponents on council. But not Mulroney. One could not play the partisan political game and remain everybody's friend. So at the weekly council meeting, he silently watched the two sides slug it out, then at the eleventh hour weighed in with an articulate compromise. Although he belonged to Jean Bazin's group, he sided with it only when pressed. More often than not he shuttled between the antagonists in search of agreement, and generally found one. Some students thought he was too superficial and too smooth, but nobody disliked him, although sometimes he straddled the fence so much that his own team complained it could never count on his vote.

That year the National Federation of Canadian University Students was financing a month-long trip to western Canada for two Laval students to be chosen by the student council. The pair were to act as PR ambassadors for Quebec on campuses from Winnipeg to Victoria. Mulroney wanted this plum more than anything, and lobbied hard, extolling his expertise on the West acquired as assistant to Alvin Hamilton. Privately, he told one student that the trip was tailor-made for him, and that he was the only candidate who fit the prerequisites perfectly. In the end it came down to Mulroney and two others, but the final verdict went against him. He never forgave his fellow executive members for passing him over, and his bitterness spilled out occasionally at council meetings in the months that followed. Losing was still something he could not swallow.

Fourth year at a Quebec law school was a watered-down version of the articling year required in other parts of Canada. Students prepared for their bar admission exams while spending part of their time working for a law firm. The work was easy: filing briefs, getting papers stamped, and occasionally doing some research.

Most of Mulroney's closest friends, including Peter White, Michel Cogger, and Michael Meighen, had lined up their off-campus jobs in Montreal and transferred over to McGill or the University of Montreal. But Mulroney stayed in Quebec City and latched on with Gravel, Thomson & Gravel, whose offices were conveniently located halfway between his rooming-house and the university, inside the only highrise office building in the Old City. More than a century old, the firm had participated in some of Quebec's most famous cases, such as the *Empress of Ireland* shipwreck near Rimouski in 1914, which killed more than a thousand people, and the renowned trial of Wilbert Coffin, convicted of murdering three Americans in the Gaspé forest in the summer of 1953. One of the early partners had been the minister of militia under Prime Minister John A. Macdonald.

Although it was small, the firm had big clients such as CPR and Bell Telephone. Overall, Mulroney had done well.

During his time at Laval, Mulroney had not opened many textbooks nor spent much time in the library, but then neither had many of his classmates. Studying was important, yet other things, such as being on hand when cabinet ministers arrived in town or spending time with JoAnn Ross, were more important. Nonetheless his Dalhousie experience had taught him a lesson, so he studied, but only enough to get by. Along the way he misjudged a few times and was forced to rewrite some exams but he successfully passed each year with reasonably good grades.

By fourth year Mulroney had shored up his academic record but showed little evidence of intellectual growth. He possessed extraordinary skill in communication but he still needed a message to deliver. He was by nature a doer, not a thinker. For him politics was a matter of strategy and tactics, not policy. Abstract talk bored him. His notion of profound discussion was defending John A. Macdonald's protectionism against Wilfrid Laurier's call for free trade. Given a choice, Mulroney preferred to gossip about personalities — who was up and who was down — political parties, sports, and which women made the best dates.

When it came to issues, he showed little sign of graduating past the pep-talk stage. He came to Laval believing that Confederation's most pressing need was more goodies for the Maritime provinces. Then he adopted Quebec as his cause and concluded that the solution to the Conservative Party's woes in Quebec lay in the appointment of big-name Quebec cabinet ministers. He did not dig into the philosophical roots of issues. In fact some people suspected he simply lacked the intellectual octane. He had no overview, no program, no ideas of his own. Mulroney could sift, assimilate, and implement, but he could not originate. It was one of the few areas where Joe Clark was clearly his superior. Clark loved ideas and discussed them ad nauseam. Already he was forming the foundation of his vision of Canada as a community of communities, an idea heavily influenced by his recent reading of Wallace

Stegner's *Wolf Willow.* To Mulroney, ideas and theory meant nothing if he could not see some fast and concrete results.

However, Mulroney understood this major shortcoming. He knew that street smarts and grassroots pragmatism were not enough to carry him all the way to the top. A politician needed a good sense of mechanics, but a leader needed vision. A leader had to rise above his peers, otherwise he was no leader. As much as he disliked intellectual thought, he realized that a successful political leader needed substance — or at least the appearance of substance. He had always been adept at absorbing other people's thoughts and running with them, and Laval gave him much to run with. The place surrounded him with intellectuals and gave him access to scholarly debate beyond anything he had seen at St. FX and Dalhousie. But in his final year at Laval, Mulroney turned to two men in particular for intellectual inspiration. The more important of these was Lucien Bouchard.

Bouchard, a square-jawed student from Chicoutimi, was easily the smartest guy in Mulroney's class. A strong nationalist, some said a separatist, Bouchard spoke no English and refused to learn. Whenever Mulroney muffed his French, even a little, Bouchard promptly corrected him. In the early years, the two for the most part kept their distance, but in fourth year, after Peter White, Michael Meighen, Michel Cogger, and other friends all left for Montreal, Mulroney and Bouchard socialized a little and, odd as it seemed, became good friends.

While Mulroney viewed politics as the art of the deal, Bouchard saw it as a set of ideas. Bouchard lived in a world of the mind. He spent his spare time in the library poring over learned articles. If he wasn't reading them, he was writing them. Despite his bookish habits, Bouchard could be delightfully funny. As the year progressed the two formed a special bond. Mulroney rarely bared his inner self to friends, but he confided deeply in Bouchard. L. Ian MacDonald, Mulroney's biographer, described Bouchard as someone who could "look into his soul." Mulroney revered him and trusted him implicitly. On matters of fundamental principle nobody influenced him more. He accepted everything Bouchard said. In short, Bouchard became Mulroney's intellectual surrogate.

Mulroney also turned for guidance to his fourth-year procedure professor. Although he routinely skipped classes, especially lectures in the afternoon, in his final year there was one afternoon class that he rarely missed. It started at 5 P.M., the most deadly time slot of all, and covered practical procedure, the most dreary of subjects. Yet the professor managed to breathe life into the study of law and frequently ventured off into broader issues. When the class went past 6 P.M. nobody made a move for the door. This academic who did not lecture so much as perform was Robert Cliche.

The fact that Cliche happened to be a high-profile executive member of the New Democratic Party, and was soon to become its leader in Quebec, did not matter. Nor did it matter that Cliche, like Bouchard, supported special status for Quebec. Mulroney soaked up whatever Cliche had to say. He admired him unabashedly. Bouchard ranked as Mulroney's number one intellectual source, and Cliche as a strong second.

During his years at Laval, Mulroney tapped other intellectual reservoirs as well, most notably his classmates Raynold Langlois and Paul-Arthur Gendreau. Langlois was a prominent campus Liberal and Mulroney's chief rival in Laval's Model Parliaments. Gendreau had a strong personality and a gifted mind and placed high on Mulroney's list of intellectual heroes. And he still relied on Peter White, his political cohort and fellow Tory schemer, for intellectual substance.

But Bouchard and Cliche gave him more than intellectual ballast. They provided ethical guidance. They were his consciences, alerting him to moral danger. When Mulroney became enthusiastic about some project and started going overboard, as he was prone to do, Bouchard could look him in the eye and tell him it was not a wise thing to do. Laval gave him thoughtful friends who drew moral boundaries for him. Their counsel spared him grief in law school and would spare him grief again and again in later life.

While Mulroney had very much found his place at Laval, Joe Clark

was still searching. Although needing to write only a simple supplemental exam, he had surprised many of his friends when he failed to
return to Dalhousie in September 1963. Instead he surfaced in
Vancouver and entered first-year law at the University of British
Columbia. Like Mulroney, Clark had found Dalhousie Law very
tough and painfully boring, and wanted to escape. He also wanted
to be at the side of Davie Fulton, who had quit Ottawa to become
leader of the Conservative Party in British Columbia.

Clark, who was flat broke, got west that summer partly by driving
a yellow school bus from its manufacturing plant in Ontario to its
purchaser in Alberta. A few days before the start of classes at UBC,
British Columbia premier W.A.C. Bennett called an early election.
Clark became Fulton's speech-writer and campaign aide, and still
kept on top of his duties as president of the student federation, which
left him little time for the study of law. (Fulton was trounced in the
election, failing even to win his own seat.) By the end of the year he
was once again in academic trouble, as described by Clark's biographer David Humphreys:

> He decided to try to bluff his way through final exams with his
> writing skill. He realized property law was too tough to bluff.
> His only hope, he decided, was to write the paper so illegibly
> that he would buy time while he prepared better for an oral
> interrogation. He scrawled twenty-five pages, and waited. Sure
> enough, in a few days the professor called him to say the paper
> was unreadable. In the oral exam Clark failed to show enough
> grasp of the subject to salvage a pass mark. Joe took some
> comfort from knowing that in constitutional law, a subject that
> truly interested him, he scored the highest mark in his year.

According to Humphreys, flunking law school had made Clark
"decidedly downcast." In the late spring of 1964, he returned home
to High River and briefly worked on his father's newspaper. He
pondered his future, what there seemed to be of it, and wrote

melancholy, searching letters to friends. He concluded that he wasn't prepared to pay the price to get through law school, and returned to the University of Alberta as a graduate student in political science. So, just as Mulroney was leaving Laval after four successful years, Clark was at his lowest ebb, having flunked out of law school for the second time, and was questioning his own worth.

Mulroney's four years at Laval were extraordinarily happy ones that he would forever recall with affection. "Of all the times in my life," Mulroney told biographer L. Ian MacDonald, "Laval was the golden years." After fleeing Dalhousie in full retreat, he had found Laval to be a welcoming haven when he most needed it. And his experience there augured well for his future, for he had made a remarkable comeback that showed the kind of resilience successful political leaders need during the long, bumpy climb to the top. It was all the more impressive because he seemed to have recovered every ounce of his former confidence, cockiness, and panache. Still he had been lucky to land where he did.

As it turned out, Laval also proved crucial to his later ascent. It added more weapons to an already impressive political arsenal and pointed his career in the right direction. St. FX had given him his original political network. Laval gave him a second, wholly separate one based in French Canada. The Laval network included men who would be among his most faithful and valuable disciples in later years. Michel Cogger, Jean Bazin, and Peter White would introduce him to the right people, organize political meetings, rally the troops, and in every way help smooth his way. But they were only the start of what he got out of Laval.

Above all else at Laval he made himself into a truly bicultural Canadian, equally at home in French and English, equally at ease in French-Canadian and English-Canadian society. His fluency in French was unusual for an anglophone; in 1964 few English politicians could speak more than a few words. This advantage would grow more valuable than anyone, including Mulroney himself, could envisage at the time.

But Mulroney's cultural transformation was much more than a

linguistic achievement. During his years at Laval he watched the Quiet Revolution unfold and changed his outlook on Confederation. He now thought like a Quebecker. Although he still valued a strong central government with no special status for any province, Quebec's priorities had become his priorities.

The most profound evidence of the distance Mulroney had travelled from Baie Comeau and St. FX was the degree to which he had been accepted by his francophone classmates, without discrimination and without jokes; after a while they stopped seeing him as an anglophone. He was simply one of them, a Québécois. Although Peter White and Michael Meighen spoke excellent French they never crossed that cultural line. All the more remarkable then that the anglophones continued to see Mulroney as one of *them*. In fact he was both; he had one foot in each society and could move back and forth at will. He was now a Québécois first and an anglophone second. Wherever he went, Mulroney always conformed to his environment and adopted the values of the people around him. At Laval he had managed to do this with two groups of people at the same time.

As Mulroney prepared to leave Laval and enter the larger world, he had much to feel satisfied about. He had erased the memory of Dalhousie, formed a solid political base in Quebec, and built up a network of contacts across the country. Although he had not distinguished himself as a student, he had a passable academic record. More important, in people like White, Bouchard, and Cliche he had found intellectual counterweights for his pure political passion. Virtually all the pieces of the man who would become prime minister were now in place. It seemed as if nothing could now stop his political ascent.

PART TWO

AMBITION
DENIED

CHAPTER EIGHT

LEGAL HURDLES

EXACTLY WHERE MULRONEY planned to launch his career as a lawyer was unclear. His friends did not really know his intentions and neither, it seemed, did Mulroney himself. If he did know, he was being coy about it. He had several options and probably he just couldn't make up his mind.

One option was to return to Baie Comeau. Mulroney had already discussed this possibility with his father. Some saw it as a natural next step, since it would lead easily into a run for Parliament in his home town. From a purely political point of view this was his best move. Baie Comeau had made huge strides since shaking off its shackles as a company town. Now a ferry crossed the Saguenay River, giving it a direct route to Quebec City. Although still remote, it was not nearly as isolated as when he'd been a boy. And the town continued to grow and expand, which meant there was a demand for lawyers.

Other friends figured he would start off his legal career in the shadow of the Quebec legislature. That too made sense. Quebec City had become his adopted home and continued to be as alluring as ever.

Still others pointed out that Mulroney seldom settled for less than the top. They spotted within him a longing to play in the big leagues of the legal world, and that meant Montreal, which in 1964 was still the largest city in Canada and by far the most exciting and dynamic.

Baie Comeau, Quebec City, or Montreal — each choice had its

pluses and its minuses, and Mulroney seemed uncertain over what to do. It was not like him to be unsure of anything.

Meanwhile, unknown to Mulroney, some of his friends were already promoting the Montreal option by talking up his name in the proper circles. In the spring of 1964 the prestigious law firm Howard, Cate, Ogilvy, Bishop, Cope, Porteous and Hansard had hired McGill graduate Claude Fontaine in its latest round of recruitment. The firm asked Fontaine if he knew any other bright, ambitious law students looking for work. Fontaine happened to be studying for the upcoming Quebec bar exams with Mulroney's friend Michel Cogger. "Why don't you try Mulroney?" Cogger advised him. Fontaine did not know Mulroney but had heard much about him through mutual friends like Jean Bazin and Gary Ouellet, a Loyola student and PC youth activist, so he passed along Mulroney's name to his new employer.

Howard Cate Ogilvy, as the firm was known, also hired Laval grad Paul Amos that spring. As one of Laval's eight invading anglophones of 1960, Amos knew Mulroney well and personally urged Tom Montgomery, a member of Howard Cate Ogilvy's hiring committee, to snap him up. By this time the firm had already hired its quota of spring recruits and seemed set for the year, but with more than one positive recommendation it decided to take a look.

Although Amos had recommended Mulroney, he was not certain he was even available. So he called Bernard Roy to make sure. Mulroney had known Roy at Laval, but they were not particularly close then. (Roy played on the hockey team and didn't have as much time to spend hanging out in the Quartier Latin.) But they liked and respected each other, and during their final year, when Roy articled with a Montreal firm, they kept in touch.

Roy told Amos that he too did not know whether Mulroney had a job and called him in Quebec City. "There seems to be a position here," Roy advised. "Would you be interested?" Indeed he was.

Mulroney's marks in law school in no way stood out, which probably explained his availability so late in the hiring season, well past the time when his classmates had found jobs. But his network of friends and not his academic record had opened the door to Howard Cate Ogilvy. Cogger to Fontaine to Howard Cate Ogilvy, with an assist from Jean Bazin and Gary Ouellet along the way. That was one branch of Mulroney's network in action. Amos to Roy, back to Amos, and on to Howard Cate Ogilvy was another branch. His friends had done it all — well, almost all. He still had to go through an interview.

On the appointed day in April, Mulroney, dressed in blue pin-stripes, arrived for the interview at Place Ville-Marie, the dominant office complex in downtown Montreal. He was well groomed as always and his hair — no longer a brushcut — was slicked down perfectly. On the seventh floor, Tom Montgomery and John Kirk-patrick, impressed that he had studied law in a francophone milieu, poked him with questions for nearly an hour. As Mulroney recounted his background, he made sure to highlight his involvement in politics and student affairs. To every question he responded with crisp, clear, and intelligent answers, never once getting rattled. Barely twenty-five, but showing the maturity of someone ten years older, he quickly convinced Montgomery and Kirkpatrick that he could handle him-self just about anywhere. But most of all, they could not help but admire his extraordinary self-confidence. Mulroney so impressed his two-man audience that he walked out with a job in the largest law firm in the British Commonwealth. The firm had a long list of blue-chip clients and was known in the Quebec legal world as "the Factory." It was a great place for an ambitious young lawyer to make a name for himself.

Howard Cate Ogilvy carried an impressive reputation built up over a long and distinguished history. It opened for business in June 1879 as Carter, Church & Chapleau. A month later Joseph Adolphe Chapleau, one of the founders and a spellbinding criminal lawyer with a reputation for rescuing clients from the gallows, was sworn in as premier of Quebec. When he stepped down as premier in 1882 to join Prime Minister John A. Macdonald's cabinet in Ottawa, he stayed with the firm until he became lieutenant-governor of Quebec in 1892. Carter and Church, the other two founders, who were also Tories, both sat in the Quebec legislature at one time or another. On its hundredth anniversary the firm would publish an official history acknowledging that the seeds of the original partnership "were planted not in the court house but on the floor of Quebec's Legislative Assembly." Although the firm had long since discarded all remnants of political partisanship, everybody who joined it was made to understand the obligation that went with such a long and lustrous tradition.

Mulroney now had a job with a prestigious firm, but his most difficult test still lay ahead: the Quebec bar exams on June 22 and 23. On those two days he would have to pass five brutal written examinations if he wanted to practise law in the province. It meant memorizing the Quebec Civil Code and the Quebec Code of Civil Procedure. Merely thinking about such a dreary exercise horrified Mulroney, but he had no choice. It would take weeks of cramming and time was already short. Most students had started studying long ago. With two months left, he had no time to waste.

When confronted by monumental or daunting tasks, Mulroney instinctively turned to others for help. He had done it in high school for Latin, at St. FX over his missed Canadian history lectures, and at Dalhousie for just about all his courses. Now, facing the need to commit to memory thousands of densely worded legal articles, he turned to Bernard Roy, who had started studying in February and was already well advanced. Mulroney had chosen wisely in Roy, who had excellent work habits and great self-discipline. For the next two critical months Mulroney would count on Roy to be his model and taskmaster.

Late in April Mulroney joined Roy at his mother's cottage at Lac Saint-Joseph, a summer resort outside Quebec City, and started to cram. Each morning at Lac Saint-Joseph, Roy would wake up, then awaken Mulroney, and together they would listen to the 8:00 news on CBC Radio. Then the daily grind began. Roy moved to one corner of the room and Mulroney to the other, and for the rest of the morning they studied in silence. Only the occasional question or comment broke the quiet. It was boring, dreary, and most of all painful. Mulroney had never been able to stand abstract concentration, so memorizing thousands of useless articles stretched his pain threshold beyond anything he had endured before. Even the usually studious Roy was suffering, and they often joked about their life in Stalag 17. Each night they took a little break and tuned in radio station WNEW from New York City, but the only real release came on Saturday night when they piled into Roy's Volkswagen and drove the twenty-five miles into Quebec City to see their girlfriends.

By this time Mulroney's relationship with JoAnn Ross had become quite serious. In fourth year they were often seen walking hand in hand and were always together on social occasions. He had even been known to accompany her to the little chapel at Laval, although he was ordinarily no churchgoer. JoAnn had gotten under his skin like nobody before her, not even Rosann Earl. The quarantine up at Roy's cottage was all the more painful because it meant seeing her only once a week.

After nearly two months of sweating over the Code of Civil Procedure, time finally ran out. Mulroney and Roy had to write the exams, ready or not. They packed up their books and drove to Montreal, bunking down in the basement of Mulroney's uncle's house in the east end of the city. On the morning of June 22, 1964, they showed up at the old Sir Arthur Currie Gymnasium at McGill University along with every applicant from across the province.

Each exam lasted precisely three hours; there were two exams the first day and three the second. There was never enough time: everybody simply scribbled furiously in a race against the clock, going flat out until the end. At noon they broke for lunch, and they started over again in the afternoon. A June heat wave had turned the unventilated gymnasium into an oven. Only the on-and-off outbursts of a marching band practising on the football field next door for the upcoming Saint-Jean-Baptiste Day parade broke the silence in the hot, sticky, and deathly quiet room.

The torture mercifully ended at 9 P.M. on Tuesday. Their memories stretched like elastic bands, many had survived on coffee and some on pills. As they filed out of the gymnasium with their heads spinning, they hoped and prayed they had not blown it. Their careers depended on passing.

Most students learned their fates from a special notice board displayed inside the court-house in Montreal, the official posting place for results. But Mulroney and some of his Laval classmates managed to short-circuit the system. Edgar Gosselin, one of their fourth-year instructors, who also sat on the marking committee, had agreed to call Raynold Langlois with the Laval results. Langlois in turn would pass them along to individual students. A week later an ecstatic Langlois learned that he had made it; so had Bernard Roy. Brian Mulroney had not.

The news of his failure devastated him. Bar admission setbacks were hardly uncommon. They were embarrassing but not the biggest disgrace in the world. People recognized the exams for what they were, a test of memorization and not much else. Sometimes a quarter or a third of all applicants failed. But these facts did not console Mulroney. After four years of academic indolence, he had studied hard for once in his life and had come up short.

He knew that flunking meant he would not be able to practise law at Howard Cate Ogilvy or anywhere else. Gaining admission to the bar had been a condition of his employment, a condition that was assumed to be a mere formality. Howard Cate Ogilvy recruits did not fail the bar exams — no one at the firm could remember such a thing happening before. It was true that Mulroney could rewrite the tests in six months, but how the firm would react in the meantime was anyone's guess.

Miraculously he was granted a reprieve. The senior partners had not hired him for his academic prowess and remained dazzled by his winning manner. They told him not to worry and to report to work in mid-July as planned. He could write the next set of exams in January. Meanwhile he would work as a glorified legal assistant instead of a lawyer. He wouldn't be able to give advice or sign documents, but he could keep his $400-a-month salary. A portion of this went towards his share of the $125 rent he and Roy were paying for a two-bedroom furnished apartment on Claremont Avenue, near the Westmount Theatre, just off Sherbrooke Street.

When Mulroney reported for work at Place Ville-Marie, the firm assigned him to the general litigation section, where most of the new boys started, and gave him a small office in the north wing on the seventh floor. There for the next several months he dutifully filed court briefs and did odd jobs, mostly working on what were known as "bumper" cases. The firm represented the Wawanesa insurance company; prior to Quebec's introduction of no-fault automobile insurance, every fender-bender was litigated. Mulroney did what he was asked and worked hard, but the people around him could tell immediately that he was not cut out for litigation. It was often technical, usually tedious, and full of legal minutiae, which tested his patience now as much as it had back at Dalhousie.

A young staffer who flunked his bar exams and did not shine in general litigation could not expect to go far. But Mulroney adapted quickly to the culture of a big law firm, and he was fun to have around. He behaved as if he were going places. At that time Tom Montgomery, one of the partners who had hired Mulroney, held a fancy dinner for a group of legal dignitaries from across the country and invited Mulroney, even though he was at least a decade younger than anybody else. He was sure Mulroney would shine in a social setting and was proven right. He seemed to have the knack for hitting it off with older people and soon took charge of the evening, leading everybody in a rousing singsong. The firm's junior gofer had made himself the master of the room. Everybody liked him, especially the wives. Mulroney brought intangibles to the firm, and the senior partners were fully aware of it. They thought this young man would make a compelling lawyer.

While running errands by day, Mulroney soon started gearing up for his next shot at the Quebec bar, scheduled for early January 1965.

This time he vowed he would be ready. However, while visiting Baie Comeau for the Christmas holidays with only weeks to go until the exams, he learned that his father had cancer and only months to live.

Nothing could have hit him harder. He had always adored his father. He had continually looked for heroes — Stanfield, Diefenbaker, Fulton, and Kennedy — but his biggest hero of all had always been Ben Mulroney. His father personified his idea of a truly good person — conscientious, unassuming, and a solid family man. He would never let anybody down. His father was simply one of the most admirable people he knew, and now he would lose him. Ben Mulroney had convinced his son to leave Baie Comeau and make it in the world outside. Now he would not be there to share his son's success. It all seemed unbearably cruel.

The horrible news shook Mulroney deeply, and yet he could not skip the bar exams. His job — his whole career — depended on it, so he steeled himself and struggled through. This time he passed everything except Civil Procedure, exactly the kind of legal mechanics that had always tormented him. Memorizing the Code of Civil Procedure proved little except maybe one's determination to be a lawyer, and at this point Mulroney was beginning to think that law was not worth the trouble and had started looking at alternatives.

As if he did not have enough problems already, he now had to break the news that he had flunked again. Once was bad enough, twice exceeded the bounds of mercy. He had already been given a second chance. All he could look forward to now was a handshake, two weeks' pay, and an expression of sincere regret that things had not worked out.

How Mulroney handled this situation would truly test his mettle. In the event, he acted decisively, promptly writing out his letter of resignation, which landed on the desk of one of the ruling partners, Angus Ogilvy. Resigning — instead of going in and pleading for another six months — was the proper course, and he had done it with dignified dispatch. It also dropped the curtain on his legal career — or so it seemed.

With law seemingly out of the question, Mulroney started rethinking his future. But one evening soon after he'd handed in his resignation, Tom Montgomery, the lawyer who had hired him eight months earlier, unexpectedly dropped by his apartment. "Brian, don't worry about it," he counselled. "You've had a bad time. You'll write the bar exam again and you'll pass." His future with the firm was secure, Montgomery assured him. Mulroney had weathered the crisis all right, not attracting so much as a mild rebuke. Resigning turned out to have been shrewd as well as proper.

Ben Mulroney died on Tuesday, February 16, 1965, six weeks after his son's latest bar failure. The funeral was a sombre affair, a Requiem Mass at Sainte-Amélie Church in Baie Comeau. The whole thing left Mulroney decidedly depressed. Fate had cheated Ben Mulroney in death as well as life. He had raised six children on an electrician's wage and had spent much of his life sacrificing his personal comfort for the benefit of his family. Now, with the kids mostly gone, he should have been able at last to start living for himself. The unfairness of it all deeply angered his eldest son. In later years Mulroney would think about it often and would sometimes break down and cry.

Long after the funeral, his father's death continued to drag Mulroney down. And a morbid incident soon afterwards only exacerbated the trauma. Ben Mulroney, it turned out, had been laid to rest in the wrong plot, and needed to be dug up and reburied. The task of identifying the decaying body fell to Mulroney. The experience was almost more than he could bear.

Mulroney's whole life seemed to be going nowhere — his career was on hold, his father was dead, and his life was dull. Each morning he got a lift from the Claremont Avenue apartment downtown in Roy's car to spend the day in boring clerical tasks. (Roy was working at the firm of Byers Casgrain.) After work Roy picked him up and they came home to their dowdy digs and Kraft dinner or bacon-and-cheese sandwiches. On Friday night they might whoop it up at a downtown bar or get into Roy's newly acquired yellow TR3, line the canvas roof with plastic to plug the biggest leaks, and bundle themselves up for a frosty two-hour drive to Quebec City and a brief visit with JoAnn. Life as a legal assistant in a law firm was anything but glamorous.

To make matters worse, his professional plight became something of a joke in the office. At the firm's annual dinner that year, Mulroney happened to sit beside Wilbert Howard, the firm's most senior partner, who light-heartedly tossed off a quip about "Mulroney's Procedure" in his speech that evening. One or two other speakers also got off similar cracks. Mulroney, who normally could not stand being the butt of jokes, no matter how good-natured, took it in stride and chuckled along. What choice did he have? He was lucky still to be around to hear the gibes.

Joking aside, Mulroney's predicament was no laughing matter. According to Quebec law no applicant could write the bar exams more than three times, except by special act of the Quebec legislature. That meant his final shot was coming up in June 1965. Flunking again would finish off his legal career for good, unless he moved to another province and started law school over again. The exam date hung over him like a death sentence.

At least this time Mulroney would have to write only the Civil Procedure exam. And his firm gave him time off with pay to get himself ready. As he had for his first attempt, Mulroney left town to study. He settled into a cottage at Saint-Sauveur in the Laurentians that belonged to Yves Fortier, a colleague in the firm. And once again Mulroney recruited a study partner. This time it was Jean Bazin, his former classmate and student council mate at Laval who had taken a year off to be president of Canadian University Students. Bazin had started to study too late for the January bar exam and had failed.

Knowing it was now or never, Mulroney pulled out all the stops, and so did Howard Cate Ogilvy, which made it an office objective to get him through. First Tom Montgomery popped up to the cottage for half a day of tutoring, and later Jacques Laurent, one of Howard Cate Ogilvy's whiz kids, arrived for a lengthy session. Laurent drilled them on key sections of the Code of Civil Procedure, asking questions to which Mulroney and Bazin spat back the answers. All the preparation paid off. On June 28, 1965, a year after he had first applied, Mulroney was formally admitted to the Quebec bar (as was Jean Bazin).

In later years, Mulroney would rewrite this chapter in his career just as he did the Dalhousie episode. He couldn't deny that he had failed, since everybody at his firm knew about it, but he could obscure the truth and depend on the passage of time to dim the memories of those who were there.

"Quite frankly," he told biographer L. Ian MacDonald in *Mulroney: The Making of the Prime Minister*, "there was illness in the family, and there were amendments. If you go back and look you will see there were amendments to the code, nothing complicated. . . . Very straightforward amendments. Nothing complicated. I didn't have the amendments. Three or four questions out of ten were on the new amendments. Right on. Just a stroke of luck. Nothing complicated about it. Strange exams as I remember. My guess as best as I can reconstruct is that I was just preoccupied with other things, and just paid no attention to the fact that there had been these amendments, not complicated, not difficult at all, that had been snuck through the Legislative Assembly in sort of like a burst of final activity. Not major things, because the Code of Procedure is not major. A ten-day delay rather than thirty, that kind of stuff. I didn't have the damn amendments, and they happened to ask four questions right on them. So that was it."

The fatal amendments, MacDonald's book explained, passed the Quebec legislature while Mulroney was preoccupied, still mourning his father's death. But others who wrote the same exam would later recall nothing about any amendments — and for good reason. The new Code of Civil Procedure did not clear the Quebec legislature until August 6, 1965, seven months after Mulroney's second failure. Contrary to his later claim, Mulroney wrote the exam entirely on the old code.

In revising what happened, Mulroney had also rolled his two

failures into one. Thus his father's illness, which had not yet been diagnosed when he first wrote the exams, helped explain his failure. Over the years the story of the last-minute amendments and the single failure came to be accepted as fact by almost everyone. All three books about Mulroney, including Claire Hoy's acerbic account, accepted Mulroney's version that he had failed only once.

For the time being, however, Mulroney's main concerns were much more immediate: he had decided to move his mother, Irene, and his youngest sister, Barbara, to Montreal. In the wake of his father's death he had suddenly found himself the man of the family. For a while Irene stayed on in Baie Comeau and tried to make ends meet, but the small life insurance payment combined with her husband's meagre pension just wasn't enough. Besides, all the children except Barbara had moved away and she spoke only a little French, leaving her lonely and isolated. The town was no longer the harmonious society of old. Quebec nationalism had arrived, and by 1965 most of the small anglophone élite had left.

After passing his bar exams, Mulroney left the apartment he shared with Bernard Roy and rented the upper half of a duplex at 5456 Notre-Dame-de-Grâce Avenue. The household included his mother, Barbara (now sixteen and planning to attend nursing school), and his younger brother, Gary (now twenty-one), who was in Montreal training to become a hairdresser. (The brothers were totally unlike and had never been close.) It was an abrupt change from his heedless bachelor life, but it was the only way the family could pull through on a junior lawyer's salary. Although taking care of the family severely cramped his style and left him virtually without spending money, it never occurred to him to do otherwise. About the only thing that mattered more to him than politics was his family.

The other three Mulroney kids were now on their own. Olive, the oldest daughter, had married an engineer named Dick Elliott. Peggy, the next oldest, had entered a convent five years earlier. Doreen, three years younger than Brian, was working as a laboratory technician at the Montreal General Hospital.

Initially Mulroney considered quitting the firm and looking for a better-paying job, but he decided to persevere at Howard Cate Ogilvy now that he was finally able to practise law. The partners noticed soon enough that Mulroney did not excel as a legal technician and concluded he was not cut out for precise fields like corporate law, tax law, or patent law. They figured he would do better in what would later be called soft law. It happened that the firm's fledgling labour section, so small that it did not rate as a separate department but was treated as part of litigation, needed help.

Labour law, still relatively new, had not yet found its niche in the legal profession. At Howard Cate Ogilvy, Paul Renault had first dabbled in the area in the 1950s and found the field lucrative. By 1963 he was doing nothing else and hired Marius Bergeron from the Quebec Labour Relations Board to handle his overload. In 1966, when Mulroney became the third member of the section, the demand for labour lawyers was taking off. Unions were becoming more sophisticated in their demands and tactics, so employers were increasingly calling on lawyers both to advise them and to help negotiate.

Labour law would not stay too "soft" for long. Within a decade it would become highly specialized, complex, and riddled with statutes. But in 1966 it was governed provincially mainly by the Quebec Labour Code, a relatively simple and straightforward act. Mulroney's potential worth as a labour lawyer rested not on his knowledge of the law but on his skills at conciliation and negotiation, and on his ability to make friends on both sides of any issue. And Mulroney's arrival in the labour group coincided with increasingly difficult labour relations in the province. As would happen so often during his career, his timing was perfect.

On May 9, 1966, not long after Mulroney moved to the labour section, thirty-five hundred members of the International Longshoremen's Association (ILA) went on a wildcat strike, paralyzing the Port of Montreal. The walk-out started spontaneously when some longshoremen received parking tickets in a restricted area on the waterfront. But this incident was only the spark that ignited a series

of long-smouldering grievances — on both sides. The employers —
the shipowners — were not in a conciliatory mood. Unloading a ship
took three times longer in Quebec than elsewhere. The work gangs
were bloated in size and pilferage was rampant. The shipowners
wanted to introduce new technology and reduce the number of men
in the work gangs, but the ILA would not hear of it.

With both sides intransigent, what started as an ad hoc work
stoppage soon escalated into the worst maritime strike in Canadian
history. It got so bad that at one point ILA goons roamed the
waterfront in broad daylight, vandalizing everything in sight and
raiding the shipowners' offices. After thirty-eight days Prime Minister
Lester Pearson personally intervened to negotiate a settlement. The
shipowners gave in to most of the union demands in return for
Ottawa's promise of a special inquiry into the obsolete system of
stevedoring in Quebec's ports.

The Inquiry Commission on the St. Lawrence Ports, as it was
officially called, held its first hearing in a Montreal courtroom on
August 19, 1966. Laurent Picard presided as a one-man commission
with binding authority to do what he wanted. Representing the
Shipping Federation of Canada — the shipowners — was Mulroney's boss, Paul Renault. And sitting next to him at the shipping
federation table as his assistant was Brian Mulroney.

Somebody with Mulroney's junior status would ordinarily expect
to remain very much in the shadows, but it did not take him long to
catch the attention of the shipowners. After two or three weeks of
hearings, Renault started to let Mulroney question witnesses. He
made an immediate impact, particularly with his ability to switch
easily between languages, questioning the longshoremen in French
and the managers in English. With Renault increasingly needing to
attend to other business — and with no more senior labour lawyers
available at the firm — he recommended to the shipowners that
Mulroney take over. They had been so favourably impressed with his
performance that they readily agreed.

Suddenly Mulroney was one of the star players in one of the biggest labour cases the province had ever seen. Here he was, a mere twenty-seven-year-old, who had been a member of the bar little more than a year and had no experience with the issues at hand, handling a case that would have been a plum for a much more senior lawyer.

Whatever doubts the shipping federation had about putting their case into such young hands evaporated almost immediately. Mulroney stepped into his new role as though born to it. The shipping federation's case for higher labour productivity was long, complex, and hard to explain, but he made it simple, repeatedly driving home the point that the owners needed better labour productivity on the waterfront. During cross-examination of witnesses, he seemed to know intuitively when to attack, when to hold back, and when to retreat. Watching him perform was a delight. The attributes that had made him flashy as a student debater — the easy command of facts, the quickness with a retort, the sense of theatre — turned the Picard commission into the Brian Mulroney Show. His speed on his feet, his colourful turns of phrase, and the clear sense that he was having fun left everyone dazzled and made him look downright invincible.

But good as he was, Mulroney met his match in Phil Cutler, the surly but formidable lawyer for the ILA. On opening day Cutler had challenged the commission's right to sit; when that failed he dragged out the proceedings by calling an endless string of witnesses. Cutler liked to bully and used intimidation as a tactical weapon. Although this was not Mulroney's preferred style, he refused to be intimidated. When Cutler yelled at him, he yelled back just as loudly.

The two adversaries outdid each other in hyperbole. Cutler exaggerated the shoddy practices of the shipowners, and in retaliation Mulroney exaggerated the excesses of the longshoremen. While Cutler harped on job losses, unsafe working conditions, and the miserliness of the shipowners, Mulroney cited the poor productivity, featherbedding, and pilferage of the workers. Both stretched the truth on their sides of the argument to the limit in order to gain ground at the centre. It was a form of discourse in which the younger man, full of blarney in the Irish tradition, had an edge. Exaggeration came naturally to him; it was his normal mode of daily speech. Facing off against Cutler he just turned it up a few notches. In many respects it was a game for Mulroney, one at which he excelled. (One day he would appoint Cutler a judge.)

Skirmishing with Cutler often proved easier than keeping his own clients united. As fierce competitors in the marketplace, they had trouble rising above their petty quarrels in a common cause. The situation taxed all Mulroney's talents for conciliation. He constantly found himself exhorting the management players to stick together and maintain a united front. Otherwise, he warned, the longshoremen would exploit their rifts.

But Mulroney's greatest challenge lay in keeping the stevedoring contractors onside. These were the companies that actually hired the longshoremen and then contracted them out to the shipowners. Although these middlemen had agreed to join forces with the shipowners, who, it was agreed, would speak for both, the pact constantly teetered on the brink of break-up. The root of the problem was that the mostly foreign-owned shipping companies believed that the Canadian-owned stevedoring contractors overcharged them. Despite the constant vigilance of Mulroney and Alex Pathy, the chairman of the shipowners' labour committee, this somewhat unholy alliance actually collapsed once or twice, but somehow the two managed to patch things up.

Mulroney quickly realized that one way to keep the stevedores happy was to make friends with their lawyer, David Angus. Fortunately Angus, a McGill grad only two years his senior, was a Tory. Although they had met only in passing a few times at YPC conventions, it didn't take long for Mulroney to turn this connection into a strong commitment. In fact Angus would prove an important part of Mulroney's political network.

The Picard commission finally wrapped up in September 1967 — fourteen months, ninety-five hearing days, seventy-two witnesses, and 12,528 pages of testimony after Mulroney first set foot in the hearing room as Paul Renault's lowly assistant. "Employers must be given a relative free hand to revise obsolete and unreasonably restrictive work rules provided that the revision creates no unsafe conditions or unduly onerous workloads," Mulroney argued in his prepared summation. He also flattered the commissioner with the prediction that his report would "bring about the dawn of a new era in labour-management relations."

Whether this prediction would prove true or not, one thing was already certain. The Picard commission had provided a new dawn in the legal career of Brian Mulroney. He had been transformed from a faceless junior assistant to a leading Quebec labour lawyer. And it had given him his first blue-chip client. He was soon to become the regular lawyer for the Shipping Federation of Canada with responsibility for legal work pertaining to ports all down the St. Lawrence and into the Maritimes. His relationship with the shipowners would be long and rewarding; it was a remarkably auspicious beginning to a legal career.

CHAPTER NINE

THE CIVIL WAR

DURING MULRONEY'S EARLY apprenticeship at Howard Cate Ogilvy, he had continued to pull strings in the backrooms of the Conservative Party while trying with increasing unease to stay neutral on the question of Diefenbaker's leadership. Only his charm allowed him to pull it off. Most of his friends had long concluded that the Chief could never win again and was dragging the party down with him. As time wore on, Mulroney found it more and more difficult to straddle the fence. Soon after he was finally called to the bar in June 1965, matters moved rapidly to a head. In the spring of 1966 the party's national president, Dalton Camp, began calling within party circles for a formal leadership review at the party's biennial convention the coming November. After wavering for so long, Mulroney was finally forced to choose sides.

Camp, whom Mulroney had known since the 1960 Nova Scotia election, had been elected party president in 1964 as a Diefenbaker loyalist, replacing Egan Chambers. Chambers earned Diefenbaker's enmity when he conducted a country-wide mail canvass of all Tory candidates and constituency presidents in the wake of the 1963 election disaster. The poll revealed that only half the party's leading members stood behind their leader. When the Chief got wind of it he was apoplectic and refused to speak to Chambers again.

When Camp took over he found Diefenbaker increasingly testy, erratic, and irrational. He began to wonder if he was wise in backing him for another election. Now past seventy and growing more crotchety with each passing month, Diefenbaker obstinately dismissed any talk of retirement as "utter nonsense" and carried on as if oblivious to the swelling discord from the rank and file. The campuses, which half a dozen years earlier had treated him like the Messiah, now laughed him off as a joke. And whenever Tories of any age sat down together, talk always turned to the question: "When is the old man going to go?" Still, no one dared to challenge him outright.

The event that finally turned Camp against Diefenbaker happened in April 1966. While the party president was vacationing on the Bahamian island of Eleuthera, Diefenbaker abruptly fired Flora MacDonald, the woman who kept party headquarters running like clockwork. Diefenbaker considered her disloyal. Camp was furious because Diefenbaker had moved while he was out of town. More fundamentally, it violated an understanding he thought he had with Diefenbaker. It was war, he concluded, and he knew it would be messy.

By chance Camp was scheduled to speak the following month to a closed-door gathering of Conservatives at the Albany Club in Toronto, a bastion of the WASP establishment. And it was in this sedate setting that he fired his first salvo. He told his audience that the time had come for the party to reappraise its leadership. Coming from the president of the party, it was easily the most serious challenge so far to Diefenbaker, but he simply ignored it. Since the speech was private and off the record, most Tories never heard about it. Then in September Camp delivered the same speech to the Toronto Junior Board of Trade, and this time he sent an advance text to the *Globe and Mail*, which splashed it on the front page. Now finally the shooting war was on, and Mulroney could no longer duck the issue.

Other than his father, there was nobody in the world Mulroney wanted to challenge less than the man who had been his first political idol. Once in a moment of rhetorical fancy Mulroney had proclaimed

177

Diefenbaker one of the greatest men in the history of the earth. That was some claim, even for a master of hyperbole like Mulroney. Of all his political heroes, starting from Lowell Murray at St. FX, nobody had influenced him as deeply as John George Diefenbaker. During only Mulroney's second year at university, it had been the Chief who had made him hungry to be prime minister. If Mulroney's psyche could be laid out on a computer screen, Diefenbaker would pop up all over. So turning against Diefenbaker turned him against parts of himself. The process would inevitably be painful. Mulroney always leaned towards sentimentality and was especially sentimental about Diefenbaker. However, when he was forced to choose between sentiment and hard-headed pragmatism, pragmatism always won out eventually.

Mulroney had in fact already done a lot of thinking about the party's problems and had always arrived at one inescapable answer: the Tories could not win elections without Quebec — the province always voted as a bloc and always calculated collectively how to vote — and they could not win again in Quebec with Diefenbaker, who had never understood Quebec and clearly never would. If there was any lingering doubt in Mulroney's mind, it was dispelled by the 1965 election, when Diefenbaker lost a second time to Pearson, whom Mulroney regarded as punchless. It was a troubling conclusion, but Mulroney accepted it entirely. Before the Tories could win another national election the leader had to go. Mulroney had believed this for some time, but his sense of loyalty had always kept it bottled inside.

Dalton Camp's phone started ringing the day after he made his controversial September 1966 speech to the Junior Board of Trade, and one of the first calls came from Mulroney. He wanted Camp to come to a private meeting of Montreal Tories. The party president accepted, and a few days later he was explaining his actions to a small group that Mulroney had hastily assembled. "Well, that's all very well for you to say," Lionel Jenks said afterwards, "but what are you going to do about it?" The question stopped Camp cold for a moment. He

RIGHT: Since Baie Comeau did not offer English-Catholic schooling beyond Grade 10, Mulroney finished high school at a private Catholic all-boys boarding school in Chatham, New Brunswick. He graduated in 1955 at sixteen, a year younger than most of his classmates, and looking it. (*Fredericton Daily Gleaner / Michael Nowlan*)

BELOW: This autographed picture hung on Mulroney's wall in residence at St. FX. Mulroney had many political heroes, but none greater than John Diefenbaker. He frequently called the Chief in Ottawa and visited his Parliament Hill office whenever he could. (*The Progressive Conservative Party of Canada*)

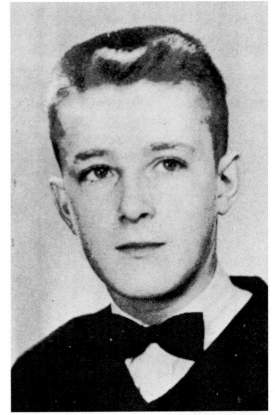

As a seventeen-year-old, Mulroney went to the 1956 Tory leadership convention to vote for Davie Fulton but became enraptured by Diefenbaker, the prairie populist, and tagged along as part of his entourage. His devotion to Diefenbaker would later cause him much agony when the Tory leader fell out of touch with Quebec and the party's youth. *(City of Ottawa Archives, Andrews-Newton Collection 47308 No. 18)*

Mulroney became leader of the campus Conservative Party at St. FX in his third year but lost the Model Parliament election to Don Keenan, a hockey star whom the Liberal Party had crassly recruited at the last minute to win votes. However, a twist of fate saw to it that Mulroney and not Keenan became prime minister that year.

RIGHT: Mulroney's deep voice, mellifluous delivery, quick wit, relaxed disposition, and extraordinary stage presence quickly made him one of St. FX's best debaters. He won the Oratorical Contest three years in a row and never lost an intervarsity debate.

BELOW: The St. FX intercollegiate debating team: Bill Wiseman, Mulroney, Paul Creaghan (Mulroney's predecessor as campus Tory leader), Rick Cashin, Tom Concannon, and René Patry. Good as Mulroney was, he was no match for Cashin.

In February 1958 Mulroney became prime minister in the most grandiose Model Parliament the Maritimes had ever seen. It was here that he got the itch to become a real prime minister. Next to him, from left to right: Gordon Churchill, Diefenbaker's minister of trade and commerce; Paul Martin, the former minister of health and welfare; student opposition leader Dan Hurley; CCF MP Doug Fisher; and Leo Nimsick, the student CCF leader.

Ben and Irene Mulroney never felt prouder than in the spring of 1959 when their son graduated from St. FX with a BA. All their sacrifices had been justified. *(Rosann Cashin)*

Mulroney's graduation photo in the St. FX yearbook said, "Future plans point to Laval University and a career in Law."

Mulroney took Rosann Earl to the graduation dance and in his final days at
St. FX fell madly in love with her. When Rosann attended Mount St. Vincent
University in Halifax that fall, he impulsively abandoned Laval and enrolled
at Dalhousie law school to be near her in Halifax. The move would seriously
complicate his academic and career plans. *(Rosann Cashin)*

Despite twice failing the Quebec bar exams, Mulroney joined the prestigious law firm Howard, Cate, Ogilvy, Bishop, Cope, Porteous and Hansard, then the largest firm in the British Commonwealth, and quickly made a name for himself.

LEFT: The similarities between Brian Mulroney and Joe Clark, the two-term president of the Progressive Conservative Student Federation, were striking. They were the same age; both possessed remarkable debating skills and lived and breathed politics. Furthermore, both harboured big political ambitions. But otherwise they could hardly have been more dissimilar, and they pursued their political goals in very different ways. *(Canapress Photo Service)*

BELOW: Joe Clark ran for Parliament in 1972 and was elected. Here he poses with Conservative leader Robert Stanfield shortly after being sworn in as an MP. Meanwhile Mulroney, practising law in Montreal, declined overtures to run for office. *(Canapress Photo Service)*

had not thought out a strategy, did not even know his next step. "I plan to go across the country and talk to Conservatives and see what they want to do," he quickly improvised. Born that instant was the notion of a national tour to sell the idea of a leadership review. Camp set out almost immediately on what Diefenbaker would derisively call "the pilgrimage." Meanwhile, Mulroney operated undercover as his key contact in Quebec, updating him on local developments. Other important members of Camp's informal dump-Diefenbaker organization were Lowell Murray, Flora MacDonald, and Norman Atkins, Camp's brother-in-law and political sidekick.

Not wanting to clash with the old man, Mulroney looked for ways to soften the impact of Diefenbaker's departure, even as he worked for Camp. "We have to do it in a very nice way," he told a hawkish friend. "We do not want to humiliate him." He also wanted to avoid alienating Diefenbaker and to preserve all his friendships, even among the remaining loyalists. This explained why he never took a public stand against the leader, as friends like Michael Meighen and Peter White did. While others fought openly, he would remain discreet and covert, running the risk that sooner or later Diefenbaker would find out.

Camp had toyed with the idea of putting Diefenbaker's leadership before a general vote of the next party convention, but he decided against it. General resolutions were decided by open votes, which were highly susceptible to manipulation. He announced instead that he would run for re-election as party president in November and make leadership review the only issue. Party presidents were elected by secret ballot, and he told everyone that a vote for him was a vote for leadership review.

Craftily, during his seven-week "pilgrimage," Camp spoke only about the principle of leadership review. Not once did he utter the leader's name, although backstage he often referred to "Charlie" — which was Diefenbaker's code-name. Camp kept refining his message and ultimately reduced it to a matter of party democracy: whether the leader is above the party. He argued that a democratic party must have a formal periodic review of its leader, or a leader could hang on until he died. The message seemed to be hitting home: everywhere he went he attracted full houses, and many of the party members who came out expressed the view that a leader had no right to rule for life and endorsed the notion of a periodic leadership review.

Throughout the whole exercise Camp continually encouraged provincial associations to pass resolutions supporting the review concept. British Columbia and Prince Edward Island had already done so when Camp arrived in Beauport, Quebec, on October 1, 1966, where provincial Tories were gathering for one of their rare conventions. Camp stayed away from the convention floor itself while Mulroney — his messenger and *agent provocateur* — shuffled in and out of his motel room with developments. Surprisingly, the news was not good. Despite all the bad blood between Diefenbaker and Quebeckers, the leader still commanded strong pockets of allegiance in the provincial party. It looked as though Camp would not get his resolution after all.

To make matters worse, Diefenbaker himself was scheduled to put in a personal appearance at the convention. His plan was to fly into nearby Quebec City, make a well-publicized visit to Daniel Johnson, the new premier of Quebec, and then arrive at the convention with great fanfare. Diefenbaker hoped an embrace from Johnson would impress the delegates and shore up his support.

Alarmed at this prospect, the Camp forces were lobbying Johnson to cancel the meeting. Lately premiers everywhere had been steering clear of the unpopular Tory leader. Mulroney, whose friendship with Johnson went back to those late nights at the Château Frontenac bar during his years at Laval, assured Camp that the meeting would never take place. "Forget it," Mulroney said, "he won't do it." Mulroney had good reason to be certain. Not only was Johnson an old pal, but his law school buddy Peter White was Johnson's executive assistant, and he was in on the plot too. Nonetheless, in the end Johnson agreed to see Diefenbaker, explaining that he could not refuse a former prime minister.

However, the Johnson meeting actually turned into a blessing for

Camp. Diefenbaker loved to have a welcoming audience wherever he went. So about a hundred loyalists left the convention floor to cheer their leader's arrival at the airport, then followed him downtown for his thirty-minute meeting with Johnson, removing from the convention the core group of Diefenbaker supporters for a couple of critical hours. During this time the leadership resolution came before the convention, and Mulroney and his group — principally Peter White, Jean Bazin, and Michael Meighen — controlled the floor long enough to ramrod it through. The players behind the vote claimed the timing was coincidental, but the Diefenbaker loyalists later accused them of engineering the whole thing. In any event, with the Diefenbaker loyalists absent, the convention passed the toughest leadership resolution of all, one that became pivotal in legitimizing Camp's case.

Another promising development at the convention was the election of Paul O. Trépanier as president of the Quebec party. A millionaire architect, Trépanier arrived in Beauport in a Lincoln convertible complete with male and female secretaries and his own Gestetner. His immediate entourage occupied six hotel suites. He was bigger than the provincial party, and better organized. He also favoured a leadership review, or so Mulroney and his cohorts had been led to believe. Prior to the convention they had invited Trépanier to a private meeting in Montreal in order to size him up and had been given assurances that he supported renewal in the party. On this basis the Mulroney group fell behind him and now expected that he would help them rally the review forces.

To Mulroney's dismay, however, Trépanier started to waffle the very next day. The Quebec executive remained split on the Diefenbaker issue, and Trépanier was clearly trying to walk down the middle. Meanwhile Diefenbaker courted the new Quebec Tory president, phoning him regularly and calling him the next George-Étienne Cartier. The wooing succeeded in weakening Trépanier even more on the leadership question. One day he leaned towards review, the next day towards the status quo, undermining the whole insurrection.

This behaviour absolutely enraged Mulroney and made him determined to bring the wayward president back into line. With help from his extensive Quebec network, Michael Meighen and Jean Bazin especially, Mulroney called a most unusual meeting of the party and summoned Trépanier to attend. Although it was convened without the authority of the executive and was therefore completely unofficial, virtually every important Quebec Conservative showed up, over the protests of Diefenbaker loyalists such as Jean Bourguignon. Mulroney and others told Trépanier to stop waffling over the issue of leadership review. Trépanier protested feebly that as president he had to represent all the Tories in Quebec and needed to keep an open mind. But the message had gotten through, and Trépanier shifted to the review side, or so it seemed.

With the November showdown in Ottawa two and a half weeks away, the Diefenbaker side made its cleverest move of all. It announced that Arthur Maloney, the former MP and renowned criminal lawyer, would be the Diefenbaker candidate for president. The Diefenbaker people could not have picked a more effective adversary for Dalton Camp. Maloney was virtually a cult figure in the party. He had also been one of Mulroney's special friends since their meeting during the summer Mulroney worked for Alvin Hamilton.

Maloney's entry shook up the race and tore at the loyalties of some delegates. When Roy McMurtry, a young Toronto lawyer and committed Camp worker, learned that Maloney had jumped into the race, he spent the evening pacing around his house and muttering to himself, unable to decide what to do. His two closest political friends were Arthur Maloney and Dalton Camp. At one point he'd decided to drop out and not even attend the convention, but finally he screwed up his resolve to stay with Camp. He wrote Maloney a letter proclaiming his undying affection while explaining his stand on principle. A few days later McMurtry bumped into Mulroney and discovered that he had suffered through the same anguish and had written Maloney a similar letter.

A week before the convention, Camp briefly dropped out of sight to rest and retool. He and his wife checked into a resort in the Laurentians north of Montreal and invited along two collaborators, Michael Meighen and Mulroney. The four of them spent a relaxing dinner discussing final strategy, but the tranquillity was shattered by the news that Trépanier had once again said something sympathetic to the Diefenbaker side, stating that he was considering supporting Arthur Maloney for party president. This apparent defection seriously undermined Camp's forces at a critical time.

Both thoroughly incensed, Mulroney and Meighen hastily drove back to Montreal and summoned Trépanier to explain himself. Trépanier was mayor of the town of Granby, an hour's drive away, and protested that he had to attend a council meeting, offering instead to appear the following evening. But Mulroney wasn't interested in excuses and ordered him to come immediately after the council adjourned. When Trépanier reached Montreal around 11 P.M., he was greeted icily by a small group of angry young Tories — the Westmount group, as he called them, the same people who had called him to task earlier. The whole thing had the formal atmosphere of an inquisition, with Brian Mulroney as Grand Inquisitor.

Mulroney spoke first and came directly to the point: What was the meaning of Trépanier's latest statement? The Quebec president once again explained that he was trying to keep both sides happy but agreed that this time he had gone too far. "Look," Trépanier promised, "I won't do it again. I am with you — for sure." Having received this commitment to cooperate, Mulroney phoned Camp to assure him that the fire had been put out. "Everything's fine," Mulroney said. "They're all with us."

Mulroney arrived in Ottawa on Saturday, November 12, two days before the start of the convention, to help Camp marshal his troops. When he compared notes with Roy McMurtry, who arrived the same day, it was clear that the next several days would be tough. The Château Laurier, the site of this impending civil war, was being armed for battle with posters and buttons. After talking it over, Mulroney and McMurtry decided to drop in on their old friend and new adversary Arthur

Maloney for a drink. They wanted a friendly chat before things got really rough. Maloney welcomed their overture but warned them to come late at night, after his workers were gone.

The pair arrived at Maloney's suite after midnight, but this was not late enough. A few Maloney workers were still hanging around and did not like this brazen sortie from their opposition. In fact they started catcalling and hurling insults, and Maloney had to intervene to cool things down. Eventually the Maloney workers left and Mulroney and McMurtry spent a few convivial moments alone with their friend, but the incident was a portent of things to come.

It seemed only two kinds of Tories came to Ottawa that third week of November 1966: emotional loyalists and hard-headed pragmatists. The loyalists only remembered that Diefenbaker had once led the party out of the wilderness — many of them had joined the Conservatives because of him. The pragmatists like Mulroney agreed that Diefenbaker had taken the party out of the wilderness but also believed he had led it straight back in again, and was now keeping it there. For them the only route out of the current wilderness was to change leaders. But there was agonizing on both sides: many Diefenbaker stalwarts saw it as a matter of loyalty to the leader. Many of them lined up behind Diefenbaker, knowing full well they were standing in the wrong spot. It was the most passionate, intense, and painful convention in the history of the Conservative Party.

In a civil war there are many casualties, as Mulroney soon discovered. On one occasion when he ventured into unfriendly territory wearing his Camp button, he got into a scrap and was punched in the nose. He returned to Camp headquarters with blood on his face from a minor gash between the nose and eye. Apparently his assailant had been wearing a ring that had nicked his skin. For the rest of the convention Mulroney wore the cut on his face like a medal and laughingly claimed to be the only person to have shed blood in the cause of leadership review.

Diefenbaker, the master orator, could still rouse an audience, a fact that made the Camp forces decidedly nervous, particularly since the

Chief was scheduled to speak on Monday night, the first evening of the convention. Normally the leader's speech would wind up the convention, but the Diefenbaker brain trust hoped he would work some miracles early in the proceedings to give Arthur Maloney a boost. Camp also feared that in the emotion of the moment someone would propose a "spontaneous" vote of confidence — by a show of hands, of course — that would undercut the meaning of the presidential vote. He determined to do what he could to thwart Diefenbaker's plan.

The strategy was simple but devastatingly effective. An hour before Diefenbaker's speech the student and youth delegates — all firmly in Camp's corner — arrived at the Château Laurier ballroom and filled up the front rows. When Diefenbaker entered the room, the front one-third of the audience pointedly refused to stand. And throughout the speech, the front section of the room refused to applaud — even once — and eventually heckled and booed the Conservative leader. One huge University of Toronto student, about six-foot-six, sitting directly in front of the podium with his arms resolutely folded, glared at Diefenbaker throughout his speech. Knocked off stride, Diefenbaker implored the convention to support the leadership of the party and briefly seemed to rally the crowd at the back. But then things went wrong again. "Is this a Conservative meeting?" an exasperated Diefenbaker finally sputtered. "Yes, yes," the youth delegates shouted back. At that moment the man who could hold an audience in the palm of his hand lost control of the room and of his own party.

The stoning of Diefenbaker, dramatic as it was, threatened to backfire for the Camp forces. Pillorying a seventy-one-year-old former prime minister did little to sell the case of the insurgents. The next day Arthur Maloney delivered an electrifying speech, including one of the most widely remembered lines in the history of Canadian political conventions. "When the Right Honourable John Diefenbaker, former prime minister and leader of this party, walks into a room," he said, "Arthur Maloney stands up." Maloney's speech gave

Diefenbaker new life and made the vote for president closer than expected. But Camp squeaked through, 564 to 502.

The narrow margin formalized the divisions in the party for everyone to see. The dumping of John Diefenbaker had spewed out venom that would poison the Tories for much of the next two decades. Bitterness hung in the air. Diefenbaker, now mortally wounded as leader, refused to attend the closing banquet. Wisely the party quickly cancelled the event and refunded the money. The delegates, in no mood to celebrate, quickly fled the scene of the crime, leaving an eerie emptiness in the suddenly deserted Château Laurier.

Before Mulroney departed he paid a visit of consolation to Arthur Maloney, a move that was typical of him. Accompanied by Claude Harari, a PC student leader, he made his way up to Maloney's suite, where the wake was still in progress. On the way they were accosted in the hallway by an abusive Jack Horner, the young MP from Alberta. Livid with rage and teetering on the edge of violence, Horner blamed both of them for bringing Diefenbaker down. But they neatly slid past him and out of sight. When they arrived at Maloney's suite they found it filled with sadness and pain. Maloney, always the statesman, received them gracefully. Most of the others in the room glared at them with looks that could kill.

Mulroney visited Maloney often in the following years. Whenever he was in Toronto the two would get together and kibitz as jovially as before. "Walk into the room, Arthur," Mulroney would joke. "I want you all to notice that when Arthur Maloney walks in a room, Brian Mulroney doesn't stand up," he would continue, and then break into uproarious laughter. The battle at the Château Laurier had not diminished their friendship at all.

The same could not be said about Mulroney's fallen idol. After his downfall, Diefenbaker rarely mentioned Mulroney or referred to him, although Diefenbaker did not launch into tirades at the mention of his name, as he did with Joe Clark and many others. But those still close to him knew that he had been deeply wounded by what he saw as Mulroney's betrayal. Mulroney had tried to be discreet and had tried to keep out of Diefenbaker's sight, but he had not fooled the Chief one bit. Diefenbaker had spies everywhere and kept a blacklist. The young man he had treated like a son had become blinded by vaulting personal ambition and defected to the enemy. He had committed treason, the blackest of the political sins. And once Diefenbaker registered a grudge, he never forgave.

Mulroney would long be haunted by his part in the dumping of Diefenbaker. It was difficult to square his actions with his strongly held belief that you could judge a person's worth by his loyalty to his friends. He often bragged about his own loyalty and said that he could not imagine ever abandoning a friend, yet he had abandoned Diefenbaker. Somehow he had to deal with the fact that he had not been loyal to his former mentor. He could tell himself — as some suspect he did — that he had not been disloyal, that he had not worked *against* Diefenbaker but *for* the principle of leadership review. If so, deep down he remained unconvinced, because he would be touchy on the subject for years. And as the events of November 1966 moved further into the past, Mulroney would deny ever having been involved in Diefenbaker's downfall.

That Diefenbaker would be replaced as leader was now a foregone conclusion. After narrowly re-electing Dalton Camp as president, the party rather anti-climactically and very easily passed a resolution calling for a leadership convention before the end of 1967. Once the party set September 1967 as the official date and Maple Leaf Gardens in Toronto as the site, candidates started throwing their hats into the ring, until the number reached eleven. The first to declare was Davie Fulton, who announced his candidacy on January 19, 1967, nearly nine months before the convention.

Even before Diefenbaker fell at the Château Laurier, Mulroney had been pushing Davie Fulton to run. Fulton had long had the look of a leader. His maiden speech in the House of Commons in 1945 had so impressed Prime Minister W.L. Mackenzie King that he sent him a congratulatory note predicting that some day he would lead his party. A Rhodes Scholar, a major in the Canadian army reserve, and a distinguished former justice minister, he was also a leading Conservative intellect, spoke passable French, and was accommodating towards Quebec. In short, he was everything Diefenbaker was not, and Mulroney had sized him up as pretty well perfect.

Ever since losing badly to Diefenbaker in 1956, Fulton had been waiting for another chance at the leadership. But after a fierce falling-out with Diefenbaker in the waning months of his last government, Fulton quit federal politics and made his ill-considered stab at reviving the moribund Conservative Party in British Columbia. In the wake of his humiliating loss in 1963, he limped back to Ottawa as an opposition MP. If not for the B.C. débâcle, Fulton would have been crowned automatically as Diefenbaker's successor. But his image as the thinking man's Conservative disguised a number of weaknesses. He lacked natural political instincts and, as the B.C. adventure showed, often displayed terrible judgement. He also drank too much and occasionally cracked under pressure. These character flaws would prove professionally fatal in later life and were readily apparent to those who knew him well; only three or four caucus colleagues initially came out in support of his candidacy. However, Mulroney did not see the flaws, or maybe he did not wish to.

Flawed or not, Fulton was a strong candidate and an early favourite to win. A lot of speculation had Robert Stanfield making a run, but the Nova Scotia premier kept dashing the rumours, even saying once that he was as inclined to get into federal politics as he was to take up ski-jumping. Duff Roblin, the premier of Manitoba, loomed as another potential frontrunner, but he too appeared to be backing away. (The other major candidates who soon declared were former Diefenbaker cabinet ministers George Hees, Wallace McCutcheon, and Alvin Hamilton.)

Before declaring, Fulton had phoned Mulroney to ask him to assemble a campaign team in Quebec and to raise some money. Mulroney quickly agreed. By this time he had already talked his Laval buddy Michel Cogger, heretofore a passive Liberal, into working as

Fulton's executive assistant. Now he would himself be one of the main players in the Fulton campaign.

Of all the candidates, Fulton claimed the bulk of the fast-rising young Tory up-and-comers — including Lowell Murray, Hal Jackman, Alan Eagleson, and not least Joe Clark. Ottawa had not seen much of Clark since the summer following the 1962 election. He had kept at his graduate program in political science at the University of Alberta but continued to let politics get in the way of his education. When a Calgary lawyer turned businessman named Peter Lougheed ran for the leadership of the dormant Conservative Party in Alberta, Clark joined his team as an organizer and became part of his brain trust.

Clark toiled diligently on Lougheed's behalf, arranging meetings across the province and getting out crowds, and capped the experience by running as one of his candidates in the May 1967 Alberta election. Clark had wanted to run in his home town of High River, but Lougheed believed the party stood a good chance of victory there and decided to increase the odds with a name candidate. So Clark dutifully parachuted himself into Calgary South, where his prospects were near hopeless since the riding rested firmly in the grip of the Speaker of the legislature. But Clark never allowed the odds to daunt him and poured everything into the campaign, canvassing non-stop from door to door — until he injured his knee three days before the election. In the end he made a race of it, losing by only 462 votes. From that narrow defeat in Calgary he went straight to Ottawa as a salaried worker on the Fulton campaign.

Like Mulroney, Clark regarded Fulton as embodying the future of the party, as a leader who would broaden the Conservatives' electoral base, particularly inside Quebec. But in philosophy Clark had far more in common with Fulton than did Mulroney, since Clark was the planner type, full of concepts for Canada in the coming decades, and Fulton was the idealistic, intellectual leader. In contrast, Mulroney was a logistics man who concentrated on the how rather than the what. Clark and Fulton were made for each other.

As first vice-president of the Alberta PC Association, Clark quickly proved his value to the campaign by delivering fifty Alberta delegates to Fulton, including MPs Bill Skoreyko and Marcel Lambert and Edmonton mayor Vince Dantzer. This gave Fulton the majority of Alberta votes. But Clark's major contribution was as an idea man who spent most of his time writing speeches and developing policy while Mulroney was raising funds and twisting the arms of Quebec delegates.

As in the past the two seldom intruded on each other's turf. In the five years since they had competed for the job as Alvin Hamilton's assistant, each had continued to build networks that often overlapped, but each gave little hint that he saw the other as a serious future rival. Mulroney continued to look down at Clark as a strait-laced klutz who spent all his time debating boring issues. In return Clark saw Mulroney as a bit of a dilettante who showed up for all the social events but overlooked the important policy committees. Clark still worked twice as hard as anyone else and displayed an almost childlike faith that discipline and effort would triumph in the end. Mulroney continued to project the image that everything came easily to him. However, on the Fulton campaign they were united in their total devotion and loyalty to their candidate.

In supporting Fulton, Clark was following the protocol of political loyalty, which dictated that ex-aides always rallied behind their old bosses, whereas Mulroney was doing no such thing. Technically Mulroney should have joined Alvin Hamilton, the former minister of agriculture who had treated him so well in the summer of 1962, but Hamilton had taken too long in jumping into the race, declaring long after Mulroney had committed himself to Fulton. It would not have mattered anyway. Hamilton had hardly a prayer of winning, and Mulroney wanted a winner.

Mulroney's loyalty to Fulton was sorely tested only seven weeks before the convention when Robert Stanfield, after much arm-twisting, changed his mind and decided to take up ski-jumping after all. Dalton Camp agreed to act as campaign manager. The Stanfield entry devastated Fulton's campaign. Most of the Tory caucus declared their support for Stanfield and Tories across the country instantly flocked to his banner, pushing him instantly to the front of the pack and Fulton into second place. Gerry Doucet, Mulroney's friend from St. FX and now a Stanfield cabinet minister in Nova Scotia, urged Mulroney to switch horses. His appeal was powerful. Stanfield's election in 1956 had been Mulroney's first real election campaign, and in 1960 he had operated as Stanfield's *sub rosa* intelligence agent and advance man. But Mulroney resisted even though Stanfield looked like a winner. "We stand for the same things," he told Doucet, "and we'll be together in the end no matter how it goes, Gerry." He did promise, however, to jump to Stanfield if Fulton fell off the ballot.

After being bushwhacked by Stanfield's late entry, Fulton was rudely jolted again when Duff Roblin unexpectedly joined the race at the eleventh hour. Now Fulton had to fight to hang onto second spot. Roblin came from the West, spoke French, and had strength in Quebec, which made him a formidable adversary. But he did not impress Mulroney, who dismissed him as a wimp. "Roblin sits down to pee," he sneered.

As the weekend of the convention approached, only one potential candidate remained inscrutable — John Diefenbaker. Events had passed him by, but would he finally accept the inevitable? The answer came after the delegates had arrived in Toronto. Just ten minutes before the filing deadline, Diefenbaker declared his candidacy. He had no organization and no strategy and was sure to be humiliated.

To the surprise of nobody, Stanfield jumped out in front on the first ballot with 519 votes. Next came Duff Roblin with 349, and in third place, a scarce six votes behind Roblin, was Fulton. It was a major let-down for the man who had led the contest most of the way. With Roblin and Fulton in almost a dead heat, the real race was for second. Both sides scrambled to see who could emerge as the solid number two — the prize being the opportunity to challenge Stanfield down the line. Diefenbaker got just 271 votes on the first ballot, fifth in a field of eleven, and would slip to 172 votes on the second. It was a pathetic final defeat for a once-great politician.

Donald Fleming, the runner-up to Diefenbaker in 1956, finished a devastating eighth with a paltry 126 votes. In search of loose votes, Mulroney, Lowell Murray, and Michel Cogger rushed over to the Fleming section hoping to swing a deal — anything to propel their man past Roblin. But Fleming would not listen. Elsewhere they fared little better, although Mulroney managed to lock up some Quebec delegates for subsequent ballots. All the scurrying around by the Fulton forces netted him exactly three more votes on the second ballot, while Roblin jumped by 81 and Stanfield by 106, effectively knocking Fulton out of it. The race was now between Stanfield and Roblin, and the Fulton workers suddenly found themselves being chased by agents for the two leaders.

When the third ballot dropped Fulton still further back, even an eternal optimist like Mulroney no longer could deny defeat. Fulton himself retreated to the directors' lounge to contemplate his options. Here Mulroney bumped into Dalton Camp. "Is there any danger that Fulton might not come our way?" Camp asked. "Don't give it a thought," Mulroney assured him. He told Camp to stand by for a decision after the next ballot.

Hoping against hope, Fulton futilely hung in for the fourth ballot — losing enough votes to fall to less than half Roblin's total. Now he could stay in the race for only one more ballot even if he wanted to. After the vote, Roy McMurtry came by and plopped a Stanfield hat onto Mulroney's head, but Mulroney yanked it off. He was not switching until Fulton officially made his move.

Fulton retreated to the Toronto Maple Leafs' dressing room and polled his key advisers over what he should do. "I want to hear what you people have to say first," he said. Mulroney, Murray, and Cogger urged him to quit and support Stanfield while he still could be the kingmaker. Most of the others, including Alan Eagleson, remained neutral. Fulton thought about it briefly, called in his wife, and told his supporters to vote as they wished — he was going over to Stanfield. The decision locked up the convention for the Nova Scotia premier. Without wasting a moment, Mulroney went straight to the floor to scare up votes for Stanfield.

The next morning Richard Holden, a Montreal lawyer, spotted his friend Mulroney walking down the street with Stanfield and Dalton Camp. "You look at that," Holden whistled to his wife. "Mulroney is already one of the senior consultants to Stanfield." In twenty-four hours Mulroney, the Fulton man, had joined the Stanfield team and become an insider. He would just as quickly emerge as the new Tory leader's man in Quebec. The ease with which Mulroney moved into the Stanfield camp made sense on closer inspection. He had supported Stanfield as far back as 1956 and knew all his close aides. Some would later argue that Mulroney was more helpful to Stanfield as a Fulton supporter. For when the time came, Mulroney helped convince Fulton to publicly announce he was going to Stanfield.

One of Mulroney's first acts as Stanfield's Quebec broker was to bring the new leader together with his old friend Premier Daniel Johnson. In a lunch arranged by Mulroney, the two politicians struck an informal alliance in the tradition of the Diefenbaker-Duplessis pact of a decade earlier. Mulroney soon expanded his middleman role to include relations between the Conservative Party and the Union Nationale from top to bottom. Tory prospects in Quebec had seldom seemed better.

With Stanfield as leader, the Conservatives nipped ahead of the Liberals in public opinion for the first time in years. For once the party actually looked forward to the next election, but the honeymoon would not last. A few months later Prime Minister Lester Pearson announced his retirement; a political neophyte named Pierre Trudeau swept out of nowhere and, with all the momentum in the world, called a quick election.

As the 1968 election campaign got under way, Stanfield phoned Angus Ogilvy in Montreal and asked if Howard Cate Ogilvy would give Mulroney six weeks' paid leave to help with the campaign.

Ogilvy quickly agreed. As assistant to the chairman of the Conservative Party's Quebec election campaign committee, Mulroney did a little of everything. He recruited candidates, worked on Stanfield's tours in Quebec, raised money, and called on the Union Nationale for help. He was always in the thick of the action.

Quebec Tories — Mulroney particularly — at first believed their party was finally making serious inroads, especially when financier Marcel Faribault resigned as president of Trust Général in Montreal to become a Tory candidate. (Mulroney, of course, had negotiated his entry.) In fact the Conservative Party fielded many fine candidates, but they might as well have stayed at home.

Trudeaumania caught fire in the spring of 1968, and nothing could stop it. The suave iconoclast, doing back-flips on the trampoline and nifty dives into the swimming pool, had captured the irreverent spirit of the sixties. By comparison the ponderous Stanfield looked like a mortician, thinking slowly, speaking slowly, and moving slowly. For the first time in Canadian history an election had turned into a beauty contest. Mulroney discovered that he could extol Stanfield's virtues until he was hoarse, yet nothing would sink in.

"We're going to get three or four seats," one of Mulroney's buddies predicted on election night.

"Oh," replied Mulroney, "I hope not. I just spoke to Mr. Stanfield — I told him he was going to get a minimum of sixteen seats in Quebec."

"Brian, what the hell did you tell him that for? You know it's not true."

"I didn't want him to feel too bad."

That evening the Trudeau steamroller flattened Tories across the country. The party in Quebec suffered its worst beating in two decades, emerging with a paltry four seats, exactly half the number the thoroughly discredited Diefenbaker had picked up last time.

CHAPTER TEN

DEALMAKER

IN OCTOBER 1967, a month after Robert Stanfield had won the leadership of the Conservative Party, the Picard commission delivered its report. But instead of fixing the problems of the Montreal waterfront, it offered only Band-Aids that left both sides complaining. After coming away almost empty-handed, Mulroney's clients, the shipowners, started looking elsewhere for long-range solutions. Mulroney now found himself professionally preoccupied with waterfront reform.

Nothing had really changed on the docks: the International Longshoremen's Association continued to block improvements while the temporary alliance between the shipowners and the stevedoring contractors remained fragile and impotent. However, the more progressive shipowners began realizing that the fundamental problems would never be solved until the bosses merged into one cohesive team. The idea for amalgamating the shipowners and the stevedoring contractors into one administrative unit originated with Alex Pathy, the chairman of the Shipping Federation of Canada's labour committee, but Mulroney liked the idea and began touting it as the best solution available.

Amalgamation looked great on paper, but the two management groups continued to distrust each other. Mulroney, as the shipowners' lawyer, started the conciliation process by exhorting both parties to set aside their petty differences for their greater common good. After selling the principle of amalgamation to management, he had to sell it to the ILA, which disliked it from the start. Naturally the powerful longshoremen's union opposed any arrangement that promised management more bargaining leverage.

When Mulroney put amalgamation onto the bargaining table during the 1968 contract talks, the ILA came out swinging. Leading the attack once again was Phil Cutler, the ILA's hard-boiled negotiator, and once again Cutler confronted issues directly whereas Mulroney came in on the flanks, always trying to avoid head-on collisions. Whatever else Mulroney did, he kept the lines of communication open. No matter how far apart the two sides might be, as long as they continued to talk he had a chance for spotting an opening and making something out of it. Sooner or later something had to break. It became his first principle of negotiating.

Although Cutler again proved a formidable adversary, there was one crucial department where Mulroney simply could run circles around his opponent. He could go over Cutler's head any time he wanted, seemingly with impunity. His network by now included most of the top labour leaders in the province, and he could pick up the phone and talk to them directly. It gave Mulroney an edge, but he took care never to flaunt it.

The contract talks stretched on for weeks, then months, ultimately involving Fédération des Travailleurs du Québec president Louis Laberge and federal labour minister Bryce Mackasey. With arbitration help from Judge Alan Gold, of the Provincial Court of Quebec, the two sides finally hammered out a three-year deal that achieved management's primary goals — the much-sought-after amalgamation and elimination of the ILA-controlled hiring hall. The newly created Maritime Employers' Association (MEA) would be the sole bargaining agent for management. But the pact came at a hefty price. The shipowners agreed to give Quebec longshoremen the best waterfront working conditions in the world and a ground-breaking grievance procedure, as well as a generous wage hike and longer vacations.

They also had to buy off redundant workers with a generous compensation package and set up a job security fund guaranteeing the remaining three thousand longshoremen forty hours' pay a week whether they worked or not.

Paying off displaced workers would cost millions and had to be done up front. A fledgling organization like the MEA simply did not have that kind of cash. Private banks were willing to make loans but wanted some kind of government backing. Cutting through all the red tape became Mulroney's next big task and put him in even closer touch with Bryce Mackasey in Ottawa. Happy Irishmen both, the two passed many hours together during the negotiations and became fast friends. For years to come Mulroney never forgot Mackasey's birthday, and if perchance the cartoonist Aislin featured Mackasey in the newspaper Mulroney would get him the original drawing as a gift.

The search for agreement took the players — Mackasey, Gold, Cutler, and Mulroney — around the clock on more than one occasion. Sometimes Gold would disappear strategically while the parties stayed up all night, to let them dicker alone. Mulroney did not mind all-nighters. In fact he liked them. He got stronger by the hour and could outlast everybody else. He also discovered that solutions came more easily in the wee hours. Non-stop bargaining exhausted people and sapped their resistance. Gold had introduced Mulroney to the power of negotiation by exhaustion; Mulroney took the lesson to heart and incorporated it into his arsenal.

Mulroney emerged from the process with his status as a hot young labour lawyer enhanced and his network expanded to include some of the major players in Quebec organized labour. He had picked the right field to begin his legal career. Quebec in the late 1960s and 1970s boiled with labour strife, and labour law became the fastest-growing segment of the legal profession. Companies that formerly had conducted their labour negotiations in-house started calling lawyers. And as a new specialty, labour law was almost without senior practitioners, which further boosted Mulroney's already rapid rise.

By the end of the 1960s the fledgling labour group at Howard Cate

Ogilvy had doubled in size to six lawyers and moved into separate offices on the ninth floor of Place Ville-Marie, away from the rest of the firm. This gave Mulroney even greater freedom to come and go. The practice of labour law followed no timetable and set no hours. It meant running from one crisis to the next, fighting many fires with few firemen. As a bachelor, Mulroney could leave town on a moment's notice and stay away however long it took.

For somebody who had essentially lost his first year of legal practice by failing the Quebec bar exams, he was now more than making up for lost time. He took full advantage of the opportunities that came his way. He seemed to know how to pick the right case, and he always handled himself superbly, inevitably outperforming his peers. His amazing personal charm, his understanding of people, and his intuitive feel for hatching deals fit his line of work beautifully.

By now he had left the personal and professional troubles of his first few years at Howard Cate Ogilvy far behind. He had long since moved out of the apartment where his mother still lived and into his own place in an old building at 331 Clarke Avenue, across the street from the St. Lyons de Westmount Church on de Maisonneuve Boulevard. It was a lovely place, tastefully decorated, with a den. He had gotten the lease and all the furnishings — even the cutlery and the bedsheets — for next to nothing from a woman leaving town in a hurry. Once again life was good.

Nick's Restaurant, also in Lower Westmount, became a weekly gathering spot for his closest circle of friends. On Sunday morning Mulroney would pick up the *New York Times*, the *Toronto Star*, and an assortment of other fat newspapers from Oxford Stationery, his favourite news shop, and adjourn across the street to Nick's, where he would sooner or later be joined by Michel Cogger, Lowell Murray, and Bernard Roy. Cogger, who lived up the hill, was now practising law in Montreal with the firm of Geoffrion Prud'homme. Murray, who also lived conveniently close, now worked for CNR in Montreal. Roy not only lived close by, he had recently joined Mulroney's firm. When the boys showed up, Mulroney folded his papers and started to banter and gossip. They compared notes on everything, but mostly they talked politics. They also swapped tales about the media and how it covered politicians and political issues. Mulroney, more than the others, talked about the American political scene, which fascinated him no end. He amazed his friends with how much he knew about the minutiae of events south of the border.

Mulroney's real home base was not his apartment or Nick's, but a bar called the Carrefour. On Fridays, around 5 or 6 P.M., he took the elevator down to Place Ville-Marie's underground shopping level and headed straight into "the Swamp," as it was popularly known. With its big circular bar the place had the kind of atmosphere that could sandbag people who had stopped in for a quick one after work and hold them late into the night. Hundreds of desirable young singles of both sexes showed up, and half of them would table-hop.

For $2.95 he would order a bathtub Martini nicknamed the Conrad Hilton Special — four and a half ounces of gin and Cinzano. One of these monsters could make just about anybody walk funny. Mulroney loved Martinis and before the evening was over would order several. Invariably he would spot the prettiest girl in the whole place, lock onto her, and, with his deep, honey-coated voice, begin coming on. His Irish charm worked well on women. He hit a lot of home runs but also struck out from time to time. This was one form of rejection that did not seem to bother him.

Sometimes Mulroney would start a pub crawl and thoroughly impress everybody with how deeply he had infiltrated the night-life of Montreal, which he had come to love. No matter which bar he entered, he knew the bartenders, the bouncer, the owner, and, it seemed, half the patrons inside. The same went for restaurants and nightclubs. Wherever he turned people would flag him down and say hello. He felt at home in every milieu, as if he'd been brought up an urbane bilingual Montrealer rather than an Irish Canadian from the outback.

Mulroney had long since stopped trekking back to Quebec City on weekends to see JoAnn Ross, but friends sensed that his feelings for her still ran deep, that he still considered her his woman. That changed abruptly when JoAnn called one day from Quebec City to inform him that she was marrying a psychiatrist, "a doctor," as she put it. Although the news caught Mulroney by surprise and hurt him — for a while at least — it did not flatten him the way his break-up with Rosann had at Dalhousie. This time he hardly stewed at all. Life was too much fun. Loads of beautiful young women filled the Carrefour every night of the week and he could virtually take his pick.

On one occasion, after eyeing an available beauty, he moved in for the kill. She explained she could not go out to dinner with him because she was catching the overnight train to Toronto. Without tipping his hand, Mulroney phoned the CN ticket office and booked himself a spot on the same train, then returned to announce he would accompany her. He had a hearing the next morning, so he planned on going only to Cornwall. But he got carried away and stayed the whole trip, catching an early-morning flight back to Montreal in time for his appearance.

On Friday nights in the winter he and Bernard Roy sometimes drove north into the Laurentians and spent the weekend in a rented house or cottage. They usually met first at the Carrefour for some lubrication before setting off, but somehow they always successfully navigated the hour-and-a-quarter drive without calamity. They billed these outings as ski weekends, although at first neither Mulroney nor Roy skied. Mulroney took up skiing for a while. He had strong legs and was absolutely fearless on the slopes but lacked any semblance of style. He would charge straight down the hill without a zig or a zag, not even a wiggle. And once down he was in no hurry to get back up. People could usually find him in the chalet, surrounded by a crowd.

The rented ski house was never anything fancy. Newspapers would pile up on the floor, which endlessly annoyed Roy, who was always picking them up like a housemaid. Regardless of where Mulroney was, he needed constant fixes of the latest news. He would devour five newspapers a day, and half his time out of town was spent looking for them. He was addicted to radio and television news as well. At times he would sleep with a radio playing under his pillow; he had conditioned himself to wake up at the sound of the CJAD news chime at the top of the hour. After a five-minute shot of news, he would drift off for another fifty-five minutes of sleep.

When Mulroney and Roy were in the Laurentians, friends from Montreal would often barge in and throw together a party. The core group was always the same gang — Mulroney, Roy, Cogger, and Jean Bazin — all single and all out for fun. Sometimes they invited women and got home-cooked meals. Otherwise they hit the local restaurants, which were very good. In the summer they sometimes rented a cottage on Nantucket off Cape Cod.

Mulroney was a Yuppie long before the term was coined. He drove a mammoth convertible — picked up at a bargain price from a friend — and dressed conservatively and impeccably, always wearing the best suit he could afford. (It was during these years that he started the habit of changing shirts several times a day, like his idol John F. Kennedy. In the middle of a negotiation he would break for twenty minutes and take a shower and change his shirt.) He started buying Canadian paintings, and eventually he would acquire quite a collection. Like many boys from poor backgrounds, Mulroney was impressed by money and what it could buy almost as much by as power — some argued more.

Montreal offered a rich cultural life, but Mulroney never spent ten willing seconds listening to an orchestra or watching ballet or a live play, unless for social or political reasons. He read the books on the bestseller list, but high culture bored him. Besides, he had better things to do, carrying on most of the night and staggering into bed at 4:00 or 5:00 in the morning, rising early for work the next day. His social life never stopped. After work, he would drop down to the Carrefour for a drink, bump into a friend, and go out to dinner. Or meet a woman. It was a simple period in Mulroney's life: he lived the role of the carefree bachelor to the hilt and had a wonderful time.

But sceptics saw more to all this pleasure-seeking than the exuberance of youth and a naturally fun-loving nature. They noted that while having a rollicking good time, Mulroney was methodically expanding his professional network. For these cynics his easy bonhomie and irrefutable charm masked unmistakable ambition. Still, they couldn't deny that he was enjoying himself and that he genuinely put his heart into each friendship. Cold networking it was not.

Mulroney brought many social talents to his networking, but one in particular made him stand out. It was his amazing knack for injecting himself into the centre of any gathering. Whether the occasion was formal or informal, business or social, involved friends or strangers, he always made sure he made a good entrance. As soon as he walked in the door he was greeting people by name, shaking hands, patting backs and talking. He was full of jokes and stories and would throw off punch lines as he made his progress. He managed to project the aura of a celebrity. Heads would turn as soon as he arrived. Soon a group would form around him as he spun yarn after yarn. Since the loudest laughs always came from his group, others would drift over and form a circle around him. Before long he had taken over the party.

If someone was already occupying the spotlight, that was where Mulroney would head. The first time Earle McLaughlin, the president of the Royal Bank, showed up at one of the firm's receptions, Mulroney headed straight for him while all the other junior lawyers deferentially kept their distance. In five minutes he was eyeball to eyeball with McLaughlin, and in fifteen minutes it was "Brian" and "Earle."

People could not really explain exactly how Mulroney insinuated himself into the confidence of big hitters. Charm played a huge role, and so did the quick wit, the engaging repartee, the subtle flattery, and the sense of fun. But it went beyond all these. He had a way of engineering a special rapport, of making other people comfortable with him, of making them feel he was on their side. It flowed out of his own gift for feeling at home anywhere, but nobody could quite put a finger on it. Whatever it was, it seemed like magic.

Mulroney had arrived in Montreal in 1964 with one good suit and not a penny to his name but knowing every political heavyweight in the province. Not even the senior partners at Howard Cate Ogilvy could match his political reach, but the same did not hold true in the world of commerce. He had started out with few business connections, but had taken care of that quickly enough. By the beginning of the 1970s, Mulroney had attached himself to an array of rich and famous people.

One of his early conquests was Angus Ogilvy, who had become his law firm's most senior partner in 1968 (the firm was thereafter known as Ogilvy Cope — short for Ogilvy, Cope, Porteous, Hansard, Marler, Montgomery & Renault). Ogilvy had a tendency to be crusty but absolutely doted on Mulroney and pulled him into his office for long chats on politics while the other young lawyers wondered enviously what in the world was going on. Angus Ogilvy treated Mulroney like a favourite son. In fact many of the senior partners gave him special treatment. A rising lawyer was privileged if one senior partner took a shine to him. Mulroney had a string of father figures.

He had the cultivation of mentors down to a science. "He was an attractive protégé," an Ogilvy Cope partner later explained. "Older men enjoyed instructing and helping him. It's an invaluable quality, and he had it." Without being sycophantic, he could signal his request for help, demonstrate a willingness to learn, and show total allegiance. And since he was also fun to have around, Mulroney frequently got invited to the homes and cottages of the senior partners. No other junior lawyer dared call a senior partner by his first name, not at a starchy firm like Ogilvy Cope, which had some real dinosaurs among its upper crust. Mulroney was on a first-name basis with almost everyone.

In Ogilvy Cope's stable of dinosaurs, none was more feared than Jack Porteous. An old-fashioned Tory, yet a bit of a maverick, Porteous was grouchy, mean, exacting, and unforgiving. He loathed junior lawyers and enjoyed humiliating them in front of their peers. After Porteous was dead, one partner would call him the most hated member of the firm, then quickly add that this was an understatement. Even Mulroney, who could sweet-talk a fire-breathing dragon, had to think twice before taking him on.

According to the firm's folklore, Mulroney had early on run afoul of the irascible old crank. One version of the story concerned a tiny washroom next to Porteous's office, which also happened to be adjacent to the library where the students worked. Porteous claimed this as his personal facility, so students ordinarily took the long trip to a more distant washroom. Porteous caught Mulroney coming out of "his" washroom and fired him on the spot. The incident forced the firm to manoeuvre a delicate retreat that allowed Mulroney to keep his job. If he could somehow turn around Porteous, then nobody anywhere would be safe from his charm.

Despite their differences in temperament the young lawyer and the senior partner had one thing in common, an insatiable curiosity about the backroom intrigues of Quebec City. Provincial politics fascinated Porteous, especially the machinations inside the Union Nationale. Porteous soon discovered that Mulroney knew everything, often before it happened, and was simply staggered by Mulroney's easy camaraderie with Premier Daniel Johnson and virtually everybody in his cabinet. Playing his cards perfectly, Mulroney fed Porteous morsels of the latest political scuttlebutt about the Union Nationale. Amazed and fascinated, Porteous invited Mulroney into his office for many little chats. Before long, to the astonishment of everybody, he took Mulroney out for a drink, then invited him to his home. In no time at all they were political cronies, and Mulroney was calling him "Jack." He had pulled off a truly astounding turnaround.

As a prestigious Montreal securities lawyer with a streak of professional brilliance, Porteous acted for some of the firm's big clients, like the Royal Bank. By the time Mulroney was emerging as a top labour lawyer, one of the biggest was Paul Desmarais, a French Canadian from Sudbury who had parlayed a small bus line into an industrial empire (he took control of Power Corporation in 1968). Porteous had helped clear Desmarais's legal path to the top and continued to act as his legal adviser. When Voyageur bus lines, one of Desmarais's companies, needed help on a labour issue, Porteous dispatched Mulroney to see what could be done.

Desmarais owned many companies, including a string of daily and weekly newspapers, the jewel of which was Montreal's *La Presse*, the largest French-language daily in North America and an institution carrying deep social and political weight in Quebec. For years *La Presse* had operated as a money-making machine, but recently labour troubles had darkened its fortunes. It seemed that labour and management could not agree on anything, from reporters' salaries to the paper's editorial stance. During contract negotiations the two sides quarrelled and moved further apart until finally, in the fall of 1971, after months of guerrilla warfare from some of the unions, the newspaper locked out everyone and suspended publication. With more than a thousand workers on the picket line, and feelings running high, the city of Montreal slapped an immediate thirty-day ban on all street demonstrations around the newspaper office in the hope of averting violence. Two days later, on October 29, 1971, it came anyway. A crowd of more than ten thousand demonstrators stormed police barricades, injuring nearly two hundred people, almost half of them police officers.

Meanwhile, the contract negotiations had reached a complete standstill, with neither side showing an inclination to compromise. The showdown dragged on for weeks and started to pinch both sides, especially the newspaper. Desmarais was swallowing millions of dollars in losses and watching his dominant share of the advertising and circulation market disintegrate. Normally a hands-off manager, he decided to intervene by inviting Mulroney to the table.

Desmarais had good reason for going to the thirty-two-year-old lawyer. After performing well in the Voyageur bus lines dispute, he had done equally well at Canada Steamship Lines, another Power Corporation subsidiary. But aside from being a top-flight negotiator, he could come into the talks without baggage. And as an insatiable busybody, he had been hovering on the edges of the talks, so he was practically up to speed on the issues. But what really sold Desmarais was Mulroney's high-level connections in the Quebec labour movement. Desmarais felt he needed some pull with the upper ranks of organized labour, and Mulroney could reach higher into labour's upper echelons than anybody else he could get. Mulroney had, as one Desmarais executive later put it, a "high-quality relationship" with Louis Laberge, the head of the Fédération des Travailleurs du Québec (in English, the Quebec Federation of Labour).

Indeed, Mulroney and Laberge got along famously. Since the marathon waterfront negotiations of 1968 they had locked horns several times and now understood each other perfectly. Mulroney knew that beneath Laberge's bluster was a pragmatic dealmaker — just like himself. Neither allowed ideology or principle to get in the way of a transaction. On one occasion when they became absolutely deadlocked over a waterfront issue they phoned Minister of Labour Bryce Mackasey in Ottawa and asked him to play the role of Solomon. Mackasey thought over the issue, rendered his decision, and that was that. Without missing a beat Mulroney and Laberge moved on to the next item of business. The *La Presse* talks needed that kind of high-level lubrication. Six of the eleven unions at *La Presse* belonged to Laberge's umbrella group. The other five fell under the jurisdiction of the Confederation of National Trade Unions, headed by Marcel Pepin, who was more dogmatic and combative. But Mulroney knew him too. Desmarais, a highly astute judge of character, concluded that Mulroney possessed the personal qualities and contacts needed to kick-start the stalled talks.

To Desmarais's surprise, Mulroney turned him down. Given the labour climate at *La Presse*, Mulroney could not envisage any settlement being reached without a complete change in atmosphere. If he was going to get involved, Mulroney told Desmarais, the talks had to start afresh with him at the helm. This was too much for Desmarais. But several weeks later, as losses kept mounting and as

Desmarais's problems multiplied, the financier changed his mind and offered Mulroney the scope he demanded.

That meant removing André Bureau, *La Presse*'s chief negotiator. As executive vice-president of *La Presse*, Bureau symbolized the legacy of animosity and distrust that Mulroney wanted to dispel. But Desmarais took it one step further, firing Bureau outright — not only as chief negotiator, but as a company executive. However, he left it to Mulroney to break the bad news. Mulroney hated swinging the axe. He found that kind of thing extremely tough and distasteful. His modus operandi was to make friends, not enemies. But he had to do it, and did.

As the new chief negotiator for Desmarais in the *La Presse* talks, Mulroney moved swiftly and decisively, bringing Louis Laberge and Marcel Pepin directly into the negotiations and relocating the whole works into a confined set of suites in the Queen Elizabeth Hotel. It was a repeat of the negotiation-by-exhaustion tactic that he had learned from Alan Gold on the waterfront, only this time he added an extra twist — everybody became a hostage. Mulroney later told biographer L. Ian MacDonald that "nobody went home" until they produced a deal. MacDonald wrote: "With the amount of wine and cognac that was consumed — 'none of us was a slouch' as Mulroney could later confess — the room service bill substantially contributed to the hotel's revenues for the entire year." A week later, in early February 1972, Mulroney called Desmarais with news of a deal.

Mulroney had put *La Presse* back on the street — but at a considerable price. The company agreed to generous pay hikes, longer holidays, and employment guarantees against technological changes. All in all the unions had come out of it very well. Louis Laberge called it "a complete victory." In his biography of Paul Desmarais, *Rising to Power: Paul Desmarais and Power Corporation*, Dave Greber concluded that "Desmarais had been humbled." Greber quoted *La Presse* journalist Jean Pelletier as saying: "He gave the strikers everything they wanted." Furthermore Mulroney had not even come close to achieving the workforce restructuring that management so dearly wanted. On this matter the company backed down completely. But in fairness to Mulroney, the kind of reform the company wanted was not doable in the climate of the day.

Although Mulroney had not exactly worked magic, the *La Presse* deal still stood out as quite a feat. In the space of a week he had overcome months of accumulated acrimony and distrust, squeezing an intricate set of agreements out of eleven different unions. And expensive as it was, the settlement cost less than a continued strike. Defenders of the deal pointed to the company's books. Almost as soon as the presses started rolling again *La Presse* started making money, which made the settlement good for the company.

Whichever way one tallied the final score, Mulroney was seen to have performed a miracle. It mattered little how he got the unions back to work; he had succeeded when no one else could. He already had a hot reputation before *La Presse*, but nothing like what he enjoyed now. The *La Presse* settlement did more for his name than any dispute he would ever handle. It gave him the image of the super-negotiator who could march into a deadlock and pull out a deal. He would engineer better and more dramatic agreements than this one, but none that gave him as much renown. It also secured the patronage of Paul Desmarais. At thirty-two, Mulroney became Desmarais's special envoy, his chosen instrument for conflict resolution, and his supreme labour adviser.

The *La Presse* settlement also brought Desmarais into Mulroney's current stable of patrons. All his life Mulroney had enlisted mentors, beginning with Colonel McCormick in Baie Comeau. Anybody who saw Mulroney and Desmarais together in the early seventies could not help but notice that the chairman of Power Corporation had joined the long list. Their mutual fondness in some ways resembled Mulroney's old relationship with Diefenbaker.

Paul Desmarais's empire now accounted for much of Mulroney's workload. Through Power Corporation, he owned four daily newspapers, five weeklies, a string of radio and television stations; he had full or partial ownership of another thirty or so companies and kept adding to the total. With Quebec in the midst of a decade of labour turmoil, the dispute docket at Power Corporation was seldom empty. And Mulroney's image as a rainmaker put him in demand throughout the Quebec corporate community, affording him the luxury of picking and choosing his cases.

When handed a labour crisis, Mulroney always began by assembling the facts and identifying the underlying problems. First he talked to corporate management and got their reading. Then, in violation of normal procedures, he called up contacts within the union and got their informal assessment. Scouting the opposition was not a technique taught in law school, but it corresponded with Mulroney's notion of what a negotiator should do. He viewed a labour dispute in the same way he viewed life in general — a web of human relationships in which people could help themselves by helping one another. It was the same approach he brought to politics. He believed a good negotiator or politician worked out from the centre of the web, helping all parties resolve their differences.

Having pulled together the basic facts, and having gotten a feel for the people involved, he laid out a general strategy, which was solid, logical, and above all practical — and always reduced to a tactical level. Sometimes this meant giving employers advice they did not want to hear. By the time he met face to face with the union he had laid out his options with each possible scenario plotted out: if the union did this, then he would respond that way, and so on. He always knew where he wanted to end up, although the path to his goal was flexible. Success, he told his clients, came from hard work and superior preparation. However, his preparation did not extend to the legal technicalities involved. It was one of his few deficiencies as a negotiator; another was his lack of technical familiarity with the law. Legal research bored him now every bit as much as it had in law school. Somebody else could check the statutes and chase down legal precedents.

The negotiating room was where he shone brightest. He excelled at maintaining dialogue in the most trying conditions. Successful bargainers know how to manoeuvre and Mulroney had mastered the art. If he started butting against a solid wall, he quietly stepped back and contrived a way around the obstacle. The ultimate objective of swinging a deal always took precedence.

Normally Mulroney could not control his hyperbole or his quick Irish temper, and often he paid the price. He could work up a terrible head of steam when provoked, but the bargaining room was different. Here he remained cool and unruffled even in desperate situations, and he was forever counselling clients to bite their tongues for fear of inciting reprisal. When provoked during a negotiation, he would retaliate not with anger but with humour. "C'mon, let's go have a beer," he would say. "We'll sort it out in the tavern." In no time the tension would be broken and the whole gang would be laughing at his anecdotes. Even hardbitten adversaries found it difficult not to like him. He used alcohol as an accessory but drank sparingly himself while negotiating so it would not dull his mind or undermine his control.

A labour negotiation is like an ocean tide — it ebbs and flows, and astute negotiators take advantage of the constant change. Mulroney had a flair for seizing the moment and knew when to give concessions and when to seek them. He would listen silently for an hour, not saying a word, seemingly preoccupied, and then suddenly — bang, bang, bang — he struck. The others in the room then realized he had been listening all along, biding his time and waiting for the right moment.

Time never seemed to matter: two days, a week, two weeks — however long it took. His patience seemed infinite. But once he shook hands on an agreement his patience simply evaporated: he could hardly bring himself to write up in legal form the deal he had so painstakingly negotiated. The man with the patience of Job offloaded that chore to a junior whenever he could.

Perhaps his single greatest bargaining talent was his ability to go outside the room. If the key ingredients to a settlement lay elsewhere he would return to his office and figure out who he knew and what could be arranged. The answer might lie with a senior bureaucrat who could cut some red tape, or with a cabinet minister who could undo a pesky regulation to save the company money it could then give to the workers. Put pejoratively, Mulroney was a fixer. For him the art of negotiation included the option of going upstairs, sometimes in alliance with his opponent across the table, sometimes behind his opponent's back, as he had done to Phil Cutler. "You've got a very good guy up there," he would tell the union boss. "He's doing a good job." When he started complimenting his opponent like that, it usually meant he was up to something.

Going over his opponent's head was not illegal and, depending on one's point of view, not necessarily unfair. More important, it could be highly effective at getting to the real decision-makers for purposes of flying a trial balloon, disseminating information (or misinformation), planting the seeds of a later proposal, engaging in simple reconnaissance, probing the depth of his opponent's internal support or maybe undermining his position, or trying to discredit a particular strategy. Amazingly, Mulroney never alienated anyone. He always got on well with the person behind whose back he went, partly because of his charm, and partly because he genuinely sought solutions and never used his access to destroy his opponent. The people most miffed at the way he bent the rules were, ironically, his colleagues back in his own law firm. The sheer audacity of moving behind the play of negotiations appalled them a little and impressed them a lot. It skirted the borders of ethical behaviour. But more than anything they envied his finesse and wished they could get away with what he did.

Mulroney's ability to wander at will behind enemy lines without hazard went beyond charm, connections, and good intentions. More than anything it had to do with his amazing lack of boundaries. He had no trouble crossing enemy lines, because for him such lines did not exist; he was everybody's friend. It was the same brand of ingenuous self-confidence that had enabled him to get so close to Diefenbaker, to become Angus Ogilvy's or Jack Porteous's confidant, to move effortlessly from being Fulton's man to being Stanfield's. It had repeatedly led him to success, except at Dalhousie. But that unhappy experience lay long behind him. He now stood on top of the social and business world of Montreal.

By the early 1970s he had acquired a truly impressive stable of contacts, and he could always be found at the centre of the action. Before game time in the 1972 Soviet-Canada hockey series, there he was in the VIP lounge of the Montreal Forum, smack between Paul Desmarais and Sam Pollock, general manager of the Montreal Canadiens. In a way it was an extension of the same impulse that had made him seek out every VIP who came to Baie Comeau. Now he rubbed shoulders with the Bronfmans and the Molsons. Virtually no famous, rich, or powerful figure in Montreal escaped the reach of his charm, including Montreal's legendary mayor, Jean Drapeau.

Almost nobody said "tu" to the ultra-formal Drapeau, not even Lucien Saulnier, his long-time friend and right hand during his most important years at city hall. Brian McKenna, Drapeau's biographer, reports that even Drapeau's wife addressed him with the formal "vous" until they were married. Mulroney quickly worked his way up to a "tu" relationship with the mayor and was invited into his private little betting pools before each election. (Mulroney usually did quite well in those pools whereas Drapeau, the master politician, always lost.) Drapeau found Mulroney enchanting and loved his company.

As Mulroney moved up into the stratosphere of Quebec society, he could have been forgiven for allowing some of his lesser friendships to slip away, but this was not his style. He hung onto old friendships and tended them like a shepherd tending his flock. And keeping up with old friends who soon numbered into the thousands would have been impossible without that favourite instrument of John Diefenbaker, the telephone. It was true that he routinely bumped into his Montreal friends as he moved around the city, but his pre-Montreal networks would have slowly withered away were it not for Bell Canada.

When Mulroney was still in his twenties he had already left Diefenbaker, that past master of networking, far behind when it came to nurturing old ties. Whereas Diefenbaker networked more or less randomly, Mulroney introduced procedure and organization to the process, and practised it in a manner approaching systems science. Old connections were broken down into separate networks, the key ones being Baie Comeau, St. FX, and Laval (with a cluster of new networks emerging in Montreal). When Mulroney picked up the telephone, these different networks took him all over the map — Ottawa, Toronto, Halifax — wherever old buddies happened to be. "How are things?" he would ask off the top, not needing to identify himself. He was mainly calling to say hello. He might have an item to pass on or a favour to ask, but it would wait. He wanted the other guy's stuff first, and he would never interrupt — never, ever. Cutting somebody off was a cardinal sin. Aside from being impolite, it broke the flow of intelligence. Only when his interlocutor was done would he say what was on his mind.

Each network had several hubs and many spokes, wheels within wheels. The spokes were too plentiful to call every week or month; he called them maybe once or twice a year. The hubs formed a select group and were the key to his system. Hubs got called frequently, as often as every week or two, and sometimes more. "How's Father Mifflen?" he would ask Fred Doucet, a member of the St. FX network. Doucet was a hub and Father Mifflen a spoke. Doucet would fill him in on Father Mifflen. "How's old Doc Somers?" Another spoke. "How's the Moose [Father Macdonell, a Canadian history professor at St. FX]?" Down the list of spokes he would go, as many as one or two dozen at a time. Thus one call to a single hub could update him on one of his St. FX wheels. "Make sure that you say hello to them," he would remind Doucet before hanging up. Doucet, now an administrator at St. FX, would pass along Mulroney's greeting to the university community and bring back greetings in return — and messages. "Did you talk to Father Mifflen?" Mulroney would ask on the next call if Doucet failed to raise it. Doucet was a major hub. Other important hubs in the St. FX network were Sam Wakim, who updated him from Toronto, Pat MacAdam, who did it from Ottawa, and Lowell Murray, from wherever he happened to be living. St. FX had less important hubs too, but all acted as a big feeding system.

Whenever one of the spokes changed jobs or got promoted or was mentioned in the newspaper, Mulroney would hear about it before long and make a special phone call of congratulations. Sometimes he would drop a note. When there was a death in the family he would offer condolences and ask if he could help. He frequently performed favours — an unsolicited letter of praise, a message, a little gesture — things that most people never bothered with or never got around to doing.

Sometimes the favours were not so small. When St. FX dismissed its long-time director of public relations — a man with six children, one with Down's syndrome — and ordered him out of his university-owned house, Mulroney indignantly flew down to Antigonish, pronounced himself the fellow's lawyer, and talked the university's administration into a settlement that gave his "client" a pension and allowed him to stay in the house. When Gerry Doucet, Fred's brother and the minister of education in Nova Scotia, needed money badly for a run at the leadership of the Nova Scotia Conservative Party in 1971, Mulroney came to Halifax and, ensconcing himself in the Nova Scotian Hotel for a week, worked the telephone to raise money from his corporate connections across the country. "Gerry," he exclaimed, "it's there. We're getting it. Go do your job. We'll win this. Don't worry about the money." He was helping an old friend, and getting a kick out of it. (Doucet ran second to John Buchanan.)

Friends swore up and down that he performed such deeds without ulterior motive, that his sense of loyalty and the thrill of helping out were his only reasons. They argued that he simply liked doing people a good turn. And he never overtly extracted mileage out of these generous actions. Mulroney could brag when he wanted to, but he never boasted about coming to the aid of a friend.

However, just as Mulroney had dipped into his networks on behalf of Gerry Doucet, he would be able to do the same for himself some day. The yen for high political office had not left him, and ten or twenty phone calls to select hubs would mobilize an army of spokes across the country — if he ever needed one. In the meantime his network fed him everything from political intelligence to the latest gossip. It also functioned as an informal public opinion poll and kept him on top of everything going on behind the scenes in law, in business, and in government.

Running such a system demanded a fat address book and a forty-megabyte memory, and Mulroney had both. Like Diefenbaker, he rarely forgot a name or face, no matter how peripheral the meeting or how lowly the person. Once he met somebody, no matter how inconsequential, and spoke to him however briefly, that person was locked into his memory bank. Often he remembered the names of a person's kids and even the colour of his shirt and the design of his necktie. By fixing certain details in his mind he was able to use these to trigger his memory. Command of second-level information, such as birthdays and details of their families, made him seem closer to his contacts than he really was and helped maintain his network.

Between making calls and receiving them, he lived on the telephone, and the quality of the intelligence he gathered helped make him a very useful person. The other lawyers at Ogilvy Cope — the astute ones at least — plugged into Mulroney's remarkable network of contacts. If they needed some pull in Quebec City, Ottawa, or just about anywhere, they went to Mulroney, and he cheerfully called one of his operatives on their behalf. "I was acting on behalf of a company in Montreal and we needed some kind of response from the Quebec government," a former colleague relates. "So I got hold of Brian. In those days the Union Nationale was in power. And Brian got hold of the minister in charge of that department. We had an appointment the next day. And the next day Brian was talking to him just like I'm talking to you. He said, 'Now listen. I need this and I'm going to get this. And there's no if or buts.' I was sure we were going to be thrown out of the office. So he told me, 'Why don't you go for a walk with the deputy minister while I talk to the minister?' And we did. And we came back and he said, 'The problem has been solved.' About a week after, I was in Ottawa, and he phoned me. He said, 'We have our new codicil.' And I said, 'Brian, what does it say?' It involved taxation, and he read it to me and I said, 'Brian, it says exactly the opposite of what we want.'

'Okay,' he said, 'we'll have it changed.' So about two days later he had the whole situation rectified."

Journalists as well as legal colleagues tapped into this rich vein. Or did Mulroney tap into them? He made a special effort to befriend reporters everywhere, as well as their editors. It was a true love-love relationship — he loved the media and they loved him back. Reporters always found him a motherlode of information, especially of the political kind. Over dinner he would regale them with tales of the goings-on in Ottawa and Quebec City or of the latest longshoremen's dispute and the classic crooks on the docks. And while he amused them with his jokes and stories, they gave him intelligence in return.

Mulroney exploited his network adroitly, but he also thoroughly enjoyed it for its own sake. He loved the camaraderie even without the information. Captivating people regardless of their rank fulfilled his need for approval, even adoration. Every labour agreement achieved, every favour bestowed, and every phone call made notched him one more approval.

More and more he lived the life of a celebrity. When he arrived for lunch at the Beaver Club — a swanky restaurant in the Queen Elizabeth Hotel that became his midday home just as the Carrefour was his after-hours headquarters — a reserved table along with a copper plate engraved with his name and a Martini inside a chilled tumbler awaited him. (Ginette Pilotte, his secretary, would call ahead.) Sometimes he needed fifteen minutes of handshaking and hellos to get from the door to his table. A minute after he sat down the maître d' would bring a telephone — another important call. He could not escape the telephone, nor did he want to. Office colleagues joked that the receiver was permanently welded to his ear. The boy from Baie Comeau had become the ultimate insider in the big city.

CHAPTER ELEVEN

THE WAGNER
RECRUITMENT

THE ONE THING Mulroney hated most about being a lawyer was logging his time charges. For purposes of billing, all the lawyers at Ogilvy Cope had to account for their time on an hourly basis. It was the plague of private law practice and the bane of Mulroney's life. He hated the picky detail of fussing over lists of figures and usually avoided doing it. But he always made sure the client received an invoice for his services, preferring to operate more intuitively. He simply did a rough calculation of what his intervention was worth to the client, and submitted his bill accordingly. Often the value he assigned to his work exceeded the number of hours logged, something the legal fraternity called "premiuming."

Mulroney could afford to "premium" some of his bills. His clients were big corporations and his performance directly affected their bottom lines. His instincts told him how far he could go without appearing greedy or overstepping the line of propriety. It was an art form that he quickly mastered. When it came to billing, he was far ahead of his colleagues in getting the most out of wealthy and sophisticated clients.

He also sometimes discounted his work, or refused to send a bill at all, as he did in 1972 when the graduating class at the University of Montreal law school rose up in protest against the archaic Quebec bar examinations, the very same exams that had once nearly aborted his own law career. Claiming that five Herculean exams in two days constituted wicked and inhuman punishment, about four hundred students voted in favour of challenging the Quebec bar in court, and picked Mulroney as their lawyer. Before the case came to trial Mulroney negotiated a new format — one exam a month for five months — and then refused to submit an invoice. "The firm will do that free for all the young lawyers," he said.

But most of the time Mulroney billed, and did so handsomely. Sometimes he billed more than seventy hours a week, a remarkable figure for a lawyer. Thanks in good part to his efforts, Ogilvy Cope's labour department usually led the firm's annual performance review. It helped that the department was a natural revenue producer. Cases in litigation could drag on for years, which made it difficult for lawyers to charge high fees, while the labour department's cases rarely lasted more than a few months, allowing the firm to count every hour and charge top rates.

As a huge firm with many blue-chip clients, Ogilvy Cope had money to throw around, but it did not lead the way in salaries. In fact the pay was comparatively frugal, almost niggardly. Junior and middle-ranking lawyers earned progressively more as they moved up the line, but huge disparities remained. The senior partners, a handful of men at the top, called the shots and took home most of the revenue.

When Mulroney joined the firm in 1964 he received the princely salary of $4,800 a year, the standard going rate for starting lawyers. By the third year he had advanced a couple of rungs up the ladder to $9,600, along with everybody else from his year. For the first three or four years the firm advanced everyone in lockstep. After that the scale became slightly more flexible — but not much. The senior partners met once a year to decide the non-partners' remuneration, and then Angus Ogilvy called them into his office one by one to render the verdict. "I don't want you to discuss it with anyone else,"

Ogilvy would counsel them. "You know how important it is that these figures remain confidential." If the word got out it would only create rivalries and jealousies.

The vow of silence meant that two lawyers working side by side were not supposed to know each other's earnings. But Mulroney by his very nature always had to know everything, and before long he started exchanging salary data with colleagues. Once he knew exactly where he stood in the pecking order, he came to believe he was being underpaid — badly. It was hard to argue with his claim. In billings Mulroney usually stood in the top 10 per cent, which was quite an achievement for a still relatively junior lawyer in a firm seventy-five strong. His billings for 1971 came to nearly $200,000, a huge sum for the day, and more than double the output of most lawyers with his seniority. He outperformed even some of the heavyweights. In short, the amount of money he brought into the firm bore little relation to the amount he took out on his paycheque.

Although no longer strapped for cash, Mulroney still lived on a fairly short leash, which cramped his style, at least the kind of style he wanted to live. He became determined to get more money. At first he tried stroking Angus Ogilvy into loosening the purse strings. This approach succeeded in getting him a small raise but not nearly what he was worth. So he tried a more aggressive approach. One year he entered into an informal pact with David O'Brien, another impatient young lawyer. Before Angus Ogilvy's annual little salary chat, they promised each other not to nod their heads like sheep. Instead they pledged each other to fight for more money; maybe together they could get some justice. Mulroney faithfully upheld his end of the bargain — O'Brien knew he had because he could hear Mulroney's voice shouting through the walls of Angus Ogilvy's office. Even their gang-up did not work. Nothing ever did. The firm took the old-fashioned view that it was a team and that even star performers like Mulroney had to put in their time.

The irony of the situation did not escape him: he, the ultimate negotiator, could not negotiate for himself the kind of compensation he deserved. Mulroney always felt underappreciated at the firm. At times Ogilvy Cope seemed oblivious to the reality that he could have landed another more lucrative job in a minute, if not with another law firm then with one of his clients, who all saw Mulroney as a wunderkind. On at least two occasions, clients warned the firm to protect Mulroney, or he would be stolen away.

The question of Mulroney's salary went deeper than money. It had to do with his formal status within the rigid hierarchy of a stodgy firm. A rising star like him would reach the top some day, but it would not happen for a good while yet — not the way Ogilvy Cope operated. He would have to advance step by step. For the moment Mulroney was still a salaried lawyer. The next step was to become a partner, which would take about eight years. Getting to the exalted level of senior partner, where the really big money was made, would take at least another decade beyond that — and even then it was no sure thing. Mulroney had all the makings of a senior partner, being a good biller and a star performer, and would probably get there some day — if only he had the patience to wait that long.

Running from crisis to crisis on behalf of clients and living the adventurous life of a fun-loving bachelor took up most of Mulroney's time, but he never let it interfere with his passion for politics, which remained his first love. As he emerged as one of Quebec's top labour lawyers, he continued to enlarge his political constituency and that of the Conservative Party. He lived and breathed politics as much as he ever had as a student — loving the celebrity, the wheeling and dealing, the strategy, and just the playing of the game. Whenever Stanfield or some other ranking Tory passed through town he made a point of showing up. As a result, his office hours were completely scrambled.

It got worse during election campaigns. As soon as an election was called, Mulroney headed straight for the political trenches and went to work, simply disappearing from the office. During these periods his colleagues usually had no idea where he was, although they could always track him down by calling the PC campaign headquarters. He would still talk to clients and give advice, but not from the ninth floor of Place Ville-Marie.

Between elections he sat on the policy committee of the federal PC Party and the finance committee of the Quebec Conservative Party, and always cut a fine figure at party conventions, where he could invariably be seen wearing a delegate's badge and working the rooms or the floor. He stood out particularly at banquets, where he would make one of his patented entrances. From the moment of his arrival all eyes focused on him and followed his progress as he wended his way among the tables, stopping — or being stopped — every few feet to shake a hand and exchange banter. Wherever he turned, someone grabbed his arm and said hello. "That's Brian Mulroney," people would whisper, "a great mover and shaker in Quebec."

The Conservative Party did not have many movers and shakers in Quebec, and among the precious few it did have, Mulroney clearly stood out. Hard as Robert Stanfield tried and as well as he meant, Quebeckers never took to him. He simply could not penetrate the ethos of French Canada. His French was painful to hear — all his normal slowness and circumlocutions in English were multiplied and, having jumped into French lessons at age fifty-three, he butchered the language almost as badly as Diefenbaker. This made Mulroney invaluable to the party in Quebec. Just as he had been a bridge between the French Catholics and the English Protestants in Baie Comeau, he now acted as a bridge to French Quebec for a Conservative Party that was still an Anglo bastion.

He always answered the call to help, doing everything that was needed, whether finding candidates, arranging meetings, giving speeches, or travelling. When travelling for the party he sometimes reached into his own pocket — or the pockets of his business friends — since the Tories in Quebec could not afford to pay expenses. When anybody in the Quebec party needed something, Mulroney, articulate, good-looking, and impressive, was the guy to do it. He could always be counted on to lend a hand. The repeated electoral defeats sapped the Tory spirit in Quebec but Mulroney remained optimistic, always believing the breakthrough was just around the corner. The party's plight in Quebec was no worse than in Nova Scotia when he arrived at St. FX in 1955, and Nova Scotia had turned around. Quebec had gone Tory in 1958 under Diefenbaker, but then the party had let its beachhead slip away. Mulroney believed the province could go Tory again. He was adamant about it. Others worked too during the long wilderness years, particularly Claude Dupras, the party's chief organizer and also an organizer for the Union Nationale, who did more work than anyone. Michael Meighen also put in thankless hours. But Mulroney, with his genius for being noticed, at times seemed like the only Tory in Quebec. Along with Dupras and a few others, he kept the Quebec Conservatives alive.

Mulroney did one other thing, and did it very well: he raised money. He had been a fundraiser in Davie Fulton's leadership campaign in 1967 and seemed natural at it. After Fulton lost, Mulroney organized a successful fundraising dinner to pay off Fulton's huge debts, which had not been easy. Few people were willing to raise funds, but Mulroney excelled at it and enjoyed it. It was also another means of building and consolidating his network.

The 1968 election disaster — returning only four Conservatives against fifty-six Liberals — had left the Quebec Tories with no money, no budget, no office, and precious few members. The Quebec wing of the federal party survived merely as a decaying shell, with only a handful of its seventy-four riding associations continuing to function as anything more than names on a piece of paper. While Mulroney roamed this wilderness, the Liberal lawyers were making an easy fortune from government legal business and garnering prestige appointments to boards, commissions, and task forces. Quebec had less pretence and hypocrisy about patronage; not only were the Tories blackballed, everybody laughed at them as fools. Few could understand why Mulroney continued to stick with the losers, but few understood the depth of his loyalty to his chosen party. Nonetheless it rankled and strengthened his resolve to right the balance some day.

This historical grievance would help explain his attitude towards patronage later on when he found himself in a position to dole it out.

Despite his hatred for Grits, Mulroney admired Pierre Trudeau, and not always grudgingly. Trudeau knew how to communicate, had mastered the media, and had lifted the Liberal Party out of the squabbling minorities of the sixties to a parliamentary majority, the first in a decade. That alone deserved admiration. As much as Mulroney revered Stanfield, always wholeheartedly and without a whisper of complaint, he wished the Conservative leader could do half as well. However, a year after Trudeau's big win in 1968, it appeared that Canada's love affair with the bachelor prime minister had started cooling down, and by 1970 there were signs of frost. Internal Tory polls suggested that the Liberals were vulnerable, even in their stronghold of Quebec. Mulroney had not heard such good news in a long time.

More than ever Mulroney lived by the political theorem that had dominated his thinking ever since Laval: the Conservative Party had to win Quebec to take over Ottawa. The Liberal Party had ridden the formula to victory time after time since 1896; it had made the Liberals Canada's governing party. After the lopsided 1968 results it seemed as if they could not lose. But if the Conservative Party could somehow make inroads in Quebec it could topple the Trudeau government in the next election, expected in 1972. That was how Mulroney saw it.

In the summer of 1971 Peter White told Mulroney that Judge Claude Wagner, the former strongman of the Lesage government, might be persuaded to run as a Tory. The news immediately pricked Mulroney's interest because Wagner was exactly the kind of candidate he was looking for, someone well known and widely respected. He had been a crimebusting Crown attorney, then a tough no-nonsense sessions court judge, and later a popular hard-line cabinet minister who in January 1970 came within a hair of succeeding Jean Lesage as leader of the Quebec Liberal Party. The majority of elected Liberal delegates had voted for him, but the ex officio delegates appointed by the party establishment flocked over to Robert Bourassa and tipped the balance. Bitter at having had the leadership stolen from him, Wagner quit politics and was reappointed to the bench on the day the Union Nationale government called an election in 1970, which Bourassa won.

Wagner was not happy in his exile on the bench and had almost been persuaded to run for the now-vacant leadership of the Union Nationale. White and his business partner Conrad Black (the two purchased the *Sherbrooke Record* together in 1969) had tried to recruit him but after much agonizing, Wagner declined to run. The October Crisis of 1970, especially the murder of Pierre Laporte, had scared him off. Nevertheless Wagner told White he might consider federal politics, so White brought Mulroney and Wagner together for lunch at the University Club in Montreal on July 27, 1971. The lunch went well, and although Wagner made no promises, Mulroney could tell he was interested. From that moment recruiting Wagner into the Conservative Party became his top political priority. He believed it could transform the Conservatives into a vibrant force in Quebec.

The prospect of landing Wagner also excited Claude Dupras, who headed a triumvirate that ran the Tory apparatus in Quebec. (The other members were Mulroney and Claude Nolin, a prominent lawyer.) The Conservative Party had been hunting for a strong Quebec leader practically since George-Étienne Cartier had ruled the province on behalf of John A. Macdonald back in the nineteenth century. Unable to build an effective organization in Quebec, the party had tried wooing every big shot it could over the years, including Mayor Jean Drapeau — anyone with coat-tails. Mulroney detected in Wagner a certain star quality that could break — finally — the Liberal stranglehold on Quebec. He saw the recruitment of Wagner as presenting a historic opportunity.

The flirtation with Wagner created interest all the way to Ottawa. Stanfield, who was touring Quebec monthly, hoping to start something, was curious, but wary of Wagner's image as a hanging judge. Mulroney advised Stanfield to meet with him personally, arguing that

Wagner had changed in the last few years. Gone was the austere brushcut and the stern manner. Wagner now came across as fatherly. Stanfield agreed and Mulroney arranged a private tête-à-tête at his own apartment. In order to create a relaxing, homey atmosphere he brought over his mother to cook the meal. While Stanfield, Wagner, and Mulroney were dickering in the living room, Mulroney's mom was bustling in the kitchen.

The get-together lasted several hours and yielded a meeting of minds, of sorts. Stanfield and Wagner both agreed that the Conservative Party had to do better in Quebec, and could do so under the right circumstances. But Wagner proved a prickly, standoffish fellow, terrible at small talk, just as cold and distant as his reputation. Moreover, he sounded as though he wanted Quebec as his personal fiefdom, and no party leader in his right mind could accept that, not even one as easygoing as Stanfield.

The evening took an interesting twist when Richard Hatfield, the premier of New Brunswick, who happened to be flying by in his airplane, unexpectedly radioed down to tell his friend Brian that he wanted to stop by for a drink. Soon after Hatfield arrived, it was time for Mulroney to drive Stanfield to the airport. The New Brunswick premier stayed behind to entertain Wagner and formed an instant dislike for him. As a result, Hatfield joined the faction opposed to Wagner's recruitment.

Despite the shaky start, Mulroney kept at Wagner, always staying in touch, always keeping the pipeline open while Wagner waffled and played hard to get. Wagner's character flaws did not escape Mulroney, but his potential to win in Quebec overshadowed everything else. "I hate to think how much money I spent buying lunches for that guy," Mulroney says in Geoffrey Stevens's biography of Robert Stanfield. Mulroney worked on Stanfield too, telling him that Wagner was the best the party could come up with. Still uncertain, Stanfield asked Dalton Camp to meet Wagner and report back. Mulroney brought Wagner and Camp together in a Montreal hotel room, made introductions, then discreetly left.

There is no record of what Camp thought of Wagner, but he gave the recruitment his blessing. However, another barrier still blocked the way; it concerned the crass question of money. All along Wagner had insisted on receiving some sort of financial guarantee in case the bottom fell out of his bold move. Wagner had a wife, a mother-in-law, and three children to support, and life in Quebec as a Tory was a big risk. Once he defected he could expect nothing from the Liberals again. Mulroney searched for a solution, even canvassing major Montreal law firms about accepting Wagner as a partner, but one after another they turned him down. Wagner was too unorthodox and too much a publicity seeker for their tastes. "If you want him," Mulroney finally told Ottawa, "you're going to have to give him security." The response to this suggestion was decidedly cool.

Mulroney had originally thought that the wooing of Wagner would take a matter of weeks, but it had stretched into months and still was at an impasse. It was already 1972 and a federal election was expected before the year was out.

"We can't miss," Mulroney assured Claude Dupras.

"Well," Dupras responded, "let's make a poll to demonstrate to us and to Mr. Stanfield that Wagner is good for us."

But first they needed some cash since Ottawa insisted that Quebec pay. A simple poll by Bob Teeter, the Republican pollster in Detroit who doubled as the Conservative Party's pollster in Canada, cost $5,000, which was big money for Quebec in those days. Mulroney went out and raised it from Power Corporation.

The Teeter poll tested Wagner against a group of prominent Quebec figures and the results were amazing, even astounding. On the question of who was "best qualified to represent the interests of Quebec in Parliament," Wagner scored ahead of everybody else — Créditiste leader Réal Caouette, Jean Drapeau, even two percentage points ahead of Pierre Trudeau. It was all the more remarkable considering Wagner had been out of politics almost two years. Respondents were also asked if switching parties would undermine a politician, and the answer was no.

The poll changed everything. Mulroney could now convincingly promote Wagner as the great hope for the Tory party in Quebec. As far as he was concerned the poll removed the last vestige of doubt. The stalled recruitment talks had revived Ottawa's interest enough to talk money.

Up to this point Mulroney had done most of the spadework, but a waterfront strike involving a long-time client, the Maritime Employers' Association, took him out of the picture in the early summer of 1972. With Ottawa ready to put up some money, it was now mostly an issue of working out an agreeable price, and that matter was being handled by Finlay MacDonald, the incoming Tory campaign chairman, whom Mulroney had first met when they worked under Dalton Camp during the 1960 Nova Scotia election. Buying a candidate with big chunks of money was perfectly legal, but unusual, and would raise political eyebrows the minute it leaked out. Stanfield's advisers wanted to keep their man clean and made a conscious decision to keep the Tory leader in the dark over the question of money for Wagner.

The deal was to be struck over lunch in the Château Champlain in Montreal. Wagner arrived looking dapper and exotic with his coat hanging from his shoulders like a cape. Over lobster salad and a bottle of Pouilly-Fuissé they discussed the size of a trust fund to be set up in Wagner's name. MacDonald assured Wagner of how anxious the party was to have him, and that everybody accepted the fact he was making a sacrifice, and after some friendly sparring they settled on $300,000. The Tories had purchased their star.

Now they had to raise the money, draw up the papers for a legal trust, and appoint trustees. That whole matter fell into the hands of Toronto lawyer and Tory backroom ace Eddie Goodman. The George-Étienne Cartier Trust Fund, as it was called, would give Wagner an estimated income of $30,000 a year before taxes. Contrary to the original notion of a safety net, even if he won a seat he would collect it on top of his MP's salary.

On September 1, 1972, Prime Minister Trudeau finally called an election for October 30. Five days later Wagner called a press conference and announced he was quitting the bench to seek the Conservative nomination in Saint-Hyacinthe. "I have no need of, I have not asked for, nor have I been offered any pension fund or financial compensation," Wagner announced.

Wagner's claim of financial virginity surprised many people — from the small circle of Tory operators who knew what had really happened, to ordinary outsiders who did not but who suspected a money deal of some kind. Rumours of Wagner's recruitment had been swirling in the press for months and had usually included reports of a purported trust fund, but reporters could never pin them down. Now Wagner had flatly denied the rumours, and by doing so he had crossed an important ethical line.

Politicians are no strangers to bending the truth. Even the most upright and above-board among them sometimes fudge issues and muddy the record, occasionally doctoring the facts to suit their purpose. Political survival demands it. Most politicians have perfected the art of appearing to say things they are not, and vice versa. But most wander only so far into the land of deception before reaching a line beyond which they will not go, the boundary between misleading the public and lying to it. With his bald-faced lie Wagner had boldly, voluntarily, and without shame crossed the forbidden line, an act that would ultimately deny him the leadership of the Conservative Party. But for the moment the people around him who knew the truth could do nothing but swallow hard and stonewall. "Mr. Wagner was very explicit in saying there was no compensation of any kind," they would reply to the questions, and thus play the game the accepted way, by misleading the questioner with a factual statement. (Stanfield still had not been told about the trust fund, although he suspected something had been done.)

As campaign chairman, Claude Dupras ran day-to-day operations, but Mulroney became the campaign's chief troubleshooter, logistics man, motivater, fundraiser, and, when needed, speech-maker. He started the campaign with sky-high hopes — predicting something like thirty seats in Quebec — but soon had to scale back his expectations. Even somebody as eternally optimistic as he had to admit that, while the Tory campaign in the other nine provinces had taken off, the campaign in Quebec was dissolving into another disaster.

Despite Wagner's strong image, he was not pulling big crowds or injecting any excitement into the contest. He proved to be a superficial candidate and a weak campaigner, shy and hopelessly cautious, anything but a man of the people. He insisted on touring Quebec in his own bus, with the reporters in a separate bus following behind, and never said anything worth repeating. (He talked only law and order, even though it was not a big issue in 1972.) He was autocratic and remote, decidedly not a team player, who fussed over his title and his status on the campaign and clearly resented Stanfield's supremacy as party leader. He refused to acknowledge Stanfield on the stump and eventually forbade his people to mention Stanfield's name. Voters could easily get the impression that Stanfield and Wagner were leading separate parties.

Behind the scenes it was worse. Wagner's bent for sticking the knife into Stanfield reached its epitome on an open-line radio show in Chicoutimi. The occasion was one of their few joint campaign appearances and, in addition to cementing the Stanfield-Wagner connection in the public mind, Wagner was to help Stanfield field questions in French. Before arriving at the radio station, Wagner stopped to lunch in a nearby restaurant with Peter White, who had agreed to work as his executive assistant for the campaign. (White had developed a relationship with Wagner after unsuccessfully wooing him to run for the Union Nationale provincially.) White ordered a fancy dessert called *poire au Pernod*, which was made in a skillet at table-side, and took lots of butter and plenty of preparation time. The maître d' forgot to mind the slowly melting butter and let it burn. He apologized profusely and promised to make a new batch, but White waved him off. There was no time. However, Wagner told the maître d' to go ahead and melt a new stick of butter. White protested, saying that it would make them late for the radio station.

"Peter," Wagner persisted, "I absolutely insist. You wanted *poire au Pernod*, we're going to stay here until you have your *poire au Pernod*."

Wagner arrived at the radio station thirty minutes late, with the program half over and Stanfield struggling manfully in fractured French while his entourage fumed behind the studio glass. Wagner had deliberately shafted his leader and everybody knew it, but he pretended nothing had happened. Then, at their joint rally that evening, Wagner droned on and on in a transparent attempt to keep Stanfield off stage. Wagner's only success during the whole campaign seemed to be in undermining his party leader.

As it became more obvious that the Tory campaign in Quebec was floundering, Wagner started to crack. First he wanted to throw out the whole television advertising campaign with its carefully crafted three-part theme and substitute an all-out blitz on law and order. Then, with about ten days left, he panicked, abandoned his bus in the Gaspé, and flew back to his own riding in Saint-Hyacinthe, stranding the reporters' bus and reneging on a string of campaign commitments. Headquarters in Montreal begged him not to desert the tour, pleading that he was shirking his duty as Quebec leader and hurting himself as well — but to no avail. He could think of nothing except his personal survival in Saint-Hyacinthe. Soon he petitioned headquarters to move its province-wide force of workers — about seventy-five people in all — into a door-to-door blitz in his riding.

The vote count on election night confirmed all the worst premonitions. The party elected exactly two MPs — Wagner himself and long-time MP Heward Grafftey, who could not stand each other. The Liberals took fifty-six seats, with another fifteen seats for Crédit Social. The result outdébâcled even the 1968 disaster and made Diefenbaker's worst Quebec showing of four seats look positively princely by comparison. The highly touted Stanfield-Wagner team had led the Conservative Party to its worst showing in Quebec since the end of World War II.

While losing badly in Quebec the Conservative Party was surging ahead in English Canada. When ballot-counting reached British

Columbia the Tories and Liberals were still see-sawing back and forth. Tories in Halifax went to bed with their party out front 109 to 107 and woke up the next morning having lost 107 to 109. (The outcome probably would have been reversed had Wagner not talked Stanfield out of asking Marcel Masse and Armand Russell, both former Union Nationale ministers with strong regional followings, to run. Both were prepared to run and almost certainly would have won their ridings. Instead both those seats — Joliette and Shefford — went to the Liberals.) Nationally, the Liberal Party had clung to power by the narrowest of margins. And if Quebec had voted like the rest of the country Stanfield would have swept to an easy majority. Outside the province the Conservative Party had trounced the Liberals 105 to 53. Once again the Conservative Party had been stymied by Quebec.

In the let-down that followed, most of the supporters of the Wagner recruitment reluctantly accepted that the party had blundered. The dream candidate had delivered nothing and had barely hung onto his own riding, the safest seat in the province. The strongman had shown himself to be anything but strong; if anything he had set the party further back in Quebec. The Wagner recruitment would stand as one of the biggest miscalculations of modern Canadian politics, and Mulroney had been its chief architect. He never forgave Wagner for behaving so badly and letting down the party.

Although he continued to defend Wagner publicly, he would soon regret ever having heard his name, let alone enticing him into the party. He had spent much of the election campaign covering up for his falling star and knew all the stories. Most unforgivable of all was that while Mulroney had rolled up his sleeves and gone all out, he believed Wagner had not. As far as Mulroney was concerned Wagner was a political whore who had taken the party to the cleaners. "I distrust people who never swear, never drink, never smoke," Mulroney later told reporter John Gray. "There was always something there between us." He came to despise the man.

But what rankled for Mulroney more than anything was the fact that Wagner, as the official Quebec lieutenant, now refused to consult him. And Mulroney needed above all else to be consulted, to be kept informed, to be an insider. Instead, in the wake of the election Wagner cut him off. Being touchy, jealous, vain, and insecure, he saw Mulroney as a threat and set out to replace him with his own group of loyalists.

Mulroney was not about to surrender his role without a fight. He still had direct access to Stanfield and could go around Wagner any time he wanted, a fact that continued to enrage Wagner as he went about making Quebec his personal fiefdom. Both Mulroney and Wagner needed to prevail, no matter what the stakes.

Given the way their feud developed, it could easily be forgotten that Mulroney had championed Wagner and recruited him into the party. Once Mulroney got locked onto his target, he had given little thought to whether he really wanted Wagner as the Quebec strong-man, and particularly little to how it would affect his own political future. Wagner was a potential rival: the more successful he became, the more difficult it would be for Mulroney himself to emerge as leader. Yet even when the man's character flaws began to intrude, Mulroney never stopped to reconsider. As sometimes seemed the case in his labour negotiations, the act of swinging the deal had become more important than the final result.

CHAPTER TWELVE

THE PERFECT WIFE

BACK IN APRIL 1972, when the Wagner recruitment was temporarily bogged down, Mulroney had taken off to Europe for a much-needed respite. He and Michel Cogger planned to wander the Mediterranean resorts of the Côte d'Azur and rub shoulders with the Continental jet set for a carefree five weeks. However, they had not been there long when a middle-of-the-night telephone call to Monaco roused Mulroney from his sleep. It was his first big client, the Maritime Employers' Association, dispatching an SOS. Labour trouble had broken out on the docks again, and the MEA needed him home post-haste.

Back in Montreal Mulroney found the waterfront in turmoil. The longshoremen had walked off the job illegally, and somehow he had to coax them back. Carefully feeling his way about, he found the union surly and unresponsive. For once neither his flair for conciliation nor his labour connections got him very far. Finally, under pressure from the MEA, whose patience had snapped, he filed a formal grievance against the International Longshoremen's Association. The ILA fought him at every turn, arguing that the walk-out was justified by management's violations of the collective agreement. However, the mediator, the same Alan Gold who had mediated the earlier dispute, ruled in Mulroney's favour, and eventually the longshoremen were forced back to work. It had not been pretty and was not a typical Mulroney negotiation, but the battle had been won.

The waterfront crisis had monopolized Mulroney's time for weeks on end. He entered the mess in early May and only emerged in early July. Now he needed a vacation more than ever. This time he decided to stay in Montreal for a while and do nothing except play some tennis, the only sport with which he maintained even a nodding acquaintance. Most days he could be found at the Mount Royal Tennis Club, more often reading a newspaper on the veranda than dashing around the courts. One day he looked up from his reading to spot a dazzling brunette next to the swimming pool down below. As she walked by he put down his newspaper and stared. What he saw was a five-foot-nine Slavic beauty, with high cheekbones and a svelte figure.

"I was sitting there reading the *New York Times* before having a swim," Mulroney later told biographer L. Ian MacDonald, "and Mila goes by. Bikini, what have you. Well, so I arranged to get myself an introduction, and by that I found out that Thursday was her birthday. She was just turning nineteen, for heaven's sake."

Mila Pivnicki seemed far too mature to be eighteen going on nineteen. Perhaps it was a certain European poise and sophistication inherited from her Yugoslav parents, or maybe it was the experience of having been uprooted at an early age and resettled in a new and strange country. She had been four when her father, Dr. Dimitrije Pivnicki, a psychiatrist, left his native Bosnia for Canada, and five when she and the rest of the family joined him in Montreal. Dr. Pivnicki prospered in Canada and rose to become prominent in his field, numbering among his more famous patients Margaret Trudeau, the wife of the prime minister. Meanwhile the Pivnicki family had rooted itself in Westmount and now lived near the tennis club.

After successfully enticing her up to the veranda for a closer inspection, Mulroney discovered that Mila possessed more than physical beauty. An engineering student with plans to become an architect, she was vivacious, engaging, intelligent, and positively bubbling with life. Perhaps her most winsome feature was her smile.

It had warmth and friendliness and melted anyone in its path, as it did Mulroney that day. In truth, he had met his match: Mila packed every bit as much personal charm as he did and dished it out to the same disarming effect. He was smitten.

Mulroney made his opening moves, but Mila politely spurned his advances. She was not nearly as dazzled by him as he was by her; after all, he was thirty-three, and it seemed a bit much to date somebody that old. But Mulroney persisted, as he always did with women, and invited himself to her birthday party. Although she gave no encouragement, he did not admit defeat. He would call her on the phone and announce he was coming by to pick her up, then hang up before she could say no. His moxie paid off, and finally he began to win her over. "Brian made me laugh," Mila would later tell MacDonald. "He had a fantastic sense of humour." On their first real date she accompanied him to a party at old pal George Archer's place, where he introduced her around. (Archer had been a regular at the bachelor weekends in the Laurentians during the sixties.) His friends were duly impressed, and understood his attraction. On his way out he gave Archer a nudge. "Hey, what do you think?" he asked, signalling that she was no ordinary girlfriend.

Indeed Mila was different. She immediately became his fixed companion and, for a change, the only woman in his life. Mulroney often went overboard in quest of the things he wanted, and Mila was no exception. He pursued her the rest of the summer and into the fall. Their romance even messed up his schedule during the 1972 election campaign, and he did not seem to mind. He always found time for her, no matter how hectic the campaign grew.

Montreal's social world could not help but notice that Mulroney seemed to be anchoring himself exclusively to one woman. His relationship with Mila became the subject of all kinds of gossip. "She's so young," was the big whisper, and indeed more than fourteen years separated them. In some ways it was not surprising, for it was not the first time Mulroney had been infatuated with a teenager.

In January 1971, shortly before Mulroney turned thirty-two, a musical act called the Golddiggers had swept into town amid much fanfare. Dean Martin had spotted them and made them semi-regulars on his Thursday-night television show, and NBC then gave them their own show as Martin's summer replacement. The exposure took them to Vietnam with Bob Hope, and now they filled nightclubs from Las Vegas on down. That January ten gorgeous women, aged eighteen to twenty-one, burst onto stage twice nightly in the Queen Elizabeth Hotel's ornate Bonaventure Room across the street from Mulroney's office, dancing and singing their way into the hearts of male Montrealers — including Brian Mulroney. The *Montreal Gazette* said they sang with "the sweetest little voices you've ever heard," and they always closed with a rousing rendition of "Let the Sun Shine In" from the musical *Hair*. Everyone agreed it was a smashing performance.

Every night during the Golddiggers' four-week run, Mulroney visited the Bonaventure Room and stayed for both shows, arranging through an executive with Hilton Hotels for front-row seats. As an old crooner he enjoyed the beauty of the human voice, but the beauty that stirred him here was not musical. He was especially taken with a six-foot-tall, brown-eyed brunette, the tallest member of the troupe. After one of the first performances he sent her a note backstage proposing a drink. The object of his interest was Paula Cinko, a nineteen-year-old from Akron, Ohio, who had joined the Golddiggers through a talent search in New York City. House rules forbade Paula from dating while she was a member of the troupe, especially dating patrons, but she was a free-spirited young woman and liked the flowers he sent. She found him amusing and extraordinarily nice, and she went out with him anyway.

Before the Golddiggers finished their Montreal run on February 6, he had made friends with all of them. On one occasion he delivered the lot to a party in Michel Cogger's apartment. After their final show they presented him with a silver beer mug autographed by the entire cast. Then he said goodbye to Paula, who was quitting the troupe and heading off to New York City to chase the glitter of Broadway. But he did not say goodbye to the Golddiggers. His relationship with

Paula had been an enjoyable little interlude. However, his budding attraction to another Golddigger, Francie Mendenhall, was much more serious.

During the next few months, Mulroney would sometimes get up from his desk on a Friday afternoon and head for the door. "Well, I'm off to Detroit tonight," he would explain on his way out. Whichever city the Golddiggers were in, Mulroney would visit, see the show, and spend time with Francie. To Mulroney's delight, the Golddiggers returned to Montreal on October 11 that year for a six-week engagement, which gave him lots of time to pursue his latest passion.

Once again he had fallen into love, or at least had become fixated in the way he had with Rosann Earl and JoAnn Ross. Francie had the same kind of arresting beauty that Elizabeth Taylor had in her youth, and his was the kind of infatuation that leads men to do goofy things. The relationship got serious enough that Francie's mother, Phyllis, came up to Montreal and met Mulroney. Phyllis hardly conformed to his image of a mother, being closer to his age than he was to her daughter's. She looked too gorgeous to be a mom. "I had my eye on the mother too," Mulroney joked to a friend afterwards. Mulroney gave Phyllis and Francie a tour of the city and showed them a lovely time, thoroughly impressing them both.

Motherly approval from Mulroney's side was another matter. Irene Mulroney did not so much meet Francie as encounter her — in a state of undress during an unannounced visit to her son's apartment. It was not the way to be introduced to the woman who might become her daughter-in-law. "She should have known better than to come over without warning," Mulroney later quipped, half in jest and half in complaint.

For a while it looked like Francie would take Mulroney all the way to the altar, but their romance ultimately went nowhere. When Francie left town with the Golddiggers on November 20, their relationship died. He had boasted to her that he would be prime minister some day, and therein lay the root of the break-up. No matter how crazy he was about her, he could never marry a Golddigger, not with that kind of ambition.

The fling with Francie dramatized Mulroney's quandary with women: those he wanted to date were not the ones he wanted to be formally associated with; the ones who made suitable escorts did not excite him. The Westmount women he brought to proper social functions bored him, and he treated them like ornaments, but the wives of some of the senior partners might frown if he turned up with the wrong kind of girl. His mother would disapprove too.

Every once in a while a woman came along whom he found both sexually attractive and socially acceptable. Rosann Earl and JoAnn Ross fell into this category, but he'd met them both before he was ready to settle down — and they had each dumped him first. For a time, Katherine Morrow, the daughter of Robert Morrow, a law partner at Ogilvy Cope, looked like a good prospect, but she dropped him too. The few women of substance he dated seriously in Montreal did not last.

Undoubtedly part of the problem was his old-fashioned attitude towards women. Women were an object of conquest, not a source of intellectual stimulation. He could usually engage them, charm them, and make them laugh. He could be gallant and helpful; he could flatter them and pamper them, but he could not treat them seriously or discuss weighty issues without being patronizing. Never did he bring a woman friend into his inner circle in those years; even in later life, long after the fight for female equality had flowered, it was rare.

In sum Mulroney was a male chauvinist extraordinaire at a time and in a place where male chauvinism was still the norm. In a city that seemed to be teeming with beautiful and available women, Mulroney had the personality and social status to turn it into a male chauvinist's paradise. He became a sexual glutton, sometimes boasting boorishly about his latest success. He once openly bragged while still at a wedding how he had engineered a successful seduction — he put it more crudely than that — between the ceremony and the reception. Sometimes he would drink too much and gaze across the

Carrefour's expanse of tables and blurt out that he could have any woman in the room.

Ironically, however, beneath this surface playboy sensibility lay the old-fashioned values he had learned in Baie Comeau. He believed in the family unit and the institution, if not the sanctity, of marriage. He believed in — but did not practise — the orthodox version of Catholic sexual morality: chastity before marriage, fidelity after it.

But now that he had reached his thirties, the swinging bachelor life had lost a little shine. Going through women like names in a telephone book no longer satisfied even an out-of-control thrill seeker like himself. Furthermore he knew intemperate sexual behaviour could foul up his political ambitions. Pierre Trudeau had become prime minister as a swinging bachelor, but that happened during a special time in the sixties, when the convention was to be unconventional. That kind of thing could not last — and did not. Three years later Trudeau got married. Sooner or later Mulroney would have to get married too if he was to climb higher on the political ladder.

When Mulroney did eventually get married, it would be to no ordinary woman. His wife would have to be beautiful — that went without saying — sexually desirable, and a member of the establishment he had worked so hard to penetrate. She would need style, personality, and class. She would have to be personally ambitious but willing to realize that ambition through him. Moreover, she would have to be able to adapt to the many idiosyncrasies of an ambitious political addict with erratic work habits. Finally, in keeping with his Baie Comeau concept of marriage, she would have to be a virgin — at least up until the beginning of their relationship.

Mila fulfilled all these criteria and more. She spoke good French, was a dedicated social climber, and had a similar drive to succeed. Moreover Mulroney had come to a stage in his career where the right wife would help him climb up the political ladder. He also happened to be head over heels in love with this very mature nineteen-year-old. She made him comfortable in ways other women did not. Despite her youth, he was impressed with her intelligence and common sense.

Here was a woman he actually respected in her own right. One friend would later say they were meant for each other. In many ways they were a perfect match.

That fall of 1972 Mulroney's old gang rented a ski house up north again, but this year Mulroney didn't participate. Occasionally he came up as a guest, and when he did he always brought Mila. "Brian's behaving abnormally," they would say. In November Mulroney, with Mila as co-host, threw a champagne engagement party for Graham Scott, a senior aide to Stanfield, and Gail Scott, an Ottawa reporter with CTV. By this time the word had spread that Mulroney himself might be in need of an engagement party. He displayed no doubt that he had found the right woman, and by the end of the year they were engaged. "I've just met a nineteen-year-old virgin," he told one of his law colleagues, "and I'm going to marry her."

A few weeks before the wedding Michel Cogger and Lowell Murray threw a party for Mulroney and Mila and invited friends and acquaintances from across the country. Among the many guests was, somewhat surprisingly, a rookie MP named Joe Clark, who came in from Ottawa. A lot had happened since Clark and Mulroney had worked together on the failed leadership campaign of Davie Fulton back in 1967. Both had done very well for themselves in the intervening years. Mulroney had gone on to make a name for himself as a lawyer and labour negotiator in Montreal, and Clark had gotten himself elected to the House of Commons.

Following the let-down of Fulton's defeat, Clark had stayed in Ottawa and caught on as Robert Stanfield's number two assistant, working under Lowell Murray. Michel Cogger, another Fulton worker, also remained in Ottawa as associate national director of the PC Party, and the three of them shared a terribly messy apartment.

With only a small staff — House of Commons budgets were not as large as they would become a few years later — Stanfield relied heavily on his two senior aides, who were responsible for much of his effectiveness as leader of the opposition. Clark and Murray, who were already good friends, combined to make a proficient team and between them did most of Stanfield's speech-writing, correspondence, caucus liaison, itinerary management, and policy work. As speech-writer, Clark wrote quickly and well. He even drafted letters at high speed, using a Dictaphone and always spitting out his replies in perfect paragraphs. Clark coined the phrase "the incentive society," which gave Stanfield a lot of political mileage, although for the most part Clark complained that the ever-cautious Stanfield threw away his best lines.

As a stage manager, Clark proved himself innovative, creative, and forever aggressive in trying to put harder edges onto a careful and sometimes reluctant leader. Already working on the "community of communities" philosophy that would represent his small-town view of Canada, Clark pushed Stanfield to identify actively with ordinary citizens inside some of these communities. Clark staged a number of public events in the late sixties, before politicians routinely pulled such publicity stunts, in an attempt to carve out a new identity for Stanfield, one that would overcome his loser image from the terrible 1968 election. He had Stanfield living in an apartment in Toronto's St. James Town for a couple of days to experience the hardship of fixed-income life in a poor pocket of the city. Then he put him onto a cattle farm in northern Alberta, where for four days he got up at dawn and did chores. Next he had the Conservative leader climbing onto combines on a wheat farm. He also organized a pollution tour of Toronto during high-smog days. Gradually the strategy paid off, and Stanfield's image improved steadily during this period.

As high-strung as ever, Clark seldom stood still and almost never slowed down. He tackled everything at full tilt and often overwhelmed the slow-moving Stanfield with sheer nervous energy, but nothing quite matched the zeal with which he attacked learning French. He signed up for the House of Commons French program and devoured every bit of written French he could lay his hands on. At home he would lie in bed reading sophisticated French novels that were clearly beyond his comprehension and plod along page by page with a couple of dictionaries by his side. He wanted to become fluent.

Moreover, his roommates suspected, he wanted to avoid an accent as dreadful as Diefenbaker's.

Clark's pursuit of bilingualism was typical. He approached everything logically, and with his focus always directly in front of him — to the point where people could predict his next move. His goal was to become prime minister. Since this journey would take a long time, he broke the whole process into stages and pursued each stage one step at a time. First he would capitalize on his roots, then build a base, then pick up Parliament Hill experience and learn French, then find a riding, then run for Parliament, then become party leader and finally drive the Liberals out of office. As he moved from step to step, he threw himself totally into each phase and did not rest until finished.

Working for Stanfield showed him how a leader ran the party machinery and how he led his caucus into parliamentary battle each day. It also gave him an inside view of Parliament Hill that would smooth his landing as an MP. In spring 1970, after two and a half years of choreographing Stanfield, Clark concluded he had learned enough and was ready to move on. "I decided my usefulness to him was expiring and his to me," he would later tell biographer David Humphreys. "I wanted to be elected. I think my talents are greater in the front room."

Few at the time shared Clark's self-assessment, including Stanfield and Peter Lougheed, the two party leaders for whom he had last worked. Whatever conspicuous qualities one needed to be perceived as a potential leader, Clark by popular consensus lacked them. People instinctively underrated him and continually dismissed him as a speech-writer, a technician. Not unduly worried, Clark accepted his image problem matter-of-factly and could even joke about it, although it bothered him enough to ask his girlfriend, Christine Forsyth, whether he walked funny and whether he could pass as a prime minister.

After leaving Stanfield, Clark spent the rest of 1970 in Europe, taking time off and sharpening his French. On returning to Canada he went straight to Alberta, and for the next year immersed himself in a squabble for the PC nomination in Rocky Mountain, traditionally a Liberal seat. In March 1972 he beat out two other hopefuls to become the Tory candidate. Desperately short of money, he worked at odd jobs, including a stint in public relations work, while he waited for Prime Minister Trudeau to call a general election. When the call finally came that fall, Lowell Murray took up a collection back east on Clark's behalf and hit up Mulroney among others. Mulroney routinely donated small sums to PC candidates he knew, so he chipped in on the Clark fund. On October 30, 1972, Clark, with help from an anti-Trudeau swing in the West, pulled an upset by winning perhaps the Liberals' safest seat in Alberta by five thousand votes.

In Ottawa, Clark brought all his zeal and frenetic energy to the floor of the House of Commons and quickly emerged as an aggressive and extremely partisan MP. He could still laugh at himself but showed no sense of humour or charity towards the Liberals. They were the awful Grits, and he attacked them with unremitting belligerence. Clark's surliest barbs were always directed at Pierre Trudeau, whom he despised. He regularly denounced the prime minister far beyond the call of partisan duty and in later life would never disavow a thing he said. Apart from such excesses of zeal, he delivered some highly effective speeches in Parliament and soon joined that small group of caucus members who rose early in the morning to shape the Tory strategy for the daily attack in question period. There was no doubt that Clark was an MP in a hurry. So when he showed up at the party for Mulroney in the spring of 1973, he had already gained a reputation as a politician on the rise.

Although Clark and Mulroney continued to keep their distance, their networks overlapped now more than ever, and they had many close friends in common. Clark's invitation had come from Michel Cogger and Lowell Murray, the co-hosts, his roommates from their days as assistants to Stanfield.

Clark and Mulroney were still as different as they had been in their younger years. Now people could see it in their dating practices. Clark exhibited a "liberated" attitude towards women before it became fashionable, preferring smart, independent, and career-oriented women. While at Dalhousie he had dated Judith McMahon, who later, as Judith Maxwell, would go on to become the chairman of the Economic Council of Canada. A couple of his other girlfriends became lawyers, including Catrina Gibson, who graduated at the top of her class at Queen's. Clark and Catrina dated a long time, leading friends to think they might marry. Then, in 1969, while Catrina was studying for her master's degree in Toronto and Clark was working for Stanfield in Ottawa, they arranged a rendezvous in Huntsville, Ontario. It was the last time Clark saw her alive. En route back to Toronto Catrina was killed in a car accident. The loss absolutely shattered him.

Although Mulroney was formally engaged and being fêted at this party, a lot of people still had trouble believing that such a consummate bachelor was actually succumbing to marriage. Now Clark unveiled his own little surprise: he too was getting married, and he had brought with him to the party his fiancée, Maureen McTeer. He used the occasion to introduce her to the Montreal PC crowd. Like Mulroney, Clark was marrying a woman from a younger generation. Maureen was thirteen years his junior. Moreover Joe and Maureen would be tying the knot only thirty-five days after Brian and Mila.

One could not help but compare Maureen McTeer and Mila Pivnicki, two young women of barely voting age in a crowd of mostly over-thirties. Only a year and a half separated them in age. Unlike many political wives, they would support their husbands' quests for high public office from day one, and in so doing both would profoundly affect the course of their careers. Beyond that the similarities ended. Mila and Maureen were as different as the men they were about to marry.

At the time it looked to some people as if Clark had chosen more wisely. Although not beautiful like Mila, Maureen possessed more naked intelligence. She was also a political animal, who had worked for the Conservative Party since age twelve and kept up to the minute on political issues, which Mila did not. Maureen had won debating scholarships in high school and over the years had done enough volunteering in PC youth circles to give her a political base of her own. After marriage, she would enrol in law school, whereas Mila would drop out of university. Somebody with Maureen's brains, experience, contacts, and savvy seemed the ideal match for a rising political leader in the 1970s.

Actually Mulroney's choice of Mila confounded some of his friends, who saw her potential political shortcomings. She was neither French nor English, but an immigrant teenager from the Serbian community in Montreal, and she hardly knew a soul outside the city. She did not even pretend to have any expertise in political matters. They argued that Mulroney could have married into some of the country's leading families. He had dated the daughters of people such as Jean Lesage, Dalton Camp, Bill Bennett (the president of the Iron Ore Company of Canada), and several of the upper-crust law partners at Ogilvy Cope. Although well established by 1973, the Pivnicki family was neither rich nor famous. For someone who had climbed so high on society's ladder, Mulroney was marrying down. However, the early Mila doubters would soon change their minds. To a person they would agree that the choice of Mila had been not just good but brilliant — even inspired. Before long they would sing her praises as one of the best things that ever happened to Brian Mulroney.

The wedding was set for late May 1973, and as the day approached Mulroney began to have second thoughts. Just what was he getting into? He was surrendering his beloved bachelor's freedom and would now have to live up to the traditional morality he believed in. The fourteen-year age difference began to cause him anxiety. As wonderful as Mila was, she was not a fully formed person. Was he making a terrible mistake? He confided his doubts to a friend. "What if I wake up one day and say, 'Oh my God, what have I done?'" The friend told him that he wanted to be more sure of the outcome than was ever possible, and assured him that his doubts would pass. One look at Mila and they always did.

As it turned out, however, Mulroney was almost late for his own wedding on May 26, 1973. With everything almost set to go,

Mulroney and Bernard Roy, his best man, raced up to the church and dashed inside a side entrance. They had a genuine crisis to sort out. For a while it looked as though they had no cleric to perform the marriage. The honour had been given to a priest Mulroney had sentimentally brought in from St. FX, even though he was known to enjoy a drink or two too many. The priest had arrived the night before, promptly gotten into the sauce, and now was completely looped. Frantic rescue efforts had sobered him up somewhat, so Mulroney crossed his fingers and hoped that everything would be okay. The congregation soon twigged to the priest's delicate condition and, expecting him to collapse at any minute, let out a sigh of relief when he made it through to the end of the vows.

Except for that bit of excitement, the wedding went off smoothly, and the reception at McGill University's Faculty Club proved to be a glittering occasion. Joining Mulroney's old gang — led by best man Bernard Roy and ushers Michel Cogger, Lowell Murray, and Yves Fortier — was a good sampling of the social élite of Montreal. Everybody from his mother to the mayor of Westmount was on hand. "If you guys had won the '72 election," author Peter C. Newman quipped to lawyer Richard Holden, "all the bums around here today would be judges and cabinet ministers." Holden looked around and had to agree that Newman was right. Indeed, dozens of the guests would someday enhance their careers through Mulroney's generosity.

Speaking from notes on the back of a cigarette package, Mulroney amused everybody with a string of jokes. He had not lost his touch at the podium. Then he turned serious and dropped his voice, as he always did in solemn moments. "I would particularly like to thank the person who has made this wonderful day in my life all possible," he said, "without whose intervention it would not have come about — Marshal Tito." After a beat, the whole place erupted into a fit of laughter. It was a good line, well delivered, and the hit of the evening. The entire room stood up and toasted the Yugoslavian dictator for driving the Pivnicki family to Canada.

Eventually any doubts Mulroney had had about marriage and his choice of wife would disappear. Mila would prove to be an ideal domestic partner — a superwife. Cheerful and well-balanced by nature, she had the emotional strength to lift him up in weak moments and gently bring him down when he flew too high. Equally important, she developed into a captivating public figure who could work a room better than her husband, which was saying a lot. Marrying her would ultimately stand out as the single best decision of his career. But the early years of their partnership would not all be smooth going, and before their marriage took flight it would come close to crashing.

While the jury remained out on Mila's value as a political wife, Maureen McTeer's early boosters soon began to see her flaws. She would not be an easy spouse for Canadians to like. Unlike Mila, she had not the slightest intention of giving up her career for her husband or keeping her opinions to herself. Whereas Mila understood that there can be only one political leader in a family, Maureen saw it differently. For starters she never became Maureen Clark, neither literally nor figuratively, and that symbolized their differences as much as anything. Her decision to keep her birth name broke new ground for political wives and made it easier for other women to follow in her footsteps — but would later cost Clark support among the core Conservative constituency. She spoke her mind, sometimes lost her composure, and often put people off. She fought public battles — especially feminist ones — and stirred up controversy, but occasionally came across as an unguided missile. The cumulative effect of her behaviour left the impression that Clark could not control his wife. It made him look weak, which, although unfair, was an image he would never really shake. While Mila in time became an enormous asset, Maureen became a liability who would hurt her husband's career.

CHAPTER THIRTEEN

CRIMEBUSTER

DURING HIS FIRST decade in Montreal, Mulroney rarely allowed the depth of his political ambition to surface, and few of his contemporaries suspected that he had the prime-ministerial itch. Apart from close friends like Sam Wakim and Michel Cogger, who had known him since university, most people saw only the successful labour lawyer, who was hooked on politics and loved to dabble in tactics and strategy, who thrived on power and privilege but showed no interest in running for public office.

Once in a while, however, his prime-ministerial ambitions would emerge, mostly in the company of a girlfriend he wanted to impress but occasionally in less-guarded moments. It happened once in the late 1960s at a buffet dinner capping off Power Corporation's annual shareholders' meeting. Mulroney showed up and, as a fledgling executive in the Power Corporation empire, so did Paul Martin Jr. The two of them started to talk, and Mulroney said something Martin would never forget. He declared that he would be prime minister some day, and proclaimed it with such conviction that he left Martin incredulous. Mulroney did not say he wanted to be prime minister, or hoped to be prime minister, but that he *would be* prime minister. His pronouncement carried the tone of inevitability. Martin had heard other people trot out prime-ministerial ambitions, but never like this.

Why Mulroney confided his ultimate ambition to a prominent Liberal is puzzling. Martin, the son of the minister of external affairs, would some day demonstrate prime-ministerial ambitions of his own, and maybe that explained Mulroney's sudden candour. Perhaps he saw the day coming when they would sit opposite each other in Parliament and wanted to establish a fraternity of sorts. Whatever the reason, it was one of a series of isolated incidents that revealed his underlying purpose. Another occurred in 1969 when he and several of his bachelor buddies, Bernard Roy, Jean Bazin, George Archer, and Leon Bailey, went to Mexico for a two-week vacation. While in Mexico City Bazin and Archer got the bright idea of taking a side trip to Cuba, since the Mexican capital had one of the few commercial air links from North America to Havana. It was exactly the kind of adventure that usually excited Mulroney — but not this time. A visit to Cuba, he warned, could come back to haunt them in later life. Canadians — unlike Americans — were not forbidden from visiting the Communist country, but in 1969 it was still frowned upon and Mulroney wanted to keep his political slate clean. So he stayed behind.

Except for incidents like the skipped Cuba trip, the desire to be prime minister rarely surfaced in Mulroney. What most of his contemporaries saw was the breezy charm, the camaraderie, and a passion for fun, not the steely discipline of someone with his eye on a high political prize. He did not come across like Joe Clark, who pursued his political goals openly, single-mindedly, and at the expense of other interests. Mulroney craved influence and success, certainly, always aimed for the highest target, and was seen to be reaching for the top in his career, but still the majority of his friends and acquaintances did not place these aspirations into the prime-ministerial context.

However, there were those outside his inner circle who saw through the façade. Some of Mulroney's colleagues at Ogilvy Cope always figured that some day he would run for Parliament and then reach for the top. Frank Common, a senior partner with Ogilvy

Cope, predicted to his son-in-law as early as 1967 that Mulroney would become prime minister. Robert Cliche, Mulroney's intellectual mentor at Laval, later ribbed him publicly about his ambitions. "Why don't you buy yourself a prime minister?" he once good-naturedly joked to Paul Desmarais in reference to Mulroney. And once at a party at the Ritz-Carlton, Charles Bronfman saw Mulroney and Paul Martin Jr. talking together in a corner. "See those two over there," Bronfman said. "Two future prime ministers."

People who paid attention to Mulroney's career noticed that he had made all the right moves — except for one: he had almost completely failed to make himself a public figure. It was not for lack of trying. Shortly after arriving in Montreal he had applied for a part-time job as host of a new local public affairs television show on CBC called *Seven on Six* (seven o'clock on Channel Six); he made the short list but ultimately lost out to a young journalist named Peter Desbarats. Mulroney had been in the news during the waterfront hearings, and again in the *La Presse* strike, but that kind of spot coverage did not filter down to the man in the street. It seemed clear that to achieve his ambition Mulroney would first have to get himself a seat in the House of Commons, and acquire public standing just as Joe Clark was doing.

During the early seventies people had repeatedly petitioned Mulroney to run for Parliament, but he always declined. Running for Parliament simply did not appeal to him. First, running as a Tory in Quebec was a great risk, and he was not interested in losing. Second, being a backbench member of an opposition party would mean starting over again at the bottom of the ladder, even if it was the House of Commons. Besides, he already had as much access to Stanfield as any MP. Third, he lacked a political agenda; there was no burning idea or set of ideas he wanted to bring into the public arena. Fourth, and most important, he could not countenance the required pay cut: a rookie MP earned a fraction of his salary as a lawyer. He still helped support his mother and now was newly married with a child on the way.

When reduced to the basics, his dilemma was whether to chase money or political office. He could not see how he could have both great wealth and a top-level political career. Money mattered a lot to Mulroney, partly for what it could buy, but even more for what it represented. Money measured one's success. His prosperous lifestyle told the world how far he had come. The conflict endured within him without resolution, and by not choosing he actually sided with the safe option, the acquisition of wealth. When close friends urged him to run for office, he explained that he wanted to build up a nest egg before jumping into the ring. In reality he was temporarily satisfied by his status as a mover and shaker in Montreal.

In January 1973, when his law firm made him a partner at last and gave him better money than ever, his quandary only worsened. The higher he rose at Ogilvy Cope, the harder it became to let go. The super-rich years of a senior partnership were still to come, and yet he could not become leader of the Conservative Party without running for Parliament. The cost of his ambition exceeded the price he was willing to pay, and still the desire burned within. He was caught in a trap.

There seemed little hope for a resolution to Mulroney's dilemma when, in the spring of 1974, events started unfolding to change it all. The sequence began at the massive hydroelectric development at James Bay, which made the far north of Quebec resemble the turn-of-the-century Yukon, with high-paying jobs rather than gold attracting the rush of southerners. Following on their heels was plenty of liquor, smuggling, and a bitter knock-down fight between competing unions for the right to represent these latter-day prospectors. The Fédération des Travailleurs du Québec claimed most of the James Bay jobs, but its rival, the Confederation of National Trade Unions, tried to muscle in. Soon unions from the two umbrella groups started sabotaging each other, and before long the contest grew violent, reaching the stage where one side set fire to a camp to deny rival workers a place to live. Finally on March 21, 1974, the day after Mulroney's thirty-fifth birthday, the warfare crossed the limit for even the wild north when Yvon Duhamel, a business agent for an FTQ local, rammed a bulldozer into one of the James Bay generators, causing a fire and forcing a mass evacuation of the site.

At first both sides blamed the blow-up on worker dissatisfaction, but that lame excuse quickly broke down. Fed up with the shenanigans, Premier Robert Bourassa appointed a royal commission to get to the bottom of the union violence and gave the commission real investigative teeth. Determined to deny his critics the claim of a Liberal whitewash, Bourassa went all out to be non-partisan, picking as chairman Robert Cliche, Mulroney's lovable former law professor and the former leader of the provincial NDP, now a respected judge. Cliche was a demigod of sorts in Quebec, a personage beyond reproach. To avoid charges of union-bashing, Bourassa appointed Guy Chevrette, a leader of the professors' union and known Parti Québécois supporter, to sit alongside Cliche. For the third and final member of the commission Bourassa wanted a representative from management and, with Cliche's recommendation, settled on Brian Mulroney.

Once again Mulroney's network had come through. Mulroney happened to be a buddy of Bourassa's, and the premier was not averse to giving his friend an appointment. Not that Mulroney didn't fit Bourassa's requirements perfectly. He was a Conservative, so the premier couldn't be accused of patronage, and he was a management player whom the unions respected. Since Mulroney had a reputation for negotiating deals that made both employers and unions happy, who better to sit on a commission tackling such an explosive issue? Mulroney's affiliation with the Conservative Party gave the commission perfect non-Liberal political balance — one New Democrat, one Péquiste, and now one Tory. For once in his life being a Conservative in Quebec had worked to Mulroney's advantage.

Ogilvy Cope did not like losing one of its top billers, even if only temporarily, but such a prestigious appointment reflected well on the firm. The senior partners speedily approved a leave of absence with full pay. Mulroney would keep his partner's salary while the firm would collect his $200-a-day stipend from the Quebec Ministry of Justice.

Mulroney took charge of recruiting the commission staff, wasting no time calling up old friends with offers of positions. He immediately phoned Lucien Bouchard, his former confidant from Laval. Brilliant as he was, at the time Bouchard happened to be down on his luck. He had returned home to Chicoutimi to practise law at a respectable firm, but had alienated his colleagues by joining the Parti Québécois and publicly supporting separatism. Now he was practising law alone and struggling. Mulroney, who liked nothing better than bucking up a friend with a favour, offered Bouchard a big fat plum — the post of associate counsel of the Cliche commission. Bouchard accepted on the spot.

Mulroney had rescued Bouchard when he really needed a job — but the favour was far from selfless. Mulroney knew he would need both Bouchard's intellect and his high-minded idealism in the coming battle. Hostile witnesses would be subpoenaed, and some would be stripped of their civil rights and grilled without mercy. The construction wing of the FTQ was going to be kicked around, and Mulroney would have to do some of the kicking. In addition to Bouchard he recruited Paul-Arthur Gendreau — another guiding light from Laval who had influenced him more than any other student except Bouchard. His only rebuff came from Raynold Langlois, another influential brain from Laval, who declined to become the commission's chief counsel. Mulroney tried to coax him with the argument that the exposure from the commission would launch him into a political career, but Langlois, a Liberal, still refused. Nevertheless, Mulroney would be surrounded by his top three intellectual heroes from law school.

The Cliche commission officially got down to work on May 3, 1974, and spent the next four months quietly digging into the events behind the James Bay mess. The picture that began to emerge deeply disturbed the three commissioners and forced them to conclude that the Mafia had infiltrated the construction unions. Now resolved more than ever to clean house, they began to contemplate an extraordinary decision: to shift the burden of proof from the state to the accused. The presumption of guilt contradicts one of the fundamental tenets of the Canadian legal system. Yet the commission's sweeping judicial powers allowed it to force all the witnesses to prove their innocence. The commissioners considered this drastic move only because they feared that without such coercive power they would never be able to expose the full extent of criminal activity.

The three commissioners debated the issue for hours on end. At the outset Chevrette, the union voice, flatly opposed it; Cliche, the judge and former law professor, had strong reservations but straddled the fence; and Mulroney supported it. The fact that organized crime had penetrated deep into Quebec's union structure troubled him, largely because — as he would later explain — the wayward union leaders were setting up a separate system of social standards. The legal or philosophical issues simply did not concern him nearly as much as the need for abnormal measures — because "a cancer had to be excised." So persuasively did he argue his case that ultimately he brought both Cliche and Chevrette around. The three commissioners unanimously agreed to place the burden of proof on those who were accused of wrongdoing.

The commissioners also approved a broad wiretapping program called "Operation Raymond." The wiretaps unveiled new horrors and underlined their worst fears. They provided evidence that union warlords had forced workers to join a particular union at gunpoint, and that votes at union meetings had been taken with guns on the table. There were tales of union leaders extorting as much as 25 per cent of a worker's weekly wage. Later one gruesome story emerged of a union official going out to beat up a rival and, not finding him there, beating up his fourteen-year-old son instead — badly enough to put him in hospital for a week — and strangling his dog. "It curled my hair in every way," Mulroney would later tell the CBC's Barbara Frum.

Before formal hearings started in September 1974, the commissioners made perhaps their most important and smartest decision:

they threw the whole process wide open to the public and welcomed media coverage. So through the fall of 1974 and early months of 1975, the Quebec public was treated to a rivetting daily soap opera. The hearings were carried live on the province-wide cable television system, every morning Quebec newspapers replayed the events on their front pages, and every evening the 6:00 television news opened with highlights from the day's proceedings. Soon the whole province was hooked and outraged. One witness, the victim of a loan-sharking racket in which he ended up owing $1,800 on a $75 loan, had to testify from behind a screen. No sooner had the public absorbed one horror than it got hit with another. Even supermarket tabloids could not compete. Quebeckers had never seen anything like it.

The steady stream of jolts did not flow so swiftly, so consistently, and so dramatically by accident. Almost every shock was stage-managed. Witnesses were pre-interviewed by investigators before going under the lights, and the commissioners always knew what revelation was coming next, timing it for maximum impact. A successful royal commission influences public opinion, and the Cliche commissioners made that their primary goal. The hearings were geared to the daily media feed. "We were supposed to ask our good questions before the deadlines," Lucien Bouchard later told L. Ian MacDonald. If Bouchard got long-winded in front of a deadline he would look up and "see Brian or Cliche pointing at his watch."

The man orchestrating this publicity campaign was none other than Mulroney. He leaked stories shamelessly and would often call up a particular reporter just before deadline with a few extra nuggets to give him an edge on the competition. The next day he would do the same favour for the reporter who had lost out the day before. He loved to take a reporter confidentially aside for a little tête-à-tête, soliciting his views on what the commission should do next, then offering some inside information. He often gave a journalist a preview of upcoming events and got him to sit on the news until he gave the signal. When *Le Devoir* reporter Louis-Gilles Francoeur was about to break a story the commission knew nothing about,

Mulroney persuaded Francoeur to hold off until the commission could investigate, and then returned the favour by leaking him a far bigger story. He had mastered the art of making deals with the media, and the reporters liked him for it. They found him a reliable source, straight up, and always true to his word. This cosiness with the press epitomized the way Mulroney liked to operate: everybody came out looking better — the commission, each individual reporter, and of course Mulroney himself.

Mulroney acted as the commission's troubleshooter. Whenever a problem arose behind the scenes — whether a witness was griping, or a police officer sulking, or a reporter jumping the gun — Cliche would always nod to Mulroney and ask him to look into it. A little later Mulroney would return saying everything had been settled.

The hearings adjourned each day at 5 P.M., and the commissioners retreated under police escort from the hearing room in the Quebec Safety Board building on Parthenais Street to their working headquarters in the Queen Elizabeth Hotel. Nothing made them happier than finishing the day with a star witness. After pouring a couple of scotches, they watched themselves on the supper-hour television news, then started sifting through the incoming evidence for next day's show, a process that usually lasted late into the night. Then, since most members of the commission came from out of town, they retired to their rooms in the Queen Elizabeth. Except for the public hearings themselves, they ate, slept, and worked on their police-protected floor. As a Montrealer, Mulroney went home each night, but always with a bodyguard. The police slept in his house and accompanied Mila and him everywhere. "I developed a very healthy respect for some of these fellows," Mulroney would later tell Barbara Frum, "in a fearful sort of way."

For those confined to the hearing room and the hotel, the regimen was reminiscent of a boarding school. The commission was implicating some tough characters and had received threats, so it was taking no chances. But one evening Cliche and his wife slipped off to a movie to escape the strain. "What is playing?" he asked the young girl at the

256

ticket booth. "*Ne bouger pas s'il vous plaît*" (Don't move please). Cliche froze. A look of terror crossed his face — until he realized the girl had given him the title of the movie and not a security warning.

The fear and stress the commissioners felt never showed up in the hearing room. If they showed anything it was strength and defiance. Here Mulroney had a platform and a chance to shine, and usually he took full advantage of it. At times he would sit back in his seat and let Cliche or Chevrette take the spotlight. Other times he seemed hardly able to sit still, his body radiating energy and his eyes darting around the room. When the commission caught corrupt union officials red-handed Mulroney would pounce, firing off a round of moralizing questions often followed with a punchy speech. The other two commissioners knew how to milk a scene too, but Mulroney was the best. He gave off the right combination of outrage and integrity and was clearly the most exciting performer. It didn't hurt that Mulroney spoke smooth, colloquial Quebec French. When an Anglo testified in less-than-perfect French, the Québécois reporters covering the hearings would nod and smile knowingly to one another. This never happened when Mulroney was talking. They regarded him as another francophone, as one of them.

In only one area did he restrain himself: invariably he went easy on the business leaders who took the stand, calling them "sir" and treating them with visible deference. He maintained this attitude even though evidence emerged that management had often made sweetheart deals with the FTQ, or at least turned a blind eye to its corruption.

As the commission burrowed deeper into the seamy underside of construction union life, it unearthed what seemed to be a connection between the construction wing of the FTQ and the Quebec Liberal Party. Eventually the link led all the way into the premier's office. Paul Desrochers, the premier's top aide, testified that he had asked André Desjardins, a notorious FTQ construction despot, to maintain peace and order during a by-election in Sept-Îles. This was at the same time that the government was in the process of granting the FTQ a ten-year union monopoly in James Bay. It looked like a clear exchange of favours — a government concession in return for political help from the union, which would be illegal.

This revelation shifted the attention of the commission from union thuggery to how much the government, including Premier Bourassa, knew. The sense of political intrigue heightened when testimony from Minister of Justice Jerôme Choquette contradicted an earlier claim by Bourassa of ignorance about a case of influence-peddling by a civil servant. For a while it looked like Bourassa would be called to take the stand, a spectacle that would surely embarrass him and might destroy him.

L. Ian MacDonald, in *Mulroney: The Making of the Prime Minister*, succinctly describes what happened next: "The question of whether the premier of Quebec could, and should, be summoned before the Cliche inquiry had precipitated a major crisis within the commission. In an argument that went on for several evenings, Mulroney made it perfectly clear to his colleagues that if they insisted on issuing a subpoena to the premier, he, Mulroney, would quit. This set him on a collision course with his close friend Bouchard, by now the commission's chief counsel. 'My plan was to put Bourassa in the box,' Bouchard acknowledged. 'It was the logical follow-up to Choquette.'" Commissioner Chevrette favoured issuing Bourassa a subpoena, and Cliche once again took a neutral position.

Mulroney, a traditionalist who believed in executive privilege, took it upon himself to protect Bourassa. He felt that an elected figure like the premier should not have to account to an appointed body like the Cliche commission. Nor did he think it right to put Bourassa in the same witness box as union thugs. "I just said absolutely no, that this was improper, that that was in excess of the jurisdiction of the commission," Mulroney told MacDonald, "and that I had no intention of going along with that request under any circumstances." In the end Cliche sided with Mulroney, and by a vote of two to one the commission decided to pass on Bourassa as a witness. Mulroney had thus done the premier a favour he would not likely forget.

The Bourassa flap came and went, and the commission continued to dredge up shocking revelations. After a run of eighty hearing days and 279 witnesses, the show that had started in the fall of 1974 finally dropped the curtain in March 1975, then produced a six-hundred-page report on May 2, 1975, that got high marks for being hard-hitting, far-reaching, and courageous. When pressed by reporters, Cliche confidently predicted that Quebec City would accept the findings. How could he be so sure, journalists asked. "I just know," Cliche grinned.

Just as Cliche predicted, in no time at all Bourassa announced broad changes along the lines recommended by the report. Among other things, the commission recommended a restructuring of the Construction Industry Commission, creating a strong and unified management body, and placing four union locals in trusteeship. Once again Mulroney's deft hand behind the scenes had achieved the desired result. During the course of the hearings Mulroney had often jumped aboard a government aircraft for a quick hop to Quebec City and an evening parley with the premier. While the commission thrashed out its final report, he consulted more closely than ever and nailed down Bourassa's agreement in advance. The report criticized the government hard enough to be credible and to make an impact, but not so hard that Bourassa would reject it. Mulroney had brokered the deal in his classic style.

By all accounts the Cliche commission had executed its mandate well and been a major success, but only at considerable cost to civil liberties. Such a soap opera could not happen under today's Charter of Rights and Freedoms. No commission could haul suspects into the witness box and, under the threat of jail, force them to incriminate themselves in front of television cameras. The process flagrantly violated the rights of an accused and the right to privacy. The Cliche commission was a show trial in the guise of a public inquiry. Nonetheless, there was no question that it had performed a valuable public service in exposing a nasty underside of Quebec trade unionism and purging the FTQ of its Mafia element.

Remarkably, through it all Mulroney had managed to preserve his friendship with Louis Laberge, the head of the FTQ. The Cliche commission's report treated the FTQ brutally for what had gone on in its construction wing and made life dreadful for Laberge, but Mulroney and Laberge got along as well as ever.

Quebeckers who had followed the Cliche commission came away with the impression that the provincial Liberals were a gang of crooks in league with a gang of thugs. Bourassa had acted honestly and was personally untouched by the scandal, but he came through as weak and naïve. Combined with other sins, that would cost him dearly when the voters unceremoniously threw him out of office the following year. (The night of Bourassa's defeat Mulroney phoned to give him his heartfelt sympathy and tell him not to despair, that there would be another day.) Robert Cliche would suffer a worse fate. Three years after the commission delivered its report, a heart attack would strike him dead — he was worn down, some people would say, by the after-effects of the constant stress, late hours, and unrelenting pace of the commission.

Most of the other players went on to prosper. Guy Chevrette, the trade union commissioner, was elected to the Quebec national assembly in the same election Bourassa lost; he would eventually become a cabinet minister in René Lévesque's government and a senior Parti Québécois figure. Lucien Bouchard became the Lévesque government's chief negotiator with its public servants. Others did well too, but nobody would ride the coat-tails of the Cliche commission farther than Mulroney. The commission transformed his political prospects and resolved his political dilemma.

It takes talent, ambition, hard work, and discipline to become prime minister, but more than anything it takes luck, one crucial turning-point to break open the way. The Cliche commission gave Mulroney exactly that kind of boost. By putting him on the front page every morning and on the 6:00 news every evening, it made him a celebrity to the man in the street, with an image as a clean, heroic investigator rooting out union corruption. An aspiring politician could not wish for a better public profile. Mulroney would profit from many lucky breaks over his career, but never one that advanced him farther in one shot. The Cliche commission cleared the big obstacle in his path. Now he could leapfrog over the usual House of Commons apprenticeship in order to reach for the top political prize.

One night shortly after the Cliche hearings had ended, Mulroney bumped into Bill Devine in the shopping concourse beneath Place Ville-Marie. Devine, a St. FX schoolmate he hadn't seen in years, remembered him as a can't-miss politician from his Model Parliament days, and asked when he was getting into politics. "When the time is right," Mulroney replied.

CHAPTER FOURTEEN

THE CADILLAC CANDIDATE

MULRONEY'S INVOLVEMENT WITH the Cliche commission had forced him to sit out the July 1974 election, the first federal contest he had missed in two decades. Despite high expectations it turned into a disaster for Robert Stanfield and the Tories, who won only 95 seats against 141 for the Liberals. In Quebec the Liberals took 60 seats, the Conservatives 3. After coming achingly close in 1972, the Conservatives faced another bleak term on the wrong side of the aisle in the House of Commons. Almost immediately rumblings began in the grassroots and in the Tory caucus that after three losses it was time for Stanfield to go.

In August 1974, a month after the election, Stanfield invited his closest advisers to Stornoway and asked for their advice: should he quit as Tory leader or hang on? All but one urged him to stay. Stanfield was not eager to bow out on a losing note, but after reflecting for a few days he concluded that now was the time to withdraw. Unlike Diefenbaker, he had too much grace to cling to his job over growing opposition. Accordingly he notified the party and country that he was stepping down as Tory leader.

Pat MacAdam, Mulroney's first friend at St. FX, who was now part-owner and operator of a double-decker-bus sightseeing tour company in Ottawa, happened to be in his kitchen when the news flashed over the radio. "I hope Bones goes for it," he told himself, and he immediately called Mulroney in Montreal to tell him so. However, the Cliche commission's public hearings would begin in a few weeks — and Mulroney was locked in. Other old friends broached the idea too, but Mulroney always shrugged it off, and not just out of duty. "Our time is not yet," Mulroney told Peter White. "There is going to be one more leader and then it will be our time." Mulroney, only thirty-five, had never held public office, and the celebrity of the Cliche soap opera was still ahead of him. The notion of his jumping into the leadership race was outlandish.

However, by July 1975, when the Conservatives finally got around to setting the convention date for February 1976, the situation had changed dramatically. The public hearings were over and Mulroney was now a star — in Quebec. At least one observer saw him as a natural contender. "So the Tories have finally set a date to send off Robert Stanfield," *Vancouver Sun* columnist Allan Fotheringham wrote the day after the convention date was announced. "The new leader of the party will turn out to be, next February, one Brian Mulroney, a young Montreal lawyer with the gift of the gab who was a former aide to Davie Fulton and is now on the Cliche Commission. Remember, you read it here last." Fotheringham had never met Mulroney, but word of him had reached his ears in Vancouver.

Fotheringham aside, nobody in the media was touting Mulroney, and the party biggies in Ottawa did not include him on their short list. When speculation turned to the subject of Stanfield's replacement, very few people threw out his name. Still, the race was wide open. Stanfield's caucus had produced no heir apparent. The only strong contender was Premier Peter Lougheed of Alberta, who could have had the job for the asking but appeared uninterested. Yet there was no shortage of pretenders who had been positioning themselves and testing support in the year since Stanfield had announced his intention to resign. Soon they would have to come out into the open and declare themselves.

Mulroney immediately found himself fielding calls from friends urging him to go for it. Sam Wakim, who back in the fall of 1955 had been more responsible than anyone for making him a Tory in the first place, became one of the first to twist his arm. "Look," Wakim counselled him over lunch at the Beaver Club, "this is the right time. There's an opening here. These things are generational. You better take a good assessment and start to think about it." Jean Bazin also urged him to chase the federal leadership. Bazin had spent the last year seriously considering the idea of taking over the Union Nationale, renaming it the Quebec Conservative Party, and persuading Mulroney to become leader (Mulroney had shown no enthusiasm for running provincially). Others in the Mulroney network also urged him to jump in, including Jean Lesage and Robert Cliche. The friend pushing hardest of all was Michel Cogger, who made Mulroney's candidacy his personal mission.

Mulroney downplayed all the overtures. He had just come off a year-long leave from his law firm and could not reasonably expect his partners to indulge him with more salaried time off so he could tilt at political windmills. Nonetheless, he didn't close any doors. And late in June his political stock rose considerably when he appeared as a guest on Barbara Frum's summer television show on CBC. The network wanted five minutes on the Quebec construction scandal, but Mulroney told the stories from the Cliche commission so colourfully that the network let him roll for half an hour. It made great television, garnering favourable reviews and a ton of viewer mail. It had also given him priceless prime-time exposure across the country.

That summer, as Tories everywhere speculated about who would ultimately show up in the ring, an old friend suddenly re-entered Mulroney's life. Don McDougall, president of Labatt Breweries, happened to be driving through Quebec en route to Sept-Îles when he and his passengers started reviewing potential candidates. McDougall said the party needed somebody young and fresh, and the more he surveyed the field, the more he liked the man who had recruited him into the party in the first place. McDougall had been part of a St. Dunstan's championship debating team that had lost to the team of Rick Cashin and Mulroney, representing St. FX, in Charlottetown in 1958. A snowstorm had postponed the debate twenty-four hours. On the night it was supposed to have been held, McDougall and his partner entertained their St. FX guests by bringing a case of beer into their hotel room and spending the evening swapping stories. When it was over, McDougall, a Liberal if anything, was a Tory thanks to Mulroney, and would remain one for life. Now, seventeen years later, as McDougall drove through the Quebec countryside, he settled on Mulroney as the party's answer to the future, having no idea that he was not the first to think of it. The more he thought about it, the more sense it made, until finally he stopped in Baie Comeau, of all places, and phoned Mulroney in Montreal to arrange lunch for the express purpose of leaning on him to run.

The following Friday Mulroney heard McDougall out, then spent part of the weekend at Michel Cogger's country house in the Eastern Townships with Mila and one-year-old Caroline. It was a beautiful summer Sunday, and while the wives supervised their kids in the baby pool, Mulroney and Cogger took a stroll in the countryside and talked Tory leadership. Once again Cogger urged him to go for it, but this time Mulroney revealed a strong reason to do otherwise. The Iron Ore Company of Canada, an American-owned company operating two huge open-pit mines in Quebec and Labrador, was offering to make him its executive vice-president while grooming him to become president in a year or so. The company was talking big money, and once again the allure of wealth seemed likely to win out over political ambition. Mulroney had wanted to be prime minister, but this deal would fix him up for life. It seemed too good to ignore.

Cogger acknowledged that the offer sounded great, but what was the rush? The Iron Ore job would not go anywhere while he ran for the leadership, but the post of party leader would wait for nobody. Cogger advised him to declare his candidacy and give the leadership race a good shot, establish himself as a contender for next time, and then take the Iron Ore job and wait for the next leadership contest in five or ten years.

Mulroney gave Cogger little encouragement but agreed to think it over yet again. Nor did he object when Cogger proposed to start testing the level of support for a Mulroney candidacy. Cogger went away relieved. At least he had stopped his friend from rushing headlong into the Iron Ore job.

Meanwhile McDougall had launched his own parallel scouting drive and was busily phoning friends from coast to coast. Before long he and Cogger had teamed up, dividing the phone calls between them and comparing notes every Sunday at 5 P.M. Although Cogger and McDougall were officially only testing the waters, both were behaving more like salesmen than disinterested pollsters. They received lots of encouragement and nobody told them they were out of their minds, although the notion of Mulroney as party leader had not previously clicked in the heads of a lot of people. A few weeks later McDougall reported back to Mulroney that while he would not win, neither would he be embarrassed. He predicted a third-place finish, which for someone virtually unknown outside Quebec who had never been elected to anything seemed a highly optimistic assessment.

While he did not want to be seen to be chasing the crown, Mulroney had started warming up to the idea of running. Playing the role of the reluctant candidate catered to his need for adoration, and it also helped him deduce just how far people were willing to go on his behalf. But his reticence was more than merely tactical. He did not like taking chances now any more than he had as a student politician. He had not risked an election since leaving St. FX in 1959 and he still recoiled at the prospect of defeat. But this time nobody expected him to win, not even Cogger and McDougall, who were pushing him to run. Still, he had to be sure he would not fall flat on his face and be embarrassed. Above everything else, he wanted to avoid ridicule, not only for the sake of his own ego but for his political future.

Despite the encouragement from Cogger and McDougall, he still questioned whether he could make a credible showing. Could a backroom boy who had never even run for Parliament appeal to a broad spectrum of the party? Before going any further he wanted his own reading from his own network. So while Cogger and McDougall continued taking soundings and hatching plans, Mulroney, the consummate networker himself, got on the telephone and, being both casual and systematic, started taking his own soundings to see whether he had enough credibility and enough of a national base for a serious run. It was a big step for a thirty-six-year-old and he wanted to be thorough.

Not everyone responded enthusiastically. When Michel Cogger first asked Lowell Murray, he said, "Aw shit, the man is not ready." Murray put it somewhat more diplomatically when Mulroney called him personally. Murray told him flatly to stay out of the race, saying he could not win and would find the whole thing bruising and hurtful. Coming from one of Mulroney's earliest political heroes, this warning did nothing to calm his fears, nor did it bode well for their friendship. Neither did the report from Richard Holden, one of the hubs in his Montreal network, whom he asked to sniff around on his behalf. Holden encountered a lot of people who, like Murray, did not think Mulroney was ready; he wrote him an affectionate note saying that he and his wife wanted him to do whatever he thought best.

But the more Mulroney thought about it, and the more he networked, the less he worried about being embarrassed and the more the notion of running grew on him. It was not just the romantic idea of leading a great campaign; two other forces drove him. One of them was named Claude Wagner, and the other was named Joe Clark.

Wagner had not declared yet but was clearly gearing up. Anybody could see it. Despite his failure as the Quebec strongman, he was picking up support at an alarming rate and showing every sign of dominating the pack. Wagner's emergence as the man to beat made no sense until one looked at the convention arithmetic. Quebec accounted for only three Conservative MPs, but only Ontario would send more delegates to Ottawa. And while Ontario and the West would each spread their votes among several candidates, Quebec would do its tribal dance and deliver almost all its votes to Wagner. (Heward Grafftey, another Quebec MP, would be running too but would get only a handful of delegates.) The Quebec bloc gave Wagner such a big head start that he might be unstoppable. The thought of Wagner taking over as leader of the Conservative Party was enough to make Mulroney choke. Nothing but poison flowed between these former allies. Mulroney figured that the last three years had shown Wagner unfit to lead the Conservative Party, or any party for that matter.

Wagner had proved to be as bad an MP as he was a campaigner. After the 1972 election he had behaved as if he regretted ever leaving the bench. He became moody and morose, withdrawing into himself and often causing trouble in the caucus, a constant thorn in Stanfield's side. As well as being vain and venomous in his dealings with anyone who rubbed him the wrong way, he was lazy and dominated by his wife. Speaking invitations from across the country would pour into his Ottawa office and he routinely turned them down. The party almost had to dynamite him out of the capital, assuring him in advance that the troops would be lined up and waiting to prostrate themselves before him. Otherwise he refused to lift a finger for a party that was dying for a French-Canadian saviour. The minimum grassroots politicking would have turned the upcoming convention into a cakewalk for Wagner. Instead he behaved as if the leadership were his by divine right.

As Mulroney contemplated his prospects the importance of saving the party from Wagner grew.

"Brian, you can't possibly win," Richard Holden had warned him.

"I know," Mulroney answered, "but I've got to stop Wagner."

"You're a little late to figure that one out," Holden replied, referring to the fact that he had created the monster in the first place.

"I know," Mulroney acknowledged, "but I've got to stop him."

The fact that he had worked so hard to recruit somebody with obvious leadership ambitions of his own had now come back to haunt him. But it was too late to undo the past. As a fellow Quebecker Mulroney believed that only he could siphon off enough delegates from Wagner's Quebec base to pull him back into the pack. Jules Lesage, son of the former premier, even offered to dig up dirt on Wagner, presumably in retaliation for all the frustration Wagner had caused his father as a member of the Lesage cabinet. "Anything you want on Wagner," he promised Mulroney, "we'll give it to you."

The other catalyst was the news that Joe Clark was sounding out his own leadership prospects. If Mulroney's chances appeared far-fetched, Clark's seemed almost laughable. Yet whereas Mulroney was coyly leaving the drum-beating mostly to others, as soon as the date for the convention was set Clark had begun blatantly beating his own. After meeting with Peter Lougheed and being assured that the Alberta premier would not enter the race, Clark called his most likely supporters to a July 30 meeting at the Bristol Place Hotel in Toronto. Fourteen people arrived; aside from Clark himself and Maureen, only MPs Allan McKinnon and Harvie Andre thought he should get into the contest. A few sat on the fence, but most of the rest were leaning towards other candidates and would consider Clark only in the event their first choice stayed out. The group of naysayers included Michel Cogger and Jean Bazin, both of whom openly declared their first allegiance to Mulroney, saying they were urging him to run. The mention of Mulroney drew some snickers. "Aw, come on, Cogger," somebody cracked, "you can't be serious. He is not even a member of Parliament." Clark, who was taking notes, cut off the snickering. "If Brian decided to run," Clark said matter-of-factly, "he'd be a very formidable opponent." As usual, Clark was showing more charity to Mulroney than vice versa. Mulroney still felt superior to Clark and, like a lot of others, did not take his candidacy seriously. For his part, Clark respected Mulroney's abilities and never knocked him but felt he had no business running for leader. He shared Lowell Murray's assessment that Mulroney lacked a grasp of the issues and did not know the country well enough.

By now Mulroney was close enough to running to call on a friend for a special favour. He had been close to David Angus ever since they had been fellow lawyers at the Picard hearings, where Angus had represented the stevedoring contractors and Mulroney the shipowners. Mulroney reached Angus at his country place in Magog, Quebec. "Goose," Mulroney said, "I want you to come to town." Angus protested that a long weekend had just begun and the last place he wanted to be was in the city. Mulroney assured him it was important and Angus grudgingly agreed.

Over lunch at the Beaver Club, Mulroney recruited Angus as his fundraiser, dismissing his friend's protests about having no experience at that sort of thing. He promised to introduce him to the likes of Paul Desmarais and Earle McLaughlin of the Royal Bank, and a host of lesser potential contributors. Angus's first assignment was to raise money for a week-long trip Mulroney and Cogger were making to western Canada in October so they could feel the mood and drum up support. Mulroney gave Angus a list of names to call, and a few days later a cheque for $500 arrived. It came from Terry McCann, the lawyer in Pembroke, Ontario, whom Mulroney had once informally tutored in debating technique while they were students together at St. FX. It was one of the thousand favours he had performed over the years, seemingly for the pleasure of it. Many more cheques would soon arrive. Angus had no trouble raising the money needed for the Western swing.

Before going out to the West Mulroney planned to stop off in Toronto on October 15 and speak to the prestigious Empire Club. The invitation had been arranged by Sam Wakim, now a Toronto lawyer, and promised to be a big step for him. For the first time Mulroney was sticking out his neck in public. He gave the whole thing a push the day before by telling Richard Cleroux of the *Globe and Mail* that he was making the speech to sniff out his prospects, and the paper reacted the next morning with a front-page story touting Mulroney's appearance as a major PC leadership event.

The *Globe and Mail* story had turned the speech into a campaign spectacle. Reporters flocked in to look over the latest potential contender. Mulroney responded with an engrossing and thoughtful talk about his experiences at the Cliche commission and the decay of the rule of law in the country. "Good laws are of little value unless they are enforced," he said. "Non-enforcement is an insidious thing because it breeds a gentle but progressive suspicion in the minds of the governed that a statute need not apply at all, that exceptions can be made, that demonstrations can supplant debate, that Parliament is in fact somewhat less than supreme." Cleverly modulating this theme, he closed with a suggestive call for renewed national leadership by those who "respect Parliament and its institutions." He won over both his business audience and the press. "He touched all the right nerve ends," *Maclean's* editor Peter C. Newman remarked afterwards. That night the local Toronto television newscasts gave him nearly five minutes of coverage — an amazing length for television news — and one station said he combined the oratorical flair of John Diefenbaker with the wit of William F. Buckley. His Western tour could not have gotten off to a better start. Now the whole country had started looking him over.

By the time Mulroney reached Vancouver on October 24, the press had started treating him as a declared candidate. *Le Devoir, Montréal Matin,* the *Montreal Star,* and the *Montreal Gazette* had all started to feature him. In Vancouver he met with some of the leading Tory lights, addressed a group of businessmen, and gave an interview to Allan Fotheringham, who gave him his stamp of approval. Mulroney, Fotheringham wrote, was the "suddenly interesting factor in the four-month stretch run to inherit Mr. Standstill's limp crown." Edmonton — where Don McDougall had opened doors — Calgary, and Regina all went well. (Mulroney pointedly skipped Manitoba because a vicious provincial leadership battle had split the party in two, and winning the support of one side would only alienate the other.)

Although Mulroney returned to Montreal with the decision all but made for him, he still hesitated. By now (the end of October) all the name candidates had declared or were about to, and to Mulroney's eye they did not make up a particularly distinguished field: Heward Grafftey, the lonely Quebec MP, who entered the race first and would finish dead last; Flora MacDonald, one of the reddest of the Red Tories; John Fraser, the favourite son from British Columbia; Sinclair Stevens, the right-wing businessman from Toronto; Paul Hellyer, the disaffected former Trudeau cabinet minister; Jack Horner, the Alberta rancher who was seen as Diefenbaker's stalking-horse; Jim Gillies, the academic economist from Toronto; Patrick Nowlan, a regional candidate from Nova Scotia who leaned to the right; and of course Joe Clark and Claude Wagner.

Knowing how Mulroney felt about the competition, Michel Cogger had taken to going down the list of contenders and comparing their qualifications with his. Half the list — Wagner, MacDonald, Stevens, Gillies, Fraser, and Clark — came from Ottawa's class of '72 and had spent fewer than three years in the House of Commons. Mulroney felt superior to them all, but the mention of Clark stirred him up the most. He knew that despite Clark's wobbly start, he had kept persevering and appeared to be gaining ground.

Still he wanted one more reading. So he instructed Cogger to arrange a meeting of core supporters at the Bristol Place Hotel in Toronto. It was now late October and about thirty people showed up, representing every province including tiny P.E.I. McDougall and Charley McMillan came from Ontario, Don Hamilton from B.C. Newfoundland produced two sitting cabinet ministers, Bill Doody, the minister of finance, and Joe Rousseau, the minister of transportation. (Frank Moores, the premier, would come aboard later.) Representing Nova Scotia was lawyer Stewart McInnes, who had boarded an airplane in Halifax the day before only to meet his law partner George Cooper on the same flight. "Where the hell are you going?" Cooper asked. To a meeting in Toronto with Brian Mulroney, he replied. Thereupon Cooper revealed that he was flying to Toronto for exactly the same kind of meeting with Joe Clark — also at the Bristol Place. Of the thousands of hotels in the country, the Clark and the Mulroney teams picked the same hotel in the same city at the same time for their organizational powwows. When the two camps arrived for their respective meetings the next morning they found themselves in adjacent rooms, plotting strategy on opposite sides of the same wall, and bumping into each other on trips to the washroom and during breaks. The hallway, and particularly the hotel bar afterwards, looked like a reunion of the PC Student Federation of the 1960s.

On November 13, 1975, after testing the water for three months, Mulroney finally took the plunge. He had put the Iron Ore offer on hold and taken an extended leave from his law firm. "I undertake this challenge with confidence I am in this race to stay," he told a press conference in the Queen Elizabeth Hotel. "I am in this race to win." His ubiquitous network, built up over twenty years, had come together to launch him as a candidate. He declared his candidacy with support from both the party élite and the rank and file.

By the time Mulroney declared, the serious candidates officially in the race were Clark, Fraser, Grafftey, Horner, MacDonald, Nowlan, and Stevens. Wagner, Hellyer, and Gillies soon joined the long list of hopefuls. (Dr. R.C. Quittenton, the eccentric president of St. Clair College in Windsor, would become a candidate too and then withdraw the day before the vote.) It was a crowded field and Mulroney's quest seemed a touch quixotic, but no more than that of at least half the others. The *Toronto Star* gave him a one-in-ten chance of winning.

However, there was one area where Mulroney was at least the equal of the other candidates: the ability to raise money. Now that he had formally announced, the contributions began to pour in. And David Angus proved himself a most proficient fundraiser, not only in loosening other people's purse-strings but in assembling a team of bagmen across the country. "Just remember," Angus told his local fundraisers, "the slogan is MINO." Angus pronounced it "minnow" but meant M-I-N-O, as in Money Is No Object. MINO was not only a slogan but an ethic, and nobody — from those who raised the money to those who spent it — spared any expense. MINO meant spending whatever was needed, no matter what it took. The high-rolling Angus machine gave Mulroney all the money he would need to get started.

The networks Mulroney had built over the years gave him the resources to build a credible national organization and finance a campaign, but finding delegates was another matter. He had dithered too long, especially for Quebec support. By November most of the Quebec delegates were safely tucked into Wagner's pocket, ostensibly destroying Mulroney's strategy for undermining his candidacy. In fact Wagner had conquered Quebec so completely that Mulroney himself was shut out as a delegate, although for that he really had only himself to blame. Expecting to be named a provincial delegate-at-large, Mulroney had not bothered to run at the delegate-selection meeting in his Westmount riding, where he would have been easily elected, only to discover later that Wagner had locked him out at the provincial council. The fact that he could not vote at the convention did not disqualify him as a candidate, but it embarrassed him mightily. Although he raised a stink at what he considered dirty tactics, he had no grounds for appeal. Mulroney, the ultimate backroom organizer, had been outmanoeuvred by Wagner in the backrooms of Quebec. Of all the things Wagner ever did to him, this one incensed him the most.

With Quebec pretty much settled and out of reach, Mulroney turned quickly to the other provinces, where the majority of delegates were still uncommitted. He set off on a long and arduous tour, meeting mostly small groups of delegates in semi-private receptions, often in small communities. No professional handlers cleared his path. No entourage travelled with him — just his young aide Stephen Leopold and usually a local Mulroney organizer to meet them. Sometimes a reporter or two would tag along for a few days and then drop off. At this point Wagner was the clear frontrunner; after him the field remained wide open.

The biggest strike against Mulroney was his lack of parliamentary experience. In fact he had more political experience than half the candidates, but neither his long years toiling behind the scenes for the party in Quebec nor all the favourable publicity from the Cliche commission could hide this blemish. He did not belong to that private club called the Conservative caucus, and now he was dismissed as an outsider, an opportunist, even a kind of arriviste. The elected MPs did not like outsiders who tried to take the short cut into their exclusive enclave. As far as most of them were concerned, he had a lot of gall to run for party leader without ever having run in an election, and not a single Tory caucus member supported him when he declared. (Later, when his fortunes improved, MPs Jim McGrath and Heath Macquarrie would fall in behind him.) The other ten candidates — nine sitting MPs and one former MP — continually took shots at his audacity. "Would you go to sea on a ship with a skipper who's never been off the land?" Patrick Nowlan asked an all-candidates meeting in Halifax. Again and again Mulroney would run into his lack of a parliamentary record and have to defend himself, saying, "But Robert Stanfield was not a member of the House of Commons when he became national leader. . . . Neither was Mackenzie King." He repeatedly pointed out that most of the other contenders had little parliamentary experience and would lamely add, "We all have our handicaps. What can I say, except it's true — I've never been elected."

His youth also worked against him, as did the fact that the bulk of his political experience came from Quebec, which was out of the party mainstream. But apart from his lack of parliamentary experience, his biggest weakness was policy. He essentially had none. Patterning himself on a long-time hero, Mulroney projected himself as a Kennedyesque figure — a vigorous and articulate representative of a new generation, who was successful outside public life. He had the image down cold but came across a little glib and short on substance. At the same time he played heavily on his hard-hat upbringing, talking frequently about how people in the real world of time clocks and lunch-boxes had trouble meeting monthly payments to the finance company. His speeches contained a lot of clichés and buzzwords, but his only real theme — which he kept repeating ad nauseam — was that the country was in danger of becoming a "one-party state" under the succession of Liberal governments unless the Conservative Party got leadership that could win. In town after town he would start off his talk by telling delegates that he would beat Pierre Trudeau in the next election.

But if Mulroney had weaknesses, so did all the others, and as the campaign unfolded in late November it soon grew apparent that none of the name candidates was catching fire. Most of them did not speak French, nor did they work much magic on the stump. All had well-known flaws. Flora MacDonald had too many old enemies from the Diefenbaker wars and leaned too far to the left at a time when the country was shifting right; and the party did not seem quite ready for a woman leader. Sinclair Stevens had a solid core of committed supporters but leaned too far to the right to be able to capture the centre. Paul Hellyer could not overcome his turncoat image. And so it went. All had some unsightly scar that disfigured their public visage.

The only candidate who continued to stand above this lacklustre crowd was Claude Wagner, thanks to the mystique of Quebec and to his huge bloc of delegates. With the bulk of Quebec's delegates sewn up, he needed only a little momentum to go over the top. Instead he was absolutely failing to consolidate his lead. He was campaigning poorly, and the trust fund rumours had now resurfaced more strongly than ever. Wagner could not seem to put the issue to rest. Despite his unequivocal disclaimer in 1972 that no money had been involved in his decision to run for the Tories, the media remained sceptical. The worried look on his face only fuelled the speculation. It did not help that Wagner struck people as having a shady quality. There was something slightly sinister about him that unnerved even some of his defenders. With the frontrunner so widely distrusted, some sort of coalition seemed likely to spring up against him. If not, some Tories felt the party would knock off the front-runner simply out of its normal urge for self-destruction. So despite Wagner's lead, as the year drew to a close the race was still wide open and it looked as though anyone who stitched together the right coalition could win.

The failure of the name candidates to generate any excitement or momentum helped the dark horses, particularly Mulroney and Clark. Among the lesser-knowns, Mulroney packed the most star quality. Just the fact that he sparkled on television gave him a leg up on the others. Young, handsome, charismatic, impeccably bilingual, with a beautiful wife and a remarkable private career, a doer rather than a professional politician, with the glow of the Cliche commission behind him — he was quite a contrast to Stanfield and looked like he had the stuff to lead the party on to victory. The same charm that had scored friends for him in the backrooms all these years now helped him snare delegates on the campaign tour. Once delegates got past his lack of parliamentary experience, they saw many of the qualities they were looking for.

As always, he came across best in a small group, with his remarkable ability to command a room. At one campaign stop Mulroney had lunch with about twenty-five senior British Columbia businessmen in the Hotel Vancouver. The audience was made up largely of hard-nosed chief executive officers, and yet in no time they were hanging on his every word. It was not so much what he said but his presence, and the measured tonality of his deep voice, his ability to make everyone feel as though he was truly interested in what they thought.

"I'm here asking for your assistance," he told a breakfast audience in Halifax, sounding like Kennedy while conjuring up the image of Diefenbaker. "I need your guidance. I need your counsel. And if at some point down the line you feel that my candidacy is worthy of your support, I would be honoured to have it. And in return I guess I can give you but one promise. That if you decide to support me I'll never violate your trust. I'll always conduct myself as our present leader has, and as Mr. Diefenbaker did, I'll always conduct myself in the finest and the highest traditions of Conservative leadership. I'll always conduct myself in such a way as to enable you to say: 'He may be wrong sometimes, but he's never on the side of wrong.' With your help and your counsel and, as I say, your guidance, after the twenty-second of February, I think we'll go all the way in ridding this country of a national disaster, Mr. Trudeau. Thank you very much."

By the Christmas break, with the convention only two months away, Mulroney was scoring better than anyone had expected. Although not profound, his speeches were full of graphic images and expressions of hope for the future. One of his greatest political skills turned out to be his way of convincing people he shared their opinions even when he did not. This allowed him to bridge normally unbridgeable issues like the death penalty, then being hotly debated as the Trudeau government was moving to abolish the noose. Mulroney remained a strong abolitionist, and capital punishment was one of the rare issues on which he stood on principle, but even here he performed a little dance. "When people across this country talk about capital punishment, they're talking about more than just the death penalty," he would reply when the issue was raised. "They're talking about a national parole system that is a national farce, a bail system that is a revolving door for criminals, and a system which grants criminals pardons even as they are in the act of committing other crimes." What the country needed, he would say, was a mandatory, non-reviewable thirty-five-year sentence for premeditated murder. His other unshakeable conviction was in the rightness of the policy of official bilingualism. Here he defended the Official Languages Act but denounced the heavy-handedness and callousness of its implementation. On other issues where any firm stand was sure to annoy large numbers of delegates, he was equally adept. He defended immigration but saw no reason why immigrants should not be required to spend their first two or three years in areas where workers were needed. He defended labour unions but condemned labour violence. He defended unemployment insurance but attacked its abuse. It seemed he could sugar-coat any view to make it palatable.

Where Mulroney scored highest was on the issue of Quebec. Louis Riel had been dead almost a century, and still the party was a joke in *la belle province*. Candidates continued to pay lip service to making a breakthrough in French Canada, but few sounded credible and some did not mean it. When Mulroney insisted that Quebec could be won over, he did so with absolute conviction, and that alone set him apart from the others, including Wagner, who had fared dismally in two elections as Quebec leader. Mulroney's campaign featured him as an attractive Quebecker with total access to both cultures, and the message was getting through. Party members started to muse about maybe winning fifteen seats in Quebec and what it would do for their chances in the next election, and that led them to toy with the idea of taking a flyer on Mulroney. Many delegates liked the notion of Cinderella arriving suddenly on the scene to try on the glass slipper. The Liberals had found their Cinderella in Pierre Trudeau, so why shouldn't the Conservative Party find one too?

The informal polls showed Mulroney surging forward. Every week Mulroney's crowds got bigger and warmer, and every week brought another high-profile endorsement or two. He had picked up more than his share of the unattached delegates, and was now shaking loose delegates previously committed to other candidates, proving the situation to be more fluid than anybody thought. Mulroney had even chipped into Wagner's solid block, stealing perhaps as many as a quarter of his delegates, which did nothing to lessen the name-calling that had characterized relations between their organizations since the beginning. It was clear that Mulroney had inflicted heavy damage on the frontrunner.

As Mulroney's campaign gathered steam, it also attracted more media attention. In mid-December a group of reporters accompanied the candidate and his wife on a campaign swing up to Baie Comeau. The party gathered in a private lounge at Dorval Airport from where they were to take the IOC corporate jet. While they waited to board, several of the reporters fell into conversation with Mila, then expecting another baby. Mila recounted that earlier that day, her husband had irritably awakened her from a nap with the shout "Where are my shirts?" (By now he couldn't get through a day without changing shirts several times.) The *Montreal Gazette*'s Don MacPherson later reported the incident in a feature story that appeared at the end of January. The piece horrified Mila; absolutely distraught, she promptly called her husband to tell him what in her view was bad news.

Only twenty-two years of age and only three years married, Mila took little part in the 1976 leadership campaign. Aside from the Baie Comeau trip she seldom accompanied her husband on his travels and showed scant evidence of the political talent that would later emerge. She was still maturing, still learning to cope with the demands of marriage and child-rearing. At this stage, it was clear that Mulroney did not view her as an equal or depend on her for advice and support.

By early January the aura of excitement around the accelerating Mulroney campaign even generated some mini-Mulroneymania. "His eyes," the *Edmonton Journal* had reported earlier, "are Paul Newman blue, his hair has the swoop of the Robert Redford style, and his voice the resonance of a Lorne Greene school of broadcasting grad. The jaw is by Gibraltar. It is hard to believe, as the television film whirs away and he pumps the hands of everyone in the hotel suite but the engrossed camera crews, that this man could have been lumped in with The Dismal Dozen, that bland bunch of candidates doing the old treadmill trot toward the Tory leadership convention." In a month and a half he had come from nowhere to being a serious contender.

The once-implausible had become plausible. Newspapers were billing him as one of the frontrunners. Global Television and the CBC's *the fifth estate* both assigned camera crews to his campaign and started working on documentaries about him in anticipation of victory. This was more than the media falling victim to their own bandwagons. Although the race remained wide open, by mid-January the smart money was betting on Mulroney.

At the convention in Ottawa delegates would be choosing from among eleven potential leaders, but between two broad philosophical groups of candidates: the right-wing pool of Wagner, Hellyer, Horner, Stevens, and Nowlan, and the centre-left pool of Mulroney, MacDonald, Clark, Fraser, Gillies, and Grafftey. Both groupings would probably arrive in Ottawa with about the same number of delegates, although the centre-left moderates were expected to flex a little more muscle. As candidates started dropping off the ballot, right and left would each coalesce around their strongest member — and at the moment Mulroney was leading the progressive pack. If the moderates had more delegates and if they acted rationally, then logic dictated that Mulroney would emerge as the new party leader. When viewed through this prism, Mulroney's prospects for victory looked absolutely tantalizing. For someone who had started out as a long shot, given little chance by his own organizers, he had achieved a remarkable turnaround. It said a lot about his skill as a campaigner. As the convention approached, Peter White, who had originally felt Mulroney did not have a prayer, took the unusual step of writing Mulroney a letter congratulating him on his imminent success on becoming party leader and prime minister.

Meanwhile the trust fund scandal continued to plague Mulroney's chief adversary. By this point Wagner had been forced to admit to its existence, explaining away his original denial with another lie: the trust fund had been set up after the election, he explained, and therefore after his original disclaimer. But the new version sounded even fishier than the first one. Delegates had to ask themselves why a party that went $2 million in debt losing an election would award $300,000 to someone who had flopped so badly.

One of the people most upset by Wagner's behaviour was Peter White, who had been his executive assistant during the 1972 campaign. White had been horrified by Wagner's original denial of the trust fund's existence, but said nothing until shortly before Wagner joined the leadership race. White sent Wagner a letter advising him he "should not seek the party leadership without first terminating connection with the trust fund." If he failed to do so, White could not support him. In the letter, White predicted that Wagner would be faced with "perfectly legitimate demands" to make a clean breast of the whole affair. But White received no reply and subsequently threw his support to Mulroney.

Then, in mid-January, just six weeks before the convention, Jonathan Manthorpe of the *Globe and Mail* dug up the fact that Wagner's wife had received the first payment from the trust fund four days *before* the election in 1972. But Wagner continued to stonewall even after this revelation, leading White, on February 7, to confirm to the *Toronto Star* the story about the first payment to the trust fund, thus exposing Wagner as a barefaced liar. It now appeared as though Wagner's campaign was permanently crippled.

The problem for Mulroney was that, as Wagner's chief recruiter, he became implicated in the whole messy affair. The more the press probed into Wagner's recruitment, the more Mulroney's name emerged. After all, it was he who had introduced Wagner to Finlay MacDonald for the purpose of negotiating the size of the trust fund. At the time of the recruitment Mulroney proudly took the credit, even bragging about what a tough job it had been. It became clear to anybody who followed the scandal that Mulroney had been mixed up more deeply than he cared to admit. Yet now he dodged and weaved and downplayed his role to that of a bit player. It just did not sound right that the man who engineered the recruitment would vanish whenever the talk turned to money. Moreover some factions blamed Mulroney for allowing the gory details to leak out in the first place. So while White's revelation had hit its target, it boomeranged. Soon some delegates saw only two candidates airing their dirty linen in public, and they washed their hands of both of them.

The Wagner trust scandal had set Mulroney back — no question. However, he was losing even more momentum because of the increasing lavishness of his campaign. By now Mulroney had abandoned commercial flights and was shooting around the country in a leased executive jet; he was the only candidate who could afford this luxury. It allowed him to drop into far-flung spots whenever he wanted and to pursue delegates wherever they happened to live. And this was only the latest extravagance of a campaign that was increasingly giving him an image as the Cadillac candidate. For example, the Mulroney campaign office was exquisitely headquartered in a tastefully furnished office in a beautiful red-stone building in Old Montreal.

Thanks to his network and David Angus's fundraising machine, Mulroney was now better financed and more slickly packaged than any of the other candidates, and he seemed to spend dollars twice as freely. This need not have been a problem. Candidates must have money if they are to make their faces known and get their messages across. And the ability to raise money makes them credible, proving that others think highly enough of them to contribute hard currency. However, being seen to have too much money damages a candidate's credibility. It raises questions as to whether the candidate is his own man or belongs in somebody's pocket. By flaunting his wealth Mulroney had made people wonder to whom he was beholden.

Campaigns are full of rumours, and in no time Mulroney's prosperity caused people to speculate that Paul Desmarais was bankrolling him. It sounded plausible enough, given Desmarais's untold millions and his close friendship with Mulroney. Leadership campaigns cost megabucks and even Desmarais did not throw around that kind of money, but that did not stop the rumours from growing. They gathered so much momentum that Mulroney was finally forced to address them publicly. "Paul Desmarais was a client of our firm twenty-five years ago when he was driving a bus in Sudbury, Ontario, and twenty-five years ago I wasn't practising law," he declared. "And he's a good and a valued client of our law firm, and I've had the occasion to represent him in the past. And he's a decent and an honourable Canadian. And he's got another quality. His brother was a Conservative candidate for Bob Stanfield in 1968. I make no apologies. I make no apologies for that. And needless to say I hope that all of you, and I trust that all of you, when this rumour is raised,

I hope that you will ask the person to whom you're speaking exactly for his source. And you'll find that the source is absolutely faceless and groundless and nameless."

The Desmarais rumour never shrivelled and died as Mulroney had hoped, but dogged him for the rest of the campaign. He later confirmed that Desmarais had contributed $10,000 and was his biggest contributor. He promised to open his books and disclose all contributions over $1,000 after the convention. (Meanwhile Angus was telling prospective contributors that there was no need to worry about being named, because Mulroney was going to ignore the party rule about disclosing the source of funds.) But if Desmarais wasn't the source of the seemingly endless money, people wondered who was. Mulroney's lavish spending style had branded him with the image of the establishment candidate, the handmaiden of the financial élite. It was ironic for someone who had entered the race as such a long-shot outsider.

Given Mulroney's political astuteness, it seemed strange he would make such a fundamental strategic mistake. As a campaigner, two impulses seemed to overcome him: as the new boy on the block, he and his advisers felt that he had to come on strong and impress upon the world that he was indeed a serious candidate. The big money and the glitz were his way of making people take his candidacy seriously and giving himself a chance to catch up to the frontrunners. But the lavish style also came naturally to him and his friends. To him, flashing money around was a mark of success. It showed that an Irish Catholic from the wrong side of the tracks had made it.

Both Mulroney and Michel Cogger, the campaign manager, enjoyed spending money. Mulroney had always gone flat out in everything he did all his life and was not going to pinch pennies on something as big as his first leadership campaign. Mulroney and Cogger decided to go first class and the hell with it. When it looked as though they could win, they pulled out all the stops.

His catch-up strategy made sense in theory. It was how he went about it that defied common sense. Once again he had gone beyond the acceptable boundaries. His campaign had become so loud, so flashy, and so expensive that it had become an issue in itself. Delegates began to believe that he was trying to buy the leadership of the Conservative Party. This image problem, combined with the fallout from the trust fund scandal, soon slowed Mulroney's campaign to a crawl. He was still seen as one of the frontrunners, but like Wagner he was now going nowhere.

Compared with the Mulroney Cadillac, Joe Clark's campaign was a Volkswagen — and one that badly needed repairs. From the outset he paid his financial needs little heed, following a pay-as-you-go philosophy. Instead of raising money, his tactic was not to spend it. So frugal had the Clark operation become that he managed without a campaign headquarters until January, somehow running everything out of his House of Commons office. The candidate doubled as his own campaign manager, which was virtually undoable and certainly unhealthy. But if anybody could pull it off, it would be Clark.

Leading a children's crusade of mostly student volunteers, Clark tackled his assignment at his usual frenetic pace, but by mid-campaign even Clark himself had to admit that he could not ride both these horses. Already a string bean without an ounce of visible fat, he had started losing weight and, 15 pounds later, would eventually bottom out at a scraggly 145. Meanwhile duties went undelegated, decisions were left unmade, and costly misunderstandings cropped up constantly, until before long almost the whole organization languished in disarray. The campaign headquarters finally moved into a one-room office in a second-storey walk-up, but it quickly became a shambles as the campaign teetered on bankruptcy. By mid-January, as the Mulroney campaign was reaching its peak, Clark appeared to be on the ropes. "I don't think Joe is going to be able to finish the campaign," Flora MacDonald reported to Lowell Murray while campaigning in Saint John, New Brunswick. "I think he is going to run out of money." Murray, although supporting MacDonald, quickly sent Clark a personal donation. However, Clark needed a major infusion of capital or else everything would collapse beneath him.

Despite the organizational chaos, Clark had been doing rather nicely out on the stump. His endless travel on behalf of the PC Student Federation a decade earlier now gave him years worth of IOUs to collect. And he was making a solid impression on delegates, to the surprise of many, pulling himself firmly into the middle of the pack. Unlike Mulroney and Wagner, he had avoided big mistakes and revealed a solid grasp of policy. He was showing up unexpectedly well as delegates' second or third choice. During the previous months nobody except Mulroney had picked up more ground than he had. He had a chance to emerge at the convention as the compromise candidate. But he would never have the chance if he was unable to raise some money fast.

In late January, Clark learned that he had the next week or so to raise $42,000 or his campaign would be forced to shut down. He hastily assembled his fundraisers, who committed themselves to raising the money. Each signed a personal promissory note with the Toronto-Dominion Bank, which then advanced the money, thus giving Clark some fast cash and some breathing room. Within a few days they had added fifteen names to the promissory note, each person promising to raise enough money to cover his or her share. The $42,000 shot in the arm kept the campaign on its feet long enough to last until the convention.

Now something had to be done about the administrative mess. Here Clark's friend Jim Hawkes, a psychologist at the University of Calgary, came to his rescue. Hawkes, who would later became an MP, stepped in to run the campaign so Clark could concentrate on being a candidate.

Aside from Wagner and Mulroney, Clark was the only candidate who could boast any semblance of organization in Quebec. It had been one of the aces he had planned on playing in the campaign, but Mulroney's candidacy had thoroughly loused up his Quebec strategy. Michel Cogger, Jean Bazin, and a throng of other educated Quebeckers of his generation — the ones who would never support Wagner — all flocked over to Mulroney. Otherwise most of them would have come his way.

If Mulroney gave Clark nothing but problems, Clark gave Mulroney a mild headache or two in denying him support in western Canada. Yet Clark posed a bigger threat to Mulroney than the simple arithmetic of committed delegates would suggest. As the campaign entered its final weeks, it was beginning to look as though the ultimate winner would be the contestant who could best rally the anti-Wagner vote. And that in turn was looking even more like a battle between Mulroney and Clark — with the outcome being far from certain.

The fates had shifted. Mulroney's Kennedyesque image had become tarnished as the February 19 opening date of the convention neared. It seemed he had peaked too early. Going from dark horse to frontrunner had changed his status from exciting outsider to the man to beat, the principal target of his opponents. Tory caucus members started to bad-mouth Mulroney to their riding delegates, saying he did not understand the system and that caucus would be damned if it would be led by a greenhorn. Some caucus members privately told delegates that the party would be throwing away the next election with him as leader. There was even talk of having a group of caucus members issue a statement threatening to bolt the party rather than serve under a neophyte. It was only talk. There would never be a statement, much less a walk-out. The talk had been started for the purpose of sending a message that Mulroney was not welcome, and to impress upon delegates that Mulroney represented a risk.

At the same time the media started cracking down on Mulroney with the kind of tough, substantive questions that are normally thrown at leaders — questions that demanded more than big words, a good voice, and some breezy charm. Mulroney's lack of depth started to show more than ever and left reporters wondering whether his campaign was anything more than image. Mulroney had deliberately avoided committing himself to much in the way of policy. His whole strategy was to sneak up the middle, between left and right, and slip through unnoticed. It had worked relatively well until he became a serious contender. Now it became obvious, as one observer put it, that Mulroney was a mile wide and an inch deep.

On the other hand Clark, the veteran of a thousand student PC policy debates, sounded increasingly formidable the more the spotlight shone on him. Since his earliest days as a perpetual member of PC youth committees, he had always practised politics as a vehicle for establishing policy, and now he was coming on strong with well-thought-out positions on just about every issue. He looked more credible every time somebody popped a weighty question at him. One CTV national news report referred to him as "a Brian Mulroney with brains and experience."

As the two youngest candidates, Clark and Mulroney both appealed to the same moderate youth wing of the party. Both had started as long shots and had gained strength. However, the glare of late-campaign scrutiny did opposite things to them. Mulroney started to slip even more, while Clark moved up even faster.

With three weeks to go, Graham Scott, still a senior Stanfield aide, gave reporters an off-the-record background briefing about what they might expect to see at the convention. Just as the session was breaking up, someone asked Scott who he personally thought would win. A month earlier Scott would have been prepared to lay down a bet on Mulroney with better-than-even odds, but recent events had caused him to doubt Mulroney's ability to pull in the later-ballot votes he would need. With no strong frontrunner, the victor would emerge after several rounds of balloting and be the one who could assemble a minimum winning coalition. The trend was not firm, but the more Scott thought about it the more he could see Clark, the popular second and third choice, putting together the magic essential formula. Clark's performance had amazed him, and as a Westerner who could speak decent French, with support in every region of the country, he was beautifully positioned. Scott told his audience of journalists that he could see a scenario developing in which Clark would go over the top.

CHAPTER FIFTEEN

OPPORTUNITY LOST

ALTHOUGH LONG GONE as Tory leader, John Diefenbaker, now eighty and wobbly and more cantankerous than ever, continued to sit in the House of Commons and to fight old battles. He boycotted caucus meetings under Stanfield's leadership and spent his days on the telephone devouring gossip from across Parliament Hill and across the nation, the juicier the better, and then recycling it with malicious intent and poisonous effect, cackling gleefully with every bull's-eye. He had made life hell for Robert Stanfield, and now that a new wave of pretenders was reaching for the crown that had been stolen from him a decade earlier, he had a new opportunity to stir things up. Diefenbaker would surely find it impossible not to meddle, a fact that made Mulroney decidedly nervous. He could expect nothing but trouble from his erstwhile idol.

The Mulroney campaign knew it could never bring Diefenbaker around, but it could try to neutralize his venom. Accordingly, the Mulroney organization produced a pamphlet featuring the 1956 photo of Diefenbaker posing with the boyish Mulroney. It also enlisted Arthur Maloney, Diefenbaker's hand-picked candidate against Dalton Camp in 1966, to help in the cause. It had to be careful because Maloney was now ombudsman for the province of Ontario and could not endorse political candidates, so they distributed widely an old Maloney quote that Mulroney was the finest stand-up speaker to come along since Diefenbaker. Things like that helped create a good impression among Diefenbaker loyalists, whom Mulroney did not want to antagonize.

But everyone knew that Diefenbaker could destroy all such efforts with a single public rebuke. So Mulroney's handlers urged him to arrange a meeting with the Chief. It would be showing proper respect for a former party leader and prime minister, and might just keep the old man in check, Michel Cogger and the others argued. However, Mulroney demurred, and the more his advisers pressed, the clearer it became that he just did not want to do it. The response seemed uncharacteristic. Seldom in his life had he shown the least inhibition about meeting anyone.

His advisers did not know that over the last several years Mulroney had already tried to patch things up with Diefenbaker and been snubbed. Back in 1973 at the annual parliamentary press gallery dinner Mulroney had persuaded Sean O'Sullivan to try to reopen the door. O'Sullivan was now an MP but recently had been Diefenbaker's executive assistant and remained close to him. "You know, Sean," a contrite-looking Mulroney told O'Sullivan during the post-dinner reception, "way back in '66, when we all thought we were being so smart, the Chief was right." Maybe the partying had overfilled him with drink, but Mulroney looked truly remorseful and impressed O'Sullivan with his earnestness. O'Sullivan passed along Mulroney's comments to Diefenbaker, but they did not soften the old man's attitude. Instead of offering forgiveness, he merely harrumphed and quickly changed the subject.

In 1975, before entering the leadership race, Mulroney had tried making amends once again, this time seizing the opportunity presented by the publication of the book *Conversations with Kennedy* by

Ben Bradlee. Bradlee, the executive editor of the *Washington Post,* had been a confidant of John F. Kennedy during his White House years and authoritatively quoted the late U.S. president as denying he had ever scrawled the letters "S.O.B." on the infamous State Department briefing document that fell into Prime Minister Diefenbaker's hands during a state visit to Ottawa in 1961. The S.O.B. incident became an international affair that epitomized the friction between the two leaders. "At that time I didn't think Diefenbaker was a son of a bitch," Bradlee quoted Kennedy as saying. "I thought he was a prick."

Mulroney had gotten an early copy of the Bradlee book and knew only too well that little nuggets of vindication always pricked Diefenbaker's interest. Diefenbaker had always believed JFK was out to get him, and the book at least proved the American president had disliked him. In any case it gave Mulroney a shot at rebuilding the connection. He phoned O'Sullivan and promised to send the reference, and O'Sullivan in turn undertook to pass it along. "While you're at it," Mulroney added, "will you indicate to the Chief I would really welcome the opportunity of coming up and chatting with him." Strangely, when O'Sullivan presented him with the Bradlee material, Diefenbaker showed not the slightest interest and failed even to acknowledge Mulroney's overture. There was a brief silence, then Diefenbaker started sifting through papers on his desk to suggest he was busy. Forgiveness remained out of the question.

Mulroney gave up further attempts at rapprochement, but Michel Cogger kept nagging and by mid-campaign finally convinced Mulroney to drop into Diefenbaker's office. The entrée this time was Peter Stursberg's recent book *Diefenbaker: Leadership Gained, 1956-62.* Mulroney would bring it along and ask him to autograph it for Mila's father.

Diefenbaker received Mulroney civilly and obligingly signed the book. He even showed his old spunk by bad-mouthing Mulroney's leadership rivals but made no comment about Mulroney's own campaign. Through the whole meeting Diefenbaker said not a contrary word about him until Mulroney was making his exit. "One more thing," Diefenbaker barked, as Mulroney headed for the door. "Don't think for one minute I've forgotten about your treachery in '66."

Since Diefenbaker was holding onto his grudge, Mulroney could only take solace in the fact that Diefenbaker blamed practically everybody for his downfall, including half of the current leadership contenders. Diefenbaker hated Flora MacDonald, whose firing in 1966 had turned Dalton Camp against him. "Flora MacDonald is one of the finest women ever to walk the streets of Kingston," he would snicker. He had raw contempt for Joe Clark, who had once advised him to resign. "Mr. Clark," Diefenbaker sneered, "walks hither and yon, talking in low monotones for fear that his genius might be overheard by others." He loathed Sinclair Stevens too, not for disloyalty but for having crossed swords with him over Stevens's failed attempt to establish a bank of western Canada. As a spent force, Diefenbaker could no longer deliver delegates — but he could still inflict damage, as Stanfield had already discovered. Within Diefenbaker's small cadre of loyalists were some of Parliament Hill's most proficient rumour-mongers, people who would sabotage anybody suspected of having connections with Dalton Camp. Sooner or later Diefenbaker was bound to let loose in public. The question was which unlucky candidate or candidates would be his target.

Diefenbaker saw the hand of Dalton Camp in just about everything sinister and believed Camp was once again busily stirring the leadership pot. Deep down in his heart he believed Camp was sponsoring not one but four or five candidates, as one might do in a pony race, so that when one pony stumbled, the others would keep his conspiracy alive. Diefenbaker even went so far as to conjure up a plot that had Camp hiding upwards of one hundred delegates on the first ballot so that he could create a bandwagon on the second ballot by swinging them behind his strongest pony. Diefenbaker was being heavily influenced by his executive assistant, Keith Martin, a Hellyer supporter and an anti-Mulroney plotter. He became convinced that Mulroney was the thoroughbred Camp ultimately wanted.

In fact, throughout the campaign, Mulroney had been dogged by the allegation that he was Camp's front man, but he repeatedly denied having any backing from the former party president. "I haven't spoken with or heard from Mr. Camp in three years," he claimed when he announced his entry into the race in November, "but he's definitely not supporting my candidacy." He was right about Camp's position. The former Dief-slayer ended up voting for Flora Mac-Donald on the first two ballots, then throwing his support to Clark.

Given that the party had neither requested nor really wanted a speech from Diefenbaker, it seemed a little curious that the convention opened on Thursday night, February 19, 1976, with Diefenbaker making the first major address. But Diefenbaker had it in his mind to give a speech, and through his network of loyalists he cowed the powers in the party into making the opening-night ceremonies a tribute to the former prime minister.

That evening the delegates who had gathered in the hockey arena of the Ottawa Civic Centre waited somewhat nervously to see what damage the unpredictable Diefenbaker might inflict. However, it seemed he had decided to take the high road. Instead of settling old scores, he delivered a philosophical speech that sparkled with grace, wit, charm, and sentiment while packing a lot of good punch lines. He talked about his concerns for the underprivileged and downtrodden, and the need for freedom and minority rights, and he did not seem to be endorsing any candidate. His timing and his mannerisms were perfect, and the crowd cheered him on like the old days.

"Today," he thundered, "members of Parliament, for all their effectiveness, might just as well be in exile. Parliament has lost its control over expenditures. And since the Trudeau party came into power it's increased them by three or four times. This year they will have increased the expenditures of Canada to an extent seven times what it was under my administration. When I think of these members of Parliament supporting the Trudeau party — and I don't call it the Liberal Party any more, he's taken it over. And he's reshaped it in his own image. He shows a continuing contempt for the institution he does not understand. He only had about a year and a half or two before he became prime minister."

Then he uncorked the stinger. "In the British parliamentary tradition, those that achieve the prime ministership must have had years of experience. He did not have that experience."

The crowd exploded into applause. It had been interrupting him all along, but this time the audience simply went wild — everybody except the wedge of delegates forming the Mulroney section. The Mulroney people sat on their hands and looked uncomfortable. Along with the entire convention they knew that Diefenbaker had trained his sights not so much on Pierre Trudeau as on Brian Mulroney, who wanted to be party leader without ever entering Parliament. Diefenbaker was announcing to the convention that Mulroney lacked the qualifications to be prime minister. In case anybody missed his point, Diefenbaker drove it home again as the cheering died down. "He did not have it," Diefenbaker shouted.

Bewilderment and disbelief rippled through the Mulroney section, followed by a sense of gloom that could be read on every face. It had only been one line in a long speech, but it had scored a direct hit on its intended target.

"Honey," Mulroney said, turning to Mila, "we're dead in the water."

The crowd kept cheering Diefenbaker as he moved along, laughing at his quips and finally bidding him farewell with a standing ovation that lasted so long that Diefenbaker, clearly touched, came back for a few more words. Then the stadium broke into a chorus of "For He's a Jolly Good Fellow." The scene could not have been more different from the humiliating heckling he had endured at the Château Laurier a decade earlier.

Meanwhile up above, the CBC Television booth was hailing the speech as a triumph. "I thought it was great," gushed Peter C. Newman, an old Diefenbaker thorn. "And I think if you'd had a vote right after it, he would have won on the first ballot." The CBC camera soon panned onto reporter Tom Leach, who had nabbed Diefenbaker on the convention floor. "A lot of people," Leach said, "expected you to be partisan about the candidates tonight but you were not. Would you care to tell us why?"

"It's no time for partisanship, narrow partisanship," Diefenbaker replied. "I'm concerned over my country." Leach asked him about Paul Hellyer, and Diefenbaker cited historical precedent to show why having been a Liberal did not disqualify someone from becoming Tory leader.

"Well, what about Brian Mulroney?" Leach asked next. "You seem to dislike him almost as much as you dislike Mr. Trudeau."

"Well, I would not have anything to say about that," Diefenbaker huffed. "I want to know where he stands, with whom he stands, and who supports him." That was that. The subject was over as far as Diefenbaker was concerned. The interview moved on to other matters.

After a quick interview with Flora MacDonald, who made the point that Diefenbaker himself had sat in Parliament for only two years when he first ran for party leader, the camera switched over to reporter Ken Colby next to Mulroney.

"Brian Mulroney," Colby said, "Mr. Diefenbaker appeared to take a little bit of a shot at you when he talked about the prime minister being in such trouble because he became prime minister when he lacked experience. And then in an interview with Tom Leach he said specifically, 'I have no comment on Brian Mulroney, I don't know who he is, I don't know what he stands for, I don't know who his backers are.' Does this cause you concern?"

The expression on Mulroney's face showed that the question had caught him off guard. Although subdued, he looked visibly perplexed. "Well, it caused me a little surprise," he replied, "because I first came to this city in nineteen hundred and fifty six as vice-chairman of the Youth for Diefenbaker committee. I knew Mr. Diefenbaker pretty well then. And when I supported him in '57 and '58 and '62, '65, and so I'm a little surprised that he would say that. But with regard to his position on elected experience, I respect his point of view on that. He's a great parliamentarian. He's had long experience in the House. And in fairness to everybody, most of the candidates in this race, who are members of Parliament, were only elected in 1972. And they were sworn into the House in '73. So they've got about a year and a half, two years' experience. And perhaps Mr. Diefenbaker was speaking of them as well."

Mulroney spoke calmly and without excitement, not giving up hope, but plainly worried. The look on his face suggested that he sensed tragedy ahead. He recovered quickly and by the end of the interview was boasting that there would be no kingmakers. "This is a convention where the delegates are going to be king," he said. Nevertheless, damage had been done. He had been singled out of the crowd and was now fair game for cheap shots from anybody.

As people started filing out of the arena, Senator Allister Grosart, a diehard member of the small Diefenbaker entourage who had always been friendly with Mulroney, came over to console him. "I'm sorry, Brian," he said. "I tried to convince the Chief not to do it." The Diefenbaker assault was hashed over far and wide that evening, and Mulroney supporters had no choice but to shrug it off, although they resented it intensely. Diefenbaker scorned Clark and Mac-Donald every bit as much, so why had he singled out their man? Mulroney himself took it personally. He had not expected any favours, but neither had he expected a public rebuke.

The mischief-making of a former prime minister had inflicted damage mainly because Mulroney was already vulnerable. Many delegates had become deeply suspicious of the Cadillac candidate, and Diefenbaker had given them an outlet for their disapproval. A good number of delegates had already started holding their noses whenever Mulroney's name came up. With the speech, what had been an image problem now exploded into an image crisis fed by the overt extravagance of his convention presence. The delegates had heard the allegations, but it was hard to see the evidence of opulence during Mulroney's quick stopovers on the campaign trail. From the moment of Mulroney's arrival at the convention they could not help but notice.

Mulroney, accompanied by Mila, had arrived in Ottawa by train and was greeted loudly by a huge reception at the station with waving placards and lots of cheers. The scene happened all over again as Mulroney reached the Skyline Hotel. (The Mulroney car made a long detour to allow his recycled welcoming group to get there first.) After disappearing into an elevator and changing his shirt upstairs, Mulroney came back down to the lobby to repeat the charade a third time because the CTV cameras had missed it earlier. The next day a Donato cartoon in the *Toronto Sun* was circulated widely among the delegates. It showed a delegate shaking Mulroney's hand and breaking off his arm, like a robot — playing to the notion that Mulroney was a plastic man and an artificial candidate.

There was no disputing that the Mulroney presence was brassy, brazen, and gauche. Wherever he went, men with walkie-talkies cleared his path and an entourage followed along with the fanfare and razzmatazz of an American presidential race. His campaign had bands, streamers, girls with Mulroney mini-skirts, and its own security crew. Mulroney workers scurried about everywhere in their blue-and-white costumes — skirts for women and jackets for men — with Mulroney's handsome face imprinted in the fabric. Mulroney's supporters wore huge octagonal badges that were bigger than anyone else's, indeed bigger than anyone had ever seen. The Mulroney forces had more of these goodies than anybody. The campaign not only was rich but looked rich, and deliberately so. The overkill of his convention display had put many delegates off and only enhanced his negative image as the candidate from Power Corporation. (Later some people would take to folding his campaign signs so that "Mulroney" spelled "Money.") Yet Mulroney and his closest advisers still didn't see it this way. Long after the convention was over he still couldn't understand what the money fuss was about.

Had his campaign been sensitive to the mood of the party, it would have changed gears before the convention. The delegates in 1976 were mostly rural or small-town folk, and contrived ostentation did not go down well with these kinds of Tories, not when the party had been out of power thirteen years and when many of them were struggling to keep their riding associations afloat. The Tories wanted a modern, dynamic, charismatic leader, but in a party accustomed to the quiet dignity of Stanfield, Mulroney was simply too slick.

So when Diefenbaker delivered his sneak attack, the cheer that convulsed the crowd had less to do with Mulroney's parliamentary experience than with his glitzy style. It was a visceral reaction against a candidate perceived as too ambitious, too pushy, and too well-monied. In reality Diefenbaker had swung fewer than twenty-five first-ballot votes. Mulroney's delegates were committed and would stick with him. But Diefenbaker had helped sour the mood of all those still thinking about supporting Mulroney on the second and third ballots, precisely the support he would need to grow and win.

Although Mila had joined her husband in Ottawa, she was in no state to boost his candidacy; her second child was due any day and she made few public appearances. In fact, Mulroney's handlers were on a Mila watch. Every time she got up to go to the bathroom they figured she was going into labour. A doctor was waiting on stand-by, and the campaign had worked out a contingency plan to rush her to the hospital. Heightening this general sense of expectancy, the Mulroney camp included two other pregnant wives: Madeleine Roy and Erica Cogger. (As it turned out, Benedict Mulroney was born on March 9, sixteen days after the convention ended.)

The policy sessions that lasted all day on Friday did nothing to improve Mulroney's tarnished image. The candidates rotated through four meeting rooms in the Skyline Hotel, each room dealing with a different broad topic, for four half-hour sessions during which delegates were free to ask questions. At the forum on social justice and social order, Mulroney tried straddling the fence on abortion, not an issue naturally amenable to fence-straddling. Mulroney survived the encounter but afterwards ran smack into John Gray of the *Ottawa Citizen*, who kept at him like a terrier. Mulroney stiffened up and grew defensive and visibly irritated as Gray honed in. At one point he looked like he wanted to plough Gray in the chops, but the television cameras were rolling, and all he could do was grit his teeth and force a smile.

It wasn't that Mulroney did badly at the policy sessions; he was, as always, poised and polished. But the delegates, still looking for a Messiah who seemed not to be there, asked thoughtful and expectant questions, and found Mulroney wanting. After listening carefully, they concluded he did not have any real positions on most issues. The candidate who impressed them most was Joe Clark. Never hedging and always crisp, forceful, and full of conviction, Clark gave sparkling performances at all four sessions and came away the clear-cut winner. Even people who disagreed with him acknowledged that he knew what he was talking about.

For Clark, who had been coming on strong the last few weeks, the policy sessions brought it all together. Conventions, once they get off the ground, take on a life of their own and generate their own trends. Delegates talk to one another, and as the 1976 delegates talked the name that came up more and more often was Clark's. Many emerged from Friday's policy session with their feelings confirmed, namely that Mulroney was sinking and Clark was rising. Clark seemed to be hitting his stride at the perfect moment.

That night Mulroney's image dropped even further. His organization rented the Coliseum, next door to the convention hall, and paid Quebec singer Ginette Reno $10,000 to perform, serving all comers free pizza and beer. The event left people to wonder once again how much the campaign was costing and who was really paying.

By day three, Saturday, Mulroney's chances of picking up new delegates had dropped almost to zero. In forty-eight hours he had gone from frontrunner to probable also-ran. With victory palpably slipping from his grasp, Mulroney knew he had one last shot at turning things around, and that was his speech to the convention that afternoon. It would be his only chance to address all the delegates and show them what he could do. A stellar performance could repair at least some of the damage, and maybe even get him enough later-ballot support to win. Delegates had heard glowing reports of him as the greatest stump speaker since Diefenbaker. Despite the bad image of his convention machine, Mulroney still carried the mystique that suggested he could win an election. Delegates were prepared to overlook a multitude of faults if somebody could lead them to power. A powerful speech could change everything.

When Mulroney stepped to the podium, he was greeted by the biggest floor demonstration of the convention. "This afternoon at this great convention," he began, "history and opportunity meet. At a single time and a single place we have come to choose our next leader. We are here to reaffirm our party's unswerving faith in a Canada free and indivisible. This nation was built in spite of alien voices prompting us to forsake our dream. A dream of a great Canadian nationality, diverse and unique on the northern half of this continent. We are now a country of different communities, a people of many cultures. And so this afternoon, ladies and gentlemen, friends of the Conservative Party, I speak for the unity of our nation, the destiny of our democracy."

High-minded stuff, but terrible for generating excitement. As the speech continued the audience sat stone-faced and lifeless, not yielding even a smattering of applause. Mulroney, looking nervous and uncomfortable, plodded on. The speech, beautiful and noble, offered a great vision, but did not ring true coming from a candidate who had been attacked during the campaign as a backroom operator without substance. The fact that he kept looking down to read the text told delegates he was reading somebody else's words, that he was not giving a speech as much as reading a script.

"Our next leader must continue our common resolve to give this party a lasting sense of unity. It is a commitment that will require patience and tolerance, reception and endurance. But it is a commitment that must be renewed immediately." He was now one-third through and had managed to generate exactly two ripples of polite applause.

"Where's the stemwinder?" people wondered. The person they were witnessing bore not the slightest resemblance to Diefenbaker, whose oratorical mastery was fresh in their minds. Everybody had expected a barn-burner and instead they were getting watered-down Plato. Even Mulroney's own people were giving one another looks and shaking their heads. He was bombing and they all knew it. One of the most surprised people in the hall was Peter Desbarats of Global Television. A week earlier, at David Angus's country retreat on Lake Memphremagog, he had heard Mulroney deliver a dry-run version of this very speech and it had sounded great. What had gone wrong?

After being criticized for lacking substance during the campaign, Mulroney and his advisers had decided on a thoughtful speech to the convention, the kind of idealistic address that John F. Kennedy would have given. Before coming to Ottawa Mulroney had dropped out of sight to the Eastern Townships of Quebec to work on his address. Roy Faibish, who had recruited him to work for Alvin Hamilton back in 1962, came down to do the actual drafting. Lucien Bouchard arrived to write the French part, and Carl Beigie, an economist who headed the C.D. Howe Institute, came in for one afternoon to advise on energy policy. Mulroney, with a rather premature sense of history, brought in a photographer to take pictures.

Working in the quiet countryside, the highly literate Faibish took a few lines from a speech of Lyndon Johnson's on civil rights that seemed as fitting for a prime minister coming out of Baie Comeau as it had been for an American president rising from the Texas boondocks. He borrowed two or three lines from a speech Adlai Stevenson had delivered in Chicago in 1953 and used Maxim Litvinov's phrase at the old League of Nations about peace being indivisible and applied it to Canada. These and other fine phrases and lofty sentiments were stitched together into what was surely one of the most idealistic and gracious speeches a Canadian leadership convention was ever likely to hear. It seemed certain to shoot down the claim that he had no substance.

On the afternoon of the second day, with the speech virtually finished, Desbarats arrived to film footage for Global's upcoming documentary. Mulroney wanted to know what he thought of the speech and took him into a bedroom upstairs and delivered the whole thing line by line. Desbarats thought it sounded simply terrific — and so did everybody else on the premises. After arriving in Ottawa several days later, Mulroney told his team not to worry about the speech because it was great. However, now, in a noisy hockey arena filled with pumped-up delegates, it sounded totally out of place. The literate phrasing combined with Mulroney's sonorous delivery made him seem pompous and formal. As he went on the audience began to murmur restlessly.

"The time has now come. The challenge is great. We can and we shall together, as Conservatives, we can and we shall meet it with vigour and a firm resolve. That is my commitment to you. I can offer no more and you deserve no less. Thank you very much." Finally it was over. The ending gave him the only decent applause of the entire speech.

Nobody had ever seen Mulroney give a bad speech before. It had none of the emotion and none of the partisan rhetoric that normally flowed so easily. It did not sound like him. Mulroney left the stage knowing the speech had backfired badly — how badly, he would soon discover. In the campaign office in the Coliseum annex he sat with his handlers and watched the television commentary. "I think Brian Mulroney lost the convention this afternoon at a time when he could have won it," opined long-time party member John Bassett on the CBC. "His task obviously was to show these delegates that his lack of experience in the House of Commons didn't matter, that he could excite the people of Canada and win the general election. He couldn't even excite a crowd of Conservatives who were dying to be excited — who wanted to get up and cheer. I think he blew it." One after another, commentators dumped on him. It was his third setback in three days. Voting would start the next afternoon and time had run out.

Mulroney and his advisers all realized the magnitude of the blunder. With hindsight it was clear that he should have come out bashing Grits rather than playing the unaccustomed role of philosopher-statesman. Everyone in the room felt terrible: in half an hour they had seen the whole campaign come crashing down, and now all their hopes lay in ruins. Mulroney and Cogger were devastated. Alex

Konigsberg, Mulroney's convention manager, broke into tears and started to sob uncontrollably (a doctor was brought in to calm him down). Elsewhere Mulroney delegates wept openly too, both in the stands and later on the way back to the hotel. For their candidate all hope had vanished.

While the Mulroney forces bemoaned their fate, Clark came through with a good speech, and then Wagner rose to deliver a show-stopper. It was the best speech of the convention, revitalizing his limp standing. Other than Mulroney's the only bad speech came from Paul Hellyer, who slit his own throat with an off-the-cuff jab at Red Tories that actually attracted boos and effectively knocked him out of the race.

Early that evening, when most other candidates were gearing up for the next day's vote, the Mulroney headquarters at the Embassy Hotel resembled a funeral parlour. Cogger, the campaign manager, called everybody down from their rooms for a pep talk in an attempt to rekindle morale. A few hundred sombre-looking people dutifully elbowed their way into the small hotel lobby. It was Saturday night, but one woman arrived in dressing gown and curlers. Cogger, all five feet of him, climbed onto a table and announced that nobody was going to bed yet. "Tonight we work," he proclaimed, "delegate by delegate, room by room. No small incident like this is going to stop us from winning this bloody election."

Then Mulroney arrived and got up on the reception counter. Standing there in his shirtsleeves and looking contrite, he told his followers that he had screwed up — but would make it up to them. The negative reaction to his speech had laid him low for an hour or two, but now he was stirring up the crowd and ready to fight again. He exhorted the troops to fight on with him, this time showing the passion that had been so patently missing a few hours earlier when he really needed it. "This candidate is going flat out," he shouted. Mulroney urged his workers to go to the Château Laurier, the Skyline, the Four Seasons, and the other hotels to rustle up some more delegates.

Mulroney donned a jacket and coat and headed straight for a car to tour the hospitality suites in the major hotels while his now-fired-up troops went back to their rooms for their coats. So many of them crowded the elevator that it overloaded and jammed, requiring the fire department to be called. But by 10 P.M. everybody was on the road in one of Ottawa's worst snowstorms of the season. The Mulroney campaign had a hospitality suite in each major hotel, and all were active on that final night. The plan was for the Mulroney delegates to infest the major centres and look for undecided delegates and steer them into one of these hospitality suites, where they would get a drink and be introduced to Mulroney.

After hitting all the hospitality suites, and doing some extraneous glad-handing, Mulroney hunkered down at the Skyline, the main convention hotel, and hatched a novel scheme. It was now late, and delegates were returning to their rooms for the night. Mulroney's handlers stood at the main entrance to the hotel lobby, snared delegates coming in, and steered them into a nearby meeting room. When the room filled up Mulroney arrived with jacket off and tie loosened to deliver an impassioned "Let's beat the Grits" ripsnorter. After ten or twelve minutes he disappeared to lie down and rest in a room upstairs while aides rounded up another roomful of delegates, broadening their recruitment venues to include the bar, the street, the hospitality suites — wherever delegates could be found. Then Mulroney reappeared for another humdinger. This cycle repeated itself every thirty minutes into the wee hours. Behaving as if he truly believed he could still pull it off, Mulroney kept going until the last delegate had gone to bed.

On the morning of the vote, the Mulroney campaign tried to lure their delegates into the arena early with free coffee and doughnuts, but the heavy overnight snowfall had fouled up that bit of strategy. Nonetheless the eager Mulroney forces were still the first to show up. Soon Mulroney arrived with Mila and his mother and took his reserved seat at the front of the Mulroney bleachers already filled with his delegates. The Mulroney section overlooked the convention floor between the blue line and the goal line. Immediately to the right, closer to the goal line, was the Hellyer group, and off in the corner, mostly behind the goal line, was the Clark contingent, which, in contrast to the feisty Mulroney group, was strangely quiet. Far off at the other end of the arena, nearly the full length of the rink away, sat the Wagner delegation.

While delegates waited for the polling booths to open, copies of the Sunday edition of the *Toronto Sun* began flooding the convention. "Mulroney and Hellyer Blew It," screamed the headline. Mulroney gave CBC Television a quick interview expressing himself confident of victory and saying he was pleased with his speech despite the *Toronto Sun* headline. It was typical campaign bravado; only Mulroney believed he could still win.

Michel Cogger and Don McDougall, the two men most responsible for bringing Mulroney into the race, sat up near the roof in a booth with special telephone lines and walkie-talkies. Down below the Mulroney workers scurried around in white hard hats with numbers on top so that Cogger and McDougall could spot them from above. Two hard hats canvassed each queue of delegates waiting to vote, and all had plenty of Mulroney badges and scarves to give out on the second and third ballots.

The foul weather had delayed the start of voting, and during the wait the Mulroney campaign got a much-needed break from a CBC poll. It put Mulroney on top of the delegate count. Mulroney workers quickly produced a makeshift placard proclaiming the key numbers — Mulroney 14 per cent, Wagner 11, Clark 11, and MacDonald 9 — and paraded it around the convention floor, making no mention of the fact that it pre-dated yesterday's speeches. "Take it with a grain of salt," CBC anchorman Lloyd Robertson warned viewers about his own network's poll. It just happened that the two candidates who had been the most vilified and disliked were leading the pack. How well they would hold up in the later ballots was a different matter.

"We picked up delegates all night last night," Mulroney told the CBC after the poll came out. "I think that's obvious. And I'm very,

very delighted with the way things are going. That poll, you know, is not inconsistent with the ones we've been conducting as you know. And they're basically, all these polls are basically pretty accurate. And so I'm reasonably confident as to the outcome."

Candidates can usually predict how well they will do long before the votes are tallied, but this convention was too volatile to forecast. Even supposedly committed delegates do not always tell the truth, and commitments waver after the first ballot. Although candidates can make deals to support one another as trends emerge, they can't force their delegates to go with them. In a convention with no clear frontrunner and many candidates, almost anything can happen.

Finally, two hours later than scheduled, voting began. And the opening ballot produced the first of several surprises to come.

FIRST BALLOT

Wagner	531	Stevens	82
Mulroney	357	Fraser	127
Clark	277	Gillies	87
Horner	235	Nowlan	86
Hellyer	231	Grafftey	33
MacDonald	214		

Mulroney had expected more votes, but then so had everyone. What really counted was the fact that Mulroney had come in a competitive second and led all moderate candidates. Wagner, now the undisputed frontrunner, had hoped for 650 and was clearly disappointed, but an analysis of the results showed he was now positioned to win: the right-wing candidates (Wagner, Horner, Hellyer, Stevens, Nowlan) had outpolled the moderates 1,265 to 1,095. The big loser appeared to be Clark, whose organization was reeling from shock. Clark had expected four hundred votes and had not even come close.

Between the first and second ballots things started to shift. Wagner's showing had been strong enough to make him the undisputed

As a young, successful, and attractive lawyer who loved to party, Mulroney could have his pick of women, and through most of the sixties and into the early seventies he was playing the field. In the summer of 1972 he met Mila Pivnicki; he married her the following spring. This snapshot, taken in the fall of 1972 at a ski chalet in Saint-Sauveur, Quebec, is one of the first photos of them together. *(Jean A. Savard)*

It was Mulroney's appointment to the Cliche commission on union thuggery in the construction industry that gave him a reputation as a crimebuster and opened the door for him to run as leader of the Conservative Party without ever having held a seat in the House of Commons. Here he is seen conferring with commission chairman Robert Cliche. *(The Gazette)*

On the road and, as always, on the phone, during the 1976 leadership race. Stanfield announced his retirement as Tory leader in the summer on 1975; both Mulroney and Clark decided to enter the race. *(Canada Wide)*

RIGHT: Lucien Bouchard was the smartest student in Mulroney's class at Laval and was bookish by nature. Yet he and Mulroney formed a special bond in their final year of law school. Bouchard became Mulroney's intellectual surrogate. One of the first things Mulroney did upon being appointed to the Cliche commission was to bring Bouchard on staff as associate counsel. *(Canapress Photo Service)*

BELOW: Mulroney was the most glamorous of the dozen candidates vying to replace Robert Stanfield as Tory leader in 1976. He was also the most extravagant and became known as the Cadillac candidate, an image that would undermine and help defeat him. *(Canapress Photo Service)*

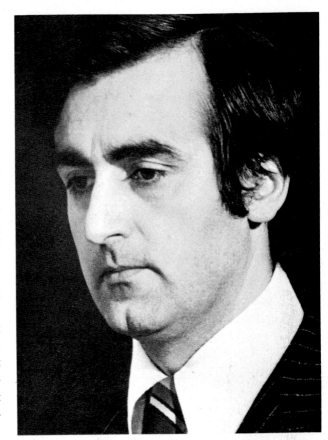

Mulroney's main rival in 1976 was Claude Wagner, who grabbed most of the delegates Mulroney needed to form a Quebec base. Ironically, it was Mulroney who had recruited Wagner for the party in 1972, a political blunder he came to regret.

After losing to Joe Clark, Mulroney was named president of the Iron Ore Company of Canada and moved into a stately house at the top of the mountain in Westmount, determined to forget politics and live the comfortable life of a corporate executive.
(Above: Canapress Photo Service; below: Canapress Photo Service / Obenrauf)

RIGHT: Rodrigue Pageau acted as a double agent trying to undermine Clark's leadership in the aftermath of his defeat as prime minister in 1980. A professional political organizer, Pageau was supposed to be shoring up Clark's strength but was actually working to recruit delegates to vote against him. After the initial damage was done, Pageau became Mulroney's chief organizer in Quebec. *(Canapress Photo Service)*

BELOW: Mulroney posing with one of the many groups of buddies whom he regularly took up to the Iron Ore Company's fishing camp in Labrador. From left to right: Tim McGrath, Finlay MacDonald, Mulroney, Pat MacAdam, Sam Wakim, Terry McCann. *(Pat MacAdam)*

Smiling rivals, Mulroney and Tory leader Clark exchange greetings at the
Joe Clark dinner in Montreal in November 1981. The $175-a-plate dinner
teetered on the verge of collapse for lack of ticket sales until Mulroney
and his troops came in and sold more than a thousand tickets in the final
weeks. Some Clark supporters alleged that Mulroney had earlier
sabotaged ticket sales so that he could save the event.

(Canapress Photo Service / MacAlpine)

Clark started building his own organization in Quebec at the same time as Mulroney was building his. At a press conference in Montreal in September 1981, he introduced Marcel Danis (centre), a former Mulroney worker, and MP Roch LaSalle as key members of his Quebec team. *(Canada Wide)*

In a highly controversial move, Mulroney called a press conference at the Ritz-Carlton Hotel in December 1982 and, with Clark sitting at his side, announced he was supporting Clark's reconfirmation as Tory leader at a party general meeting the following month. At the same time his supporters continued to work to bring Clark down so that Mulroney could run for Tory leader again. Later, harassed and worn down, Clark called a leadership convention after receiving two-thirds of the votes. *(Canapress Photo Service / Poling)*

In 1983, with another leadership contest imminent, Mulroney's most
serious handicap was the fact that as president of the Iron Ore Company
he had been forced to shut down the town of Schefferville, Quebec. Before jumping into the race Mulroney faced a public hearing and
dazzled his audience and critics. *(Canapress Photo Service / Poling)*

leader of the rightists. In second place, Mulroney stood poised as the obvious choice for the moderates. His fate would be decided in the next twenty minutes as candidates at the bottom withdrew from the race and threw their support to one of the leaders, in attempts to play kingmaker. As lowest vote-getter, Grafftey automatically dropped off, freeing up thirty-three votes, but he showed no signs of going any-where. Everyone in the packed arena waited tensely for the first move.

After what seemed an eternity but was in reality a matter of minutes, ninth-place finisher Jim Gillies walked over to Clark, shook hands, and pinned on his yellow-and-black campaign button, bringing most of his eighty-seven delegates with him. Dejection in the Clark camp was suddenly transformed into jubilation as, back in the Gillies section, his delegates could be seen tying on Clark's yellow bandanas. Meanwhile the Mulroney camp wondered what to make of it.

Now Grafftey, a fellow Quebecker to the left of centre, made his move, getting up and also moving over to Clark, bringing with him most of his small band of supporters. A mini-bandwagon now seemed to be rolling for Clark, stunning the Mulroney camp. Their candidate was paying the price for his slick, lavish campaign that had alienated everybody but his own delegates. Just as Mulroney had feared, it looked as though the caucus was ganging up on him. Suddenly Clark was challenging him as the moderate alternative to Wagner, but it was still too early to predict the outcome. And Wagner still had the edge over both of them.

Mulroney was still expecting to snare Flora MacDonald and John Fraser, both of whom were bigger catches than the consolation prizes Clark had landed so far, but MacDonald had decided to stay put for another ballot and Fraser was still dithering as the second ballot was about to begin. Sinclair Stevens, far over at the Wagner end of the arena, had formally withdrawn after finishing a disappointing seventh but remained glued to his seat. Clark and Mulroney now seemed in a virtual dead heat.

Finally, after an agonizing reappraisal, Fraser was talked by his supporters into joining Clark — and most of his 127 votes followed suit. The Clark camp was delirious: their man now had a clear edge over Mulroney. But where would Sinclair Stevens go? As a right-wing Tory his support should logically have gone to Wagner, 182 votes that could shift the momentum back to the conservative side. Without warning, Stevens suddenly got up and started to trek down the length of the arena away from Wagner. Reporters, microphones, and cameras followed him step by step through the crowded convention floor, but Stevens was not talking. He seemed headed straight towards Mulroney, who now desperately needed a break, but continued to walk straight past him and on to Clark. As Stevens and Clark shook hands and the Clark section erupted into pandemonium, Mulroney and his supporters watched in shock and disbelief.

Up in the spotters' booth Cogger turned to McDougall: "You have just seen the extreme right embrace the extreme left," he said. Within the narrow ideological range of the Progressive Conservative Party of Canada, Cogger's analysis was accurate. Given that Stevens evidently did not like Wagner, it made more sense for him to go to Mulroney than to somebody like Clark, since Mulroney was perceived as straddling the ideological centre. Mulroney had been positive that Stevens was coming to him, and he would think about Stevens's dramatic walk for years to come, never pretending to understand it. Claude Wagner was even more aghast, since he had been abandoned by a clear ideological ally. Now the delegate balance appeared to have shifted from the candidate of the right to the candidate of the left, but only the results of the next ballot would confirm this.

One thing was clear, however: the Stevens "defection" had devastated Mulroney's chances and installed Clark as the leader of the stop-Wagner alliance. Stevens had delivered Clark not only a crucial bloc of delegates, but an overwhelming psychological lift. Had Stevens hung in for another ballot, maybe Mulroney could have built up strength, but now Clark was moving too fast. It would take a miracle for Mulroney to recover.

Hellyer, his delegates wedged in between the Clark and Mulroney sections, cringed at this sudden twist of events. He felt he had to stop the moderate faction at any price, even at the cost of his own candidacy. Although the second ballot was already under way, Hellyer abruptly bolted to Wagner's section, neglecting even to consult his supporters. Ultimately only about one-third of his delegates followed his lead. Another third went to Jack Horner and fully a third went next door to Clark. Thus the disintegration of the ill-fated Hellyer vote helped consolidate the very trend Hellyer was trying to reverse. With Hellyer sitting with Wagner, the former Hellyer seats became filled with the burgeoning yellow-and-black of Clark. Half an hour earlier Clark's colours had been sequestered in the corner behind the goal line. Now they had spread towards the centre until they bumped into the blue of the Mulroney section.

During a campaign stop in Windsor, Mulroney had predicted that the second ballot would reveal what delegates really felt about other candidates, and the results proved him right. (Hellyer and Fraser had pulled out too late for their names to come off the second ballot.)

SECOND BALLOT

Wagner	667	MacDonald	239
Clark	532	Hellyer	118
Mulroney	419	Nowlan	42
Horner	286	Fraser	34

To nobody's surprise, the second ballot had pushed Mulroney back into third place and, for practical purposes, out of the race. Regardless of how many names remained on the third ballot, it had become a two-way contest between Clark and Wagner. Without hesitating, Flora MacDonald stood up and led a long procession of supporters to Clark. While she was embracing Clark in his box, the back end of her parade was passing in front of Mulroney and shouting, "Come over, Brian." Meanwhile Horner and Nowlan joined Wagner at the other end of the arena. Now the field was Wagner, Clark, and Mulroney. Wagner's only hope lay in convincing

Mulroney to drop out and swing behind him, a prospect roughly akin to John Diefenbaker pledging himself to Dalton Camp. Mulroney and Wagner loathed each other and, for the most part, so did their delegates. While Mulroney contemplated his decision, Wagner and Clark partisans were screaming at him to come their way. The scene encircling the Mulroney box was one of utter madness.

In the midst of this mayhem Mulroney talked animatedly with advisers Alan Eagleson and Claude Dupras, sweat rolling down the foreheads of all three. Eagleson, the president of the Conservative Party in Ontario, urged him to go to Clark, while Dupras, the president of the Conservative Party in Quebec, plumped for Wagner. MP Roch LaSalle came over as an emissary from Wagner but got nowhere. "I have always said there would be no kingmakers at this convention," Mulroney told reporters as LaSalle left empty-handed. "I am in this to the finish." A few minutes later Horner came around to try his luck on behalf of Wagner, but with the same result. One of Clark's ambassadors, Jim Gillies, looked like he would literally climb into the Mulroney box, but to no avail. "No deals," Mulroney said afterwards. "No way. I owe nothing to the caucus." Jim McGrath and Heath Macquarrie, the only MPs in Mulroney's contingent, moved over to Clark.

By now the yellow-and-black of Clark had more than tripled its original extent, jumping over the Mulroney section and reaching all the way to the centre of the arena, where it met the blue-and-white of Wagner. The colours told the story of the convention. One end of the rink was yellow and black, except for an island of Mulroney blue; the other was blue and white.

THIRD BALLOT

Wagner	1,003
Clark	969
Mulroney	369

"Obviously I've been eliminated by the convention," Mulroney told a crowd of reporters awaiting his reaction. "But I accept that." He said he had no regrets, and that he had fought a good and clean fight. Now that he was officially bumped from the ballot, his delegates had to choose between Clark and Wagner and thus anoint the winner. They had shown tremendous loyalty through three ballots and would probably follow him now. How they decided would greatly depend on whom he supported. He was in a position to choose the next Conservative leader, which faced him with a true dilemma: of his two choices he despised one and did not respect the other. He could not support Wagner, but neither could he bring himself to endorse Clark, whom he had always seen as the lesser man. How could he swing the convention to someone he regarded as only half as good as himself? His only way out of this quandary was to endorse nobody. "I am hereby liberating those magnificent people who have worked so hard in my campaign," he announced a few minutes later. "I have no vote myself and I believe my supporters should have the right to vote for the man of their choice now that I have left the race." For the first time he was happy he did not have a vote.

Having dealt with the media, Mulroney turned around to address his delegates and, without a megaphone, strained to make himself heard. His voice, weakened from a long and tiring campaign, valiantly tried to project itself up into the bleachers. Everybody in his end of the arena grew hushed as they struggled to hear. Striving to bellow and yet maintain his dignity, Mulroney thanked his delegates for loyally supporting him and counselled them to vote according to their consciences. He said he was not making any deals or joining any alliances. His little speech, only a few minutes long, was one of the most touching scenes of the convention and Mulroney's finest moment. Suddenly he stopped looking like the slick, well-monied mouthpiece of the upper class and seemed to become a man of principle who could rise above the morass of dealmaking. In defeat he looked almost heroic.

Sitting on the fence may have been the only palatable choice, but it was also politically astute. If he planned to run again, he could not be seen to have brought down Wagner, a fellow Quebecker. Quebeckers did not betray one another in this manner. However, just because Mulroney was officially neutral did not mean that the Mulroney campaign would not influence the outcome. When asked which candidate he personally favoured, Mulroney kept repeating that he had no vote to cast — and that was the tip-off. It was his subtle way of reminding people that Wagner had blocked him from becoming a delegate, of sending the message that Wagner was worse than Clark.

On the convention floor Mulroney's true intentions were not so veiled. His hard-hatted workers all had both Wagner and Clark buttons in their pockets, and they pressed their walkie-talkies to their ears for instructions. The voice of Jean Bazin, Mulroney's Quebec chairman, crackled over the air with instructions to move the delegates to Clark. So as Mulroney's supporters lined up to vote, the Mulroney workers took out Clark's yellow-and-black buttons and started handing them around.

As Clark waited for the fourth-ballot results, he hastily penned his victory speech on a scrap of paper on his knee. Meanwhile Mulroney handled himself in exemplary fashion. It was easy to fall apart in such circumstances, to allow a harmless remark to trigger an outburst, especially for someone with his tendency to react impulsively, but his conduct was immaculate. Mulroney remained composed and gracious in defeat, and carried himself with statesmanlike poise. During the sad wait both he and Mila could hardly suppress their tears, but there were no histrionics. While the delegates lined up to vote, a few buddies dropped down from his bleachers to lift his spirits, but words failed them. There was nothing anybody could say. Everybody in the Mulroney entourage felt shell-shocked and bitter. Nobody could explain the ideological about-face of Sinclair Stevens. Nobody could swallow the blatant gang-up by the caucus. They felt outraged, hurt, and cheated, as if the outcome were morally and ethically wrong.

The fourth ballot gave Clark the victory by a mere 65 votes, 1,187 to Wagner's 1,122. Mulroney's delegates had gone to Clark two-to-one and, depending on how one viewed it, had either propelled Clark to victory or pushed Wagner into defeat. So Mulroney had ended up doing what he set out to do when he first entered the campaign, which was to stop Wagner. But in the end Wagner had also stopped him. Together they had split the Quebec vote and denied each other the Tory leadership. Either one of them would likely have won without the other.

Although Clark had performed well, he had not captured anybody's imagination. He simply happened to be the most popular second and third choice — the least offensive candidate to the largest number of people. Although he had won honestly, it looked more like an act of alchemy than the calculated decision of a century-old political party. Clark had ridden the wave of a chain reaction that a roomful of nuclear physicists could not have reproduced.

As the delegates applauded the surprising result, Mulroney joined the other defeated candidates on stage in a show of unity and to endorse the party's choice. Then Clark gave a solid victory speech, whose most memorable line was: "We will not take this nation by storm, by stealth, or by surprise. We will win it by work." The same words could as easily have described his whole approach to politics.

After Clark's victory speech the delegates left to fight another snowstorm. Mulroney stayed a while to thank his workers and then walked alone across the convention floor, through the litter of the campaign signs, cigarette butts, and trampled paper cups towards an exit tunnel. He had almost made it when the *Globe and Mail*'s Jonathan Manthorpe and a few other reporters spotted him and rushed up for his final thoughts. Mulroney stopped to answer their questions. "When I saw Sinc [Stevens] go to Joe, it reinforced my belief that politics does indeed make strange bedfellows," he said sardonically. His eyes were red from exhaustion and maybe tears. As the impromptu interview was picking up steam, Bryce Mackasey, the postmaster general of Canada, incongruously appeared on the scene and pushed his way into the group. Strange that a Liberal cabinet minister would be haunting a Tory convention, but Mackasey had been a commentator in the CTV booth. He had been practically the only pundit not to pan Mulroney's speech. Mackasey wrapped his arm around his old friend.

"Come on," he said, waving off the reporters, "leave him alone. He's had a tough day."

With that he led Mulroney outside and away.

"The day John Kennedy was shot," the reporters could hear him telling Mulroney on their way out, "Patrick Moynihan was interviewed on television. He said, 'If you are Irish you know that at some point the world is going to break your heart.'"

PART THREE

ASCENT TO
POWER

CHAPTER SIXTEEN

AFTERMATH

AFTER BEING USHERED out of the Civic Centre by Bryce Mackasey, Mulroney made his way to a party in the basement bar of the Beacon Arms Hotel in downtown Ottawa. It had been hastily organized by his campaign workers; just getting there in the snowstorm proved an ordeal. It was Sunday evening and all the liquor stores were closed, but the various Mulroney hospitality suites yielded more than enough booze to supply the occasion. Meanwhile the Clark revellers over in their headquarters at 200 First Avenue could not get enough to quench their celebratory thirst and had to ask the Mulroney people for help. The sombre Mulroney organizers obligingly sold them their surplus.

Several hundred delegates and volunteers showed up at the Mulroney wake, all of them weary to the bone and deeply depressed. They believed that victory had been theirs and then allowed to escape. Mulroney gallantly addressed his faithful troops one last time, and again carried himself with model civility. Exhausted and hoarse, and fighting to maintain his voice, he graciously congratulated Clark and urged everybody to get behind him now that he was leader. He humbly acknowledged that mistakes had been made in his own campaign, but he did not dwell on these, concentrating instead on the good that had come out of it and how he had been stirred by the

317

support of his hard-working supporters and Conservatives across the country. It was a moving performance. Mulroney stayed on the scene for a while and mingled, but he did not linger. But then neither did most of his supporters.

The next morning Mulroney, in shirtsleeves and suspenders, with his tie slightly askew, stood alone and silent in front of the hotel room window, staring wistfully out at Parliament Hill. He gazed straight ahead at the profile of the Peace Tower and kept gazing until a couple of people walked up and broke the mood. Once he started to talk he cursed those responsible for his defeat — above all, the friends he felt had been disloyal.

Later that morning nobody showed up at the station to say goodbye as he boarded the train back to Montreal. Five days earlier in the same spot a crowd of three hundred — including cheerleaders — had welcomed him with streamers, signs, and a band. He could not do anything or go anywhere without being surrounded by a herd of handlers, admirers, and media and security people. Everywhere he went he was introduced as the next prime minister of Canada. Now the reporters who had swarmed around him were off chasing down Joe Clark, who really might get to be the next prime minister. Now his only company was the rump of his entourage — Alex Konigsberg, his convention manager, Michel Cogger and his wife, and David Angus. As far as the world was concerned they were ordinary passengers catching the train to Montreal. In contrast to the scene five days ago, this one was dramatic for its very ordinariness. The only goodbye wave came from his driver, Mark Maloney, Arthur Maloney's nephew, the last reminder of his moment in the political spotlight. Mulroney was back to being a private citizen and, in the mind of the public, a nobody. It would be worse when he got back to Montreal.

Earlier that day, at 3:15 in the morning, after most delegates had gone to bed, Richard Cleroux of the *Globe and Mail* had stuck his nose into a tenth-floor suite in the Embassy Hotel. It was here that the Mulroney organization doled out cash to delegates to reimburse them for their rooms and meals. Operations like these were not exactly above board, but neither were they uncommon. While no-body talked about such payments, most of the major candidates did the same.

As Cleroux stepped inside he encountered Pierre Gauthier, an overwrought Mulroney worker who held up a series of white enve-lopes. He had spent the weekend stuffing such envelopes with cash and dispensing them to Mulroney delegates. "They all wanted to be paid," Gauthier sobbed. "I'm ashamed to say that most of them were from Quebec. I had delegates demanding $150 to pay for their rooms or they wouldn't stay around for the vote. They'd say, 'You pay my room, you pay my meals, or I'm going home.' I must have paid for four hundred rooms." What angered Gauthier was not the ethics of the transactions but the fact that Mulroney had polled fewer votes than the number of white envelopes dispensed. A number of delegates had taken Mulroney money and then voted for one of his competi-tors, and Gauthier thought it was dishonest and disloyal; he was beside himself with outrage.

Too late for Monday's paper, Cleroux filed the story for the following day. "Delegates Paid, Aide to Mulroney Says; 'Pay My Room or I'm Going Home,'" proclaimed the *Globe and Mail* headline in the middle of page one. The story recounted the scene with Gauthier, then went on to blame Mulroney's loss on his ostentatious display of money. "The Mulroney campaign was a media myth, plastered together with dollar bills, free lunches, paid organiz-ers, lots of hoopla and little content," Cleroux wrote.

When the paper hit the street on Tuesday morning Mulroney called Cleroux from Montreal and unleashed a long, rambling, and painful diatribe that was full of swear words and brimming with self-pity. He flatly denied the story and accused Cleroux of betraying him. He told the reporter he had been open with him during the campaign, and now Cleroux was quoting somebody without first checking with him for an explanation as to who the person was and whether he was telling the truth. "How could you do this to me?" he demanded as more profanity poured out. He also challenged

Cleroux's contention that the campaign had been overly lavish. He still did not understand what the spending fuss was about.

As he rambled on, switching from French to English to French and back to English, he showed more hurt and sorrow than anger. His voice cracked with emotion and left Cleroux wondering about his psychological stability. Cleroux had written a perfectly accurate story and had betrayed no confidences, but now he felt sorry for ever having done so. He had never encountered Mulroney in such a state before and realized that he had caused deep injury.

In fact the story, published after the campaign was over, came and went with hardly a hiccup. All eyes were focused on Clark, not on the ten losers. Yet Mulroney was unable to let it go. The first thing he did was drop Cleroux as a media contact. He kept him on his grudge list for months.

When Mulroney returned to his desk at Ogilvy Cope, he tried to act as though everything was normal — but it clearly was not. For one thing his phone, which ordinarily never stopped ringing, now sat deathly silent. The odd call came in, one of the first, strangely enough, from Prime Minister Trudeau, who merely wanted to wish him well. (Trudeau and Mulroney weren't friends, but they knew and respected each other and talked from time to time.) A similar call came from Sean O'Sullivan, the Diefenbaker MP who had supported Hellyer. "Well, at least you told me the truth that you weren't going to support me," Mulroney told O'Sullivan, before taking a swipe at "all these sons of bitches who lied to me about their support." But most of the time his phone just sat there like a piece of broken equipment.

As much as Mulroney tried to pretend that nothing had happened, colleagues could tell from one quick look that he was not his old self, and certainly not the same man who had marched off into battle the previous fall. The loss had left him numb and sapped his morale, and even his bravest face could not disguise it. Outwardly and in public he had been dignified and gracious in defeat. Among friends there was nothing dignified or gracious about the feelings he expressed.

One colleague dropped into his office to ask about the campaign, and as Mulroney talked he could hardly hold back his tears.

L. Ian MacDonald, Mulroney's friend and biographer, recorded in *Mulroney: The Making of the Prime Minister* the impressions of Tommy Montgomery, Mulroney's mentor at Ogilvy Cope: "He was up and down, reliving it," Montgomery told MacDonald. "He couldn't leave it alone. I thought he might be permanently damaged by it, though he managed to function all right. But he did have a period of black depression." According to MacDonald, he occasionally worried about "kicking the bucket" and once told Montgomery he had a dream he was going to die and that he had checked into a hospital for general tests.

For one of the few times in his life, Mulroney felt meek and lowly. The fact was that the majority of delegates had voted against him as their leader. He had always had a glass jaw when it came to personal criticism, and he took his defeat very personally. It was as if each and every one of those delegates had rejected him, had told him he was not good enough. For someone in constant need of approval, even adoration, it was devastating.

Losing was bad enough, but the suddenness of his fall had caught him totally unprepared. One moment he was grasping victory and the next he had crashed without warning, without any time to adjust. Having avoided every election going back to his days in law school, he had just suffered the biggest defeat the Conservative Party could give him. He had no immunization against defeat and simply lacked the emotional fibre to cope. Suddenly he felt like a has-been, an outcast. In the aftermath of the convention he swore off politics, vowing never to seek high office again.

Had he looked at his failure rationally, the way he urged his corporate clients to do when they suffered setbacks in a labour negotiation, or if he had looked at the bright side, as he had done most of his life, Mulroney would have returned from Ottawa a happy guy, for he had done remarkably well. He had finished third in a field of eleven candidates and could legitimately brag about catching a lot of people by surprise. What's more, he had exceeded his own goals and almost won the whole thing. As an unelected thirty-six-year-old virtually unknown outside Quebec, he had had no right to do as well as he had done. But he was not viewing events rationally and could not recognize the size of his accomplishment, only how he had fallen short. That he had achieved his original goals — to stop Wagner and promote himself for a future candidacy, and done so without ever looking back — did nothing to soothe his deeply wounded ego. His original goals had long ago been overtaken by the belief that he could win.

To make matters worse, Mulroney now had to face the bill for having splurged so heavily on his leadership campaign. Losers are always saddled with debts, but Mulroney had run wide open and spared no expenses. The reckoning came one day that March over lunch at the Beaver Club. Montreal lawyer Jean Bruyère and Liberal businessman Benoît Mailloux, who had sat with Mulroney on the Laval student council in 1963, had totalled up the numbers and now gave him the news that contributions had fallen drastically short of expenses — somewhere between $250,000 and $275,000 short. Big money had supported him, but he had badly overspent. (By comparison Clark's pay-as-you-go campaign had finished free of debt.) Mulroney now faced a bigger mess than he had ever thought possible. "Okay, that's the situation," Mulroney said grimly. Mailloux, citing examples of foolish spending, berated him for not containing expenses, adding that nobody had been put in financial control. Mulroney listened stoically. "I'm going to have to find ways to settle this," he said quietly.

As if a quarter-million-dollar debt were not enough, the Tory convention committee soon gave him some more bad news: it was denying him a campaign subsidy. The committee had earlier adopted a rule requiring all candidates to file a financial return disclosing how much they had spent and the names of everyone who had contributed more than $100. Mulroney had promised to comply when he was being harassed over his connection with Paul Desmarais. But later he changed his mind to protect many of his contributors from Quebec who feared ever seeing their names pop up on a Conservative donors' list. It was widely rumoured that these people were also contributors to the provincial Liberal Party and did not want to be blacklisted for government business.

Flaunting the disclosure rule would have been easy for Mulroney had the convention not turned a handsome profit. Left with a potful of money, the convention committee decided to thank all leadership candidates for the effort and expense of running by granting them a subsidy on their expenses. But there was one hitch — they first had to submit a proper disclosure return. Mulroney could still ignore the regulation, but he would be walking away from $30,000, and he needed the money badly.

Mulroney responded to this predicament by refusing to file a return while still putting in a claim for his share of the subsidy pool. He argued that the rules did not require public disclosure, only internal disclosure to the party. No other candidate dared make such a claim, but, weak as it was, it was the only leg Mulroney had to stand on. (Claude Wagner had also raised funds heavily in Quebec and yet had complied with the disclosure rule.) After deliberating, the convention committee stuck to its decision and disallowed his claim.

Mulroney, his feathers ruffled, protested vehemently and launched an appeal, taking his case directly to the president of the party, who happened to be his old friend from Laval law school, Michael Meighen. He was already upset with Meighen, who, despite their old bonds, had run the convention by the book, scrupulously avoiding favouritism towards anybody. He felt that Meighen should have found ways to use his position as convention chairman to help his candidacy. With Mulroney now kicking up a fuss, Meighen took the issue back to the convention committee, which once again refused to back down on its original decision. Mulroney, now sizzling with rage, directed his wrath at Meighen, who felt bad for him but said he could do nothing as long as Mulroney refused to file a proper return. But Mulroney wasn't capable of understanding why, and he held Meighen personally responsible for his loss of the subsidy, cutting him out of his life, just as he had done to Richard Cleroux. Meighen was one more friend who had betrayed him.

When the Conservative Party formally published the spending figures, Mulroney's were the only ones missing. Sinclair Stevens topped the spenders' list at $294,107. Clark came in debt-free at $168,354. Don MacPherson of the *Montreal Gazette* reported that Mulroney spent $345,000 — more than double Clark's, and $50,000 higher than the champion Stevens. However, Bill Fox in the *Toronto Star* reported that unofficial estimates put Mulroney's spending spree in the $500,000 stratosphere. Different theories abounded about how much he had spent and where his money had come from; but apart from Paul Desmarais his donors remained a matter of speculation. The whole affair reinforced the public suspicion that a few wealthy backers had bankrolled him.

Meanwhile the campaign debt somehow had to be retired. Mulroney pulled together his bagmen, led by David Angus and Guy Charbonneau, the chief Tory fundraiser in Quebec. The three met fortnightly and went down the list of payables, divvying up the names. They talked to creditors about accepting discounts and talked new donors into making contributions. Raising money was not easy for a defeated candidate. It would take six months to clear the books, and even then Mulroney would have to dig into his own pocket.

Just as Lowell Murray had warned, the leadership campaign had been a bruising affair. Time usually heals emotional wounds, but for Mulroney the passage of time only aggravated the hurt. Once the shock of the initial trauma wore off, the real inner devastation hit him like a second wave, followed by a third and a fourth and many more. Michel Cogger had urged him not to form his own version of John Turner's 195 Club, which had enshrined the memory of those faithful delegates at the 1968 Liberal leadership convention who had scrupulously stuck with Turner on the last futile ballot. Mulroney agreed with him, realizing on an intellectual level that he had to put the memories of the campaign behind him so he could move on to other things. However, as hard as he tried, the memories would not quit. He had come too close. Never given to reflection before, he became pensive and even a little philosophical as he wondered whether the opportunity of a lifetime had passed him by. The more he thought about it, the more certain he became that he should have won. With the inroads he could make in Quebec, clearly he had been the right man and the party had not recognized it. If only his friends hadn't betrayed him.

Michael Meighen now ranked high on the list of friends who had let him down, but Mulroney reserved his strongest vitriol for Lowell Murray. From the beginning, Murray had tried to talk him out of running, saying he was not ready. Then he had promised to remain neutral and ended up supporting Flora. On the final day of the convention Mulroney had watched in horror as his old friend from St. FX, his first political mentor, had followed Richard Hatfield and Flora MacDonald as they marched to Clark for the third ballot.

In fact Murray had not even been a convention delegate and had wielded virtually no influence on the outcome, but that did not matter. Mulroney had expected Murray to swing behind him from the start, automatically and without thinking, and he treated his behaviour as a personal betrayal on the order of a Cold War defector crossing from West to East. It never occurred to him that Murray might support someone else. If the shoe had been on the other foot, Mulroney would have regarded it as a matter of duty to rally behind him. As a friend, he would have done anything for Murray — absolutely anything. Since they had graduated from St. FX, Mulroney had done him any number of favours, including securing him his job as executive assistant to Davie Fulton. When Murray moved to Montreal Mulroney found him a gorgeous old apartment with high ceilings and fireplaces, the kind nobody could get without pull. Murray had been an usher at his wedding. He simply could not believe Murray could have sided with Clark. It did not matter that Murray and Clark were former roommates who had once run Stanfield's office together. He had been Murray's friend long before Clark. Murray had a duty to him in his hour of need. Paul Creaghan,

Mulroney's predecessor as leader of the St. FX Conservative Party, who had since gone on to become the minister of justice in New Brunswick, had also joined the rush to Clark, but that was nothing by comparison. He and Creaghan had never gotten on particularly well. Mulroney spelled "loyalty" in capital letters, and what he interpreted as Murray's double-cross traumatized him.

Just as Mulroney was devoted to friends who were loyal, he could be hard on those who were not, and he gave Murray the same treatment he gave Meighen and everybody else who failed his loyalty test: he cut them out of his life. Only with Murray it was worse. For a time he refused even to acknowledge Murray's existence, and friends feared mentioning his name in Mulroney's presence. Later, when Mulroney could not ignore him any longer, he could not mention Murray's name without coupling it to the F-word. "That fucking Lowell. I'm going to get that son of a bitch" — his voice would begin to crescendo — "and that fucking goddamn queer Hatfield." And "Flora, that fucking whore." He always called Flora MacDonald a "fucking whore." Ironically, Mulroney was treating Murray and the others exactly as his former idol, John Diefenbaker, had treated him when he himself had been disloyal.

Mulroney's bitterness towards Murray would reach its peak on Christmas Eve 1976, when his former friend became the godfather to Clark's daughter. At Catherine Clark's christening the proud father asked Murray to be his national campaign chairman for the next election. Seeing Murray move in as Clark's chief political adviser — the one assembling Clark's election machine — was almost too much to bear.

Just how deeply Mulroney was hurting in the wake of his defeat became apparent later that spring at a black-tie dinner at the Garrison Club in Quebec City for former party leader Robert Stanfield. Despite his avowed repudiation of politics, Mulroney could not refuse an invitation to such an alluring political event, a farewell tribute with a very select guest list for somebody he greatly admired. About thirty men — no women were invited — representing the cream of the party from both Quebec and the Big Blue Machine in Ontario showed up that evening. Dalton Camp, Roy McMurtry, Norman Atkins, and Paul Curley, soon to be a campaign organizer, were all there. So were Lowell Murray and Michael Meighen, but Mulroney refused to acknowledge either of them. Actually Mulroney emanated hostility to half the people present.

Everybody had a few drinks, posed for a photograph, and then sat down to dinner. During the speeches afterwards Camp good-humouredly needled Mulroney for disowning him during the leadership race, when the Diefenbaker supporters had tried to paint him as a Camp candidate. Camp's remarks, in which he satirized Mulroney for having claimed that he had not seen him in three years, drew a big laugh — from everyone except Mulroney, who saw no humour in this or in many of the other jokes that evening. He even indulged in some minor heckling at the dinner table, but kept himself in check as long as Stanfield was present.

The whole occasion was bittersweet because Stanfield had never become prime minister, and everyone in the room felt bad for him. Stanfield made a gracious speech and left shortly after everybody adjourned for liqueurs. With the guest of honour gone, the boys let down their hair and started to have themselves a real party. Before long, most people were drunk and the jokes and political war stories were flying. Everybody was having fun, except Mulroney, who looked — in the words of one reveller — suicidal. At parties like these Mulroney was usually the epitome of fun and attracted crowds around him. This time people kept their distance. He radiated hostility and seemed to be spoiling for a fight.

Accounts of what happened next varied in later years, as people tried to reconstruct events through memories blurred by alcohol. However, everyone recalled that at some point Mulroney made a scene by shouting rude remarks about a variety of people and insisting that the Conservative Party had screwed itself by picking a loser like Clark. His harangue also included some of the people in the room, making it necessary for him to be pulled outside and calmed down before he went further. Later, Dalton Camp took him for a walk and advised him to bury his bitterness, but Mulroney was unrepentant, saying he would never forgive the SOBs for what they had done, and vowing that their time would come.

Nobody in that group had ever seen Mulroney behave this way. It was completely out of character for him to make a fool of himself, or to be so obviously mean-spirited and uncharitable. His performance at the Stanfield dinner was unlike the Brian Mulroney they had all known, and it shattered the image he had forged over the years as an uncomplaining happy warrior in the loyal service of the party. But the Garrison Club flare-up would not be the last time many of them would witness such misbehaviour. The venue would change and so would the chance remark that triggered the outburst, but not the spewing forth of thoughtless and indiscreet venom — against Clark, against friends he believed had betrayed him, and against a party that showed no gratitude to somebody who had given so much. Mulroney was sliding into a personal hell from which he would not emerge for the next three years.

Friends tried to soothe his pain by reminding him how far he had come, but then had to listen to him replay the imagined injustices and betrayals over and over. "Ya dance with the lady what brung ya" had always been his credo, and he could not forgive any of his old friends who had danced with other partners. People who promised money had not come through. Quebeckers had not flocked to him when the trust fund scandal crippled Claude Wagner. The grievances were endless.

And then there was the matter of the gang-up that drove Clark past him on the second ballot. Years later he would tell journalist Parker Barss Donham that he had been stopped by "the biggest gang-bang in history." He kept asking himself why Sinclair Stevens had made the move he did. If Stevens was going anywhere it should have been to Wagner or Horner, or else to him. More than anybody else he blamed Flora MacDonald, whom he'd known since his YPC days, when she worked as a secretary in party headquarters. Over the years they had collaborated in all kinds of common causes in the name of the Conservative Party, including the effort to topple Diefenbaker from the leadership. He thought he had worked out a deal for her to come his way, and he considered her move to Clark a betrayal. Mulroney would never forgive MacDonald, not even years later when she became one of his cabinet ministers.

Other things played on his gloom too. All the shots that the other candidates and their troops had taken — about his money, his lack of depth, his plastic campaign — haunted him. Even the memory of the television commentators who panned his convention speech still rankled.

If only he had been an MP. If only Flora MacDonald had gotten sixty-four more votes on the first ballot, then Clark would have fallen early and things would have turned out differently. MacDonald would have been in third place, and Sinclair Stevens never would have gone to her, and neither would some of the others, making him the leader of the moderates. Or if the final ballot had come down to himself versus Clark rather than Clark versus Wagner, then he would have emerged the winner — if only he could have gotten past Wagner. If only . . .

Everybody was a double-crosser, a sell-out, a liar. Every grudge was magnified and exaggerated. Sometimes he named names, and other times he just dismissed his enemies as "they." These were the people who had turned against him. "They" did not support Clark as much as oppose him. Like a little child, he focused only on himself and failed to understand that his friends had other friends as well, their own worlds and their own space, and that these interests might not always coincide with his. He could not rein in his emotions, and all the rehashing, the second-guessing, and the bitterness only deepened his despair.

Devastating as it was, the loss would have hurt less had the winner been somebody older and more established. Being struck down by a contemporary he considered his inferior was the ultimate indignity. Hard as he tried he could not understand what had possessed the delegates to do it. Clark simply didn't have what it took to lead the Conservative Party and hadn't a hope of making the breakthrough in Quebec that the party needed to topple the Liberals. Clark was a loser. Mulroney just could not believe that the Conservative Party could choose Joe over him. For the life of him it made no sense.

Meanwhile Mulroney continued showing up for work in Place Ville-Marie each morning and putting in his hours, but he seemed unable to settle back down into the practice of law. He had been away nearly two years — on full salary — and had ceased being a factor in the operation of the firm. He did no significant legal work and clearly had his mind on matters other than the affairs of Ogilvy Cope. After the excitement of the Cliche commission and the glamour of political stardom, his heart wasn't in the daily grind of a lawyer's life. His files had long since been taken over by others, and his partners noticed that his enthusiasm and desire had dissolved. If he continued to drift much longer they would have to do something, but somehow it did not seem likely he would be sticking around very long.

When Mulroney had decided to run for the leadership, he had turned down the opportunity to become vice-president of the Iron Ore Company of Canada and heir apparent to the presidency of one of the biggest mining operations in Canada. But that job remained unfilled, and now he reopened negotiations by calling the Cleveland head office to tell them he was still interested.

Ironically, Mulroney's professional stock had never been so high. Outsiders did not know about his inner turmoil, but they did know about his extraordinary record as a labour lawyer. And that, combined with his exposure from the Cliche commission and the leadership campaign, now made him hot property for the corporate world — hot enough that several career opportunities were dangled before him, among them the presidency of the National Hockey League, an executive post with Standard Brands, and an executive position in the Desmarais empire. All offered fatter salaries than Ogilvy Cope, but the Iron Ore job appealed to him the most.

The Iron Ore Company of Canada, a mining giant formed in

1949, happened to be the biggest user of the St. Lawrence Seaway, each year sending millions of tons of ore into the Great Lakes system from its two huge mines. The company operated open-pit mines in Schefferville, Quebec, and Labrador City, Labrador, a huge shipping terminal in Sept-Îles, Quebec, a railway connecting the three centres, and two hydroelectric power stations. It had seven thousand workers and assets worth a billion dollars. The Hanna Mining Company in Cleveland managed IOC on behalf of five corporate shareholders — mostly U.S. steel producers — and had the responsibility of buying the year's output of iron ore. IOC had once made big profits but, because of depressed commodity prices and increased international competition, had fallen on hard times in recent years and had sunk badly into the red. It had not paid a dividend in nearly a decade.

The company had no control over world markets, but it could do something to straighten out its terrible labour problems at home, which were the product of nineteenth-century management attitudes and militant unions. As many as two dozen wildcat strikes had poisoned operations in the previous three years. Even though IOC paid top wages, the company had suffered a work stoppage every other month over the past ten years and had one of the worst strike records in the country. If the mining operations were ever going to turn a profit, the turmoil had to stop.

Bill Bennett, the old-line president, was a gifted administrator, but his expertise lay in tax law and transportation, and he had never taken the time to tackle the labour problem. He rarely visited the operational centres, and when he did he was seldom seen by ordinary workers. Bennett would be retiring in the summer of 1977, and Hanna Mining had made it a top priority to find a new president who was a conciliator with great people skills. He had to be bilingual, but above all he had to speak the language of the everyday worker. Mulroney seemed the perfect candidate.

Mulroney had first come to IOC's attention during a heated strike in 1969 when the company sought to cut the pay of its railway workers by reducing the work week to forty hours. Mulroney was called in as the company's behind-the-scenes legal adviser, and he initiated some moves that helped the parties find a settlement. So impressed was Bennett, the president, that he gave him a big television set, compliments of IOC.

Bennett came from a different management era, but he had a good eye for up-and-comers and thought he had spotted one in Mulroney. Like so many had done before him, he took the young man under his wing and treated him like a son. For a time the two were very close; Mulroney had even briefly dated one of Bennett's daughters. Bennett particularly liked what he saw when Mulroney was probing union coercion in the construction industry as a member of the Cliche commission. IOC had some big construction projects going in Quebec and in Labrador, and Bennett followed Mulroney's progress closely. When Hanna Mining in Cleveland began looking for the next IOC president, Bennett proposed Mulroney and gave him a glowing recommendation. Soon Cleveland became convinced it had found the right man. If anybody could bring labour onside it would be Mulroney. He also had better connections in government — in Ottawa, Quebec City, and St. John's, Newfoundland — than anybody else they could imagine.

However, by the spring of 1976, when Mulroney called Cleveland to reopen the pipeline with Hanna Mining, the situation had changed. Bennett now opposed Mulroney's appointment, and the reason was simple: Mulroney's decision to run for the Tory leadership. Himself no stranger to politics, Bennett had worked as Liberal cabinet minister C.D. Howe's executive assistant during World War II (in fact, he was the first ministerial executive assistant in Canadian history). But he was a traditionalist who firmly believed that the head of IOC should avoid political partisanship. Mulroney's decision to run for leader had caught him by surprise — he had no idea his protégé harboured grand political ambitions — and caused him to notify Cleveland that he was withdrawing his recommendation.

But Cleveland — not Montreal — called the shots, so Mulroney simply went over Bennett's head and renewed negotiations directly with the parent company. True to its American business culture, Hanna Mining saw nothing wrong with partisanship and remained very interested. Bob Anderson and Carl Nickels, two of the company's top guns, came to Montreal and met him over dinner at Ruby Foo's, an upscale Chinese restaurant.

As he had done so often, Mulroney thoroughly charmed his dinner companions. They already knew his record as a labour lawyer and were impressed with his political connections, but it was Mulroney's personality that convinced them he could solve IOC's labour problems. Both Anderson, Hanna's chairman, and Nickels, a senior executive, left Montreal with their minds made up that they wanted him in spite of Bennett. It took several more meetings and some tough negotiations — Mulroney got an assist from a couple of Ogilvy Cope lawyers, particularly Arthur Campeau — to clinch the deal. The result was most advantageous for a man whose only previous management job had been the St. FX Co-op in 1959 and who knew not the first thing about extracting ore from the ground and processing it for shipment.

As Mulroney saw it, he had found the near perfect position. When he ascended to the presidency he would hold one of the three or four most prestigious jobs in Quebec. His dominion would cover his native North Shore of Quebec, making him Mr. Big in Baie Comeau, where he would now outclass even the mill manager who lived on top of the hill. And not only was it a great corporate plum, but it paid big money.

Mulroney could not have dreamt up a much better employment package. In 1976, when Calgary oil company presidents were lucky to be making $100,000 a year, Mulroney had stepped into a job that paid $180,000 in U.S. funds. And that was only his base salary, and only for his first year. He had a five-year contract that got progressively richer. A lot depended on how well the company did, but as things worked out his total annual income, including all the extras, would eventually eclipse $300,000 and nudge into the $350,000 range. The fringe benefits alone beat out his lawyer's salary, which, down in the $70,000 range, now looked positively puny. The perks included big subsidies towards the purchase of a suitable house in Westmount. Finally he would be earning the kind of salary he always wanted, enough to make him a very wealthy man.

For weeks before Mulroney arrived on the scene that summer, talk about the new vice-president floated around the office of the Iron Ore Company's headquarters in Montreal. People were curious, and not a little apprehensive, at the prospect of an outsider parachuting into the top executive ranks. Rumour had it that he was slated to become president when Bill Bennett retired the following summer. Everyone knew who Mulroney was — star of the Cliche commission, almost-leader of the federal Progressive Conservatives — but not what sort of boss he would make. When he finally showed up for work at the beginning of July 1976, he quickly dispelled most of their concerns. He arrived immaculately dressed, as usual, and immediately went around and shook everybody's hand. As so often in the past, people were especially struck by his extreme self-confidence: he gave off the aura of knowing exactly what he was doing and where he was going.

The only person not charmed by Mulroney's arrival was Bill Bennett. That first year Mulroney spent his time getting to know the company and meeting the other key people in the organization he would be taking over. He travelled to the company's operational centres, building bridges wherever he went, doing his best to establish the image of someone who would listen and who cared about everyone at every level of the company. He was good at making himself popular: just his daily ritual of saying good morning to all the staff who worked at headquarters set him apart from Bennett, the epitome of the old guard.

For a company as big as IOC, its so-called headquarters was a joke. It had three offices, a conference room, and a secretarial pool on the eleventh floor of the Standard Life Building on Sherbrooke Street in downtown Montreal. The whole thing took up little more space than a two-bedroom apartment. In all never more than ten people worked there, including the three or four secretaries, among them Mulroney's secretary of many years at Ogilvy Cope, Ginette Pilotte. There was no accounting division or personnel department: virtually all the hiring took place at one of the company's three operational centres — Sept-Îles, Schefferville, and Labrador City. It lacked even a sales staff. IOC had no sales reps — anywhere. Hanna Mining in Cleveland did all the marketing. It also contracted the ships to carry the ore away. IOC merely dug the stuff out of the ground and turned it into pellets for shipment — and even that process came partly packaged from Cleveland.

The Montreal head office was little more than a storefront designed to give the company a Canadian look. In reality, Hanna Mining ran the show. At one time, the most senior IOC executive living in Canada had been a general manager based at Sept-Îles, whose huge shipping terminal was the heart of the operation. When Cleveland finally appointed a Canadian president, he had refused to live in the outback and set up office in Montreal. Although incorporated in Canada, IOC was only slightly more Canadian than the Statue of Liberty.

The new job had changed Mulroney's career; the salary and the perks that went with it irretrievably changed his lifestyle. Soon after coming to IOC he joined the Mount Royal Club, the most exclusive private club in Montreal. The club was next door to his office, and the swanky Ritz-Carlton Hotel was just across the street. On most days he could be seen at either of these places for lunch, although he still sometimes patronized the Beaver Club in the Queen Elizabeth Hotel. In the evenings after work, he often dropped in at the Ritz-Carlton bar.

The most noticeable sign of his new executive status was his new house. Since marrying Mila, he had lived in a comfortable but unpretentious home in a nice area on the western slope of fashionable Westmount. Now he lived at 68 Belvedere Road in Upper Westmount. One reporter who ran into him at the Mount Royal Club soon after his IOC appointment asked where he was living. "You know the mountain?" Mulroney shot back. "Right on the top. Right on the fucking top." Although not a mansion, it was a beautiful six-bedroom house on 17,556 square feet of land. His employment contract eased him into it with a 4-per-cent mortgage and a buy-back guarantee. (He bought the house in 1976 when real estate prices were depressed and took advantage of the contract provision to sell it to the company in 1981 after prices had climbed. IOC paid Mulroney $500,000 — giving him a non-taxable capital gain of more than $350,000 — and rented it back to him for $1,100 a month.)

Mulroney's comfy new lot in life left him with ample time to dabble in politics, but he still recoiled at the thought. To hear him tell it, he had changed his outlook. As far as he was concerned, politics was full of dirt, double-dealing, and back-stabbing, and he was glad to leave it behind. John Turner had recently retreated into temporary exile on Bay Street, but Mulroney claimed he had abandoned politics for good. Hard as it was to imagine, he said he had lost interest in becoming leader of the Conservative Party. His friends and his colleagues at IOC heard the avowals many times, always offered with the pious conviction of someone who had undergone an almost religious conversion.

Mulroney may have meant every word, but almost nobody believed his conversion would last. He sounded too much like a freshly jilted lover who has renounced all women for the rest of his life. Even his new colleagues at IOC, most of whom were apolitical, felt that his disclaimers did not ring true. They could see that he remained an inherently political animal; the fact that his networking continued unabated underscored it. Despite his protests, politics still gave him more kick and excitement than anything else. Mulroney had not lost his desire — only his hope.

Certainly Joe Clark looked to be around a long time as leader of the Conservative Party. At thirty-six, he presented a young fresh alternative to Pierre Trudeau and had scored an early hit with the public. Within two months of his convention victory he had pulled the listless Conservative Party into first place in the public opinion polls, with a

15-point lead over the Liberals. By the summer of 1976 it looked as if it would be only a matter of time before Clark became Canada's sixteenth prime minister — even more so that fall when television came to the House of Commons. The Commons debates showed Clark at his best. Each day the whole country got to see him stand up and drill one of his machine-gun bursts at Trudeau. Mulroney's chances of ever becoming prime minister seemed non-existent.

Even while swearing he had renounced politics for good, Mulroney had actually been unable to resist a chance to do a little backroom bargaining. Back in April 1976 Bryce Mackasey had impetuously quit the federal cabinet, and it was Mulroney who acted as the fixer who delivered him to Robert Bourassa's team in Quebec City. Over the following summer Mulroney, although he had just started at IOC, took time to shuttle back and forth between the two Liberal camps until the deal was done, all the while consoling the mercurial Mackasey for having walked out on Pierre Trudeau. He saw nothing extraordinary about helping out the hated Liberal Party by brokering a deal between two Grits like Mackasey and Bourassa. Then in November 1976 Bourassa himself needed consoling after falling ignobly to René Lévesque and the Parti Québécois in an electoral rout. Defeated both across the province and in his own riding, Bourassa felt humiliated and believed he was politically finished. During these gloomy days Mulroney boosted his spirits and, contrary to popular wisdom, assured him that a second chance would come. Bourassa could just as easily have been saying exactly the same thing to him, but Mulroney never would have seen the irony. Mulroney was helping a friend. Any connection between the advice he was giving and his own need for it escaped him completely.

Lévesque's sudden rise temporarily reversed the fortunes of the two major parties in Ottawa, sending Trudeau's stock up and Clark's down. After nearly a year on top, the Tories fell back to second place in public opinion polls. As much as the public continued to dislike the ruling Liberals, it wanted Pierre Trudeau rather than Joe Clark to handle separatism in Quebec. By the summer of 1977 the Liberals led the

Tories by a whopping margin of 51 per cent to 27. The unexpected turnabout seemed to defy gravity: once again the Conservative Party's historical irrelevance in Quebec had come back to haunt it.

The Quebec crisis was not the worst of Clark's problems. Not long after taking over as Conservative leader, he began to stumble, and questions started surfacing about his ability to lead the party. No single incident had caused it. First he unwisely became entangled in a public squabble with fellow Tory MP Stan Schumacher about who would get to run in the new riding of Bow River. Redistribution had redrawn the electoral map of Alberta and had moved Clark's home town of High River into the riding, which also included Schumacher's home town. Clark wanted to foster an image as the man from High River, but he failed to make a deal with Schumacher, who announced he would challenge him for the nomination. An embarrassed Clark ultimately backed down and picked the riding of Yellowhead instead. The unwritten rules of politics hold that a party leader should never be forced to submit to one of his backbenchers. The whole episode hurt his image badly; it was the first sign that Clark could not control his caucus. A better leader would have fixed the problem behind closed doors. Meanwhile Maureen had made statements that suggested he could not control his wife either. And before long, Jack Horner, who had placed fourth on the first ballot at the February convention, bolted across the floor to join the Liberals, citing his incompatibility with Clark as the driving factor. Before much longer the sulking Claude Wagner would allow himself to be bought off with a Senate appointment from Pierre Trudeau, reducing the Tories to two seats in Quebec. As well, Clark was too stiff of manner and too formal in language; what played well in the House of Commons played less well in television interviews and other more casual settings. After a promising start it now looked as though the Conservative Party was going nowhere under Clark.

As Clark's fortunes fell, Mulroney started ridiculing him more openly, indiscriminately repeating all the most disparaging anti-Clark jokes. He would deride Clark for having failed law school — conveniently ignoring the fact that he had once failed law school himself — and for never having held a regular job outside politics. Each time Clark stumbled, Mulroney became more convinced the party had blundered and he unleashed more anti-Clark vitriol. Usually his indiscretions were assisted by alcohol. Most evenings Mulroney could be found holding court in the Ritz-Carlton's Maritime Bar, and as often as not his main topic was Joe Clark.

When Mulroney was in his cups and savaging Clark, the performance was something to behold. "The vituperation was quite breathtaking," remarked one journalist after watching a vintage performance. "Mulroney can be quite funny, and he was actually being quite funny about Clark, as well as being vituperous. And none of them who had seen this performance before were surprised at all. I was kind of shocked, actually, at the degree of the contempt that he held for Clark at that point. Clearly he regarded Clark as the lesser man who had no business winning the leadership."

Politics keeps few secrets, and news of Mulroney's behaviour drifted back to Ottawa, at least some of it to Clark. Although he knew exactly how Mulroney felt towards him, Clark never retaliated in kind and chose to keep his feelings about Mulroney to himself. Even in private nobody ever heard him utter a bad word about his rival. Despite his bruises as leader, Clark retained most of his idealism and took the view that it was more important to do his job on Parliament Hill than to worry about rumblings from Quebec.

Although Mulroney had always liked to drink, he had never been a drunkard. He did not ordinarily imbibe excessive amounts but had never held liquor particularly well. In better times it made him more convivial: after he'd had a few he might tell some off-colour jokes when perhaps he shouldn't have, but he rarely crossed the line to unacceptable behaviour. Now, however, as he continued to wrestle with the despair released by his devastating defeat, alcohol seldom improved his mood. It removed his inhibitions and loosened his tongue, exposing the depth of his bitterness. A few hard drinks inevitably pulled him back to February 1976 and caused him to relive the anguish of defeat.

Occasionally his drinking led to trouble. On one of his first trips back to Ottawa for the annual parliamentary press gallery dinner he got so drunk he became involved in an ugly little scuffle with CTV reporter Jim Munson. Munson was the instigator, and normally Mulroney would have ignored the provocation, but this time he could not hold back. The incident caused such a flap at CTV that it looked as though Munson might lose his job, but Mulroney later intervened with the network to prevent the firing.

That first year at IOC, Mulroney kept his drinking under control well enough that few if any of his new colleagues were aware of how serious it had become. Although he occasionally drank fairly heavily at lunchtime, he always pulled himself together and put in a full afternoon at the office. With the exception of his performances at the Ritz, he kept up appearances. Only a few of his closest friends — and his wife — knew the truth of the situation. This was a very difficult time for Mila; with two young children — Ben in diapers and Caroline now three — and a husband who had suddenly lost his way, she found life almost as trying as he did.

Word that Mulroney could not stomach Clark as leader soon reached the ears of the Liberal Party. On one occasion when Mulroney ran into his old Laval classmate André Ouellet, now the minister of urban affairs in Trudeau's cabinet, he promptly gave Ouellet an earful about the Tory leader. Ouellet also happened to be the deputy Quebec lieutenant in the Liberal caucus; after checking with his boss, Marc Lalonde, he offered Mulroney a Liberal nomination in an upcoming Montreal by-election. For practical purposes getting a Liberal nomination in Montreal amounted to winning a seat in Parliament. "You come," Ouellet promised him, "and you'll be a minister in our party."

Mulroney would have fit the Liberal Party like a glove. He often sounded like a Liberal, especially on the subject of Quebec's place in

Canada, and was sometimes mistaken for one. But no matter how much he suited the part, it went against his nature to switch sides. Mulroney saw the political parties as groupings of people and loyalties, rather than groupings of principles and platform planks. He could change his position on most issues easily enough, but he could not abandon his loyalty to the party he had fought for since St. FX. He detested the fat-cat Liberals as a group (although as individuals most of them were his friends). Mention of the word "Liberal" still triggered an automatic profanity like "the goddamn Grits" or "those fucking Grits." As far as Mulroney was concerned, once a Conservative, always a Conservative. "For me, for example, to leave the Conservative Party is absolutely inconceivable," he had said during the 1976 campaign when putting down Claude Wagner and Paul Hellyer for abandoning the Liberals. "It would be like shooting myself. It's part of my life."

In the aftermath of his 1976 defeat he had temporarily closed down this part of his life. In the tug of war between politics and money, the acquisition of wealth had won out. Although lacking political fulfilment, his IOC job gave him most of the prosperity and status that he had always wanted in his professional career. Few jobs could have been closer to perfect. No matter how down he got, he was not about to admit that he wanted anything more.

CHAPTER SEVENTEEN

THE NEW MAN

WHEN BRIAN MULRONEY took over as president of the Iron Ore Company of Canada as scheduled in July 1977, the event did not go off entirely smoothly. Instead of retiring gracefully, Bill Bennett had decided to remain with the company. The outgoing president had made an arrangement with the Hanna Mining board of directors to stay on indefinitely as a "consultant," and he showed no eagerness to move the thirty-five feet from his old office to his new one. Meanwhile Mulroney could hardly wait to move in. It was important that he be perceived as the boss but, given the delicacy of the situation, he hesitated about confronting his former mentor. The problem remained awkward and unpleasant. By the time Bennett finally did vacate the president's quarters, their relationship had deteriorated to the point where they hardly spoke to each other.

Bennett showed up for work every day and remained highly respected throughout the company's management ranks. (Sometimes IOC officers arriving in Montreal to brief Mulroney would talk to Bennett first and get briefed themselves.) By all rights Mulroney should have treated his predecessor as a precious resource — after all, he knew more about the company than anyone else and had a phenomenally detailed memory of corporate history — but Mulroney refused to consult him. Bennett's continued presence rankled. The new president would sometimes drop into the old president's office with tidbits of news, but it was only a show and both of them knew it. "You know," Bennett later told a colleague, "that SOB never once walked in that door and asked for my opinion on anything."

The fact that the retired president disagreed with his successor's way of doing things made matters worse still. The thing that irked Bennett most about Mulroney was how lavishly he spent company money both on himself and on employees. The first thing Mulroney did upon becoming president was to give the office staff in Montreal exactly the same salaries as office workers in the operational centres. The company had always paid the others more as compensation for their higher cost of living, but that rationale carried no weight with Mulroney. The employees in Montreal, he said, were just as good as the other office workers and deserved the same pay.

The decision made him instantly popular at head office, but what he did for the handful of Montreal staff hardly compared to his generosity towards senior managers across the company. He made sure they got paid well — exceedingly well, boosting not only their salaries but their management bonuses as well. Later, when IOC was earning record profits, his managers routinely pulled down annual bonuses of $25,000 and more, and Mulroney's own bonuses reached into the $150,000 range. The higher salaries and the enriched bonuses did wonders for morale in the senior ranks. Everything had to be approved by the Hanna board of directors, but Mulroney was good at getting money out of Cleveland.

He even had tax professionals concoct a deferred income program to shelter the bonuses from the tax collector. Under this scheme IOC managers could choose to have the company put all or part of their bonus money into special accounts, where it would earn tax-free interest until they retired and went into a lower tax bracket. In effect it was an RSP with no ceiling on annual contributions. (The Department of National Revenue later outlawed this tax dodge.) Since the company could do little to shelter Mulroney's base salary, he started investing in tax shelters, not all of which panned out. Like most high-income earners, Mulroney was always in search of loopholes.

One perk that did not come with the president's job was a chauffeur. Bennett did not think a driver was necessary or even justifiable and had never had one in all his years with IOC. However, he did keep a handyman in the office, an elderly fellow named Frank Raymondo, who did a few odd jobs and brought in the mail in the morning and picked it up at night. He had been the janitor in the company's previous building and took care of the heating, but that was years earlier. After Mulroney took over, Raymondo, who was past retirement age, was fired, although the new president delegated that piece of dirty work to an underling. Raymondo was replaced by Joe Kovacevic, a carpenter who became Mulroney's personal chauffeur and general factotum. Each day Kovacevic drove Mulroney in to work and back. Sometimes he chauffeured Mila and the kids, and sometimes he filled in as nursemaid for the Mulroney children (the Mulroneys kept losing nannies). He also did the odd bit of carpentry work on the house.

Being driven to and from work each day was a nice luxury, but the real pay-off for having a personal chauffeur came in the form of status. Being chauffeured looked even better than it felt. It gave Mulroney an élite ranking that very few citizens could claim, offering incontrovertible proof that he had really arrived.

The only thing now missing was a corporate jet. From the time he arrived at IOC, Mulroney had been unhappy with the state and the availability of the company's aircraft. IOC owned three aircraft, but between dropping supplies into Schefferville and Labrador City and bringing back employees to Sept-Îles, they were tied up most of the time. (IOC had a contractual obligation to take employees out of Labrador City and Schefferville to Sept-Îles at least once a year so they could catch commercial flights.) One of the planes, a Grumman Gulfstream, also ferried IOC personnel to Cleveland. It was a lovely, spacious aircraft, able to seat nine or ten people very comfortably, but it was always in use and flew slowly. Depending on the wind, a trip from Montreal to Cleveland took about four hours, whereas an executive jet would do it in less than half the time. The senior officers of IOC had talked about getting an executive jet before Mulroney arrived, but under Bennett it had never happened.

Mulroney had flown around with Paul Desmarais in his private jet, which had a sofa, a bar, a kitchen, and a stereo system, and now he wanted one of his own. Once he became president he picked up the jet issue, arguing that too much executive time was being wasted flying down to Cleveland, and that the Gulfstream consumed a lot of fuel and was too expensive to justify a passenger load of one or two people for trips to Cleveland. Before long he had convinced the Hanna board of directors to buy a dandy de Havilland Hawker 125 from Nelson Skalbania, the Vancouver real estate speculator. The plane sat seven and could get Mulroney from Montreal to Cleveland in an hour and a half. It also allowed him to drop into Sept-Îles or Schefferville on a moment's notice. Moreover it flew not out of Sept-Îles but out of Montreal and was under Mulroney's control, so that he could use it for a whole variety of interesting purposes that had nothing to do with the Iron Ore Company of Canada.

Over the next several years he would deploy the jet shamelessly for social purposes and to dispense favours. When Robert Morrow, a former partner at Ogilvy Cope, needed a triple heart bypass operation in the United States, Mulroney had the company plane fly him there. When Paul-Arthur Gendreau, his old classmate from Laval, was made an assistant deputy minister of justice in the PQ government, Mulroney gathered together Michael Meighen, Peter Kilburn, Yvon Marcoux, and a couple of other Laval alumni for a flight to Quebec City to celebrate. Frank Moores, the former premier of Newfoundland, became a frequent flyer. The jet had all sorts of uses.

As the firing of Raymondo demonstrated, Mulroney wasn't afraid to occasionally ruffle a few feathers. When he moved up, so did his secretary, Ginette Pilotte, to the dismay of Bennett's long-time secretary, who had expected to retain her seniority. Pilotte did not get on particularly well with the other secretaries; she was a private person, completely loyal to him, handling both his business and personal affairs with absolute discretion. Telling her something confidential was like putting it in a safe. She always referred to him as "the Boss," as in "The Boss wants to see you." Soon everyone in the office started referring to him as "the Boss," and the nickname stayed with him all the way to the prime minister's office.

For someone based nine hundred kilometres from the nearest centre of operation, Mulroney moved quickly and boldly to make his presence felt. He visited the centres often, particularly Sept-Îles, cultivating an image as a hands-on, shirtsleeves president. Unlike his predecessor, Mulroney often ventured out into the workplace and did walkabouts, as if campaigning for votes, in the days before this was common among chief executive officers. He needed no pretext to shake hands and exchange banter; it was one of the things he did best. He was equally at ease with truckdrivers, mechanics, heavy equipment operators, labourers, or the local mayor. Nobody had ever seen the stodgy Bennett or any other IOC manager behave like this.

He always asked the person's name, what he did, and what he thought. He always listened carefully to what the workers said. Everyone got his personal attention and was made to feel important. And the next time he always seemed to remember their names, which impressed them no end. As a result he became well liked — as well liked as a president presiding over an unpopular management could be.

Although Mulroney looked like a hands-on president, he did not even try to intrude into the day-to-day operations of the mines. "Look," he told Richard Geren, the executive vice-president stationed in Sept-Îles, "I don't know anything about mining, and I'm not interested in knowing anything about mining. That's not why I'm here. That's why you're here. You look after that." Mulroney said he would handle labour relations, public relations, legal issues, and finance, although he soon backed down partly on the last one. After one internal budget meeting, he stopped going, even though it was here that the company thrashed out its big spending decisions. Finance bored him, but Mulroney proved good on his word about labour relations. Improving them became his personal mandate. His forays into the workplace seemed to be soothing the feelings of hostility at least somewhat, and this gave him cause for optimism. He had reason to feel good about himself.

The house, the big salary, the chauffeur, and only thirty-eight years old. Mulroney was awfully young to be living like a tycoon, but he did not think so. There were still a few status symbols that he craved. One thing about his job that did not measure up to his expectations or to his new status as one of Quebec's leading businessmen was the calibre of his physical surroundings. Not only was the head office small, but it clearly lacked prestige. Visitors walked directly into the secretarial pool because there was no proper reception area. It all looked a bit tacky.

Soon after becoming president, he engineered a move from the eleventh to the sixteenth floor into a much more impressive space. The new quarters offered more room, a spacious reception area, two entrances, and a much bigger corner office for the president. And now he could boast with a smirk of satisfaction that the headquarters of the Quebec North Shore Paper Company, his late father's long-time employer, was one floor below him. The move also gave Mulroney an opportunity to refurbish from top to bottom. Mila bought the furniture and chose the décor, an elegant brown-and-beige colour scheme. The effect was simple and understated, with antique desks and marble tables to enhance the look of quiet luxury.

But despite all these trappings of success, Mulroney continued to drink as heavily as ever. All too often, after a long lunch in the Ritz he would return to the office in mid-afternoon, walking thoroughly erect and with a deliberateness that made him look — in the words of one of his employees — as if he was being pushed by a wave. Once inside the main door he would head directly to his own office without stopping and, once safely inside, remain there for the rest of the day. At such times he did not even try to dictate a letter and often even stayed off the telephone, a dead give-away that something was not right. Frequently he would stay at the Ritz through the afternoon and into the evening. (On visits to the operational centres or to Cleveland he drank at social occasions, but only moderately. He always cleaned up his act before leaving town.)

Although he still wore the well-cut navy-blue suit, the crisp white shirt, and the gleaming black shoes, Mulroney no longer looked quite so immaculate. The clothes still hung perfectly on his frame, but the physique on which they hung had deteriorated a little, a combination of too much drink, careless eating habits, and general neglect. He looked slightly unwholesome. The old spark flashed less often, as did the optimistic and confident grin. He could still turn on the juice when needed, which explained how he continued to impress the IOC workers below him and the Cleveland bosses above him, but it no longer gushed out as it had in the old days.

It was Mila who had to bear the full burden of Mulroney's periodic bouts of depression. When he finally dragged himself home after a long evening at the Ritz, he was not the entertaining man she had married only a few years before.

It was during this period that Mila's penchant for power shopping really surfaced. Actually she alternated between the life of a practical, down-to-earth young mother on the look-out for bargains and the habits of a high-society fashion plate who could not get enough designer dresses or expensive jewellery. When she and her husband were first married, she had haunted pawnshops in search of good deals and found a store where she could get seconds of designer clothes (she had always managed to dress well, even when they were courting). But as her husband began to make more money, her acquisitions became more expensive. Later, her shopping habits would sometimes embarrass him — occasionally even strain his financial resources — and raise questions about whether she could control her need to buy things.

Despite having a beautiful wife and two young children, Mulroney had not lost his eye for beautiful women or his desire for conquest, and drink both made him amorous and lowered his resistance to temptation. His frequent travels introduced him to plenty of enticements, and often enough he could not resist sampling the forbidden fruit. In the period after becoming president, he engaged in liaisons with a variety of women from a variety of places.

Mulroney did not always make it home at the end of a long day. One morning the IOC office received a phone call from an utterly distraught Mila, asking the whereabouts of her husband. Apparently he had gone off to one of the company's operational centres and not returned. The office checked on her behalf but could only report that he was nowhere to be found. Mila could not hold back her tears. However, she behaved in public as if nothing was wrong.

L. Ian MacDonald's sympathetic biography hints at the strains on the marriage. "In the days after his defeat in 1976, the fairy-tale aspect of their life came suddenly to a halt, and ahead there was the hard struggle of building a solid marriage. There were times in the next three years when even his most loyal friends wondered at [Mila's] seemingly inexhaustible fund of forbearance and good cheer. For one thing, he was bitter; for another, he was sometimes bored silly by the job at Iron Ore. Because of either or both, he could be a damn unhappy man and a difficult one to be around. In those years, it was Mila who made the extra effort, sometimes simply by biting her tongue, and in so doing may have saved their marriage and helped him get his career back on a steady and promising course."

Although still wrestling with personal demons, Mulroney continued to expand his network. Networking kept him in touch with his friends. One of his more recent pals was Nick Auf der Maur, then a left-wing journalist and Montreal city councillor who met Mulroney during the Cliche commission and, like so many others, become absorbed into his circle of friends. So when L. Ian MacDonald, a *Montreal Gazette* columnist who had also met him at the Cliche commission and very quickly become a good friend, organized a stag dinner for Auf der Maur, who was about to get married, Mulroney was one of the thirty people invited. The dinner was held in the private upstairs dining room of Les Halles, a fancy restaurant on Crescent Street in Montreal. The evening began with each guest standing up to roast Auf der Maur for five minutes. While many people found this difficult, for Mulroney it was a breeze. Without working up a sweat, he rattled off a flawless piece of wit that entertained the whole room. However, within half an hour his smooth, easygoing façade would crumble into a thousand little pieces.

Somebody made the mistake of seating Mulroney next to Patrick Brown, a bit of a madcap journalist who would go on to distinguish himself as a foreign correspondent for CBC Television. Along with Robert Chodos and Rae Murphy, Brown had co-authored an instant book on the 1976 Tory convention called *Winners, Losers*. If the book struck readers as being amusing and irreverent, that was because the authors had intended it exactly that way. Political science it was not. The slender paperback gave the Conservative Party and its candidates a good poking. Robert Stanfield read the book and promptly denied having done so. None of the candidates escaped the author's barbs.

Unfortunately Mulroney had also read *Winners, Losers* and was not denying it. "Were you part of that book?" he demanded of Brown as soon as they were introduced. When Brown admitted his guilt Mulroney launched into a full-scale assault. The book had actually been tougher on Clark, who read it on an airplane and found it funny. Mulroney saw nothing funny about it. He told Brown that the book had upset his mother and made her cry. Furthermore, he added, he had counted the inaccuracies and had come up with seventy-six. "It's full of errors," Mulroney sputtered, adding that Mila agreed. Brown, who had by now downed a few drinks, took the whole thing as a joke and challenged Mulroney to name one error. An expert needler even when sober, Brown started needling Mulroney when clearly Mulroney was in no condition for it. Soon the sparring match had reached the shouting stage and had attracted the attention of the rest of the room. "I don't wear Gucci shoes," Mulroney was overheard blurting out. He grew more and more fed up with Brown's refusal to take his complaints seriously and finally, beside himself with rage, got up in the middle of the main course and stormed out, never to return. Virtually all the others had been finding the scrap amusing and were surprised that such a substantial political figure had such a thin skin.

Most of the time during Mulroney's first three years at IOC, he maintained his self-imposed exile from politics, but once in a while he emerged briefly. The first occasion was in March 1978, and he did it as a special favour to his old friend Sam Wakim, who had won the federal Tory nomination in Toronto's Don Valley East and needed to raise money for the coming campaign, expected that spring. At Wakim's request, Mulroney agreed to be the star speaker at a fundraising dinner and stole the show merely by showing up. The media came out in force to greet him and immediately started querying him about his future political plans, asking whether he thought that he rather than Clark should be leading the Tories. Mulroney quickly endorsed Clark as leader and denied reports of a rift between them, adding that he felt the Conservative Party had chosen wisely and well in picking Clark. That night Mulroney raised $20,000 for Wakim.

"Brian Mulroney," the *Globe and Mail* reported the next day, "re-emerged as a politician last night for the first time since that Sunday afternoon in February, 1976, when he lost in his bid for the leadership of the federal Progressive Conservative party. What he said was that Joe Clark was the best man to lead the Tories to victory in the next election. It was an admission that was a long time coming. Yet, there still is an inclination not to take Mr. Mulroney at his word."

Later that spring, the *Globe and Mail's* evaluation was borne out in a shockingly public manner. No matter how badly Mulroney trashed Clark in private, so far none of his bad-mouthing had ever gotten into print — for which he could thank the Montreal media, who listened to his Ritz-Carlton rants without reporting them. But all that changed in April of 1978 when Ottawa freelance journalist Stephen Kimber interviewed Mulroney on behalf of the *Financial Post's* monthly, the *Financial Post Magazine*.

Kimber was putting together a feature profile on Mulroney. What particularly interested him was how Mulroney had switched professions in mid-career and come out on top in the business world. So it was business and not politics that by prearrangement brought Kimber to the Château Laurier in Ottawa on April 11, where Mulroney had just emerged from a meeting. But instead of doing the interview in the hotel, as they had arranged, he invited Kimber to drive with him to Montreal. The two climbed into the back seat of Mulroney's black Buick, with Joe Kovacevic at the wheel, and settled into the plush red velvet upholstery. While Kimber scribbled notes, Mulroney started to talk.

Ottawa was expecting Trudeau to call an election any day now, and that clearly was on Mulroney's mind. He had hardly loosened his tie and lit up a cigarette when he started talking about Clark's prospects in the coming campaign. "I look at the numbers, you know, and I just can't see it," Mulroney said. "God bless him if he can do it, but the way I look at it, Clark is going to get wiped out in Quebec. Without Quebec there's no way he can win the election." A great quote, but not the story Kimber had come to get. "The Liberals took a poll during the leadership convention and it showed that with me as leader, there were only two safe Liberals on the whole island of Montreal, Trudeau and Bryce Mackasey." Mulroney would not get off politics.

Then he launched into a description of how the "private little club" — as he called the Tory caucus in Ottawa — had conspired against him during the leadership race. On and on he went with graphic descriptions of how they had screwed him at every turn. "I can still remember after the first ballot Jim Gillies and Heward Grafftey came over and they were standing in front of me — Heward's eyes bulging right out of his head — and they were screaming at the top of their lungs that for the good of the party I had to go to Clark. Here I was the number two candidate and they were telling me I had to go for number three." Mulroney kept pouring it on while Kimber, now a somewhat frustrated note-taker, tried to squeeze in the odd question.

"You know what they called me?" Mulroney asked rhetorically. "Now this is the unkindest cut. They said I was the candidate of big money, that I was trying to buy the leadership. I had to laugh." He added: "It wasn't an easy thing to go through. You work so hard and you come so close only to have all these people gang up on you for no reason. I mean, I haven't been a criminal or anything. If my father had been alive, all that stuff about being the money candidate would have given him a good laugh. We were broke all our lives. Anything that I've gotten in life, I've worked damned hard for." Once again he repeated his well-worn claim that he was finished with politics. "I know you shouldn't say that, but that is my decision. I can't conceive of any circumstances that would change my mind."

From there he started unloading directly onto Clark, saying he himself had not run for the leadership because he needed a house and a job — a venomous dig at Clark for not having a career outside politics and for having moved into Stornoway from a tiny Ottawa apartment. "I ran because the Conservative Party needed a winner," he added. The acid test for Clark, he declared, would be the outcome of the next election. "Then we'll see who's a winner and who's a loser."

Why was Mulroney picking this particular moment to bare his soul to a journalist he had never met before? By now the shock of René Lévesque's victory was wearing off and the public was becoming accustomed to a separatist government in Quebec. Voters were once again starting to loathe Pierre Trudeau more than they feared Quebec sovereignty — all of which had resurrected Clark's political standing, but he still looked like a long shot. Another part of the reason may have been magazine lead times. Kimber's article would not hit the stands until after a late-May election. If Clark did as badly as Mulroney figured he would, he would appear prescient in the aftermath of defeat. That was the best sense Kimber could make of it. Only later did he learn from other journalists that slamming Clark was a regular ritual for him. Actually Mulroney's interview was more a visceral reflex than a calculated political plot.

It was dark by the time the car reached Mulroney's house in Westmount. Mila was home, but she was preparing to go to the symphony. Once she was gone, the Swedish housekeeper put the kids to bed, then served Mulroney and Kimber dinner while Mulroney continued venting his frustrations. "If Joe Clark wins the election," he said, tapping his plate with a fork, "I'll eat this plate. I mean, let's look at it. Can you see any way that he can win? Any way at all?" Through it all Kimber scrawled notes, even during dinner.

After the meal they moved into the living room and Mulroney poured a drink for Kimber but not for himself. Kimber had noticed that he had not had a drop the entire time. Mulroney explained that he had quit drinking a while back. (In fact this was a brief, failed attempt to go on the wagon. Not long after the Kimber interview, he was drinking as much as ever.) Every word he uttered was perfectly sober. "The PQ wouldn't have won that election if I was the leader," he said. "It's true. The Quebec people were looking for an alternative to a profoundly unpopular provincial government. I would have given them that alternative. It's all in my platform. I can show it to you. You know who would have been the provincial Tory leader if I had been elected?" He paused for dramatic effect. "Claude Ryan, that's who. . . . He would have taken the job . . . I'm sure of it. Look at the Union Nationale and how they came back to life. With [Rodrigue] Biron, for Christ's sake. From zero to eleven seats. Imagine what would have happened if there'd been a Tory party in Quebec with a credible leader." After a moment he checked himself. "Look, change that about how if I was leader the PQ victory wouldn't have happened. I didn't mean it the way it sounded. It's just that the people needed a provincial federalist alternative, and the Conservative Party didn't provide one."

As much as Kimber had come for a business story, he was leaving with a political story, and a pretty hot one at that. However, a lot would change before the article appeared in the magazine's June issue. The spring election that seemed like a sure thing never happened. Pierre Trudeau decided to postpone the vote despite pleadings from his backroom advisers, giving the resurging Joe Clark more time to recover in the polls, and a much better shot at winning. Realizing how bad his words would now look, Mulroney phoned Kimber in

Ottawa a month later to see if he could postpone the article until after the election, saying that they could then talk again and this time he would be more open. But the *Financial Post* said no. Shortly before publication date, in a last attempt at damage control, Mulroney tracked Kimber down on vacation at his mother-in-law's place in New York. "Did I seem bitter?" he asked. "I didn't mean to seem bitter. Maybe we should talk about this some more." But it was too late.

"After Joe, Who?" read the headline of the article, which answered its own question in smaller type below: "Brian Mulroney, perhaps. He's bitter as hell, but he does say he's only 39." In the text Kimber said that talking to Mulroney about the leadership convention was "like scraping sandpaper over an exposed nerve."

During the following storm Mulroney categorically denied making the statements quoted in the article. In fact he went a step further and in an interview with the *Montreal Star* denied ever meeting Kimber. It was an astonishing claim. Yet whether anybody believed him did not matter as much as the fact that it gave him an escape. If anybody accused him of disloyalty he had only to disown the statements. Then his accuser had to either back off or prove him a liar, which was difficult. It was a crude but effective tactic, yet it almost backfired because Mulroney had forgotten one detail that undermined his whole cover-up.

After spending the evening in Mulroney's house in Montreal, Kimber had suddenly realized he didn't have enough money to get back home. Mulroney had kindly come to the rescue, calling the airport and booking him on the last plane to Ottawa and putting the ticket on his own credit card. Kimber later reimbursed Mulroney, and that transaction formed irrefutable evidence that they had met. The *Montreal Star*, which was checking out Mulroney's denial that he had ever met Kimber, asked him to produce the documentary proof. But luckily for Mulroney, before Kimber could do so the *Star* went on a long strike and the story died. Mulroney would later shift his defence to the claim that the interview was off the record and that Kimber had broken a confidence, an allegation Kimber strongly denied, citing the fact he had been taking notes the whole time, including at the dinner table.

The Kimber article had finally revealed to the world just how much the leadership loss continued to torment Mulroney. He would continue to vehemently deny that he was bitter, but nobody believed him any more. From then on, when Tories talked about Mulroney they always mentioned the magazine article. It certainly confirmed all the rumours that had reached the ears of Joe Clark. Although Clark said nothing in public, their official relationship, already formal, became frostier still.

In fairness Mulroney was hardly the only loser from 1976 who had trouble handling defeat. Virtually all defeated leadership candidates replay the events and blame others for their misfortune. What separated Mulroney from the other losers was how long he stayed down. After a year or so the other defeated candidates seemed to have turned the corner — except for Claude Wagner, who continued to make life miserable for Clark until accepting a Senate appointment in 1978. Like Wagner, Mulroney descended into a personal abyss and stayed there.

There would be periods when he seemed to be okay, when it looked as if he had finally put 1976 behind him. Then a chance remark at a party would set him off again, and all the bitterness would well up and spill over. He seemed destined to become a tragically unfulfilled figure like Davie Fulton, a young man with a brilliant past who never realized his promise.

After being humbled in the 1962 election, John Diefenbaker, suddenly a minority prime minister, retreated to Harrington Lake and spent most of the summer in seclusion. While there he twisted his ankle in a gopher hole and was forced to hobble physically like the semi-invalid he had become politically, which only deepened his despair further. Churchill went into what he called his "black dog days." Lloyd George, Roosevelt, and other great leaders all endured bad periods. Even Pierre Trudeau, one of the hardest emotional rocks in the landscape of Canadian political history, suffered through the odd low, particularly after his marriage started unravelling and western Canada kept rejecting him. He worked his way through down periods by snowshoeing, canoeing, walking, and — in his earlier days — motorcycling. Trudeau needed serenity and most of all needed to be alone. Isolation and tranquillity recharged his batteries and restored his equilibrium.

Mulroney, on the other hand, needed to keep busy and needed to surround himself with friends. Action left him little time for reflection on past injustices. Friends repelled his biggest fear, which was rejection, and satisfied his need to be popular. Both distracted him from his inner agony. Idleness and solitude were his enemies. Activity and company were the only things that kept him from drinking and brooding.

His need to keep himself occupied explained a lot of things. It explained why in the aftermath of the greatest defeat of his life he could switch careers and prosper. In fact the bigger the challenge the better. The more he had to overcome, the less time he had for self-examination and the better he performed. It explained why during the darkest days of his life his networking never missed a beat — the telephone was the biggest and most therapeutic diversion of all. As he had at Dalhousie after flunking first-year law, when he threw himself into the Nova Scotia election campaign, Mulroney once again performed splendidly — at least in public. He jumped eagerly into fundraising drives on behalf of the United Way, the mentally handicapped, the elderly, and the liver foundation. He even took charge of an ambitious campaign to raise $7 million for capital projects at St. FX. And he continued to display an overwhelming personal concern for the welfare of his galaxy of friends, just as he had always done. (When Al Larson, one of IOC's managers at Sept-Îles, received the news at 4:00 A.M. that his twenty-year-old son had been killed in a car accident, Mulroney and Mila travelled from Montreal and were on his doorstep at 10:00 A.M. to offer condolences.) He still lived on the telephone, networked endlessly, and surprised people with unexpected favours. That this was an often deeply depressed man would have amazed most of those who saw him in action during his first two years as president of IOC.

In May 1978, while Mulroney was worrying about the impending publication of the Kimber interview, he was jolted by a sudden and unexpected strike at IOC. The union had been in a legal strike position for months, but he had just finished assuring Cleveland that the workers were not going out and was caught completely off guard. His only solace was that the union leaders were equally upstaged. They woke up in the morning to learn that a picket line had been thrown up by some of their members, and that other workers were honouring it. Before long the whole company had shut down, railway and all.

Mulroney had been hired to prevent work stoppages. Now, less than a year after becoming president, he was facing his first company-wide strike. It did not reflect favourably on his rapprochement with labour or portend well for the future. However, the roots of the strike went back well before his time as president. How he handled it would tell his American masters a great deal.

Summer is the prime season for mining, and the shut-down was costing dearly, but despite his history as a hot-shot negotiator, Mulroney stayed away from the bargaining table. The company had proper labour personnel to do the negotiating, and he knew from experience that a president must keep out of the line of fire. His job was to give the marching orders, approve strategies, and define the limits. But he was far from invisible; indeed, he showed his face at a few picket lines.

The strike stretched from May to August, and its settlement marked a turning-point in labour relations at IOC. The company agreed to wage increases and a hike in its pension plan contributions, and it agreed to maintain the clause in the contract tying wages to the cost of living. But the most important aspects of the deal were primarily symbolic: the union wanted measures to improve safety in the workplace and the right to investigate accidents itself. It also wanted limits on the amount of contracting out by the company. Mulroney persuaded his bosses in Cleveland to go along with these demands, and in so doing laid a foundation of good faith that would serve him well in the next few years as he worked to improve communication between management and labour.

Despite the work stoppage, IOC emerged at the end of the year with — of all things — a profit, a most surprising turn of events. In his first full year as president Mulroney had taken a chronic money-loser from a $78-million loss to a $19-million profit, a $97-million turnaround in a single year. The profit was tiny for an outfit as big as IOC, but finally the company had crawled over to the right side of the ledger.

The dramatic about-face in company fortunes made Mulroney look like a miracle worker. But the real miracle belonged not to Mulroney but to the suddenly red-hot base metals market. In 1978 the Lake Erie price for iron ore pellets took off and went through the roof, in turn driving IOC's income sky high. At virtually the same time the Canadian dollar, which had spent the last number of years hovering a few cents above the American dollar, dropped dramatically, and that boosted IOC's income by another 10 to 20 per cent. As had been the case so often in his career, Mulroney was lucky as well as skilful. He could not have timed his arrival better.

Moreover, the shift towards profitability had only begun. From 1979 to 1982 IOC would amass much bigger profits. In fact, profits would grow so monstrously that during these years the company would make transfers south of the border in the order of $310 million. IOC shareholders would collect more dividends during Mulroney's four years as president than they had in the previous twenty combined.

IOC's string of good years would peak in 1981 with a whopping $104.8-million profit. Late that year, when it looked as though IOC would be reaching a milestone, Mulroney showed up at a regular board meeting in Cleveland and made an unusual proposal. He recommended giving every IOC employee, unionized or not, a $250 Christmas bonus. It was his way of cutting the workers into the company's good fortune. The directors, clearly caught by surprise, squirmed a little. What kind of precedent would it set? How would it affect the existing labour contracts? What would the union hierarchy say? What would the other mining companies on the North Shore say? Mulroney brushed their concerns aside, promising to take care of any problems. It would cost about a million and a half dollars but would help labour relations, and certainly the company could afford it. After ten minutes' discussion the directors gave the plan their blessing, agreeing to treat the bonus as profit-sharing. It proved to be an astute move, raising the standing of the company in the eyes of the workers while lowering the stock of the union leaders.

The Christmas bonus was exactly the kind of grand gesture that Mulroney liked to make; he was good at symbolic acts, whether large or small. Throughout his tenure as president he made a point of flying up to the operating centres so he could be there personally to present gold watches to twenty-five-year employees or press the flesh at retirement parties. In his mind such events were anything but frivolous. Not unlike his first role model, Colonel McCormick, he would drop into Sept-Îles, Schefferville, and Labrador City dispensing favours and receiving homage. The politician in him enjoyed these public events — they fed his ego — but he also understood the practical value of putting a human face onto management, especially when the face had long been as cold and unsmiling as IOC's. "If people aren't working for you," he would say, "they're working against you."

In the years following the 1978 strike Mulroney went beyond using personal charm and astute public relations to soften up his labour constituency. Some of his measures were both substantive and progressive, reflecting a fundamentally enlightened approach to organized labour. The first thing Mulroney did was to start involving workers more deeply in the affairs of the company by telling them what was going on. As a private company with only five shareholders, IOC had always believed workers were supposed to wield the wrench, not understand why. The attitude had endured for so long that the workers themselves expected it and knew no other way. Under Mulroney, consultants were brought in, new programs were launched, and full-time public relations people were put on the ground in both Sept-Îles and Labrador City. From now on supervisors sent thank-you notes to employees, employees' families got plant tours, and the company took out ads in local newspapers congratulating its employees for community volunteer work. The company newspaper, *Dialogue*, was upgraded and turned into a quality publication. Mulroney believed workers needed to know the goals of the company and the state of the iron ore business, and he told them.

After years of ignorance and distrust, many of the workers at first reacted with cynicism. And many of Mulroney's managers resisted the new approach. The old adversarial relationship was easy and predictable and required no imagination. Mulroney pushed for change, constantly reminding his employees that the company was one big family and that everybody, no matter his or her level, contributed to its success. He kept hammering away at the theme that the whole could not function properly without healthy parts.

Without question Mulroney profoundly influenced the atmosphere at IOC, but he did not do it alone. Dick Geren, the executive vice-president who ran the operations of the company from his base in Sept-Îles, deserved much credit too. A long-time mining man and a straight-shooter who was widely respected by workers, even to the point of being a bit of a father figure, he had been brought in a year before Mulroney to help clean up the mess. Together they hammered away at their theme: the company had to change its attitudes. As a result IOC moved from the Dark Ages to the leading edge of labour relations ahead of most other big corporations. Mulroney particularly encouraged the development of a new generation of progressive, innovative managers.

He also worked especially hard at winning over the union leaders. He invited them to company parties, something previously unheard of, and consulted them before taking action. At the same time he let union officials know they could phone him any time. Occasionally he convened special full-day meetings between key union people and key managers. With Mulroney as moderator, both sides delivered reports and set out their goals. When a conflict arose, Mulroney would encourage the adversaries to talk it out, always leading the discussion towards a happy conclusion. Whatever the outcome, he treated the unions with respect and deference.

Mulroney's reforms went a long way to restoring at least some measure of trust and respect between labour and management. The 1978 strike was the last serious labour disruption during his presidency. In the ten years before Mulroney, strikes had cost the company approximately a year's worth of lost production. For the first time in recent memory IOC had achieved something resembling labour harmony.

The turnaround in labour relations showed up directly on the bottom line. IOC's operations were designed to run at 100-per-cent capacity; anything less was inefficient. With iron ore prices reaching record-high levels, labour peace made the profits fatter. One could make the case that Mulroney was the best thing that could have happened to IOC.

Although he was flying high professionally once the 1978 strike was settled, Mulroney continued to battle with drinking and depression. At times he would start drinking in the mornings. The fragility of his emotional state made a rare public appearance on September 15, 1978, the day his dear friend and long-time mentor Robert Cliche suddenly dropped dead from a heart attack outside a restaurant in Quebec City. After the Cliche commission ended, they had remained close friends. Mulroney had regularly phoned him every couple of weeks to talk about politics and business, and to seek advice. Now Cliche was gone.

Mulroney heard the news around 2 P.M. By 3 o'clock he had phoned Cliche's widow to offer his condolences. Although upset, he maintained his composure while expressing his sorrow. Around 8 o'clock he called again. He had clearly been drinking and was now in quite an emotional state. "I don't believe it," Mulroney told Madeleine Ferron (Cliche's wife had kept her birth name). "I am totally destroyed."

When he called again at 11:00 that night he was drunk and in tears — really out of control. "My friend Robert passed away," he sobbed. "I don't believe it. I talked to him last week and he was joking. I don't believe it. I'm very down. We're losing a great man. I'm losing a great friend." After the conversation ended, Ferron told her children that Mulroney was now probably one of the saddest people in Quebec.

At the office, Mulroney continued to perform well, although a petty, vindictive streak occasionally surfaced. After the 1978 strike was settled, the employees who had been laid off from the Montreal office were called back to work — everyone except a secretary named Evelyn Larocque. Behind that decision was a little story. When Mulroney was still vice-president, Larocque had been the keeper of the company hockey tickets, a set of four choice season's seats located right behind the Canadiens' bench in the Montreal Forum. Bennett, to his credit, gave first priority to IOC employees visiting Montreal from the field, although everyone at headquarters dipped into them when available. But Mulroney liked taking friends to the games and became miffed when Larocque once refused to give him tickets because they had already been assigned to somebody else. Either he was unaware of the house rules or he simply chose to ignore them. "I think Evelyn didn't quite understand when Brian came in as vice-president that he was going to be president when Mr. Bennett retired," one headquarters staffer later said. Although other factors may have been involved in the decision not to rehire Larocque, the hockey ticket incident seemed to be at the root of it. (After becoming president he forestalled any potential clash over tickets by buying two more season's seats — behind the goal and not nearly so good. But no employee coming to the big city from the bush was likely to complain.)

Mulroney almost invariably got what he wanted out of Cleveland. The only time his relationship with his corporate masters came to a serious test was during the period leading up to the 1980 Quebec referendum on sovereignty-association. At a company meeting at the

Auberge aux Gouverneurs in Sept-Îles, Mulroney gave a speech sizing up the current political situation in the province. He warned his audience, which included representatives of IOC's major shareholders such as Bethlehem Steel and a large group of the Canadian company's senior managers, that there was a real danger Quebec would go its own way. As a Quebecker who had watched the reawakening of Quebec nationalism from his privileged vantage point in Quebec City during the 1960s, and who kept in touch with the major players in the Parti Québécois government, including Premier René Lévesque, Mulroney could claim some authority on the subject.

However, after the meeting broke up, Mulroney discovered that his analysis had deeply offended Mike Monaghan, IOC's vice-president of operations and the number three man in the company. Monaghan angrily told Mulroney that he had totally misrepresented the Quebec situation and did not know what he was talking about. Quebec would never separate, he maintained. If Monaghan had stopped there, Mulroney might have let the matter rest. But the vice-president then went around the room loudly repudiating his boss's remarks, calling Mulroney a separatist and trying to enlist others — including the Americans present — onto his side. It caused quite a scene.

Monaghan's astonishing outburst did not overly surprise the people who really knew him. He was an outspoken Irishman given to such eruptions. He also was married to a French Canadian, kept abreast of the political scene, and considered himself an authority on Quebec politics. Monaghan had spent his whole career on Quebec's North Shore and knew the company inside out, but what really irked him was that he had been passed over when Cleveland chose Bill Bennett's successor. The fact that the new president had not the slightest interest in the practical side of mining had rubbed salt in his wounds. He had come to hate Mulroney's guts.

How did a president deal with a vice-president who branded him a separatist in front of about forty top company figures? Mulroney could get along with anybody — if he chose to — but being conciliatory did not include permitting open insurrection. When he had to, he didn't hesitate to launch a counter-strike. Mulroney took the matter right to the top — directly to Hanna Mining's chairman, Bob Anderson, angrily demanding Monaghan's head, or else. The board would have to choose between him and Monaghan; if it did not sack the vice-president, then Mulroney was gone as president.

Anderson did not want to fire Monaghan — he was too good an operating man — but there was no question that he had to keep Mulroney. So word quickly came down that Monaghan was out. It later emerged that he had been transferred kicking and screaming to Cleveland and been made Hanna Mining's senior vice-president of operations. Then, soon after Monaghan's strategic reassignment, Mulroney was appointed to Hanna Mining's board of directors, which solidified his position more than ever. Only one other major corporate challenge would confront him during his years at IOC, and that was the fate of the town of Schefferville. But that problem was still in the future.

As president of a major Canadian company, Mulroney increasingly entered the world of corporate directorships. He already sat on the board of directors of IOC and its subsidiary, Quebec North Shore and Labrador Railway, and would eventually be invited onto the boards of Provigo, Québec-Téléphone, United Provinces Insurance, Labrador Mining and Exploration, TIW Industries, CJAD, and Ritz-Carlton Hotel Company. One of his friends was Conrad Black, a rapidly rising industrial baron based in Toronto, who was one of IOC's major shareholders and sat on its board. Although Black had supported Claude Wagner in the leadership race, he liked Mulroney enough to put him on the boards of several of his own companies, most notably Standard Broadcasting and Hollinger North Shore Exploration Ltd. (However, their friendship became strained at one point when Black made a hostile but ultimately unsuccessful attempt to take over Hanna Mining, and Mulroney — torn between two loyalties — tried to tiptoe down the middle.) Mulroney was also invited onto the board of the Canadian Imperial Bank of Commerce by its chairman, Russ Harrison, whom he had befriended when Harrison was the head of the bank's Quebec region and Mulroney was a rising labour lawyer. When Mulroney threw a party soon after joining IOC and moving into his new home on Belvedere Road, Harrison made a point of getting into the bank's plane and flying down for it. Mulroney had truly made it as one of Canada's business élite.

Although the IOC president did not have the full range of authority of a traditional chief executive officer, being basically a front man for the company's American owner, Mulroney wielded more authority than Bill Bennett ever had. He never hesitated to take on the Cleveland directors in fighting for what he felt IOC needed, and he knew how to get his way — all of which gave him more independence than IOC had enjoyed in the past. He also liked to dabble in new areas, such as the search for new markets for iron ore, and he made several trips abroad after the 1978 settlement. The first trip took him to Venezuela in early 1979 but yielded him nothing except a pesky virus that plagued him for months afterwards. The antibiotic prescribed by his doctor reacted badly with alcohol, temporarily forcing him to stop drinking whether he liked it or not.

The virus did not stop him from going on more overseas trips, although it continued to bother him during a week-long trade mission to Romania in June. This foray into Eastern Europe had been engineered by Mulroney's old friend from his summer working for Alvin Hamilton, Tory MP Robert Coates (now president of the Conservative Party), who knew the Romanian ambassador in Ottawa. Joining him were both Coates and long-time Mulroney insider Pat MacAdam, now a parliamentary aide to two Tory MPs and part-time Parliament Hill agent for IOC. The oppressively hot weather in Bucharest promptly laid Mulroney low (the guest-house where the Romanians put them was primitive and lacked air conditioning). The first thing Mulroney did upon arriving was go to bed. He recovered the next day, but despite endless shuttling from meeting to meeting and bureaucrat to bureaucrat, the trip ended in failure. The Romanians had no hard cash to pay for iron ore pellets, and, after thinking it over, IOC was not interested in a barter deal.

The only positive note during his stay came on the last day when he received an audience with President Nicolae Ceausescu, who greeted Mulroney wearing purple lattice-weave shoes, purple socks, a purple suit, and a tartan shirt that would have done Don Messer proud. "Mr. Mulroney," Ceausescu said through his translator, "twelve years ago Richard Nixon sat in that very same chair you are sitting in. Now, he didn't give up. And look where he went. And don't you give up either." "Oh Jesus," Mulroney said afterwards, "he's well briefed." The meeting went smashingly well, lasting forty minutes — twice as long as scheduled.

Ceausescu may have been well briefed, but he couldn't have known what was happening inside Mulroney's head. For the first time since the February 1976 leadership convention, he was considering a return to politics. The first evidence that something had changed came the day after his return from Romania, when he picked up Coates and MacAdam in the IOC jet. Coates and MacAdam had just returned to Montreal's Mirabel Airport after staying in Europe an extra day for sightseeing, and Mulroney was taking off to a board meeting in Cleveland; he offered to drop them in Ottawa. Shortly after take-off, Mulroney, who had drunk very sparingly in Romania, casually mentioned to his two guest passengers that he was finally feeling much better. "Well, boys," he chirped, "I made up my mind. I'm going on the wagon. I'm going to play a lot of tennis this summer and get myself back in shape."

Mulroney had dispensed the news so offhandedly that it did not seem especially significant at the time. Within minutes it was forgotten as the plane flew into a terrible electrical storm that bounced them around like a cork in water. They all thought they'd had it and Mulroney himself turned absolutely white. (They landed safely in Ottawa, then Mulroney continued on to Cleveland.) But it was true enough that Mulroney had stopped drinking altogether; in future he would spurn even a little wine at dinner. No one would ever see him touch a drop of alcohol again.

Mulroney's casual mention that he was giving up drinking was the first sign that his long dark night was finally coming to an end, that he was ready to put the bitterness and recrimination from his 1976 defeat behind him. During the past three years he had changed careers, networked endlessly, and generously donated his time to charity, but all this conspicuous activity had failed to banish his inner demons. Now he was ready to confront them. But why now?

The single most important force behind his determination was Mila, whose patience with her errant husband had practically run out. She later revealed, when talking privately about the divorce of Mulroney's sister Doreen, that she had threatened during this period to walk out on him and take the kids with her (their third child, Mark, was born in the spring of 1979). He doted on his children and depended on Mila for emotional support. Although he fooled around on his wife, he never expressed the slightest desire to leave her.

Mila also knew her husband better than anyone, knew that despite his public protests to the contrary the political flame still burned deep within. Through the dark days she salved the wounds of defeat, reassured him that all was not lost, and ultimately encouraged him to think again about entering the political arena. Although Mila almost never gave reporters any secrets, she later let slip a revealing comment to the *Toronto Star*: "I told him we had to build up our strength and go again." Mulroney had come to realize she was right, and he decided to take another run at the Conservative Party leadership.

His great success at IOC just wasn't enough. He had tried to believe that he could be happy with the money, prestige, and perks of a corporate president, but the job simply did not fulfil his need for political power. The country had lots of high-salaried corporate leaders but only one prime minister. He knew deep down that this was the only job he really wanted, the only one that would ever truly satisfy him. Mila reinforced this belief. Politics not only ran in his blood but seemed imprinted in his genes.

Given his decision to return to politics, it was clear that he first had to abandon alcohol. He could not continue to drink and still expect to conquer the political world. Sir John A. Macdonald, one of his enduring heroes, had pulled it off, but that was a century ago. On this matter his role model was not Macdonald but Maurice Duplessis, the villain he had so enthusiastically attacked in St. FX oratorical contests twenty years earlier. As much as he had vilified him, he had come to admire the genius with which Duplessis had made himself the invincible leader of postwar Quebec. He had been whipped in 1939 after one relatively undistinguished term in office and looked finished. During his five-year exile in opposition, the lifelong bachelor, a notorious drinker and womanizer, took stock of himself and swore off alcohol and restrained his sexual appetites. All the time and energy he had wasted on drinking he then dedicated to politics, and from that moment he became unstoppable, winning every election until his death fifteen years later.

Like Duplessis, Mulroney would make himself a new person and pursue his goal of becoming prime minister single-mindedly. Nothing would get in his way or divert him, not liquor and not women. No longer would he hold court at the Ritz, and no longer would he play around. But he knew it wouldn't be easy.

It was clear from the April 1978 interview with Stephen Kimber that Mulroney had tried to stop drinking at least once before. This time he got outside help. He had never admitted to anyone that he had a drinking problem and was too proud to join an Alcoholics Anonymous group. AA believed in group sessions, but Mulroney could no more stand up before a bunch of people and utter the words "I am an alcoholic" than he could join the Liberal Party. Fortunately he did not have to.

Alcoholics Anonymous recognized that high-profile people could not be truly anonymous in the usual AA sessions, so its Montreal chapter provided private one-on-one counselling for local notables. This informal service was run by prominent Montreal developer Maurice Mayer, who had quit drinking himself in the early 1970s and now devoted considerable time to helping others do the same. Mulroney first met Mayer in the Nassau villa of Peter Thomson, the

Montreal financier who was the principal owner of Power Corporation until he sold it to Paul Desmarais. Exactly how Mulroney and Mayer got together remained unclear. What would eventually emerge to a select few of Mulroney's closest friends was that Mayer was there to counsel him when things got tough. (Mulroney would later do the same for others.)

The first people to observe the turnabout were the staff at IOC headquarters, who could not help but notice the change in his work habits. He would still drop into the Ritz for lunch — and order a bowl of soup — but then he'd head straight back to the office. ("You have no idea the amount of time you waste drinking," he confided to a friend. "You can go back to your office at one o'clock and it's amazing how much work you can get done during the afternoon.") Office gossip had it that he had been called onto the carpet in Cleveland over his drinking and that he had checked into an institution to dry out.

Mulroney said nothing about his decision to his IOC colleagues. Apart from his throwaway comment to MacAdam and Coates, he seems to have said almost nothing to anyone. In fact, his statement on the airplane came about as close as he ever got to making a public announcement, and even then he might not have said anything at all had not MacAdam himself become a teetotaller ten months earlier. He never explained why he had gone on the wagon, beyond leaving the impression that alcohol made him susceptible to the kind of viruses that had been dragging him down lately. Whenever pressed on the subject, he dismissed it as nothing at all.

Why did Mulroney so downplay his decision to quit drinking when many ex-drinkers wear their conversion to sobriety on their sleeves? Forswearing booze for good showed real strength and self-discipline. But telling people he had done so meant admitting to a drinking problem in the first place, and he simply could not confess to such personal failings. It all went back to his need for adoration. He could not be full of flaws and blemishes and still be revered. Therefore he had to hide all personal deficiencies. This explained why he could not laugh at himself or tolerate others laughing at him. He simply could not understand that it was possible to admit failings without surrendering the esteem of others. He could not believe that people would respect him for being open and honest. To him, admitting that he had formerly had an alcohol problem would ruin him once and for all.

Whether he was admitting to anything or not, his friends soon saw the difference. Quitting drinking refashioned every corner of his life. He stopped sitting in bars and brooding about the injustices of 1976. He spent much more time working, and no longer did he repeatedly drag his closest friends through a blow-by-blow account of all his betrayals, real or imagined. He became much more like the Brian Mulroney of old, in private as well as in public. He continued being tolerant about the drinking of others, and he continued to stock liquor in his house and offer it to guests. But from now on he would drink mainly two beverages: coffee and soda water.

Perhaps the biggest turnaround was in his marriage. Although Mila had been important to him before, from now on she would be essential to his personal and political well-being. Her toughness of character had helped him through his depression and helped him find the will to give up alcohol. The girl he had married had grown into a strong woman in her own right. From now on Mila would be a full-time partner, whose strengths neatly balanced her husband's weaknesses, the one person he knew he could always rely on. She would calm him down when he lost control, would prick his conscience when he lost his moral bearings, and would put his defeats and rejections in perspective. In fact, she became so central to his life that he hated to leave town without her.

As Mulroney re-entered the world of politics, Mila emerged as the perfect political wife few people would have expected at the time of their marriage six years earlier. In public she always looked like a million dollars, always sparkled with irrepressible good humour, and became a veritable dynamo on social occasions. She disarmed people with her looks and her charm. When she and her husband worked a room together they were irresistible. In the next few years they became a matched set, a picture-perfect political couple.

But Mila brought more to the partnership than a beguiling surface. She also turned into an astute, determined, and disciplined operator — Madame Dispatch in the form of Mary Tyler Moore. Larry Zolf would later call her "an engineer" — a reference to her technocratic manner of organizing everything. She brought a new level of organization to Mulroney's life. The strength that had emerged when their marriage seemed in danger of breaking up stemmed in part from her remarkably healthy attitude towards politics; she understood that politics brought with it both highs and lows, good and bad. This outlook allowed her to endure the setbacks and defeats with an uncommonly level head while Mulroney continued to take them hard. Mila was exactly the kind of political partner he needed.

Perhaps her greatest contribution was in learning how to help him control his impulses. He still went flat out and seemed not to know when to rein himself in. She established the limits — the boundaries — he had so often lacked. She became not only his strongest supporter but his toughest critic, one of the very few who could tell him he was plain wrong without threatening his ego.

Mila had learned how to restrain her husband's excesses while catering to his needs and idiosyncrasies. Even after he gave up drinking, Mulroney could never be an ordinary husband who went shopping with his wife to pick out a dress. Married or not, he still had to spend half his weekends on the phone and attend political events at all hours. Mila now accepted this reality, came to terms with his compulsions, understood his lack of control over them, and was able to lay out a family life around them. She thereby gave him the semblance of normality that provided a level of serenity that had previously escaped him. From now on, Mulroney's marriage would become his rock of stability, and Mila the first person he turned to for support.

Giving up booze stands out as one of the major mileposts in Mulroney's life. It not only saved his marriage, it showed he had the fibre necessary to mount a political comeback. After three dark years he had emerged tougher and more determined than ever.

In August 1979, two months after Mulroney had sworn off alcohol, John Diefenbaker died suddenly of heart failure at age eighty-three. The final years had transformed him into an object of public affection and even something of a cult figure. People across the country had turned out in masses to see him wherever he travelled, and now thousands came to see him lie in state in the Hall of Honour on Parliament Hill. Befitting his overblown sense of his historical importance, Diefenbaker had laid meticulous plans for his funeral, the biggest burial pageant Canada had ever seen, and called it "Operation Hope It Never Happens." After the funeral his coffin would be placed on a special train for a long ceremonial ride to Saskatoon, stopping at little towns along the way, before coming to final rest at the John G. Diefenbaker Centre at the University of Saskatchewan.

On the day of the funeral, as the casket was being moved from Parliament Hill to the site of the service three blocks away, crowds of watchers lined the sidewalks to pay their last respects, while the long procession snaked from side to side to avoid droppings from the RCMP horses up front. And there on Wellington Street among the mourners was Brian Mulroney. In an earlier time Mulroney would have been marching along with the official procession on the other side of the barrier.

Diefenbaker had done as much as anyone to derail his former protégé's chances of winning the 1976 convention, but Mulroney would have the last laugh. Only guests on the official list had received tickets to the funeral ceremony, and only individuals with tickets were allowed into Christ Church Cathedral. Diefenbaker had set it all out before he died. However, Mulroney had outsmarted the Chief, getting a ticket from Pat MacAdam, who was on the funeral committee. So while all the Diefenbaker loyalists were taking their seats, Mulroney quietly slipped in and joined the faithful near the back of the church, an invasion that almost seemed capable of bringing

Diefenbaker out of his coffin for one final tirade. The only thing that would have irked the old man more would have been the knowledge that Mulroney would eventually join the board of directors of the John G. Diefenbaker Foundation.

CHAPTER EIGHTEEN

THE

GUERRILLA WAR

MULRONEY'S DECISION IN the third week of June 1979 to swear off alcohol and resume his pursuit of the Conservative Party leadership made little sense in light of recent political events. Only a couple of weeks earlier — on June 4, the day before his fortieth birthday — Joe Clark took the oath of office as Canada's sixteenth prime minister, the youngest in the history of Canada.

In the long-awaited election of May 1979, Clark had beaten Trudeau 136 seats to 114, six precious seats short of a majority. The New Democratic Party under Ed Broadbent, with 26 seats, and the dying Social Credit Party, with six, held the balance of power. It was heartbreaking. Another half percentage point in the popular vote would have pushed Clark over the top.

Clark should have done better. Given Trudeau's unpopularity, any leader of the Conservative Party should have been able to deliver a majority. The fact that Clark had fallen short pointed to a couple of problems. First, he could not shake his image problems from earlier foul-ups and had never quite gotten the public's confidence. Also, Clark had failed to solve the problem that had bedevilled every Tory leader of the twentieth century: how to overcome Quebec's dislike and distrust of the Conservative Party. Clark, who had gotten into terrible jurisdictional squabbles with the impossible Claude Wagner before Wagner accepted the Senate appointment from Pierre Trudeau, had made no impression on Quebec voters. The province had surrendered only two of its 75 seats to him, while awarding 67 to Trudeau. A mere handful of Quebec seats would have given Clark a firm grip on power. As it was, he had to reach into the Senate to find enough Quebec bodies to give his cabinet a national look.

Having to patch together his cabinet with appointed Quebeckers was exactly the stitching job Clark had wanted to avoid, and it explained why he had turned to Mulroney before the election and asked him to join his team. Politics makes strange bedfellows, especially when one of the bedfellows desperately needs seats. Clark knew Mulroney was one of the few Quebeckers who could help. Without question he could have boosted Clark's strength in Quebec; if he had run and brought five Tories into Parliament with him, any asking price would have been worth it. Clark wanted Quebec seats so badly he was prepared to do almost anything.

Mulroney briefly mulled over the idea of running and then politely declined, explaining that his contract with IOC had locked him in until 1981. It was backloaded so that only if he stayed the whole five years would he reap full benefits. Although he did not mention it, there was also the matter of the steep pay cut he would suffer with an MP's salary, or even a cabinet minister's. Leaving IOC early would cost him hundreds of thousands of dollars. However, Mulroney promised to work on behalf of the party and proved true to his word. In February 1979, the month before Trudeau called the election, Mulroney organized the annual Joe Clark dinner in Quebec and did a splendid job. He and his volunteers sold 2,133 tickets at $125 a plate, making it the biggest such dinner the party had ever held in the province. As chairman, Mulroney formally introduced Clark at the affair and told everybody that in picking Clark as leader "the party chose wisely and chose well."

Now, despite his failure to win a majority, Clark's future as prime minister looked promising. Conventional wisdom had him limping along for a year or two and then dissolving Parliament at an opportune time and winning big, as Diefenbaker had. Barely forty, and on the threshold of a new era, Joe Clark looked like he would be around as prime minister for some time.

Clark grasped the complexities of government with remarkable quickness and gained the respect of most of the bureaucrats around him. He also ran one of the most open governments in modern Canadian history and quickly introduced a system for controlling government spending that the Liberals would later adopt. In administrative terms Clark ran a good ship and could rightly challenge the prevailing notion that only the Liberal Party was competent to govern.

However, in political terms Clark began stumbling twenty-four hours after taking power. Trying to look firm, and hoping to show the Department of External Affairs that the politicians and not the bureaucrats were deciding government policy, Clark took advantage of his first press conference as prime minister to announce that Canada would be moving its Israeli embassy from Tel Aviv to Jerusalem. Although this had been an election promise, nobody — including Clark's own staff — had expected action so soon and so irrevocably. The jolt caused a nationwide furore that bogged down his government for weeks; Clark eventually appointed Robert Stanfield as a special envoy to study the issue so his government could back down from a bad policy while saving face. At the same inaugural press conference, Clark announced that his government would take steps that would inevitably lead to a quick sell-off of Petro-Canada, the government-owned oil company, thereby stepping into a second quagmire. At the time the public liked the Crown corporation and wanted to keep it. On his second day in office Clark had seriously mishandled two volatile issues, a performance that would help deny him the honeymoon traditionally accorded a new government. More blunders were to follow. Lowell Murray had refused to support Mulroney in 1976 because, in Murray's words, Mulroney was not ready. From the look of things, neither was Clark.

One move that caused no controversy or surprise was the appointment of Murray to the Senate on September 13, 1979. Canadian prime ministers have a long tradition of keeping their backroom political advisers within easy reach through appointments to the upper chamber. But two weeks later, when a couple more senators were sworn in, one of them raised a few eyebrows. Guy Charbonneau, the Tories' long-time Quebec bagman, had done more for the Conservative Party in Quebec over a longer period of time than anybody — he had been the party's Quebec fundraiser since the mid-1950s and was the one who kept the books. By traditional standards he was perfectly suitable for the Red Chamber, but he was definitely a Mulroney man. Mulroney had leaned on Clark and somehow talked him into awarding Charbonneau the ultimate political plum.

Not long after Charbonneau's appointment, Senator Lowell Murray talked to Michel Cogger, his old roommate from their Stanfield days who was now practising law in Montreal, about the possibility of bringing Mulroney to Ottawa and into the cabinet. Murray, still in Mulroney's bad books, wanted to know whether he could be enticed into making the shift if a cabinet post was assured. Although it had political appeal for both sides — a cabinet portfolio was an ideal launch pad for a future leadership bid — Mulroney remained reluctant to leave his lucrative IOC post. As well, all kinds of logistical obstacles blocked the way. He could be sworn directly into the cabinet, but political tradition would require him to enter Parliament shortly thereafter, either by winning a by-election for the House of Commons or by getting an appointment into the now-overused Senate. Still Murray planned to pursue it further and would have done so had his attention not been distracted by more pressing matters.

Since its early missteps, the Clark government had continued to squander its public good will. Instead of calling Parliament into session and presenting his program, Clark waited four long months while his inexperienced cabinet learned the ropes. He had said at the outset that he would govern as if he had a majority, and once the

House of Commons finally convened in October he stubbornly acted according to his rhetoric, even though it soon led him into a crisis that threatened his government's survival.

In early December John Crosbie, the blunt-mannered minister of finance, brought down his first budget, with the theme "Short-term pain for long-term gain." It introduced some harsh measures, the harshest being an 18-cent-a-gallon boost in the excise tax on gasoline. The public from coast to coast detested the measure, and the two main opposition parties, after stoking public resentment still further, threatened to join forces in Parliament to defeat the budget and the government along with it. At the same time Clark refused to be intimidated and stood his ground. He was in no mood to make compromises, believing that if he was defeated the voters would punish his opponents. He even turned down a chance at acquiring a slim parliamentary majority through a working alliance with the tiny Social Credit Party.

Until this point the Clark government had forked out only a handful of the usual patronage plums that came with power. But after sixteen years in the wilderness many Tory stalwarts wanted some early dividends and started pressing. Clark explained that it took time. His office was compiling two lists: a compendium of all the jobs to be awarded, and a comprehensive list of people to fill them. The objective was to match the available skills to the appropriate jobs so that in awarding patronage he could make the best appointments. However, the work of compiling all this data into centralized lists had mushroomed in scale, and the team had only just started pumping out its first big batch of names when the Crosbie budget landed in the House of Commons. On the evening of Thursday, December 13, when Clark defiantly called the opposition's bluff, the Liberals and the NDP made good on their threat and finished off the Clark government by a vote of 139 to 133. Clark had committed an unpardonable parliamentary sin: he had failed to make sure he had the bodies needed to defeat a non-confidence motion.

The defeat of the government riled a lot of Tories, but it infuriated no one more than the jilted bridegrooms of patronage. What Clark did after the defeat raised their dander even more. On December 14, he had been slated to meet with former MP Jean Pigott, a member of Clark's office staff who was in charge of patronage, to dole out 150 appointments. Ever the idealist, Clark took the position that, having lost the confidence of Parliament, he would be wrong to carry through with the appointments in the nine weeks before the general election. He would go through with them only after the public had reaffirmed his government at the polls. Michel Cogger, a member of the Tory executive in Quebec, came to Ottawa and pleaded with the government to process the appointments for the good of the party. He argued that since approval in principle had been given before the defeat, the processing was a mere formality. His appeal fell on deaf ears.

But the worst of Clark's problems was his party's lack of preparedness for an election. Not having polled since August, the Tories went into the campaign blind and only now learned how deeply they had antagonized the public. In half a year Clark had become almost as unpopular as Trudeau had ever been.

The Conservatives had to scramble just to plug candidates into all the ridings, and nowhere was this task tougher than in Quebec. Once again the party leaned on Mulroney to run, and once again he thought it over and said no — and this time nobody could blame him. After the smoke had cleared from the parliamentary vote, anybody could see that the Tories were heading straight for defeat. During the rush of events Trudeau had reversed his earlier decision to resign and now the Liberals had rallied behind him. If Mulroney won a seat he faced a long wait in opposition. In fact he had little chance of getting that far. In Quebec, Tories everywhere were racing for cover. It made no sense to quit his job at IOC only to be left with nothing.

In the early weeks of the election campaign the Liberals and the NDP hammered the Clark government over the detested 18-cent gasoline tax, arguing that a Tory victory would cause much higher gasoline prices. At first the Tories appeared headed for a total rout but, never giving up, Clark fought back with heart and true savvy, and in the role of the underdog he led his party on a late-campaign comeback. He started narrowing the gap but too late. On election night Pierre Trudeau returned to power with 147 seats — a workable majority — while Clark hobbled in with 103. Quebec once again made the difference. Trudeau swept 74 out of 75 seats in the province, wiping out Social Credit and leaving the Tories with one lonely MP, the unsinkable Roch LaSalle, who survived by 389 votes.

As far as Mulroney was concerned, the February 1980 débâcle only proved his point: that Clark was a born loser. He could not understand why the prime minister had simply watched his government fall apart without rustling up some concessions on the budget. A little strategic backtracking and shuffling could have split the opposition and saved the day. Clark's stubborn refusal to make a deal was stupid, even arrogant. But it had given Mulroney an unexpected opening. Now he might have another chance at the Tory leadership before the next election. Clark would surely cling on, but Mulroney knew the party and understood the internal damage that had been inflicted. He figured that Clark's days as party leader were numbered. Party loyalists, who had waited for most of a generation only to see Clark squander victory in nine short months, would not forgive easily. There would be another leadership race in a year or two, maybe three — and Mulroney would be ready. The election defeat had changed everything for him.

It changed everything for Clark too. The party had not turned to him in 1976 with joy and enthusiasm, and later never fell in love with him; in weak moments like this he became vulnerable. The last four years had been hell for Mulroney; now it would be Clark's turn. Having risen higher and fallen further, he had more to be depressed about. But Clark did not suffer anything like Mulroney's collapse after 1976. If the loss got him down personally he did not show it. Without missing a beat, he let the world know he planned to soldier on as leader and turn things around at the next election.

In the months immediately following Clark's defeat, Mulroney started to inch back into the political spotlight, becoming active in Quebec's referendum debate on sovereignty-association as a proponent of the federalist No coalition. But he stayed mainly in the background until the night of the vote count in May 1980, when he blossomed in full but inglorious colour as a commentator on CTV's live coverage of the results. During the program he got into a horrendous slanging match with his old friend Louis Laberge, accusing the labour leader of regarding Quebec non-francophones as second-class citizens. (Laberge had just made the point that the total No vote would have to top 60 per cent before the francophone figure crossed the 50-per-cent threshold.) While Mulroney spoke, Laberge could be heard yelling off camera, accusing Mulroney of lying outright. On camera Mulroney suddenly bolted upright and became flushed with anger. From there it disintegrated into an uncontrolled shouting match, forcing interviewer Harvey Kirck to pull them apart like two fighting animals. But Mulroney did not stay furious at Laberge for long. "Harvey, may I say just before Louis goes —," he said in an apparent effort to patch things up later in the evening, but the camera had switched over to Lloyd Robertson on another set, and whatever he intended to say was cut off.

Mulroney made a more civil impression four months later, on September 25, 1980, in a speech to the Canadian Institute of Chartered Accountants in Montreal. It was his first important political speech since his 1976 defeat, and it was openly political. He wrote it weeks in advance and tested it on old friends like Michel Cogger, Jean Bazin, and Michael Meighen, whom he had forgiven at last for being unable to get him the $30,000 subsidy in 1976. (It helped that Meighen had made a personal contribution towards retiring Mulroney's debt.)

"With few if any exceptions," he told the accountants, "the Conservative Party has been consigned to the opposition benches for one reason alone: its failure to win seats in the French-speaking areas of this nation." From there he trotted out the theme he had first embraced at Laval: that the party would not become a sturdy governing force until it reached an accommodation with Quebec, and he strongly suggested it would mean putting Quebeckers into key leadership roles in the party. Mulroney took a strong centralist position on the Constitution, one much closer to Pierre Trudeau's unitary vision of Canada than Clark's provincialist concept of "a community of communities," which he had espoused during his successful 1979 campaign. It was plain to all informed observers that these were not the polite utterances of a Tory loyalist.

"Iron magnate Brian Mulroney denies he is out to knife Joe Clark," *Maclean's* magazine reported. "Yet there was unmistakably a lean and hungry look about the man last Thursday when he let fly his first public critique of Progressive Conservative policy since finishing third in the 1976 leadership contest which Clark won, partly because he was the only finalist not from Quebec."

"Reaching far beyond the demands of the occasion," *Globe and Mail* columnist William Johnson wrote the next day, "Mr. Mulroney gave a finely crafted talk, an ambitious survey of the Canadian national scene and of the Progressive Conservative Party in particular that would have done proud the Brian Mulroney of 1976, the man who was a candidate for the leadership of the party. Now Mr. Mulroney is a private citizen. But one wonders at the amount of time and care he put into yesterday's speech. He cared terribly about the message he was delivering. The kind of attention he received from print and television reporters was that usually given a candidate declaring for a party's leadership, or an elder statesman coming out of retirement to deliver a passionate address on the state of the nation."

Mulroney's speech did nothing to make Clark's life easier in living down his defeat. Clark had boldly held a series of regional meetings across the country at which he presented himself as an easy target, hoping party members would take their shots and vent their frustrations. The strategy worked only partly. He drew fire for every shortcoming, and especially for his high-minded refusal to dole out patronage when he had the chance. Too many party members had imagined their names were on the list. He became the butt of scorn for not being able to count bodies in Parliament, and by the end of the year a sizeable portion of the party felt he should be made to walk the plank.

Clark's first big test came at the Conservatives' biennial general meeting in Ottawa in late February 1981, a year after his electoral defeat. More than two thousand Tory delegates would be voting on a range of issues, but the only one that mattered was Clark's leadership. Ever since John Diefenbaker's fateful encounter at the Château Laurier in 1966, the party's constitution required what amounted to a leadership referendum at each general meeting. No matter how popular the leader was, or how well he had done in the last election, delegates were formally asked: "Do you think the Progressive Conservative Party should hold a leadership convention?" Ironically, Joe Clark — along with Mulroney and many others — had worked to bring about this very reform. And he now would have to face the test every two years. Even if he won this time, he would have to go through the whole degrading process yet again before the next election.

Nobody expected Clark to lose the vote, but he would have to handle the convention exactly right to escape without bruises. He began badly when, having misread his audience, he bungled his speech, exhorting delegates to stand behind him for the good of the party, much as Diefenbaker had in 1966, instead of giving them cause for excitement and confidence. Diefenbaker had been booed and heckled; Clark was stared at with frosty politeness. Delegates applauded decorously but the expressions on their faces remained numb and cold. It was hard to believe so many people could clap and yet create so little noise.

Although many people in the party wanted Clark out, no one of the stature of Dalton Camp had stepped forward to lay down a challenge. The only visible dissenters were a disparate collection of fringe rightists, including a group of students who slid pro-review pamphlets under hotel room doors. But they managed to embarrass the party's mainstream. Technically Clark needed a shade over 50 per cent of the vote. In reality he had to do far better to survive. He was shooting for 70 per cent and, given his lack of opposition, most observers predicted 72 to 75 per cent.

When the vote came on Sunday afternoon at the end of the convention, the results surprised everybody, including Clark. He had scored a humbling 66 per cent: a vote of confidence, but clearly a hollow one. Nobody quite knew what to make of it. Was it victory? Was it defeat? Although a solid majority of the convention had supported him, this appearance was deceiving. The party's official apparatus had lined up squarely behind him and done what it could to boost his vote as high as possible. Even so, fully a third of the delegates had voted for a leadership review, revealing the depth of grassroots disenchantment for all to see.

After his initial shock, Clark went in front of the delegates and thanked them for their support. Publicly he took the position that a clear majority had voted its confidence and had given him a mandate to carry on as leader. Strictly speaking, he was correct. But he had absorbed a stiff body blow that would leave its mark. The vote made him look vulnerable and would encourage more people to take a shot at him at the next general meeting.

Clark returned to Parliament Hill to find his caucus in a rebellious mood. About half of them wanted him replaced. At the weekly caucus session three days after the convention, his MPs formally gave him a vote of support but made it plain that they were not giving him a blanket endorsement, only a reprieve. The caucus didn't buy Clark's line about having a mandate to carry on and told him it planned to re-examine his leadership at the end of the summer. Most of them respected his scrappiness in the House, but they did not think he could win the next election.

Meanwhile, anybody sitting on the executive of the Quebec wing of the Conservative Party could tell that Mulroney was gearing up for another run at the title. Although he said little, they did not need hard evidence. One sure sign was his re-emergence as a force in the party backrooms, as he put his people into place. If things continued to develop, a showdown seemed inevitable, with Mulroney and Clark squaring off for control of Quebec.

Evidence that something was amiss in Quebec had started drifting back to Ottawa a few weeks before the February 1981 convention, when the official delegate lists began arriving back at party headquarters. The Clark people had been worrying for some time about the loyalty of their Quebec organization; the Quebec lists deepened those worries, and the convention vote confirmed them. Before the convention they had been assured that Quebec supported Clark, but when the Clark people worked through the numbers, they revealed that the Quebec delegation had not voted as promised: as many as 80 per cent had voted against Clark. The sabotaging of Clark's support had come mainly from Quebec.

The key culprit turned out to be Rodrigue Pageau, Clark's chief Quebec organizer — the man entrusted to elect pro-Clark delegates. For all practical purposes Pageau had been a double agent. While piously assuring Ottawa that Clark supporters were being selected at Quebec local constituency meetings, Pageau had in fact made sure that a majority of Quebec's delegates were pro-review. A veteran political technician with Union Nationale roots, Pageau possessed superior connections in Quebec and plenty of tenacity. Although he had spearheaded the anti-Clark drive, he had not done it alone. Pierre-Paul Bourdon, a professional political organizer, and the colourful Jean-Yves Lortie had been his key people.

Few political operators came with reputations to match Lortie's. A bailiff by profession, he was renowned within party circles, especially in the east end of Montreal, as a machine-style ward-heeler of the old school. People would later call him "the French poodle" because of his frizzy hair, fur coats, and penchant for gaudy jewellery — especially gold chains and multiple finger rings. He always drove a big, flashy car, sometimes a black Lincoln with a telephone (those were the days before the cellular phone), but more often a Cadillac — during one period, a pink one. He reportedly damaged his Cadillac at the Ottawa convention and was seen driving another an hour later. Lortie was the person Claude Wagner had most to thank for sewing up the Quebec vote in 1976. When recruiting delegates at the grassroots level, Lortie could be heavy-handed when the need arose. Subtlety was not one of his character traits.

During the entire Ottawa convention Lortie had spent only an hour or two inside the hall itself. The rest of the time he was across the river in Hull, commanding a band of 112 Quebec delegates whom he had squirrelled away in a hotel. Minutes before the big vote, he bussed the lot of them to the arena so they could vote against Clark. Unlike Pageau, Lortie never camouflaged his true colours and later bragged about his exploits to the *Toronto Star*.

Lortie and Pageau had both been Wagner loyalists, and even now, a year and a half after Wagner had died of cancer, they wanted to avenge his defeat by Clark in 1976. But what burned them up more than anything was that Clark had failed them on patronage. In fact, Lortie had been shut out of party office since Clark became leader. Now that Clark looked vulnerable, Lortie was staging a comeback. As far as he and Pageau were concerned, Clark had turned his back on fellow Tories and betrayed the party.

Mulroney had ties to all the anti-Clark plotters, including financial ones — much of the funding behind Pageau and Lortie came from Mulroney's long-time friend Peter White and from Senator Guy Charbonneau, Mulroney's political ally — but nobody could pin anything on him. He always pretended not to be interested in the leadership. During the Ottawa convention he had mouthed public support for Clark and stayed out of controversy. Up to this point Mulroney had not done anything overtly rebellious, although that would soon change. Before long Mulroney would get together with Pageau and Lortie and others and inherit much of the party organization left behind by the late Claude Wagner.

Many Wagnerites hated Mulroney's guts because of 1976, but those who had been left in the cold by Clark disliked the leader even more. In the wake of the February 1981 meeting, most of them now fell behind Mulroney. Mulroney was a Quebecker who believed in loyalty and patronage and would never forget his friends. They wanted to break the pattern of having an anglophone head of the Conservative Party. (To them Mulroney was a francophone.) So the Quebec dissidents informally adopted Mulroney as their leader.

In the meantime Mulroney had assumed the role of the reluctant bridegroom, claiming not to be involved, but nonetheless putting together the pieces for another run at the Conservative leadership. Early in 1981 he notified Cleveland that he did not plan to renew his five-year employment contract. He would continue as IOC president on a month-to-month basis. He could quit his job on short notice and jump at any political opportunity that came his way. It was no longer a question of if, but when and how.

Not long after the Ottawa convention, Prime Minister Trudeau called a by-election in the Quebec riding of Lévis. The Liberals had swept Lévis in the 1980 election by twenty-nine thousand votes, making it one of the safest Liberal seats in the country. Despite the odds, Clark decided to go all out for a win — he knew no other way — and appointed as campaign manager Denis Beaudoin, a disaffected Social Crediter who knew the constituency and had a gift for organization. Beaudoin, a Tory for less than eighteen months, shared Clark's philosophy of going all out but was astonished to learn that not everybody in the Quebec party did. Headquarters in Montreal did not want to invest in the campaign and refused to send him money, workers, speakers, and pamphlets — the normal weapons of electoral war. Half his time was spent battling not the Liberals but his own party. Montreal headquarters was now controlled by Mulroney loyalists, and Beaudoin got the unmistakeable message that they wanted Clark to lose big. It infuriated him that the Tory party in Quebec would not help its own leader.

Despite this handicap, Beaudoin came within 5,500 votes of scoring a major upset in Lévis. A 5,500-vote margin is no cliff-hanger, but considering where the Tories had started from, and the complete lack of back-up, they had achieved a moral victory. Beaudoin, believing that with proper party support he could have won, quit politics and returned in frustration to his farm in the Eastern Townships. He was so upset that he wrote a long farewell letter to Clark in which he laid out all the problems of the campaign and alleged Mulroney's duplicity in publicly supporting him as federal leader while privately sabotaging the party's campaign. A leader who let such a thing happen in his own house was somebody he did not trust, wrote Beaudoin. He would not fight for somebody who did not fight for himself.

A few days later the phone rang at Beaudoin's farm. It was Clark, who summoned him to Ottawa for some serious talking. At their meeting Beaudoin briefed him from beginning to end on the Quebec problem. "Okay," Clark replied, "I give you Quebec. Do whatever you want with it." Out of deference to Claude Wagner, Clark had never built his own machine in Quebec. Now with Wagner gone and Mulroney rapidly mobilizing his forces, Clark decided to take control of the party apparatus, then virtually non-existent, and appointed Beaudoin as Quebec's organizational boss, giving him carte blanche to fire anybody he wanted. Beaudoin soon fired Jean Dugré, the membership secretary who was working for the party but unabashedly promoting Mulroney, then dropped Rodrigue Pageau, the national director in Quebec who had worked clandestinely to bring Clark down. Beaudoin assumed both their jobs, thus giving Clark firm bureaucratic control of Quebec.

Beaudoin's first challenge as boss in Quebec was to manage another by-election in the province, this time in Joliette, which would be voting on August 17, 1981. Although this was a traditional Tory seat, held since 1968 by Roch LaSalle, the party's own polls showed the Tories losing Joliette by between five and ten thousand votes. (Roch LaSalle had been the lone Tory survivor from Quebec in 1980, but resigned from the House of Commons a year later to become leader of the Union Nationale in Quebec.)

As the by-election approached, any insightful newspaper reader could detect the ever more public animosity between Clark and Mulroney. The two were jockeying in public as to whether Mulroney would run in LaSalle's place. Clark publicly prodded Mulroney to go for it and gave him until June 30 to make up his mind.

Free of his contractual obligations to IOC, Mulroney could now seriously consider running, and the prospect was enticing. A leadership convention, he firmly believed, was only a year or so away, and his 1976 experience had taught him — rather brutally — that he had to join the cosy caucus club before it would let him lead the party. Joliette, the only seat in all Quebec to stick with the Conservative Party in 1980, gave him the perfect entry. However, he did not want to be stuck as an opposition MP under Clark, and he shuddered at the thought of being introduced as Clark's Quebec lieutenant. But most of all he feared losing. "If he ran and won, he'd be very hard to stop," Dalton Camp told journalist Parker Barss Donham at the time. "If he ran and lost, I don't think he'd be very credible." Some of his supporters suggested he was being set up by Clark to take the loss and thus remove him as a leadership threat. After thinking it over, and going back and forth a few times, Mulroney came close to running but ultimately decided not to take the risk. He still had not shaken his old fear of losing elections.

In early July Mulroney broke the news directly to Clark during an hour-long meeting on Parliament Hill. When he emerged, eager reporters shouted questions as they crowded around, wanting to know the verdict. Mulroney blamed his decision on the Liberals, saying they had called the by-election on too short notice for him to run. As reporters scurried off the hill to file their stories, a former Trudeau aide wandered by and wondered what was going on.

"Mulroney just met with Clark," he was told.

"Is he going to run?"

"No."

"But he'll be all over the television newscasts tonight," the former aide shot back. "It's amazing how he does it — he still hasn't run for elected office but he's always in the public eye."

Toronto Star reporter Bill Fox, who reported the exchange with the aide, concluded that "the net effect of the day, in political terms, was that Mulroney managed to sit out Joliette with his leadership aspirations reasonably intact." Six weeks later the Tory fears of dropping Joliette proved unfounded as LaSalle, who had lost in the recent provincial election and then decided to run again in his old federal seat, swept to victory in a landslide of more than thirteen thousand votes.

Around this time Mulroney began planting stories with Pierre O'Neill of *Le Devoir*, yet another media friend he had picked up during the Cliche commission hearings, that the Conservative Party had plunged one million dollars in debt and was in financial crisis because major donors had lost confidence in Clark. The party went on the record to condemn it as a "malicious fabrication," not knowing that Mulroney was the source. The leak served to further destabilize Clark's leadership. Mulroney was playing a dangerous game, but so far he was getting away with it.

The next clue that Mulroney was doing more than sitting meekly on the sidelines came late in the fall, with the approach of the annual Joe Clark dinner in Montreal. With only weeks to go, a mere eighty-two tickets had been sold. It looked very much like the whole thing would flop badly, to the great embarrassment of Clark and the party. As the dimensions of the coming fiasco began taking shape, Mulroney called Finlay MacDonald, his ally in the wooing of Claude Wagner, who was now at the PC Canada Fund. "Do you realize how many tables have been sold?" Mulroney asked. Unfortunately, yes, MacDonald replied. "Finlay, it's a goddamn disaster," Mulroney said. "We could have it in a telephone booth." Did he want some help? "Desperately," replied MacDonald. "All right," Mulroney said, "tell Joe that I'll call the boys." Mulroney rounded up some help, personally rolled up his sleeves, and went to work on friends and business associates. In the end he and his troops managed to sell the place out, unloading a total of more than a thousand tickets at $175 a shot. At the dinner, as Clark made his way up to the podium with the television cameras rolling, he stopped to shake Mulroney's hand. That evening Mulroney was Clark's best friend.

Mulroney had saved the day — or so it appeared. Clark had never been a big draw in Quebec. Nobody argued that. On the other hand, maybe something more than Clark's unpopularity explained the poor ticket sales. Beaudoin and some of the other Clark supporters in Quebec swore up and down that the Mulroney gang had actively sabotaged the dinner, telling people to stay away. When Clark looked bad their man looked good, especially when he later came to the rescue.

In public Mulroney remained loyal to his leader, but by late 1981 he had begun a series of secret lunchtime meetings with some of his closest friends in a private room at the top of the stairs in the posh Mount Royal Club. Usually eight or ten Mulroney confidants would pull up chairs around a big round table. They included Peter White, Michel Cogger, Jean Bazin, Senator Guy Charbonneau, and former Newfoundland premier Frank Moores, who had also served as an MP and as president of the Conservative Party. At the first meeting Mulroney, acting as chairman, explained his rationale: the party's next general meeting in Winnipeg, he said, would hold another vote on Clark's leadership, and he wanted to know how he should handle the whole thing. Mulroney, as was his style, went around the table and asked each person what he thought. It was clear he wanted to be ready for a full-scale leadership convention in case something happened to Clark. The feedback that emerged quickly confirmed his own instincts, namely that Clark was vulnerable and that his chances of replacing him were good. At this point nobody really talked of actively undermining Clark.

The meetings quickly turned into an intelligence-gathering forum. Mulroney wanted to know what was happening in each province; who was fighting Clark and what they were doing; what were Clark's chances in Winnipeg. Once everybody had given reports, they repeatedly discussed questions such as whether 70 per cent would save Clark, or how Mulroney should respond when the media quizzed him about Winnipeg.

Each meeting in the Mount Royal Club started with drinks —

Mulroney himself had club soda — and then waiters brought in lunch. Once the waiters had left and the doors were shut, Mulroney would get down to business. Whenever a waiter returned to pour coffee, the conversation stopped dead. Mulroney had made it clear from the outset that he wanted these meetings kept under wraps. Their mere existence would convince Clark's supporters of a plot and hurt them all. Once the waiter had cleared the room, conversation returned to normal.

Over the months the membership of the Mount Royal meetings expanded. Ken Waschuk of Saskatchewan, until recently a Clark aide and now a party employee, soon joined the group. Fred Doucet, from Mulroney's St. FX network, also turned up from time to time. But the greatest single breakthrough came with the arrival of Nova Scotia MP Elmer MacKay. He personally dropped in only once, but his political confidant, Fred von Veh, became a regular. MacKay had been a Clark cabinet minister and until recently chairman of the Tory caucus, but the 1980 election fiasco had convinced him that the party needed a new leader. Although not a member of the Mount Royal Club group, Mulroney's old friend Bob Coates, the former party president who had been angered at being left out of Clark's cabinet, was already actively working to discredit and undermine Clark at every turn.

The Mount Royal Club group continued to meet about once a month all through 1982. As the months passed, the group had increasing trouble sticking to pure intelligence gathering. Members continually debated whether they should get actively involved in the movement to dump Clark. Everybody agreed that Mulroney should not be seen sticking the dagger into Clark, but beyond that the group divided into hawks such as Frank Moores and doves, with the hawks urging Mulroney to become more aggressive. Michael Meighen, a dove, made the point that he had come to discuss strategy in the event of a leadership race and wanted nothing to do with any plotting against Clark; he was never invited back.

Sometimes former double agent Rodrigue Pageau, Mulroney's

chief on-the-ground organizer, would walk into the room and whisper something to Mulroney or someone else, then promptly leave.
Pageau did not belong to the Mount Royal Club group. He sat on a
second committee that was holding parallel meetings with Mulroney,
an all-Quebec team that worked in French and operated just as
secretly. However, the Quebec committee was more hands-on and
more aggressive than the Mount Royal Club group, having the aim
of wresting control of the party's Quebec executive out of Clark's
hands. Mulroney's failure to nail down control of the Quebec wing
of the party had devastated him in 1976. Claude Wagner had locked
up delegates in riding after riding clear across the province while he
watched helplessly from the sidelines. Mulroney vowed never to let
it happen again, and the primary purpose of the Quebec committee
was to see that it did not.

The Quebec committee met at various places, including
Mulroney's home on several occasions. Besides Mulroney and the
infamous Jean-Yves Lortie, it included Pierre Claude Nolin, Claude
Dumont, Jean Dugré, and the Brunet brothers, Robert and Luc, but
the main force other than Mulroney was Pageau. It met at least once
a week and concentrated on logistics. Pageau had set up the committee to mimic the Conservative Party's official executive committee in
Quebec, and it behaved as if it was the mainstream of the party, except
that it was actively working against the established leader.

Meanwhile the nation's capital was positively awash with plots and
schemes to dump Clark. Robert Coates had been holding almost
weekly meetings in his parliamentary office, whose purpose, pure and
simple, was to make Clark's leadership untenable. Apart from Clark's
failure to appoint Coates to the cabinet, he had not forgiven him for
opposing Diefenbaker back in 1966 (Coates had stuck with
Diefenbaker until the very end). Somehow Coates managed to
overlook the fact that his friend Mulroney had been more central to
the conspiracy against Diefenbaker than Clark had been. Among the
MPs holding informal anti-Clark meetings were Elmer MacKay, Paul

Dick, and John Gamble. As pollster Allan Gregg later put it, these machinations had wheels within wheels.

The godfather of all the Ottawa plotting was Frank Moores. Even though Moores lived in Montreal, his closeness to the parliamentary party allowed him to function as the main link between Ottawa and Mulroney's Quebec forces. It was he who had built Mulroney's suddenly strong inroads into the previously hostile Tory caucus. For instance, it was Moores who recruited Elmer MacKay. After resigning as premier of Newfoundland in 1979, Moores had moved to Montreal and sunk into a personal depression not unlike Mulroney's. Mulroney, who felt that a former premier deserved better, led the rescue effort by giving him a cushy IOC consulting contract. A couple of other Quebec businessmen also helped out. Now back on his feet, and deeply grateful to Mulroney, Moores pursued the dumping of Clark as a personal make-work project, doing nothing else for much of 1982. He had no quarrel with the Tory leader; he was merely trying to help the man who had helped him. When not working on disgruntled caucus members, he was travelling across the country collecting money and fomenting discontent in the grassroots.

A garrulous backslapper, Moores operated as Mulroney's front man and contact man from coast to coast. However, he fell short when it came to the administrative side of organizing. Much of the on-the-ground logistics was handled by Peter White, who was now living in London, Ontario, and working as a business associate of Conrad Black. White acted as the comptroller, administrator, secretary, and general co-ordinator. He kept track of the delegates and their ridings, and just about everything else, including the flow of money. He made sure the money was spent properly and accounted for and, like Moores, he found it took most of his time. In the coming months White would set up bank accounts for youth organizers across the country and oversee the recruitment of large sections of the party's youth wing to Mulroney's cause, a task that would later become important. In Nova Scotia, for example, when anti-Clark youth activists Andrew Demond and Chris Worthington needed money, they simply called White to have their special dump-Clark bank account replenished.

In early 1982 Mulroney's Quebec committee decided to launch a surprise attack at the Conservative Party's Quebec convention in February, aimed at taking control of the Tories' Quebec wing. The plans were worked out and the final details put into place at a party in Mulroney's home on Super Bowl Sunday in late January. Marc Dorion, Jean-Yves Lortie, Bernard Trépanier, Claude Dumont, Jean Dugré, Rodrigue Pageau, Jean Bazin, brothers Fernand and Benoît Roberge, and Jacques Blanchard were there, as well as Michel Cogger and Senator Guy Charbonneau.

On the final weekend of February 1982, about six hundred delegates crowded into an east-end Montreal Cégep, or community college. On the surface the convention unfolded as one of the most placid meetings in years. On the Saturday delegates gave Clark a standing ovation — a first in Quebec for any national Tory leader in memory — when he arrived to speak. Later, with reporters crowded around him, a confident Clark described Mulroney as "cabinet timber" and a possible Tory leader down the line, but then, breaking into a slight grin, warned that Mulroney would have to wait because he planned on being prime minister for a couple of decades at least. He left Montreal on Sunday morning feeling triumphant and in control.

As soon as Clark had gone, the Mulroney forces put a three-pronged strategy in motion. The first prong involved the election of the Quebec party president. They had persuaded the Clark forces to accept Robert Brunet unopposed as president by giving them the false impression he was pro-Clark, or at least neutral. Brunet was the law partner of retiring president Marcel Danis, a loyal Clark supporter. Only after the convention was over would the Clark forces discover Brunet leaned to Mulroney. The second prong came during the election of officers. Going into the vote, the Clark forces thought they had a deal that all nine slots would be filled by acclamation, resulting in a slight majority for the Clark faction. At the last moment, however, two additional Mulroney candidates declared, Jean-Yves Lortie and Ed Ross. With the help of bussed-in Mulroney delegates, who gave Mulroney a majority, these two scored a narrow victory. The third prong consisted of a surprise attack on Marcel Danis, who had rebuffed overtures from the Mulroney people to change sides, despite the fact that he had worked for Mulroney in 1976. The Mulroney delegates prevented Danis from sitting on the executive as past president, thus denying Clark another crucial member.

The three-pronged strike had gone like clockwork and now Mulroney's people controlled the executive, which meant he would be able to arbitrarily appoint thirty-eight delegates-at-large to the national convention in Winnipeg, now eleven months away and representing his last chance to topple Clark before the next election. As long as Clark had controlled the Quebec executive, he was assured that the at-large delegates would vote for him. Now they belonged to Mulroney. The Mulroney forces had done their homework and done it well.

Actually they had done their job a little too well. When Mulroney's troops muscled Marcel Danis off the executive, Peter Blaikie, the national Tory president, bolted from the hall, muttering, "This is war." Later, when reporters caught up with him, he was still seething. "Certain people used this convention to take control of the executive for reasons that have nothing to do with the activities of the association but which have something to do with an eventual leadership race," he fumed. "It is very clear there was an attempt by a certain group — I won't name anybody and you can draw your own conclusions — to control delegates to the next national convention, and I believe that to be premature." Blaikie might as well have named Mulroney because everybody knew exactly who he meant.

Reporters moved over to Mulroney, who countered with a shocked look of indignation while denying any nefarious involvement. "We have never had a more positive and less acrimonious convention, fully supportive of Mr. Clark and the party leadership," Mulroney told

Globe and Mail columnist William Johnson. "To impugn the motives of loyal Conservatives without identifying anyone by name is akin to McCarthyism and should be beneath the dignity of the high office Mr. Blaikie holds." Mulroney told other reporters that the party was united behind Clark, and that it was Blaikie who had the leadership ambitions. Mulroney was right about at least one thing: not a single member of the Mulroney coalition said a bad word against Clark. The group had strict rules about it. Even Lortie refused to say he opposed the Tory leader.

"Your people are really doing something or other," pro-Clark youth organizer Scott McCord shouted to Mulroney's face. Mulroney gave off an innocent look. "I don't know what you're talking about, 'my people,'" he shouted back. "I just showed up."

Clark was driving back to Ottawa when he heard the news that his candidates for the executive had been defeated and that Mulroney's people had taken over. It suspiciously resembled the 1966 coup in Beauport, when the Quebec delegates had applauded John Diefenbaker in the hall but — led by Mulroney, Peter White, and Jean Bazin — had voted for leadership review when he was not there.

Back in Ottawa a chastened but wiser Tory leader sent Mulroney a blunt warning through the press. "The party has a very long memory," Clark told reporters outside the House of Commons the next day. "It would judge very harshly anyone who is deliberately trying to cause internal difficulties that would deflect us from our very important work of replacing the government." Clark had not mentioned Mulroney's name in his warning, but, like Blaikie, he did not need to.

When responding to this salvo from Clark, Mulroney once again donned the cloak of incredulity and pleaded innocent. "[Clark] clearly is not referring to me," he retorted, "because I said nothing except extremely positive things about him, his leadership, and the party."

The hijacking of the Quebec wing taught Clark a lesson about what to expect in the coming months as the Winnipeg convention approached. He now understood that the Mulroney forces were determined to win and prepared to fight dirty. To survive as leader he would have to fight back with every weapon he could command.

The second act in Mulroney's campaign to oust Clark opened in early March when he stood before 275 Progressive Conservatives at a fundraising brunch for the St. Denis Progressive Conservative constituency association in Montreal and gave a carefully worded discourse on Ottawa's budget process that bored everyone in the audience silly. But it looked leaderly and raised his profile, enough to draw sniper fire from Lowell Murray about Mulroney "obviously going after the leadership." Murray added, "It's probably better to have him out in public so the people can see what it is, if anything, he stands for, rather than have him operating privately." Mulroney sniped back that Murray's comments were "pretty silly and self-serving."

Actually Mulroney had only started making speeches. More were to come, and for good reason. One of his major problems in 1976 was his lack of policy depth, and his public profile had practically vanished after his plunge from the political limelight. The public memory is notoriously short and so is a party's memory. After a six-year lay-off he had to remind people that he was still around and available. The Mount Royal Club group (as well as other advisers) were calling on Mulroney to fix the problem. It was decided that one of the best ways to build visibility and credibility was for him to undertake a national tour and make serious speeches on weighty issues. A few important public addresses early in the game would defuse the charge that he lacked substance and begin to establish him as the natural alternative to Clark.

To help him with his speeches, Mulroney persuaded Jon Johnson, a Royal Bank employee in Montreal, to conduct research and help write the texts. He also brought in Peter White for his knowledge of issues. Both Johnson and White, ardent Tories who had worked on his 1976 campaign, were logical choices. But Mulroney also pulled in another Tory from a surprising source — Bill Neville. Neville had until recently been Clark's chief of staff and right-hand man, closer to his political pulse than even Lowell Murray, and he was still writing speeches for Clark in his spare time. However, Mulroney had cultivated Neville all through his years with Clark; while Neville worked for and supported the Tory leader, he socialized with Mulroney. Neville, who had joined the head office of the Canadian Imperial Bank of Commerce in Toronto, now willingly helped Clark's most obvious competitor. Mulroney sat on the bank's board of directors, and every time he came to town for a board meeting he and Neville would get together. With help from Johnson, White, and now Neville, Mulroney put together a series of speeches on the country's economy and what could be done to improve it.

The first stop on Mulroney's tour, on April 22, 1982, was Ottawa. The Ottawa-Carleton Conservative Association had planned on inviting Joe Clark for its fundraising banquet but concluded he could not sell enough tickets and asked Mulroney instead. Mulroney drew a packed house and raised $20,000 at $100 a plate. He also pulled in big coverage from virtually every news organization. "I am delighted to be here tonight," he began. "I'm sorry I missed the big celebration for the Queen last week. Mr. Trudeau forgot to invite me. That's all right. The next time the Queen comes we're going to forget to invite him." It was the first of many quips before he dug into more serious matters. That evening he set out a ten-point program for boosting Canada's sagging productivity, including the establishment of a tripartite national productivity commission and the call for a "national commitment to civilize labour relations in Canada" much along the lines that he had used in turning around employee relations at IOC. Most observers judged it to be an impressive performance.

Over the next six weeks he blitzed five cities from Vancouver to Fredericton, speaking mostly at fundraisers for local riding associations. Speech after speech, the tour aligned Mulroney solidly on the party's right — ideological territory he had mostly ignored in 1976. He had always been an instinctive progressive; in 1976 he was usually lumped in with Red Tories like Joe Clark and Flora MacDonald, although he tried during the campaign to be all things to all people, carefully not positioning himself on either left or right. Now his speeches emphasized restraint in government spending, encouragement for entrepreneurs, curbing the Foreign Investment Review Agency, fostering foreign investment, and boosting research and development. Part of Mulroney's repositioning had to do with the fact that Clark had taken solid control of the progressive side of the party. If Mulroney wanted to topple him he would have to make an alliance with the right.

Yet the ideological retooling of Mulroney went deeper than that. Very late in the 1976 campaign two of Mulroney's advisers, Don McDougall and Frank Moores, conducted an informal canvass of delegates that revealed that the left side of the party simply did not take to Mulroney. The discovery shocked them because Mulroney had based his campaign on the assumption that he would be the catalyst the progressive candidates would rally behind as they dropped off the ballot. But that was not the end of the bad news. McDougall and Moores also discovered that, contrary to previous assumptions, the right outnumbered the left, which meant their candidate would lose even with left-wing support. (In fact Clark, a progressive, went on to win, but only because right-wing delegates had crossed lines rather than support Claude Wagner and because Clark was minimally offensive across the party.) McDougall and Moores concluded that Mulroney should have positioned himself on the right to pursue people like Sinclair Stevens and Jack Horner instead of people like Flora MacDonald and John Fraser. After the campaign ended it became clear that the Mulroney campaign had fundamentally miscalculated, and Mulroney decided he would not make that mistake again. Accordingly, his spring 1982 speaking tour across the country was deliberately designed to shift his appeal towards the right.

Mulroney claimed he was not a candidate for anything, but he certainly looked like one. The tour, which drew a crush of media interest wherever he landed, excited some party members and made others queasy. Mulroney insisted he was merely helping local riding associations raise needed funds. However, his most enthusiastic supporters openly debunked that piece of fiction and declared he was starting to campaign for leader. Again Clark warned Mulroney through the media that anyone who stirred up dissension over the issue of leadership was endangering his chances of ever becoming "a minister or something." Neither Clark's warning nor the general controversy seemed to faze Mulroney, who stuck to his cover story that he was just giving speeches. For the record Mulroney would always make sure to say that there was no leadership vacancy, that he was loyal to Clark, and that he was simply doing his bit to help raise money for the party. "I have been fully supportive of Mr. Clark at all times since he assumed the leadership just over six years ago," Mulroney said, adding that he was not responsible for how people characterized his tour.

While Mulroney took the offensive, the sniping from Clark's own caucus worsened. Now John Crosbie and David Crombie, Clark's former minister of health and welfare, were sticking little pins into their leader. And Crombie was also furiously studying French in anticipation of a leadership race. Some of the cruelest strikes against Clark came out of the West Block cafeteria from the so-called Breakfast Club. This infamous daily gathering consisted mostly of disgruntled MPs, their aides, and a handful of other Parliament Hill regulars. The MPs who showed up rain or shine were Gordon Towers, Dan McKenzie, and Gordon Ritchie, all from the prairies; a sizeable batch of journalists often joined the table, including Derik Hodgson, Bill Fox, Fred Ennis, and Doug Fisher. Each morning at quarter to eight, a dozen or so people would bring their breakfast trays to their standard meeting spot at a bank of tables that had been pushed together near the back; over bacon and eggs they'd begin firing off jokes and snide comments about the women's movement, Red Tories, Liberals, socialists, metric conversion, bilingualism, and anything else that irked them. But they always saved their best jokes and put-downs for Joe Clark. They loathed Clark and disparaged him endlessly as a weak-kneed left-winger. Yet nobody could dispute the entertainment value of their quips, and other West Block cafeteria patrons would strain to overhear the latest nastiness.

The catalyst for most of the Clark-bashing was the extraordinarily sharp-tongued Rick Logan, Robert Coates's top political aide, who usually sat in the middle of the group. A raconteur with undeniable panache, Logan had phoned up open-line radio programs during the 1979 election when Pierre Trudeau appeared as a guest and, in a perfect Pakistani accent, thanked the prime minister for accepting him into the country along with the twenty-eight relatives he had sponsored. Now Logan had turned his mischief-making against Joe Clark. Every morning he would fire off rude digs and tell outrageous stories that made his audience guffaw with malicious delight. In Logan's hands, Clark always emerged as a bumbling kid with his mittens on a string, or as a big turkey, or just as a plain jerk. When Clark's picture appeared on the front page of the *Toronto Sun* standing beside two Sunshine Girls, Logan passed around the newspaper and announced it was the Tory leadership loyalty test: "How many boobs do you count in this picture?" Anybody who counted only four passed the test. Every morning the Breakfast Club gave birth to another joke or another dirty rumour. "Did you hear that Maureen has finally dumped the little wimp?" Logan would chortle. "And he's living in the Beacon Arms." (The Beacon Arms was then one of downtown Ottawa's seedier hotels.) And so it went.

No matter how cheap or mean the jokes were, they always got repeated later, sweeping through the closed world of Parliament Hill like tidal water in a bathtub, back and forth, back and forth until they had splashed almost everyone. For the rest of the day on which Logan introduced the leadership loyalty test, people across Parliament Hill picked up the *Toronto Sun* and repeated his question. Yet the jokes and rumours remained beneath the surface so that Clark supporters could not refute them or mount a defence. Whether the rumours were true did not matter. What mattered was that a half-dozen MPs and another half-dozen aides and reporters walked around Parliament Hill all day repeating the scurrilous gossip. Within days the same gossip and innuendo began popping up in newspapers — un-attributed, of course, since everything said at the Breakfast Club table was off the record. For someone struggling to keep a grip on caucus and restore his image, the poison darts from the Breakfast Club were devastating. Any political leader would be wounded by such a con-certed attack.

The sessions always fell a little flat when Logan was away. He spent considerable time travelling around the country, spreading his poison against Clark. Where he got the money nobody seemed to know, but he turned up at big Tory meetings from Newfoundland to British Columbia and always returned to Parliament Hill with a fund of new anti-Clark zingers.

Like Logan, most of the people around the Breakfast Club table supported Mulroney. Pat MacAdam, another regular and now an aide to MPs Gordon Towers and Ron Stewart, still had his IOC retainer to follow developments on Parliament Hill affecting mining and northern allowances. MacAdam fed Mulroney every bit of venom that bubbled from the Breakfast Club's toxic pot. Mulroney himself never went near the Breakfast Club, but hardly a day went by when he and MacAdam did not spend time on the phone, and sometimes MacAdam would augment his reports with written briefing notes and clippings.

When the wisecracks died down and the talk turned serious, MacAdam or Logan usually brought the conversation around to Mulroney, whom they held up as the saviour of the Conservative Party, the hope for a new post-Clark order. Implicitly they compared Mulroney and Mila to the Kennedys, conveying the feeling that Mulroney would bring Camelot to Canada. All this drumbeating had its effect. Many of the same MPs who had ganged up on Mulroney in 1976 now leaned towards him. Now and then Mulroney would drop into Parliament Hill and make the rounds — always set up by MacAdam — and work his Irish charm on MPs. He had filled in his last missing link. With Frank Moores and Pat MacAdam as his front men on Parliament Hill, he would never suffer another gang-up from what he had called the "private little club."

By summer 1982 the plotting against Clark had reached such a scale that it could no longer be concealed, even from the general public. Although the newspapers had gone easy on Mulroney, their revelations undermined his periodic claims of loyalty to Clark. Mulroney owed his relatively easy ride from the press to two things. One was his cosiness with the Montreal media, most of whom relied upon him as a source; the other was that the media in the rest of the country had focused much of their attention on the public machinations of Toronto businessman John Morrison and MP John Gamble, the only two anti-Clark operators who had come into the open, not only admitting their plotting but bragging about it. But Mulroney could not expect such luck to hold forever. It would be only a matter of time before the reporters would train their sights on the conspirator who pulled the longest and fattest strings, and that clearly was him. The more he continued to mouth support for Clark, the more tempting he made it for the media to expose his hypocrisy. He was already starting to draw heat. By summer he needed to cool himself down and cultivate the image of a good party trouper.

That summer Mulroney had been ducking out of town for fishing weekends, as he had most years since joining IOC. He enjoyed fishing and took full advantage of the company's private camp north of Labrador City, located in a network of lakes in the middle of nowhere. The camp was nothing fancy or ostentatious, just half a dozen log cabins that from the air might be mistaken for an Inuit settlement. Three cabins with two metal cots each provided the sleeping quarters. Another cabin with a bar served as a lounge; a hut supplied a shower and toilet. There was also a cottage housing two married couples who looked after the place and acted as guides and cooks. It was nicely set up, but Spartan. Mulroney always stocked up on newspapers, magazines, and books before coming — he was still a dedicated news junkie. The facility offered no telephone, only a radio-telephone for emergencies, and no television. It was the only time people saw Mulroney not use a telephone, and the only time they ever saw him totally relaxed.

Since the camp boasted only six beds, Mulroney was limited to inviting five guests at a time. The invitations themselves usually came over the telephone from his secretary, Ginette Pilotte. Guests needed pack only a few clothes; everything else was provided, including their particular brand of booze and cigarettes. The IOC jet picked them up in Montreal, Toronto, Ottawa, or wherever they happened to be and flew them into Labrador City, where a float-plane ferried them the rest of the way.

Each morning, after a lumberjack breakfast, the guides would take them out among the lakes, sometimes by boat and sometimes by float-plane, to strategic spots where little aluminum outboard boats were stashed. Anybody could catch fish here: the lakes were teeming. The group would fish until noon, when the guides would fillet a few trout, bake some beans, and serve lunch on the shore. Then they would fish some more. Back at the base camp that evening, after having a shower and washing the mosquito repellent off their skin, they would sit down to a hearty dinner prepared by the guides' wives, then move over to the rustic lounge, light up the Franklin fireplace, and sit around telling jokes and swapping lies. Despite the limited accommodations, over the course of a season Mulroney managed to bring through a wide array of friends — Michel Cogger, Frank Moores, old St. FX friend Terry McCann, Newfoundland MP Jim McGrath, Pat MacAdam, Richard Holden, Jacques Blanchard (a Quebec City lawyer who had supported Wagner in 1976), and many more.

The invitations that Ginette Pilotte telephoned out for the weekend of July 24, 1982, brought together an odd concoction of guests. First there were David Angus and Sam Wakim, both old Mulroney loyalists but from different cities and different networks and not close friends. Then there were Bill Neville and Finlay MacDonald, who were both Clark people but had little to do with each other and nothing to do with Angus and Wakim. (MacDonald had recently joined Clark's office as senior adviser.) The fifth guest, Dalton Camp, was neutral. He went back a long way with both Mulroney and Clark.

And although Camp had voted for Clark in 1976, Mulroney had so actively distanced himself from Camp at the time that he could not possibly include him on the list of traitors. In political terms the guests were evenly split between Mulroney and Clark. Except for Mac-Donald and Camp, who were good friends, none of them ordinarily saw one another socially.

Mulroney had a reason for bringing this somewhat incongruous group of Tories together, a hidden agenda that his guests initially did not appreciate, since much of the first evening was spent playing bridge while Mulroney, who did not play cards, sat around. Once the card-playing ended, Mulroney, cold sober in a room full of drinkers, got his chance to steer the talk to politics, eventually launching into a discourse about the economy. Leveraged buy-outs had recently arrived on the corporate scene in a big way and, to the surprise of his guests, Mulroney denounced them as a drain on society, and did so most forcefully and eloquently. He said they sucked money out of the system for the sake of putting profit into somebody's pocket. Furthermore they did not create jobs — "not a fucking job," as he put it — or contribute a dime to the economy. He went on to declare that he would do something about it if he ever got the chance. It was an impressive performance and convinced his guests that he had some strong convictions. It also told them that, despite his big-business connections and his right-wing speeches about the need for government to step back and give the private sector more room to create wealth, he still belonged to the progressive side of the Conservative Party. "This is the first time that I would take you seriously as prime minister," Dalton Camp remarked to him afterwards.

With Winnipeg six months away, Mulroney had to make a decision about how to handle the simmering issue of the Conservative leadership as it got hotter, and soon the talk focused on that subject. "Well, what do you guys think I should do?" Mulroney asked, making it clear he wanted his guests to level with him. Camp advised Mulroney to get out of the line of fire because he was fast becoming the "point man" in the war against Clark. In armed battle the point man is the soldier in front of the charge, the one who draws the fire. "All you've got to do is just keep this up," Camp warned, adding that if he did so the media would quickly cast him in the role of prime conspirator against Clark, a status that would destroy his future chances. He advised him to support Clark, or at least not overtly oppose him, in the best interests of both himself and the party.

Both MacDonald and Neville agreed that if he wanted to become party leader he could not be the one to lead the anti-Clark forces. Mulroney could find reasons to ignore their advice, but he could not dismiss Camp. After all, Camp possessed the ultimate credentials when it came to replacing a leader; his part in the overthrow of Dief had branded him for life, making him a Typhoid Mary in some Tory circles. On any other occasion Mulroney, by this point in the discussion, would have been vehemently protesting his innocence and piously reaffirming his loyalty to the leader. But here, deep in the wilderness, he uttered not a squeak of protest. Instead he listened intently and said little, as he always did when he faced a critical decision. His political instincts, razor sharp as usual, told him Camp was right. He had been around the Conservative Party long enough to know what happened to the one who wielded the knife. Even if the plot succeeded, and even if the deposed leader deserved it, the man who did the deed was rarely welcomed afterwards. If he got fingered for bringing Clark down, he could kiss goodbye to any hope of ever becoming leader.

Mulroney had other reasons to follow Camp's advice and fall loyally behind Clark. Despite all the knocks from the Breakfast Club and the other detractors, in the past year Clark had shown himself to be amazingly tough and resilient. Every day the media nitpicked at him and his caucus stabbed him. He could seldom pick up a newspaper or turn on the radio without getting a blast, and rarely did he hear any good news. Yet he persevered, outwardly unscathed, never complaining or seeming to feel sorry for himself over the unfairness of it all.

Since frittering away his prime ministership Clark had matured dramatically as a political leader and demonstrated that he had learned from his mistakes. Stumping the country, slamming the Liberals and chiding Tory dissidents, he was performing at his lifetime best, showing confidence and even cheerfulness in adversity, and endearing himself to audiences with his self-deprecating wit. "Please wait for my punch lines," he told an Edmonton audience that had cheered too quickly. "I don't want this spontaneous applause — it's not caucus." Clark's was a classic case of someone rising too fast and reaching the top too soon. He was not ready to lead the party in 1976, but six tough years of on-the-job training had changed him. He had always been a skilled performer in the House of Commons, but now he cut a truly impressive figure. When a Tory colleague fumbled the ball in Parliament he could step in and turn things around with one short thrust. Even his critics — most of them anyway — conceded that since his defeat he had run one of the most effective oppositions anybody could remember. He had acquitted himself admirably in the tricky constitutional debate and had forced the government to back down in the infamous bell-ringing incident of March 1982, when the entire Tory caucus walked out of Parliament. All this while continually shaking off the attacks from his detractors. Nobody could say Clark had not shown his mettle.

Furthermore the tide seemed to be turning in Clark's favour. Lately the Gallup poll had become his best friend. Back in September 1981, he had sneaked past Trudeau by one percentage point; by December he had run up his lead to four points. Now in the summer of 1982, as Canada headed into its worst recession in half a century, he had stretched his margin to a stunning 19 points, putting to shame the notion that he could not win again. Even Quebec had started to shift; the polls there rated him the most admired non-Quebec politician in the country. It made no sense to bump the leader of a party so far ahead in public opinion. In fact, some argued that a leadership convention would be the worst thing for the party. As 1982 wore on, Clark looked like he would be a majority prime minister after the next election and maybe become a Canadian legend for tenacity and guts.

Clark's resurgence should have driven his critics underground and out of business, but in fact it hardly slowed them down. Too many Tories still rejected him as their leader. Despite the polls, these people refused to discard the notion that Clark was a loser. Hatred of Clark had almost become a religion. They believed his underlying image problems were incurable, and that ultimately the public would not buy him, and no numbers, analyses, or events could change their opinions. The polls showed Clark beating an unpopular Trudeau. "Wait until Trudeau resigns and is replaced by John Turner," they argued. They were spooked by the vision of the ever-devious Trudeau lying low until Clark was reconfirmed as leader in Winnipeg and then suddenly stepping down in favour of Turner. They maintained that Turner would clean Clark's clock. "We want to win the next election, dammit," his detractors would say, making the point that Clark should not be permitted to drag down the entire Conservative Party another time. Leading the chorus of doubters and denigrators, the Breakfast Club continued its daily poisoning of the wells, pumping out the theme of Clark as a loser. Its campaign gave Clark-bashing such wide currency that it helped rally the dissidents in caucus and helped make it acceptable to vote against the leader in Winnipeg despite his standing in the polls.

Clark might have been able to turn this situation around had he been willing to reach out more on a personal level, but he never initiated a phone call anywhere. It never entered his mind to call people up to see what was doing, which was the foundation of telephone networking. Unlike Mulroney, he simply was not a telephone man and seemingly nothing could make him one. His aides in the opposition leader's office had tried various schemes. First they encouraged him, then advised him, and finally implored him to call key people. When that failed they resorted to preparing lists of crucial contacts for him to call. Clark would sometimes make the effort, but he never felt comfortable at it and never did it for long. Once his staff even resorted to giving him colour-coded cards with names to call —

blue cards for once a month, and red cards for once a year — and then blocked off time in his schedule and rotated the cards for him. But the scheme didn't work. It was not his style. Networking was not in his blood.

Who knows what would have happened had Clark done a little networking, a little soothing of bruised egos? People like Rodrigue Pageau and Jean-Yves Lortie were working against him because they felt abandoned, as did Robert Coates and a number of the other anti-Clark conspirators. Even Brian Mulroney claimed he had put in calls to Clark that were not returned. He liked to recite these as examples of where he had tried to be helpful and been spurned. A little telephone blandishment would have done Clark no end of good.

Despite Dalton Camp's warning, Mulroney went ahead with a planned speech in Elmer MacKay's riding in August, where he lashed out at the Liberal "collectivist philosophy" and slammed Trudeau for running up a $25-billion deficit. He had become decidedly nervous about what lay in store for him in Winnipeg — too much had changed. However, it would take several months for him to fully take Camp's advice to heart and act on it.

Ever since Mulroney had begun the guerrilla war, Clark had been arming himself for Winnipeg. In defending his crown he would not cede an inch of territory, not even in Quebec. Since the February convention, Mulroney had controlled the Quebec party executive, but as party leader Clark retained authority over appointments, which gave him command over the party bureaucracy. He could appoint people and delegate resources. Building on this base, every weekend he toured some part of Quebec, never ducking an event, not even tiny ones in small towns. The constant visiting brought him into every corner of the province and brought him closer to Quebec than practically any outsider. Under Denis Beaudoin, his chief organizer, the party in Quebec hired eight full-time organizers (it previously had none), opened up a field office in Quebec City, launched a monthly newspaper for party members, and boosted province-wide membership from 861 in September 1981 to about twenty thousand two years later. Clark had pulled out the stops in wooing Quebec, and although he had not won its heart, he had earned some respect.

Mulroney had his own organizational muscle, and much of it hinged on his amazing ability to network. Not able to appoint salaried officers at party expense, Mulroney had to rely on his ability to call old friends and enlist them to the cause, which evened the odds considerably. That fall he networked as furiously as ever. Across the country people still picked up the phone to the familiar: "Hey, it's old Bones. . . . How ya doing?" Only now most of his calls focused on the issue of Clark's leadership, as he kept tabs on all the various plots and sub-plots brewing. In fact he was so busy maintaining his network and getting his daily fix of gossip that the staff in his office at IOC had come to accept the reality that they could not get to him before 11 A.M. The rest of the day was only marginally better.

By now Mulroney's network had become so large that he had trouble keeping his tattered address book up to date and in one piece. He often failed to add new names or update old ones, sometimes because he lacked space and sometimes because he lacked patience. The result was a mess. At one point he tried to get his old friend Peter White, who had moved into an IOC office for a few months to help with his speeches and political mail, to go through the whole thing and revise it name by name. But White took one look at the task and begged off. (Only after Mulroney became prime minister, and the PMO switchboard took over the address book, was the problem finally solved.)

That fall, as the convention drew closer, the fight for delegates between the pro-Clark and the pro-review forces quickly escalated, causing more excitement in the Conservative Party and bringing in more new members than at any time since the electric years of John Diefenbaker. Whichever side recruited the most supporters would win the showdown, a basic reality that Mulroney and Clark, two of the best organizers in the party, knew only too well. Neither side had trouble enrolling members. Young people flocked to the Tories, and in Quebec the Clark and Mulroney forces went head to head in virtually all the seventy-five ridings. The war was not one big battle but a series of little ones, each slugged out over the election of local delegates to the January meeting.

The battle for Winnipeg revolutionized the Tory delegate-selection system. Gone were the days when a cadre of faithful Tories met in their local constituencies to bestow delegateships on the hardest-working party members. Now political organizers arrived at local selection meetings with hundreds of instant Tories — often from a particular ethnic community — to seize temporary control of a constituency association that a month earlier had only 150 members. Whichever side packed more people into the room swept the entire slate of six candidates. This turned the Winnipeg delegate hunt into something resembling a series of tiny U.S. primaries, without the democratic safeguards of the primaries. It marked the beginning of a transformation of the Canadian political system. It was winner-take-all. The Conservative Party — indeed Canada — had never seen anything like it.

Because Quebec had so many vacant ridings — ridings that lacked even the semblance of a local Tory organization — organizers had a field day. The first few meetings in the province drew thirty or forty people, but soon the numbers escalated as Marcel Danis, now leading the Clark forces in Quebec, and Rodrigue Pageau for Mulroney battled to outdo each other. One night Danis would win with fifty people, and two nights later Pageau would top him with sixty in the riding next door, prompting Danis to produce seventy or eighty the next time. By November both sides were regularly turning out 250 people per meeting.

Turning out two or three hundred instant Tories from empty constituencies night after night taxed the ingenuity and resources of both organizations. Before each meeting local residents had to be found, approached, and signed up as party members and, in many cases, bussed in for the vote. Doing it across seventy-five ridings required a small army of workers and a lot of money. Early in the game both sides started offering "incentives," such as a $500 cash donation to a senior citizens' centre in return for one hundred able bodies who agreed to sign a PC membership card and vote the right way at a party meeting. The so-called incentives grew bigger as the need for votes increased. Both Pageau and Danis spent whatever they needed and neither ran short of money.

Before each meeting both the Mulroney and Clark teams posted agents at the door to challenge the credentials of party members belonging to the other side. In Hull a woman with no identification other than her PC card was refused admission until she went home to get her driver's licence, even though people who had known her for years stepped forward to vouch for her identity. In the Montreal riding of Dollard the meeting broke down into a feud over locked doors, strong-arm tactics, and questionable election logistics. In the end the Mulroney slate beat the Clark slate by six votes. On and on it went. Each side accused the other of dirty tricks and both were right. They played as rough as Maurice Duplessis, Mulroney's favorite villain, had ever done forty years earlier.

By the end of October Clark had done better in Quebec than almost anybody had predicted. The territory belonged to Mulroney, but Clark controlled the salaried positions in the party and had been organizing flat out for most of the year with a surprisingly strong and loyal group led by Denis Beaudoin, Marcel Danis, Jean Riou, Jean Charest, Robert Valcov, and Claude Boisselle. As well, a lot of old Wagner supporters had still not forgiven Mulroney for spoiling what would have been victory for Wagner in 1976. In the end Clark would take somewhat better than half the Quebec delegates.

The fact that Mulroney had failed to sweep Quebec did not augur well for his prospects in Winnipeg. If he could not win Quebec, he could not win anywhere. But this was not the worst of his political troubles at the moment. At IOC he faced a looming problem that threatened to make short work of his political comeback: it looked like the town of Schefferville would have to be shut down.

Not long after Mulroney gave out his dramatic $250 bonus to all

IOC employees, the world market for iron ore suddenly slumped. After several bumper years, 1982 was shaping up as a disaster for the steel and mining industries, and soon the market collapsed completely, turning Schefferville, already an inherently uneconomic production unit, into a huge drain on the company. In the quarter-century since Schefferville had begun producing ore, its output had shrunk from more than 10 million tons a year to less than 2 million, and its population had shrunk from a peak of nearly 5,000 to 1,700. Meanwhile the ore from its sister mine near Labrador City was cheaper to produce, easier to sell, and closer to the port of Sept-Îles. Even greater damage had been inflicted by the high-grade natural ore from mines in Australia and Brazil. With the market in recession, and major IOC shareholders like Bethlehem Steel reluctant to take Schefferville ore, the town was merely sucking profits from Labrador City. It could not go on forever.

Over the years IOC had put together several committees to examine Schefferville's future viability — as early as 1980 rumours of the town's imminent closing had circulated — but only in the deep recession of 1982 did the company finally take action. Mulroney had seen the writing on the wall; his world travels since 1979 had been attempts at finding new markets for Schefferville ore. In the end nothing had worked, but not for lack of will on his part. "We forestalled that decision for, I would say, at least two years," said one former IOC officer, "hoping that something would enter the picture that would make the project more viable."

Earlier in the fall Al Larson, IOC's senior financial officer in Canada, and three of his accountants had undertaken a complete audit of the mine's present worth and future prospects. So secret was their undertaking that the Sept-Îles foursome checked themselves into the Château Champlain in downtown Montreal, where for two weeks they worked through the numbers, rehashed them several times again, and always came up with the same bottom line: Schefferville was costing the company millions. Furthermore, the deficit was getting bigger every year.

Armed with hard numbers, Larson reported his findings directly to Hanna Mining chairman Robert Anderson, briefing him on the company jet en route from San Francisco to Cleveland. Larson's evidence helped convince Anderson that Schefferville had to close. At the next board meeting, on October 22, a meeting in Cleveland that Mulroney attended, the board members of Hanna Mining voted to shut down the town.

It was no reflection on Mulroney that Larson took his findings directly to Cleveland rather than Montreal. In reality IOC's Canadian president had little say in the basic decision to close the town. When faced with the inevitable bad news he paced from one end of his office to the other, as he always did when he felt cornered and helpless. "He was like a lion in a cage," Jean-Pierre Maltais, IOC's public relations director, would later say. "He was saying, 'What are we going to do? What are we going to do?'"

The thought of shutting down Schefferville — or any town for that matter — violated most of the community values that Mulroney held dear. He had grown up in a company town and could picture what it would mean for the local populace. Worse, he knew the closing could finish him politically. He had not wielded the axe, but as company president he would have to accept the responsibility and take the blame. Clark would no doubt cast him in the role of the man who closed a town and hit him with it in the remaining weeks before Winnipeg. If he survived to become Tory leader, he could visualize the devastating Liberal television ads at the next election: a movie camera pans slowly across a deserted main street of a ghost town as the odd bit of tumbleweed blows across the screen; then an announcer breaks the silence with a solemn warning that what Mulroney did to Schefferville he would do to the country. Clark's image problems would look trivial compared with his. It would cripple Mulroney's political comeback and maybe kill it. Not that he could complain. As IOC's chief executive officer he had enjoyed too much credit when good fortune struck in the late 1970s, and now he had to shoulder more blame than he deserved when times turned bad.

Although powerless to keep Schefferville alive, Mulroney could push hard for a fair settlement, and that he did with his usual gusto. He strove to make it not only fair, but more than fair, seeking the best shut-down settlement in the history of Quebec, even Canada. When the subject of separation benefits came up at the Cleveland board meeting, one of the vice-presidents argued against doing anything. "They've had a good job for a number of years," he said. "We've paid them well, we don't owe them anything." Mulroney pounded his fist in response. "I'll tell you what we're going to do for them," he shot back. "We're going to give them two weeks' pay for every year of service." Then he checked off a list of other things the company could do. Pretty soon he had won everybody over, including the unwilling vice-president. Mulroney took control of the team drafting the settlement package and made it as generous as possible.

He also moved swiftly and skilfully to minimize the impact of the bad news. His first manoeuvre was to delay the public announcement several days so he could brief key politicians in Quebec City and Ottawa. As soon as the Hanna board had made its decision, he arranged a meeting with Quebec's labour minister, Pierre Marois. Mulroney had not spelled out the reason for the visit, but Marois smelled the news and pulled the IOC file before he arrived. He also instructed his secretary to make Mulroney wait in the reception area so that he would have to cool his heels in the lobby like anybody else. Marois's little ploy fell apart completely. Mulroney slipped through an open door and started making the rounds of Marois's staff, glad-handing his secretaries and everybody else in sight.

Once Mulroney was inside Marois's private office, the labour minister suggested he might use his ministerial powers to order a parliamentary inquiry into the Schefferville closing. "You don't have to do that," Mulroney replied. "I agree to it." He promised to participate wholeheartedly and offered to pay part of the cost. Marois got the impression that Mulroney was nervous and trying awfully hard to convince him he wanted the best settlement for the workers, even if it meant fighting with higher-ups. On the whole Mulroney hit it off well with Marois, which was important. Part of his strategy for minimizing the fallout was to get all the key politicians onside before the public announcement.

His mission to Ottawa went well too. Mulroney enlisted Pat MacAdam, who was still on an IOC retainer, to make the Ottawa rounds with him while he paid visits to Minister of Employment Lloyd Axworthy and Minister of Mines Judy Erola, as well as to Joe Clark and Ed Broadbent, leaders of the two opposition parties. Early in the morning when MacAdam took delivery of a chauffeur-driven car that Mulroney's office had rented for the day, he almost choked. There in front of him was the biggest stretch limousine he had ever seen. "Holy shit," he whistled to himself. "We've got to get rid of this baby." Mulroney could not go around closing a town in a white stretch Cadillac. It was one time the Boss could not afford to go first class. MacAdam quickly shooed the limo away and ordered a regular Buick.

The Schefferville shut-down, when it came, happened swiftly and suddenly. The news got into the newspapers on Monday, November 1, 1982 — the same day the mine gates closed for the final shift. Some workers could not believe it and reported to work anyway, and were turned away. People had heard all the rumours, but nobody really thought the whole town would close for good. There had been no consultations with unions or the town council, and almost everyone felt anger, shock, and worry.

On Wednesday, November 3, Mulroney flew up to Schefferville to meet the town, giving a lift up on the IOC plane to Schefferville mayor Charles Bégin. Bégin happened to be in Montreal for an appearance on CTV's *Canada AM* about what it was like to lose his town. Upon touching down, Mulroney and Bégin went straight to the town hall, where more than one hundred townsfolk were waiting, many of them businesspeople who were about to see their livelihoods disappear. From behind the mayor's table in the council chambers, Mulroney spoke in a sombre voice and blamed the closing on dwindling demand for Schefferville's ore. "Everywhere we go we are confronted with the realities of rich natural ores from Brazil," he said.

He talked about giving the workers a good settlement, which he said would total about $10 million for 450 workers; then he went a step further and made a move that was classic Mulroney. He announced the establishment of an economic development committee for Schefferville, with Mayor Bégin and himself as the two co-chairmen. The committee would look for ways to create new industries to keep the town alive. The announcement put a new slant on the news. It cost nothing and promised nothing and would ultimately not delay Schefferville's inevitable doom by as much as a day, but it held out hope to a stunned local populace that the town might survive.

Although Mulroney had stage-managed the Schefferville announcement to the best of his ability, he could not escape bad press. The first story, by Canadian Press reporter Larry Black, hit the newswires on November 5: "The Iron Ore Co. of Canada's corporate shareholders received a quarter of a billion dollars in dividends in the three years before the mining firm shut down its operations in the town of Schefferville, Que.," the story began, then went on to point out that this figure exceeded the $186 million in profits the company made during the same period.

The next day the *Gazette* in Montreal ran an even more damning piece by Jennifer Robinson, who believed the IOC president was more concerned with his image than with the concerns of the people of Schefferville. "Doomed Schefferville Is Angry and Afraid After Mine Shutdown," read the headline. "The bitterness against Iron Ore and Mulroney is very close to the surface," Robinson wrote. "'Brian Baloney. . . . A little more and he would have needed a box of Kleenex,' said one union man of about 35, drawing roars of laughter from his drinking buddies at the hotel." She also described the exquisite meal Mulroney had put on for the visiting journalists, with whom he spent the evening following the announcement. "Drinks, wine, pinwheel crystal, scallops in a white wine sauce, more wine and a thick ribeye steak, brussel sprouts, baby carrots and baked potatoes, and for dessert, a creamy mixture topped with strawberries. Definitely superior to the local cuisine."

Mulroney was furious with these and the other critical stories that followed, and he counter-attacked with letters to the editor and telegrams to the federal party leaders stating his side of the issue. Soon, however, the furore died down. On balance he had succeeded in his primary aim of minimizing the immediate political impact of the town's closing.

Mulroney had cleared his first big hurdle. The next and bigger hurdle would come when the Quebec parliamentary inquiry opened its hearings and called him as a witness, but that would be after Winnipeg. In the meantime the annual Joe Clark dinner was fast approaching. It fell on November 21, five days — as it later turned out — after the last constituency battle in Quebec had ended. Hoping to paper over the ever-widening gulf between Clark and Mulroney and present at least the veneer of party unity, Claude Dupras, one of the event's organizers, invited Mulroney to formally introduce Clark at the $175-a-plate affair. It seemed like a good idea all around, but Mulroney wavered. He gave an excuse about having business in Cleveland that evening but promised to think it over and get back. After not hearing anything for several days Dupras gave up and got MP Roch LaSalle.

Then, with a week to go, Mulroney met Dupras for lunch and announced he would happily introduce Clark. Somewhat taken aback, Dupras explained that LaSalle had now been given the honour. Mulroney protested vehemently, saying he had already written a unifying speech that would support Clark. It was too late, Dupras insisted. The program had been printed and mailed. However, if Mulroney would make a "full endorsement" of Clark he would reconsider. Mulroney pulled out the prepared text and read it aloud at the table. "This is not the type of speech I was thinking about," replied Dupras, who thought Mulroney's support of Clark was too wishy-washy. Mulroney retorted that the endorsement was plenty strong, but Dupras remained adamant. The meeting ended cordially, but Mulroney promptly leaked a story to the *Montreal Gazette* about how he had wanted to introduce Clark and had been snubbed.

The alleged snub did not annoy him as much as losing an important forum in which he could pull himself out of trouble. Despite Dalton Camp's warning in July, the ugly battle for control of Quebec's delegates had made him the flashpoint in the guerrilla war against Clark. Furthermore his numbers told him that Clark was headed to victory in Winnipeg, making it even more urgent that he get out of the line of fire. Denied the opportunity to cheer for Clark in public at the dinner, and with the convention two months away and Schefferville coming upon him as well, he had to plot out his next several steps carefully.

Actually stepping back from his role as Brutus was proving to be more difficult than he had imagined. The day after the Joe Clark dinner, *Le Devoir* denounced him as an anti-Clark conspirator. He had recently spoken in Oakville at Otto Jelinek's tenth anniversary as an MP, sounding as usual like a leadership candidate. "Brian Mulroney makes long speeches in the best social clubs of the country," the paper proclaimed in an editorial. "One day he talks of the need for dramatic reform of the fiscal system; the next he accuses, attacks, and counter-attacks. Like the prose he uses in his function as president of Iron Ore, the method is direct but complex. Perhaps one day he may explain his strange behaviour in his memoirs, which could well be titled *Me, the Candidate.* For that is his one true role despite his sleights-of-hand and his denials." The editorial went on to say that it was Joe Clark who had renewed Tory credibility in Quebec, and he had done it at considerable risk and despite the Quebec Conservatives themselves. "If Mulroney could put his ego aside he would find in such work a vast area in which to prove his mettle. It would be much better for the party, the country, and his own political future."

Now more than ever he had to do something. His instincts told him that if he did not pull out of the leadership traffic, and do it fast, his escalating image as the spoiler would destroy him. He had to take the high road and somehow work out a non-aggression pact with Clark.

Mulroney mulled over his prospects and spent a couple of days examining his options. That same week he put in a call to Finlay MacDonald in Ottawa and finally tracked him down in Toronto, where, by coincidence, Mulroney himself would be the next day. As a trustee of the Schenley Awards, he was coming to Toronto for Grey Cup weekend and asked MacDonald if he minded staying over a day to meet him for lunch. MacDonald was Clark's senior adviser, and as Mulroney's long-time friend he happened to be his best line into Clark's office.

On Friday, November 26, at Winston's, the favoured lunch spot of the Toronto business élite, Mulroney quickly came to the point, telling MacDonald he wanted to pull himself out of the leadership controversy and do his part in bringing the party back together. He explained he had given the matter much thought and was willing to endorse Clark publicly at a joint press conference. MacDonald did not need convincing. In July at the fishing camp weekend he had agreed with everything Dalton Camp had said. After they discussed the form the endorsement should take, Mulroney pulled out of his breast pocket a piece of foolscap with some handwritten notes and read them aloud, stopping occasionally to mark in minor changes as he went.

"In 1966," he began reading, "the principle of a review of the party leadership by secret ballot at regular intervals was included in our party's constitution. Both Mr. Clark and I supported the principle at that time in the sincere belief it was healthy for democracy. We are still of that view today. No other political party in Canada has provided such a democratic opportunity to its members. We should be proud of this ennobling instrument. It must, however, be used with care and its proper exercise demands both reflection and prudence. Because of this I long ago decided that I would listen carefully to people in this country, in this party, on this and related issues and make my own determination at an appropriate moment. I have learned to take such responsibility seriously. It's my practice to deal first-hand both with people and policies that affect them. Judgements in this regard are too important to be arrived at in any other manner.

"I therefore made it my business to travel to various parts of Canada and to speak out clearly, as best I could, on the problems facing this country, and to bring forward some programs that might help resolve them. This was my privilege as a Canadian, it was my duty as a Conservative. Perhaps more importantly, I had the opportunity to visit with people, Conservatives and non-Conservatives alike, many of whom generously shared with me their views concerning both the future of this party and this country. Two things are abundantly clear: Canadians want a change in government and orientation at the earliest possible moment. The best manner of achieving this is by electing a truly representative majority Progressive Conservative government. I'm in full accord with these views and will do everything I can to help bring them about. Mr. Clark's reconfirmation as leader of this party is an important part of this process and his subsequent re-election as prime minister will be good for Canada. Our fellow delegates to the Winnipeg convention must now make their decision freely and thoughtfully, as was intended by the reform we introduced in 1966."

Mulroney continued. "Much has been written, perhaps too much has been written, about the difference between Joe and me. I suppose that in as much as we both sought the leadership of our party at a convention that was very vigorously contested in 1976, the presumption of an ongoing adversarial relationship between us is somewhat natural. Of late, however, little has been written of our friendship and warm mutual regard that began when we were both nineteen years of age and persists to this day.

"In a political party such as ours there will always be differences of views and ongoing debates on matters of substance and strategy and style. This is as it should be. Our overriding obligation, however, is to Canada. And our paramount obligation is to provide Canadians with a genuine and a reasoned basis for hope. This is our highest duty and at this time in our history I think we discharge it best by proceeding with the confirmation of Mr. Clark and getting on with the business of forming a government capable of recapturing the greatness on which this nation was built."

While not exactly a heart-rending testament of loyalty, it was an endorsement nevertheless. Mulroney was officially advising delegates to vote for Clark in Winnipeg, a massive shift from his behaviour over the past twelve months. Visibly pleased, MacDonald promised to inform Clark immediately. After lunch he caught the next flight back to Ottawa, but not before calling in the news to Clark and Lowell Murray. As it happened, Clark and Murray were about to fly out of Ottawa for the weekend and arranged to meet MacDonald at the airport. "I bring you peace in our time," MacDonald quipped upon arriving as he waved a copy of Mulroney's statement. But after reading it over, Clark and Murray did not see as much promise in the news as had MacDonald. At this point neither of them could imagine the leopard changing his spots. Clark was suspicious, Murray outright hostile.

As Clark and Murray were shooting holes in the offer, Mulroney's friends were doing exactly the same thing — for totally opposite reasons. The overture mortified them — most of them anyway. In one act Mulroney risked destroying everything he had planned and worked for over the past year. They could accept some tactical manoeuvring, and might even swallow a strategic cease-fire, but not an out-and-out surrender to the other side. "Look," argued Pat MacAdam, "if you want to be perceived as being loyal to the leader, why don't you take him to a hockey game at the Forum? You're going to be sitting behind the Canadiens' bench. You can tip off the television crew and they'll pick you out of the crowd. You can be seen buddy-buddy with Joe at the Forum. Do something symbolic like that."

In contrast, as Clark began to consult more widely, he got more positive feedback. Dalton Camp, for one, encouraged Clark to accept, as did others. Initially reluctant to buy what seemed like an obvious sham, he ultimately decided to take Mulroney's offer. He was fighting for survival, and his chief adversary had offered to lay down his arms and stay safely on the sidelines, removing the single biggest obstacle on the road to Winnipeg. At the moment the Quebec dissenters gave him nothing but problems. Now he could hope to focus his attention elsewhere. Meanwhile Mulroney's backing would enhance his credibility and shore up his support. The more major players who lined up behind him the better. A public endorsement from somebody like Mulroney could only do him good. And maybe, just maybe, Brian meant it.

Ironically, by the time Clark, the sceptic, had swung over to Mulroney's side, Mulroney was having serious second thoughts. A joint press conference had already been scheduled for Monday, December 6, when Mulroney, hearing nothing but warnings from friends all week, started to weaken. On the Saturday night before the event, Mulroney called Finlay MacDonald at his home in Ottawa to suggest that maybe he should not go through with it. MacDonald, a tremendous cook who loved to entertain, took the call in the kitchen while his guests looked after themselves in the living room. After some time Dalton Camp, one of the guests, joined MacDonald and helped him work on Mulroney. Dinner kept being delayed — the guests were getting hungry — but finally, forty-five minutes later, Mac-Donald and Camp emerged triumphant from the kitchen. The deal had been saved.

On Sunday, December 5, the day before the big performance, Mulroney called together his Mount Royal Club group for Sunday brunch at Senator Guy Charbonneau's apartment and told them his intentions. He then read aloud his prepared statement, just as he had done to Finlay MacDonald nine days before. Some knew what was coming; others were caught by surprise and pounced immediately. Peter White argued that suspending operations was one thing and embracing Clark in public was quite another. He opposed it if for no other reason than because it looked hypocritical and would reflect badly on him. Others chimed in with other objections, but Mulroney held firm. His mind, he said, was made up.

Mulroney ran into even stronger opposition later that afternoon when he broke the news to a group of twenty-five or thirty supporters assembled in his own home. The group comprised the Quebec committee along with an assortment of anti-Clark organizers and friends. Present were Rodrigue Pageau, Jean-Yves Lortie, David Angus, Brian Gallery, Pierre Claude Nolin, Roger Nantel, Jean Bazin, Fernand Roberge, Pat MacAdam, Sam Wakim, and nearly two dozen others. After Mulroney dropped his bombshell and made it clear he did not want anybody working against Clark on his behalf, the group lapsed into momentary silence. The news hit everybody hard, but nobody harder than Jean-Yves Lortie, who had been gearing up for his next strike at Clark since the Quebec wing meeting nearly a year earlier. Suddenly Lortie had lost his candidate.

With his gold jewellery flashing and fire in his voice, Lortie stood up in Mulroney's living room and declared that the leadership review movement had come too far to be stopped now. Nobody, he declared, could tell him what to do. "Me, I continue to work," he announced. Lortie's words sparked a minor revolt. Roger Nantel, Mulroney's PR man in the 1976 race, also delivered an impassioned speech, as did Rodrigue Pageau. The only thing restraining them from going further was the fact that they were guests in Mulroney's house. When Pageau invited people over to his place for further talks, most of the activ-ists — Lortie, Nantel, Marc Dorion, Pierre Claude Nolin, Jacques Blanchard, Jean Dugré — got up and went. At Pageau's place they convinced themselves that Mulroney was still going to run. "If Brian does not go," Lortie defiantly proclaimed, "we find somebody else."

The next day a pack of reporters and cameramen surrounded by television lights waited expectantly in a small salon in the Ritz-Carl-ton Hotel in Montreal while Mulroney and Clark entered together and sat down behind a green table full of microphones. Mila stood off in the background. Without introduction, Mulroney started reading his scripted statement, first in French and then in English. He read the words well but the endorsement sounded hollow and contrived. The problem was not the delivery but the content. None of the reporters believed a single word.

"Brian was good enough," Clark kicked in when he started making his statement, "to give me advance notice of the statement that he was making today and was kind enough to schedule this news conference at a time when I was going to be in Montreal and could attend. Needless to say, I appreciate the expression of his renewed commitment to our common cause and his kind references to me personally. As a Canadian, as a Quebecker, as a respected business leader, and as a Conservative who has been active in this party for a long time, Brian speaks with experience, with authority, with sincerity about the need for a change in government and a change in direction for our country. This statement reflects not only his own belief, but the views and concerns expressed to him by Conservatives and other Canadians across the country. Those same concerns have been expressed to me in my travels everywhere in Canada, and I can only state my full agreement with Brian's assessment of public sentiment and of party sentiment in this regard.

"For almost a year and a half now the Progressive Conservative Party has held a commanding lead in public opinion polls. It's a lead that's enough to ensure the election of a strong majority Progressive Conservative government whenever an election is called. I am determined, as Brian is, that our party show itself worthy of this support to win an election. To govern this country effectively we have to be a cohesive, united political force. Brian's statement in this regard is most timely. It's very constructive. It's helpful to me and helpful to our party. And I warmly appreciate it."

With that Clark had finished. Now came the questions.

Reporter: Does this mean an end to the backbiting that has been going on in the party leading up to the Winnipeg convention? Your troops, Mr. Mulroney, have been anti-Clark up to now. What are you going to do with those delegates?

Mulroney: Oh, I think you're somewhat mistaken. You characterize the activity that way. I think the characterization is somewhat inaccurate. As I understand it, there are delegates not only in the province of Quebec but elsewhere who vigorously and sometimes with a great deal of enthusiasm seek to be elected as delegates. They are opposed here, they are opposed there. Some win, some lose. My view is that the winners from across the country will go to Winnipeg and will make that determination as both Joe and I were together in 1966, very much together in the elaboration of this principle. And one of the keys to the principle of this was that it be done thoughtfully and with a great deal of concern. I don't remember that it was the intention that it be conducted any other way. And so I am satisfied that that is the way the delegates will and perhaps should conduct themselves.

Reporter: Do you see any further threat when you come to Winnipeg, Mr. Clark?

Clark [*chuckling*]: Well, have you ever been in Winnipeg in January? [*General laughter*] There will be a lively winter atmosphere there.

Let me just pick up on something Brian said in his statement and referred to again now. The review provision is there in the constitution of the Progressive Conservative Party with good cause. And Brian and I were among the people who worked to put it there. It helps ensure that the Progressive Conservative Party remains an open and a democratic party. That involves a responsibility for the individual members of the party to come to careful decisions as to what is in the long-term interest of the party.

Mr. Mulroney has, himself, over the last little while, because he is a very prominent Progressive Conservative, been canvassing not just opinion but attitude in the party. He has been taking his responsibilities as a Progressive Conservative very seriously. I trust that will set a standard for other Conservatives, and they will consider both the interest of the party and the interest of the country as seriously as Brian Mulroney has when they come to make their decision at the end of January. I don't expect to win 100 per cent — I won't cite any more figures — I think that if any leader ever did, that would indicate that the device was not particularly useful — it wasn't serving the democratic interest. I think what it does provide is for the Progressive Conservative Party to have, on all levels, including at its grassroots levels, a responsibility and an opportunity for individual Progressive Conservatives to consider seriously how we best act to serve the party and serve the country. Mr. Mulroney has and I am sure that other Progressive Conservatives will act in the same far-sighted spirit.

Reporter: Mr. Mulroney, just two weeks ago, you felt slighted or extremely slighted that Mr. Clark did not acknowledge your presence at a fundraising dinner in Montreal. What has happened in the interim?

Mulroney: I didn't feel slighted. The fact of the matter is. . . . Let me deal quickly with a tempest in a teapot — just so there is no mistake about it. I was invited to introduce Mr. Clark. I think there was an error in communication somewhere along the line for which neither Mr. Clark nor I — as it turns out — is responsible. I was prepared at that time to introduce him with the same degree of generosity as I think I have today and in other circumstances. Someone made a decision which, I suspect, if they had to make over again today they wouldn't make. It is a tempest in a teapot. My nose wasn't out of joint. I have always — for twenty-seven years — tried to do the right thing for the party, and I think I am trying to do that today.

Reporter: Mr. Mulroney, are you just shelving your leadership plans pending the review, or have you given up on the possibility of ever becoming leader of the Tories?

Mulroney: Not at all. Mr. Clark, in March or so, said that he fully expected that I would make an attractive candidate for the leadership in, say, ten or fifteen years. [*Slight laughter*]

Reporter: If there is a Conservative government in power next time, can we expect to see Mr. Mulroney in the cabinet?

Clark: Brian will answer the question about the candidacy and I will say that, to use the French word, that Brian Mulroney is eminently "ministrable."

Mulroney: With regard to the other thing, I can't answer it and I will tell you why. I have come to the conclusion that Mr. Trudeau is never going to call another election. I am seriously wondering whether he will ever dare face the people again. If he does, I imagine it will be by extending his mandate to the ultimate, which will be in a couple of years, and we will be waiting for him. When he issues the writ, any time he wants to issue the writ, please come and see me. I think I will have something to tell you.

The questions and answers rambled on, switching between English and French. Near the end one reporter asked both of them what was their excuse to kiss and make up.

"Just a second, hold the phone," Mulroney replied. "In 1976 Mr. Clark was elected leader of the party. I have consistently been supportive of him. In 1979, I chaired the largest fundraising dinner, and organized the largest fundraising dinner ever held in the history of the Conservative Party in the province of Quebec. I did it again in 1981. I have consistently been supportive of both the party and Mr. Clark. I take the leadership review question seriously for the reasons that we have talked about. I wouldn't at all want to leave you with the view that I am reluctant to kiss Mr. Clark. [*Laughter*] But I assure you there is no need for it."

Within an hour the news from the Ritz Summit — as Heward Grafftey would later call it — had spread across the country. Just down the road from the hotel, Francis Hooper, one of Mulroney's front-line foot-soldiers, heard it over his car radio while driving down Sherbrooke Street and nearly hit the sidewalk. He could not believe what he thought he just heard. He was off to Quebec City that evening to organize a youth meeting and now suddenly did not know whether to go. Everything had collapsed. John Balkwill, a Kanata, Ontario, dentist who sat on the Tory national executive and coordinated much of the Ontario movement against Clark, was absolutely despondent, believing that Mulroney had set back the cause of leadership review by at least four months. He tried to phone Mulroney to find out what was going on but could not get through. On Parliament Hill Elmer MacKay was absolutely furious. "Christ,"

430

MacKay growled, "he is screwing us. We are on the front line here, fighting for him, and he is screwing us, stabbing us in the back, saying he doesn't want it."

Other Mulroney supporters said worse things. The entire Mulroney team was a highly demoralized bunch.

CHAPTER NINETEEN

THE BATTLE OF
WINNIPEG

AFTER HEARING THE terrible news that Mulroney had pulled himself out of the battle for Winnipeg, twenty-two-year-old Mulroney youth organizer Francis Hooper felt let down and forsaken. Nor did he know what to do about the coming youth meeting in Quebec City that evening, which he was supposed to help organize. "Continue the same way," Rodrigue Pageau advised him when he phoned for instructions. "We'll know more later." Hooper did exactly as Pageau said. Not only did he attend the Quebec City meeting as planned, he continued organizing against Clark after that and would keep on organizing all the way to Winnipeg. "Nobody ever told us to stop," he explained later. "I figured that Brian went a little too far in what he wanted to say. I'm not sure he wanted to say that."

Likewise, Elmer MacKay and Ontario organizer John Balkwill, once they overcame their initial shock, continued to throw bombs in Clark's direction as if nothing had happened — and so did virtually all the conspirators in Mulroney's corner. Mulroney had told his key operatives to get out of the traffic, but they simply had not passed on the message to the troops — not Pageau, Jean-Yves Lortie, Frank

Moores, Peter White, Michel Cogger, Guy Charbonneau, Ken Waschuk, or any of the other members of the core group. Quite the opposite. They got onto the telephone and told delegates across the country that nothing had changed. "Don't pay any attention to it," they counselled, explaining that Mulroney was merely engaging in a strategic manoeuvre. Even his most senior people cautioned others not to believe the Ritz Summit and ventured the opinion that he was still in the game. Since most of Mulroney's partisans were looking for an excuse to disregard it anyway, they did not need much convincing.

When allegations began to surface that Mulroney's public endorsement of Clark had not changed a thing in the trenches, Mulroney flatly denied any impropriety, claiming that any anti-Clark sniper fire did not come from his troops. When shown evidence to the contrary, he merely threw up his hands and said he could not stop free people from exercising their political prerogative.

By early January 1983 — a month after the Ritz Summit and a few weeks before Winnipeg — Joe Clark had come to realize that he should never have agreed to accept Mulroney's half-hearted peace offering. In hindsight his aides agreed that Clark at the very least should have staged the event on Parliament Hill. The Ritz-Carlton was Mulroney's turf, run by his good friend Fernand Roberge, the place where he had done much of his leadership plotting. Going into Mulroney's territory made it look like the Conservative leader had gone cap in hand in search of loyalty. Clark already had trouble getting people to respect his leadership. In retrospect the Ritz-Carlton press conference made him look less a leader and Mulroney more. It actually enhanced Mulroney's status as the alternative to Clark, since Clark himself had made a special arrangement with him. It made many people take Mulroney more seriously. Furthermore it had allowed Mulroney to shed the dreaded conspirator's cloak. Despite Mulroney's last-minute doubts, he had definitely won this round.

For the Ritz Summit to mean something to Clark, it would have had to have been held several months earlier. Quebec had wrapped up its delegate-selection meetings on November 16, 1982 — three weeks before Mulroney publicly pledged his support to Clark. It meant that the sides were drawn and the flavour of the convention set prior to the summit. With half the Quebec delegates already committed to voting for a leadership review, a press conference in downtown Montreal wasn't going to change very much.

Clark remained stoic as usual and did not complain about having been hit by a sucker punch. But shortly before Winnipeg he dropped a public hint to a French radio reporter that Mulroney had not been on the level. His own office staff quickly advised him to drop the matter. "It's one thing to be conned," he was told. "But it's quite another to admit that you were conned."

By the eve of the convention, the anti-Clark forces had recovered much of the momentum lost following Mulroney's formal with-drawal. They knew they had half the Quebec delegates committed to a leadership review. Elsewhere in the country Clark remained in control but faced strong pockets of resistance in a number of places, particularly Ontario, Nova Scotia, and Newfoundland. Through it all it looked like Clark would survive, although those who had been working so long and hard to bring him down had convinced them-selves they still had a chance. And Mulroney, almost by default, had managed to position himself to come out a winner no matter which way the party faithful voted in January.

The most graphic proof that Mulroney had merely rented Clark his loyalty, rather than given it fully, came on the eve of the Winnipeg meeting when the Mulroney forces paid to fly anti-Clark delegates to the convention. All pro-Mulroney delegates from Quebec had their expenses covered, including airfare, hotel, and registration fees (the Clark delegates got the same treatment from Clark's campaign). Once everything was added up, the bill for their expenses came to about $1,000 a head — a hefty amount of money for a group that had ostensibly pulled out of the race. Both the pro-Clark and pro-Mulroney camps chartered DC-9s from Montreal. In Quebec City neither Clark organizer Marcel Danis nor Mulroney organizer

Rodrigue Pageau could fill a plane by himself, so the two arch-rivals chartered one together and split the costs.

The delegates who gathered in Winnipeg on Thursday, January 25, did not need to worry about being bored. When the convention opened the next day the agenda would include few dreary policy resolutions. As in 1981, the real order of business was leadership. Delegates could not wait to see what percentage of the vote Clark would get on Friday night when they had to answer the simple question: "Do you wish to have a leadership convention?" In 1981 he had received barely more than 66 per cent. Given the organized opposition and the wide-open fights for delegateships, especially in Quebec, a two-thirds vote of support this time would represent a much more solid victory than in 1981, when dissent still rumbled beneath the surface.

But Clark had undermined his position by promising his caucus that he would resign if he did not go beyond 66 per cent. Lowell Murray had hedged this slightly. According to Murray, 50 to 60 per cent would require a leadership convention; 60 to 70 per cent was the grey area; and over 70 per cent was the comfort zone. But Clark and Murray knew that anything less than 66 per cent would likely cause a caucus revolt.

This time the party establishment had gone even further than in 1981 to choreograph everything to tilt Clark's way. Positive literature and positive images of the leader inundated delegates the minute they arrived on Thursday. Forty-foot screens showed Clark in the image of a strong and decisive leader for tomorrow; the printed material spoke of the new era in party fortunes, of the fact that Clark led the polls and the party was getting fat from political donations.

But while the official party apparatus hoisted Clark up, his detractors were busily tearing him down. As delegates rode up the escalator of the convention centre they ran smack into early anti-Clark activist John Morrison handing out leaflets. The big hitters in the leadership review movement — Coates, MacKay, Moores, and especially Mulroney — were keeping their heads down, but "Clear the Air" buttons

435

and "Go, Joe, Go . . . Please" buttons were visible on lapels everywhere. All the official pro-Clark hype could not hide the fact that the Conservative Party was a bitter, squabbling family. The two sides had come together for this weekend, but their mutual antipathy filled the air with tension. The Conservative Party was at war with itself, just as it had been in 1966.

So much was happening below the surface that nobody could predict how the vote would go. Rumours and lies permeated the premises — as they did at all conventions — and merely compounded the confusion. The consensus had not changed since December, when Mulroney "officially" endorsed Clark: namely, that the embattled leader would again survive. The computers and personal contacts and fieldwork all added to the same conclusion: Clark had made it across the 70-per-cent barrier. The Clark forces looked confident and even cocky, whereas the review forces, especially the youth, looked uncertain but defiant. As more and more delegates arrived, the Clark people were scouring every nook and cranny of the Winnipeg convention centre and the surrounding hotels for every last vote, holding breakfast and lunch rallies and collaring delegates in the corridors.

Late on Thursday afternoon, the inimitable Jean-Yves Lortie strutted up to the convention's registration desk in his big fur coat. Close on his heels was a herd of 186 party members from Quebec, all of whom had come to register for the convention. Normally delegates pre-registered by mail and arrived in a steady stream of ones and twos to pick up their badges. But nobody in Lortie's throng had pre-registered or paid the fees, and that fact alone drove the registration office to distraction. Only Lortie would dare pull such a tactic.

After following Lortie in, the would-be delegates, all of them openly anti-Clark, lined up against the wall, choking the ordinarily spacious area. Lortie had decided to pay their registration fees on the spot and, in a gesture befitting his backroom style, plunked down two cheques totalling nearly $56,000 to cover the whole gang. To Lortie's chagrin, the registration officials refused to accept the cheques, saying they would not handle cheques of that size unless certified. Lortie started to argue and promised to sign his name and personally guarantee the worth of the cheques, but the registration desk refused to relent and all hell broke loose. "Pourquoi pas?" he shouted, demanding to know what was wrong with his money. Eventually Lortie retreated and miraculously returned later with twelve certified cheques totalling $40,870, plus $15,000 in cash — mostly in hundred-dollar bills. Nobody knew how he had done it so fast.

However, Lortie's quick fix still failed to satisfy the registration staff. Throwing up one roadblock after another, they used any technicality to block him. First, they argued there were too many people to handle. Then they said they had to pull the file on each one to verify their bona fides. Next they insisted that the delegates had to pay individually. Then it seemed that the computer was down, and finally the registration desk was closing for dinner. Things threatened to turn ugly, but the two sides finally reached a truce: Lortie's 54 youth delegates would return after the dinner break that evening; the 132 regular delegates would be registered the next morning. Lortie promised to be back and threatened to stage a demonstration on the convention floor itself if the registration did not go smoothly.

But when the youth delegates came back around 9 P.M., the registration desk remained openly hostile. While it began processing the applications, it made each person produce two sets of identification, then sign his or her name twice so that beady-eyed officials could compare the signatures. The registration staff claimed that since these people had not pre-registered, they had to verify who they were. The line-up moved at such a sluggish pace that most of Lortie's young delegates missed Clark's speech to the party's youth wing.

While Lortie's troops waited impatiently in the registration area — it would be about 2 A.M. before all of them were registered — Clark spoke to a packed room of youth delegates and drew a wildly enthusiastic response, although not unanimously so. Ken Zeise, Randy Bocock, Andrew Demond, and a handful of other pro-review youth leaders had come early and charged through the doors to commandeer the three tables at the very front. Their tactic reminded many of the older Tories of the front rows of silent youth when Diefenbaker spoke at the Château Laurier in 1966. When most of the room stood and cheered, the three tables at the front sat sullenly with their arms folded. No one in the room could miss the dissidents' display.

The next morning, Lortie's youth delegates, the ones who had registered late the previous evening, found themselves locked out of the room where pro-Clark and pro-Mulroney candidates were fighting for control of the youth executive. The start of the meeting had been moved up from 10:30 to 9:20, but nobody had told Lortie's delegates about the change; an official notice of the new time had been quietly slipped into the youth registration kits the previous day, before the registration table had closed for dinner. The Clark supporters who had engineered the change had locked the door at 9:20 sharp. The disenfranchised Quebec delegates, who gathered outside the locked door, deemed this subversion the death of democracy and generally raised hell. Meanwhile, inside the room, voting was being held up while the delegates debated whether to let the latecomers in. Eventually the chairman ruled in favour of keeping the door locked and the voting began. The Mulroney forces lost the election for the youth presidency, further aggravating the animosities.

In the meantime Lortie had returned to the registration desk with the rest of his regular delegates, who were once again lined up along the wall in the registration area and were still getting the same runaround. The night before, the party had demanded a delegate list broken down by riding, complete with all the vital data. Lortie and his colleagues had stayed up all night to assemble the list, finally finishing at 6 A.M. Now the registration desk had changed its mind and wanted the list in alphabetical order. On the verge of going berserk, Lortie started shouting insults and making a scene. In the meantime the television cameras had discovered this unfolding drama and were swooping in on the scene.

"They're up to something," complained a young woman wearing a "Go, Joe, Go . . . Please" button. "They do not like us. Ever since we've been here we've had problems."

"Are you basically Mulroney supporters?" asked the reporter.

"Not necessarily," she replied, sounding defensive.

"You are though — a lot of you are," pressed the reporter.

"No, we just want to be — it doesn't matter who we're for. We just want to vote. It makes no difference who we're voting for."

Minutes later Mulroney rode up the escalator to the registration desk. As he arrived, with Mila, Pat MacAdam, and Sam Wakim in tow, Lortie's crowd burst into cheers and applauded him like a conquering hero. Mulroney rhymed off some cheery remarks as the television cameras swarmed around, but his sunny smile instantly evaporated when he learned what had happened.

Suddenly flushed with righteous anger, Mulroney erupted. "We are all legitimate delegates," he declared to the sound of applause. "These officials are bureaucrats. Their salaries are paid by donations from us. They have no right to prevent any delegate from voting." With the entire crowd cheering him on, he strode in full fury to the registration desk and demanded to see the functionary in charge, then disappeared into the registration office to give them all hell. In short order the line started to move. To Lortie's delegates he suddenly looked like a knight on a white charger.

At an impromptu press conference in front of the registration desk shortly afterwards, Mulroney denounced the whole incident as "absolutely scandalous." The party bureaucrats, he said, were treating party members like a herd of cattle and were guilty of "a remarkable abuse of authority." However, Mulroney had arrived in Winnipeg as an official Clark supporter, and the media wanted to know what he was doing to support the leader.

Reporter: Mr. Mulroney, are you urging your supporters to go with Clark as you go through the crowds like this?

Mulroney: I don't have supporters in the Conservative Party. I only have friends.

Reporter: Well, your friends, are you urging them to go with Clark?

Mulroney [*either ignoring or not hearing the question*]: And I made my position clear. I've done it many times.

Another Reporter: Are you urging your supporters here to vote against review?

Mulroney: Pardon me?

Reporter: Are you urging those people who support you to vote against review?

Mulroney: I have consistently urged my friends in the party to support Mr. Clark.

Reporter: Are you making phone calls and the like on behalf of Mr. Clark?

Mulroney: Oh, I've done many things on behalf of Mr. Clark.

Reporter: Are you going to work on his behalf today, for example, with delegates?

Mulroney: I do what I'm asked to do. That's for sure.

Reporter: Have you been asked to do anything?

Mulroney: Oh, a few things, yeah.

Reporter: Such as?

Mulroney: Oh, I'll tell you about them after I've done it.

Reporter: Have you got any more information on this problem with the meeting here?

Mulroney: No, I have no more information on the problem of the meeting except to tell you that it's a very disturbing problem. It's a problem that would disturb any reasonable and thoughtful man. And the Conservative Party has to be very concerned about ever attempting to indulge in exclusionary politics. And it is very bad politics. I don't know how people propose to vote. But if you're holding a national convention where you invite people to come from Sainte-Anne-des-Monts or from Burnaby, you don't ask them to be herded like cattle for nine hours while the party bureaucrats decide whether or not they are going to allow people to vote. That is outrageous conduct by the Conservative Party and it ought not to have happened, and I hope it never happens again.

The delaying tactics aimed at a large group of anti-Clark delegates looked bad and tarnished the image of the Clark people, especially after the television cameras arrived. On the other hand Lortie's arrival with nearly two hundred delegates and a fistful of hundred-dollar bills made Mulroney look neither pure nor loyal. Everyone knew Lortie was Mulroney's man. Mulroney later dressed down Lortie for drawing attention to the continuing anti-Clark operations with which Mulroney was inevitably linked in people's minds. Since he was supposed to be supporting Clark, he wanted everybody associated with him to keep a low profile in Winnipeg. Even Frank Moores, the natural glad-hander, was keeping out of general circulation.

Other than his pious posturing at the registration desk, Mulroney pretty much kept out of the limelight, usually staying in his suite at the Westin Hotel and receiving visitors. Meanwhile Pageau, Lortie, Pierre-Paul Bourdon, Charbonneau, Cogger, and others looked after Quebec. Elmer MacKay was in charge of pulling together the Maritimes, Ken Waschuk rallied Saskatchewan, and MP Tom Siddon handled British Columbia. Frank Moores coordinated the whole operation by walkie-talkie from his hotel room. By this point the work had been done and the seeds had been planted. There was no need to campaign. The less show the anti-Clark forces created, the better.

That Friday evening, shortly after 7:00, Clark launched into his major speech of the convention. How he performed would help make or break him. "I believe I can open by saying 'my friends,'" he began, then came out fighting. If his leadership was confirmed, he warned, "I will have the right to expect that the party and the caucus will accept the discipline we need to win and to govern." That particular statement — or threat — drew the loudest applause of the night; it showed a toughness the party had rarely seen before. But Clark was not so aggressive that he could not admit having made mistakes. "I've learned a lot as leader of the party and leader of a government. I want to put that knowledge to work to win a decisive national election for this party and start a national recovery for our country."

Clark had delivered an effective speech, marred only by the fact that at thirty-five minutes he had gone on a bit long. After he had finished speaking, Mulroney left the convention hall and by doing so unintentionally stole a little limelight. When he descended from his seat in the bleachers, a mini-wave of supporters stood up and cheered him as he passed. This spontaneous pro-Mulroney outburst notwithstanding, Clark had good reason to be optimistic: the mood of the convention had swung sharply in his favour. The review forces had arrived in Winnipeg more defiant than confident but now, as delegates queued up to vote, their defiance had clearly wilted. The Clark people were now wearing the confident expressions. They even looked a little smug as they patrolled the convention floor, proclaiming that their man had the magic 70 per cent in the bag.

Once the polls closed and the sealed ballot boxes were carted off for counting, delegates could do little but wait. Flora MacDonald jumped to her feet and started dancing in the aisle to the tune of "I'se the B'y That Builds the Boat," swirling her skirt and throwing up her hands while people cheered. Enthusiasm — at least a certain level of it — started building for Clark on the floor. Some adversaries could be seen shaking hands and exchanging assurances of no hard feelings — as if the party had decided to shake off the trauma of the last few years. Then CTV released the results of an exit poll showing Clark scoring a commanding 76 per cent, which would have lifted him well into Lowell Murray's comfort zone. Word of the poll spread like wildfire across the floor and further subdued the already quiet forces favouring a leadership review.

Off in a corner on the second floor, where Clark was holed up in the convention centre's boardroom, sipping Coke in the company of Maureen and a core of key advisers, the atmosphere was very different. Unknown to the waiting crowd, at 9:35 P.M. Clark had been handed the results in a sealed envelope. He stared at the paper for a second and then his hand began to shake. "Sixty-six point nine," he said. The room remained silent. "Jesus Christ," blurted out Terry Yates, Clark's chief fundraiser. Maureen, who had always been far less charitable towards Mulroney and Clark's other adversaries than was Clark himself, burst into tears.

Clark consoled his wife and then turned to his colleagues for advice. Still unsure, he called for additional counsel from those outside the room and asked for a delay of the convention announcement so that he could consult more widely. As he pondered his next move, the delegates on the floor waited for some news — first thirty minutes, then forty-five, then an hour had passed since the balloting ended. The counting could not take that long: what could be causing the hold-up? The confidence of the Clark supporters began to wane. Something must have gone wrong. Good news would have come out faster. Now rumours began to swirl.

Wanting to stay out of sight, Mulroney had voted and then retreated to his hotel suite to watch the coverage on television. When the delay overran the deadline for the CBC's *The National,* he too figured the vote must have fallen apart. Finally, Jean Guilbeault and MP Pat Carney, the co-chairs of the convention, stepped to the lectern. They announced that 2,406 delegates had voted and there were four spoiled ballots. "The number of votes 'No' were 1,607, which is 66.9 per cent, and the number of votes 'Yes' were 795, or 33.1 per cent." At 66.9 per cent, Clark had risen only fractionally over his 66.1 per cent of 1981 — but he *had* done better.

"Well, that's it," declared pro-review worker Dave Dawson. "It's over. They've won." Many of the anti-Clark people were stumbling around the convention floor with long faces. Some were in tears. Ken Zeise, the whiz-kid Ontario youth president whom some later credited with mobilizing 6 or 7 percentage points of the 33 per cent against Clark, walked around aimlessly. "All you can do now is make peace with them," counselled Richard Smith, another pro-review worker from the Ontario youth. A despondent Elmer MacKay, sitting in a hotel room with Frank Moores and Bob Coates, had completely given up hope.

An overwhelming mandate it was not; nevertheless Clark had won. He had kept his promise to his caucus and done better than last time, if only by a hair. More important, virtually every person in the hall — including those who had worked so hard for a leadership review — accepted the reality that he had won. They all expected him to lead the party into the next election, and only the most hard-core Clark-bashers now seemed to doubt that he would again become prime minister, almost certainly leading a majority government. He had survived his ordeal by fire and would have a second chance.

Clark's arrival at the podium a minute later with Maureen standing at his side was greeted by triumphant cheers. "Ladies and gentlemen, mes amis," Clark responded. "I've just heard, as you have, the co-presidents indicate the results of the vote on the review. I remind this party that we cannot be seen as a government or as an alternative if we are seen to be divided in the country. This country needs an alternative government, and it needs that alternative government urgently. I asked tonight for a clear mandate to carry the party to victory. I received the support of a clear majority of the delegates voting here."

Then, as he shifted into what appeared to be the standard victory proclamation and appeal for party unity, he turned a startling corner that took him and the party where nobody had expected. "But my friends, my friends," he continued, "that mandate is not clear enough." Cheers and whoops of joy rang out. "It is not clear enough," he pressed on, "to enforce the kind of discipline and to achieve the kind of unity that this party requires. My friends, we know that the greatest enemy this party faces is uncertainty about our unity. Un-certainty about the Progressive Conservative Party is damaging to this party. Uncertainty about the future of the Progressive Conservative Party is deeply damaging to this country. Consequently I will be recommending to the national executive —"

A pleading chorus of "No, no, no" now interrupted Clark, mixed with more cheers. "I understand that feeling," Clark responded. "My friends, I have been struggling to hold this party together for the last two years." There was applause. "We have done very well in establishing ourselves as a fighting opposition, but until we have silenced all the serious critics in these ranks, we will not prove our capacity to form a government to the people of this country, and consequently I will be recommending to the national executive that they call a convention at the earliest possible time."

The moment was one of the most emotional in the history of the Conservative Party. The convention hall filled with a noise as confused as the emotions Clark's words had unleashed: people were too stunned to know how to react. After a brief pause, Clark continued. "I want to take this occasion to announce that if the national executive calls a leadership convention, I will be a candidate for that leadership." Then he quickly stepped away.

All around the podium people had tears in their eyes. Clark's abrupt about-face had caught everybody off guard. His supporters had flip-flopped from celebrating a victory to staring at defeat in a few dramatic seconds. The pro-review supporters were equally stunned. Clark had missed the magic 70 per cent by a mere sliver. Every bloc of twenty votes moved him one percentage point closer. A swing of sixty-five votes would have pulled him safely across the threshold and put him beyond the reach of any possible dispute. Bill Kempling, the normally jovial caucus whip, shook his head in despair and muttered: "What more does a guy have to do?"

As the dramatic 180-degree shift sank in, the pro-review delegates began celebrating deliriously. Jean-Yves Lortie, wearing his heavy fur coat despite the indoor heat, uncorked a bottle of champagne and pranced a few dance steps in front of the national television cameras. But the anti-Clark revellers were mere islands dotting a big sea of shock and dismay. When they noticed the rising anger of the Clark majority around them, they quieted down. One young pro-Clark delegate started screaming a string of profanities at John Morrison, who, along with MP Otto Jelinek, bolted the convention hall to escape harm. (Later, as he partied in a private room at the Holiday Inn, Morrison was advised to keep out of the hallway for his own safety.) A sobbing young woman smacked review worker Jim Crossland on the back and started shrieking abuse. "I hope you're happy about yourself now," she screeched. Richard Smith, another pro-review worker, sidled up to Gordon Walker, the Ontario minister of industry and trade, figuring nobody would punch him out in front of a cabinet minister. For the next twenty minutes the pro-review forces left the hall as unobtrusively as possible, a good many of them choosing the rear exit. Youth organizer Ken Zeise retreated to a hotel room that he had wisely registered under a different name in anticipation of trouble; it became a refuge where the anti-Clark youth could celebrate in safety.

As Clark left the podium, a group of loyalists lifted him to their shoulders and carried him off like a victorious coach, as crowds of well-wishers flocked around to shake his hand or just touch him. After he was lowered to the floor, the crowds continued to press around while a protective group of caucus members formed a shield to guide him and Maureen out of the building. Bystanders applauded as the moving troupe cut through the throng — except one man in shirtsleeves who called out: "Joe, you're stupid."

Stupid is how Clark's decision looked to many among both his friends and foes. It was the first time in the history of Canadian politics that a leader had quit after winning a clear majority. Twice as many delegates had voted for his leadership as had voted against. He had led the polls for the last seventeen consecutive months, most of them by lopsided margins. Clark had pulled many flubs in seven years as party leader, but this one beat them all.

What possessed Clark to do it? He thought he had little choice. Although he had technically bettered his 1981 vote, he believed this would not satisfy the caucus rebels. He knew that Elmer MacKay had collected between forty and fifty letters from MPs calling for a leadership convention if he did not better his 1981 vote. These lay in MacKay's safe, waiting to be used against him at any time. The caucus had already stripped away many of the leader's traditional prerogatives, such as naming the executive members of caucus, including the chairman. It had taken away his appointments to the PC Canada Fund. Already reduced to living from Wednesday to Wednesday, when caucus met, Clark was drained by the never-ending harassment. Now he expected more of the same.

Besides, Clark had become sick of being compared with a perfect mythical leader who did not exist. He had grown tired of battling phantoms. He wanted somebody real to fight. No serious rival had dared challenge him in broad daylight; only a leadership convention would force the pretenders to the throne out of the shadows. In sum, Clark had worked himself into such a state of mind that — in the words of one of his closest advisers — he wanted "to have it out with these guys." Even before the big vote he had had half a mind to call a leadership convention.

Most observers — including the majority of Clark's opponents — felt that he could have survived with 66.9 per cent, that he should have thanked the convention for its majority endorsement and urged it to prepare for battle against the Grits. An election loomed on the horizon, a fact that would increasingly divert his enemies from internal battles. Soon they would have to start firing at the Liberals and the NDP or else risk losing their own seats. (At a formal dinner for Prince Charles later in the year, the heir to the British throne would remark to him, "What I don't understand was why 67 per cent was not enough.")

Mulroney himself took the view that 66.9 per cent would have been enough for him, and he said so quite openly. "I was flabbergasted," he would later tell L. Ian MacDonald. "I was absolutely stunned. It never, never once occurred to me that that would be the decision." Mulroney understood Clark's thinking no more than he had understood his behaviour leading up to the defeat of his short-lived government. Now Clark had chosen to fall on his sword again. It raised the question of his judgement. Mulroney believed that Clark had been silly to make 70 per cent the magic number when the rest of the world measured a win at 50 per cent plus one. In most circles 67 per cent constituted a landslide, one that would make a normal politician downright proud. After the convention Dalton Camp called it "the new math." He had never conceived of demanding 70 per cent from John Diefenbaker in 1966. With 67 per cent, Diefenbaker would have stepped up to the podium and thanked delegates from the bottom of his heart for the tremendous outpouring of support, which is exactly what Clark should have done this evening. Mulroney had never held a high opinion of Clark, but he would not have believed Clark could do anything this dumb.

But that evening, as Mulroney watched Clark make his amazing announcement on his hotel television set, he said almost nothing. He realized Clark had given him a gift. He would be getting another shot at the leadership. After three years of covert manoeuvring aimed at exactly this result, it had arrived suddenly and when he least expected it, yet strangely his face betrayed hardly a flicker of reaction.

What made him so guarded? Perhaps it was a simple case of shock. Some people would later attribute it to his highly developed sense of history. In moments of lasting importance, he kept cool in order to savour them. Others felt that with a leadership campaign coming on, he faced an entirely new political chessboard and was too preoccupied with contemplating his next move. But more likely it had to do with the number of visitors in his suite. People had been coming and going all evening, and not all were welcome. Better not to gloat in such circumstances.

Meanwhile, down on the convention floor, reporters were busily sweeping up the fallout from Clark's dramatic decision. When the *Globe and Mail* approached Clark loyalist Roch LaSalle, he put the blame squarely on Mulroney. "He was behind it," LaSalle complained. "He is the master of consummate hypocrisy. He has lost perhaps half the support that he would have because of what he has done. I am sure Mulroney will run, but I will not support him, even though it would be nice to have a leader from Quebec."

The aftershock from Clark's surprise announcement was such that delegates hardly paid attention the following morning when they voted to virtually eliminate the concept of a leadership review, the very constitutional provision that had felled Clark only hours earlier. Although done hastily, the decision was not made without good reason. What had started in 1966 as democratic reform had turned itself into a democratic nightmare that drained both the leader and the party. From now on a leader who kept winning elections would never face a review vote, and a leader who lost would be reviewed only once between elections. It meant that no future Tory leader would suffer Clark's ordeal of being reviewed twice for a single defeat.

Over the final day and a half of the convention, the full meaning of Clark's act began to sink in and take hold. Within hours Michael Wilson, a Clark loyalist, revealed on national television that he would be giving serious thought to running for leader. By calling a convention Clark had thrown the leadership issue wide open. People who had flown into Winnipeg scowling at the pro-review activities were already beginning to fit themselves into different camps. Many delegates who had stood four-square behind Clark in the biennial review would now look elsewhere. By the end of the convention much of the bitterness of the rank and file had disappeared, which could only work to Mulroney's advantage.

Mulroney did not stay around to join any victory celebrations. Later that evening he hopped on board the waiting IOC jet. But in the short time he had been there, Winnipeg had changed everything for him, every bit as much as it had for Clark. He now had a clear shot at the leadership of the Conservative Party, without having been caught with the knife in his hand. However, any thoughts about assembling a campaign would have to wait. In only ten days, on February 10, he was to appear before the Quebec government's parliamentary inquiry into the closing of Schefferville. What happened there could derail his leadership bid in a matter of hours. The hearing could not have come at a worse time.

Over the next week and a half he would have to chart his course carefully as he worked simultaneously to shed the millstone of

Schefferville and don the cloak of a leadership candidate, a task that would tax even his considerable talents. Schefferville would have killed the career of any normal politician. Unless he put Schefferville to rest and got good media reviews, he had hardly a prayer of becoming Tory leader. So when Mulroney boarded the IOC jet out of Winnipeg he flew not home to Montreal, but south to Florida. There he would have the time and seclusion he needed to work up a Schefferville strategy.

The details of IOC's compensation for the Schefferville workers — which Mulroney had been touting since the very beginning as a $10-million package — had by now been worked out and released. He had unveiled the particulars of the package two days before the convention opened. The separation pay amounted to an average of $16,400 for the 151 regular or full-time workers, and $6,000 for the 375 seasonal workers. Employees could buy their houses from the company for one dollar, and those who had already bought their homes could sell them back to the company for their paid-in equity. IOC had set up a centre in Schefferville where workers looking for work could get secretarial help and make free long-distance phone calls. As well it had lined up federal government assistance to help them relocate to new areas. Meanwhile workers would keep their fuel subsidies and free travel eligibility until July 31. On and on the goodies went. The package could not have enough bells and whistles for Mulroney.

Some Hanna Mining executives had thought the settlement a bit too steep, but Mulroney lined up the board of directors behind him. He called it one of the most generous packages in Canadian history, and virtually all his potential critics agreed. Even the steelworkers' union, which rarely saluted the company for anything, was complimentary. The favourable publicity — coming virtually on the eve of Winnipeg — helped Mulroney both at the convention and beyond by shifting public attention away from the pain of the shut-down and towards the generosity of the company.

The settlement package looked very good but offered less than met the eye. For one thing, under the terms of the existing collective agreement IOC was already required to pay much of the money anyway. And a year later unionists would cite the Hanna Mining annual report to claim that the deal cost the company $6.9 million instead of the claimed $10 million. As well, many of the catchy bells and whistles proved to be trivial or worthless. Offering to sell occupants their houses for one dollar sounded great until they realized the houses would soon be in a virtual ghost town. While good and generous, the settlement package yielded less than Mulroney had made it seem.

However, all Mulroney's damage control up till now would be futile unless he cleared the big hurdle, the Quebec parliamentary inquiry, where he, as the star witness, could expect to be grilled. If he flopped in front of the townsfolk of Schefferville, everything would come undone, and he could forget about the Tory leadership — all of which explained why he made such a fast exit from Winnipeg and headed south.

In Florida Mulroney ensconced himself in a comfortable hotel at Delray Beach and started preparing for February 10. "A stream of company officials and assistants paraded through," biographer L. Ian MacDonald wrote, "bearing enough documents and data to load an iron-ore train. Mulroney's job was to synthesize all this material, to tell the company's story, to put the best possible slant on the closings, and to make some constructive suggestions for the future of the town. . . . By the time he returned from Florida at the beginning of the second week in February, he was carrying a fifty-five-page brief. And by the time he flew into Schefferville on Wednesday, February 9, the eve of the two-day hearing, he was ready to put on a show."

On the evening of February 9, 1983, Quebec's forlorn North Shore was enduring a typically cold and stormy midwinter day when the sleek IOC jet touched down on Schefferville's modest landing strip and taxied to a stop on the snow-covered tarmac. When Mulroney emerged he found Claude Arpin of the *Montreal Gazette* waiting for him. A tenacious reporter, Arpin had discovered Mulroney's arrival time and showed up to meet him. Now he had the IOC president all to himself when plenty of other reporters were also in town. Mulroney greeted Arpin in his usual friendly manner and invited him into his waiting limousine, in which they drove to the IOC guesthouse. There they were served a lavish meal while Mulroney talked.

Arpin, who had gotten to know Mulroney over the years, had never seen him so nervous. Ordinarily Mulroney repeatedly straightened the knot in his tie when something was bothering him. This time he was pouring down one Virgin Caesar after another, completely preoccupied with the next morning's hearing. "What would happen if . . . ," Mulroney would begin to ask, and then conjure up a question that could trip him up. Usually Mulroney shut out negative thoughts, but on this occasion he could not hide his fear of being ambushed with a loaded question either from one of the fifteen politicians on the parliamentary committee or from somebody in the audience. Over and over again, Mulroney pored over his speech and thumbed through his briefing documents. "Jean-Pierre," he snapped, motioning to Jean-Pierre Maltais, "get me the maps. Where are the maps? You didn't bring the maps?" He talked constantly, starting one thought, then interrupting himself with another, and then another: the national media would be there, and he would have to impress them; the town of Schefferville had to be saved. He kept repeating that the mine shut-down was not killing the town, as if to convince himself the town really did have alternatives. Throughout this rambling discourse Arpin just sat and listened. Mulroney was directing his message mostly to himself anyway. It was not the same confident, commanding Brian Mulroney that Arpin had seen so often.

The next morning while local native leaders, town councillors, and concerned citizens said their piece in the high school auditorium, Mulroney waited his turn outside in the hallway, now more nervous and high-strung than ever. With reporters looking on, he lifted up an imaginary rifle as if to hunt game in the woods. "If I ever catch any Marxist-Leninists," he crowed in earthy French, referring to an earlier scrap with radical elements in the steelworkers' union, "I'll shoot them." He took aim and pretended to fire. "If I had my way I'd set them out running in the woods and pick them off like flies." Then he held his hand up in the air and shouted "Pshu! Pshu!" and walked down the hall. Larry Black, the Canadian Press reporter who witnessed this little scene, thought it most strange, but chalked it up to the stress and anxiety of the moment.

Mulroney's turn came after Mayor Bégin finished delivering the town report. He arrived at the front of the gymnasium trailed by assistants carrying graphs and charts, and easels to put them on. Suddenly the television cameras turned on their floodlights and the entire audience of three hundred sat up. In an instant the room had moved from drowsy boredom to hushed expectation.

Mulroney began by sketching out a brief history of the company and what it had done for the region over the years. A few boos rippled out. Although well-mannered, the audience was irritable and tense and did not need much to stir its anger. Mulroney had gotten off to a rocky start but, showing none of his earlier nervousness, he coolly ignored the boos and started to delve into the numbers behind the closing. Using a three-foot pointer, he zeroed in on the graphs and charts and showed the hundreds of millions of dollars that IOC had lost in past years. Through it all he sounded honest and sincere, and in no time he had the audience following his story. Then he went on the offensive, charging that the provincial and federal governments had sucked $350 million worth of taxes out of the area without putting back a cent. "As a local union leader is fond of saying," he said, "all Quebec ever put in here was a liquor store." Meanwhile the shareholders of IOC had reaped an average return on capital investment of 4.1 per cent since 1953. "That's not exactly the behaviour of your so-called multinationals who allegedly bleed this province dry and pull out when the going gets rough," he said. By now Mulroney had full control of his audience. "You want to know why profits started improving after 1979?" he asked. "It's because we got rid of the Marxist-Leninists who had gained control of Local 5569." Chairman Jean-Pierre Bourdeleau interrupted when his twenty minutes expired, but Mulroney ignored him and continued talking. Bourdeleau tried again a few minutes later, but Mulroney kept pushing on and after another try Bourdeleau gave up. Mulroney stretched his twenty minutes into nearly an hour and a half and would not sit down until he was ready.

While telling the IOC story and showing an easy command of the facts, Mulroney listed in detail the generous terms of the settlement package, which went over well with the audience. But he went further than that and caught the crowd's imagination with a message of hope for what Schefferville could become. Just as he had talked himself into believing in the survival of Schefferville the night before, he now convinced his audience. He held out hope for new mines opening in the surrounding area and cited ample evidence. Discoveries of beryllium oxide and other ores at Strange Lake, 155 miles to the northeast, looked promising, he said. In the last several years the company had spent about $3.5 million on field development programs, and "our preliminary metallurgical test work has been very encouraging." He also talked about manganese deposits, and newly discovered nepheline syenite bodies that "appear to be larger and contain more alumina" than elsewhere in Canada. Moreover, the company would push forward with its non-ferrous exploration program because "we believe that the area will yield other interesting mineral discoveries." Mulroney did throw in the caveat that, if successful, the new discoveries could take ten years to start producing — but he had only started to wax eloquent about the possibilities.

Schefferville was full of potential, he said. It would make a great military training centre for Canadian forces or NATO troops, or it could house a correctional institute, a northern research centre, an institute of mining and metallurgy, or it could become a lodging place for caribou hunters. Mulroney absolutely glowed when he described Schefferville as a ski resort. "Seven-month winters with heavy snowfalls, combined with excellent facilities, would certainly attract the enthusiastic attention of thousands of North American skiers," he explained in his report. He had plenty of other ideas — scores of them: a manpower retraining centre, a handicraft industry for native people, a national park. He promised that the company would work with interested citizens to help bring Schefferville a new beginning. He put on a dazzling performance and turned anxiety and hostility into hope.

The members of the parliamentary committee watched this performance with fascination. Most were disarmed, although a few harboured some doubts. In the question period that followed his presentation, the sceptical minister of labour, Pierre Marois, started pressing Mulroney about when the company first learned about the need for the closing and why it had not consulted government beforehand. As Marois started to dig further, he received a handwritten note from a fellow committee member: "Don't you think it's enough? Why don't you stop?" Marois pressed on, but the bulk of the committee plainly sided with Mulroney. The minister of energy and resources, Yves Duhaime, also shot off some tough questions, but nothing Mulroney could not handle. He had done his homework and was prepared for everything. Sometimes he would call on one of the attending IOC managers for technical explanations, but Mulroney himself never lacked for a convincing explanation. Being a stickler for detail, which he could be when it counted, had paid off. He had survived the ordeal without a nick or a scratch.

Mulroney's *tour de force* had turned imminent disaster into triumph. "Mulroney Scores Political Points at Probe," proclaimed the next day's headline in the *Montreal Gazette*. "Brian Mulroney Steals the Show," said the headline in *Le Soleil.* "The Iron Ore Closing: A Responsible Decision," crowed the *Journal de Québec.* When Mulroney picked up his red pointer and started flipping through his charts, Parti Québécois backbencher Élie Fallu turned to fellow committee member Robert Dean and quipped: "Well, Bob, it's a show." A Mulroney aide overheard Fallu's remark, reconstructed it into "That guy is going to sweep the province," and passed it to the media, who included it in the generally glowing coverage.

Only Mulroney could have closed a town and come off looking

better than before. Of all his feats over the years it would rank among the very greatest. Yet the actual number of jobs lost was nothing compared with his cuts elsewhere in the company. At the same time that he was slashing 151 full-time jobs in Schefferville, he was cutting about 1,400 jobs at IOC's other mine in Labrador City. After seeing its workforce cut almost in half, that town was reeling; and since they were being laid off rather than displaced, they did not qualify for the generous compensation given their Schefferville counterparts. Meanwhile the town of Sept-Îles had already lost its concentrator and pellet plant. Under Mulroney IOC had gone on a company-wide scale-down and shed well over half its workforce.

IOC had made some tough decisions during Mulroney's tenure. When he became president in 1977, the company employed 7,500 workers. Now the number was down to about 2,700, with most of the cutting coming in his final year. Although it was not something he would brag about, accomplishing this reduction without provoking a labour backlash was no small achievement. Even with the closing of Schefferville diverting attention, few business executives could have done it so quietly. The new trimmed-down company now looked very different from the one he had joined seven years ago, but with the Conservative leadership campaign waiting for his candidacy, Mulroney would not be sticking around to see it in action.

Mulroney, whose own job at IOC fell under the axe as soon as he left, was IOC's last full-time president and the last one to live in Canada. At first Bob Anderson, Hanna Mining's chairman, assumed his duties, then he handed the job to Carl Nickels, Hanna Mining's senior vice-president. In future the executive decisions would come from Cleveland. One of the first things Cleveland did was to sell off IOC's executive jet. Soon the small Canadian head office was reduced, and eventually it closed altogether.

Mulroney also left behind the much-touted committee to search for new industries for Schefferville. Despite his grand vision for breathing new life into the town, the committee never amounted to anything, and neither did any of the projects he conjured up for the benefit of the parliamentary inquiry. Eventually the town shrivelled up into a village of fewer than three hundred, not including the local native population.

Mulroney's last visit to Sept-Îles as IOC's chief executive officer coincided with his forty-fourth birthday — March 20, 1983. The next day he would officially throw his hat into the ring for the leadership of the Conservative Party, but first some of the locals were putting on a party to bid him happy birthday and farewell. At the party he announced that he was resigning as company president effective immediately. "It was very emotional," he later told *Globe and Mail* reporter John Gray. "You know, here I'd worked like a son of a bitch to get this company turned around. The company's making money and everyone was happy. And I could really put up my feet and really have a goddamn good life with the kids. And I get on the plane, a goddamn beautiful jet, anything you want, and flying back, going to Ottawa, to announce the next morning. We leave Seven Islands and we take off and we're still into a climb when we hit Baie Comeau, and I had to burst out laughing. I said to myself, my old man'll come right up here and strangle me and say, 'You stupid bastard, what are you doing? You know, all your life you work to accomplish something, and here you just packed it in.' But, you know, there's a certain amount of ambition in these things, and there's also a certain belief that you can do something to change it. . . . And I'll tell you this, I'm going to give it a real goddamn good kick at the can. And if I make it, fine. And if I don't, at least I'll be able to say when they put me down, 'I didn't sit on the goddamn sidelines, I tried.' That's all I can do."

CHAPTER TWENTY

LEADERSHIP
GAINED

MULRONEY HAD DELIBERATELY delayed the formal announcement of his candidacy for the leadership of the Progressive Conservative Party until well after the executive set the convention date for the second week of June. He wanted to be among the last to declare, and thus avoid being seen as an opportunist in the aftermath of Winnipeg. His entry into the race not only came late but was unveiled in Ottawa. Although he planned to play up his Quebec base during the campaign, he wanted to send out the message that he was more than a regional candidate.

On March 21, 1983, when Mulroney stepped out of the Château Laurier for the three-block trip to the National Press Building, he walked into a scene that stopped him dead in his tracks. The taxi waiting in line for him happened to be a Cadillac. "Michael," he barked to aide Michael McSweeney, "I'm not going in that car. Get him out of there and get the next one." Television cameras would film his arrival at the other end, and the last thing he wanted was to be seen stepping out of a Caddie. McSweeney tried to shoo the taxi away, but the driver refused to budge. Even McSweeney's explanation that they were only going up the street could not make the cabbie surrender his spot at the head of the line. So for a brief moment Mulroney and the Cadillac stood frozen in a stand-off. "Pay him off," Mulroney finally shouted. A few seconds later the Cadillac pulled out and another taxi pulled in — this one an acceptably modest Plymouth.

The flap over the taxi neatly symbolized one of the chief differences between 1976 and 1983. This time the man dubbed the Cadillac candidate had decided to turn himself into a Plymouth. In 1976 he had overdosed on glitz, been branded the establishment's man, and paid a heavy price. In 1983 he recycled himself as the frugal candidate and took it to his usual extreme. Normal moderation would not suffice. His aides took to calling it the "rusty station wagon" campaign.

For the longest time Mulroney's handlers would not be able to get him near a chartered airplane. Whenever possible Mulroney insisted on travelling by car. Otherwise it would be regular commercial air travel, economy class, and — especially when reporters or cameras were around — he would carry his own bags. His first leadership campaign had brandished the biggest and flashiest posters of all. This time every last detail was geared down to be basic and simple. Proper computers were forbidden; they looked too slick and expensive. The campaign headquarters made do with a bank of modest Micom word processors instead. Michel Cogger, the 1976 campaign manager who had taken the heat for much of the extravagance, was kept mostly out of sight in 1983. Peter White also stayed in the background. Last time, because of his association with Paul Desmarais, Mulroney had been tabbed as the candidate from Power Corporation. This time he did not want White's business association with magnate Conrad Black to tag him as the candidate from Argus Corporation. Only much later, when there was no other way, would he start renting a plane — and then only after the other candidates had done so first. (Eventually Mulroney also relented over the use of good computers; he needed them to process the mountain of data collected about delegates.)

In sharp contrast to the freewheeling days of 1976, expenditures were carefully controlled. The campaign organization in each province submitted a budget to headquarters and then had to stick to it.

Although the campaign would still spend big dollars, the money this time would be invested in productive areas like delegate tracking, rather than cosmetics. Mulroney had learned the lessons of 1976 well.

John Crosbie, Clark's former minister of finance, also jumped into the race on March 21, bringing the field of candidates to eight — Clark, Mulroney, Crosbie, former international trade minister Michael Wilson, former health and welfare minister David Crombie, Edmonton Oilers owner Peter Pocklington, backbench MP John Gamble, and former party president Peter Blaikie (who would drop out before the convention). Later, fringe candidate Neil Fraser would also enter the race, bringing the total to nine. With a little over eleven weeks until the convention, Clark and Mulroney stood above the field as the undisputed frontrunners, and Crosbie occupied third spot above the rest. Coincidentally the big three had all once endured the cruelties of first-year law at Dalhousie Law School. Mulroney had flunked out, and Clark had technically flunked before pulling out on his own. Only Crosbie had survived the ordeal, eventually graduating with one of the highest standings in the history of the school.

After throwing his hat into the ring, Mulroney immediately returned to Montreal, where he quietly boarded a commercial flight to Vancouver. While the Clark campaign was issuing media itineraries and assigning press to the media bus, the Mulroney team virtually sneaked out of town, offering reporters no schedules and no accommodation on the tour. In fact the Mulroney camp even refused to reveal where the candidate was going. Jason Moscovitz, the CBC Television reporter assigned to follow Mulroney, tracked him down in Vancouver but lost him at the next stop in Edmonton. Moscovitz was the only reporter on that trip, and as far as the Mulroney campaign was concerned, he was one too many. Later Aileen McCabe of the Southam newspaper chain and David Lord of Canadian Press would actually hunt him down like a wanted criminal, finally locating him in Hamilton. Once found, Mulroney invited them up to his hotel suite and treated them well, but the next day the chase started over again. (Whenever McCabe got invited for a late-night chit-chat,

Mulroney would usually rant on disparagingly about Clark — all off the record.)

Most leadership candidates want publicity — the more the better. Mulroney wanted to avoid it. Taking a page from Clark's strategy of 1976, he followed what would be called the "boonie strategy" — a low-key, almost underground campaign aimed mostly at the hinterlands that deliberately kept low and out of sight. In 1976 he had been the slick media candidate. This time he would avoid the media and meet every delegate in the flesh, in small intimate gatherings that gave him a chance to unleash his winsome personality. Instead of meeting a big group in a downtown ballroom, he would show up in somebody's rumpus room in the north end of town — just he and Mila and one aide plus a local organizer. Every single delegate would be targeted for a handshake and a hello and — as he would quip — a coffee and a doughnut and two questions. Personal contact would be the key. He was trying to reach not 25 million Canadians, but the three thousand Tories who would travel to Ottawa and vote on the afternoon of June 11. Mulroney contended that a leadership convention had nothing to do with broad-spectrum politics and everything to do with meeting people face to face, something he could not do effectively with a pack of reporters hanging around. Only after he had finished going delegate by delegate and kitchen by kitchen was he planning to emerge from hiding for a traditional media-type campaign to reinforce the notion that he was doing well. Mulroney had thought up this strategy in the many bitter hours spent analyzing his 1976 defeat.

As the campaign unfolded, it quickly became clear that Mulroney had rediscovered his old zest for life. Early in the race a spring downpour dropped buckets of water onto his car as he whizzed through the Quebec countryside along with Mila, old friend George Archer, and campaign aide Peter Ohrt, who was at the wheel. Suddenly Mulroney burst into song, to the tune of "Singin' in the Rain." "I love campaigning in the rain, I love campaigning in the rain." The old excitement was back.

461

In the weeks after entering the race Mulroney virtually disappeared from television screens and newspapers. In fact the boonie strategy was working so well that it began to backfire in one crucial area: Mulroney had disappeared not only from the eyes of the media, but from the minds of contributors whose money he needed to finance his campaign. When donations started drying up, Mulroney and his advisers reluctantly decided he had to start making speeches and get on television again; he would have to run a two-track campaign that worked the media for national publicity while he stayed mostly close to the ground hunting for grassroots votes.

Meanwhile, all his careful courting of the Tory caucus, with the help of the door-opening of Pat MacAdam and Frank Moores and the inside lobbying of MPs such as Elmer MacKay and Bob Coates, paid off. Sinclair Stevens, who had irretrievably swung the convention to Clark in 1976, announced early on that he was supporting Mulroney. In 1976 only two MPs had backed him; this time nineteen ultimately came on side, most from the disaffected right wing, including some of the same people who had once ganged up against him for his lack of parliamentary experience. Among them were Tom Siddon, Otto Jelinek, Jack Murta, Steve Paproski, George Hees, and Alvin Hamilton. Only Clark, with thirty-five MPs, had more caucus members behind him. (His supporters included John Fraser, Harvie Andre, Ray Hnatyshyn, Jake Epp, Flora MacDonald, Roch LaSalle, and Jim McGrath.)

Mulroney had one more thing working in his favour in 1983: Mila. In 1976, when she was pregnant, Mila had taken little part in the campaign; this time she followed her husband every step of the way, proving herself to be a major asset. On the eve of Mulroney's declaration, she told a group of friends gathered to celebrate her husband's forty-fifth birthday, "I don't know. . . . I might make the odd trip. I don't want to leave the kids too long." But she went on the first trip to Vancouver and after that hardly missed a day of campaigning. One of the first to succumb to her charm was Vancouver television interviewer Jack Webster, who had planned a two-part interview, one with both Brian and Mila and one with just Brian. After she arrived on the set Webster quickly discarded that plan, keeping her on camera for the whole show.

Mulroney's brother and sisters also rallied around during this second run at the leadership, although not all with equal enthusiasm. His sister Doreen, a dedicated peace activist who advocated nuclear disarmament, had to be persuaded to join the Conservative Party in order to support a pro-Mulroney delegate in the riding of Westmount. His brother Gary had long lived uncomfortably in his older sibling's shadow. In their youth, the two had never been close, and their relationship had become positively icy when Mulroney found out that Gary was gay. For many years, Mulroney had rarely mentioned him, and when he did he seemed embarrassed. He had no tolerance for homosexuality and pushed his brother away because of it. But the two had recently reconciled, and Gary now became one of his most loyal supporters. (In later years Mulroney would hire him as a constituency aide.)

Only one ghost from 1976 haunted him still — the fact he'd never been elected to Parliament. Two general elections had come and gone in the last seven years and he still did not have a seat in the House of Commons, nor had he even tried to get one. The only thing he had been elected to was a board of directors. This failure caused hockey agent Alan Eagleson to switch his allegiance to Clark, and many others who might otherwise have leaned his way held back. At first, when challenged on this issue, Mulroney pointed to Grant Devine as somebody who had never held office until the day he was elected premier of Saskatchewan the year before. Or else he would recite his own twenty-eight-year history in the Conservative Party. Eventually he hit upon an answer that invariably silenced his critics. Joe Clark, he said, possessed experience and had lost power after sitting on the government benches only thirty-seven days. "We as Conservatives go out and work for sixteen years as foot-soldiers. We finally elect a Conservative government, and so-called parliamentary experience causes that government to be blown out of the water in thirty-seven days. Now, if that's parliamentary experience . . ." Suddenly the competence of the Clark government, not the inexperience of Brian Mulroney, was on trial.

Most observers agreed that Mulroney had an excellent shot at winning this time around. However, it was clear from the beginning that Clark had gotten off to a faster start. While Mulroney dealt with the Schefferville crisis, then delayed his announcement until most of the contenders had declared, Clark had started hunting for delegates virtually the day after Winnipeg.

But Clark enjoyed more than just a head start. His campaign of 1983 bore no resemblance to the children's crusade of 1976, when he kept expenses under $170,000. This time he would spend $1.9 million (and go heavily into debt). Clark also had some of the ablest workers. Bill McAleer, a low-key but highly effective organizer from the Davis machine in Ontario, was his campaign chairman; Finlay MacDonald was his chief of staff; and, as always, Lowell Murray was his strategic guru — all first-rate political men. As the leader for seven years, Clark easily outdrew Mulroney in attracting establishment figures, including some who had supported Mulroney the first time; in addition to Alan Eagleson, both Hal Jackman and Don McDougall switched to Clark. Although now a spent force, Davie Fulton backed Clark rather than Mulroney. As well Clark had a lot of support from people who felt he had been badly treated by the party.

Perhaps Clark's greatest weapon was the Gallup poll. Under his leadership the Conservative Party continued to lead the Liberals in public opinion, the margin in the spring of 1983 being about 50 per cent to 32. He seemed positioned for a smashing majority in the next election. Not surprisingly, Clark warned delegates not to change leaders when the party was doing so well.

Nowhere did Clark's organizational head start do him more good than in the many ridings in Quebec that were without strong local party organizations. These ridings had been the prime battlegrounds leading up to Winnipeg and now became the arenas of combat once again. Riding by riding, the Clark and Mulroney forces would recruit busloads of instant Tories and then slug it out. Only now, with the stakes even higher, the competition grew even more fierce and ruthless. As with Canadian general elections, the political formula for winning the Tory leadership included winning the majority of delegates from Quebec. Clark knew this basic political fact just as well as Mulroney and was not conceding him an inch of Quebec territory.

Marcel Danis, Clark's chief organizer in Quebec, knew his man could not hold his early advantage very long. Quebec was Mulroney's turf, and his campaign machine was coming together quickly. Clark's only hope for winning Quebec lay in speed and surprise. By striking early he might catch the Mulroney forces unprepared and overwhelm them before they could pick up the muscle to pack the delegate-selection meetings.

Moving abruptly, Danis scheduled sixteen meetings on March 25, four days after Mulroney officially entered the race. Another fourteen would choose delegates in the following three days, and another twelve in the three days after that, leaving all but thirty-three ridings undecided within ten days of Mulroney's announcement of his candidacy. Danis had scored a master-stroke. With more than one-third of the ridings selecting delegates on the same weekend, in constituencies spread across the province, Rodrigue Pageau, once again Mulroney's chief organizer, could not cope. He simply could not match Danis blow for blow.

In a church basement in the Montreal suburb of Longueuil, where the number of card-holding Tories jumped from 40 to 632 in three weeks, and where eight pro-Clark off-duty policemen patrolled the premises, the Mulroney representatives could not even get into the room where the votes were being counted to scrutinize the tally. "Listen," Mulroney worker Claude Dumont protested, "we got the right to have somebody to represent Brian." "Brian who?" retorted Clark organizer Michel Côté (no relation to the Michel Côté who would later join Mulroney's cabinet). The riding executive was controlled by Clark supporters who had barred Mulroney agents on the technicality that Mulroney was not a legal candidate, since he had not yet formally filed his nomination papers nor put down the required $2,000 deposit. That night Clark eked out a win even though the Mulroney supporters contended they had three times as many people in the room.

However, across town in Saint-Denis, the story was reversed. Amid the confusing crush of the packed room, Richard Holden stood up and took control of the meeting, telling all the Mulroney supporters to line up on one side and the Clark people on the other. The room divided into two halves — except for one couple in the middle who refused to budge. "We don't have to say how we're going to vote," they insisted. "Okay," replied Holden, "we have Clark, Mulroney, and we have the undecided." A less than impartial adjudicator, Holden counted children with parents and tallied a majority for Mulroney. Television cameras recorded the counting scene, which Mila saw on a newscast. "Mila thinks you're a marvellous counter," Mulroney later quipped to Holden.

As the Saint-Denis meeting was breaking up, a Mulroney worker sidled up to CBC Television reporter Jason Moscovitz and cracked: "Tonight it was our Greeks against their Greeks. On Sunday it's our drunks against their drunks." The Mulroney supporter was referring to the upcoming vote in downtown Saint-Jacques. As a Montrealer, Moscovitz knew the riding well and had a hunch that any funny business might include the Old Brewery Mission, a hostel for homeless men. On his way to the Sunday meeting he made a point of driving by the mission and happened to catch a group of derelicts boarding a private bus. He quickly learned that the Mulroney camp had signed them up in return for free beer. It would come out later that all held valid membership cards, which had been properly registered at least five days before the meeting. The only administrative oddity was that none of them had normal addresses on their membership cards, only bed and floor numbers at the mission.

Moscovitz and his camera crew boarded the bus and accompanied them to the meeting, filmed them getting off at the other end, and collared the last person off for an on-camera interview. This particular member of the Conservative Party seemed not to know what planet he was on, let alone that he had come to a political nomination meeting to vote for a slate of six delegates. It made great television. Moscovitz also interviewed a Mulroney spokesman for balance. But no explanation, no matter how well articulated, could mask the reality of what was happening. At the end of the meeting Mulroney had won by twenty-seven votes, the difference being the men from the Old Brewery Mission. (The Clark organizers brought in a busload of senior citizens from nearby Résidence Mont Carmel.) Two days later the Mulroney organization won the meeting in Verdun, ninety-three to forty-three, with twenty-five votes coming from the Dawson Boys and Girls Club. Some of these card-carrying Tories were only four-teen years old.

The television footage of residents from the Old Brewery Mission being bussed in for the promise of free beer drew headlines across Canada. But Mulroney defended the derelicts as war veterans who deserved the right to participate in democracy. Later at a stop in Cornwall, a man inquired why his organization would entice such people with alcohol. Still not yielding an inch, Mulroney attacked the CBC — the people's network — for holding those poor men up to national ridicule. "I didn't know you needed a $600 suit to join this party," he huffed, sounding his pious best.

Following that first hectic weekend, the Clark and Mulroney camps traded allegations about dirty tricks, and both were correct. Each side had bent the rules to the limit. In the delegate count, Clark had come out ahead in that first series of clashes, winning seventeen ridings to Mulroney's eleven and gaining an early delegate lead of eighty-two to sixty-two. Clark had put his early advantage to good use. However, the Mulroney organization had mobilized even more quickly than the Clark organization had anticipated, especially in the Montreal-area ridings, and had fared better than expected. After the first week the Clark supporters started finding themselves out-numbered, sometimes by lopsided margins.

The shady incidents — from both sides — were endless. Sometimes one meeting had two different membership lists. Other times the dates of meetings were changed by one side without the other side being told. Lost in the shuffle were the long-serving party faithful, who were pushed aside in the rush as the Mulroney and Clark camps tried to outdo each other. In some constituencies wounds would remain unhealed almost a decade later, long after the instant members had disappeared.

Through all the dirty work of the Quebec wars, the face of Jean-Yves Lortie was nowhere to be seen. Since the incident at the registration desk in Winnipeg, Lortie had disappeared from view on orders from Mulroney, who did not want him besmirching the image of his campaign. But he was still organizing, only now from behind the scenes. When a CBC camera spotted him at Mulroney headquarters, he fled and took refuge in the washroom, only to find the camera still waiting for him when he finally came out.

Some of the biggest scandals came with the sudden flowering of Tory campus clubs. A Conservative club attached to an institution of higher learning could send up to three youth delegates. That loophole spawned a nifty racket of clubs in some rather unusual "campuses." Paper clubs sprouted everywhere. Clark and Mulroney both did okay in the battle of phoney clubs, but not nearly as well as John Crosbie, whose organization in Newfoundland created clubs for nursing schools, flying schools, driving academies, and beauty colleges. New clubs arose as fast as the ink could dry on the registration forms. Newfoundland had more youth delegates than regular delegates and was sending as many campus delegates to Ottawa as was Ontario — and all were selected according to the rules.

Ultimately Clark and Mulroney split Quebec about fifty-fifty, with Mulroney winning most of Montreal and Clark prevailing elsewhere. Quebec had turned into a two-sided battle between the two leading contenders, forcing everybody else out of the picture.

Despite his surprising success in the Quebec wars, Clark was being dragged down by a couple of uncharacteristically intemperate re-marks. Trying to look tough, he vowed to crack down on party dissidents, promising that from now on it would be "my way or the doorway." Then later he dismissed Ontario premier William Davis, who was considering joining the race, as "a regional candidate"; neither Davis nor many of his supporters had forgiven him. At the same time Mulroney was telephoning Davis regularly, either for advice or just to talk. Mulroney had not known the Ontario premier particularly well, but now he made it his business to get better acquainted.

At the end of April, just as Mulroney was surfacing from his boonie campaign, he put in an appearance at an all-candidates meeting in Toronto and gave a smooth performance. Except for a question over his failure to run for Parliament, he emerged untouched. The same did not hold for Clark, who unwisely rose to the bait when John Gamble attacked him over a controversial proposal to allow provinces to opt out of federally sponsored programs and still keep the money. When Clark spoke briefly in French, he was booed, and most of the candidates immediately started picking on him. Mulroney — who spoke a few words of French without getting booed — enthusiasti-cally joined the gang-up by drilling home the point that the govern-ment of Quebec was "socialist and separatist." He declared, "Before I give away a nickel of Canada's money, I want to know what Lévesque's going to do with it." Mulroney had never accepted Clark's "community of communities" view of the country; the year before he had quietly supported Trudeau rather than Clark on the patriation of the Constitution. Mulroney had consistently attacked Clark on the stump for playing footsie with the Parti Québécois and being soft on separatism.

Clark's regionalism did not go down well in Toronto, but it played well in Quebec, especially with the French media, which grilled Mulroney at a press conference in Montreal the following day. During a fifteen-minute exchange, which sometimes grew heated, one of the reporters asked him how he could attack Clark's constitutional position when he lacked one of his own. "Positions that the party should adopt in constitutional matters aren't devised during leadership campaigns on a Saturday night in the back of a truck," Mulroney shot back. He was not about to "show my four aces" before negotiations had even started. "But I can tell you," he said, "that we'll find a serious and eloquent formula to meet Quebec's legitimate and historical responsibility to safeguard its language and culture. But no formula exists to satisfy a separatist government, because let's not be naïve and think for one minute that they would be interested in a formula that would demonstrate that federalism can work."

Mulroney had called the press conference not to discuss the Constitution but to launch a three-day tour of Quebec beginning the next day. During the tour, on a flight from Quebec City to Mont-Joli, he came across a French newspaper editorial slamming him for evading such a crucial issue as the Constitution. Adviser Peter Ohrt suggested he quell his critics with a formal statement of constitutional policy. On the spot Mulroney swung into action. Grabbing a Quebecair vomit bag, he began jotting down points. "Canada is a great country and Quebec is an integral and important part thereof," began point number one. Mulroney wrote down nine points in all, and later added another to make it an even ten. In Rimouski he unveiled it as his constitutional position. "Why, this could have been written by Pierre Trudeau," complained one reporter. By this time the ten points had been neatly typed on a sheet of paper. Afterwards he presented the original to Ohrt as a souvenir. "One day this will be worth something," he chuckled to Ohrt, who had it framed.

The vomit bag incident showed that Mulroney still tended to treat policy as an afterthought. However, he was determined not to be labelled this time as the candidate of all style and no substance. This time he started his campaign with the release of a book called *Where I Stand*, a slender paperback that compiled his speeches of the last three years. "Those who read this book will be under no illusion as to where I stand," read the opening line. The book, published by

McClelland & Stewart, helped give his campaign the veneer of substance.

In 1976 Mulroney had been hurt by two serious strategic mistakes in policy. First, he had said as little as possible for fear of offending delegates, making him seem like a lightweight. Second, he had lined up at the wrong end of the party's philosophical spectrum, with the progressive side of the party, when more votes were available on the right. Now as he campaigned across the country his policy statements shifted to the right. He emphasized balancing the budget and giving tax breaks to medium and small business as among his top priorities. He also championed improved productivity, research and development, export-led growth, and a new era of management-labour relations, all packaged with colourful, hard-hitting language.

As much as this more substantial Mulroney pushed his right-wing rhetoric, he remained prudently flexible. His words, though vivid, always left him more room in the centre than it seemed at first. For example, he flatly accused FIRA, the controversial Foreign Investment Review Agency, of killing investment. "In Japan," he would say, "they've never heard of Ottawa but they can spell FIRA." A graphic quote, it appeared to spell death for the agency. But when pressed for details he began to fudge, promising only to "put FIRA on the back burner." If pushed further he would fire off some more strong words about firing the first civil servant who used FIRA to stop much-needed foreign investment, without really committing himself to anything. The same applied to Crown corporations, which he promised to bring under control and make more accountable to Parliament. While vowing to crack down on government spending, he also promised to give the armed forces "first-class" treatment and advocated more funding for medicare in exchange for the removal of provincial user fees. Despite the right-wing gloss to his rhetoric, he was no soul mate of Margaret Thatcher or Ronald Reagan. He remained an innate pragmatist whose marriage with the party's right wing was more of convenience than of conviction.

Next to the ideological right, Mulroney's most important support came from the Tory youth. Peter White had identified young Tories as strategically significant and concluded that Mulroney had to win them in order to succeed. While staying discreetly out of the campaign limelight, White started to forge relationships with the PC youth leaders, who were impressed that someone of White's stature — a business associate of Conrad Black — was interested in them. Clark, meanwhile, had nobody of comparable business standing lining up youth support. Nearly one-third of all delegates were youth, so the potential was enormous.

As Mulroney crossed the country he kept repeating his campaign themes — increased productivity, labour harmony, and government restraint — but always fell back on his favourite subject, the Conservative Party's impotence in Quebec. Of the 282 federal seats in Canada, Mulroney would tell his audiences, 102 had French-speaking populations of 10 per cent or more, and in the last election Trudeau won 100 of them. "You give Pierre Trudeau a head start of a hundred seats and he'll beat you ten times out of ten," he declared. Mulroney said he was a generous man, but his generosity did not extend to giving the Liberals such a gift. His party had won exactly one seat in Quebec in 1980; it had finished behind the NDP in thirty-nine ridings and behind the Rhinoceros Party in two. As long as Quebec remained a Tory wasteland, the party would be doomed to opposition. Only he could crack the Liberals' near monopoly on Quebec and bring the Conservative Party back to power. Mulroney repeated the message over and over, sometimes delivering it as often as ten or twenty times a day. By the end of the campaign his aides could recite it in their sleep. It was one of the very few things left untouched from 1976.

The other, less formal agenda that Mulroney pursued during his campaign concerned patronage. Time after time he sent out the message that, unlike Clark, he would not forget to reward the party faithful once he reached high office. In front of a delegate meeting in Quebec City, he singled out his friends Jacques Blanchard and Jean Sirois in the audience. "What senators they'd make," he chortled.

"And I can see at least five great candidates for the magistracy." On another occasion he joked that he had promised fourteen senatorships that day alone. Once when delegates applauded him enthusiastically he retorted: "Keep this up and there's seventeen new senators there." A man in the audience shouted: "Mr. Mulroney, you're going to be prime minister," and Mulroney shouted back, "You're going to be a senator." He always promised that in fairness he would also dole out plums to Liberals and New Democrats — "after I've been prime minister for fifteen years and I can't find a living, breathing Tory in the country."

In mid-campaign, Southam News reporter Aileen McCabe hooked up with the Mulroney tour in southern Alberta, only to be told the plane was full. If she wanted to make the next stop, she would have to find a car and drive two hundred miles. That was before Mulroney heard about a Southam News poll that had projected Clark the winner. Suddenly a plane seat opened up for her that happened to be right next to Mulroney, who let her know what he thought about the poll. As the plane took off, an uptight candidate began to belittle the poll results, telling her that it was all nuts and that his polling data, which were far more detailed, projected him the winner.

The McCabe incident was not unique. Mulroney never hesitated to gripe to reporters about how they covered him, particularly reporters from the CBC. Since before the campaign had officially begun, he had believed the CBC was slanted against him. Much of his distrust had started after the "Friends of Brian" bash put on by some buddies at Montreal's Queen Elizabeth Hotel before the campaign kick-off. The Mulroney camp had staged the big party to show the world what kind of popular support he had, with the hope of creating a draft-Mulroney atmosphere. Between three and four thousand people showed up and made it into a gigantic success, dispelling any doubt about Mulroney's ability to draw an impressive crowd.

The National duly covered the big gala, but because of a desk foul-up in Toronto, the size of the crowd was reported as simply more than a thousand. When Mulroney watched the report that night he lost control. Somehow knowing the CBC studio telephone number, he caught anchor Knowlton Nash coming off the air. Mulroney told Nash that six thousand people had shown up, including more important people than the CBC reported, and he rhymed off the names of some of the big hitters who had been there. He accused the CBC of trying to kill his campaign before it started. None of Nash's assurances could soothe his suspicions or quell his anger. As far as he was concerned, one CBC story had undermined the evening's success.

Half an hour later Mulroney called again, this time more outraged still. The longer he talked the more worked up he became. Around midnight Nash, now at home, got another incensed call from an even more irate Mulroney. "I'll tell you how angry I am," he told Nash. "Here, I'll put Mila on, and she'll tell you how angry I am." Mila, quiet and gentle in contrast to her husband, told Nash she thought the story was wrong and unfair. (According to L. Ian MacDonald, Gary Mulroney, who was helping on the campaign, also called the CBC newsroom that night to register a complaint.)

About a week after the "Friends of Brian" incident, CBC Television reporters Peter Mansbridge, Mike Duffy, and Jason Moscovitz arrived at Toronto's Bristol Place Hotel for a sort of summit meeting with Mulroney on the subject. After making the trio wait in the lobby for several hours while he and his organizers put the finishing touches on his campaign, Mulroney invited them up. But after a bit of cool-headed give-and-take he let the whole matter drop. Instead he started to talk with the three star reporters about the coming campaign, and swapped stories. "You know," he said as cold clubhouse sandwiches were passed around, "if I get really lucky I can win this."

He also made sure that the reporters understood he was innocent in Clark's downfall. His proof, he proclaimed, came from Mansbridge's own mouth. Then he pulled a sheet of paper out of his wallet. It was a transcript of comments Mansbridge had made on air in Winnipeg after Clark had failed to get 70 per cent. Mansbridge had made the point that many members of provincial legislatures —

who all had a vote — had not shown up. If they had, Mansbridge noted, Clark would have hit 70 percent. Mulroney now held up this comment as evidence that he had not brought down Clark, then folded up the paper and returned it to his wallet.

As the campaign progressed there would be more complaints about the CBC's coverage and more phone calls. Mulroney's handlers tried to talk him out of calling up reporters whenever stories snagged one of his emotional trip-wires, but often it was hopeless.

Mulroney's grievances notwithstanding, the media over the course of the campaign had actually given him an easy ride and spared him much of the critical scrutiny that they had aimed at Clark. However, Mulroney believed John Crosbie was getting the easiest ride, and privately accused the press of having a love affair with him. It frustrated him that the former finance minister, his biggest competitor for right-wing votes, could fly around in a private jet without getting nailed for lavishness. He grew positively green with jealousy when, with three weeks to go, *Maclean's* magazine put Crosbie on its cover as "The Tory to Watch." The cover story reported that Crosbie was coming on fast, and Mulroney's own poll data confirmed it. A late-charging Crosbie was the last thing his campaign could afford. Mulroney needed a cushion of at least two hundred first-ballot votes over Crosbie to emerge as the undisputed choice of the Anyone-But-Clark voters. If the Newfoundland MP did too well, he would split the ABC vote, which would play directly into Clark's hands. Furthermore, polls showed Crosbie as the most popular second choice of delegates, giving him the potential to catapult ahead in later ballots, exactly as Clark had done in 1976.

The "Crosbie factor" loomed large enough to cause the Mulroney camp to consider shifting its primary attack from Clark to Crosbie. The wisecracking Newfoundlander had one overwhelming vulnerability, his inability to speak French. With two weeks left in the race, as Mulroney and his advisers debated whether to exploit this weakness, the loose-tongued Crosbie overturned his own bandwagon with an unpolitic statement on this very topic. While touring Quebec,

Crosbie dismissed his lack of French by saying he could not speak Chinese or German either and yet could still have a relationship with China and Germany. It was the Big Blunder of the campaign and destroyed his momentum on the spot. With Crosbie gravely wounded, the Mulroney campaign had no need to do anything.

Having preserved his lead over Crosbie, Mulroney could concentrate in the final two weeks on closing in on Clark, who, while still in front, remained within his reach. Mulroney closed his campaign with an evening appearance in Montreal on Friday, June 3. It went off well but he looked exhausted. For two and a half months he had driven himself eighteen hours a day, living on a diet consisting mainly of cigarettes, coffee, and chocolate bars, reaching 268 of the 282 ridings in the country and holding up to eight or nine meetings a day. Now he took a four-day rest, which did wonders for him. When he arrived in Ottawa the following Wednesday he looked refreshed and perked up. This time his arrival in Ottawa carried none of the overblown hoopla of 1976. He and Mila and a couple of aides rolled unnoticed into the Château Laurier parking lot in Mila's grey Phoenix.

The convention itself opened on Thursday, June 9, 1983, with the formal introduction of the eight leadership hopefuls. Clark got the loudest cheers from the three thousand delegates but also drew a few boos, the only candidate to do so, which pretty well summed up where he stood with the party and the convention. He had both the most delegates and the most diehard opponents. Anti-Clark feeling hung all around, and many people openly flaunted their disdain. One button featured Clark's face underneath the words "The Who — Farewell Tour." Another asked the question "Why Limp with the Wimp?" As one delegate told *Toronto Star* columnist Richard Gwyn: "He's a loser. He won't win the election, he looks funny, and anyway I just don't like him." Nevertheless, Clark would top the field on the first ballot, no question about it. Polls gave him from 35 to 40 per cent of the votes.

The only question was how long he could stay on top. Clark would have to pick up new delegates on subsequent ballots, and his ability to grow remained perhaps the biggest question mark of the convention. Without new delegates he would begin to sputter and stall as he approached the finish line. Clark's biggest competitor was not Mulroney or Crosbie but the Anybody-But-Clark factor. Clark had to find another 10 or 15 per cent of the vote before the ABC delegates coalesced into a single bloc, and this would not be easy. On the other hand, the ABC coalition would have to form fast.

The Clark campaign had a sophisticated buddy system to get him those last delegates. Committed Clark delegates paired themselves off with the delegates of other candidates — not a new idea, except that the Clark campaign did it by computer. If a Crombie delegate had recently suffered a marriage separation, that person would be matched up with a Clark buddy who had recently gone through the same experience. The Clark team had the best managers, who were leaving no stone unturned.

Mulroney also drew a boisterous cheer at the candidate introductions. Throughout the convention he attracted the most curiosity and the most enthusiastic supporters. Twenty-seven years earlier Mulroney had worked furiously for the youth forces that had helped make John Diefenbaker the leader. Now, two leaders later, more young Tories backed him than any other candidate. Primed and full of fight, they poured into the convention hall with air-horns, cheered the loudest at every rally, and on pre-arranged signals started "spontaneous" demonstrations for the benefit of the television cameras. The Mulroney youth had their own separate delegate-tracking system. They felt they were part of something important, and nobody worked harder or had more fun.

The candidate who had the spirit of youth on his side held an advantage. Half the Quebec delegates and 35 to 40 per cent of the total youth vote gave Mulroney a strong foundation to build on. Nevertheless signs had started to emerge of a looming ABM movement — Anybody-But-Mulroney. While about half the delegates were ABC, perhaps as many as one-third were ABM. Some did not trust him; others thought he lacked experience. And a not insignificant group viewed him as disloyal.

Most delegates arrived in Ottawa with their minds made up, which made the speeches on Friday less important than the ones of 1976. Mulroney would have to either bring down the house or fall completely flat before he started shifting many votes. Only after the shake-out following the first ballot on Saturday afternoon — when delegates of losing candidates would be looking for alternatives — would the speeches begin to kick in as an important factor.

Mulroney had drawn the lot to speak first, which was both a break and a curse. This time he played it safe with a careful, moderate address that stuck to his campaign theme of tolerance and understanding between haves and have-nots, West and East, and French and English. "With modest exceptions," he said, "we as a party have excelled at winning conventions and losing elections, and we have to ask ourselves why. Our area of weakness in French Canada, time after time, decade after decade, election after election, has staggered this party and debilitated the nation." Citing Sir John A. Macdonald as his authority, he called on delegates to recreate the old grand alliance of West and East. Some of his loudest applause came when he stressed the need for party unity. "We must henceforth live by the party's eleventh commandment, which is: 'Thou shalt never speak ill of another Conservative.'" The speech had not won him any votes, but neither had it lost him any.

Speaking fifth, Clark found himself facing a minor crisis before he uttered his first syllable. His floor demonstration had dragged on too long, draining off valuable minutes of speaking time. He stood helpless behind the podium while down below his organizers frantically shouted and waved their arms in an attempt to herd their group off the floor. The culprit was not bad planning or mismanagement, but a partly though not accidentally blocked exit. John Balkwill, the Kanata dentist who had helped sabotage Clark's leadership as a member of the Tory national executive, had pulled another one of his tricks. As a convention official, Balkwill had brought in extra security people and posted them strategically so as to make it difficult for the Clark demonstration to get off the floor. As a result, Clark started three minutes into his allotted time, but nonetheless he delivered a solid speech that clearly outshone Mulroney's. Looking relaxed and confident despite a severe head cold earlier in the week, Clark sounded statesmanlike and looked prime-ministerial. "We have come a long way together," he told the audience. "The Liberals alone did not just put us at the top of the Gallup poll."

Clark performed well, but not as well as Crosbie who, with nothing to lose, went all out to make up for his earlier gaffe. Already the winner of the workshop sessions, he now rose to the occasion with an "I shall overcome" speech in which he promised to speak French by 1985. He had wrung more enthusiasm out of the arena than any of the eight candidates, and had indisputably won the battle of the speeches. Crosbie's performance threatened to slow down the consolidation of the ABC vote around Mulroney, which for the moment brightened Clark's prospects a little.

At noon the next day, Saturday, party president Peter Elzinga explained the voting procedure over the din of competing chants of "Brian, Brian" and "Joe, Joe" and "Crosbie, Crosbie" and then declared the polls open. The casting of votes went uneventfully and, as planned, ended right at 1 P.M., but the counting of votes crawled along at a snail's pace, seeming to take forever, particularly since the sweltering June weather outside had turned the Ottawa Civic Centre into a steam bath. At times the noise grew deafening as the various camps broke into competing cheers. As the wait grew ever more intolerable, Mulroney kept prodding the supporters sitting in front of him to stand up so he could catch a quick smoke without being caught on national television. It turned out that the party's squeaky-clean voting procedures had caused much of the delay (the RCMP had been asked to sweep the counting room for electronic bugs before the counting could start).

None of the candidates were to know a thing before the official announcement, so nobody would get a head start on canvassing for the next ballot. However, Mulroney would get a tiny signal. If Bernard Roy, his scrutineer, was wearing glasses when he walked onto the stage for the official announcement, it meant that he had won. Shortly before 3 P.M. the counting crew finally trooped onto the stage and Roy emerged without his glasses.

FIRST BALLOT

Clark	1,091	Crombie	116
Mulroney	874	Pocklington	102
Crosbie	639	Gamble	17
Wilson	144	Fraser	5

The results surprised almost nobody, since the candidates had finished pretty much in their expected order. Mulroney had forecast his own vote almost dead on. He had predicted 875 at the start of the convention; with 874, more than 200 votes more than Crosbie, he had reason to feel satisfied.

By contrast Clark — flanked on one side by Maureen and his mother, Grace, and on the other by his brother, Peter, and with his number one adviser Lowell Murray close by — did not look at all happy. He had placed first, but with almost 1,500 votes needed to win it was generally conceded that he needed 1,200 votes on the first ballot in order to crush his opposition and go over the top in two or at most three ballots. At 1,091, more than 100 votes short of his first-ballot target, it simply did not look possible for him to pick up the additional 400 votes. Crosbie's failure to come within striking range of Mulroney compounded Clark's problems, making it look as though the ABC alliance would form around Mulroney faster than expected.

Officially the first ballot did nothing more than bump fringe candidates John Gamble and Neil Fraser out of the race. Unofficially it eliminated everybody except Clark and Mulroney, and left Crosbie clinging to a thread. Any hopes that Wilson, Crombie, and Pocklington had of rising out of the pack as Clark had done in 1976 now lay in ruins. They were simply too far back. All three now had some serious decisions to make. They could hang in until they were officially eliminated in another ballot or two, or they could salvage some influence by dropping out voluntarily in favour of another candidate.

David Crombie needed no time to decide. The pint-sized former mayor of Toronto, who had delivered his convention speech standing on a box to get high enough above the lectern, nursed giant hurts over Clark's failure to make him the political star he felt he deserved to be; now he could never endorse him, although he was closer to Clark philosophically than to any other candidate. With Clark disqualified, Mulroney stood the next-best chance, but he had eliminated himself two nights earlier. On a prearranged visit to Crombie's campaign tent in a downtown Ottawa park that was supposed to be a quiet meeting, Mulroney had brought with him a busload of supporters and a television crew. The commotion not only caught Crombie by surprise, it caused his wife to be inadvertently pushed around, which left him seething and dashed any hope Mulroney had of cementing a deal. Now Crombie was going to nobody. His decision to stay in the race until the bitter end would add another ballot to the vote and give Crosbie more time to gather some momentum, which could only hurt Mulroney. Crosbie's ability to siphon support away from Mulroney was the only silver lining in an otherwise doomsday scenario for Clark.

Peter Pocklington, on the other hand, was looking to make a deal. He had already done Mulroney a lot of good simply by entering the race. Like Mulroney, he too had never run for office, which helped defuse criticism of Mulroney's greatest weakness. But more important, most of Pocklington's 102 delegates came from Clark's home province of Alberta and would have ordinarily gone to Clark, a crucial shortfall that had seriously weakened Clark's prospects coming into the convention. Furthermore, Pocklington's delegates had been recruited through right-wing Amway sales agents, which meant they would never vote for a Red Tory, even one from Alberta. So as

Pocklington decided what to do next, the only thing he had to resolve was whether to support Crosbie or Mulroney.

At the start of the campaign the right-wing Alberta businessman had promised to fall in behind Crosbie if he himself dropped off the ballot. Of the big three candidates Crosbie was the closest to him ideologically. However, Mulroney had been working on Pocklington throughout the campaign, using all his persuasiveness and making reassuring philosophical noises. This wooing process culminated in a personal visit to Pocklington's hotel suite Friday evening, the night before the vote, where he convinced Pocklington to support him if he finished higher than Crosbie on the first ballot. Mulroney could now rightfully expect to see Pocklington arrive in his box in the next ten or fifteen minutes, starting the tide he believed would take him over the top.

Michael Wilson had also decided to drop out and was taking counsel from advisers over where to go. He had always been stead-fastly loyal to Clark, having come into Parliament under him and having been fast-tracked in caucus, most recently replacing Crosbie as the party's finance spokesman. The fact that he was running against Clark had in itself raised some eyebrows. But as the campaign wore on it grew evident that Wilson also harboured some grudges against his leader, most notably Clark's failure to make him minister of finance during his short-lived government.

Bizarre spectacles can unfold at leadership conventions when losing candidates rush their decisions in the pressure of events. Sinclair Stevens had stunned the 1976 convention by going to Clark. This time Wilson and Pocklington astonished the convention by performing an unprecedented act of political collusion. Leaving their respective boxes simultaneously, they rendezvoused in the swarm of bodies on the floor and, after shaking hands, started to walk in Mulroney's direction. Never in convention history had two unsuc-cessful candidates ganged up so brazenly. Dead sure they were coming his way, Mulroney started making room in his box. Then he got a serious shock. Instead of turning towards the steps leading to his section, both candidates continued walking past him, seemingly heading off in Crosbie's direction. "My God," gasped Mila. "Michael's going somewhere else." Mulroney could not believe it. The gang-up of 1976 was happening all over again. It was the worst-case scenario, the prospect he had dreaded most. "I didn't know what the hell was going on," Mulroney would later tell L. Ian MacDonald. The fright lasted only seconds. Wilson and Pocklington turned around and quickly joined Mulroney in his box. It turned out that the whole detour had been a mistake. In the crush, Wilson and Pocklington had lost their way and accidentally overshot the Mulroney stairway.

The Wilson-Pocklington trek had all but sealed Clark's fate. Mulroney had collected a pile of new votes and polarized the convention between him and the embattled Tory leader. Now he had the momentum. As the delegates began lining up to vote on the second ballot, the anti-Clark gang-up seemed sure to gather around him. The gods had reversed the fates of Mulroney and Clark. In 1976, Mulroney had been the one standing still, while Clark came from behind.

SECOND BALLOT

| Clark | 1,085 | Crosbie | 781 |
| Mulroney | 1,021 | Crombie | 67 |

Each camp always greeted the announcement of its vote with a rousing cheer, but the sound coming from the Clark section hardly qualified. The second-ballot numbers had confirmed their worst fears, and, try as they did, they could not hide their disappointment. Worse than simply stalling, Clark had actually dropped six votes. As he watched his lead slowly fade towards defeat, Clark clapped and cheered on his supporters while his aides scrambled in search of a last-minute miracle, but his lieutenants could see no hope.

Although Mulroney had picked up 174 votes, the top decision-makers in the Mulroney camp were not yet celebrating. They had expected Clark to slide, but not so soon, and now they were worried about Clark falling too fast. Because of Crombie's decision to stay in the race, thus forcing an extra round of voting, a complete Clark collapse, which now seemed possible, would pit Mulroney against Crosbie on the final ballot. All their planning was predicated on a Mulroney-Clark showdown — which they knew they could win. The ABC factor alone would take care of it. But against Crosbie, the most popular second-choice candidate, the outcome could be very different.

The second ballot had pumped new hope into the Crosbie supporters and lifted their spirits — almost to the point of giddiness. They knew they could win it all if only they could somehow overtake Clark. Their candidate had jumped 142 votes, giving him practically as much momentum as Mulroney. Crosbie soon got another boost when Crombie, now officially eliminated, marched over to his box. Looking for a way to stem this late tide, the Mulroney camp briefly toyed with the idea of instructing some of their delegates to vote for Clark on the next ballot in order to prop him up, but ultimately rejected this strategy as too risky. The loss of votes might defuse Mulroney's own momentum.

Crosbie was still 240 votes behind Mulroney and would be eliminated in the coming ballot if he did not overtake either Mulroney or Clark. Even a candidate with momentum could not overcome a margin of 240 votes in a single ballot — unless he could somehow get Clark to drop out in his favour. Although bizarre, this thinking made perfect sense to the Crosbie people. If Clark could not win anyway, why shouldn't he support the opponent who had been the more loyal? Only the enmity between Clark and Mulroney made it plausible — at least in the minds of the euphoric Crosbie supporters, who now started buttonholing Clark delegates to come their way. Clark himself received a hard-sell pitch from Newfoundland premier Brian Peckford, who visited his box and implored him to accept the inevitable. "We're going up right now," Peckford pleaded while television cameras watched. "You're not." Meanwhile Crosbie over in his box at the other end of the convention hall was telling reporters, "Joe cannot win. They've got a choice to make. They can choose me. They can choose Mulroney." At this stage only a Crosbie-Clark alliance could derail Mulroney.

It seemed strangely fitting that Clark faced the same kind of dilemma that had confronted Mulroney in 1976, when emissaries from both Wagner and Clark begged him to come their way. Unable to win himself, Mulroney had been the kingmaker who could anoint either Claude Wagner or Joe Clark as the leader of the party. Ultimately he had favoured neither and so had chosen Clark by default. Now, in the same arena seven years later, Clark knew he himself could not win, but he possessed the power to choose between Crosbie and Mulroney. He had maintained his poise and dignity all afternoon while watching his leadership slip from his grasp. With Peckford hounding him to his face, he merely shook his head and said no, leaving the Newfoundland premier to trudge back to the Crosbie box empty-handed. By doing nothing he had chosen Mulroney as his successor.

Although victory now seemed assured, Mulroney felt too apprehensive to relax. While the third-ballot votes were being counted, he retreated to the hockey dressing room for his third shower and shirt change of the afternoon. Meanwhile back at his suite in the Château Laurier, Pat MacAdam was making endless trips to the hotel ice machine with a plastic bucket to cool down a case of Dom Pérignon in the bathtub. His victory preparations were interrupted by a frenzied phone call from Sonny Mass, a member of Mulroney's Laval network. Mass was calling from the dressing room in the convention centre. Without so much as a hello, he told MacAdam to get two pairs of Jockey shorts out of the dresser in Mulroney's bedroom and bring them over in a cab on the double. While showering, Mulroney had left the curtain slightly open and had thoroughly soaked his briefs. So as the rest of the convention awaited the results of the third ballot, Mulroney was trapped below without underwear. Fifteen minutes later, with the crisis resolved, Mulroney was back in his box to await the results of the vote.

THIRD BALLOT

Clark	1,058
Mulroney	1,036
Crosbie	858

Although Mulroney had picked up a scant fifteen votes, Clark had fallen back another twenty-seven, leaving the two virtually in a dead heat. Crosbie had gained 104, but now automatically dropped off the ballot. Finally Mulroney and Clark would face each other head to head, something that had never happened before, not in their student days, and not in 1976. Now the Conservative Party would have to choose one or the other.

John Crosbie, the sharp-tongued Newfoundlander who might have been king had he been bilingual, had become the potential kingmaker. He and his aides retreated to a dressing room, escorted through the crowds by police, and emerged fifteen minutes later to do exactly what Clark had done an hour earlier and what Mulroney had done seven years before: he announced he was supporting nobody. "I think it's best for the future of the party and the unity of the party if I keep my counsel," he explained, adding that the turning point came when Clark refused to come his way. How Mulroney and Clark carved up his 858 votes would decide the winner. Both their organizations invaded the Crosbie section like vultures scavenging a fresh carcass. One quick glance at the Crosbie section told it all. Mulroney's signs were popping up twice as fast as Clark's.

With the votes all in, Clark and Mulroney could do nothing but wait for the final announcement. The afternoon had given way to evening but the sweltering heat refused to quit. As everyone waited, Clark got up and with Maureen beside him spontaneously walked towards Mulroney's box for a symbolic handshake. The scene on the floor was so crowded that a TV commentator remarked that it looked like Clark was running the gauntlet. It was an extraordinary gesture from a candidate who had every reason to sink into a bitter sulk, for in approximately thirty minutes his leadership ambitions would be wiped out. Once again he was showing remarkable character and class. But, befitting his image as the leader who couldn't shoot straight, he had neglected to phone ahead and arrived on the outskirts of his opponent's territory only to discover that Mulroney wasn't there. Mulroney had been watching this little scene unfold on television from his dressing room while writing his victory speech. He had a towel wrapped around his waist after his fourth shower of the day. Hastily he dispatched Mila to intercept Clark. When Joe and Mila met, they kissed and exchanged a few words before he and Maureen returned to their end of the rink. When Mulroney emerged a few minutes later onto the convention floor, he and Mila headed straight for the Clark section, then paused to wait for Clark and Maureen to come out to meet them halfway. There, surrounded by a crushing crowd, the rivals shook hands and congratulated each other on a well-fought campaign.

Back in his seat following the ceremonial handshake, Mulroney surrounded himself with some of the old friends who had helped bring him here. Sam Wakim, Terry McCann, and Fred Doucet from St. FX; Michel Cogger, Jean Bazin, and Michael Meighen from Laval; David Angus from his lawyer days; Rodrigue Pageau and Roger Nantel from the dump-Clark campaign. (Pat MacAdam was back at the hotel and Bernard Roy was in the counting room. Peter White and Frank Moores were on the floor.) Seated behind him were scores of others. They were a mere sliver of the political network that had helped him reach this moment. A historic announcement was imminent, and he wanted them at his side. At 9:20 P.M. the vote-counting team trooped onto the stage for the last time, and Bernard Roy was finally wearing his glasses.

"Ladies and gentlemen," convention co-chair Pat Carney proclaimed, "we have a winner." Giving the results in alphabetical order she announced: "Joe Clark, 1,325." The arena broke into a deafening roar — almost all coming from the Mulroney section. For the first time all day Mulroney supporters cheered the Clark vote. "Brian Mulroney, 1,584." Mulroney's box erupted again. This time Mulroney stood up and raised his arms in triumph, gratefully acknowledging the hundreds of delegates who had helped him fulfil his long dream. Shaking hands with every buddy within reach, he was now the leader of the Progressive Conservative Party of Canada.

He and Mila plunged into the crowd and began working their way towards the podium. Meanwhile Clark, in shirtsleeves, gave a small, fatalistic shake of his head. For several seconds he sat impassive and unblinking with one hand cupped under his chin and the other resting on his knee. If only 130 of the 2,909 voting delegates had voted differently then he, not Mulroney, would be saluting the crowd. It had been that close. Nobody in the Clark box breathed a word until Clark broke the silence. "That's it," he finally said, first to his mother, then again to Maureen. A minute later he and Maureen stood up and made their way up front to join the other defeated candidates on stage. Meanwhile many of his supporters sobbed, and some shouted, "We love you, Joe."

As the runner-up, it was up to Clark to move the ritual motion to make the vote unanimous. "Let me begin by congratulating Brian Mulroney for a strong, successful campaign," he led off, his voice hoarse and at one point cracking. He then went on to plead for all party members to rally behind the new leader and pledged himself to do the same. "Our party has made its choice," he said. "The party has a duty to make sure that choice is supported in every corner of the land. From my heart . . . I intend to ensure that happens." He likened the Conservative Party to a family, "a family with occasional differences, but as a family we have to work together." Afterwards party president Peter Elzinga commended Clark for his "courage and compassion" and arch-opponent David Crombie walked over with a big smile and planted a kiss on Clark's cheek. Then House leader Erik Nielsen, the party's interim leader for the last four months, beckoned Mulroney on stage. After a divisive battle, the push was on for party unity.

Mulroney and Mila had stopped in the middle of the crowd while Clark spoke. Now they worked their way to the podium. The stage was crowded — with Clark and Maureen, and all the other candidates as well as Elzinga and Nielsen. Mulroney shook hands with everybody as the audience applauded. But the biggest applause and the loudest cheers broke out when Mulroney and Clark shook hands at centre stage. Then Mulroney kissed Maureen on both cheeks, her face frozen into a half-smile that hid her true feelings. For once, delegates from both camps happened to be cheering together.

"Chers amis, dear friends," Mulroney began his acceptance speech, directing his first words to Clark, who "has served this party with dignity, honour, and courage." The arena broke out in sustained applause, and Clark, never so popular as in defeat, walked from the end of the stage to shake Mulroney's hand again. "I salute him as a friend and as a colleague-in-arms and as a distinguished and most thoughtful Canadian," Mulroney continued. Clark, he added, must continue to play a major and prominent role in the party leadership. "I count on your support and loyalty at all times as we build a new country and a new government."

During the rest of his nineteen-minute speech the crowd repeatedly interrupted him with applause. His voice, even more hoarse than Clark's, almost disappeared several times, but he positively glowed with poise and self-possession. Near the end, he changed gears slightly to thank all the members of his family — including his mother, Irene — who were in the hall. Then he turned to his wife, who throughout the speech had been standing demurely just one step away from the podium and slightly behind him. "I want to thank one person very much," he continued. "Mila, who has made such a contribution to my life and to the campaign." As the crowd once again erupted into cheers Mila waved and smiled and blew a kiss but kept her place.

"And now we go on to the business of building a country that is more generous, more tolerant — tolerance — more equitable and more just," Mulroney went on. "This is our obligation to Canada, to provide the basis for an opposition which will command the respect — as ours does now in the growing confidence of the Canadian people. We reach out to Canadians and together — *ensemble* — together, we're going to build a brand-new party and a brand-new country."

CHAPTER TWENTY-ONE

INSIDE THE TENT

"NOT BAD FOR A COUPLE of raggedy-assed kids from eastern Nova Scotia," Mulroney quipped hoarsely as he gave Pat MacAdam a big bear-hug back in his Gold Key suite at the Château Laurier. A small group had gathered in his fourth-floor rooms to share the moment of his triumph: Mila, MacAdam and his fiancée, Janet Terris, Senator Guy Charbonneau and his wife, Yolande, Sam Wakim and his wife, Marty, and Michael McSweeney, the family friend who had acted as his campaign aide. As well, columnist Allan Fotheringham showed up with date Janis Johnson. (Fotheringham had been the first journalist to tout Mulroney as a potential leader during the 1976 campaign and now claimed — only half-jokingly — that he had discovered him.) While the Dom Pérignon that had been cooling in the bathtub was being served, the victor himself sipped his standard soda water and coffee, betraying few signs of having an hour earlier fulfilled the ambition of a lifetime. He was quiet and business-like, already planning the next day's events. (Actually the planning had started in the car that carried him from the convention centre to the Château Laurier — Mulroney was on the car telephone the whole way.) The entire room, although festive, remained strangely subdued.

After about half an hour, long enough to change his shirt and mingle a little, Mulroney made his farewells as he and Mila prepared to leave this small celebration for a much larger and more raucous one down below. Nearly a thousand of his supporters had packed into a rented ballroom on the main floor of the hotel, the excess spilling out into the hallway. As they waited for their new leader they kept breaking into chants of "Bri-an, Bri-an." But before going down to celebrate with the masses, Mulroney placed a telephone call to Baie Comeau, to his old boyhood friend Gilles Lachance, his earliest tutor in the French language. In his moment of victory he had not forgotten his roots.

When Mulroney finally appeared, he was mobbed on sight and had to inch his way to the podium. Once again poised and in command, the perfect picture of a triumphant candidate, he thanked them all for their support, apologized for being late, and, in a raspy voice now threatening to disappear completely, invited them to drink another beer to their success. He grabbed a microphone and hoarsely crooned a few numbers with the band while Mila banged a tambourine. Then he plunged back into the crowd to shake the hands of the people who had worked and voted to make him leader.

In another rented room in the same hotel, Joe Clark stood behind a microphone and spoke to a very different throng of loyalists. Although they were surrounded by a band, balloons, and lots of free booze, the accoutrements of victory were altogether out of place. What was supposed to have been a celebration had become a wake. The Clark volunteers had believed in their cause and worked their hearts out, and now they felt angry and bitter. A few of them had booed earlier when Mulroney's picture flashed up on the giant television screen replaying highlights from the convention.

Clark, always proper and formal on stage, especially in circumstances such as this, tried to console his followers. He began somewhat woodenly, thanking them for their efforts and, as he had done a couple of hours earlier, pledging his loyalty to the new leader. The mere mention of Mulroney's name drew a fresh chorus of boos, but Clark instantly cut it off. "I meant what I said tonight about party unity," he admonished them. "If there is anyone in this party who knows about the need to support the party leader, I do. And I expect all of us to extend to Brian the kind of loyalty that —" He never finished his sentence. Chants of "Joe, Joe, Joe" drowned him out. Once these had died down he promised not to tolerate recriminations against any supporter of his for working on the losing side. Now as he continued, his stiffness started to bend. He paraphrased Diefenbaker's famous words following his loss to Dalton Camp seventeen years earlier. He would "lie down and bleed a little," he said, but he would not quit. "I'll be back in the House of Commons. . . . I'll be back fighting for the interests of the people of Canada. . . . I love this party deeply, and I love this country deeply." Nobody had ever seen him publicly reveal his emotions so openly before. His supporters allowed him to go no further by drowning him out again with chants of "Joe, Joe, Joe."

Mulroney and Mila mingled with their supporters into the early morning hours. When they finally returned to their suite around 2 A.M., they found the party still going strong. It continued for another hour.

Later that morning, at 7:45, Pat MacAdam arrived back at Mulroney's suite to find his boss had long been up and ready to go. He had already made several phone calls, one of them rousing a startled Ray Hnatyshyn from his sleep. It was the last thing Hnatyshyn, the MP for Saskatoon West and a Clark loyalist, had expected. Mulroney said the party had to go forward and he wanted him on his team. A long, full day lay ahead, but Mulroney would squeeze in a phone call or two whenever he could catch a moment, for the purpose of touching base with Tories across the party spectrum and beginning the process of reconciliation. MacAdam took him to an 8:30 A.M. taping of CTV's *Question Period*, which Mulroney had consented to as a thank-you to the show's host, Bruce Phillips. (Phillips had invited him to the parliamentary press gallery dinner following his 1976 defeat and had always treated him fairly.) Later that morning he met the Conservative Party's national executive —

its board of directors — for the first time as party leader. It would be almost noon before he returned to the Château Laurier, and by then a mob of reporters was waiting for him in the parking lot.

Since it happened to be his daughter Caroline's ninth birthday, lunch was a private party including his other children, Ben (now seven) and Mark (now four), his mother, sisters Olive, Peggy, Doreen, and Barbara, brother Gary, and Mila's parents. After lunch, his exhaustion began to show through, but he had no time for rest, not even for a quick nap. Too much needed to be done. "Get Mazankowski on the phone," he told MacAdam. "What?" asked MacAdam, remembering a poignant scene from the day before when a television camera had caught MPs Don Mazankowski, Erik Nielsen, and Bill McKnight huddled in the football stadium above the arena, apparently looking for a last-minute way to derail the Mulroney Express. Not sure the call was a good idea, MacAdam hesitated. "Get Mazankowski on the phone," Mulroney barked, somewhat impatiently. A few minutes later Mazankowski was tracked down in his office on Parliament Hill. "I need you," Mulroney told him. Next was Bill McKnight, another of the stop-Mulroney plotters. Earlier that morning Mulroney had already met Nielsen at the national executive meeting and convinced him to stay on as interim leader of the opposition. Most of his phoning that afternoon would be devoted to healing rifts and building bridges.

Actually the phone calls were a sideline. The afternoon was mainly devoted to meeting the top five defeated candidates. Over the next few hours Peter Pocklington, John Crosbie, David Crombie, and Michael Wilson all walked down the long corridor leading to Mulroney's hotel suite, each for a private twenty-minute session. The only major candidate who did not show up was Joe Clark. In the tradition of the gracious winner, Mulroney was going to him. So at the end of the afternoon he left the hotel and had Michael McSweeney chauffeur him to Stornoway, the residence of the leader of the opposition, which was soon to become his new home. Joe and Maureen were spending the day at home catching up on playtime with six-year-old Catherine, their only child, and visiting with Clark's mother, Grace, who had come in from High River for the convention. Clark was going back to being a regular MP without official residence, without chauffeur, without car, without extra office staff, and with a salary cut from $105,600 to $67,100. As if to emphasize his misfortune, a fire earlier in the day had gutted his leadership campaign headquarters a few miles away.

Mulroney had carefully withheld the timing of the visit from reporters in order to spare Clark unnecessary publicity. The defeated former leader was already down; he did not need a clutter of microphones and television cameras on his front lawn. So no members of the press waited in ambush when Mulroney and McSweeney pulled into the driveway of 541 Acacia Avenue in Rockcliffe Park, the residential village within Ottawa favoured by the diplomatic, political, and civil service élite. While McSweeney stayed in another room, Mulroney and Clark sat down for a private chat. They had come a long way since that first meeting as eighteen-year-olds at a PC Student Federation convention in Ottawa in 1958.

Too much had happened in the ensuing twenty-five years for the encounter to be easy. Harsh charges from a bitterly fought campaign still rang in the ears of both men. Mulroney's shadowy but undeniable role in helping destabilize Clark's leadership remained a raw sore for the loser, the latest chapter in a long rivalry. But beyond everything else they both coveted a prize that could not be shared. If not today, then in the next few days they would have to discuss messy details of the transfer, such as when Clark was moving out of Stornoway so Mulroney could plan his move in. None of Mulroney's quick wit nor his fabled charm could help him here. In fact, the less he said the better.

How the tables had turned. In retrospect, losing the leadership in 1976 had turned out to be a blessing while winning had become a curse. Clark, who had turned forty-four one week earlier, had been elected Conservative leader at least five years too soon. Of the many misfortunes that had befallen Clark, that was perhaps the greatest.

The job did not forgive mistakes, and by the time he'd moulded himself into a true leader, it was too late. In later years Mulroney would acknowledge that he had not been ready in 1976 either. Luckily, his defeat had given him a period of grace, an opportunity to become older, wiser (and richer), to get his personal life in order and to mature as a human being. He had survived the biggest crisis of his life and emerged tougher and more resilient. Mulroney could never have imagined it a few years earlier, but losing in 1976 was the best thing that could have happened to him.

What took place inside that room at Stornoway would for the most part stay private. Only the two men alone facing each other and their pasts knew what was said. Later neither would talk much about it. However, a few scraps soon filtered out. For one thing, Mulroney told Clark not to hurry in vacating Stornoway, and to keep the limousine until September. (Mulroney would soon be leaving town to fight a by-election and would need neither.) For the rest of the summer Clark could keep all the perks that went with being leader of the opposition. Mulroney wanted his defeated adversary to go out with dignity, partly to soothe his own conscience and partly out of respect for the office. Whatever he thought of Clark, he was a former prime minister, and former prime ministers deserved respect.

They also discussed what role Clark, as an ex-leader, would play in the party under Mulroney, and here too the new leader was accommodating. Clark made it clear he did not want to be a parliamentary critic for any particular government department, but preferred to take some time off to think about his future. The two agreed that he would pull together some recommendations for the caucus on international arms control and world peace initiatives, a handy arrangement that suited them both. The assignment gave Clark something to do and a ticket out of the country, so he could relax and recuperate and consider his next move. More than anything he needed time off, and he needed to be out of the spotlight.

After an hour they reappeared from their private chat, both playing the roles of perfectly chivalrous gentlemen, both thankful this awkward episode was over. The next time Mulroney came to Stornoway he would be moving in.

The next morning, Monday, June 13 — Mulroney's first business day on Parliament Hill as Conservative leader — the two former rivals walked together into the theatre of the National Press Building for a joint press conference. As if the last two years had never happened, they told reporters about how they would work together to elect a Conservative government. "Brian and I are old friends," Clark said. "I look forward to serving with him on the floor of the House of Commons. I look forward to playing an active and prominent role in Parliament and in the country on behalf of the Progressive Conservative Party, at Brian's side and in the interest of electing Brian Mulroney as prime minister of Canada. Exactly what that role will be we haven't defined." For his part Mulroney referred to Clark as "my friend Joe"; he even called Maureen his friend, which took political hypocrisy to new heights since the two despised each other with a visceral and unconcealed hatred. The last time Mulroney and Clark had pretended to be old friends was at the infamous Ritz Summit.

After the press conference Clark and Mulroney walked side by side to a special Tory caucus meeting, beaming ear to ear as photographers snapped pictures. That afternoon, Mulroney and his whole family sat in the gallery of the House of Commons while Erik Nielsen, the interim leader of the opposition, stood up on the floor to introduce him. The entire chamber rose to its feet and applauded.

Joe Clark's introduction as Conservative leader seven years earlier had been far different. He had simply moved up a couple of parliamentary rows to his new pew, directly across the aisle from Pierre Trudeau. After receiving some words of congratulation, he had started firing off his first questions. That Mulroney had to be introduced from the gallery underlined his most glaring weakness: he was not yet the leader of the opposition, a title that could be conferred only on an elected member of Parliament. So his first order of business was to get himself a seat in the House of Commons. Where he would run had been a subject of talk weeks before he won the convention.

Mulroney wanted to run in Quebec, but that was out of the question. The Tories had only one seat in the province, and it belonged to Roch LaSalle, a Clark partisan openly antagonistic to Mulroney. The other seventy-four seats all belonged to Liberal MPs who would not likely cut short their political careers to help the new Tory leader.

The first Conservative to offer Mulroney his seat was Gordon Towers, the MP from Red Deer and one of the Breakfast Club regulars. He had won his central Alberta constituency by more than twenty-five thousand votes in 1980, making it one of the safest Tory ridings in the country. It would be a painless route into Parliament but would also put Mulroney right next door to Clark's riding of Yellowhead. Only a bit slower in offering Mulroney his seat was Elmer MacKay, whose early support had helped turn the tide in the Tory caucus. MacKay represented the Nova Scotia riding of Central Nova, which came within forty miles of Antigonish, the home of St. FX, the root of one of Mulroney's primary networks and the birthplace of his dream to become Conservative leader. Mulroney had other choices too, but none he considered seriously. Although MacKay had won by fewer than five thousand votes, Mulroney's heart made Central Nova the choice. Nobody could say he had not maintained his local connections, having sat on St. FX's board of governors and been given an honorary doctorate of laws from the institution; a couple of years earlier he had spearheaded the campaign to raise money for new campus buildings. He had set out to raise $7 million and ended up with $11 million worth of pledges. Many of his old St. FX friends were now community leaders in Pictou County, which was part of the riding, so it was almost like going home.

While Mulroney waited for Prime Minister Trudeau to call a by-election in Central Nova, he stayed in Ottawa and lived comfortably in his luxurious suite in the Château Laurier. He had a huge living room, a dining room, two bedrooms, two baths, and a fireplace.

ABOVE: After bitterly fighting each other for delegates, and often stooping to the corruption and dirty politics of an earlier era, Mulroney and Clark engaged in a ceremonial handshake shortly before the results of the 1983 convention's final ballot were announced. (*Canapress Photo Service / Bregg*)

RIGHT: Leader at last, Mulroney exulted in the announcement that declared him the winner over Clark by a margin of a few hundred votes. (*Canapress Photo Service / Deryk*)

Up on stage, Maureen McTeer, the wife of the loser, congratulated the
wife of the winner. Maureen and Mila disliked each other
as much as their husbands did. *(The Gazette)*

Joe Clark proved to be much more gracious in defeat in 1983 than Mul-
roney had been in 1976, and immediately rallied to Mulroney's side.
On the Monday morning after his loss, he affably escorted
Mulroney to his first caucus meeting as Tory leader.

(Canapress Photo Service / Bregg)

Not an MP, Mulroney could not take a seat in Parliament and was introduced to the House of Commons from the Speaker's Gallery.
(Canapress Photo Service)

RIGHT: Mulroney's first priority as new leader was to get himself into Parliament. He began campaigning in a by-election in Central Nova, in Nova Scotia. After ruminating over his loss for several weeks in Europe, Clark came to New Glasgow to help Mulroney get out the vote. (*New Glasgow News*)

BOTTOM: On the day of his by-election, Mulroney spent time relaxing with two of his closest friends, Fred Doucet (left) and Pat MacAdam, both of whom he would name as political aides in the following days. (*Canapress Photo Service*)

As a new MP, Mulroney was formally escorted into the House of Commons by Tory veterans George Hees (left) and Erik Nielsen, as Prime Minister Trudeau leads his Liberal caucus in non-partisan applause. *(Canapress Photo Service)*

Within twenty-four hours of Mulroney's induction as an MP, Trudeau confronted Mulroney with the troublesome Manitoba language issue in hopes of splitting Tory ranks. Following his maiden speech three weeks later, Mulroney was congratulated by his own MPs after putting the Tory position on record. He managed to avoid party disunity while taking a strong stand. *(Canapress Photo Service / Mitchell)*

Days before John Turner, the new prime minister, called the 1984 election, Mulroney and Mila campaigned in Alberta. Ever since rededicating himself in 1979 to becoming prime minister, Mulroney had accepted Mila as his full political partner and his equal in life, and together they formed an awesome team. At the grassroots level, Mila usually campaigned more effectively than he did. *(Canapress Photo Service / Ball)*

On the campaign bus during the 1984 election, Mulroney talks with Pat MacAdam (seated with his elbow against the window), Toronto lawyer Brian Armstrong (behind MacAdam), Charley McMillan (on Mulroney's left), and Bill Fox, far right. *(Pat MacAdam)*

LEFT: Flanked by Terry Mc-Cann on his right and Charley McMillan and Roger Nantel on his left, Mulroney watched the election results in the former mill manager's house on the top of the hill in Baie Comeau. *(Canapress Photo Service / Grant)*

BELOW: Later that evening Mulroney changed into his customary dark blue suit and along with Mila visited the local hockey arena to salute his triumph. A noisy, adoring crowd of six thousand kept him from speaking for seven minutes. *(Canapress Photo Service / Chartrand)*

Here in his living room he sat down and resigned his corporate directorships, about a dozen in all, including big companies like Provigo and the Canadian Imperial Bank of Commerce. "Another ten grand here, ten grand there," he sighed as he wrote out the letters. In the next few days Mulroney rented an adjoining suite and set up an office where two young women hired at party expense replied to all the well-wishers' letters and telegrams. He expressly refused to settle into a Parliament Hill office until he was elected, telling people he had no right to be there until he had earned proper admittance.

On a beautiful, sunny Saturday two weeks after Mulroney's big win in Ottawa, Michel Cogger staged a victory party at his plush summer home in Knowlton, Quebec. However, early in the morning vandals had slashed his big tent on the lawn and dumped a load of horse manure into his swimming pool. Too late to clean the pool, Cogger pulled a tarpaulin over it and went ahead with the party.

Walter Wolf, an Austrian-born naturalized Canadian who had helped finance the dump-Clark movement, arrived at the controls of his personal black helicopter. Wolf was a jetsetting millionaire in his mid-forties who had made a fortune in oil and construction. Cogger had been his lawyer since 1974, and in the fall of 1982 had invested $500,000 on Wolf's behalf in East Coast Energy, a highly speculative oil exploration company of which Mulroney's old friend from St. FX, Fred Doucet, was one of the principals. (Mulroney himself had put in $5,000, and a number of other prominent Tories also bought shares.) However, by the spring of 1983 Mulroney wanted to distance himself from Wolf, who had publicly acknowledged having given $25,000 to help bring down Clark. And although Cogger stopped acting as Wolf's lawyer soon after the leadership win, his close association with the controversial businessman would make him a political liability.

Moments later Mulroney and Mila arrived, also by helicopter, courtesy of Jacques Blouin, the president of a group of helicopter companies who also happened to be the president of the PC riding association for Manicouagan, the Quebec constituency that included

Baie Comeau. About two hundred guests greeted Mulroney's dramatic arrival on that Saint-Jean-Baptiste weekend. In a brief speech that reprised his favourite lines from the leadership campaign, he jokingly promised half of them patronage appointments. So-and-so would be a judge on the Supreme Court, so-and-so a senator, and somebody else a cabinet minister, and on he went.

A week after the Cogger party Prime Minister Trudeau called two by-elections for August 29, one in Mission–Port Moody, British Columbia, and the other in Central Nova. The Liberals were eager to get the neophyte leader into the House of Commons, where they figured he would prove an easy target. Mulroney soon departed for Nova Scotia to start campaigning. After winning the nomination unopposed on July 12, he stayed in the riding for the whole fifty-five-day campaign, except for one quick trip to British Columbia to help Tory candidate Gerry St. Germain in his by-election. Elmer MacKay, his "chief adviser" in Central Nova, fixed him and his family up in old Pictou Lodge, a pleasant seaside resort outside the town of Pictou. A series of log cabins with a big dining room and a dance hall, the lodge had once been a vacation spot for rich Americans but had fallen out of favour and been allowed to deteriorate. It was now being restored. Mulroney and Mila set up housekeeping in a three-bedroom cabin with a fireplace and kitchen. They were later joined by Pat MacAdam, who became his personal campaign aide. The kids moved into the cabin next door with Michael McSweeney, who was now like a sixth member of the household. With no housekeeping help, and with Mulroney barely capable of boiling water, Mila did the cooking.

On a clear day Mulroney could see right across to Prince Edward Island. It was midsummer and the circumstances were idyllic, but he was not on holiday. Taking nothing for granted, he started each day at 7:00 with a visit to a local factory gate and then kept on the move all day, attending coffee parties, going door to door, and occasionally even trekking from farm to farm. It was a typical constituency campaign. "It's great to be home again," he would say, thereby letting residents know he had once lived in the vicinity. In the course of his stumping he met a lot of people. One person who befriended him was the local provincial MLA for Pictou East, Donald Cameron, who lent Mulroney his own campaign manager. Although former hockey great Bobby Orr made an appearance on his behalf, Mulroney relied primarily on MacKay's local organization, not wanting to be seen parachuting people in. Even old college friend Fred Doucet, a long-time resident of next-door Antigonish and a hub in his St. FX network, was kept in the background, although he did work on the campaign. (Doucet was now director of development at St. FX; Mulroney had engineered the promotion when the school had asked him, and he agreed, to spearhead the school's recent fundraising drive.)

The Liberals had originally talked about letting Mulroney run unopposed, but the NDP would have nothing to do with it. After deciding to run a candidate after all, the Liberals went flat out to deal the new Tory leader an embarrassing defeat. They nominated Alvin Sinclair, a fifty-one-year-old high school principal who had already run twice against MacKay, and sent in a wave of eleven cabinet ministers to help his campaign, including Jean Chrétien.

While Mulroney campaigned in Central Nova, Joe Clark returned from Europe and wrote his report on world disarmament, a report that never would be made public. He still showed utter loyalty to Mulroney and breathed not a word of bitterness. Where others would have fallen into a deep and vengeful depression, he continued to behave with a generosity and good temper that could only be described as remarkable. His psychological toughness amazed his harshest critics and even his admirers. Few saw how much he was hurting inside. Most of his detractors now acknowledged that, image to the contrary, he was no weakling. In the aftermath of defeat, the notion of Joe Clark as wimp died a quiet and unlamented death. Now, in one of his lowest moments, Clark enjoyed greater goodwill than ever before. In defeat he had gained the respect that had always eluded him as party leader.

Although outwardly he had borne up magnificently, he had not survived unscathed. When he had left for Europe he had gone alone, while Maureen took her own trip to the United States. Although they continued to share the same house, raised their daughter jointly, and always publicly supported each other's goals, they would henceforth lead separate lives.

In Central Nova, Mulroney continued to put in long days as the August 29 election date approached. Elmer MacKay had given him a tough schedule. Weary to the bone, he would return to Pictou Lodge around 11:00 each night, sometimes without having changed his shirt even once, and then would cap his day by turning on the CBC Television news.

In the final days of the campaign Mulroney would often turn to Pat MacAdam after Knowlton Nash had signed off for *The National* and tell him to get out "the book." The book was a spiral-bound steno notebook containing candidates for his shadow cabinet. The two of them would then spend hours going over the names and the positions, trying to figure who would go where. Credentials were taken into account, but so were geography, seniority, and religion. They also spent time working on his office staff. It was during these late-night planning sessions that Mulroney decided to make Fred Doucet his chief of staff, a choice that would become highly contentious. Doucet, a career academic administrator of no particular distinction, did not know the players on Parliament Hill and lacked experience with parliamentary machinery. Many, including MacAdam, questioned his suitability. However, Mulroney insisted on his old friend. His second in command had to be someone fiercely loyal, someone he knew he could trust. Soon after Clark's defeat in the 1980 federal election, when Mulroney was already beginning to think about another run at the leadership, he told Peter White that he would have to meet Doucet. "Let me tell you something about Fred," Mulroney continued, then pointed out of his IOC office window. "If I asked Fred to move that skyscraper two inches by tomorrow morning, Fred would find a way to do it."

Deputy chief of staff went to Lee Richardson, a Westerner from

Peter Lougheed's entourage. Elmer MacKay would become his senior adviser; Charley McMillan, a university teacher and policy adviser during the campaign who had helped out in 1976, would be his special assistant for policy and research; MacAdam himself would be a special assistant for caucus liaison. Others who would be joining his office were Bill Pristanski, executive assistant (English); Hubert Pichet, executive assistant (French); and Ian Anderson, press secretary; as well as Tom Van Dusen, John Diefenbaker's former executive assistant, special assistant (legislative). Notably absent from the list of key staff members was Michel Cogger, whose association with Walter Wolf had now come back to haunt him. Although Cogger would be given the title of chief counsel to the leader, he would be consigned to an office across the street in the Wellington Block, where the less important members of the opposition leader's staff worked, and would find himself increasingly shut out of Mulroney's inner councils.

Mulroney's organizers knew he would win easily but had not figured on amassing 60 per cent of the popular vote on August 29. Mulroney outpolled Liberal candidate Alvin Sinclair by eleven thousand votes — more than double MacKay's 1980 margin — and the other candidates forfeited their deposits. The next morning Mulroney, his family, and his political entourage drove to Halifax to catch the afternoon flight to Ottawa. Having finally made it into Parliament, he could assume his new position. A car came with the job, and one of Mulroney's first acts as leader of the opposition was to call "Brother Bert," his old friend Bert Lavoie from St. FX, now a successful GM dealer in Sainte-Eustache, northwest of Montreal. Brother Bert leased him a dark blue four-door Buick sedan.

Now that he had finally taken physical possession of Joe Clark's old corner office on the fourth floor of the Centre Block, the same office where he had visited Diefenbaker as a student, and truly deserved the title of Leader of Her Majesty's Loyal Opposition, Mulroney's first task was to unite the party behind him, a job that would require all his considerable talents for conciliation. He had already applied first aid, but he had to go beyond that and heal the wounds, or else be disabled by the same internal fighting that had crippled Clark, Stanfield, and Diefenbaker. The Tory caucus had a tradition of undermining its leaders. On the other hand, if he brought his fractured troops together and welded them into a cohesive force, he had a good chance of becoming prime minister. Given the widespread disenchantment with the long-ruling Liberals, he could found a Tory dynasty.

One of Mulroney's first telephone calls as opposition leader that long Labour Day weekend of 1983 went to the man whose behaviour had hurt him the most in 1976, Lowell Murray. Murray had stuck with Clark to the very end, and soon after Clark lost, he sent in a letter resigning as Conservative Party campaign chairman. Mulroney tracked him down in a Halifax hospital, where his newborn son was undergoing major surgery of the esophagus, and invited the surprised Murray to join MP Marcel Lambert in heading up a caucus task force on industrial productivity, one of five special committees created to examine issues from youth to tax simplification. The nature of the assignment did not matter nearly as much as the request itself. The proper signals had been sent. Murray accepted the job. The Murray rapprochement showed that Mulroney wanted to forgive and forget.

Next on the list was Roch LaSalle, who had once vowed never to cooperate with Mulroney. The following weekend Mulroney dropped in at a corn roast in LaSalle's riding. LaSalle quickly came onside. "We want everybody inside the tent pissing out," Mulroney would say, paraphrasing Lyndon Johnson's oft-repeated line. "We don't want people outside pissing in."

Finally Mulroney invited his entire troupe of MPs, along with their spouses and staffs, to spend a late summer weekend in the resort town of Mont-Sainte-Marie, Quebec, about seventy miles north of Ottawa. Here in shirtsleeves they hammered away at party policy, with every caucus member getting a say. The event — including a big social on Saturday night — went over big and would be repeated again in the spring. Mulroney would never allow himself to forget that the caucus had ultimately caused Joe Clark's demise; he was determined not to let it happen to him. Every year he would hold a black-tie dinner for all the Tory MPs in Parliament Hill's Hall of Honour, and there would be plenty of parties at Stornoway for smaller groups. In later years, when his popularity would plummet far lower than Diefenbaker's, Stanfield's, or Clark's ever had, his caucus would stick behind him and his leadership would remain strong. Almost every MP was assigned some kind of job, with the main purpose of giving everyone the sense of being involved and being valued. It seemed he could not set up enough task forces or commission enough studies. In all, 87 of 103 Tory MPs had special responsibilities. Clark, who had started lecturing part-time at York University in Toronto, was left out at his own request.

On September 12, exactly two weeks after winning Central Nova, Mulroney made his début in Parliament. Wearing a dark suit and a blue-and-white carnation, he was formally led down the centre aisle of the House of Commons, as is the custom for new MPs. The galleries were packed and the media out in force as he took his rightful seat opposite Prime Minister Trudeau. Clark, in grey pinstripes, watched from several seats away on the front bench. Both Trudeau and NDP leader Ed Broadbent welcomed Mulroney with courteous speeches, although both got in some friendly digs. Trudeau mentioned the procession of Tory leaders that had passed through Parliament during his time as an MP, and Broadbent could not help but note Mulroney's lack of policy orientation despite his long association with the former NDP leader in Quebec, the late Robert Cliche.

Looking perfectly at home in his new surroundings, Mulroney responded by praising the prime minister as a man of great accomplishment and distinction, and then launched a few digs of his own. He welcomed Trudeau back from Greece, and he welcomed the cabinet back from Central Nova. "The Liberal candidate in Central Nova," he continued, "persistently referred to a candidate from Quebec who did not live in his riding, but lived in a million-dollar house rent-free — and I defended you, sir, regularly." Trudeau smiled throughout Mulroney's performance, clearly enjoying himself. Before sitting down Mulroney facetiously urged the prime minister not to quit despite urgings from portions of his own benches. Then the House got back to business.

Mulroney had clearly won the day. "Mulroney a Big Hit in Commons Debut," read the headline in the *Ottawa Citizen*. "Mulroney Outbarbs PM During Commons Debut" was the headline in Allan Fotheringham's column. Worry about Mulroney's lack of parliamentary experience was temporarily put to rest. However, the true test was yet to come.

In his opening remarks Mulroney spoke warmly of Trudeau. "I was honoured by the thoughtfulness and the generosity of his words today," he told Parliament, then quickly added, "I wait with bated breath for tomorrow." His wariness about what lay in store for him proved to be well founded. The next afternoon, Mulroney's second day in the House, the Liberals laid a trap during question period. Robert Bockstael, the Liberal MP from St. Boniface, rose with a question. "Madam Speaker," the Manitoba MP began, "my question is directed to the Right Honourable Prime Minister." It had to do with delivering French-language services in Manitoba, a highly controversial issue dating back to the birth of the province. As part of the terms for entering Confederation in 1870, Manitoba gave French the same official status as English, but in later years reneged on its commitment. A 1979 Supreme Court decision had ordered the return of institutional bilingualism, and Howard Pawley, the NDP premier, was earnestly trying to comply. But he found himself blockaded by the Tories, the official opposition in the Manitoba legislature. The federal government had already gone on record as supporting the Manitoba government, and now Bockstael was mischievously asking Trudeau whether Ottawa planned "to reinforce its support" and, if so, in what manner.

The question was a plant. Although directed to the prime minister, the intended target was the new leader of the opposition, whose caucus was deeply split over the issue. Although the Conservative Party was officially committed to bilingualism, many individual Tory

MPs strongly opposed it, especially those from Manitoba. Trudeau replied that he was thinking perhaps of proposing an all-party resolution of support for the Manitoba government and would seek an appointment with the leader of the opposition to discuss the wording, thus throwing the issue squarely into Mulroney's lap. Trudeau knew he could rally his caucus to support bilingualism at any time — and he also knew that Mulroney could not. Bilingualism had always divided and tortured the Conservatives. If one issue could tear the party apart, this was it. The Liberals had set the stage for a showdown over the most divisive issue they could find.

Mulroney found himself in a tight spot. By supporting the Liberal resolution he would alienate the provincial party in Manitoba and parts of his own caucus in Ottawa. Within hours some of his own MPs had publicly advocated keeping out of the issue. Already the fragile caucus unity he had forged threatened to disintegrate. But not to support Trudeau would be to betray his belief in bilingualism, one of his very few bedrock convictions. And he would be seriously injuring if not killing his hopes of a Quebec breakthrough, the political goal he most cherished. Whichever way he went spelled trouble. "Here I am," Mulroney later told L. Ian MacDonald, "not twenty-four hours in the place, I don't even know my way to the can, and the Liberals play their trump."

Mulroney would have about three weeks to decide how to handle the coming parliamentary resolution. The Liberals, chortling with delight, half expected the Tory caucus to come apart. It was hard even for Tories to see how he would stickhandle his way through the trap. Mulroney worried and waited for the Liberals to table their time bomb.

The Liberals expected a parliamentary rookie like Mulroney to stumble quickly upon entering the House of Commons, just as Clark had done. The proceedings of the House of Commons were a game unlike any other. Only nine days after his début the inevitable happened. During the daily question period Mulroney rose, wearing his hat as the MP for Central Nova, to ask Minister of Transport Lloyd Axworthy whether he would renew the subsidies for Maritime freight rates. "Can the minister give his assurances to the House — I hope that he can — that there will be no cut-back of any kind of subsidies going to producers, the small and medium-sized businessmen, in the Maritime provinces? Can he give us that assurance today, please."

The most surprised person in the chamber was Axworthy, who could hardly conceal his delight at being handed such a gift. (Pat MacAdam, Mulroney's caucus liaison officer, would later liken it to a college student writing home for ten dollars and getting back twenty.) Chiding Mulroney for asking the question seven hours too late, he gleefully revealed that earlier in the morning he had announced in Moncton the renewal of the subsidies, to the tune of $67 million. Mulroney had committed one of the biggest mistakes an MP could make. The basic rule of question period, as defined by John Diefenbaker himself, is that nobody should ask a question without knowing the answer in advance. Parliamentary tacticians used question period not to draw out information but to embarrass the government. It was a forty-five-minute daily tug-of-war between government and opposition for public favour. Instead of embarrassing the government, Mulroney had embarrassed himself. It was difficult to imagine Joe Clark ever making such a slip.

After Axworthy's put-down, Mulroney should have cut his losses and let matters drop. Instead he bounced back to his feet to counterattack. Thanking the government for "the smallest of blessings," he said that Maritime producers needed much more than meagre subsidies. From here on in, Axworthy merely toyed with him, like a cat playing with a condemned mouse. "The Honourable Leader of the Opposition may ask, 'What's $67 million?'" Axworthy declared. "We happen to think it is a lot of money." And then he needled Mulroney for also wanting to cut the deficit. Again the opposition leader rose to retaliate, and again Axworthy slapped him down, citing his quick conversion from somebody who wanted to cut government spending to somebody who wanted to spend more. When Axworthy triumphantly sat down for the final time, the Liberal backbenchers had broken into laughter and were whooping a chorus of "Joe, Joe" while others were shouting over to Mulroney for "More, more." Mulroney had been thoroughly trounced. It was the worst blunder he would ever make from the opposition benches.

Actually, Mulroney's office had known about Axworthy's announcement, but the information had not gotten through. And for that, Fred Doucet shouldered the blame. Doucet oozed loyalty from every pore and would do whatever Mulroney asked, but he had no experience with House of Commons strategy. Tory veterans would soon start complaining that Doucet had no business being chief of staff. This would be the first sign that packing his staff with old buddies was a mistake, although it would take many more foul-ups for Mulroney to learn the lesson that the people who helped him achieve high office were not necessarily the best ones to keep him there.

Despite the odd miscue, Mulroney quickly settled into the House of Commons and soon dispelled the notion that he was a novice. People who had made much of his lack of parliamentary experience did not know about his stellar past in Model Parliaments and college debates. Looking confident and assured, and as quick on his feet as ever, he looked as though he had been in the place for years, matching the best parliamentary performers blow for blow. In fact, Mulroney could be too comfortable and too quick. On his second day in the House, Minister of Health Monique Bégin, a lady of considerable girth, heckled him with the word "Accouchez!" — meaning literally "Give birth" but idiomatically "Get to the point." Without a pause Mulroney shouted back: "Ça s'en vient, Monique. En parlant d'accouchement, Monique, ça s'en vient?" ("It's coming, Monique. Speaking of childbirth, Monique, is it on the way?") The retort caused an immediate flap. The House of Commons had few limits, but joking about personal matters such as another MP's weight problem was a no-no. Compounding the *faux pas*, Mulroney had spoken directly to Bégin by name rather than addressing the Speaker and referring to her as the Honourable Minister of Health and Welfare, as the House rules require.

Mulroney later tried to explain away his gaffe by telling people that earlier in the day Bégin had said "Accouchez" to him when he pressed her on her health care legislation on the way into question period; now he was merely using it back. But Bégin refuted the story. "Without wanting to dwell on the impropriety of the incident, I'd just like to say since the House opened I've never met with the leader of the opposition coming into question period," she told the Commons. "I accept his apologies but I also like the truth." Three days later House leader Erik Nielsen apologized to the House on Mulroney's behalf. By then Mulroney had already changed the official printed version in Hansard to "I can assure the Hon. Minister of National Health and Welfare that I will get there in due time."

While Mulroney and his staff waited apprehensively for the Liberals to table their resolution on the protection of French in Manitoba, the new opposition leader settled into a routine more punishing than any job he'd held before. After waking up around 6:30 he would start to read the morning papers — at least five — and would scan other articles, reading in detail the ones that struck him as important. At about 7:30 he would head to the shower; he'd be dressed and out the door by 8:30. Sometimes an early meeting would bring him into work by 8:00.

Once on the Hill, his attention turned to administrative matters, particularly committee meetings and policy items. Early on he had appointed a raft of caucus committees; now he insisted on following their progress, studying their interim reports, and plotting out the implications. For the first time in his life he devoted serious time to policy generation — when the election call came, he would be ready. At IOC he had been famous for delegating, but now he could not let go even of the tiniest details and seemed to be overextending himself, to the point that his office staff worried that he was driving himself into the ground.

Policy work consumed a good part of his morning. The rest of it went to getting ready for question period, which began at around 2:15. A team of advisers, both staff members and MPs, briefed him every day. Sometimes the preparation for question period would tie up half his schedule. Mulroney told his aides that the chief parliamentary purpose of the leader of the opposition was to exploit question period. As opposition leader he usually asked the first set of questions, setting the theme of the Tories' daily attack. The entire exercise lasted little more than forty-five minutes; his opening questions — usually one question followed by two supplementaries — lasted only a few minutes. But often his few minutes would form the footage on the evening television news. Question period was only a tiny slice of parliamentary life, but it happened to be the one the country got to see each evening.

After question period ended, around 3 P.M., he returned to his office upstairs and for the next hour met with individual caucus members to iron out the inevitable personnel problems. Then he met other people in the hour that followed.

Whenever a speaking engagement drew near — which seemed almost every day — his already tight schedule got thrown into a shambles. Mulroney took speeches seriously and spent hours preparing them — too much time, some would say. In theory speech-writers were supposed to save him hours of preparation, but in reality it did not work that way. Each speech went through four or five drafts, whether or not it was considered important. Since he was putting himself on the record with his views, he gave every speech equal attention. Every word had to convey his thoughts exactly. By the time his script had cleared all the hurdles, he had practically written it himself.

Each day he tried to get out of the office and home to Stornoway by 6 P.M. for dinner, committing the next two hours to his family. But by 8 — especially if a speech beckoned — he would move to the study and buckle down until midnight. If he had two or three speeches to work on at once, he became even more intense. To let off steam he would interrupt his labours by picking up his favourite instrument to call old buddies. He still loved to network; it was his only hobby, and the evening was his favourite time to phone around.

In early October Prime Minister Trudeau finally tabled his proposed multi-party resolution in support of French-language rights in Manitoba. It invited the government and legislature of Manitoba "to take action as expeditiously as possible in order to fulfil their constitutional obligation and protect effectively the rights of the French-speaking minority of the province." Mulroney and Trudeau had twice met privately to work out the content. Trudeau continued to treat his parliamentary opponent with respect — in private the two got on well — and Mulroney talked the PM into forgoing a recorded vote and allowing only the party leaders to speak. The arrangement allowed Mulroney's Manitoba MPs to avoid taking a public stand, which gave him the break he needed. When he got back to his office after their deal, Mulroney couldn't help chuckling at having outfoxed Trudeau.

On October 6 Trudeau led the one-day debate with a truly impressive speech, in which he brilliantly laid out the logic of his case. Then Mulroney, in what was his first formal address in the Commons, rose to state the Tory position. He had spent far more time than usual preparing his remarks and, except for some notes from Lowell Murray, had not used a speech-writer. Mulroney did not speak from the heart on many political issues, but on bilingualism he did. Some would later call the speech his finest.

"The purpose of this resolution is one which has touched the soul of Canada for decades," he said after a few introductory remarks. "When I was very young in Baie Comeau, we were taught at the local school the sad story about some of our francophone brothers outside of Quebec. Even at that young age, we knew that an injustice had been committed in Manitoba. We did not know why or how, but we knew that certain basic rules — which we Quebeckers, anglophones as well as francophones, could benefit from — had been broken. A francophone minority, which had enjoyed an historical protection of its language in Manitoba, was suddenly cut off — amputated — from this guarantee which was so vital. We knew also, Madam Speaker, without being able to really evaluate its consequences, the less than glorious role some of our Quebec leaders had played in the outcome of this very painful situation."

Invoking the name of the late Robert Cliche, "a great humanist," and expressing sympathy for the problems of the people of Manitoba, he declared pride in announcing the unanimous support of his party for the resolution. Since there was no recorded vote — it was a resolution and not a bill — and only the three party leaders would speak, he had persuaded his Manitoba MPs to remain silent, and by so doing he had met the government's challenge.

Mulroney had won over his Manitoba caucus through a combination of flattery and threats. He strongly hinted that any MP who crossed him on this issue would very shortly be sitting as an independent. Mulroney could afford to be tough with his dissidents. The caucus above all respected a leader who was a winner, and Mulroney already very much looked like one. In September the Tories had reached a landmark 62 per cent in the Gallup poll, giving them an unprecedented 39-point lead over the second-place Liberals.

"This resolution is about fairness," Mulroney concluded twenty minutes later. "It is about decency. It is an invitation for cooperation and understanding. It speaks to the finest qualities in this nation. I say to you on behalf of my entire party on this or any great issue that affects this nation that we stand before you, Madam Speaker, united in the sunlight, ready to work for a better Canada." When he sat down, Joe Clark and other MPs left their seats to shake his hand. He had made a great speech and scored a great parliamentary victory — standing on principle and still keeping his party together.

In early December the Liberals once again tried to squeeze the Tories over what looked like a good campaign issue, this time medicare. Minister of Health Monique Bégin, no more a friend of Mulroney's now than in September when he had made fun of her weight, tabled the new Canada Health Act, which would impose penalties on provinces that tolerated user fees and extra-billing by doctors. The banning of extra-billing was popular with the general public, but the right wing of the Tory caucus strongly opposed it, as did most of the Tory premiers. Mulroney wanted to keep his party harmonious, but he was even more determined not to be caught on the wrong side of so important an issue. Otherwise the Liberals would be able to cast themselves as defenders of the health care system against the invading Tories.

Once again he cajoled his caucus into supporting a measure that a large part of it did not like. As he had done as a young lawyer at the Picard hearings back in 1966, exhorting shipowners and stevedore contractors to stick together against the longshoremen's union, Mulroney told his MPs they had to stay together in the face of the Liberal challenge. If they didn't, they would all go down together. It was caucus division, he told them, that had kept the party out of power all these years (the party's current popularity in the polls didn't hurt his case). "I must say I'm surprised," Bégin said after Mulroney announced Tory support for speedy passage of the bill. Neither she nor Trudeau had expected him to unite his caucus on an issue so contentious and so intrusive on provincial jurisdiction.

Early in the new year, the pesky Manitoba language problem flared up again. Much to Mulroney's chagrin, the Conservative members of the Manitoba legislature had begun filibustering the Pawley government's French-language-rights bill, resorting to a series of bell-ringing and walk-out tactics to block approval. To make matters worse, a couple of Mulroney's own MPs, Dan McKenzie and Ron Stewart, had gotten into the act by launching a trust fund to help a federal civil servant in Manitoba fight the bill. Mulroney privately told them he would not tolerate any dissent on this issue, and once again he pulled his caucus into line. "I told these guys that it's my way or the way out," Mulroney told journalist Jean Pelletier at the time, in an interview for *Maclean's* magazine. "I have not been elected just to earn instant popularity today or tomorrow. I am here, among other things, to protect the fundamental rights of the Canadian people and to provide my party with a vision of the country that will reflect at all times a faithful image of my thinking and my heritage." Pelletier could tell that Mulroney cared deeply about the issue. "Hell, what are these guys thinking about?" Mulroney said of his caucus. "That's what being an opposition party for too long does to you, you tend to confuse prejudice and policies. Bilingualism is the goddamn law of the land. We are either for it or against it, and as long as I'm the leader we are for it!"

As tough and uncompromising as he was being, Mulroney also showed some empathy for the view of his Manitoba MPs. "They don't understand that we are all hostages of our environment and prisoners of our childhood," he said, sounding like a true small-l liberal. "I don't see the history of Canada in the same way as somebody from the north of Manitoba. They have lived in a different historical current than mine. So I can understand very well some of the reactions I witness in western Canada. I understand — but I cannot share them because I witness them with a totally different appreciation."

On February 23, 1984, the eve of the last day in Parliament before a midwinter break, Mulroney flew to Toronto on party business. Then he planned to fly directly to West Palm Beach for a holiday with Mila and the kids. However, shortly after 6 P.M. a hand-delivered letter from Trudeau arrived at Mulroney's Parliament Hill office, informing him that the PM would be introducing another resolution the next day. Trudeau explained that since the Manitoba government appeared ready to prorogue the provincial legislature — and thereby let the bilingualism bill die — he wanted Parliament to pass an immediate resolution urging the Manitoba legislature to vote on its bill "without further delay." Trudeau's letter inquired whether the Conservatives would support his resolution, and asked for a reply the next morning.

Promptly postponing his Florida trip, Mulroney caught a late flight back to Ottawa to deal with this latest language crisis. When he arrived in his Centre Block office around 11:00, most of his advisers were already waiting for him — Fred Doucet, Lee Richardson, Pat MacAdam, Ian Anderson, Elmer MacKay, Charley McMillan, Bill Pristanski, Tom Van Dusen, and Hubert Pichet — and they all wore sober looks. So far the rebellious MPs had grudgingly kept quiet, but this time it would be tougher keeping them in line. For months they had been hearing from irate constituents who didn't want to spend millions of dollars institutionalizing French in their province.

Mulroney took off his overcoat as he strode to his desk. First he asked for a cup of coffee; then he asked for a summary of the situation. As caucus liaison officer, MacAdam gave him a breakdown of the whereabouts of the five Manitoba MPs. Jake Epp was on a trip. Charlie Mayer and Jack Murta were in their ridings. Lee Park would be leaving shortly for a NATO meeting, and Dan McKenzie was about to go down south for the parliamentary break. Other aides gave short reports of their own. After a while MacAdam slipped out of the meeting and around midnight called all five Manitoba MPs. He told Charlie Mayer and Jack Murta to stay in their ridings, that there was no need for them to return to Ottawa. He gave Dan McKenzie good wishes for a nice trip south. Jake Epp was told not to break off his trip. Lee Park, who was flying out of Mirabel the next evening, was persuaded to leave Ottawa in the morning, before the House met. The meeting broke up around midnight and the aides all scattered, leaving Mulroney alone at his desk as he started to write out in longhand the speech he would deliver the next day.

"I acknowledge, Mr. Speaker, that the view in some areas of western Canada is different," he told Parliament. "It is neither pernicious nor benighted. It is simply different. It is different because the evolution of western Canada did not in some very important respects parallel the evolution in the east."

The resolution sailed through Parliament without the presence of his Manitoba MPs. It was a combination of idealism and pragmatism — he had stuck in principle to his belief in bilingualism but had survived the experience by being flexible. Despite the Commons resolution, the Pawley government prorogued the legislature and let the bill die, but Mulroney had escaped another potential disaster.

After Parliament had recessed, three of the five Manitoba Tories — Jack Murta, Lee Park, and Charlie Mayer — went public, saying the controversy was a matter for the province to settle on its own. Jake Epp could not be reached for comment. Dan McKenzie later issued a statement saying that bilingualism threatened to turn anglophones into second-class citizens. But Mulroney did not discipline them. The following week he announced he was willing to tolerate a "modest divergence of view" among his caucus members on French-language rights in Manitoba now that an all-party resolution on the question had passed in the House of Commons. He said the important thing was that the party had supported the resolution. Although Mulroney did it partly with mirrors, he had pulled the Tory caucus together in a way not seen since the early days of Diefenbaker.

With the Manitoba language issue resolved yet again, Mulroney left for his delayed Florida vacation. The break proved restful but did not come without some real agony, for while there he tackled one of the most vexing challenges of his life: without warning, he stopped smoking, and he did it as quickly and with as little explanation as when he had quit drinking nearly five years earlier. Smoking had become a liability for politicians in the 1980s. The only heavy smoker who had flourished in recent memory was René Lévesque, whose cigarettes seemed almost an extension of his personality. Lévesque aside, smoking conveyed the wrong image, particularly in a leader.

Living without cigarettes proved more difficult than going without a drink. Mulroney's tobacco addiction went back more than a quarter of a century; he had smoked heavily since his teens. During the leadership campaign he had gone through two or three packs of filter-tip du Mauriers a day. It would take Mulroney many months to wean himself off his prescription of Nicorette chewing gum.

Mulroney had settled down in West Palm Beach for only a few days when some big news arrived from Ottawa — news that would profoundly affect his political future. Pierre Trudeau, after taking a walk through a big snowstorm and pondering his alternatives, announced he was stepping down as prime minister and Liberal leader. "I went to see if there were any signs of my destiny in the sky," he quipped. "There weren't. There were just snowflakes."

The turn of events, long expected but still dramatic, held both good and bad omens for Mulroney. With Trudeau gone, the Conservative Party finally might win some seats in Quebec. However, with Trudeau out of the way, the Liberal Party was also shedding an unpopular leader, the man most responsible for lifting the Tories so high in the Gallup poll. For the next several months the country would be watching the race to become Trudeau's successor, and Mulroney knew that very soon his massive lead in the polls would start to shrink.

Sixteen days later, on March 16, John Turner emerged from political retirement to jump into the leadership contest. Seven candidates would ultimately join the campaign, but only Turner and Jean Chrétien had a real shot at winning, and even Chrétien faced fairly long odds. From the outset the race looked to be a Turner coronation, a prospect that frightened some members of the Tory caucus. Some Tories believed Turner would sweep the country, but Mulroney preferred the candidate from Bay Street to the "p'tit gars" from Shawinigan. He knew that Chrétien would be much harder to fight in Quebec. With Turner as Liberal leader, Quebeckers for the first time in history would choose between a native-son Tory leader and a Liberal leader from English Canada.

Turner had another weakness that Mulroney and many others soon saw: he had been out of politics too long. Eight years as a fat-cat lawyer in Toronto had made him rusty, but even Mulroney, who knew something about the ill effects of a political lay-off, did not realize how rusty Turner had become until he flubbed the Manitoba language issue on the day he announced his candidacy. "On the Manitoba question," Turner told reporters at his first press conference, "I support the spirit of the parliamentary resolution, but I think we have to recognize that what is at issue here is a provincial initiative, and that a solution will have to be provincial, and I would hope that it would be resolved by the political process and not by the judicial process."

The Liberal frontrunner had just done Mulroney a big favour. By soft-pedalling French-language rights in Manitoba, Turner was swinging the Quebec door open to the Conservative Party, and Mulroney moved quickly to keep it ajar. The next day he attacked Turner for deserting Liberal principles out of "political greed." Forces within the Liberal Party quickly coerced Turner into agreeing that Ottawa must intervene "at times" to protect minority language rights, but the tide had already turned. "When Mr. Turner announced his candidacy," Mulroney exclaimed on Montreal radio station CJAD, "he was asked what set him apart from Mr. Mulroney and he said: 'Why, my experience.' And if by experience you mean declaring your candidacy on a Friday, disavowing positions in regard to protection of minority rights on Saturday, repudiating decades of Liberal policy by Monday, reversing yourself by Tuesday, and swallowing yourself whole by Thursday — if that's experience, I'll have none of it." Now the infighting Liberals were on the defensive over the Manitoba language issue, and the Tories had become the defenders of bilingualism. It was a remarkable turnaround.

Mulroney had always demanded high performance from his staff, and as the Liberal leadership fight unfolded and the inevitable election drew nearer, he grew even fussier and more exacting, especially with his speeches. "Now don't tell me there's five hundred thousand people unemployed," he would say. "Translate that into something. Tell me that there are four thousand unemployed in Hamilton." Or he would say: "Don't tell me the debt is $33 billion a year. Tell me what that means in terms of $200 in the pocket of every man, woman, and child in Canada." He liked to popularize statistics. "Give me facts that can sing," he would say. "Make it relevant. Simplify it." Everything had to be made simpler, but at the same time his tendency towards hyperbole often collided with his desire for simplicity, leaving his speech-writers baffled. Economic speeches underwent few revisions because he did not know the material so well, but purely political speeches would get torn apart and reconstructed phrase by phrase in the search for relevance, poetry, and drama. Sometimes the final revisions did not come back from word processing until 3 or 4 A.M., putting big demands on his staff. Many of these long hours and extraordinary efforts were pushed onto a new cadre in his office, young speech-writers like Jon Johnson, Peter Burn, Ian Shugart, Geoff Norquay, and Jocelyne Côté-O'Hara. On the issues and substance of government, it was not the old boys from his network who carried the load but these bright newcomers.

Hard as he pushed his staff, as difficult as he could be to work for, and as little as he realized what hell he often put them through, nobody really complained. Mulroney genuinely appreciated their efforts, and he always pushed himself even harder. For him the "singularity of purpose" — as one staffer put it — of winning the coming election took precedence over all the other considerations. In building up to the next campaign, nothing was going to distract him from his goal of winning.

The job of leader of the opposition had already begun to change him the way nothing else ever had, affecting some of the basic elements of his character. He became more disciplined and more serious. He apportioned his time carefully and became more circumspect in dealing with people — even his old buddies. He still called old friends regularly, and he liked to think things between them were just like the old days, but they were not. He was the leader of a political party and everything had to fit around his schedule. There was simply no time for the kind of casual get-togethers with old friends that had been so important.

One thing that had not changed was his dreadful eating habits. Food had never interested him; meals had always been a social tool or a distraction. He still ate candy to sustain himself (licorice was his favourite), and when travelling always had candy bars waiting for him in his hotel room. He continued to drink too much coffee. If it weren't for his ritual dinner with Mila and the kids, he might never have eaten a proper meal.

In the late winter of 1984, Joe Clark was still frequently absent from Parliament, causing many people to wonder whether he would run in the next election. Those Clark loyalists who looked for signals from their former leader as to how they should behave still saw nothing other than total loyalty to Mulroney. Clark continued to astound everyone in the aftermath of his defeat. Even close friends never heard him take any cheap shots at the new leader, never saw any evidence of bitterness. Clark truly believed the party had the right to depose him, even if he did not like the decision. His idealistic outlook helped him live with what had happened.

After leaving Stornoway, Clark and Maureen had bought a stucco house a few blocks away, but they were not happy there and soon regretted the move. Before long they settled across the river in Aylmer, Quebec. For a long time Clark and Mulroney had almost no contact, but gradually they started improving their relationship, at least professionally.

As the Liberal leadership campaign heated up, the national media soon forgot about the Tories. Shortly after returning from his Florida vacation in early March, Mulroney took to the road and began criss-crossing the country from Salmon Arm, B.C., to Charlottetown, campaigning at every stop as if fighting an election. It was the boonie strategy revisited. While the Liberal leadership race preoccupied the national press, Mulroney scored big in small centres and regional media coverage. It was a dress rehearsal for the coming campaign, a chance to work out the glitches and fine-tune the machinery.

Sooner or later his road show would have to come to Manitoba and face the language issue head-on. Having taken a stand on principle, Mulroney had decided to enter the lion's den itself. He expected to be heckled and jeered, but he was determined to confront his critics in a public meeting in Winnipeg. However, he had trouble screwing up his resolve to carry through. He knew it was a risk. An ugly incident could badly stain his image just before an election. On the other hand a courageous performance would enhance his image as a strong leader. Either way such a confrontation would help shape his public identity.

On March 29, after procrastinating for weeks, Mulroney finally went to Winnipeg, appearing before a spillover crowd. Tensions were high in the hall; members of the RCMP watched the audience because of death threats, and a sprinkling of Tories in the crowd wore buttons saying "No Official Bilingualism." He was so nervous that soon after he began to speak, he lost his place in the twenty-page text. "It's coming, I'm getting there," he laughed as he fumbled through his papers. As he pleaded for French-language rights in the province, calling on Manitobans to help him begin a "new dialogue of understanding" among Canadians, he was several times interrupted by shouts of "Go home to frog country!" and "Get out of here!" Occasionally he seemed shaken by the ugliness of it all, but apart from his early fumble he plodded on to the end without fudging or backing down.

"It is my fundamental belief, as it was Sir John A. Macdonald's, that real national unity will never be achieved until French-speaking Canadians living outside Quebec enjoy no less rights than English-speaking Canadians in my native province," he said. "That was Macdonald's message 114 years ago. It is my message tonight. I am not here to order or direct anyone along this road. I am here to encourage and persuade." Once, when the heckling from the rear became especially loud, he shouted back, "I'm not going to sell Sir John A. Macdonald down the river, not here, not today." Mulroney had showed true grit in confronting his opponents. Even reporters who did not like him gave him full marks for guts.

From his hotel suite the next morning Mulroney anxiously chased down every bit of reaction he could find, wanting to know what everyone thought. But most of all he was dying to know how his speech had played in Quebec. The word coming back made him feel ten feet tall. Quebec — the entire province, it seemed — had loved it and loved him. In fact, right across the country the reaction was tremendous. The Manitoba language issue had established his authority over caucus and made him look like a good political manager while dividing the Liberals and opening the door to Quebec. Much more he could not ask. As Mulroney had done before — and would do again — he had taken a crisis and turned it into a triumph.

CHAPTER TWENTY-TWO

THE FRUITS

OF AMBITION

WHENEVER BRIAN MULRONEY grew uneasy, one could literally see the tension overtake his body. His posture stiffened, his back and shoulders grew rigid, and his shoulders lifted, as if hydraulically, to obscure at least part of the back of his neck. His entire backside from neck to buttocks became an unpliable sheet of unimould, while his arms, hanging straight down, swung stiffly as if from hinges at his shoulders. With half his moving parts locked in a state of semi-paralysis, he walked with a slight waddle. The overall effect looked unnatural and definitely uncomfortable.

The dramatic political events of the spring of 1984 caused the back of Mulroney's neck to virtually disappear. In the course of a few weeks the party's two-and-a-half-year reign atop the Gallup poll collapsed. With John Turner poised to inherit Trudeau's mantle, the Liberals suddenly rebounded into public favour. The turnaround stunned even the most optimistic Grits. In March the Tories still sat comfortably on top by a whopping 54 per cent to 32 per cent; in April they were trailing 46 to 40. In the history of Canadian polling no one had ever witnessed such a collapse. At this point Mulroney could only hope the abrupt reversal was an unexplainable blip — but he grew increasingly worried.

The next poll, in May, with the Liberal convention only a month away, made him and his staff more nervous still. The Liberals' lead seemed to be holding firm. Now hard-won caucus solidarity began to show early signs of stress: the front-line troops knew their jobs grew more tenuous with every drop in the Gallup poll. Swallowing hard over the Manitoba language issue was not nearly as difficult as watching the party's standing sink through the floor. Some questioned Mulroney's absence from the national media during the Liberal leadership race. The leader assured them the polls were just a blip, patiently explained his boonie strategy, and sent every caucus member copies of the laudatory clippings from the local press. His soothing words calmed the alarmist mood, but the polls had to change — and soon. Mulroney sounded confident, but his body language told a different story.

Mulroney could not help but wonder whether he was about to suffer the same fate as the unlucky Robert Stanfield in the spring of 1968. He too had been leading the polls since becoming Tory leader (in September 1967); then the Liberal Party replaced Lester Pearson with Pierre Trudeau, and the rest was painful history that every Tory knew by heart. John Turner was no Pierre Trudeau, but the Liberals seemed to have a way of making history repeat itself.

Turner coasted to an easy second-ballot victory at the Liberal convention on June 16, then began to wrestle with the mechanics of putting together a cabinet and assuming office. Finally Mulroney made his first counter-move, flying to Washington to meet President Reagan in the Rose Garden. The Liberal Party had basked in four months of saturation coverage from the national media. A trip to Washington would get Mulroney back into the news and depict him as a statesman. He also wanted to dispel the popular impression that the Tories could not organize a two-car funeral, a myth created by Joe Clark's fumble-strewn world tour in 1979. Mulroney and Reagan, two charming Irishmen, instantly hit it off.

Mulroney had hardly arrived back in Canada when, on June 30, 1984, John Napier Turner took the oath of office as Canada's seventeenth prime minister. But when he would call an election was anybody's guess. The Liberals, already into the fifth year of their term, could technically hold off until early 1985 but would almost certainly send the country to the polls in 1984. It seemed likely that Turner would either drop the writ immediately or wait until fall. Although neither prospect now looked particularly good for the Tories, Mulroney was betting on a fall election.

Having finally reached 24 Sussex Drive, Turner was not without problems of his own. Trudeau, whom he despised and who had little use for him, had left behind a logistical mess. In two weeks the Queen would begin a thirteen-day visit to Canada; on September 9 the Pope would arrive for an eleven-day national tour. Both leaders had a policy of avoiding any move that could be construed as interference in a country's affairs, so coming during an election campaign seemed out of the question. And there wasn't enough time for Turner to shoe-horn an election in between their visits. Yet delaying either tour for an election carried serious political risk. Nonetheless a couple of Mulroney aides speculated that Turner would postpone the Queen's visit and call a quick election. "Turner is smarter than that," Mulroney said. "He's got the Queen coming and he's got the Pope coming, and he's going to wrap one arm around each, and he's going to walk up and down the country for three months, and then he's going to call an election." He was absolutely certain the vote would be put off until the fall.

Adding to Turner's problems, he had inherited one of the most worn-out and tired cabinets anybody could remember, a weakness he compounded by reappointing it with only minimal changes. With each of the three party leaders struggling to position himself as the representative of change, Turner had unwisely sent a message that he belonged to the same old Liberal gang. It was his first stumble, and more were to come.

A few days after Turner took office, Mulroney left for a tour of the

West in another effort to get the Tories back in the news. "If I were John Turner I would have appointed the cabinet he named at midnight, not during the day," he told an audience in Weyburn, Saskatchewan. "Here we have the same faces that destroyed the Canadian economy standing again beside the prime minister." All through his Western tour he perfected a string of jokes about the "new" Turner cabinet.

The only thing the new prime minister could take solace in was his continued buoyancy in the Gallup poll. A week after taking office he had boosted his lead over the Tories to 11 points, 49 per cent to 38 per cent, with a paltry 11 per cent for the NDP. Another poll by another company (Thompson and Lightstone Co. Ltd.) produced almost identical results. Clearly his surge was not a blip. For Mulroney the news could not have been worse. Although the pollsters warned that the Liberal lead was soft, it looked as though a quick election could crush the Tories for another four years and shatter his carefully crafted image as a winner. Even Mulroney's normally indomitable confidence began to fray at the edges.

Mulroney happened to be in Regina when the early-July Gallup poll appeared, and reporters immediately pressed him for reaction. It meant nothing, he insisted, because it followed on the heels of the Liberal convention. "Hang onto your hat," he warned, "you're going to see a campaign like you haven't seen in twenty-five years" — referring to Diefenbaker's campaign of 1957. Whenever Mulroney travelled west he started talking about John Diefenbaker and his vision of "One Canada" — and now he did it again. "In 1957," Mulroney said, "with the odds stacked against him, facing a government that had been in office for two decades, John Diefenbaker set off from Saskatchewan in the face of adverse polls and he carried a message of hope and renewal across the country, which on the 10th of June, 1957, made him prime minister and the Progressive Conservatives the new government of Canada. I set off from Saskatchewan this morning in similar circumstances, and I'm going to carry that same message of hope and renewal and courage across Canada."

While Mulroney stumped for support in the West, Turner had made up his mind to call an early election. He flew to London to talk the Queen into going through with her visit as planned, but she could not be persuaded. Turner returned to Ottawa late on Sunday, July 8, and the next day called a general election for September 4. At the same time he announced patronage appointments for nineteen former Liberal ministers and MPs, the most controversial one being the appointment of MP Bryce Mackasey as ambassador to Portugal. Most of the appointments really belonged to Trudeau, but in order to preserve the Liberal majority in the House of Commons, Turner made them on Trudeau's behalf after Parliament was dissolved. Coming on the heels of his old-look cabinet, his patronage appointments made him look like Trudeau's puppet.

Mulroney immediately pounced. "It's something out of an Edward G. Robinson movie," he said at a press conference an hour later. "You know, the boys cuttin' up the cash. There's not a Grit left in this town. They've all gone to Grit heaven." He also promptly challenged Turner to meet him in at least two nationally televised debates — one in English and one in French. "We're going in as the underdog, but we'll close that gap," Mulroney promised.

In Turner's patronage appointments Mulroney recognized a gift-horse political issue, and immediately he jumped onto the offensive. He accused the Liberals of having "dishonoured the system" and vowed, "It shall never, never happen again under a Conservative government." The campaign, Mulroney insisted, was about change, and Turner had now shown himself to be part of the old gang. The government, he declared, had grown old and needed to be thrown out. The reporters who watched him could tell he was striking a chord with the public.

A few days before the election call, friends of Joe Clark threw a party to celebrate his forty-fifth birthday. Clark dutifully attended but clearly was not enjoying himself, and when he departed he left his gifts behind. (Only months later did he bother to pick them up.) His birthday fell within a week of the first anniversary of his loss of the leadership. Although he always remained gracious and never whispered a word of grievance, he still had not bounced back to his old self. It seemed he was having more trouble than he let on coming to terms with his defeat.

During the leadership campaign he had privately mused that it would be a mistake for him to stay in Ottawa if he lost. Perhaps he would join an international organization or maybe edit a small-town newspaper as his father had done in High River. His reasoning made sense. A former prime minister in his forties could do a lot better than languish in the political shadows. However, despite rumours that he had been offered six-figure jobs with at least two insurance companies, among other options, Clark had decided to stay in politics.

Clark's decision reminded one political watcher of the story of the kid who ran away from home to join the circus. He was assigned all the unpleasant tasks, like cleaning out the elephant cages. When his worried parents finally found him, they begged him to come home where he was loved and wanted. Malnourished and covered in manure, the boy replied tearfully: "You mean, leave showbiz?" Tough as politics could be, Clark could never be an insurance executive or go into rural exile. He simply could not bring himself to leave politics. It was the only thing he had done in his career, and perhaps the only thing he knew how to do. So after Turner called the election, Mulroney's list of 282 Tory candidates included the name of Charles Joseph Clark.

The Conservative election machine had been ready and waiting for months. Mulroney's caucus committees and task forces had delivered their reports, which had since been worked into the Tory platform — every candidate had binders full of policies. The Conservative Party had a policy on everything. But from a strategic point of view the only policy that really mattered was their policy of hammering the Liberals. Mulroney believed that oppositions don't win, but governments lose, and he planned to stay away from policy whenever he could.

The first three weeks of the campaign had been completely mapped out months in advance. Campaign chairman Norman Atkins, a leading force in the famed Big Blue Machine in Ontario, was a master of logistics and left no detail to chance. With him the trains always ran on time. Atkins merely had to flip a switch to set his machinery rolling. The Conservatives knew exactly where Mulroney would go and what he would do. The candidate himself was already campaign tough, having cut his teeth in Central Nova and more recently gone through a full dress rehearsal during the boonie tour. All the logistics that make a campaign look professional — for instance, coordinating the visuals with the policy message — had long ago been worked out.

About the only thing that remained unsettled was which riding Mulroney would pick. Turner had already announced he would run in British Columbia in the Vancouver riding of Quadra, whereas the Tory leader had been procrastinating. He had staked his political career on winning Quebec and could not duck out of running there — nor did he want to. For him it was a case of where in Quebec, not if. Baie Comeau seemed like a natural choice, especially since he had so romanticized his home-town roots over the years, but from a hard-headed political point of view Baie Comeau was a lousy choice.

His home town sat in the southwest corner of Manicouagan, an isolated 320,000-square-mile constituency that was the second-largest riding in the ten provinces. A party leader already had enough to do without being burdened with a huge and remote riding. To further complicate matters, redistribution was slated to move Baie Comeau out of Manicouagan after the next election, which would force Mulroney to change ridings yet again. Manicouagan also happened to contain Schefferville, now down to 275 non-Indians and 900 natives from its peak population of 4,000. Full of boarded-up houses and empty streets, the town and its emotions were best left unstirred. Sept-Îles, the riding's biggest population centre, had also been wounded in the IOC cut-backs, so there would be resentment there too. But the worst mark against Manicouagan was its political history. The riding had always been Liberal and was represented by André

Maltais, a popular MP and a good constituency man. Maltais had triumphed in 1980 by a whopping 16,655 votes, and nobody — not even the local Tories — had an unkind thing to say about him.

Campaign chairman Atkins advised Mulroney to run elsewhere. So did Bernard Roy, Mulroney's long-time close friend, now the Quebec campaign chairman. Roy knew about Mulroney's desire to represent his home town, but after visiting the riding for three days and talking to voters, he concluded the risk was too great. Manicouagan was a suicidal mission. And if he lost there, it would be a blow for the entire party.

Mulroney's advisers unanimously argued for choosing Brome-Missisquoi. It had as much going for it as Manicouagan had against it, being a convenient one-hour drive southeast of Montreal and having a long tradition of voting Tory. Since 1958, under Heward Grafftey, who was not running again, it had voted Tory seven out of nine times. Brome-Missisquoi was about as close as the Conservative Party would get to having a sure seat in Quebec. Furthermore Mulroney's presence would spill over and boost Tory prospects in several neighbouring ridings.

After hearing out his advisers, Mulroney declared his decision — he was picking Manicouagan. After saying for years that he could turn Quebec around, he had come to believe his own legend. His advisers tried to dissuade him, but he had made up his mind. "I'm from Baie Comeau," he proclaimed, "and that's where I'll be running." He also said that people would call him a coward if he chose a safe seat rather than his home town. He had chosen with his heart, and in so doing he had elected to gamble.

On July 13, with the constituency issue resolved, Mulroney flew to New Glasgow, Nova Scotia, and bade an emotional farewell to Central Nova. "This has been an exceptionally difficult decision," he told voters, in tears. He explained that he felt an obligation to run in Quebec and spearhead the drive for Conservative seats in *la belle province*. "It's not every day that a Conservative walks away from a

twenty-thousand-vote majority," he said with characteristic embel-
lishment. His margin had actually been 11,024. (The figure of twenty
thousand was based on a prediction from the pollsters.)

The next day Mulroney arrived in Manicouagan, landing in
Sept-Îles. There, before an audience of two hundred, he drew bursts
of laughter and applause by reading off the entire list of Turner's
nineteen patronage appointments. All the taxes of the voters of
Sept-Îles will go "to the end of your days" to send "a bunch of tired
Liberals to their golden retirements." Campaign workers helped stir
up the audience by distributing printed lists of the names and salaries
of the Liberal appointees. Mulroney had found his issue and was now
milking it for everything he could.

Then his rented Boeing 727 touched down in Baie Comeau. He
had returned there many times over the years, but never to a welcome
like this. People treated him like a conquering hero. He took reporters
down Champlain Street and pointed out his boyhood home at
number 99. The town had grown all around, but Champlain Street
had remained much as it had been, except for new paint on the
houses. He got the biggest charge of the day when he settled into the
mill manager's house at the top of the hill, the same house and the
same hill that had been in the centre of his adolescent universe and
had once defined his notion of success. The mill manager had long
since moved out, and the house had been converted into a VIP
guest-house, but that took nothing away from the thrill. Over dinner
that evening he described how he had felt walking into the house of
his father's boss. "I said to myself, 'This isn't bad,'" he told guests.
"Being prime minister is one thing, but it's something else to be able
to sit in the home of the mill manager, put your feet up on the table,
and say: 'Yep, this ain't bad.'"

The campaign had started off gloriously. Earlier that day a new
poll released by Southam News had buoyed him up further. It showed
the Liberals and the Conservatives virtually neck and neck. Already
Turner's stumbles had taken their toll. And a tie in the popular vote

automatically translated into a Tory win because the Liberals wasted many votes accumulating huge pluralities in Quebec. If the Southam poll stood, the Tories would win 136 seats outside Quebec and would require only a half-dozen seats inside Quebec for a majority. He had arrived in Manicouagan as the Conservative leader and, it seemed, was leaving as the next prime minister.

For Mulroney the only let-down about the triumphant homecoming was that he had to depart so quickly. He had to leave that same evening. It was a tired but exuberant candidate who boarded his 727 — soon to be christened *Manicouagan I* — and headed off to a stop in Montreal. He had reason to feel good as he settled back into his seat in the first-class section. The days of the "rusty station wagon" campaign were long behind him. He now jetted around with a staff of more than a dozen and a horde of reporters.

The seating arrangement aboard the aircraft followed a strict order of precedence. Mulroney, Mila, and key staffers filled the first-class compartment. (The key staffers were Charley McMillan, Pat Mac-Adam, Peter Harder, Bill Pristanski, Bonnie Brownlee, Bill Fox, and Pat Kinsella, the tour manager.) The rest of the staff of about half a dozen occupied the front of the main compartment. The roadies, who handled the more than one ton of sound, light, and backdrop equipment, sat roughly in the middle. Seated at the back were the journalists covering the tour. Although the campaign had hardly started, the hierarchy was well defined.

Mulroney had a practice of emerging from his first-class section for a shirtsleeves stroll down the aisle, bantering all the way. On this particular day a reporter was celebrating a birthday, and Mulroney came down the back to mark the occasion. As usual he made stops along the way. Someone asked him how he could reconcile his stinging rebuke of Turner's patronage appointments that morning in Sept-Îles with the speeches he had given when campaigning for the Conservative leadership a year earlier.

"What speeches?" Mulroney asked.

"The one," shot back a reporter, "where you said, 'People have asked me if I would give a job to a Liberal —'"

Mulroney finished the quote for him.

"Yes, when there isn't a living, breathing Tory left without a job in this country." It had been one of the occasions when he had looked over his audience and announced that he saw future senators in the room.

"I was talking to Tories then," he explained, "and that's what they want to hear. Talking to the Canadian public during an election campaign is something else."

Mulroney also confessed that he could not blame Bryce Mackasey for accepting his ambassadorship. "Let's face it," he quipped, "there's no whore like an old whore. If I'd been in Bryce's position I'd have been right in there with my nose in the public trough like the rest of them." Near the end he looked around and said: "I hope this is all off the record. I'm taking the high road now."

One of the reporters who had overheard the exchange was Neil Macdonald of the *Ottawa Citizen.* The following Monday the *Citizen* published a story on top of the front page proclaiming: "Mulroney Admits Altering Patronage Stand for Election." Macdonald's report bared in public what Mulroney had said during his casual stroll down the airplane aisle, direct quotes and all.

The fallout from the *Ottawa Citizen* article stopped the Tory campaign in its tracks. Every Liberal from John Turner on down denounced Mulroney as a hypocrite. Newspaper columnists, editorial writers, and cartoonists had a field day. Mulroney had spent the previous week self-righteously condemning Turner's patronage and now had been publicly exposed as somebody who wanted to do nothing more than change the colour from Liberal red to Tory blue. In a few hours what had been his most effective weapon had become his biggest liability.

Actually the damage went beyond the normal ups and downs of an election campaign. Mulroney's unguarded comments about patronage tended to confirm people's lingering suspicions of him. The public had never quite trusted him. There was something false about him, something insincere. He was a bit too smooth, a bit too slick, and a bit too flexible — in a word, slippery. Public scepticism of his genuineness had hurt him back in 1976 and had lurked beneath the surface throughout the 1983 leadership race, even among Tories — but they kept their doubts buried because he looked like a winner. Now Mulroney's patronage comments had brought all people's misgivings back to the surface.

Completely floored, Mulroney, chewing even more Nicorettes, agonized over what to do. Some advisers counselled him to stonewall and ride out the storm, while others told him to cut his losses and apologize so that the campaign could move on. For a while he dithered, unable to decide what to do.

Mulroney's sole consolation was that John Turner had gotten himself into a mess of his own. In the last several days the new prime minister, ignoring the pleas of his handlers to quit his disagreeable habit of slapping women on their derrières, had patronizingly patted the behinds of two Liberal women in public. One of them happened to be party president Iona Campagnolo, who had not so good-naturedly returned the favour — all in front of a CTV camera. Turner's pat and Campagnolo's retaliation made a great television clip that was played and replayed on sets across North America. Then Turner absolutely infuriated women's groups across the country by steadfastly refusing to apologize. As the country was trying to decide which leader to entrust with the affairs of state, two issues had captured its emotions — patronage and bum-patting.

However, Mulroney faced the more serious crisis, one that under-mined his fundamental credibility. He and his aides knew that something had to be done to get the Tory campaign back on track. People like Bill Fox, Pat MacAdam, and Charley McMillan huddled together, and the campaign's formal strategy committee, including campaign chairman Norman Atkins, Bill Neville, Lowell Murray, pollster Allan Gregg, Finlay MacDonald, and Mulroney staffer Jon

Johnson, convened in emergency session in Ottawa. Finally a consensus emerged that Mulroney had to confront the issue. Since he could not deny his remarks, the best way of controlling the damage was to apologize for joking about patronage.

On July 18, two days after the story broke, Mulroney called a press conference in Sault Ste. Marie, Ontario. With Mila at his side, he nervously read out a prepared statement: "During the course of an informal conversation with certain members of the media last Saturday night while flying to Montreal from Baie Comeau, certain casual and bantering remarks on the subject of political patronage were attributed to me. I do not deny having made these remarks, but I say simply they were made without any serious intent since they clearly do not represent either my attitudes or my position with respect to this important matter of public policy. I was mistaken to treat so important a matter in a way which might be misunderstood and I very much regret having done so. As I have said since the outset of this campaign, I am committed to the attainment of new standards of quality in making public appointments and that remains my commitment to the people of Canada."

During the question-and-answer period that followed, Mulroney declared that the Liberal appointments had caused him to reconsider his attitude towards political patronage. He now felt the whole system needed overhauling. A Conservative government would appoint quality candidates from labour, business, and political parties — and, he added tantalizingly, he hoped they would be vetted in advance.

The apology (although it stopped short of a full apology) and the suggestion (although not a promise) of patronage reform had at least moved Mulroney off the defensive on the issue, possibly enough to allow his campaign to get back on course. He had moved quickly to put out the fire. Meanwhile Turner kept stonewalling over the bum-patting issue. "I apologized for what I said about patronage," Mulroney would say later. "I knew I had to do it. But I never really appreciated how important it was until Turner did not [apologize]."

In political terms Mulroney had survived, but he was still bruised.

His early momentum had collapsed, and now he had to start over and rebuild. The Tory game plan, which had been so well laid out months in advance, had been knocked off the board. No longer could he gleefully attack Turner's patronage appointments. An apology could not make him pure again nor allow him to reoccupy the moral high ground. From now on he would be more careful and would start paying more attention to the pros who were handling him.

After his public apology in Sault Ste. Marie, Mulroney moved on to Winnipeg for his first visit since being heckled in March over institutional bilingualism. This time he received polite applause as he publicly embraced the same Tories who had caused him so much trouble over the language issue. Bud Sherman, one of the Manitoba ringleaders, had become a Conservative candidate in this election, and Mulroney now helped kick off his campaign in Winnipeg–Fort Garry. He proclaimed that Winnipeg and the country needed Sherman to play a major role in the next government of Canada. "Bud and I have disagreed in the past," Mulroney quipped, as a crowd of five hundred laughed and applauded, "but in the spirit of Isaiah we have reasoned together."

By the time Mulroney reached Vancouver, the next stop in his three-day Western swing, he had returned to the attack, playing the role of stand-up comic and outraged politician to cheering crowds. Never did the crowds cheer as enthusiastically as when he resurrected the image of John Diefenbaker and linked his underdog status to Diefenbaker's. "John Diefenbaker in 1957 was behind in the polls, running against an entrenched Liberal Party," he began softly as his voice started to rise. "And some of the wise journalists from eastern Canada said, 'It can't be done.' But Mr. Diefenbaker went out confident and committed — as I am in your strength and your support and counsel — preaching unity, and tolerance, and fairness. Preaching one Canada, home for equal opportunity for men and women. He formed a government in September 1957 based on those fundamental principles. We're going to form another in September

1984 based on exactly those same principles." His audience exploded into a frenzy of applause and sign-waving. Mulroney was back in stride.

On July 21 Mulroney returned to Ottawa and lost little time getting ready for what loomed as the most important event in the campaign — the upcoming television debates between the three party leaders. The format had been struck at a negotiating session in the Four Seasons Hotel in Ottawa. Figuring that Mulroney could easily outduel the still-rusty Turner, the Tories had pressed for a series of five regional debates, staged late in the campaign for maximum impact. The Liberals would agree only to one debate in English and one in French, and then only if held early (they calculated that an early debate would be forgotten by voting day). It had been offered as a take-it-or-leave-it proposition. Desperate for any debate, the Tory negotiators went along, and agreed to debate in French on July 24 and in English the following day.

In the French debate the three party leaders came out about even on matters of substance. But in the eyes of Quebec voters, who had traditionally valued tribal loyalty above political philosophy, Mulroney had swept the field, easily knocking aside both Turner and Broadbent. What Mulroney said mattered little. He spoke in flawless, idiomatic French and sprinkled in references to the Beauce, the Gaspésie, and the Saguenay, leaving no doubt that he was a real Québécois. The debate had cast Mulroney as the native son and relegated Turner and Broadbent to the status of outsiders. To Quebeckers it was clear that Mulroney could best represent the interests of French Canada.

The English debate the next evening, like the French, was divided into three sections. In the first segment, Mulroney would go head to head with Broadbent. Then he would step aside for a Turner-Broadbent encounter before returning to face Turner. Throughout, a panel of journalists would ask questions. The patronage issue came up in the first segment with Turner off camera, meaning the man responsible for the controversy was not on the firing line. Both Mulroney and Broadbent promptly condemned the government's appointment record and moved on to other concerns.

In the third segment, for all his rust, Turner seemed to be handling himself surprisingly well against Mulroney. A quick study, Turner had come well prepared. Good coaching had even enabled him to waltz around the bum-patting issue without damage by stressing his record of commitment to women's issues. As Mulroney and Turner sparred away, it looked as though the debate would end in a draw, which was all the Liberals had really wanted. Then Turner inexplicably turned to his opponent and started scolding him on the issue of patronage, accusing him of saying one thing to his party and another to the country.

"I have been saying the same thing to my party on all the issues that I say to the country," Turner said. "We have this patronage issue brought up earlier. Mr. Mulroney has not been dealing with the issue in the same way. He told his party last year that every available job would be made available to every living, breathing Conservative."

"I beg your pardon, sir," Mulroney interjected.

"I would say, Mr. Mulroney," Turner retorted, "that on the basis of what you've talked about — getting your nose in the public trough — that you wouldn't offer Canadians any newness in the style of government. The style that you've been preaching to your own party reminds me of the old Union Nationale, it reminds me of patronage at its best. Frankly, on the basis of your performance, I can't see freshness coming out of your choice."

According to L. Ian MacDonald, Mulroney then told himself, "I just got lucky." Mustering all his reserves of self-righteousness, and reaching deep into his bag of debating skills, which went all the way back to St. FX, he launched his retaliation.

"Mr. Turner," he responded with the prissy outrage of a schoolmarm, "the only person who has ever appointed around here, for the last twenty-odd years, has been your party, and 99 per cent of them have been Liberals. And you ought not to be proud of that. Nor should you repeat something that I think you know to be inaccurate. You know full well that that was a figure of speech that was used and I don't deny it. In fact I've gone so far — because I believe what you did is so bad I've gone so far, sir, as to apologize for even kidding about it. I've apologized to the Canadian people for kidding about it. The least you should do is apologize for having made these horrible appointments. I've had the decency, I think, to acknowledge that I was wrong in even kidding about it. I shouldn't have done that and I've said so. You, sir, at least owe the Canadian people a profound apology for doing it. The cost of that, $84.4 million, is enough to give — the cost of that to the ordinary Canadian taxpayer — we could pay every senior citizen in this country on the supplement an extra $70 at Christmas rather than pay for those Liberal appointments. And I say to you, sir, two things: (a) you should produce that letter because you keep coming back to this situation. Please produce the secret letter you signed that you undertook to make these appointments, and (b) may I say respectfully that I think that I felt I owed it to the Canadian people — and I did — an apology for bantering about the subject. You, sir, owe the Canadian people a deep apology for having indulged in that kind of practice with those kinds of appointments."

Mulroney's outburst had caught Turner by surprise, so much so that he started back-pedalling.

"I told you and told the Canadian people, Mr. Mulroney, that I had no option," Turner insisted, his voice raspy and defensive.

"Mr. Trueman," the moderator interjected, "your next question, please." Mulroney ignored the moderator and continued his attack.

"You had an option, sir," Mulroney shot back, his voice rising and his pace quickening. "You could have said, 'I'm not going to do it. This is wrong for Canada and I'm not going to ask Canadians to pay the price.' You had an option, sir, to say no and you chose to say yes to the old attitudes and the old stories of the Liberal Party. That, sir, if I may say respectfully, that is not good enough for Canadians."

"I had no option," Turner sputtered. "I was able — "

Mulroney cut him off.

"That is an avowal of failure. That is a confession of non-leadership and this country needs leadership. You had an option, sir. You could have done better."

Turner remained frozen, his face with the look of a terrified deer caught in the headlights of an oncoming car.

"Mr. Turner, your response, please," the moderator announced in an official voice.

"I — I've just said, Mr. Moderator — taken the Canadian people through the circumstances," Turner replied, now completely withdrawn into a defensive shell. "Mr. Trudeau had every right to make those appointments before he resigned. In order that he not do so, yes, I had to make a commitment to him, otherwise I was advised that, with serious consequences to the Canadian people, I could not have been granted the opportunity of forming a government."

Never before had the country witnessed such a spectacle. Mulroney had scored a knockout punch in front of seven and a half million people. "I hit him once," Mulroney would later recount, smacking his open hand with his fist. "I hit him again, pow" — Mulroney smacked his hand again — "he went down."

That night an ecstatic Brian Mulroney walked on air as he returned home to Stornoway. Over the years he had conquered many debating opponents, but never one so big — the prime minister of Canada — and rarely so decisively. In the course of a two-minute clip he had sold himself as the better, more upright leader. While he had come across as strong and decisive, Turner, stumbling and stuttering, had apologized for the past. But it was not just debating points that he had scored that evening. He had turned around the patronage issue and regained the moral authority he needed in order to exploit it again on the stump. The image of Mulroney lecturing Turner on the ethics of patronage became burned into the consciousness of the nation; Turner would never recover.

In the past Mulroney had almost always come up big when it counted, often turning defeat into victory. Flunking law school at

Dalhousie had flattened him like nothing before in his life, but he rebounded during his golden years at Laval. Similarly the 1976 leadership loss had utterly routed him, but ultimately he learned from his failure and turned it into success in 1983. Without Mulroney's ill-considered walk down the airplane aisle, Turner would not have challenged him on patronage, and the debate would have ended in a draw. He had found a way to convert the most damaging mistake of his campaign into a triumph.

After the debate Mulroney left for a campaign swing through southern Ontario. Now radiating confidence and enthusiasm, he delivered one barn-burner after another, always hitting Turner hard over patronage. Once again he started reading out the names of Turner's appointments and their salaries and job descriptions. He always drew a laugh by calling Turner "Mr. New," but his little vaudeville routine got the biggest howls when he mimicked Turner at the debate: "I had no option. The devil made me do it." It brought down the house. Turner's first act as prime minister, he said, was not to help the unemployed or the elderly but to reward fellow Liberals. "Worst of all," he said, his voice rising, "the prime minister in the debate stood there helpless like a baby and said, 'I had no option.' I say he had an option. The option of honour was to say, 'No, I will not do it. It's wrong. It's bad for Canada.' Instead he said yes to the old Liberal ways. He made Canadians pay the price and now Canadians are going to make him and his party pay the price on September 4."

It took people a while to notice, but in milking the patronage issue Mulroney was pulling his punches a tiny bit. When reading out the Liberal names he never quite made it to the end of the list. Now he always left out the name of his old friend Bryce Mackasey, who had consoled him after his loss in 1976. Mulroney had already phoned Mackasey to apologize for any embarrassment he had caused, and for the rest of the campaign he would shame him no more.

In hammering home his message, Mulroney constantly played fast and loose with numbers. He routinely costed Turner's patronage appointments at precisely $84.4 million, forgetting to mention that this figure represented the accumulated cost after twenty years. (The one-year figure that Canadian Press used was $4 million.) The deficit, projected at $29 billion by the government, but at $32.7 billion by the Conference Board of Canada, became $34 billion according to Mulroney. Later he stretched it into $36 billion. And he had not lost his knack for popularizing statistics. He told a Toronto audience that if Canada's unemployed lined up shoulder to shoulder they would stretch from John Turner's office in Ottawa to Saint John, New Brunswick. And if Turner "drove past them in his limousine to look at their faces it would take sixteen hours."

By the end of July, the Liberal campaign, such as it was, teetered on the edge of collapse. In less than three weeks it had become obvious to everyone, especially the Liberals themselves, that Turner should never have called an early election. He had not overcome his fatigue from the leadership race, and neither had his party. Lagging behind in every organizational detail — whether fundraising, policy generation, polling, candidate recruitment and training, or media relations — the Liberals simply were not ready. That in turn had led to administrative disarray, foul-ups, internal bickering, and turf wars, culminating in the mid-campaign departure of campaign manager Bill Lee, replaced by — of all people — that old Trudeau hand Keith Davey. The decision to bring in a ghost from the past merely compounded the Liberals' woes. Now the party had publicly reverted to the Trudeau legacy and abandoned all pretence of being new and fresh. Thereafter Turner went into a free fall in the polls, dropping as much as a percentage point a day.

In contrast to the hapless Liberals, the Tory campaign now looked invincible and Mulroney carried the aura of triumph. (On August 3 in Chicoutimi Mulroney turned to Pat MacAdam and told him to call Gordon Osbaldeston, the top civil servant in Ottawa, to tell him to freeze the invitation lists for the Queen's visit, which had been postponed to September. He didn't want a bunch of Liberals at the formal events during her tour.) His crowds kept growing bigger and more enthusiastic and more admiring. People started turning out to see not a political candidate but a future prime minister. Mulroney played to their expectations with uplifting rhetoric, saying the campaign was about small towns and big dreams, about a bright, new, prosperous tomorrow, and about cooperation across the country. He promised "hundreds of thousands" of new jobs to be produced through increased research and development and through increased productivity in Canadian industry. A Tory government would bring good economic times. Investors would be welcomed to the country and would start investing again, and Canada would again march forward into prosperity.

Each week Mulroney and his entourage left Ottawa for five or six days and returned at week's end for one or two down days. Sometimes the group would spend its down day in Manicouagan. Each morning he would be up at 6:00 to scan the latest newspaper clippings that his staff had assembled. Then the unremitting daily grind of travel and public appearances would begin. One day he started in Montreal, made stops in Kingston, Toronto (where Bill Davis joined him on the stump), Thunder Bay, Kenora, North Bay, and Gatineau, and ended the day back in Montreal. Sometimes the number of his daily appearances reached double digits. Before he retired for the night, Sam Wakim would call from Toronto to read him the early edition of the next morning's *Globe and Mail.*

The campaign tour rolled along almost flawlessly. The electronic mail, the buses, the planes, and all the nuts and bolts fitted together perfectly. Scheduled times were met. Before disembarking from the plane or bus, Mulroney read a briefing report on the riding and a short biography of the local candidate. His briefing book even contained a map of his route into the building where he would speak. When he and his entourage stopped at the end of the day, their hotel keys were passed out on the bus. They would go straight to their rooms, where a basket of fruit was always waiting. No glitches and no gremlins plagued their progress. At this point it seemed nothing could derail the Mulroney Express. From now on Mulroney only had to avoid mistakes. Playing it safe, he ran his campaign off a single speech, repeated over and over with the same lines shuffled and reused, always adjusted to reflect the concerns of the audience.

Good as Mulroney was, he was not the best Tory campaigner on the stump. That laurel belonged to Mila. Especially in unscripted settings — mainstreeting or working a room — when she could interact with people, Mila's engaging personality could transform a knot of doubtful onlookers into a group of fans faster than anyone. When she sat on stage her vivacity, freshness, and enthusiasm made him seem a little brighter, a little better. She always laughed at his jokes with such sparkling delight that the audience never guessed she had heard them a hundred times before.

Mila remained glued to her husband's side throughout the campaign. Whenever they got separated in a crowd, even if only for a minute, he grew visibly uncomfortable and would look around for her. "Where's Mila? Where's Mila?" he would ask, a touch of panic in his voice. Always she had to be with him and always within sight. Only now did it become evident to outsiders to what degree they had become a team, in life as well as on the campaign trail. Until now only friends and staff had known how close they were. He no longer felt whole or settled without her nearby. In the eleven years of their marriage Mila had grown into a true personal and political partner. Mila had become a haven for Mulroney, and without her he was lost.

In early August a Southam News–Carleton University poll gave the Conservatives a startling 51 per cent of the decided vote, compared with 32 for the Liberals and 16 for the NDP, the ingredients for a sweeping majority. Even more dramatic were the numbers in Quebec. They showed the Tories at a breathtaking 49 per cent, compared with 37 for the Liberals, a remarkable turnaround for a party that had mustered only 12.5 per cent of the Quebec popular vote in 1980. Quebec had climbed aboard the Tory bandwagon with a vengeance.

Manicouagan, which a month earlier had seemed such a risk, had flipped faster and further than the rest of Quebec, and not without reason. Mulroney repeatedly told the North Shore voters they could choose either a backbencher or a prime minister as their MP. As prime minister he said he would not have to go through fourteen civil servants to get something done. "The problems of the riding will get, I don't say preferential treatment, I say priority treatment, since they have been neglected for such a long time," he said at his nomination meeting on August 6. Throughout his riding he was introduced as the next prime minister of Canada. "The dossiers of Manicouagan will be studied at interesting levels," he promised. Local polls showed Mulroney scoring over 60 per cent. The once impossible seat was taking Mulroney to easy victory.

Among the outside troops brought into Manicouagan during the campaign was Michel Cogger, now far from the corridors of power. In April, as the Liberals were racing to nominate John Turner, Cogger had come to the conclusion he was no longer wanted, packed up his Ottawa office, and moved back to Montreal, where he pitched in to help the Quebec Conservatives prepare for the coming campaign. But he remained on the margins, even in Quebec. In fact he spent most of his time in Manicouagan, and a good part of it fishing with his friend Jacques Blouin, president of the local Tory riding association.

Mulroney had always supported Trudeau in patriating the Constitution and, unlike Joe Clark, believed that the 1981 deal was fundamentally sound. "Trudeau did what had to be done and it serves no purpose to fight him on that," Mulroney told Jean Pelletier of *Maclean's* magazine not long after he became opposition leader. "Let's face it, Trudeau is one of the most impressive political figures in the world." But in his nomination speech in Sept-Îles he did a complete flip-flop on the Constitution and came out attacking Trudeau for abandoning Quebec. "One thing is certain," he told his constituents. "Not one Quebecker authorized the federal Liberals to take advantage of the confusion that prevailed in Quebec following the referendum in order to ostracize the province constitutionally." He said Quebec had to be brought into the Constitution "with honour and enthusiasm." He even promised to deal with the separatist Quebec government that he had so publicly scorned a year earlier. Now he described it as "duly and legitimately elected." All this bore little resemblance to Mulroney's platform during the race for the Conservative leadership, when he had proclaimed he would not "play footsie" with the PQ.

The guiding force in Mulroney's conversion from a Trudeau-style federalist in 1983 to an advocate of provincial rights in 1984 was none other than his old friend and mentor Lucien Bouchard, who now acted as his personal adviser on Quebec matters. He had written much of Mulroney's Sept-Îles speech, which Graham Fraser of the *Globe and Mail* described the next day as being full of code words aimed at PQ supporters and those angry at being left out of the constitutional settlement. Mulroney had really wanted Bouchard to run as a Tory candidate, but at the time Bouchard saw no chance of winning, so he stayed in the backroom.

However, other Parti Québécois sympathizers had come into the open as Conservative candidates. Pierre Ménard, a PQ supporter who strongly believed in provincial rights, was running in Hull. Before the election call Mulroney had assembled an unlikely coalition of forces to help him win seats in Quebec. This disparate group included members of the Parti Québécois, dissatisfied provincial Liberals, and members of the Union Nationale. What most of them had in common was a decidedly nationalist bent.

The campaign inside Quebec had been an operation unto itself from the outset. Now, with Pierre Trudeau gone and his anglophone successor staggering, the Conservatives played up the need for Quebeckers to pick the winning side. Mulroney reminded them that voting Tory meant voting for a prime minister from Quebec. Unlike the campaign in English Canada, which played heavily on the party name, the Quebec campaign never mentioned the word "Conservative." Other words also got left behind in English Canada. Mulroney could not tour western Canada without stirring up the vision of John Diefenbaker and voicing the phrase "One Canada," but inside Quebec the words "Diefenbaker" and "One Canada" never passed his lips.

The key words in the Quebec campaign were "Québécois," "solidarity," and "change."

Meanwhile the slumping Turner, desperately looking to turn his
fortunes around, started hurling mud. He lashed out at Mulroney for
courting the separatist vote and publicly named three Tory candidates
in Quebec with separatist leanings — Pierre Ménard, Suzanne
Duplessis, and Monique Vézina — who had all campaigned for the
Yes side in 1980. Clearly stung, Mulroney responded that it was time
to "heal old wounds, not to settle old scores" from the 1980 referendum debate. "It's time for unity," he told four hundred supporters
in downtown Sarnia. "It's time for reconciliation. It's time for
change. That's what this campaign is all about. That's what this
election is all about." Turner shot back that he would "not negotiate
the constitution of this country with a political party in Quebec that
doesn't believe in the future of this country," sounding remarkably
like Brian Mulroney, the leadership candidate of a year before.

One of the campaigners who rushed to Mulroney's aid was Joe
Clark, even though Mulroney had once denounced him for being
too conciliatory to Quebec nationalists. Starting a four-day campaign
swing through Quebec on August 12, his second foray into the
province, Clark charged that Turner did not understand Quebec and
accused him of conducting a "terror campaign" aimed at courting
votes in English Canada.

Still the ultra-faithful lieutenant, Clark had undertaken his own
mini-campaign tour in which he praised Mulroney at every stop.
(Mulroney's office was orchestrating both the leader's tour and
Clark's.) To help out the Tory cause, Clark spent six of the eight
campaign weeks on the road, visiting sixty-five ridings other than his
own, most of them belonging to the Liberals or the NDP. When
reporters asked him why he was putting himself out in such a way,
Clark would reply that he was only doing his duty.

Only one aide accompanied him and there was no travelling pack
of reporters. The backdrop behind him carried not his picture, but

posters of Brian Mulroney. Flecks of grey had begun to show in Clark's sandy brown hair; nevertheless he looked relaxed and spoke well. In cutting up the other parties he was sometimes downright funny. (He described the riding of Vancouver Quadra, into which John Turner had parachuted, as "an area that has recently been besieged by tourists, one of whom is a candidate.") Wherever Clark went, particularly in western Canada, people would tell him they wished he was still leader. "That's been decided," he told a Vancouver supporter and walked away. He always shrugged such comments off. He refused to look back. "I make a point in not indulging in 'what if,'" Clark told *Toronto Star* reporter Roy MacGregor on a flight between campaign stops. "That's all behind now."

Turner's charges about Mulroney's new-found friendliness towards Quebec nationalists were accurate, but what he said no longer really mattered. Every polling firm in the country now projected a mammoth Tory majority; Mulroney had become invulnerable. The only doubts that remained hinged on the cost of his promises.

In putting together his platform, Mulroney had not promised the moon, but he had come very close. He had pledged everything from beefing up the armed forces by 10 per cent to spending more on social programs. He even vowed to reopen VIA Rail passenger lines scrapped by the Liberal government. His commitments to the West alone would cost $5 or $6 billion, according to a study prepared for finance critic John Crosbie. When the price tags for all the Tory promises were added up, the same study suggested, the total bill would top $20 billion. The figures leaked out when a reporter saw the report under Crosbie's arm. Mulroney denied the numbers (after severely rapping Crosbie's knuckles for the leak) but sidestepped the issue of what the real costs were by promising to unveil them later in the campaign.

The fact that Mulroney was simultaneously promising both deficit-cutting and major new spending made him appear to be talking out of both sides of his mouth. Throughout the campaign Turner had been accusing him of "trying to buy voters with their own money." One of the few times that Turner scored points during the

French debate was when he called Mulroney "the $20-billion man." Turner had costed out all the pledges in his own platform and challenged Mulroney to do likewise. The media too had badgered Mulroney about it. Now finally he responded. He gave notice that he would lay out all the costs in a lunch-hour speech to the Empire Club in Toronto's Royal York Hotel on August 28, a week before election day. His staff considered it the most crucial speech of the campaign. It would be one of the few times he would depart from his canned script.

On his way in for the speech, a clearly exhausted Mulroney talked about the latest poll that had him winning 180 seats. "What do you think?" he asked speech-writer Jon Johnson on the bus in from the airport. "I think about 185," replied Johnson. Mulroney shook his head. "I don't want any more than 160 seats," he said. "We're going to have a hell of a time managing these people. Look who we've nominated in Quebec. I don't even know 90 per cent of them."

The much-awaited costing speech went off smoothly. Mulroney put the three-year price tag at $4.3 billion, large enough to be credible but small enough not to be frightening. While he spoke, aides handed out background papers full of statistics that broke down Mulroney's figures by category and year. Turner would naturally dispute the numbers, but with a week to go it was too late to do much damage. The cost issue, if not dead, was buried in a mountain of numbers.

Mulroney had been nervous before the big speech, but now he could afford to indulge in some euphoria. He had successfully evaded the last potential pitfall. In a matter of days he would win by a landslide. "Not bad for a boy from Baie Comeau," he shouted to *Globe and Mail* reporter Ross Howard as he mainstreeted along Toronto's Danforth Avenue. After all those years of losing, for once it was great to be a Tory.

After a few lightning stops in some selected last-minute seats, Mulroney spent the final days of the campaign in Quebec. His tour rolled along the St. Lawrence like an army of liberation after the occupying forces had raised the white flag of surrender. Wherever he went, crowds turned out to cheer his arrival, their size and enthusiasm astounding even the local organizers. In Trois-Rivières and in Quebec City hundreds showed up at the airport. Supporters even stood along the roadside and waved as he drove into town. For the Tories to win more than a handful of Quebec seats would be so rare that Mulroney's handlers were almost afraid to breathe a prediction, but at the same time they could not help thinking of fifty seats, the number Diefenbaker had won in 1958.

The very last days had been set aside for Manicouagan. Virtual pandemonium broke out when Mulroney landed at the Sept-Îles airport. But the ultimate triumph came on the afternoon of September 3, the day before the big vote, when *Manicouagan I* touched down in Baie Comeau. He had come to close off his campaign where, as he put it, he had first "dreamed big dreams." Pushing against a chain-link fence at the edge of the tarmac, a crowd of five hundred waited in a drizzle. They had come to dote on the next prime minister of Canada, to welcome him home, and to let him know how proud they were. Mulroney, equally proud, wallowed in the sentiment of the moment. "A boy from Baie Comeau has made a long trip," he declared in French, "and today he's coming home." He drew on the memory of the town's founders and paid tribute to their efforts in carving the community out of the wilderness. Then he linked their accomplishment to his quest for high office. "In the spirit of our parents who cleared the land here," he said, "we are modestly making a little history. If we continue to work hard, Tuesday night the member of Parliament for Manicouagan will be the prime minister of Canada." They would be electing "a son of the North Shore, the son of a Baie Comeau electrician who is proud of his roots." He always felt proud of his home town, but never so much as at this moment.

From the airport Mulroney's entourage moved into town and up the hill to the Manoir. His team of aides and the crowd of journalists swamped the fifty-two-room hotel where he had met Colonel McCormick forty years earlier. Now it was his local campaign headquarters. Mulroney himself checked into the mill manager's stone house across the way, a few hundred yards from his old home. The next morning, after casting his ballot at the local primary school, he and Mila took a sentimental walk down Champlain Street and stopped in front of number 99 for a photo opportunity as reporters tagged along.

For his victory party that evening, he had invited some of his old friends to a buffet dinner in the huge ground-floor living room of the mill manager's house, where on three television sets, elevated on tripods, they would watch history being made. Lucien Bouchard arrived from Chicoutimi, Sam Wakim from Toronto, Michel Cogger, Jean Bazin, and Roger Nantel (his PR man from 1976, who had become a good friend) from Montreal, and Terry McCann, his old buddy from St. FX days, from Pembroke. As the Quebec campaign chairman, Bernard Roy felt duty-bound to stay with his troops in Montreal, so he declined. But Fred Doucet was there and so was Pat MacAdam. Frank Buggie, a boyhood friend in Baie Comeau whose brother Tom had been in Mulroney's class at St. Thomas, came in from Quebec City. Mulroney's brother Gary was there too, as were Michael McSweeney and Peter Pocklington. Eventually Mila disappeared upstairs with the other wives and Mulroney, relaxing in a green sweater and a checked shirt open at the neck, was left with the boys.

Bill Pristanski, his executive assistant, phoned Newfoundland soon after the polls there had closed, and got back encouraging reports. Not long after 8 P.M., the returns started pouring in. The first polls in Manicouagan put André Maltais ahead of Mulroney 138 to 88, but this was merely a blip. Mulroney pulled ahead by 8:30 and soon widened his lead into a veritable landslide. Each time his lead increased, the room erupted into a cheer. At 8:50 Radio-Canada declared Mulroney elected as the MP for Manicouagan. He would ultimately amass a majority of more than eighteen thousand, sweeping all communities in the riding and winning bigger than the Liberals ever had. He had even captured two out of the three polls in Schefferville. His decision to gamble in Manicouagan had paid off big.

Before long Pristanski had Elmer MacKay on the phone from Central Nova. "Ask him what his majority was," Mulroney hollered. MacKay carefully skirted the issue since he was rolling up a bigger majority than Mulroney had a year earlier. By now the numbers from across eastern and central Canada had confirmed the Tory sweep, showing it to be even bigger than everybody had thought. Historic reversals were happening everywhere, especially in Quebec. Roch LaSalle had earlier scored the first Tory win in Quebec. Robert de Cotret, a former Clark cabinet minister, won early too, and after that a horde of Tory no-names were being declared elected one after another as once-mighty Liberals — including cabinet ministers — fell like autumn leaves. The dimensions of the sweep astonished even the Tory insiders. Mulroney had more than made good on his promise to elect MPs from Quebec; he had toppled the Liberal fortress.

When the CBC declared a Conservative majority government, the room let out a rousing cheer. Everybody erupted into some kind of celebration, punching the air or doing a little dance, or just hooting up a loud cheer — all except Mulroney, who stood motionless and quiet with his hands on his hips. The last Tory majority had been the big Diefenbaker sweep of 1958, when he'd been a third-year arts student at St. FX. Now he had repeated the Chief's feat. Only a subdued grin disclosed his delight. No champagne bottle was snapped open. No backslapping. No hugs. Just quiet congratulations all around. Victory, at long last, was anti-climactic.

L. Ian MacDonald, Mulroney's friend and soon-to-be biographer, was allowed into the room for a brief period so he could gather material for his book, but he came away with little to report. "Is that all there is?" he thought to himself afterwards. Like everybody else, he found Mulroney surprisingly detached, as if the story unfolding on the three television screens did not relate to him. He seemed either overwhelmed or completely uninterested in the scope of his victory. He was surrounded by his friends, but what was happening in his head he kept to himself.

It seemed odd that, having invested so much in becoming prime minister, Mulroney would appear distracted at the moment of his triumph. Normally he was not enigmatic; normally he wore his heart on his sleeve. Whether his mind was going back to his roots or jumping forward to what lay ahead, nobody could say. "I wish my father was here," he said at one point, which maybe held part of the answer. His father's sacrifices had given him this opportunity; if only his father had lived to see it realized.

Mulroney's emotions suddenly sparked to life when Rodrigue Pageau, his faithful Quebec organizer, arrived in the room with his wife. Pageau, looking thin and white, had dragged himself out of bed at the Manoir next door to savour this special moment. He was in the late stages of terminal cancer and had not been able to work on the election campaign. Now his skin looked like transparent parchment, but Mulroney had flown him to Baie Comeau by air ambulance to taste the victory. "Well, you're elected prime minister now," Pageau said with satisfaction. "I'm going to bed."

The reality that Mulroney had become prime minister–elect finally started to sink in among the friends gathered in the room. Terry McCann received a little jolt when Mulroney excused himself to go to the washroom and three strangers followed him in. "Holy Jeez," McCann said, when he learned they were Mounties. From now on life would be different for his old buddy Bones. Mulroney merely shrugged a "So be it." "This is a new ball game," he said humbly, "and I'm going to do the best for my country."

Around midnight Mulroney changed into a suit and drove with McCann, Wakim, and Mila to the local hockey arena to proclaim victory publicly. About six thousand sweating but ecstatic supporters stomped, clapped, and cheered his arrival. As far as they were concerned, he had shown the world that more came out of Baie Comeau than newsprint and aluminum. With Mila at his side, Mulroney took the stage and tried to begin his victory speech, but the crowd refused to let him. Three times he tried before giving up and stepping back to hold Mila's hand and sway from side to side to the lilting cheers of the crowd. "Chers amis," he finally called out again from behind the lectern. It would take eleven attempts and a full seven minutes before he could make it stick. "The country has spoken — the real country nurtured by its past sacrifices, by the latent strength of its people, and by its awareness of its place in the world," he proclaimed. "Canada has responded to the call to unity." His delirious supporters repeatedly drowned him out.

As he spoke, his seat count surpassed two hundred and continued to climb. Every province from populous Ontario to tiny Prince Edward Island had given him a majority, a grand alliance of English and French, of East and West — everything he needed to bring the country together in a way that had escaped even the Liberals during the last thirty years. With some political skill and savvy, he could hold onto the winning formula for years to come.

Meanwhile in Spruce Grove, Alberta, immediately west of Edmonton, where Joe Clark's sprawling riding of Yellowhead began, a crowd of about two hundred waited for their candidate to appear at a high school gymnasium. Clark had romped to easy victory, winning better than thirty-seven thousand of the fifty thousand votes cast. But, two time zones behind, he refused to comment until Mulroney had spoken. Election night was bittersweet for him. He fully expected to be offered an important cabinet post, even though many of the scarred veterans of the dump-Clark wars were urging Mulroney to shut him out completely. Now he watched his former rival roll up a historic win and score the breakthrough in Quebec that had eluded him as leader. Clark had tilled the Quebec soil so diligently. In the coming months and years, Quebec Tories would quietly credit him for sowing the seeds of Mulroney's 1984 harvest.

"I feel very happy, not only that we have won but that we have won in areas where traditionally it has been very difficult for us to win," he finally said, after graciously thanking his supporters. "I am also immensely gratified that the work that Bob Stanfield did before me, and I and Brian Mulroney have been able to do in Quebec has paid off and that we are a national party at a time when the country desperately needs one." At his side, Maureen McTeer wore the same stoic smile she had worn fifteen months earlier when Mulroney wrested the party leadership from her husband. The reception from the crowd was polite and subdued. One supporter started to chant "Joe, Joe, Joe," but nobody took it up. The "Re-elect Joe Clark" balloons stayed in their net close to the ceiling; Clark's organizers forgot to release them.

The next morning Mulroney was up at 6:30. With Mila still asleep, he phoned the Manoir and woke up Pat MacAdam, who had a fax machine in his room. "Are the clippings in from Ottawa yet?" he asked. Not even bothering to comb his hair, MacAdam grabbed an armful of newspaper clippings and dashed over to the manager's house. As they read the stories over toast and coffee, the true size of the victory sank in. The details of the landslide were all there in black and white. "By Jesus," Mulroney said quietly, "we did it." MacAdam himself was in awe. Twenty-nine years earlier, to the week, he had encountered a brash pipsqueak with a brushcut who wanted to know the way to the St. FX dining hall. How far that boy had come.

The Tory seat count had finally solidified at 211 — 75 per cent of the seats in the House of Commons, the third-largest majority in Canadian history. He had outperformed Trudeau, Laurier, and even Sir John A. Only Diefenbaker in 1958 and Mackenzie King in 1940 had achieved greater victories.

After an hour MacAdam excused himself to go back to his room to shave and comb his hair. "No, no, wait," Mulroney said. "President Reagan's going to be calling. Maybe you could answer the phone." Just then Rodrigue Pageau and his wife dropped by. After some bear-hugs and pats on the back, the White House call arrived. "*Chalice*," Pageau swore, "the president of the United States is phoning Bones." The conversation lasted five minutes, as Ronald Reagan conveyed his best wishes and Mulroney purred in response. They had met during Mulroney's June visit to Washington and now talked about getting together soon. They also kidded about there being a second Irish leader in North America.

Later that morning he hopped to Sept-Îles by plane to thank residents of Manicouagan's other major population centre for making him their new MP. Uniformed police escorted his bus into town. "The prime minister of Canada and MP for Manicouagan will always comport himself with dignity and courage — thanks to you," he told about two hundred campaign workers at a luncheon. Still contemplative and subdued, he paid tribute to Mila and said he would never have won the PC leadership without her. Late that afternoon he landed in Ottawa. About 150 people awaited him at the airport, but soon a squad of plainclothes Mounties surrounded him and whisked him into the black armour-plated limousine reserved for prime ministers and foreign heads of state.

Late the next morning, his second day as prime minister-elect, the formal transfer of power began when Gordon Osbaldeston, the country's most senior civil servant, arrived at Stornoway with two heavy attaché cases. The cases were full of briefing books explaining how the cabinet and the Privy Council Office worked. Osbaldeston left two hours later, leaving the cases behind. On September 17 — in eleven days — Martin Brian Mulroney would be sworn into office as Canada's eighteenth prime minister. First he would have to digest the contents of the books and tell the civil servants how he wanted to run his cabinet. He also had to pick his ministers, which meant looking down his long list of MPs and searching for the best talent while protecting regional interests, maintaining philosophical balance between blue and pink Tories, and paying off political IOUs.

He would also have to choose a personal staff that would number more than one hundred. His key decisions here would be just as important as his cabinet appointments, and in some ways more so. He was conscious of that, and even more conscious of the adage that those who do not learn from the past are doomed to repeat it. He knew the mistakes Diefenbaker and Clark had made, and he was damned if he was going to make them again. In his government everybody would sing from the same page of the hymn-book. Being prime minister would attract the eyes of the country and yet be a lonely job; he needed people around him whom he could trust, whom he could feel comfortable with — old friends who could be there to listen and encourage, to tell him that everything was going to be okay, old friends to do what he wanted done without his always having to spell it out, old friends like Bernard Roy, Fred Doucet, Peter White, and Pat MacAdam.

He had still to learn the lessons of office. Before long all the old friends — or almost all — would be gone. In the past he had proved himself a master of political adaptation, and in the years to come he would do so again and again. In the past he had repeatedly bounced back from failure, defeat, and depression to score even greater victories, somehow turning each seemingly fatal setback to his advantage. In the future, no matter how far down he sank in public esteem, those who knew him best would never count Brian Mulroney out.

INDEX

Africville (N.S.), 93-94
Alcoholics Anonymous, 369
Amaron, Bob, 91, 118
Amos, Paul, 160
Anderson, Bob, 333, 365, 416, 456
Anderson, Ian, 503, 515
Andre, Harvie, 269, 462
Angus, David, 174, 270, 273-74, 284, 301, 318, 324, 406, 426, 487
Antigonish Movement, 20, 75
Aquarium restaurant, 113
Archer, George, 235, 249, 461
Arpin, Claude, 451-52
Atkins, Norman, 92, 179, 327, 529, 530, 534
Auf der Maur, Nick, 106, 349
Axworthy, Lloyd, 418, 507-8

Baie Comeau, 3, 4, 5, 6-13, 102-3, 159, 529, 531, 550-51, 553-54
Bailey, Leon, 249
Balcer, Léon, 45-46, 116
Balkwill, John, 430-31, 432, 478-79
Ballantyne, Murray, 126
Bassett, John, 302
Bazin, Jean, 111, 131, 149, 155,
160, 168-69, 181, 182, 201, 249, 264, 269, 286, 312, 382, 392, 396, 398, 426, 487, 551
Beaudoin, Denis, 388-89, 392, 411, 414
Beaver Club, 216, 335
Bedson, Derek, 54
Bégin, Charles, 418, 419, 453
Bégin, Monique, 509-10, 513-14
Beigie, Carl, 301
Bell, Dick, 45
Bell, Tom, 66
Bennett, Bill, 331, 332, 334, 342-43, 344, 363, 366
Bergeron, Marius, 171
Bernatchez, Firmin, 118
Berry, Steve, 29
Bertrand, Jean-Jacques, 126
Biron, Rodrigue, 354
Black, Conrad, 224, 365, 459, 472
Black, Larry, 419, 453
Blaikie, Peter, 397, 398, 460
Blanchard, Jacques, 396, 406, 426, 472
Blouin, Jacques, 499, 545
Bockstael, Robert, 506

Bocock, Randy, 437
Boisselle, Claude, 414
Bouchard, Lucien, 152-53, 156, 253, 255, 258, 260, 301, 546, 551
Bourassa, Robert, 224, 252, 257-59, 260, 337
Bourdeleau, Jean-Pierre, 453-54
Bourdon, Pierre-Paul, 386, 441
Bourguignon, Jean, 182
Boutilier, Mrs. (cook), 82, 92
Bradlee, Ben, 291
Breakfast Club, 402-4, 410
Brewin, John, 119
Brian Mulroney: The Boy from Baie-Comeau (Auf der Maur, Chodos, Murphy), 106-7, 170
Bristol Place Hotel, 272-73
Broadbent, Ed, 375, 418, 505, 537-38
Brome-Missisquoi riding, 530
Bronfman, Charles, 250
Brown, Gillis, 34
Brown, Patrick, 350
Brownlee, Bonnie, 532
Brunet, Luc, 394
Brunet, Robert, 394, 396
Bruyère, Jean, 322
Buggie, Frank, 17, 71, 551
Buggie, Tom, 17
Bureau, André, 207
Burn, Peter, 520

Cameron, Donald, 501
Camp, Dalton, 91-92, 98, 176-77, 178-86, 187, 190, 192, 225-26, 292-93, 327, 328, 390, 406-8, 424, 425, 448
Campagnolo, Iona, 534
Campbell, Gerry, 29
Campeau, Arthur, 333

Canada AM, 418
Canada First Party, 66, 69
Canada Health Act, 513-14
Canada Steamship Lines, 205
Canadian Imperial Bank of Commerce, 365, 400, 499
Canadian Press, 419, 453, 460, 542
Carleton, Bobby, 69
Carney, Pat, 443, 487-88
Carrefour bar, 199, 216
Cashin, Rick, 38-39, 50, 52, 56-57, 66, 68, 70, 80-81, 83, 89, 90, 91, 106
CBC, 254, 256, 264, 280, 294-95, 302, 305, 460, 466, 467, 468, 473-75, 552
Mulroney applies to, 146, 250
CCF, 24. *See also* Model Parliaments; New Democratic Party
Ceausescu, Nicolae, 367
Central Nova riding, 500-503, 530-31
Chadwick, C.R., 48
Chambers, Egan, 176
Chaput, Marcel, 127
Charbonneau, Guy, 324, 378, 387, 392, 396, 425, 433, 441, 491
Charbonneau, Yolande, 491
Charest, Jean, 414
Charles, Prince of Wales, 447
Château Frontenac bar, 113-14
Chevrette, Guy, 252-60
Chodos, Robert, 106, 350
Choquette, Jérôme, 258
Chrétien, Jean, 501, 518
Christian Atheists, 90
Churchill, Gordon, 63, 64, 66, 67, 141
Cinko, Paula, 236
CJAD, 365, 519

Clark, Catherine, 326, 495

Clark, Charles Joseph (Joe):

after leadership defeat, 492-93,
494-97, 501-2, 505, 520-21,
527-28, 547-48, 554-55

in Alberta politics, 189-90

annual dinner for, 376, 391-92,
420

compared with Mulroney, 130-33,
143-45, 151, 189, 190, 243-45,
249, 269-70, 288

and Diefenbaker, 131, 143, 148-
49, 186, 292

education, 130, 131, 138, 144-45,
153-55, 189

first elected to House, 243

and Fulton, 131, 154, 189-90, 464

leadership campaign 1976, 269,
272, 273, 277, 281, 285-87,
288, 299, 306-13, 324

leadership campaign 1983, 460,
464-68, 472, 476-89, 492-93

learns/speaks French, 133, 241-42,
288, 469

opinion of Mulroney, 138, 190,
269-70, 376, 409, 424

as PC leader, 326, 336-39, 353,
356, 375-81, 383-92, 396-99,
402, 408-14, 421, 426-30, 433-
36, 441-49, 497

leadership review 1981, 384-87

leadership review 1983, 435-36,
441-49

movement to dump, 385, 386-
89, 391-414, 420-26, 430-35

PC party jobs, 130, 133, 135-36,
240-42

in PC youth groups, 131, 143-44,
148-49, 154

physical appearance, 132, 285, 548

policy orientation, 131, 132, 143,
151-52, 190, 288, 299

as prime minister, 375-80

speaking and debating skills, 130,
132, 299, 303, 313, 337, 441-
42, 479

support in Quebec, 286, 386, 387,
389, 396-97, 411-14, 421, 434,
464-68, 469, 554

and women, 243-45 (*see also* Mc-
Teer, Maureen)

Clark, Grace, 480, 495

Clark, Peter, 480

Cleroux, Richard, 271, 318-20

Cliche commission, 252-61, 332

Cliche, Robert, 153, 156, 250, 252-
60, 264, 362-63, 513

Coady, Moses, 20

Coates, Robert, 137, 366, 367, 393,
394, 403, 411, 435, 462

Cogger, Erica, 298, 318

Cogger, Michel, 378, 380, 406,
433, 441

bachelor days, 198, 201, 233, 236,
240, 243, 246

in dump-Clark movement, 382,
392, 396

and Fulton campaign, 188-89, 192

at Laval, 113, 124, 150, 155, 160

in leadership campaign 1976, 264,
265-67, 269, 270, 272, 284,
286, 290, 291, 303, 305, 308,
318, 324, 459

in leadership campaign 1983, 459,
487, 499

and Mulroney as PC leader, 503,
545, 551

Colby, Ken, 295

Commission of Inquiry on the Exercise of Union Freedom in the Construction Industry (Cliche commission), 252-61, 332
Common, Frank, 249-50
Comtois, Jean, 111
Confederation of National Trade Unions, 206, 251
Congress on Canadian Affairs, 124-25, 126-28
Connolly, Harold, 99
Conrad, Jim, 54, 94
Conservative Party. *See* Progressive Conservative Party
constitutional issues, 126-28, 337-38, 353, 363-64, 383, 469-70, 545-46
Conversations with Kennedy (Bradlee), 290-91
Cooper, George, 273
Corriveau, Gérard, 121
Côté, Michel, 465
Côté-O'Hara, Jocelyne, 520
Creaghan, Paul, 29-30, 32-33, 35, 40, 44, 46, 51, 52, 80, 95, 106, 325-26
Crombie, David, 402, 460, 480-81, 483, 484, 488, 494
Crosbie, John, 379, 402, 460, 468, 475-76, 479, 480-85, 486, 494, 548
Crossland, Jim, 446
CTV, 288, 297, 314, 340, 382, 418, 442, 493, 534
Curley, Paul, 327
Cutler, Phil, 173-74, 196, 197

Dalhousie law school, 80, 83-85, 100
  campus politics, 86, 90, 144

Clark at, 138, 144-45, 154
Crosbie at, 460
Mulroney at, 80-107
Danis, Marcel, 396, 397, 413, 414, 434-35, 465
Dantzer, Vince, 190
Davey, Keith, 542
David, Jean, 119-20
Davis, William, 469, 543
Dawson, Dave, 443
de Cotret, Robert, 552
Dean, Robert, 455
debating clubs:
  at Dalhousie, 88-89
  at St. FX, 36, 60, 74
Demond, Andrew, 396, 437
Desbarats, Peter, 250, 301-2
Desjardins, André, 257
Desmarais, Paul, 204-9, 212, 270, 283-84, 324, 330
Desrochers, Paul, 257
Devine, Bill, 261
Le Devoir, 139-40, 255, 271, 391, 421
Dick, Paul, 394-95
Diefenbaker, John, 40, 41-47, 54-55, 508
  later years, 191, 289-96, 373-74
  movement to dump, 138-43, 147-49, 176-88
  as prime minister, 61-64, 70-73, 86, 113-19, 121-22, 129, 135, 145, 356
Diefenbaker, Olive, 54
Diefenbaker: Leadership Gained (Stursberg), 291
Donahoe, Richard, 61
Donham, Parker Barss, 328, 390
Doody, Bill, 272

Dorion, Marc, 396, 426
Dorion, Noel, 116
Doucet, Fred, 213, 393, 487, 499,
  501, 502, 509, 515, 551, 557
Doucet, Gerry, 37, 40, 60-61, 64,
  80, 106, 191, 213
Drapeau, Jean, 212, 224
Drew, George, 39
Drouin, Marc, 111
Duffy, Mike, 474
Dugré, Jean, 389, 394, 396, 426
Duhaime, Yves, 455
Duhamel, Yvon, 252
Dumont, Claude, 394, 396, 465
Duplessis, Maurice, 25, 36-37, 58,
  114, 369
Duplessis, Suzanne, 547
Dupras, Claude, 222, 224, 226,
  228, 310, 420
Dussault, René, 122-23

Eagleson, Alan, 189, 192, 310, 463
Earl, Rosann, 78-81, 106, 238
East Coast Energy, 499
Edmonton Journal, 280
elections and campaigns. *See also*
  Model Parliaments
  Alberta 1967, 189
  British Columbia 1963, 154
  federal:
    1957, 54-55, 139
    1958, 63, 69-71, 139
    1962, 129-30, 134-36, 137, 139
    1963, 145
    1965, 178
    1968, 193-94, 222
    1972, 228-31, 235, 243, 272
    1974, 262
    1979, 375-76

    1980, 379-81, 388, 472
    1984, 527, 528-55
  federal by-elections:
    Central Nova 1983, 500-501,
    502, 503
    Joliette 1981, 389-91
    Lévis 1981, 388
  Nova Scotia:
    1956, 33-35, 98, 99
    1960, 91-92, 97-99
  Quebec:
    1960, 115
    1970, 224
    1976, 260, 337
    referendum 1980, 363, 382
Elizabeth II, 525, 527, 542
Elliott, Dick, 170
Elzinga, Peter, 479, 488, 489
Ennis, Fred, 402
Epp, Jake, 462, 516, 517
Erola, Judy, 418
extra-billing, 513-14

Faibish, Roy, 129-30, 133, 136,
  138, 301
Fallu, Élie, 455
Faribault, Marcel, 194
Fédération des Travailleurs du
  Québec (FTQ), 196, 206, 251-61
Ferguson, Ann, 12
Ferguson, Barbara, 12
Ferguson, Ernest, 12
Ferguson, Max, 97
Ferron, Madeleine, 362-63
the fifth estate, 280
Financial Post Magazine, 351, 355
Fisher, Doug, 61, 66, 127, 128, 402
Fisher, John, 12
Fleming, Donald, 40, 45, 192

Flemming, Brian, 89, 95-96, 106
Flemming, Hugh John, 45
Flynn, Jacques, 116
Fontaine, Claude, 160
Foreign Investment Review Agency, 471
Forsey, Eugene, 126
Forsyth, Christine, 242
Fortier, Yves, 168, 246
Fortin, Mademoiselle (landlady), 109
Fortin, Paul, 149
Fotheringham, Allan, 263, 271, 491, 506
Fournier, Jean-Pierre, 119
Fox, Bill, 324, 390-91, 402, 532, 534
Francoeur, Louis-Gilles, 255-56
Fraser, Blair, 119
Fraser, Graham, 546
Fraser, John, 272, 273, 281, 306, 307-8, 309, 462
Fraser, Neil, 460, 480
Freedom Fund, 48-49
Frenette, Claude, 146
Frum, Barbara, 254, 256, 264
Fulton, E. Davie, 40-41, 45, 55, 61, 70, 86, 121, 124-25, 126, 154, 187-92, 222, 464

Gallery, Brian, 426
Gamble, John, 395, 405, 460, 469, 480
Gauthier, Pierre, 319
Gendreau, Paul-Arthur, 153, 253, 345
George-Étienne Cartier Trust Fund, 227-28, 276, 281-82
Geren, Richard, 346, 361
Gibson, Catrina, 244

Gillies, Jim, 272, 273, 281, 306, 307, 310, 352
Global Television, 280, 301
Globe and Mail, 177, 271, 282, 313, 318, 319, 351, 383, 398, 448, 457, 546, 549
Gold, Alan, 196, 197, 233
Golddiggers, 236-37
Goodine, David, 17
Goodman, Eddie, 227
Gosselin, Edgar, 164
Grafftey, Heward, 230, 268, 272, 273, 281, 306, 307, 352, 430, 530
Graham, Al, 70
Gravel, Thomson & Gravel, 150-51
Gray, John, 231, 298, 457
Greber, Dave, 207
Greenspan, David, 119
Gregg, Allan, 395, 534
Grosart, Allister, 135, 296
Guerrette, Ray, 74
Guilbeault, Jean, 443
Gwyn, Richard, 476
Gzowski, Peter, 119-20

Hamilton, Alvin, 74, 86, 129-30, 133-35, 136-37, 141, 188, 190, 462
Hamilton, Don, 272
Hanna Mining Company, 331, 332-33, 335, 343, 365, 416, 450, 456. *See also* Iron Ore Company (IOC)
Harari, Claude, 186
Harder, Peter, 532
Harris, Ed, 97
Harrison, Russ, 365-66
Hatfield, Richard, 225, 325, 326
Hawkes, Jim, 286
Hayes, Lawrence, 95

Hees, George, 188, 462

Hellyer, Paul, 272, 273, 276, 281, 295, 303, 306, 308-9

Hicks, Henry, 33, 98-99

Higgins, Bobby, 22, 28, 30, 31

High River, 131, 154

Hnatyshyn, Ray, 462, 493

Hodgson, Derik, 402

Holden, Richard, 193, 246, 267, 268-69, 406, 466

Hollinger North Shore Exploration Ltd., 365

Hooper, Francis, 430, 432

Horner, Jack, 186, 272, 273, 281, 306, 309, 310, 338

Howard, Cate, Ogilvy, Bishop, Cope, Porteous and Hansard (Howard Cate Ogilvy), 160-62, 164-65, 168, 171, 193, 197-98

Howard, Ross, 549

Howard, Wilbert, 168

Hoy, Claire, 170

Humphreys, David, 131, 154, 242

Hungarian refugees (1956), St. FX raises funds for, 47-49

Hurley, Dan, 65, 66, 67

Inquiry Commission on the St. Lawrence Ports (Picard commission), 172-75

International Longshoremen's Association (ILA), 171-74, 195-97, 233

Iron Ore Company (IOC), 265-66, 330-36, 342-49, 358-62, 363-66, 395, 404, 405, 414-20, 450-57

Israeli embassy controversy, 377

Jackman, Hal, 42, 189, 464

James Bay project, 251-52, 257

Jelinek, Otto, 421, 445, 462

Jenks, Lionel, 178

Jennings, Mike, 22

Joe Clark: A Portrait (Humphreys), 131, 154, 242

John Paul II, 525

Johnson, Daniel, 113-14, 126, 180-81, 193, 204

Johnson, Janis, 491

Johnson, Jon, 399, 520, 534-35, 549

Johnson, William, 383, 398

Jones, W.S.K., 61

Journal de Québec, 455

Kane, Elmar, 109

Keating, Charles, 39

Keenan, Don, 57, 58, 59, 66

Keenan, Jenny, 109

Kempling, Bill, 445

Kennedy, John F., 142, 201, 291

Kerr, Alexander, 96, 104-5

Khattar, Joe, 81, 82, 86, 88, 92

Kilburn, Peter, 345

Kimber, Stephen, 351-56

Kinsella, Pat, 532

Kirck, Harvey, 382

Kirk, J. Ralph, 54

Kirkpatrick, John, 161

Konigsberg, Alex, 303, 318

Kovacevic, Joe, 344, 352

Laberge, Louis, 196, 206, 207, 260, 382

Labrador City, 331, 456

Labrador Mining and Exploration, 365

Lachance, Gilles, 11, 492

Lalonde, Marc, 340

Lambert, Marcel, 190, 504

Lane, Helen, 77

Langlois, Raynold, 141, 153, 164, 253

Larocque, Evelyn, 363

Larson, Al, 357, 415-16

LaSalle, Roch, 310, 381, 389, 391, 420, 448, 462, 498, 504, 552

Laurendeau, André, 126, 139-40

Laurent, Jacques, 168

Laval law school, 76-77, 108, 110, 112, 155
  campus politics, 123, 141, 146-47, 149-50
  Mulroney at, 107-56

Lavoie, Bert, 37, 51, 70, 503

Lavoie, Butch, 12

Leach, Anne, 82-83, 87

Leach, Tom, 294-95

Leach family, 81

LeBreton, Marjorie, 133

Lee, Bill, 542

Leopold, Stephen, 274

Lesage, Jean, 115, 116, 118, 124, 127, 128, 139, 264

Lesage, Jules, 111, 269

Lesaux, Peter, 48

Lévesque, René, 11, 113, 124, 127, 128, 337, 353, 364, 469, 517

Liberal Party of Canada, 25, 63, 222, 223, 337, 377, 519
  campus politics (see Model Parliaments)
  elections (see elections and campaigns)
  leadership campaign and convention 1984, 517-19, 521, 523-24
  offers Mulroney a nomination, 340
  in Quebec, 24, 114, 222, 223, 376, 381, 472, 552
  standings in opinion polls, 337,

338, 409-10, 464, 513, 523-24, 526, 531-32, 542, 544
  treatment of Mulroney as PC leader, 501, 506, 507-10, 513-14
  Turner government, 525-27

Liberal Party of Nova Scotia, 25, 34, 99

Liberal Party of Quebec, 24, 114-15, 118, 124, 139, 223-24, 257-58, 260, 323

Logan, Rick, 403, 404

Lord, David, 460

Lortie, Jean-Yves, 386-87, 394, 396, 397, 398, 411, 426, 432, 436-41, 445, 468

Lougheed, Peter, 189, 242, 263, 269

MacAdam, Pat, 75, 213, 263, 370, 373, 406
  in dump-Clark movement, 404, 424, 426, 439
  on IOC retainer, 366, 367, 404, 418
  in leadership campaign 1983, 462, 485, 487, 491, 493, 494
  on Mulroney's staff, 500, 502, 503, 508, 515-16, 532, 534, 542, 551, 555, 557
  at PC headquarters, 131, 133, 135
  at St. FX, 21-22, 40, 41, 53

McAleer, Bill, 464

McCabe, Aileen, 460-61, 473

McCann, Terry, 50, 270, 406, 487, 551, 553

McCord, Scott, 398

McCormick, Robert R., 6-7, 12-13

McCutcheon, Wallace, 188

MacDonald, Angus R., 54, 69

MacDonald, Finlay, 92, 227, 282, 391, 406, 422, 424, 425, 464, 534

MacDonald, Flora, 177, 179, 272, 273, 276, 281, 285, 292, 295, 306, 307, 309, 325, 326, 328-29, 441, 462

MacDonald, L. Ian, 13, 107, 152, 155, 169, 170, 207, 234, 235, 255, 258, 321, 349, 447, 451, 474, 483, 507, 538, 552

Macdonald, Neil, 533

Macdonell, Fr. (St. FX), 213

McDougall, Don, 264-65, 266-67, 271, 272, 305, 401, 464

MacEachen, Allan, 61, 66

MacEwen, Max, 51

MacGillivray, Red, 22

McGoughty, Brian, 22

McGrath, Jim, 275, 310, 406, 462

MacGregor, Roy, 548

McInnes, Stewart, 272-73

Mackasey, Bryce, 196, 197, 206, 313-14, 337, 527, 533, 541

McKay, Andy, 101

MacKay, Elmer, 393, 394, 395, 430-31, 432, 435, 441, 443-44, 446, 462, 498, 500, 503, 515, 552

McKee, Dave, 40

McKenna, Brian, 212

McKenzie, Dan, 402, 514, 516, 517

McKinnon, Allan, 269

MacKinnon, Bill, 34-35

McKnight, Bill, 494

McLaughlin, Earle, 202, 270

Maclean's, 119-21, 271, 383, 475, 514, 545

MacLennan, Danny, 26, 29-30, 31

McMahon, Judith, 244

McMillan, Charley, 272, 503, 515, 532, 534

McMurtry, Roy, 182, 183-84, 192, 327

MacPherson, Don, 280, 324

Macquarrie, Heath, 275, 310

McSweeney, Michael, 458, 491, 494, 495, 500, 551

McTeer, Maureen, 244-45, 247, 269, 338, 443, 444, 480, 486-87, 488, 489, 494-95, 502, 521, 555

Mailloux, Benoît, 322

Maloney, Arthur, 137, 182, 183-84, 185-86, 289-90, 318

Maloney, Mark, 318

Maltais, André, 529-30, 551

Maltais, Jean-Pierre, 416, 452

Manicouagan riding, 499-500, 529-30, 544-45, 550-51

Manitoba language issue, 506-7, 512-13, 514-17, 518-19, 521-22, 536

Manoir, the (Baie Comeau), 8, 550

Mansbridge, Peter, 474-75

Manthorpe, Jonathan, 282, 313

Marchand, Cliff, 22

Marcoux, Yvon, 345

Maritime Employers' Association (MEA), 196-97, 227, 233

Marois, Pierre, 417-18, 455

Martin, Joe, 88

Martin, Keith, 292

Martin, Paul, 61, 65-66, 67, 68

Martin, Paul, Jr., 248-49, 250

Mass, Sonny, 485

Masse, Marcel, 231

Matheson, Carrie Ann, 48

Maxwell, Judith, 244

Mayer, Charlie, 516

Mayer, Maurice, 369-70

Mazankowski, Don, 494

Meighen, Michael, 222, 393
  in dump-Diefenbaker movement,
    181, 182, 183
  at Laval, 110, 111, 113, 122, 124,
    139, 140-41, 145, 147, 150,
    156, 345, 487
  Mulroney cuts friendship with,
    323-24, 327, 382
Ménard, Pierre, 546, 547
Mendenhall, Francie, 237-38
Mendenhall, Phyllis, 237
Mifflen, Fr. (St. FX), 213
Mills, Myles, 51
Model Parliaments:
  at Dalhousie, 123
  at Laval, 123, 141
  Maritime, 60-61, 64-69, 89-91
  national significance of, 28, 129
  at St. FX, 23-31, 33, 35, 51-54, 56-
    59
Monaghan, Mike, 364-65
Montgomery, Tom, 160, 161, 165,
  167, 168, 321
Montreal Gazette, 236, 271, 280,
  324, 349, 419, 420, 451, 455
Montréal Matin, 271
Montreal Star, 271, 355
Moores, Frank, 272, 345, 392, 393,
  395, 401, 404, 406, 432-33, 435,
  441, 462, 487
Morrison, John, 405, 435, 445-46
Morrow, Andy, 17
Morrow, Katherine, 238
Morrow, Robert, 238, 345
Moscovitz, Jason, 460, 466-67, 474
Mount Royal Club, 335
Mount Royal Club group, 392-94,
  399, 425
Mount Royal Tennis Club, 234

Mount St. Bernard College, 19, 30,
  54, 59
Mulroney, Barbara (sister), 6, 170,
  494
Mulroney, Benedict (son), 298, 340,
  494
Mulroney, Benedict Martin (father),
  3-6, 9, 14, 18, 25, 47, 79, 102,
  146, 166, 167, 170
Mulroney, Caroline (daughter),
  265, 340, 494
Mulroney, Doreen (sister), 6, 18,
  170, 368, 463, 494
Mulroney, Gary (brother), 6, 170,
  463, 474, 494, 551
Mulroney, Irene (mother), 4-5, 9,
  79, 170, 198, 225, 237, 246, 250,
  304, 489, 494
Mulroney, Mark (son), 368, 494
Mulroney, Martin Brian:
  bilingualism of, 11, 14, 67, 70, 77,
    110-12, 133, 155-56, 172, 257,
    277, 279, 537
  childhood, 4-18
  depression, 94, 106, 320-22, 324-
    30, 339-40, 348-50, 356-58,
    362-63, 368
  drinking problem, 339-40, 347-
    48, 350, 354, 362-63, 367-71,
    372-73
  education:
    applies for Rhodes Scholarship,
      75-76
    articling year, 150-51
    in Baie Comeau, 10, 13-14
    bar exams, 162-64, 165-67, 168-70
    at Dalhousie, 80-107
    fails Dalhousie, 97, 99-100, 106-7
    at Laval, 76-77, 107-56

at St. FX, 19-79
at St. Thomas, 14-18
family life:
  marriage and children, 234-35,
  239-40, 244-47, 280, 340, 348-
  49, 368, 371-72, 494, 511, 544
  (*see also* Mulroney, Mila)
  relationship with father, 4, 47,
  166, 167
  relationship with mother, 170
  relationships with siblings, 6,
  170, 463
health, 92-94, 348, 366, 476
media contacts, 113, 119-21, 128,
  216, 255-56, 257, 349-50, 351,
  355-56, 391, 405
names and nicknames, 37, 52,
  131, 346
physical appearance, 11, 19, 51,
  52, 78, 83, 132, 161, 348, 523
smoking, quits, 517
speaking and debating skills, 36-
  39, 51, 57-58, 66-68, 74, 88-89,
  132, 271, 277, 300, 302, 509,
  511, 519, 537-41
summer jobs, 102-3, 129-30, 133-
  38, 146
views:
  on Constitution, 156, 363-64,
  383, 469-70, 545-47
  on death penalty, 52, 140, 278
  on official bilingualism, 27, 139-
  40, 278, 507, 512-13, 514-17,
  521-22
voice, 22, 34, 37, 66, 94, 98, 130,
  199, 277
women, 77-81, 82-83, 87, 122-23,
  163, 199-200, 235-39, 245, 348-
  49, 368

In Politics:
asked to run for Parliament, 250-
  51, 340, 376, 380, 389-90
assistant to Hamilton, 129-30,
  133-38
campus politics:
  at Dalhousie, 86, 89-91
  at Laval, 116, 123, 124-25, 126-
  28, 141, 146-47, 149-50
  at St. FX, 23-33, 35, 52-54, 56-
  59, 64-69
and Clark:
  compared with Clark, 130-33,
  143-45, 151, 189, 190, 243-45,
  249, 269-70, 288
  private views of Clark, 327, 330,
  338-39, 381, 447-48, 461
  public statements on Clark, 351,
  352-56, 376, 383, 387, 391-92,
  397-98, 402, 405, 420, 422-30,
  433, 440
and Diefenbaker, 41-47, 54-55,
  61-64, 71-73, 86, 116-19, 121-
  22, 139-41, 177-78, 289-92,
  295-96, 373-74
in dump-Diefenbaker movement,
  177-87
in federal election 1984:
  cost of promises, 548-49
  debates, 527, 537-41
  elected in Manicouagan, 529-32,
  544-45, 550-51
  patronage issue, 527, 531, 532-
  36, 537-42
  Quebec/constitutional issues,
  545-47
  staff, 532, 534-35
in federal election campaigns:
  1958, 69-72

Mulroney, Martin Brian: in federal
election campaigns (*continued*)
1962, 134-35
1963, 145
1968, 193-94
1972, 228-29
1979, 376
1980, 380
1984 (*see above*)
and Fulton, 40-41, 55, 70, 86,
121, 124-25, 131, 187-92, 222
joins Union Nationale, 114-15
leadership campaign 1976, 263-
320
balloting, 306-13
Clark factor, 269-70, 287-88
considers candidacy, 263-73
declares candidacy, 273
defeat devastates Mulroney,
319-22, 324-30, 339-40, 356,
368
Diefenbaker factor, 289-96
lavish campaign, 273-74, 282-
85, 296-98, 299, 322, 324
policies lacking, 275-76, 287,
298-99
and Quebec delegates, 274, 279,
319
speech to convention, 299-303
Stevens defection, 308, 312, 313
Wagner factor, 267-69, 274,
279, 281-82
leadership campaign 1983, 458-93
balloting, 479-88
builds Quebec support for, 385-
86, 387-90, 394
Crosbie factor, 468, 475-76,
479, 480, 481, 484-85, 486
declares candidacy, 458

low-key campaign, 458-60, 461-62
and media, 460-61, 473-75
patronage issue, 387-88, 472-73,
500
policy emphasis, 399-401, 407,
470-72
and Quebec delegates, 464-68, 477
speeches to convention, 478, 489-
90
tests support, 382-83, 392-94, 404
youth supporters, 395-96, 471-
72, 477
leadership review 1983:
backs dump-Clark movement,
387, 388, 389, 391, 392-402,
405, 411-14, 421, 432-35, 499
formally supports Clark, 407,
421-30, 439-40
and Nova Scotia provincial politics, 33-35, 85, 88, 91-92, 97-99
as PC leader:
and Clark, 489, 494-97, 505,
513, 521
elected in Central Nova, 497-98,
500-501, 502-3
in House, 505-14
Manitoba language issue, 506-7,
512-13, 514-17, 519, 521-22
policy generation, 504-5, 510,
528
prepares for federal election, 521,
524, 526
staff, 502-3, 509, 511, 519-20,
556-57
works for party unity, 493-97,
503-5, 512-15
in PC youth groups, 61, 64, 74, 75,
85-86, 91, 92-93, 118, 142, 147
prime minister–elect, 552-57

and Quebec PC organization, 180-
83, 194, 220-27, 228-29, 231-
32, 274, 312, 376, 378, 385-86,
387-91, 394, 396-98, 411, 412,
420, 546
and Quebec provincial politics,
113-16, 118, 121-22, 125-26,
180-81, 193, 204, 215-16, 257-
60, 337, 354, 364, 382
and Stanfield, 33, 74, 88, 97-99,
190-94, 224-25, 232, 326-27
and Wagner, 223-32, 267-69,
274, 279, 282, 310-13, 387
Private Career:
directorships, 365, 400, 499
at IOC, 342-49, 363-66, 370, 388,
395, 405, 412, 456-57
and Bennett, 331-32, 334, 342-
43
closing of Schefferville, 414-20,
449-57
labour relations, 343, 346-47,
358-62
offer from, 265-66, 330, 332-33
salary and benefits, 333-34, 335-
36, 343-45, 376
legal career:
after 1976 defeat, 330
becomes partner, 251
Cliche commission, 251-61
joins Howard Cate Ogilvy (later
Ogilvy Cope), 160-61
negotiator/conciliator, 171, 174,
195-97, 205-11, 233-34
Picard commission, 172-75
La Presse strike, 205-8
salary, 217-20, 333-34
Mulroney, Mila (wife), 347, 348,
353, 357. *See also* Pivnicki, Mila

as Brian's partner, 247, 371-72, 544
in campaigns, 279-80, 304, 371-
72, 439, 461, 462-63, 474, 483,
487, 488, 489, 491-92, 499,
500, 532, 544, 551, 553, 556
and children, 280, 298, 340, 344,
368
marriage difficulties, 340, 348,
349, 368
Mulroney, Olive (sister), 6, 15, 18,
170, 494
Mulroney, Peggy (sister), 6, 15, 18,
170, 494
*Mulroney: The Making of the Prime
Minister* (MacDonald), 13, 107,
169, 170, 207, 258, 321, 349,
451
Munson, Jim, 340
Murphy, Bill, 82, 92
Murphy, Rae, 106, 350
Murray, Lowell, 179, 512, 534
appointed senator, 378
bachelor days, 137, 198, 240, 246
and Clark, 131, 240-41, 243, 325-
26, 378, 424, 435, 464, 480, 504
and Fulton, 189, 192
in leadership campaign 1976, 267,
270, 285
in leadership campaign 1983, 399,
435, 464, 480
Mulroney cuts friendship with,
325-26, 327, 378
Mulroney reconciles with, 504
at St. FX, 27, 28-32, 40-41, 213
Murta, Jack, 462, 516

Nantel, Roger, 426, 487, 551
Nash, Knowlton, 474
National Hockey League, 330

National Republic Party, 24-25, 28-30, 38, 52

The National, 473-74

Neury, Gene, 22

Neville, Bill, 399-400, 406, 408, 534

New Democratic Party (NDP), 145, 153, 375, 379, 472. *See also* elections and campaigns

Newman, Peter C., 119-21, 246, 271, 294

Nickels, Carl, 333, 456

Nick's Restaurant, 198

Nielsen, Erik, 488, 489, 494, 497, 510

Nimsick, Leo, 33, 58, 65, 66

Nolin, Claude, 224

Nolin, Pierre Claude, 394, 426

Norquay, Geoff, 520

Nowlan, George, 44-45, 69

Nowlan, Michael, 17

Nowlan, Patrick, 272, 273, 275, 281, 306, 309

O'Brien, David, 219

October Crisis (1970), 224

O'Donovan, Vince, 88, 95

Ogilvy, Angus, 166, 193-94, 203, 218-19

Ogilvy, Cope, Porteous, Hansard, Marler, Montgomery & Renault (Ogilvy Cope), 203-5, 215, 217-20, 251, 252-53, 320-21, 330, 333

Ohrt, Peter, 461, 470

O'Keefe, Fr. (St. FX), 35

Old Brewery Mission, 466-67

O'Leary, Clem, 69-70

O'Neill, Pierre, 391

Oratorical Contests:

at Dalhousie, 89

at St. FX, 36-37, 57-58, 60, 74

Orr, Bobby, 501

Osbaldeston, Gordon, 542, 556

O'Shea, Mary Irene, 4-5. *See also* Mulroney, Irene

O'Sullivan, Sean, 290-91, 320

Ottawa Citizen, 298, 506, 533

Ouellet, André, 340

Ouellet, Gary, 160

Pageau, Rodrigue, 386, 387, 389, 393-94, 396, 411, 413, 414, 426, 432, 435, 441, 465, 487, 553, 555

Paproski, Steve, 462

Park, Lee, 516

Parti Québécois (PQ), 337, 354, 364, 469, 546

Pathy, Alex, 174, 195

patronage, 120, 379-80, 387-88, 472-73, 500, 527, 531, 532-36, 537-42

Pawley, Howard, 506, 514, 516

Pearkes, George, 45

Pearson, Lester, 61, 70, 145, 172, 178

Peckford, Brian, 484-85

Pellerin, Russ, 33

Pelletier, Gérard, 126

Pelletier, Jean, 207, 514, 545

Pepin, Marcel, 206, 207

Petro-Canada, 377

Phillips, Bruce, 493

Picard commission (Inquiry Commission on the St. Lawrence Ports), 172-75

Picard, Laurent, 172

Pichet, Hubert, 503, 515

Pigott, Jean, 380

Pilotte, Ginette, 216, 335, 345-46, 406

Pivnicki, Dimitrije, 234, 494

Pivnicki, Mila, 234-35, 239-40, 244-46. *See also* Mulroney, Mila

Pocklington, Peter, 460, 480-83, 494, 551

Pollock, Sam, 212

Porteous, Jack, 203-5

Power Corporation, 204-9, 226, 248, 297, 330, 370

Pratte, Yves, 146

La Presse, 205-8

Pristanski, Bill, 503, 515, 532, 551

Progressive Conservative Party of Alberta, 189

Progressive Conservative Party of British Columbia, 154, 188

Progressive Conservative Party of Canada:

campus politics (*see* Model Parliaments)

conventions, leadership:

1956, 39-46

1967, 187-93

1976, 263, 293-320, 322-24

1983, 476-93

conventions, national:

1959, 86

1963, 143-44

1964, 147, 148

1966, 179, 183-87

1981, 384-87

1983, 435-49

delegate-selection process, 413-14, 464-68

in elections (*see* elections and campaigns)

left and right wings, 276, 281, 306-9, 400-401, 471

Mulroney as bridge to Quebec for, 116, 118, 121-22, 139-41, 179, 183, 193-94, 220-22, 279, 472, 522, 530, 537

Quebec support affects national standing of, 45, 64, 71, 140, 178, 223, 231, 338, 376, 381, 382, 472

Quebec support in 1984 election, 530-32, 537, 544-47, 549-52

standing in opinion polls, 336, 337-38, 353, 354, 380, 409-10, 464, 513, 518, 523-24, 526, 531-32, 544, 548

youth role, 40-44, 147-48, 185, 288, 437-38, 468, 472, 477 (*see also* Progressive Conservative Student Federation; Young Progressive Conservatives)

Progressive Conservative Party of Canada, Quebec wing,

annual Clark dinner, 376, 391-92, 420

convention, Beauport 1966, 180-81

convention, Montreal 1982, 396-98

executive and apparatus, 180-81, 221-22, 224, 228, 324, 378, 386-89, 411-12, 530

Mulroney takes control, 386, 388, 394, 396-98, 411, 412

Wagner as leader, 223-32, 267-69, 274, 276-77, 279, 281-82, 310

weakness under Diefenbaker, Stanfield, 116, 121-22

Progressive Conservative Party of Nova Scotia, 33-35, 44-45, 91-92, 97-99, 214

Progressive Conservative Student
  Federation, 61, 64, 74, 85, 91, 92-
  93, 118, 142-44, 147-49, 286
Provigo, 365, 499

Quebec City, 108-9, 113
Quebec committee, 394, 425-26
Quebec Federation of Labour. *See*
  Fédération des Travailleurs du
  Québec (FTQ)
Quebec nationalism and separatism,
  115-16, 126-28, 139-40, 156,
  337, 353, 363-64, 469, 545-47
Quebec North Shore and Labrador
  Railway, 365
Quebec North Shore Paper Com-
  pany, 3, 6-8, 125, 146, 347
Quebec referendum (1980), 363,
  382
Québec-Téléphone, 365
Question Period, 493
Quiet Revolution, 115-16, 139, 156
Quinn, Gary, 46
Quittenton, R.C., 273

Radio-Canada, 551
Rassemblement pour
  l'Indépendance Nationale, 127
Raymondo, Frank, 344
Read, Horace, 83
Reagan, Ronald, 524, 555
Renault, Paul, 171, 172
Reno, Ginette, 299
Rhinoceros Party, 472
Rhodes Scholarship committee, 75-
  76
Richardson, Lee, 502, 515
Riou, Jean, 414
Rising to Power (Greber), 207

Ritchie, Gordon, 402
Ritz-Carlton Hotel, 335, 339, 365,
  426, 433
Ritz Summit, 426-30, 433
Roberge, Benoît, 396
Roberge, Fernand, 396, 426, 433
Roberts, Leslie, 99
Robertson, Lloyd, 305
Robinson, Jennifer, 419
Roblin, Duff, 45, 188, 191, 192
Rogers' Raiders, 41-42, 46

St. Francis Xavier University (St.
  FX), 18-21, 22, 35-36, 37-39
  campus politics, 23-33, 51-54, 56-
    59, 64-69
  Mulroney at, 19-79
  Mulroney raises money for, 357,
    498, 501
  Student Co-op, 74
St. Germain, Gerry, 500
St. Mary's University, 90-91
St. Thomas College, 15, 17, 39
St. Thomas High School, 14-18
Saulnier, Lucien, 212
Scammell, Bob, 104
Schefferville, 331, 414-20, 449-57,
  529, 551
Schenley Awards, 422
Schumacher, Stan, 338
Scott, Gail, 240
Scott, Graham, 240, 288
Sept-Îles, 331, 456, 529, 531, 550
Sherman, Bud, 536
Shipping Federation of Canada, 172-
  75, 195-97
Shugart, Ian, 520
Siddon, Tom, 441, 462
Sinclair, Alvin, 501, 503

Sirois, Jean, 472

Skalbania, Nelson, 345

Skoreyko, Bill, 190

Smith, Richard, 443, 446

Social Credit Party, 135, 145, 375,
379, 381

Le Soleil, 455

Somers, H.J., 48, 54, 213

Southam News, 460, 473, 531, 544

Standard Brands, 330

Standard Broadcasting, 365

Stanfield, Robert:
   after resigning PC leadership, 326-
   27, 350, 377
   Nova Scotia premier, 34, 44, 74,
   88, 91, 97-99, 188
   as PC leader, 190-94, 221, 224-25,
   228, 229-30, 232, 240-41, 242,
   262, 289, 524

stevedoring contractors, and Picard
   commission, 172-75

Stevens, Geoffrey, 225

Stevens, Sinclair, 272, 273, 276,
   281, 292, 306-8, 324, 328, 462

Stewart, Ron, 404, 514

Students' Political Association, 29,
   30, 33

Stursberg, Peter, 291

Teeter, Bob, 226

Terris, Janet, 491

Thomson, Peter, 369-70

TIW Industries, 365

Toronto Star, 273, 282, 324, 368,
   387, 390, 476, 548

Toronto Sun, 297, 305, 403

Towers, Gordon, 402, 404, 498

Tremblay, André, 112

Trépanier, Bernard, 396

Trépanier, Paul, 181-82

Tribune Company, 6

Trudeau, Pierre, 193, 194, 223,
   239, 320, 337, 354, 356-57, 375,
   380, 410, 505-6, 507, 512, 514,
   515, 517-18, 527, 545

Turner, John, 137-38, 324, 336,
   410, 518-19, 523, 524, 525-27,
   529, 533, 534, 535, 537-40, 542,
   547, 548-49

Union Nationale, 24, 25, 36, 58,
   114-15, 116, 125-26, 193, 194,
   204, 222, 231, 264, 354, 386,
   389, 546

United Provinces Insurance, 365

United Way, 357

University of Montreal law school,
   218

Valcov, Robert, 414

Van Dusen, Tom, 503, 515

Vézina, Monique, 547

von Veh, Fred, 393

Voyageur bus lines, 205

Wagner, Claude, 223-32, 267-69,
   272, 273, 274, 275, 276-77, 279,
   281-82, 303, 306-13, 323, 338,
   356, 376, 387

Wakim, Marty, 491

Wakim, Sam, 22-23, 26-27, 47, 52,
   53, 72, 76, 78-79, 137, 213, 264,
   270, 351, 406, 426, 439, 487,
   491, 543, 551, 553

Walker, David, 42

Walker, Gordon, 446

Waschuk, Ken, 393, 433, 441

Webster, Jack, 462

Weeks, Gordie, 22
Wells, Clyde, 96
Where I Stand (Mulroney), 470-71
White, Peter, 502, 557
  and Conrad Black, 224, 395, 459,
    472
  and dump-Clark movement, 387,
    392, 395-96, 399, 412, 425, 433
  and dump-Diefenbaker move-
    ment, 139, 147, 180, 181, 398
  at Laval, 123-24, 137-38, 139,
    140-41, 144, 147, 150, 153,
    155, 156
  and leadership campaign 1976,
    263, 281-82
  and leadership campaign 1983,
    459, 472, 487
  and Wagner, 223, 224, 229-30,
    281-82

White, Theodore, 142
Willis, Harry, 136
Wilson, Michael, 449, 460, 480-81,
  482-83, 494
Winners, Losers (Brown, Chodos,
  Murphy), 350
Winston's, 422
Wolf, Walter, 499, 503
Worthington, Chris, 396

Xaverian Weekly, 21, 28, 37

Yates, Terry, 443
Young Progressive Conservatives,
  61, 85-86, 142, 147-48
Youth for Diefenbaker, 41-42, 46

Zeise, Ken, 437, 443, 446
Zolf, Larry, 372

This book is set in Garamond, a typeface designed in 1545 by Claude Garamont, a punch cutter in Paris. Garamond gained popularity in the early seventeenth century. It is light in "colour," delicate in design, and yet smoothly legible. It is one of the finest old styles ever cut.

Design by Gordon Robertson

Type set by Tony Gordon Limited